TALES AND SKETCHES
Volume 2: 1843–1849

THE WHITMAN DAGUERREOTYPE (ENLARGED)
Brown University Library

Edgar Allan Poe

TALES AND SKETCHES

Volume 2: 1843–1849

EDITED BY

THOMAS OLLIVE MABBOTT

with the assistance of Eleanor D. Kewer
and Maureen C. Mabbott

UNIVERSITY OF ILLINOIS PRESS
Urbana and Chicago

First Illinois paperback, 2000

Reprinted by arrangement with Harvard University Press

Manufactured in the United States of America
♾ This book is printed on acid-free paper.

Previously published as *Collected Works of Edgar Allan Poe*,
volume 3: *Tales and Sketches, 1843–1849*

Library of Congress Cataloging-in-Publication Data
Poe, Edgar Allan, 1809–1849.
[Selections. 2000]
Tales and sketches / Edgar Allan Poe ;
edited by Thomas Ollive Mabbott with the assistance of
Eleanor D. Kewer and Maureen C. Mabbott. — 1st Illinois pbk.
p. cm.
Originally published as v. 2–3 of: Collected works of Edgar Allan Poe.
Cambridge, Mass. : Belknap Press of Harvard University Press, 1978.
Includes bibliographical references and index.
Contents: v. 1. 1831–1842 — v. 2. 1843-1849.
ISBN 0-252-06922-6 (v. 1 : alk. paper)
ISBN 0-252-06923-4 (v. 2 : alk. paper)
1. Fantasy literature, American. I. Mabbott, Thomas Ollive, 1898–1968.
II. Kewer, Eleanor D. III. Mabbott, Maureen Cobb.
IV. Poe, Edgar Allan, 1809–1849. Works. 1969. V. Title.
PS2612.M33 2000
813'.3—dc21 00-039217

P 5 4 3 2 1

CONTENTS

Volume II

CONTENTS

TALES: 1845–1846

TALES: 1847–1849

SOURCES OF TEXTS COLLATED

ILLUSTRATIONS

VOLUME II

TALES: 1843–1844

THE MYSTERY OF MARIE ROGET

This is a famous tale of historical importance, since it is the first detective story in which an attempt was made to solve a real crime. It has, I feel, enjoyed a higher reputation among general readers than it deserves.*

Reviewing Poe's *Tales* in the *Aristidean* for October 1845 (obviously after discussion with the author), Thomas Dunn English wrote:

> "The Mystery of Marie Roget" has a local, independent of any other, interest. Every one, at all familiar with the internal history of New York, for the last few years, will remember the murder of Mary Rogers, the segar-girl. The deed baffled all attempts of the police to discover the time and mode of its commission, and the identity of the offenders. To this day, with the exception of the light afforded by the tale of Mr. Poe, in which the faculty of analysis is applied to the facts, the whole matter is shrouded in complete mystery. We think, he has proven, very conclusively, that which he attempts. At all events, he has dissipated in our mind, all belief that the murder was perpetrated by more than one.

We may here give a synopsis of what is now known to have happened.† Mary Cecilia Rogers was employed as a cigar girl in

* Dorothy Sayers, however, in her introduction to *The Omnibus of Crime* (1929), p. 18, says that of the Dupin stories – the others being "The Murders in the Rue Morgue" and "The Purloined Letter" – she finds it "the most interesting of all to the connoisseur." [Richard P. Benton, *Studies in Short Fiction,* Winter 1969, agrees with Miss Sayers, and after recounting some of the adverse criticism of Poe's story, sets forth in detail his reasons for believing "The Mystery of Marie Rogêt" is "caviar for the gourmet."]

† In *PMLA,* March 1941, Professor William K. Wimsatt, Jr. published "Poe and the Mystery of Mary Rogers," based on his study of eight contemporary newspapers and all the many later articles he found. Through this morass of "confused and contradictory journalism" he traced the course of events by listing the principal documents in chronological sequence and by citing, with critical comments, news-

the tobacco store of John Anderson on lower Broadway. Cigar girls were usually chosen for their beauty, and Mary was thought the most beautiful in New York.‡ Visitors came from afar to see her, and she was acquainted with the leading newspapermen, whose offices were nearby. Therefore, it is no wonder her mysterious death had sensational news value in a day when the elder James Gordon Bennett had begun to print all the news, without caring if it was fit to print.

Mary's first notable adventure came when her disappearance on October 4, 1838 was sensationally reported by several newspapers the following morning. Within a few days, however, the papers announced her return to the city. There was some suspicion of a hoax, as well as of a proposed suicide, but — retrospectively — James Gordon Bennett in the *New York Herald* of August 3, 1841, said she had eloped with a naval officer.

For nearly three years after this episode, Mary's actions received no public notice. Then on July 25, 1841, after telling her fiancé she was going to visit an aunt, Mary Rogers once again disappeared. Three days later, her body was found floating in the Hudson River and was pulled ashore south of Weehawken at a

---

paper accounts of the official proceedings, as well as influential journalistic theorizing, from July 28 to October 10, 1841. It is rarely necessary to go back of this synoptic article, although I have checked all of Poe's quotations from newspapers, either in person or through librarians. Most of the files are in the New York Society Library, the New-York Historical Society, the American Antiquarian Society, or the Library of Congress. The *Courier and Enquirer* was examined for me by Miss Evelyn Nelson at the State Library, Albany; the *Sunday Mercury* by Mr. T. M. Hodges at Hamilton College, Clinton, New York. Excerpts from the newspapers are given by John Walsh in *Poe the Detective* (1968). These two studies, by Wimsatt and Walsh, are fundamental to any serious consideration of the tale; in the comment and the notes that follow they are frequently cited simply by the author's name.

‡ John Anderson is listed in the New York Business Directory, 1840–1841, as "Importer of Havana & Principe Segars in all their varieties, 321 Broadway, sign of the Indian Chief." On September 13, 1840, the New York *Sunday Morning Atlas* carried a woodcut of a dark-haired beauty proffering a cigar as "The Cigar Girl," No. 22 in an illustrated series, "Portraits of the People." The picture was accompanied by an essay on the recently adopted English practice of hiring pretty girls as clerks in cigar stores for the purpose of attracting the "men about town." Following the essay was a "brief history" emphasizing the dangers of such employment, although in the narrative the virtue of the fictional heroine triumphs and is rewarded. The *Atlas* picture was used again in that paper for August 6, 1841 as a portrait of Mary Rogers (see Walsh, *Poe the Detective*, p. 59).

resort area known as the Elysian Fields in Hoboken, New Jersey. There was a coroner's inquest, briefly noted in a New York paper on July 29, but the news of the death was first taken seriously by the New York *Sunday Mercury* of August 1, 1841.

The binding of the body strongly suggested murder. Gangs of toughs were causing much trouble, and there had been numerous reports of the molestation of women. The newsmen seized on the idea that Mary also had been the victim of a gang. Rumors abounded and were disputed; rewards were offered and increased. Several men were questioned or arrested; one, Joseph Morse, was apprehended as far away as Worcester, Massachusetts. Mary's former employer, John Anderson, was arrested but released for lack of evidence. Her fiancé, Daniel Payne, was also closely scrutinized by the police, as was her former suitor, Alfred Crommelin, whom Mary had attempted to see on the day before she disappeared. A seaman on the *U.S.S. North Carolina* was thrice questioned. He had boarded with Mrs. Rogers in 1840, and called on Mary on July 3, 1841. But he had an alibi to show he was not in Mary's company on the fatal Sunday of July 25.

The murder of so beautiful and well-known a girl was a big story, and it received national attention for many weeks. In the Philadelphia *Saturday Evening Post* of August 14, 1841, the editor, Charles Jacobs Peterson, whom Poe knew as an associate on *Graham's Magazine,* suggested the desirability of "analysis" in the investigation of the Rogers case. This is sometimes thought to have aroused Poe's attention. He went to work, using especially the material in the New York weekly *Brother Jonathan* and the New York *Evening Post.*

The police continued their investigations, and the newspapers their reports, disputes, conjectures, and editorializing. More depositions were taken; the Mayor of New York himself questioned the physician who had performed the coroner's autopsy. Early in September, fragments torn from Mary's clothing were reported found in a thicket at Weehawken, and some six weeks later a coroner's inquest was held on the body of Mary's fiancé, Daniel Payne, discovered dead or dying near the thicket, with a remorseful note nearby. *Brother Jonathan* carried the report in its issue for October 16.

Poe must have completed his story by June 4, 1842, when he wrote George Roberts, editor of the Boston *Notion:*

> It is just possible that you may have seen a tale of mine entitled "The Murders in the Rue Morgue," and published, originally, in "Graham's Magazine" for April 1841. Its *theme* was the exercise of ingenuity in the detection of a murderer. I have just completed a similar article, which I shall entitle "The Mystery of Marie Rogêt – a Sequel to the Murders in the Rue Morgue." The story is based upon the assassination of Mary Cecilia Rogers, which created so vast an excitement, some months ago, in New-York. I have, however, handled my design in a manner altogether *novel* in literature. I have imagined a series of nearly exact *coincidences* occurring in Paris. A young grisette, one Marie Rogêt, has been murdered under precisely similar circumstances with Mary Rogers. Thus, under pretence of showing how Dupin (the hero of "The Rue Morgue") unravelled the mystery of Marie's assassination, I, in reality, enter into a very long and rigorous analysis of the New-York tragedy. No point is omitted. I examine, each by each, the opinions and arguments of the press upon the subject, and show that this subject has been, hitherto, *unapproached.* In fact, I believe not only that I have demonstrated the fallacy of the general idea – that the girl was the victim of a gang of ruffians – but have *indicated the assassin* in a manner which will give renewed impetus to investigation. My main object, nevertheless, as you will readily understand, is an analysis of the true principles which should direct inquiry in similar cases. From the nature of the subject, I feel convinced that the article will excite attention, and it has occurred to me that you would be willing to purchase it for the forthcoming Mammoth Notion. It will make 25 pages of Graham's Magazine; and, at the usual price, would be worth to me $100. For reasons, however, which I need not specify, I am desirous of having this tale printed in Boston, and, if you like it, I will say $50. Will you please write me upon this point? – by return of mail, if possible.

On the same day Poe wrote his friend Dr. J. E. Snodgrass of the *Saturday Visiter,* offering the story to him. The language is similar to that used to Roberts, but Poe was "desirous of publishing it in Baltimore," at the price of forty dollars.§

Poe's dubious action in offering the tale firmly to two publications on the same day he might have justified by arguing that many editors would avoid printing so controversial an article, but it was

§ References to a similar letter to Thomas W. White seem to be based on an auction catalogue of Bangs & Co., New York, May 28, 1897, lot 2302 – actually the letter to Roberts.

the kind of thing that lost him friends when found out. On this occasion, Snodgrass and Roberts would have none of the story.

Ultimately it was taken by Snowden in New York. The first version definitely pointed to a secret lover as the murderer, and the publisher must have decided that such a person, if existing, would hardly bring a suit for libel. It appeared in the *Ladies' Companion* in three installments – November and December 1842 and February 1843.

Two installments were in print when, in November 1842, the case was almost solved by a "confession" – in reality the deathbed words of a delirious woman. On November 18, the daily *New-York Tribune* carried the following article, which was copied in the *Weekly Tribune* and formed the basis of *Brother Jonathan's* account in the November 26 issue:

The Mary Rogers Mystery Explained.

The terrible mystery . . . is at last explained . . . Mrs. Loss, the woman who kept the refreshment house nearest the scene of her death . . . was accidentally wounded by the premature discharge of a gun in the hands of her son; the wound proved fatal; but before she died she sent for Justice Merritt of New Jersey, and told him the facts. On Sunday the 25th of July, 1841, Mary Rogers came to her house in company with a young physician, who undertook to procure for the unfortunate girl a premature delivery. While in the hands of the physician she died, and a consultation was then held as to the disposal of her body. It was finally taken at night by the son of Mrs. Loss and sunk in the river where it was found. Her clothes were first tied up in a bundle and sunk in a pool on the land of Mr. James G. King in that neighborhood; but it was afterwards thought they were not safe there, and they were accordingly taken and scattered through the woods as they were afterwards found. The name of the physician is unknown, but Mayor Morris has been made acquainted with these facts by Mr. Merritt, and we doubt not an immediate inquiry after the guilty wretch will be made . . . No doubt can be entertained of the truth of this confession. It explains many things . . . especially the apathy of the mother of Miss Rogers.*

The month's delay in the publication of the last installment of Poe's story, John Walsh argues persuasively, may have been re-

* Now very well known, this notice was first called to my attention by Walter E. Peck. The sensational murder of Samuel Adams by John C. Colt (which suggested Poe's "Oblong Box"), and Colt's suicide, reported on November 19, were filling the papers, and the "confession" of Mrs. Loss did not receive the attention it might otherwise have been accorded.

quired by the author in order to adjust the text to take account of the new material brought to light through the words of Mrs. Loss. But in the first version he treated Mary Rogers only as the victim of a secret lover. All references to a possible illegal operation were added for the second printing (*Tales*) in 1845.

There is a tradition that it was John Anderson who really instigated Poe's composition of the story. This has been given little attention by my predecessors, but I have come to regard it with respect. The earliest printed reference found is in the *New-York Tribune* of May 27, 1887, in an article headed "They All Thought Anderson Sane." This is a report of the trial of a property suit brought by Anderson's granddaughter, Mrs. Mary Maud Watson. What is pertinent is the following: "Andrew C. Wheeler, known in journalism as 'Nym Crinkle,' testified that while living at Tarrytown he had frequent conversations with Mr. Anderson . . . The witness had heard him speak of the case of Mary Rogers, referring to the 'Marie Roget' of Edgar A. Poe. He did not know that Mr. Anderson paid Poe to write the story in order to divert suspicion from himself." This negative statement has a positive corollary; there must have been a notion current that Anderson did employ Poe. Since he had done nothing criminal – although he may have given Mary money at her request – Anderson certainly had good reason to desire such an "analysis" as Peterson of the *Saturday Evening Post* had suggested.

It would hardly be possible to prove the story, but several circumstances tend to confirm it. The most significant is that Anderson was on good terms with Poe in 1845, even after "The Mystery of Marie Rogêt" had been published in the revised version, with footnotes identifying the characters in the narrative with their actual counterparts. On November 8, 1845, two weeks after Poe's name first appeared as "Editor and Proprietor" of the *Broadway Journal,* the paper ran an advertisement which was carried in all later issues: "JOHN ANDERSON & CO.,/Importers and dealers in/CHOICE SEGARS, and Manufacturers of Premium/Tobacco and Snuffs – 2 Wall, and 13 and 15 Duane streets,/New York. nov 8 – 3m." The final abbreviation indicates that the advertisement was to be inserted for three months, and presumably was paid for in advance. No other tobacconist advertised in Poe's paper, and John Anderson was too keen a man of business to suppose the *Broadway Journal* would bring in much trade. It was precisely at the time Poe's magazine was in difficulty that Anderson helped the "Editor and Proprietor" financially. The case is certainly not complete, but Anderson was far too discreet to have negotiated with Poe in writing.

Anderson's connection with the case was more fully revealed in a suit in 1891–1892 brought by his daughter, Laura V. Appleton, to break the will of her late father, who had become a millionaire. His business partner, Felix McCloskey, testified that Anderson, speaking of Mary Rogers, told him that "an abortion had been committed on the girl — the year before her murder took place — or a year and a half — something of that kind — and that he got into some trouble about it — and outside of *that* there was no grounds on earth for anybody to suppose he had anything to do with the murder"; and that at another time Anderson said of her death that "he *hadn't* anything *directly, himself,* to do with it."†

Whatever the case, and despite Poe's exoneration of him in "The Mystery of Marie Rogêt," John Anderson's life was thereafter shadowed by the tragedy; so much so that because of it he refused to run for Mayor of New York, and in his declining years he became convinced that he communed with the ghost of the murdered girl.

It is natural to take an author at his word about his work and assume that Poe analyzed the case completely, as his own introduc-

† See Samuel Copp Worthen in *Proceedings of the New Jersey Historical Society,* April 1942, and in *American Literature,* November 1948. He used a copy of the testimony in the suit. Commenting on Worthen's articles, Professor Wimsatt (whose very important article in *PMLA* for March 1941 is described in the second footnote above) remarked in *American Literature* for January 1950: "Anderson's responsibility may have gone no further than that earlier push which he had given her on the downward path." Worthen, however, careful to use only sworn testimony, did not print the plain statement to him of Mrs. Appleton that her father regarded himself remorsefully as *in a way* responsible for Mary's death. Mr. Worthen told me all this, and I reveal it, years after his death, because of Wimsatt's argument that less might be implied by what Worthen printed.

tory footnote suggests, but that note is by no means unequivocal or candid. He was right in three things: he demolished the gang theory, he cleared John Anderson, and he regarded the delayed discovery of the dead girl's clothes as contrived; but he did not solve the mystery.‡

TEXTS

(A) Snowden's *Ladies' Companion* for November, December 1842, and February 1843 (18:15–20, 93–99, 162–167); *(B)* *Tales* (1845), pp. 151–199; *(C)* J. Lorimer Graham copy of *Tales* (*B*) with manuscript revisions (1849); (*D*) *Works* (1850), I, 213–261; PHANTASY-PIECES, title only, canceled.

The J. Lorimer Graham copy of *Tales* (*C*) is followed. In the table of contents of PHANTASY-PIECES (1842) "The Mystery of Marie Rogêt" is named, but crossed out, because the story was not yet completely printed. None of the printed texts use the accent in the title.

It is probable that Poe made changes for the delayed third installment, but if so we do not know what they were. We can, however, see in the variants the few ingenious deletions and additions he made for the second printing in *Tales* (*B*). We know that Poe revised carefully the twelve stories Duyckinck had chosen for this book, but the revisions in "The Mystery of Marie Rogêt" had to take account of more than the usual author's improvements. To make his story conform to the true mystery he had analyzed, Poe felt compelled to add and subtract details to suggest an abortion death, and to manufacture other details in his first footnote so that it would appear he had been right all along. Wimsatt (*PMLA,* pp. 242–243) first discovered the significance of these changes and Walsh (*Poe the Detective,* pp. 69–71) presents the deletions and additions in the text dramatically with, as he says, "some measure of admiration." He reprints the *Tales* text with the some 150 words involved in boldface type, but he does not use the Lorimer Graham copy, and thus misses Poe's last effort to make his story conform to the facts. See note 5, below.

‡ In addition to the literature cited above, there are many lesser discussions of the Rogers case, some of them eccentric or otherwise worthless. The *National Police Gazette,* November 28, 1846, suggested (with some reason) that the notorious abortionist Madame Restelle had something to do with the case (see Edward Van Every, *Sins of New York,* New York, 1930, p. 98). The *Confession* of Charles Wallace (New Orleans, 1851) includes a fictional account of how that malefactor murdered Mary Rogers. There is something on the Rogers case in *The Tale of a Physician* (1869) by Andrew Jackson Davis. J. H. Ingraham's *The Beautiful Cigar Girl* (New York, 1844) relates only remotely to Mary. An article by Will M. Clemens in the *Era Magazine,* November 1904, is perhaps deliberately misleading. Two decades later, Irving Wallace, in *The Fabulous Originals* (1955), suggested that Poe was the murderer – a bit of ironic humor, I suppose, which may have been taken seriously by some readers. Other details have come to light in recent years, but of a confession of a second person, mentioned by Poe in his introductory footnote, no trace has ever been found.

THE MYSTERY OF MARIE ROGET.* [*C*]

A SEQUEL TO "THE MURDERS IN THE RUE MORGUE."

Es giebt eine Reihe idealischer Begebenheiten, die der Wirklichkeit parallel lauft. Selten fallen sie zusammen. Menschen und Züfalle modificiren gewöhnlich die idealische Begebenheit, so dass sie unvollkommen erscheint, und ihre Folgen gleichfalls unvollkommen sind. So bei der Reformation; statt des Protestantismus kam das Lutherthum hervor.

There are ideal series of events which run parallel with the real ones. They rarely coincide. Men and circumstances generally modify the ideal train of events, so that it seems imperfect, and its consequences are equally imperfect. Thus with the Reformation; instead of Protestantism came Lutheranism. — Novalis.†

Moralische[a] *Ansichten.*

There are few persons, even among the calmest thinkers, who have not occasionally been startled into a vague yet thrilling half-credence in the supernatural, by *coincidences* of so seemingly marvellous a character that, as *mere* coincidences, the intellect has been unable to receive them. Such sentiments — for the half-credences of which I speak have never the full force of *thought* —

* On[b] the original publication of "Marie Rogêt," the foot-notes now appended were considered unnecessary; but the lapse of several years since the tragedy upon which the tale is based, renders it expedient to give them, and also to say a few words in explanation of the general design. A young girl, *Mary Cecilia Rogers,* was murdered in the vicinity of New York; and, although her death occasioned an intense and long-enduring excitement, the mystery attending it had remained unsolved at the period when the present paper was written and published (November, 1842). Herein, under pretence of relating the fate of a Parisian *grisette,* the author has followed, in minute detail, the essential, while merely paralleling the inessential facts of the real murder of Mary Rogers. Thus all argument founded upon the fiction is applicable to the truth: and the investigation of the truth was the object.

The "Mystery of Marie Rogêt" was composed at a distance from the scene of the atrocity, and with no other means of investigation than the newspapers afforded. Thus much escaped the writer of which he could have availed himself had he been on[c] the spot, and visited the localities. It may not be improper to record, nevertheless, that the confessions of *two* persons, (one of them the Madame Deluc of the narrative) made, at different periods, long subsequent to the publication, confirmed, in full, not only the general conclusion, but absolutely *all* the chief hypothetical details by which that conclusion was attained.[1]

† The *nom de plume* of Von Hardenburg.

Title: The starred footnote was omitted in A, as were all Poe's other footnotes except that on the motto and that referring to "The Murders in the Rue Morgue"; most are not noticed individually in the variants below.

Motto: gewöhnlich *is misprinted* gewohulich *(A, B, C, D).*

a Moral *(A, B, C, D) corrected editorially.*

b Upon *(B, D)*

c upon *(B, D)*

are[d] seldom thoroughly stifled unless by reference to the doctrine of chance, or, as it is technically termed, the Calculus of Probabilities.[2] Now this Calculus is, in its essence, purely mathematical; and thus we have the anomaly of the most rigidly exact in science applied to the shadow and spirituality of the most intangible in speculation.

The extraordinary details which I am now called upon to make public, will be found to form, as regards sequence of time, the primary branch of a series of scarcely intelligible *coincidences,* whose secondary or concluding branch will be recognized by all readers in the late murder of MARY CECILIA ROGERS, at New York.

When, in an article entitled "The Murders in the Rue Morgue," I endeavored, about a year ago, to depict some very remarkable features in the mental character of my friend, the Chevalier C. Auguste Dupin, it did not occur to me that I should ever resume the subject. This depicting of character constituted my design; and this design was[e] fulfilled in the[f] train of circumstances brought to instance Dupin's idiosyncrasy. I might have adduced other examples, but I[g] should have proven no more. Late events, however, in their surprising development, have startled me into some farther details, which will carry with them the air of extorted confession. Hearing what I have lately heard, it would be indeed strange should I remain[h] silent in regard to what I both heard and saw so long ago.

Upon the winding up of the tragedy involved in the deaths of Madame L'Espanaye and her daughter, the Chevalier dismissed the affair at once from his attention, and relapsed into his old habits of moody[i] reverie. Prone, at all times, to abstraction, I readily fell in with his humor; and, continuing to occupy our chambers in the Faubourg Saint Germain, we gave the Future to the winds, and slumbered tranquilly in the Present, weaving the dull world around us into dreams.

But these dreams were not altogether uninterrupted. It may readily be supposed that the part played by my friend, in the

---

d such sentiments are *(A, B, D)*
e was thoroughly *(A, B, D)*
f the wild *(A, B, D)*
g it *(A)*
h remain longer *(A)*
i moody and fantastic *(A)*

drama at the Rue Morgue, had not failed of its impression upon the fancies of the Parisian police. With its emissaries, the name of Dupin had grown into a household word. The simple character of those inductions by which he had disentangled the mystery never having been explained even to the Prefect, or to any other individual than myself, of course it is not surprising that the affair was regarded as[j] little less than miraculous, or that the Chevalier's analytical abilities acquired for him the credit of intuition. His frankness would have led him to disabuse every inquirer of such prejudice; but his indolent humor forbade all farther agitation of[k] a topic whose interest to himself had long ceased. It thus happened that he found himself the cynosure of the policial eyes; and the cases were not few in which attempt was made to engage his services at the Prefecture. [l]One of the most remarkable instances was that[l] of the murder of a young girl named Marie Rogêt.

This event occurred about two years after the atrocity in the Rue Morgue. Marie, whose Christian and family name will at once arrest attention from their resemblance to those of the unfortunate "cigar-girl,"[m] was the only daughter of the widow Estelle Rogêt. The father had died during the child's infancy, and from the period of his death, until within eighteen months before the assassination which forms the subject of our narrative, the mother and daughter had dwelt together in the Rue Pavée Saint Andrée;* Madame there keeping a *pension,* assisted by Marie. Affairs went on thus until the latter had attained her twenty-second year, when her great beauty attracted the notice of a perfumer, who occupied one of the shops in the basement of the Palais Royal, and whose custom lay chiefly among the desperate adventurers infesting that neighborhood. Monsieur Le Blanc† was not unaware of the advantages to be derived from the attendance of the fair Marie in his perfumery;[n] and his liberal proposals were accepted eagerly by

* Nassau Street.
† Anderson.

j *Omitted (A)*
k on *(A)*
l . . . l The only instance, nevertheless, in which such attempt proved successful, was the instance to which I have already alluded – that *(A)*
m "segar-girl," *(A)*
n *parfumerie; (A)*

the girl, although[o] with somewhat more of[p] hesitation by Madame.[3]

The anticipations of the shopkeeper were realized, and his rooms soon became notorious through the charms of the sprightly *grisette.* She had been in his employ about a year, when her admirers were thrown into confusion by her sudden disappearance from the shop. Monsieur Le Blanc was unable to account for her absence, and Madame Rogêt was distracted with anxiety and terror. The public papers immediately took up the theme, and the police were upon the point of making serious investigations, when, one fine morning, after the lapse of a week, Marie, in good health, but with a somewhat saddened air, made her re-appearance at her usual counter in the perfumery.[q] All inquiry, except that of a private character, was of course immediately hushed. Monsieur Le Blanc professed total ignorance, as before. Marie, with Madame, replied to all questions, that the last week had been spent at the house of a relation in the country. Thus the affair died away, and was generally forgotten; for the girl, ostensibly to relieve herself from the impertinence of curiosity, soon bade a final adieu to the perfumer, and sought the shelter of her mother's residence in the Rue Pavée Saint Andrée.[4]

It was about three years[r] after this return home, that her friends were alarmed by her sudden disappearance for the second time. Three days elapsed, and nothing was heard of her. On the fourth her corpse was found floating in the Seine,* near the shore which is opposite the Quartier of the Rue Saint Andrée, and at a point not very far distant from the secluded neighborhood of the Barrière du Roule.†[5]

The atrocity of this murder, (for it was at once evident that murder had been committed,) the youth and beauty of the victim, and, above all, her previous notoriety, conspired to produce intense excitement in the minds of the sensitive Parisians. I can call to mind no similar occurrence producing so general and so intense an effect. For several weeks, in the discussion[s] of this one

* The Hudson.

† Weehawken.

o but *(A)*

p *Omitted (A)*

q *parfumerie. (A)*

r three years/five months *(A, B, D)*

s discussing *(A)*

absorbing theme, even the momentous political topics of the day were forgotten. The Prefect made unusual exertions; and the powers of the whole Parisian police were, of course, tasked to the utmost extent.

Upon the first discovery of the corpse, it was not supposed that the murderer would be able to elude, for more than a very brief period, the inquisition which was immediately set on foot. It was not until the expiration of a week that it was deemed necessary to offer a reward; and even then this reward was limited to a thousand francs. In the mean time the investigation proceeded with vigor, if not always with judgment, and numerous individuals were examined to no purpose; while, owing to the continual absence of all clue to the mystery, the popular excitement[t] greatly increased. At the end of the tenth day it was thought advisable to double the sum originally proposed; and, at length, the second week having elapsed without leading to any discoveries, and the prejudice which always exists in Paris against the Police having given vent to itself in several serious *émeutes,*[6] the Prefect took it upon himself to offer the sum of twenty thousand francs "for the conviction of the assassin," or, if more than one should prove to have been implicated, "for the conviction of any one of the assassins." In the proclamation setting forth this reward, a full pardon was promised to any accomplice who should come forward in evidence against his fellow; and to the whole was appended, wherever it appeared, the private placard of a committee of citizens, offering ten thousand francs, in addition to the amount proposed by the Prefecture.[7] The entire reward thus stood at no less than thirty thousand francs, which will be regarded as an extraordinary sum when we consider the humble condition of the girl, and the great frequency, in large cities, of such atrocities as the one described.

No one doubted now that the mystery of this murder would be immediately brought to light. But although, in one or two instances, arrests were made which promised elucidation, yet nothing was elicited which could implicate the parties suspected; and they were discharged forthwith.[8] Strange as it may appear, the

---

t excitement became *(A)*

third week from the discovery of the body had passed, and passed without any light being thrown upon the subject, before even a rumor of the events which had so agitated the public mind, reached the ears of Dupin and myself.[9] Engaged in researches which had absorbed our whole attention, it had been nearly a month since either of us had gone abroad, or received a visiter, or more than glanced at the leading political articles in one of the daily papers. The first intelligence of the murder was brought us by G——, in person.[10] He called upon us early in the afternoon of the thirteenth of July, 18—, and remained with us until late in the night. He had been piqued by the failure of all his endeavors to ferret out the assassins. His reputation — so he said with a peculiarly Parisian air — was at stake. Even his honor was concerned. The eyes of the public were upon him; and there was really no sacrifice which he would not be willing to make for the development of the mystery. He concluded a somewhat droll speech with a compliment upon what[u] he was pleased to term the *tact* of Dupin, and made him a direct, and certainly a liberal proposition, the precise nature of which I do not feel myself at liberty to disclose, but which has no bearing upon the proper subject of my narrative.

The compliment my friend rebutted as best he could, but the proposition he accepted at once, although its advantages were altogether provisional. This point being settled, the Prefect broke forth at once into explanations of his own views, interspersing them with long comments upon the evidence; of which latter we were not yet in possession. He discoursed much, and beyond doubt, learnedly; while I hazarded an occasional suggestion as the night wore drowsily away. Dupin, sitting steadily in his accustomed arm-chair, was the embodiment of respectful attention. He wore spectacles, during the whole interview; and an occasional glance beneath their green glasses,[11] sufficed to convince me that he slept not the less soundly, because silently, throughout the seven or eight leaden-footed hours which immediately preceded the departure of the Prefect.

In the morning, I procured, at the Prefecture, a full report of

u which *(A)*

all the evidence elicited, and, at the various newspaper offices, a copy of every paper in which, from first to last, had been published any decisive information in regard to this sad affair. Freed from all that was positively disproved, this mass of information stood thus:

Marie Rogêt left the residence of her mother, in the Rue Pavée St. Andrée, about nine o'clock in the morning of Sunday, June the twenty-second, 18—.[12] In going out, she gave notice to a Monsieur Jacques St.[v] Eustache,* and to him only, of her intention to spend the day with an aunt who resided in the Rue des Drômes.[13] The Rue des Drômes is a short and narrow but populous thoroughfare, not far from the banks of the river, and at a distance of some two miles, in the most direct course possible, from the *pension* of Madame Rogêt. St. Eustache was the accepted suitor of Marie, and lodged, as well as took his meals, at the *pension*. He was to have gone for his betrothed at dusk, and to have escorted her home. In the afternoon, however, it came on to rain heavily; and, supposing that she would remain all night at her aunt's, (as she had done under similar circumstances before,) he did not think it necessary to keep his promise.[14] As night drew on, Madame Rogêt (who was an infirm old lady, seventy years of age,) was heard to express a fear "that she should never see Marie again;" but this observation attracted little attention at the time.[15]

On Monday, it was ascertained that the girl had not been to the Rue des Drômes; and when the day elapsed without tidings of her, a tardy search was instituted at several points in the city, and its environs.[16] It was not, however, until the fourth day from the period of her disappearance that any thing satisfactory was ascertained respecting her. On this day, (Wednesday, the twenty-fifth of June,) a Monsieur Beauvais,† who, with a friend, had been making inquiries for Marie near the Barrière du Roule, on the shore of the Seine which is opposite the Rue Pavée St. Andrée,[17] was informed that a corpse had just been towed ashore by some fishermen, who had found it floating in the river. Upon seeing the

* Payne.
† Crommelin.

v *Omitted (A)*

body, Beauvais, after some hesitation, identified it as that of the perfumery-girl. His friend recognized it more promptly.[18]

The face was suffused with dark blood, some of which issued from the mouth. No foam was seen, as in the case of the merely drowned. There was no discoloration in the cellular tissue. About the throat were bruises and impressions of fingers. The arms were bent over on the chest and were rigid. The right hand was clenched; the left partially open. On the left wrist were two circular excoriations, apparently the effect of ropes, or of a rope in more than one volution. A part of the right wrist, also, was much chafed, as well as the back throughout its extent, but more especially at the shoulder-blades. In bringing the body to the shore the fishermen had attached to it a rope; but none of the excoriations had been effected by this. The flesh of the neck was much swollen. There were no cuts apparent, or bruises which appeared the effect of blows. A piece of lace was found tied so tightly around the neck as to be hidden from sight; it was completely buried in the flesh, and was fastened by a knot which lay just under the left ear. This alone would have sufficed to produce death. The medical testimony spoke confidently of the virtuous character of the deceased. She had been [w]subjected, it said, to[w] brutal violence. The corpse was in such condition when found, that there could have been no difficulty in its recognition by friends.[19]

The dress was much torn and otherwise disordered. In the outer garment, a slip, about a foot wide, had been torn upward from the bottom hem to the waist, but not torn off. It was wound three times around the waist, and secured by a sort of hitch in the back. The dress immediately beneath the frock was of fine muslin; and from this a slip eighteen inches wide had been torn entirely out — torn very evenly and with great care. It was found around her neck, fitting loosely, and secured with a hard knot. Over this muslin slip and the slip of lace, the strings of a bonnet were attached; the bonnet being appended. The knot by which the strings of the bonnet were fastened, was not a lady's, but a slip or sailor's knot.[20]

---

w . . . w subjected to *(A)*

After the recognition of the corpse, it was not, as usual, taken to the Morgue, (this formality being superfluous,) but hastily interred not far from the spot at which it was brought ashore.[21] Through the exertions of Beauvais, the matter was industriously hushed up, as far as possible; and several days had elapsed before any public emotion resulted. A weekly paper,* however, at length took up the theme;[22] the corpse was disinterred, and a re-examination instituted; but[x] nothing was elicited beyond what has been already noted. The clothes, however, were now submitted to the mother and friends of the deceased, and fully identified as those worn by the girl upon leaving home.[23]

Meantime, the excitement increased hourly. Several individuals were arrested and discharged. St. Eustache fell especially under suspicion; and he failed, at first, to give an intelligible account of his whereabouts during the Sunday on which Marie left home. Subsequently, however, he submitted to Monsieur G——, affidavits, accounting satisfactorily for every hour of the day in question.[24] As time passed and no discovery ensued, a thousand contradictory rumors were circulated, and journalists busied themselves in *suggestions.* Among these, the one which attracted the most notice, was the idea that Marie Rogêt still lived – that the corpse found in the Seine was that of some other unfortunate.[25] It will be proper that I submit to the reader some passages which embody the suggestion alluded to. These passages are *literal* translations from L'Etoile,† a paper[y] conducted, in general, with much ability.[26]

"Mademoiselle Rogêt left her mother's house on Sunday morning, June the twenty-second, 18–, with the ostensible purpose of going to see her aunt, or some other connexion, in the Rue des Drômes. From that hour, nobody is proved to have seen her. There is no trace or tidings of her at all. * * * * There has no person, whatever, come forward, so far, who saw her at all, on that day, after she left her mother's door. * * * * Now, though we have no evidence that Marie Rogêt was in the land of the living after nine o'clock on Sunday, June the twenty-second, we have proof that, up to that hour, she was alive. On Wednesday noon, at twelve, a female body was discovered afloat on the shore of the Barrière du Roule. This was, even if we presume that Marie Rogêt was thrown into the river within three hours after she left her mother's house, only three days from the time she left

* The "N. Y. Mercury."

† The "N. Y. Brother Jonathan," edited by H. Hastings Weld, Esq.

x and *(A)*

y small daily print *(A)*

her home – three days to an hour. But it is folly to suppose that the murder, if murder was committed on her body, could have been consummated soon enough to have enabled her murderers to throw the body into the river before midnight. Those who are guilty of such horrid crimes, choose darkness rather than light. * * * * Thus we see that if the body found in the river *was* that of Marie Rogêt, it could only have been in the water two and a half days, or three at the outside. All experience has shown that drowned bodies, or bodies thrown into the water immediately after death by violence, require from six to ten days for sufficient decomposition to take place to bring them to the top of the water. Even where a cannon is fired over a corpse, and it rises before at least five or six days' immersion, it sinks again, if left alone. Now, we ask, what was there in this case to cause a departure from the ordinary course of nature? * * * * If the body had been kept in its mangled state on shore until Tuesday night, some trace would be found on shore of the murderers. It is a doubtful point, also, whether the body would be so soon afloat, even were it thrown in after having been dead two days. And, furthermore, it is exceedingly improbable that any villains who had committed such a murder as is here supposed, would have thrown the body in without weight to sink it, when such a precaution could have so easily been taken."[27]

The editor here proceeds to argue that the body must have been in the water "not three days merely, but, at least, five times three days," because it was so far decomposed that Beauvais had great difficulty in recognizing it. This latter point, however, was fully disproved.[28] I[z] continue the[a] translation:

"What, then, are the facts on which M. Beauvais says that he has no doubt the body was that of Marie Rogêt? He ripped up the gown sleeve, and says he found marks which satisfied him of the identity. The public generally supposed those marks to have consisted of some description of scars. He rubbed the arm and found *hair* upon it – something as indefinite, we think, as can readily be imagined – as little conclusive as finding an arm in the sleeve. M. Beauvais did not return that night, but sent word to Madame Rogêt, at seven o'clock, on Wednesday evening, that an investigation was still in progress respecting her daughter. If we allow that Madame Rogêt, from her age and grief, could not go over, (which is allowing a great deal,) there certainly must have been some one who would have thought it worth while to go over and attend the investigation, if they thought the body was that of Marie. Nobody went over. There was nothing said or heard about the matter in the Rue Pavée St. Andrée, that reached even the occupants of the same building. M. St. Eustache, the lover and intended husband of Marie, who boarded in her mother's house, deposes that he did not hear of the discovery of the body of his intended until the next morning, when M. Beauvais came into his chamber and told him of it. For an item of news like this, it strikes us it was very coolly received."[29]

In this way the journal endeavored to create the impression of

z We *(A)* a our *(A)*

an apathy on the part of the relatives of Marie, inconsistent with the supposition that these relatives believed the corpse to be hers. Its insinuations amount to this: – that Marie, with the connivance of her friends, had absented herself from the city for reasons involving a charge against her chastity; and that these friends, upon the discovery of a corpse in the Seine, somewhat resembling that of the girl, had availed themselves of the opportunity to impress the public with the belief of her death. But[b] L'Etoile was again overhasty. It was distinctly proved that no apathy, such as was imagined, existed; that the old lady was exceedingly feeble, and so agitated as to be unable to attend to any duty; that St. Eustache, so far from receiving the news coolly, was distracted with grief, and bore himself so frantically, that M. Beauvais prevailed upon a friend and relative to take charge of him, and prevent his attending the examination at the disinterment. Moreover, although it was stated by L'Etoile, that the corpse was re-interred at the public expense – that an advantageous offer of private sepulture was absolutely declined by the family – and that no member of the family attended the ceremonial: – although, I say, all this was asserted by L'Etoile in furtherance of the impression it designed to convey – yet *all* this was satisfactorily disproved.[30] In a subsequent number of the paper, an attempt was made to throw suspicion upon Beauvais himself. The editor says:

"Now, then, a change comes over the matter. We are told that, on one occasion, while a Madame B –– was at Madame Rogêt's house, M. Beauvais, who was going out, told her that a *gendarme* was expected there, and that she, Madame B., must not say anything to the *gendarme* until he returned, but let the matter be for him. * * * * In the present posture of affairs, M. Beauvais appears to have the whole matter locked up in his head. A single step cannot be taken without M. Beauvais; for, go which way you will, you run against him. * * * * * For some reason, he determined that nobody shall have any thing to do with the proceedings but himself, and he has elbowed the male relatives out of the way, according to their representations, in a very singular manner. He seems to have been very much averse to permitting the relatives to see the body."[31]

[c]By the following fact, some[c] color was given to the suspicion thus thrown upon Beauvais.[d] A visiter at his office, a few days prior

b But the *(A)*
c . . . c Some *(A)*
d Beauvais, by the following fact. *(A)*

to the girl's disappearance, and during the absence of its occupant, had observed *a rose* in the key-hole of the door, and the name *"Marie"* inscribed upon a slate which hung near at hand.[32]

The general impression, so far as we were enabled to glean it from the newspapers, seemed to be, that Marie had been the victim of *a gang* of desperadoes – that by these she had been borne across the river, maltreated and murdered.[33] Le Commerciel,* however, a print of extensive influence, was earnest in combating this popular idea. I quote a passage or two from its columns:

> "We are persuaded that pursuit has hitherto been on a false scent, so far as it has been directed to the Barrière du Roule. It is impossible that a person so well known to thousands as this young woman was, should have passed three blocks without some one having seen her; and any one who saw her would have remembered it, for she interested all who knew her. It was when the streets were full of people, when she went out. * * * It is impossible that she could have gone to the Barrière du Roule, or to the Rue des Drômes, without being recognized by a dozen persons; yet no one has come forward who saw her outside of her mother's door, and there is no evidence, except the testimony concerning her *expressed intentions,* that she did go out at all. Her gown was torn, bound round her, and tied; and by that the body was carried as a bundle. If the murder had been committed at the Barrière du Roule, there would have been no necessity for any such arrangement. The fact that the body was found floating near the Barrière, is no proof as to where it was thrown into the water. * * * * * A piece of one of the unfortunate girl's petticoats, two feet long and one foot wide, was torn out and tied under her chin around the back of her head, probably to prevent screams. This was done by fellows who had no pocket-handkerchief."[34]

A day or two before the Prefect called upon us, however, some important information reached the police, which seemed to overthrow, at least, the chief portion of Le Commerciel's argument. Two small boys, sons of a Madame Deluc, while roaming among the woods near the Barrière du Roule, chanced to penetrate a close thicket, within which were three or four large stones, forming a kind of seat, with a back and footstool. On the upper stone lay a white petticoat; on the second a silk scarf. A parasol, gloves, and a pocket-handkerchief were also here found. The handkerchief bore the name "Marie Rogêt." Fragments of dress were discovered on the brambles around. The earth was trampled, the bushes were broken, and there was every evidence of a struggle. Between the thicket and the river, the fences were found taken down, and the

* N. Y. "Journal of Commerce."

ground bore evidence of some heavy burthen having been dragged along it.[35]

A weekly paper, Le Soleil,* had the following comments upon this discovery — comments which merely echoed the sentiment of the whole Parisian press:

"The things had all evidently been there at least three or four weeks; they were all mildewed down hard with the action of the rain, and stuck together from mildew. The grass had grown around and over some of them. The silk on the parasol was strong, but the threads of it were run together within. The upper part, where it had been doubled and folded, was all mildewed and rotten, and tore on its being opened. * * * * The pieces of her frock torn out by the bushes were about three inches wide and six inches long. One part was the hem of the frock, and it had been mended; the other piece was part of the skirt, not the hem. They looked like strips torn off, and were on the thorn bush, about a foot from the ground. * * * * * There can be no doubt, therefore, that the spot of this appalling outrage has been discovered."[36]

Consequent upon this discovery, new evidence appeared. Madame Deluc testified that she keeps a roadside inn not far from the bank of the river, opposite the Barrière du Roule. The neighborhood is secluded — particularly so. It is the usual Sunday resort of blackguards from the city, who cross the river in boats. About three o'clock, in the afternoon of the Sunday in question, a young girl arrived at the inn, accompanied by a young man of dark complexion. The two remained here for some time. On their departure, they took the road to some thick woods in the vicinity. Madame Deluc's attention was called to the dress worn by the girl, on account of its resemblance to one worn by a deceased relative. A scarf was particularly noticed. Soon after the departure of the couple, a gang of miscreants made their appearance, behaved boisterously, ate and drank without making payment, followed in the route of the young man and girl, returned to the inn about dusk, and re-crossed the river as if in great haste.

It was soon after dark, upon this same evening, that Madame Deluc, as well as her eldest son, heard the screams of a female in the vicinity of the inn. The screams were violent but brief. Madame D. recognized not only the scarf which was found in the thicket,

* Phil. "Sat. Evening Post," edited by C. J.[e] Peterson, Esq.

e *Peterson's middle name was Jacobs, hence* J *is printed for the* I *of the original texts (B, C, D)*

but the dress which was discovered upon the corpse.[37] An omnibus-driver, Valence,* now also testified that he saw Marie Rogêt cross a ferry on the Seine, on the Sunday in question, in company with a young man of dark complexion. He, Valence, knew Marie, and could not be mistaken in her identity. The articles found in the thicket were fully identified by the relatives of Marie.[38]

The items of evidence and information thus collected by myself, from the newspapers, at the suggestion of Dupin, embraced only one more point — but this was a point of seemingly vast consequence. It appears that, immediately after the discovery of the clothes as above described, the lifeless, or nearly lifeless body of St. Eustache, Marie's betrothed, was found in the vicinity of what all now supposed the scene of the outrage. A phial labelled "laudanum," and emptied, was found near him. His breath gave evidence of the poison. He died without speaking. Upon his person was found a letter, briefly stating his love for Marie, with his design of self-destruction.[39]

"I need scarcely tell you," said Dupin, as he finished the perusal of my notes, "that this is a far more intricate case than that of the Rue Morgue; from which it differs in one important respect. This is an *ordinary,* although an atrocious instance of crime. There is nothing peculiarly *outré* about it. You will observe that, for this reason, the mystery has been considered easy, when, for this reason, it should have been considered difficult, of solution. Thus, at first, it was thought unnecessary to offer a reward. The myrmidons[40] of G—— were able at once to comprehend how and why such an atrocity *might have been* committed. They could[f] picture to their imaginations a mode — many modes — and a motive — many motives; and because it was not impossible that either of these numerous modes and motives *could* have been the actual one, they have taken it for granted that one of them *must.* But the ease with which these variable fancies were entertained, and the very plausibility which each assumed, should have been understood as indicative rather of the difficulties than of the facilities which must attend elucidation. I have before observed that it is by prominences above the plane of the ordinary, that reason feels her way, if at all, in her

* Adam.

search for the true,[41] and that the proper question in cases such as this, is not so much 'what has occurred?' as 'what has occurred that has never occurred before?' In the investigations at the house of Madame L'Espanaye,[g]* the agents of G——were discouraged and confounded by that very *unusualness* which, to a properly regulated intellect, would have afforded the surest[h] omen of success; while this same intellect might have been plunged in despair at the[i] ordinary character of all that met the eye in the case of the perfumery-girl, and yet[j] told of nothing but easy triumph to the functionaries of the Prefecture.

"In the case of Madame L'Espanaye[k] and her daughter, there was, even at the beginning of our investigation, no doubt that murder had been committed. The idea of suicide was excluded at once. Here, too, we are freed, at the commencement, from all supposition of self-murder. The body found at the Barrière du Roule, was found under such circumstances as to leave us no room for embarrassment upon this important point. But it has been suggested that the corpse discovered, is not that of the Marie Rogêt for the conviction of whose assassin, or assassins, the reward is offered, and respecting whom, solely, our agreement has been arranged with the Prefect. We both know this gentleman well. It will not do to trust him too far. If, dating our inquiries from the body found, and thence tracing a murderer, we yet discover this body to be that of some other individual than Marie; or, if starting from the living Marie, we find her, yet find her unassassinated — in either case we lose our labor; since it is Monsieur G—— with whom we have to deal. For our own purpose, therefore, if not for the purpose of justice, it is indispensable that our first step should be the determination of the identity of the corpse with the Marie Rogêt who is missing.

[l]"With the public the arguments of L'Etoile[l] have had weight; and that the journal itself is convinced of their importance would

* See "Murders in the Rue Morgue."

f would *(A)*
g Espanage, *(A)*
h sweet *(A)*
i the *especially (A)*
j *Omitted (A)*
k Espanage *(A)*
l . . . l "I know not what effect the arguments of 'L'Etoile' may have wrought upon your own understanding. With the public they *(A)*

appear from the manner in which it commences one of its essays upon the subject — 'Several of the morning papers of the day,' it says, 'speak of the *conclusive* article in Monday's Etoile.'[42] To me, this article appears conclusive of little beyond the zeal of its inditer. We should bear in mind that, in general, it is the object of our newspapers rather to create a sensation — to make a point — than to further the cause of truth. The latter end is only pursued when it seems coincident with the former. The print which merely falls in with ordinary opinion (however well founded this opinion may be) earns for itself no credit with the mob. The mass of the people regard as profound only him who suggests *pungent contradictions* of the general idea. In ratiocination, not less than in[m] literature, it is the *epigram* which is the most immediately and the most universally appreciated. In both, it is of the lowest order of merit.

"What I mean to say is, that it is the mingled epigram and melodrame of the idea, that Marie Rogêt still lives, rather than any true plausibility in this idea, which have[n] suggested it to L'Etoile, and secured it a favorable reception with the public.[43] Let us examine the heads of this journal's[o] argument; endeavoring to avoid the incoherence with which it is originally set forth.

"The first aim of the writer is to show, from the brevity of the interval between Marie's disappearance and the finding of the floating corpse, that this corpse cannot be that of Marie. The reduction of this interval to its smallest possible dimension, becomes thus, at once, an object with the reasoner. In the rash pursuit of this object, he rushes into mere assumption at the outset. 'It is folly to suppose,' he says, 'that the murder, if murder was committed on her body, could[p] have been consummated soon enough to have enabled her murderers to throw the body into the river before midnight.'[44] We demand at once, and very naturally, *why?* Why is it folly to suppose that the murder was committed *within five minutes* after the girl's quitting her mother's house? Why is it folly to suppose that the murder was committed at any given period of the day? There have been assassinations at all hours. But, had the murder taken place at any moment between nine o'clock in

m *Omitted (A)*
n has *(A)*
o this journal's/the *(A)*
p would *(A)*

the morning of Sunday,[45] and a quarter before midnight, there would still have been time enough 'to throw the body into the river before midnight.' This assumption, then, amounts precisely to this — that the murder was not committed on Sunday at all — and, if we allow L'Etoile[q] to assume this, we may permit it any liberties whatever. The paragraph beginning 'It is folly to suppose that the murder, etc.,' however it appears as printed in L'Etoile, may be imagined to have existed actually *thus* in the brain of its inditer — 'It is folly to suppose that the murder, if murder was committed on the body, could have been committed soon enough to have enabled her murderers to throw the body into the river before midnight; it is folly, we say, to suppose all this, and to suppose at the same time, (as we are resolved to suppose,) that the body was *not* thrown in until *after* midnight' — a sentence sufficiently inconsequential in itself, but not so utterly preposterous as the one printed.

"Were it my purpose," continued Dupin, "merely to *make out a case* against this passage of L'Etoile's argument, I might safely leave it where it is. It is not, however, with L'Etoile that we have to do, but with the truth. The sentence in question has but one meaning, as it stands; and this meaning I have fairly stated: but it is material that we go behind the mere words, for an idea which these words have obviously intended, and failed to convey. It was the design of the journalist to say that, at whatever period of the day or night of Sunday this murder was committed, it was improbable that the assassins would have ventured to bear the corpse to the river before midnight. And herein lies, really, the assumption of which I[r] complain. It is assumed that the murder was committed at such a position, and under such circumstances, that *the bearing it* to the river became necessary. Now, the assassination might have taken place upon the river's brink, or on the river itself; and, thus, the throwing the corpse in the water might have been resorted to, at any period of the day or night, as the most obvious and most immediate mode of disposal. You will understand that I suggest nothing here as probable, or as coincident with my own opinion.

q it *(A)*   r we *(A)*

My design, so far, has no reference to the *facts* of the case. I wish merely to caution you against the whole tone of L'Etoile's *suggestion,* by calling your attention to its *ex parte* character at the outset.

"Having prescribed thus a limit to suit its own preconceived notions; having assumed that, if this were the body of Marie, it could have been in the water but a very brief time; the journal goes on to say:

> 'All experience has shown that drowned bodies, or bodies thrown into the water immediately after death by violence, require from six to ten days for sufficient[s] decomposition to take place to bring them to the top of the water. Even when a cannon is fired over a corpse, and it rises before at least five or six days' immersion, it sinks again if let alone.'[46]

"These assertions have been tacitly received by every paper in Paris, with the exception of Le Moniteur.*[47] This latter print endeavors to combat that portion of the paragraph which has reference to 'drowned bodies' only, by citing some five or six instances in which the bodies of individuals known to be drowned were found floating after the lapse of less time than is insisted upon by L'Etoile. But there is something excessively unphilosophical in the attempt on the part of Le Moniteur, to rebut the general assertion of L'Etoile, by a citation of particular instances militating against that assertion. Had it been possible to adduce fifty instead of five examples of bodies found floating at the end of two or three days, these fifty examples could still have been properly regarded [t]only as exceptions[t] to L'Etoile's rule, until such time as the rule itself should be confuted. Admitting the rule, (and this Le Moniteur does not deny, insisting merely upon its exceptions,) the argument of L'Etoile is suffered to remain in full force; for this argument does not pretend to involve more than a question of the *probability* of the body having risen to the surface in less than three days; and this probability will be in favor of L'Etoile's position until the instances so childishly adduced shall be sufficient in number to establish an antagonistical rule.[48]

"You will see at once that all argument upon this head should

* The "N. Y. Commercial Advertiser," edited by Col. Stone.

---

s *Omitted (A)* t . . . t as exceptions alone *(A)*

be urged, if at all, against the rule itself; and for this end we must examine the *rationale* of the rule.[49] Now the human body, in general, is neither much lighter nor much heavier than the water of the Seine; that is to say, the specific gravity of the human body, in its natural condition, is about equal to the bulk of fresh water which it displaces. The bodies of fat and fleshy persons, with small bones, and of women generally, are lighter than those of the lean and large-boned, and of men; and the specific gravity of the water of a river is somewhat influenced by the presence of the tide from sea. But, leaving this tide out of question, it may be said that *very* few human bodies will sink at all, even in fresh water, *of their own accord*. Almost any one, falling into a river, will be enabled to float, if he suffer[u] the specific gravity of the water fairly to be adduced in comparison with his own — that is to say, if he suffer[v] his whole person to be immersed, with as little exception as possible. The proper position for one who cannot swim, is the upright position of the walker on land, with the head thrown fully back, and immersed; the mouth and nostrils alone remaining above the surface. Thus circumstanced, we shall find that we float without difficulty and without exertion. It is evident, however, that the gravities of the body, and of the bulk of water displaced, are very nicely balanced, and that a trifle will cause either to preponderate. An arm, for instance, uplifted from the water, and thus deprived of its support, is an additional weight sufficient to immerse the whole head, while the accidental aid of the smallest piece of timber will enable us to elevate the head so as to look about. Now, in the struggles of one unused to swimming, the arms are invariably thrown upwards, while an attempt is made to keep the head in its usual perpendicular position. The result is the immersion of the mouth and nostrils, and the inception, during efforts to breathe while beneath the surface, of water into the lungs. Much is also received into the stomach, and the whole body becomes heavier by the difference between the weight of the air originally distending these cavities, and that of the fluid which now fills them. This difference is sufficient to cause the body to sink, as a general rule; but is insufficient

u suffers *(A)* v suffers *(A)*

in the cases of individuals with small bones and an abnormal quantity of flaccid or fatty matter. Such individuals float even after drowning.

"The corpse, being supposed at the bottom of the river, will there remain until, by some means, its specific gravity again becomes less than that of the bulk of water which it displaces. This effect is brought about by decomposition, or otherwise. The result of decomposition is the generation of gas, distending the cellular tissues and all the cavities, and giving the *puffed* appearance which is so[w] horrible. When this distension has so far progressed that the bulk of the corpse is materially increased without a corresponding increase of *mass* or weight, its specific gravity becomes less than that of the water displaced, and it forthwith makes its appearance at the surface. But decomposition is modified by innumerable circumstances – is hastened or retarded by innumerable agencies; for example, by the heat or cold of the season, by the mineral impregnation or purity of the water, by its depth or shallowness, by its currency or stagnation, by the temperament of the body, by its infection or freedom from disease before death. Thus it is evident that we can assign no period, with any thing like accuracy, at which the corpse shall rise through decomposition. Under certain conditions this result would be brought about within an hour; under others, it might not take place at all. There are chemical infusions by which the animal frame can be preserved *forever* from corruption; the Bi-chloride of Mercury is one. But, apart from decomposition, there may be, and very usually is, a generation of gas within the stomach, from the acetous fermentation of vegetable matter (or within other cavities from other causes) sufficient to induce a distension which will bring the body to the surface. The effect produced by the firing of a cannon is that of simple vibration. This may either loosen the corpse from the soft mud or ooze in which it is imbedded, thus permitting it to rise when other agencies have already prepared it for so doing; or it may overcome the tenacity of some putrescent portions of the cellular tissue; allowing the cavities to distend under the influence of the gas.

---

w to *(B, C) misprint*

"Having thus before us the whole philosophy of this subject, we can easily test by it the assertions of L'Etoile. 'All experience shows,' says this paper, 'that drowned bodies, or bodies thrown into the water immediately after death by violence, require from six to ten days for sufficient decomposition to take place to bring them to the top of the water. Even when a cannon is fired over a corpse, and it rises before at least five or six days' immersion, it sinks again if let alone.'[50]

"The whole of this paragraph must now appear a tissue of inconsequence and incoherence. All experience does *not* show that 'drowned bodies' *require* from six to ten days for sufficient decomposition to take place to bring them to the surface. Both science and experience show that the period of their rising is, and necessarily must be, indeterminate. If, moreover, a body has risen to the surface through firing of cannon, it will *not* 'sink again if let alone,' until decomposition has so far progressed as to permit the escape of the generated gas. But I wish to call your attention to the distinction which is made between 'drowned bodies,' and 'bodies thrown into the water immediately after death by violence.' Although the writer admits the distinction, he yet includes them all in the same category. I have shown how it is that the body of a drowning man becomes specifically heavier than its bulk of water, and that he would not sink at all, except for the struggles by which he elevates his arms above the surface, and his gasps for breath while beneath the surface — gasps which supply by water the place of the original air in the lungs. But these struggles and these gasps would not occur in the body 'thrown into the water immediately after death by violence.' Thus, in the latter instance, *the* [x]*body, as a general rule,*[x] *would not sink at all* — a fact of which L'Etoile is evidently ignorant. When decomposition had proceeded to a very great extent — when the flesh had in a great measure left the bones — then, indeed, but not *till* then, should we lose sight of the corpse.

"And now what are we to make of the argument,[y] that the body found could not be that of Marie Rogêt, because, three days only

x . . . x *body (A)* y argument of the journal, *(A)*

having elapsed, this body was found floating? [z]If drowned, being a woman, she might never have sunk; or having sunk, might have re-appeared in twenty-four hours, or less. But no[z] one supposes her to have been drowned; and, dying before being thrown into the river, she might have been found floating at any period afterwards whatever.

" 'But,' says L'Etoile, 'if the body had been kept in its mangled state on shore until Tuesday night, some trace would be found on shore of the murderers.'[51] Here it is at first difficult to perceive the intention of the reasoner. He means to anticipate what he imagines would be an objection to his theory — viz: that the body was kept on shore two days, suffering rapid [a]decomposition — *more* rapid than if immersed in water.[a] He supposes that, had this been the case, it *might* have appeared at the surface on the Wednesday, and thinks that *only* under such circumstances it could so have appeared. He is accordingly in haste to show that it *was not* kept on shore; for, if so, 'some trace would be found on shore of the murderers.' I presume you smile at the *sequitur*. You cannot be made to see how the mere *duration* of the corpse on the shore could operate to *multiply traces* of the assassins. Nor can I.

" 'And furthermore it is exceedingly improbable,' continues our journal, 'that any villains who had committed such a murder as is here supposed, would have thrown the body in without weight to sink it, when such a precaution could have so easily been taken.'[52] Observe, here, the laughable confusion of thought! No one — not even L'Etoile — disputes the murder committed *on the body found*. The marks of violence are too obvious. It is our reasoner's object merely to show that this body is not Marie's. He wishes to prove that *Marie* is not assassinated — not that the corpse was not. Yet his observation proves only the latter point. Here is a corpse without weight attached. Murderers, casting it in, would not have failed to attach a weight. Therefore it was not thrown in by murderers. This is all which is proved, if any thing is.[b] The question of identity is not even approached, and L'Etoile has been at great pains merely to gainsay now what it has admitted only a moment before. 'We

z . . . z No *(A)*
a . . . a decomposition. *(A)*
b be. *(A)*

are perfectly convinced,' it says, 'that the body found was that of a murdered female.'[53]

"Nor is this the sole instance, even in this division of his subject, where our reasoner unwittingly reasons against himself. His evident [c]object, I have already said,[c] is to reduce, as much as possible, the interval between Marie's disappearance and the finding of the corpse. Yet we find him *urging* the point that no person saw the girl from the moment of her leaving her mother's house. 'We have no evidence,' he says, 'that Marie Rogêt was in the land of the living after nine o'clock on Sunday, June the twenty-second.'[54] As his argument is obviously an *ex parte* one, he should, at least, have left this matter out of sight; for had any one been known to see Marie, say on Monday, or on Tuesday, the interval in question would have been much reduced, and, by his own ratiocination, the probability much diminished of the corpse being that of the *grisette*.[d] It is, nevertheless, amusing to observe that L'Etoile insists upon its point in the full belief of its furthering its general argument.

"Reperuse now that portion of this argument which has reference to the identification of the corpse by Beauvais.[55] In regard to the *hair* upon the arm, L'Etoile[e] has been obviously disingenuous. M. Beauvais, not being an idiot, could never have urged, in identification of the corpse, simply *hair upon its arm*. No arm is *without* hair. The [f]*generality* of the[f] expression of L'Etoile is a mere perversion of the witness' phraseology. He must have spoken of some *peculiarity* in this hair. It must have been[g] a peculiarity of color, of quantity, of length, or of situation.

" 'Her foot,' says the journal, 'was small — so are thousands of feet. Her garter is no proof whatever — nor is her shoe — for shoes and garters are sold in packages. The same may be said of the flowers in her hat. One thing upon which M. Beauvais strongly insists is, that the clasp on the garter found, had been set back to take it in. This amounts to nothing; for most women find it proper to take a pair of garters home and fit them to the size of the limbs

c . . . c object *(A)*
d grisette. *(A)*
e our paper *(A)*
f . . . f *general (A)*
g must have been/was *(A)*

they are to encircle, rather than to try them in the store where they purchase.'[56] Here it is difficult to suppose the reasoner[h] in earnest. Had M. Beauvais, in his search for the body of Marie, discovered a corpse corresponding in general size and appearance to the missing girl, he would have been warranted (without reference to the question of habiliment at all) in forming an opinion that his search had been successful. If, in addition to the point of general size and contour, he had found upon the arm a peculiar hairy appearance which he had observed upon the living Marie, his opinion might have been justly strengthened; and the increase of positiveness might well have been in the ratio of the peculiarity, or unusualness, of the hairy mark. If, the feet of Marie being small, those of the corpse were also small, the increase of probability that the body was that of Marie would not be an increase in a ratio merely [i]arithmetical, but in one highly geometrical, or[i] accumulative. Add to all this shoes such as she had been known to wear upon the day of her disappearance, and, although these shoes may be 'sold in packages,' you so far augment the probability as to verge upon the certain. What, of itself, would be no evidence of identity, becomes through its corroborative position, proof most sure. Give us, then, flowers in the hat corresponding to those worn by the missing girl, and we seek for nothing farther. If only *one* flower, we seek for nothing farther — what then if two or three, or more? Each successive one is multiple evidence — proof not *added* to proof, but *multiplied* by hundreds or thousands.[57] Let us now discover, upon the deceased, garters such as the living used, and it is almost folly to proceed. But these garters are found to be tightened, by the setting back of a clasp, in just such a manner as her own had been tightened by Marie, shortly previous to her leaving home. It is now madness or hypocrisy to doubt. What L'Etoile says in respect to this abbreviation of the garter's being an usual occurrence, shows nothing beyond its own pertinacity in error. The elastic nature of the clasp-garter is self-demonstration of the *unusualness* of the abbreviation. What is made to adjust[j] itself, must of necessity require [k]foreign adjustment[k] but rarely. It must have

h journal *(A)*
i . . . i direct, but in one highly *(A)*
j accomodate *(A)*
k . . . k accomodation *(A)*

been by an accident, in its strictest sense, that these garters of Marie needed the tightening described. They alone would have amply established her identity. But it is not that the corpse was found to have the garters of the missing girl, or found to have her shoes, or her bonnet, or the flowers of her bonnet, or her feet, or a peculiar mark upon the arm, or her general size and appearance – it is that the corpse had each, and *all collectively*. Could it be proved that the editor of L'Etoile *really* entertained a doubt, under the circumstances, there would be no need, in his case, of a commission *de lunatico inquirendo.*[58] He has[l] thought it sagacious to echo the small talk of the lawyers, who, for the most part, content themselves with echoing the rectangular precepts of the courts. I would here observe that very much of what is rejected as evidence by a court, is the best of evidence to the intellect. For the court, guiding itself by the general principles of evidence – the recognized and *booked* principles – is averse from swerving at particular instances. And this steadfast adherence to principle, with rigorous disregard of the conflicting exception, is a sure mode of attaining the *maximum* of attainable truth, in any long sequence of time. The practice, *in mass,* is therefore philosophical; but it is not the less certain that it engenders[m] vast individual error.*[59]

"In respect to the insinuations levelled at Beauvais, you will be willing to dismiss them in a breath. You have already fathomed the true character of this good gentleman. He is a *busy-body,* with much of romance and little of wit. Any one so constituted will readily so conduct himself, upon occasion of *real* excitement, as to render himself liable to suspicion on the part of the over-acute, or the ill-disposed. M. Beauvais (as it appears from your notes) had some personal interviews with the editor of L'Etoile, and offended him by venturing an opinion that the corpse, notwithstanding the

* "A theory based on the qualities of an object, will prevent its being unfolded according to its objects; and he who arranges topics in reference to their causes, will cease to value them according to their results. Thus the jurisprudence of every nation will show that, when law becomes a science and a system, it ceases to be justice. The errors into which a blind devotion to *principles* of classification has led the common law, will be seen by observing how often the legislature has been obliged to come forward to restore the equity its scheme had lost." – *Landor.*

l had *(A)*

m engenders frequently *(A)*

theory of the editor, was, in sober fact that of Marie.[60] 'He persists,' says the paper,[n] 'in asserting the corpse to be that of Marie, but cannot give a circumstance, in addition to those which we have commented upon, to make others believe.' Now, without re-adverting to the fact that stronger evidence 'to make others believe,' could *never* have been adduced, it may be remarked that a man may very well be understood to believe, in a case of this kind, without the ability to advance a single reason for the belief of a second party. Nothing is more vague than impressions of individuàl identity. Each man recognizes his neighbor, yet there are few instances in which any one is prepared to *give a reason* for his recognition. The editor of L'Etoile had no right to be offended at M. Beauvais' unreasoning belief.[61]

"The suspicious circumstances which invest him, will be found to tally much better with my[o] hypothesis of *romantic busy-bodyism,* than with the reasoner's suggestion of guilt. Once adopting the more charitable interpretation, we shall find no difficulty in comprehending the rose in the key-hole; the 'Marie' upon the slate; the 'elbowing the male relatives out of the way;' the 'aversion to permitting them to see the body;' the caution given to Madame B——, that she must hold no conversation with the *gendarme* until his return (Beauvais'); and, lastly, his apparent determination 'that nobody should have anything to do with the proceedings except himself.' It seems to me unquestionable that Beauvais was a suitor of Marie's; that she coquetted with him; and that he was ambitious of being thought to enjoy her fullest intimacy and confidence. I shall say nothing more upon this point; and, as the evidence fully rebuts the assertion of L'Etoile, touching the matter of *apathy* on the part of the mother and other relatives — an apathy inconsistent with the supposition of their believing the corpse to be that of the perfumery-girl — we shall now proceed as if the question of *identity* were settled to our perfect satisfaction."[62]

"And what," I here demanded, "do you think of the opinions of Le Commerciel?"[63]

"That, in spirit, they are far more worthy of attention than any

n the paper,/our journal, *(A)* o our *(A)*

which have been promulgated upon the subject. The deductions from the premises are philosophical and acute; but the premises, in two instances, at least, are founded in imperfect observation. Le Commerciel wishes to intimate that Marie was seized by some gang of low ruffians not far from her mother's door. 'It is impossible,' it urges, 'that a person so well known to thousands as this young woman was, should have passed three blocks without some one having seen her.' This is the idea of a man long resident in Paris – a public man – and one whose walks to and fro in the city, have been mostly limited to the vicinity of the public offices. He is aware that *he*[p] seldom passes so far as a dozen blocks from his own *bureau*, without being recognized and accosted. And, knowing the extent of his personal acquaintance with others, and of others with him, he compares his notoriety with that of the perfumery-girl, finds no great difference between them, and reaches at once the conclusion that she, in her walks, would be equally liable to recognition [q]with himself in his.[q] This could only be the case were her walks of the same unvarying, methodical character, and within the same *species* of limited region as are his own. He passes to and fro, at regular intervals, within a confined periphery, abounding in individuals who are led to observation of his person through interest in the kindred nature of his occupation with their own. But the walks of Marie may, in general, be supposed discursive. In this particular instance, it will be understood as most probable, that she proceeded upon a route of more than average diversity from her accustomed ones. The parallel which we imagine to have existed in the mind of Le Commerciel would only be sustained in the event of the two individuals'[r] traversing the whole city. In this case, granting the personal acquaintances to be equal, the chances would be also equal that an equal number of personal rencounters would be made. For my own part, I should hold it not only as possible, but as very far more than probable, that Marie might have proceeded, at any given period, by any one of the many routes between her own residence and that of her aunt, without meeting a single individual whom she knew, or by whom she was

p he *(A)*
q . . . q with himself. *(A)*
r individuals *(D) misprint*

known. In viewing this question in its full and proper light, we must hold steadily in mind the great disproportion between the personal acquaintances of even the most noted individual in Paris, and the entire population of Paris itself.

"But whatever force there may still appear to be in the suggestion of Le Commerciel, will be much diminished when we take into consideration *the hour* at which the girl went abroad. 'It was when the streets were full of people,' says Le Commerciel, 'that she went out.' But not so. It was at nine o'clock in the morning.[64] Now at nine o'clock of every morning in the week, *with the exception of Sunday,* the streets of the city are, it is true, thronged with people. At nine on Sunday, the populace are chiefly within doors *preparing for church.* No [s]observing person[s] can have failed to notice the peculiarly deserted air of the town, from about eight until ten on the morning of every Sabbath. Between ten and eleven the streets are thronged, but not at so early a period as that designated.

"There is another point at which there seems a deficiency of *observation* on the part of Le Commerciel. 'A piece,' it says, 'of one of the unfortunate girl's petticoats, two feet long, and one foot wide, was torn out and tied under her chin, and around the back of her head, probably to prevent screams. This was done by fellows who had no pocket-handkerchiefs.' Whether this idea is, or is not well founded, we will endeavor to see hereafter; but by 'fellows who have no pocket-handkerchiefs,' the editor intends the lowest class of ruffians. These, however, are the very description of people who will always be found to have handkerchiefs even when destitute of shirts. You must have had occasion to observe how absolutely indispensable, of late years, to the thorough blackguard, has become the pocket-handkerchief."[65]

"And what are we to think," I asked, "of the article in Le Soleil?"[66]

"That it is a[t] pity[u] its inditer was not [v]born a parrot – in which case he would have been the most illustrious parrot of his race.[v] He

s . . . s one of observation, *(A)*
t a vast *(A, B, D)*
u pity that *(A)*
v . . . v more minute. It is easy to surmise, and as easy to assert. *(A)*

has merely repeated[w] the individual items of the already published opinion; collecting them, with a laudable industry, from this paper and from that.[67] 'The things had all *evidently* been there,' he says, 'at least, three or four weeks, and there can be *no doubt* that the spot of this appalling outrage has been discovered.'[x] The facts here re-stated by Le Soleil, are very far indeed from removing my own doubts upon this subject, and we will examine them more particularly hereafter in connexion with another division of the theme.

"At present we must occupy ourselves with other investigations. You cannot fail to have remarked the extreme laxity of the examination of the corpse. To be sure, the question of identity was readily determined, or should have been; but there were other points to be ascertained. Had the body been in any respect *despoiled?* Had the deceased any articles of jewelry about her person upon leaving home? if so, had she any when found? These are important questions utterly untouched by the evidence;[68] and there are others of equal moment, which have met with no attention. We must endeavor to satisfy ourselves by personal inquiry. The case of St.[y] Eustache must be re-examined. I have no suspicion of this person; but let us proceed methodically. We will ascertain beyond a doubt the validity of the *affidavits* in regard to his whereabouts on the Sunday. Affidavits of this character are readily made matter of mystification. Should there be nothing wrong here, however, we will dismiss St.[z] Eustache from our investigations. His suicide, however corroborative of suspicion, were there found to be deceit in the affidavits, is, without such deceit, in no respect an unaccountable circumstance, or one which need cause us to deflect from the line of ordinary analysis.

"In that[a] which I now propose, we will discard the interior[b] points of this tragedy, and concentrate our attention upon its outskirts.[c] Not the least usual error, in investigations such as this, is

w repeated what others have done, (without establishing any incontrovertible proofs) *(A)*

x *After this* Here, again, he speaks but from suspicion, and brings nothing to bear conclusively upon the matter. *(A)*

y Saint *(A)*

z Saint *(A)*

a the analysis *(A)*

b *interior (A)*

c *outskirts. (A)*

the limiting of inquiry to the immediate, with total disregard of the collateral or circumstantial[d] events. It is the mal-practice of the courts to confine evidence and discussion to the bounds of apparent relevancy.[e] Yet experience has shown, and a true philosophy will always show, that a vast, perhaps the larger portion of truth, arises from the seemingly irrelevant.[69] It is through the spirit of this principle, if not precisely through its letter,[70] that modern science has resolved to *calculate upon the unforeseen.* But perhaps you do not comprehend me. The history of human knowledge has so uninterruptedly shown that to collateral, or incidental, or accidental events we are indebted for the most numerous and most valuable discoveries, that it has at length become necessary, in any prospective view of improvement, to make not only large, but the largest allowances for inventions that shall arise by chance, and quite out of the range of ordinary expectation. It is no longer philosophical to base, upon what has been, a vision of what is to be. *Accident* is admitted as a portion of the substructure.[f] We make chance a matter of absolute calculation.[g] We subject the unlooked for and unimagined, to the mathematical *formulae* of the schools.

"I repeat that it is no more than fact, that the *larger* portion[h] of all truth has sprung from the collateral; and it is but in accordance with the spirit of the principle involved in this fact, that I would divert inquiry, in the present case, from the trodden and hitherto unfruitful ground of the event itself, to the cotemporary circumstances which surround it. While you ascertain the validity of the affidavits, I will examine the newspapers more generally than you have as yet done. So far, we have only reconnoitred the field of investigation; but it will be strange indeed if a comprehensive survey, such as I propose, of the public prints, will not afford us some minute points which shall establish a *direction* for inquiry."

In pursuance of Dupin's suggestion, I made scrupulous examination of the affair of the affidavits. The result was a firm conviction of their validity, and of the consequent innocence of St.[i]

d *circumstantial (A)*
e *relevancy. (A)*
f subtructure. *(A) misprint*
g certainty. *(A)*
h proportion *(A)*
i Saint *(A)*

Eustache.[71] In the mean time my friend occupied himself, with what seemed to me a minuteness altogether objectless, in a scrutiny of the various newspaper files. At the end of a week he placed before me the following extracts:[72]

"[j]About three years and a half ago,[j] a disturbance very similar to the present, was caused by the disappearance of this same Marie Rogêt, from the *parfumerie* of Monsieur Le Blanc, in the Palais Royal. At the end of a week, however, she re-appeared at her customary *comptoir*, as well as ever, with the exception of a slight paleness not altogether usual. It was given out by Monsieur Le Blanc and her mother, that she had merely been on a visit to some friend in the country; and the affair was speedily hushed up. We presume that the present absence is a freak of the same nature, and that, at the expiration of a week, or perhaps of a month, we shall have her among us again." – *Evening Paper – Monday, June 23.**

"An evening journal of yesterday, refers to a former mysterious disappearance of Mademoiselle Rogêt. It is well known that, during the week of her absence from Le Blanc's *parfumerie*, she was in the company of a young naval officer, much noted for his debaucheries. A quarrel, it is supposed, providentially led to her return home. We have the name of the Lothario in question, who is, at present, stationed in Paris, but, for obvious reasons, forbear to make it public." – *Le Mercurie – Tuesday Morning, June 24.*†[73]

"An outrage of the most atrocious character was perpetrated near this city the day before yesterday. A gentleman, with his wife and daughter, engaged, about dusk, the services of six young men, who were idly rowing a boat to and fro near the banks of the Seine, to convey him across the river. Upon reaching the opposite shore, the three passengers stepped out, and had proceeded so far as to be beyond the view of the boat, when the daughter discovered that she had left in it her parasol. She returned for it, was seized by the gang, carried out into the stream, gagged, brutally treated, and finally taken to the shore at a point not far from that at which she had originally entered the boat with her parents. The villains have escaped for the time, but the police are upon their trail, and some of them will soon be taken." – *Morning Paper – June 25.*‡[74]

"We have received one or two communications, the object of which is to fasten the crime of the late atrocity upon Mennais;§ but as this gentleman has been fully exonerated by a legal inquiry, and as the arguments of our several correspondents appear to be more zealous than profound, we do not think it advisable to make them public." – *Morning Paper – June 28.***[75]

"We have received several forcibly written communications, apparently from various sources, and which go far to render it a matter of certainty that the

* "N. Y. Express." † "N. Y. Herald." ‡ "N. Y. Courier and Inquirer."

§ Mennais was one of the parties originally suspected and arrested, but discharged through total lack of evidence.

** "N. Y. Courier and Inquirer."

j . . . j Two or three years since, *(A)*

unfortunate Marie Rogêt has become a victim of one of the numerous bands of blackguards which infest the vicinity of the city upon Sunday. Our own opinion is decidedly in favor of this supposition. We shall endeavor to make room for some of these arguments hereafter." – *Evening Paper – Tuesday, June 31*.‡[76]

"On Monday, one of the bargemen connected with the revenue service, saw an empty boat floating down the Seine. Sails were lying in the bottom of the boat. The bargeman towed it under the barge office. The next morning it was taken from thence, without the knowledge of any of the officers. The rudder is now at the barge office." – *Le Diligence – Thursday, June 26*.§[77]

Upon reading these various extracts, they not only seemed to me irrelevant, but I could perceive no mode in which any one of them could be brought to bear upon the matter in hand. I waited for some explanation from Dupin.

"It is not my present[k] design," he said, "to *dwell* upon the first and second of these extracts. I have copied them chiefly to show you the extreme remissness of the police, who, as far as I can understand from the Prefect, have not troubled themselves, in any respect, with an examination of the naval officer alluded to. Yet it is mere folly to say that between the first and second disappearance of Marie, there is no *supposable* connection. Let us admit the first elopement to have resulted in a quarrel between the lovers, and the return home of the betrayed. We are now prepared to view a second *elopement* (if we *know* that an elopement has again taken place) as indicating a renewal of the betrayer's advances, rather than as the result of new proposals by a second individual – we are prepared to regard it as a 'making up' of the old *amour*, rather than as the commencement of a new one. The chances are ten[l] to one, that he who had once eloped with Marie, would again propose an elopement, rather than that she to whom proposals of elopement had been made by one individual, should have them made to her by another. And here let me call your attention to the fact, that the time elapsing between the first ascertained, and the second supposed elopement, is [m]a few months more than[m] the general period of the cruises of our men-of-war. Had the lover been interrupted in his

‡ "N. Y. Evening Post."

§ "N. Y. Standard."

k *Omitted (A)*
l ten thousand *(A)*
m . . . m precisely *(A)*

first villainy[n] by the necessity of departure to sea, and had he seized the first moment of his return to renew the base designs not yet altogether [o]accomplished — or not yet altogether accomplished *by him?*[o] Of all these things we know nothing.

"You will say, however, that, in the second instance, there was *no* elopement as imagined. Certainly not — but are we prepared to say that there was not the frustrated design? Beyond St.[p] Eustache, and perhaps Beauvais, we find no recognized, no open, no honorable suitors of Marie. Of none other is there any thing said. Who, then, is the secret lover, of whom the relatives (*at least most of them*) know nothing, but whom Marie meets upon the morning of Sunday, and who is so deeply in her confidence, that she hesitates not to remain with him until the shades of the evening descend, amid the solitary groves of the Barrière du Roule? Who is that secret lover, I ask, of whom, at least, *most* of the relatives know nothing? And what means the singular prophecy of Madame Rogêt on the morning of Marie's departure? — 'I fear that I shall never see Marie again.'[78]

"But if we cannot imagine Madame Rogêt privy to the design of elopement, may we not at least suppose this design entertained by the girl? Upon quitting home, she gave it to be understood that she was about to visit her aunt in the Rue des Drômes, and St.[q] Eustache was requested to call for her at dark. Now, at first glance, this fact strongly militates against my suggestion; — but let us reflect. That she *did* meet[r] some companion, and proceed with him across the river, reaching the Barrière du Roule at so[s] late an hour as three o'clock in the afternoon, is known.[79] But in consenting so to accompany this individual, [t](*for whatever purpose — to her mother known or unknown,*)[t] she must have thought of her expressed intention when leaving home, and of the surprise and suspicion aroused in the bosom of her affianced suitor, St.[u] Eustache, when, calling for her, at the hour appointed, in the Rue des Drômes, he should find that she had not been there, and when,

n villany *(A, B, C, D)*
o . . . o accomplished? *(A)*
p Saint *(A)*
q Saint *(A)*
r meet with *(A)*
s at so/atso *(A)*
t . . . t *Omitted (A)*
u Saint *(A)*

moreover, upon returning to the *pension* with this alarming intelligence, he should become aware of her continued absence from home. She must have thought of these things, I say. She must have foreseen the chagrin of St.[v] Eustache, the suspicion of all. She could not have thought of returning to brave this suspicion; but the suspicion becomes a point of trivial importance to her, if we suppose her *not* intending to return.

"We may imagine her thinking thus – 'I am to meet a certain person for the purpose of [w]elopement, or for certain other purposes known only to myself.[w] It is necessary that there be no chance of interruption – there must be sufficient time given us to elude pursuit – I will give it to be understood that I shall visit and spend the day with my aunt at the Rue des Drômes – I will[x] tell St.[y] Eustache not to call for me until dark – in this way, my absence from home for the longest possible period, without causing suspicion or anxiety, will be accounted for, and I shall gain more time than in any other manner. If I bid St.[z] Eustache call for me at dark, he will be sure not to call before; but, if I wholly neglect to bid him call, my time for escape will be diminished, since it will be expected that I return the earlier, and my absence will the sooner excite anxiety. Now, if it were my design to return *at all* – if I had in contemplation merely a stroll with the individual in question – it would not be my policy to bid St.[a] Eustache call; for, calling, he will be *sure* to ascertain that I have played him false – a fact of which I might keep him for ever in ignorance, by leaving home without notifying him of my intention, by returning before dark, and by then stating that I had been to visit my aunt in the Rue des Drômes. But, as it is my design *never* to [b]return – or not for some weeks – or not until certain concealments are effected – the[b] gaining of time is the only point about which I need give myself any concern.'[c] [80]

v Saint *(A)*
w . . . w elopement. *(A)*
x well *(B, C, D) misprint*
y Saint *(A)*
z Saint *(A)*
a Saint *(A)*
b . . . b return, the *(A)*
c *After this is another paragraph:* "Such thoughts as these we may *imagine* to have passsed through the mind of Marie, but the point is one upon which I consider it necessary now to insist. I have reasoned thus, merely to call attention, as I said a minute ago, to the culpable remissness of the police. *(A)*

"You have observed, in your notes, that the most general opinion in relation to this sad affair is, and was from the first, that the girl had been the victim of *a gang* of blackguards.[81] Now, the popular opinion, under certain conditions, is not to be disregarded. When arising of itself – when manifesting itself in a strictly spontaneous manner – we should look upon it as analogous with that *intuition* which is the idiosyncrasy of the individual man of genius. In ninety-nine cases from the hundred I would abide by its decision. But it is important that we find no palpable traces of *suggestion.* The opinion must be rigorously *the public's own;* and the distinction is often exceedingly difficult to perceive and to maintain. In the present instance, it appears to me that this 'public opinion,' in respect to *a gang,* has been superinduced by the collateral event which is detailed in the third of my extracts.[82] All Paris is excited by the discovered corpse of Marie, a girl young, beautiful and notorious. This[d] corpse is found, bearing marks of violence, and floating in the river. But it is now made known that, at the very period, or about the very period, in which it is supposed that the girl was assassinated, an outrage similar in nature to that endured by the deceased, although less in extent, was perpetrated, by a gang of young ruffians, upon the person of a second young female. Is it wonderful that the one known atrocity should influence the popular judgment in regard to the other unknown? This judgment awaited direction, and the known outrage seemed so opportunely to afford it! Marie, too, was found in the river; and upon this very river was this known outrage committed. The connexion of the two events had about it so much of the palpable, that the true wonder would have been a *failure* of the populace to appreciate and to seize it. But, in fact,[e] the one atrocity, known to be so committed, is, if any thing, evidence that the other, committed at a time nearly coincident, was *not* so committed. It would have been a miracle indeed, if, while a gang of ruffians were perpetrating, at a given locality, a most unheard-of wrong, there should have been another similar gang, in a similar locality, in the same city, under the same circumstances, with the same means and appliances, engaged in a wrong of precisely the same aspect, at precisely the same period of time![83] Yet

d The *(A)*

e in fact,/to the philosophical, *(A)*

in what, if not in this marvellous train of coincidence, does the accidentally *suggested* opinion of the populace call upon us to believe?[84]

"Before proceeding farther, let us[f] consider the supposed scene of the assassination, in the thicket at the Barrière du Roule. This thicket, although dense, was in the close vicinity of a public road. Within were three or four large stones, forming a kind of seat with a back and footstool. On the upper stone was discovered a white petticoat; on the second, a silk scarf. A parasol, gloves, and a pocket-handkerchief, were also here found. The handkerchief bore the name, 'Marie Rogêt.' Fragments of dress were seen on the branches around. The earth was trampled, the bushes were broken, and there was every evidence of a violent struggle.[85]

"Notwithstanding the acclamation[g] with which the discovery of this thicket was received by the press, and the unanimity with which it was supposed to indicate the precise scene of the outrage, it must be admitted that there was some very good reason for doubt. That it *was* the scene, [h]I may or I may not[h] believe — but there was excellent reason for doubt.[86] Had the *true* scene been, as Le Commerciel suggested,[87] in the neighborhood of the Rue Pavée St. Andrée, the perpetrators of the crime, supposing them still resident in Paris, would naturally have been stricken with terror at the public attention thus acutely directed into the proper channel; and, in certain classes of minds, there would have arisen, at once, a sense of the necessity of some exertion to redivert this attention. And thus, the thicket[i] of the Barrière du Roule having been already suspected, the idea of placing the articles where they were found, might have been naturally entertained. There is no real evidence, although Le Soleil[j] so supposes, that the articles discovered had been more than a very few days in the thicket;[88] while there is much circumstantial proof that they could[k] not have remained there, without attracting attention, during the twenty days elapsing between the fatal Sunday and the afternoon upon which they were found by the boys.[89] 'They were all *mildewed* down hard,' says Le

f us now *(A)*
g acclammation *(A) misprint*
h . . . h I *(A)*
i thickets *(A)*
j Soliel *(A) misprint*
k would *(A)*

Soleil, adopting the opinions of its predecessors, 'with the action of the rain, and stuck together from *mildew*. The grass had grown around and over some of them. The silk of the parasol was strong, but the threads of it were run together within. The upper part, where it had been doubled and folded, was all *mildewed* and rotten, and tore on being opened.' In respect to the grass having 'grown around and over some of them,' it is obvious that the fact could[l] only have been ascertained from the words, and thus from the recollections, of two small boys; for these boys removed the articles and took them home before they had been seen by a third party.[90] But grass will grow, especially in warm and damp weather, (such as was that of the period of the murder,) as much as[m] two or three inches in a single day. A parasol lying upon a newly turfed ground, might, in a[n] week, be entirely concealed from sight by the upspringing grass.[91] And touching that *mildew* upon which the editor of Le Soleil[o] so pertinaciously insists, that he employs the word no less than three times in the brief paragraph just quoted,[p] is he[q] really unaware of the nature of this *mildew?* Is he to be told that it is one of the many classes of *fungus,* of which the most ordinary[r] feature is its upspringing and decadence within twenty-four hours?

"Thus we see, at a glance, that what has been most triumphantly adduced in support of the idea that the articles had been 'for at least three or four weeks' in the thicket, is most absurdly null as regards any evidence of that fact. On[s] the other[t] hand, it is exceedingly difficult to believe that these articles could have remained in the thicket specified, for a longer period than a single week — for a longer period than from one Sunday to the next. Those who know any thing of the vicinity of Paris, know the extreme difficulty of finding *seclusion,* unless at a great distance from its suburbs. Such a thing as an unexplored, or even an unfrequently visited recess, amid its woods or groves, is not for a moment to be imagined. Let any one who, being at heart a lover of nature, is yet chained by duty to the dust and heat of this great metropolis — let any such one attempt, even

l would *(A)*
m *Omitted (A)*
n a single *(A, B, D)*
o Soliel *(A) misprint*
p just quoted,/quoted just now — *(A)*
q the editor *(A)*
r remarkable *(A)*
s But, on *(A)*
t otner *(D) misprint*

during the weekdays, to slake his thirst for solitude amid the scenes of natural loveliness which immediately surround us. At every second step, he will find the growing charm dispelled by the voice and personal intrusion of some ruffian or party of carousing blackguards. He will seek privacy amid the densest foliage, all in vain. Here are the very nooks where the unwashed most abound – here are the temples most desecrate.[u] With[v] sickness of the heart the wanderer will flee back to the polluted Paris as to a less odious because less incongruous sink of pollution. But if the vicinity[w] of the city is so beset during the working days of the week, how much more so on the Sabbath! It is now[x] especially that, released from the claims of labor, or deprived of the customary opportunities of crime, the[y] town blackguard seeks the precincts of the town, not through love of the rural, which in his heart he despises, but by way of escape from the restraints and conventionalities of society. He desires less the fresh air and the green trees, than the utter *license* of the country. Here, at the road-side inn, or beneath the foliage of the woods, he indulges, unchecked by any eye except those of his boon companions, in all the mad excess of a counterfeit hilarity – the joint offspring of liberty and of[z] rum. I say nothing more than what must be obvious to every dispassionate observer, when I repeat that the circumstance of the articles in question having remained undiscovered, for a longer period than from one Sunday to another, in *any* thicket in the immediate neighborhood of Paris, is to be looked upon as little less than miraculous.

"But there are not wanting other grounds for the suspicion that the articles were placed in the thicket with the view of diverting attention from the real scene of the outrage. And, first, let me direct your notice to the *date* of the discovery of the articles. Collate this with the date of the fifth extract made by myself from the newspapers.[92] You will find that the discovery followed, almost immediately, the urgent communications[a] sent to the evening paper. These communications, although various, and apparently from various

u rife with desecration. *(A)*
v With a deadly *(A)*
w vicinage *(A)*
x *Omitted (A)*
y the lower order of the *(A)*
z *Omitted (A)*
a communication *(A)*

sources, tended all to the same point — viz., the directing of attention to *a gang* as the perpetrators of the outrage, and to the neighborhood of the Barrière du Roule as its scene.[b] Now here, of course, the suspicion is not that, in consequence of these communications, or of the public attention by them directed, the articles were found by the boys; but the suspicion might and may well have been, that the articles were not *before* found by the boys, for the reason that the articles had not before been in the thicket; having been deposited there only at so late a period as at the date, or shortly prior to the date of the communications, by the guilty authors of these communications themselves.

"This thicket was a singular — an exceedingly singular one. It was unusually dense. Within its naturally walled enclosure were three extraordinary stones, *forming a seat with a back and footstool.* And this thicket, so full of a natural art, was in the immediate vicinity, *within a few rods,* of the dwelling of Madame Deluc, whose boys were in the habit of closely examining the shrubberies about them in search of the bark of the sassafras. Would it be a rash wager — a wager of one thousand to one — that *a day* never passed over the heads of these boys without finding at least one of them ensconced in the umbrageous hall, and enthroned upon its natural throne? Those who would hesitate at such a wager, have either never been boys themselves, or have forgotten the boyish nature. I repeat — it is exceedingly hard to comprehend how the articles could have remained in this thicket undiscovered, for a longer period than one or two days; and that thus there is good ground for suspicion, in spite of the dogmatic ignorance of Le Soleil,[c] that they were, at a comparatively late date, deposited where found.[93]

"But there are still other and stronger reasons for believing them so deposited, than any which I have as yet urged. And, now, let me beg your notice to the highly artificial arrangement of[d] the articles. On the *upper* stone lay a white petticoat; on the *second* a silk scarf; scattered around, were a parasol, gloves, and a pocket-handkerchief bearing the name, 'Marie Rogêt.' Here is just such an arrangement as would *naturally* be made by a not-over-acute person

---

b theatre. *(A)*
c Soliel *(A) misprint*
d or disposal of *(A)*

wishing to dispose the articles *naturally*. But it is by no means a *really* natural arrangement. I should rather have looked to see the things *all* lying on the ground and trampled under foot. In the narrow limits of that bower, it would have been scarcely possible that the petticoat and scarf should have retained a position upon the stones, when subjected to the brushing to and fro of many struggling persons. 'There was evidence,' it is said, 'of a struggle; and the earth was trampled, the bushes were broken,' — but the petticoat and the scarf are found deposited as if upon shelves. 'The pieces of the frock torn out by the bushes were about three inches wide and six inches long. One part was the hem of the frock and it had been mended. They *looked like strips torn off*.' Here, inadvertently, Le Soleil[e] has employed an exceedingly suspicious phrase. The pieces, as described, do indeed 'look like strips torn off;' but purposely and by hand. It is one of the rarest of accidents that a piece is 'torn off,' from any garment such as is now in question, by the agency *of a thorn*. From the very nature of such fabrics, a thorn or nail becoming entangled in them, tears them rectangularly — divides them into two longitudinal rents, at right angles with each other, and meeting at an apex where the thorn enters — but it is scarcely possible to conceive the piece 'torn off.' I never so knew it, nor did you. To tear a piece *off* from such fabric, two distinct forces, in different directions, will be, in almost every case, required. If there be two edges to the fabric — if, for example, it be a pocket-handkerchief, and it is desired to tear from it a slip, then, and then only, will the one force serve the purpose. But in the present case the question is of a dress, presenting but one edge. To tear a piece from the interior, where no edge is presented, could only be effected by a miracle through the agency of thorns, and no *one* thorn could accomplish it. But, even where an edge is presented, two thorns will be necessary, operating, the one in two distinct directions, and the other in one. And this in the supposition that the edge is unhemmed. If hemmed, the matter is nearly out of the question. We thus see the numerous and great obstacles in the way of pieces being 'torn off' through the simple agency of 'thorns;' yet we are required

e Soliel *(A) misprint*

to believe not only that one piece but that many have been so torn. 'And one part,' too, *'was the hem of the frock!'* Another piece was *'part of the skirt, not the hem,'* – that is to say, was torn completely out, through the agency of thorns, from the unedged interior of the dress! These, I say, are things which one may well be pardoned for disbelieving; yet, taken collectedly, they form, perhaps, less of reasonable ground for suspicion, than the one startling circumstance of the articles' having been left in this thicket at all, by any *murderers* who had enough[f] precaution to think of removing the corpse. You will not have apprehended me rightly, however, if you suppose it my design to *deny* this thicket as the scene of the outrage. [g]There might have been a wrong *here,* or, more possibly, an accident at Madame Deluc's.[g] [94] But,[h] in fact, this is a point of minor importance. We are not engaged in an attempt to discover the scene, but to produce the perpetrators of the murder. What I have adduced, notwithstanding the minuteness with which I have adduced it, has been with the view, first, to show the folly of the positive and headlong assertions of Le Soleil,[i] but secondly and chiefly, to bring you, by the most natural route, to a further contemplation of the doubt whether this assassination has, or has not been, the work of *a gang.*

"We will resume this question by mere allusion to the revolting details of the surgeon examined at the inquest. It is only necessary to say that his published *inferences,* in regard to the number of the ruffians, have been properly ridiculed as unjust and totally baseless, by all the reputable anatomists of Paris. Not that the matter *might not* have been as inferred, but that there was no ground for the [j]inference: – was there not much for another?[j] [95]

"Let us reflect now upon 'the traces of a struggle;'[96] and let me ask what these traces have been supposed to demonstrate. A gang. But do they not rather demonstrate the absence of a gang? What *struggle* could have taken place – what struggle[k] so violent and so enduring as to have left its 'traces' in all directions – between a weak and defenceless girl and the *gang* of ruffians imagined? The silent grasp of a few rough arms and all would have been over. The

f enough of *(A)*
g . . . g *Omitted (A)*
h For, *(A)*
i Soliel, *(A)*
j . . . j inference. *(A)*
k *Omitted (A)*

victim must have been absolutely passive at their will. You will here bear in mind[l] that the arguments urged against[m] the thicket as the scene, are applicable, in chief part, only against it as the scene of an outrage committed by *more than a single individual.* If we imagine but *one* violator, we can conceive, and thus only conceive, the struggle of so violent and so obstinate a nature as to have left the 'traces' apparent.

"And again. I have already mentioned the[n] suspicion to be excited by the fact that the articles in question were suffered to remain *at all* in the thicket where discovered.[97] It seems almost impossible that these evidences of guilt should have been accidentally left where found. There was sufficient presence of mind [o](it is supposed)[o] to remove the corpse; and yet a more positive evidence than the corpse itself (whose features might have been quickly obliterated by decay,) is allowed to lie conspicuously in the scene of the outrage — I allude to the handkerchief with the *name* of the deceased.[98] If this was accident, it was not the accident *of a gang.* We can imagine it only the accident of an individual. Let us see.[99] An individual has committed the murder. He is alone with the ghost of the departed. He is appalled by what lies motionless before him. The fury of his passion is over, and there is abundant room in his heart for the natural awe of the deed. His is none of that confidence which the presence of numbers inevitably inspires. He is *alone* with the dead. He trembles and is bewildered. Yet there is a necessity for disposing of the corpse. He bears it to the river, but leaves behind him the other evidences of guilt; for it is difficult, if not impossible to carry all the burthen at once, and it will be easy to return for what is left. But in his toilsome journey to the water his fears redouble within him. The sounds of life encompass his path. A dozen times he hears or fancies the step of an observer. Even the very lights from the city bewilder him. Yet, in time, and by long and frequent pauses of deep[p] agony, he reaches the river's brink, and disposes of his ghastly charge — perhaps through the medium

l mind that I *admit* the thicket as the scene of the outrage; and you will immediately perceive *(A)*
m *against (A)*
n the strong and just *(A)*
o . . . o *Omitted (A)*
p long *(A)*

of a boat. But *now* what treasure does the world hold — what threat of vengeance could it hold out — which would have power to urge the return of that lonely murderer over that toilsome and perilous path, to the thicket and its blood-chilling recollections? He returns *not,* let the consequences be what they may. He *could* not return if he would. His sole thought is immediate escape. He turns his back *forever* upon those dreadful shrubberies, and flees as from the wrath to come.[100]

"But how with a gang? Their number would have inspired them with confidence; if, indeed, confidence is ever wanting in the breast of the arrant blackguard; and[q] of arrant blackguards alone are the supposed *gangs* ever constituted. Their number, I say, would have prevented the bewildering and unreasoning terror which I have imagined to paralyze the single man. Could we suppose an oversight in one, or two, or three, this oversight would have been remedied by a fourth. They would have left nothing behind them; for their number would have enabled them to carry *all* at once. There would have been no need of *return.*

"Consider now the circumstance that, in the outer garment of the corpse when found, 'a slip, about a foot wide, had been torn upward from the bottom hem to the waist, wound three times round the waist, and secured by a sort of hitch in the back.'[101] This was done with the obvious design of affording *a handle* by which to carry the body. But would any *number* of men have dreamed of resorting to such an expedient? To three or four, the limbs of the corpse would have afforded not only a sufficient, but the best possible hold. The device is that of a single individual; and this brings us to the fact that 'between the thicket and the river, the rails of the fences were found taken down, and the ground bore evident traces of some heavy burden having been dragged along it!'[102] But would a *number* of men have put themselves to the superfluous trouble of taking down a fence, for the purpose of dragging through it a corpse which they might have *lifted over* any fence in an instant? Would a *number* of men have so *dragged* a corpse at all as to have left evident *traces* of the dragging?

---

q for *(A)*

"And here we must refer to an observation of Le Commerciel; an observation upon which I have already, in some measure, commented. 'A piece,' says this journal, 'of one of the unfortunate girl's petticoats was torn out and tied under her chin, and around the back of her head, probably to prevent screams. This was done by fellows who had no pocket-handkerchiefs.'[103]

"I have before[r] suggested that a genuine blackguard is never *without* a pocket-handkerchief.[104] But it is not to this fact that I now especially advert. That it was not through want of a handkerchief for the purpose imagined by Le Commerciel, that this bandage was employed, is rendered apparent by the handkerchief left in the thicket; and that the object was not 'to prevent screams' appears, also, from the bandage having been employed in preference to what would so much better have answered the purpose. But the language of the evidence speaks of the strip in question as 'found around the neck, fitting loosely, and secured with a hard knot.'[105] These words are sufficiently vague, but differ materially from those of Le Commerciel. The slip was eighteen inches wide, and therefore, although of muslin, would form a strong band when folded or rumpled longitudinally. And thus rumpled it was discovered. My inference is this. The solitary murderer, having borne the corpse, for some distance, [s](whether from the thicket or elsewhere)[s] by means of the bandage *hitched* around its middle, found the weight, in this mode of procedure, too much for his strength. He resolved to drag the burthen — the evidence goes to show that it *was* dragged. With this object in view, it became necessary to attach something like a rope to one of the extremities. It could be best attached about the neck, where the head would prevent its slipping off. And, now, the murderer bethought him, unquestionably, of the bandage about the loins.[106] He would have used this, but for its volution about the corpse, the *hitch* which embarrassed it, and the reflection that it had not been 'torn off' from the garment. It was easier to tear a new slip from the petticoat. He tore it, made it fast about the neck, and so *dragged* his victim to the brink of the river. That this 'bandage,' only attainable with trouble and

r already *(A)*   s . . . s *Omitted (A)*

delay, and but imperfectly answering its purpose — that this bandage was employed *at all,* demonstrates that the necessity for its employment sprang from circumstances arising at a period when the handkerchief was no longer attainable — that is to say, arising, as we have imagined, after quitting the thicket, [t](if the thicket it was),[t] and on the road between the thicket and the river.

"But the evidence, you will say, of Madame Deluc, (!)[u] points especially to the presence of *a gang,* in the vicinity of the thicket, at or about the epoch of the [v]murder. This I[v] grant. I doubt if there were not a *dozen* gangs, such as described by Madame Deluc, in and about the vicinity of the Barrière du Roule at *or about* the period of this tragedy. But the gang which has drawn upon itself the pointed animadversion, although the somewhat tardy [w]and very suspicious[w] evidence of Madame Deluc, is the *only* gang which is represented by that honest and scrupulous old lady as having eaten her cakes and swallowed her brandy, without putting themselves to the trouble of making her payment. *Et hinc illæ iræ?*[107]

"But what *is* the precise evidence of Madame Deluc? 'A gang of miscreants made their appearance, behaved boisterously, ate and drank without making payment, followed in the route[x] of the young man and girl, returned to the inn *about dusk,* and recrossed the river as if in great haste.'[108]

"Now this 'great haste' very possibly seemed *greater* haste in the eyes of Madame Deluc, since she dwelt lingeringly and lamentingly upon her violated cakes and ale[109] — cakes and ale for which she might still have entertained a faint hope of compensation. Why, otherwise, since it was *about dusk,* should she make a point of the *haste?* It is no cause for wonder, surely, that even a gang of blackguards should make *haste* to get home, when a wide river is to be crossed in small boats, when storm impends, and when night *approaches.*

"I say *approaches;* for the night had *not yet arrived.* It was only *about dusk* that the indecent haste of these 'miscreants' offended the sober eyes of Madame Deluc. But we are told that it was upon

t . . . t *Omitted (A)*
u (!) *omitted (A)*
v . . . v murder, I *(A)*
w . . . w *Omitted (A)*
x rout *(A) misprint*

this very evening that Madame Deluc, as well as hei eldest son, 'heard the screams of a female in the vicinity of the inn.' And in what words does Madame Deluc designate the period of the evening at which these screams were heard? 'It was *soon after dark,'* she says. But 'soon *after* dark,' is, at least, *dark;* and *'about dusk'* is as certainly daylight. Thus it is abundantly clear that the gang quitted the Barrière du Roule *prior* to the screams overheard (?)[y] by Madame Deluc.[110] And although, in all the many reports of the evidence, the relative expressions in question are distinctly and invariably employed just as I have employed them in this conversation with yourself, no notice whatever of the gross discrepancy has, as yet, been taken by any of the public journals, or by any of the Myrmidons of police.

"I shall add but one to the arguments against *a gang;* but this *one* has, to my own understanding at least, a weight altogether irresistible. Under the circumstances of large reward offered, and full pardon to any King's evidence,[111] it is not to be imagined, for a moment, that some member of *a gang* of low ruffians, or of any body of men, would not long ago have betrayed his accomplices. Each one of a gang so placed, is not so much greedy of reward, or anxious for escape, as *fearful of betrayal.* He betrays eagerly and early that *he may not himself be betrayed.* That the secret has not been divulged, is the very best of proof that it is, in fact, a secret. The horrors of this dark deed are known only to [z]*one,* or two,[z] living human beings,[a] and to God.

"[b]Let us sum up[b] now the meagre yet certain fruits of our long analysis. We have attained the idea [c]either of a fatal accident under the roof of Madame Deluc, or[c] of a murder perpetrated, in the thicket at the Barrière du Roule, by a lover, or at least by an intimate and secret associate of the deceased.[112] This associate is of swarthy complexion. This complexion, the 'hitch' in the bandage, and the 'sailor's knot,' with which the bonnet-ribbon is tied, point to a seaman. His companionship with the deceased, a gay, but not

y (?) *omitted (A)*
z . . . z *one (A)*
a being, *(A)*
b . . . b And *who* that one? It will not be impossible – perhaps it will not be difficult to discover. Let us sum up *(A)*
c . . . c *Omitted (A)*

an abject young girl, designates him as above the grade of the common sailor. Here the well written and urgent communications to the journals are much in the way of corroboration. The circumstance of the first elopement, as mentioned by Le Mercurie, tends to blend the idea of this seaman with that of the 'naval officer' who is first known to have led the unfortunate into crime.[d] [113]

"And here, most fitly, comes the consideration of the continued absence of him of the dark complexion. Let me pause to observe that the complexion of this man is dark and swarthy; it was no common swarthiness which constituted the *sole* point of remembrance, both as regards Valence and Madame Deluc. But why[e] is this man absent? Was he murdered by the gang?[f] If so, why are there only *traces* of the assassinated *girl?* The scene of the two outrages will naturally be supposed identical. And where is his corpse? The assassins would most probably have disposed of both in the same way. But it may be said that this man lives, and is deterred from making himself known, through dread of being charged with the murder. This consideration might be supposed to operate upon him now – at this late period – since it has been given in evidence that he was seen with Marie – but it would have had no force at the period of the[g] deed. The first impulse of an innocent man would have been to announce the outrage, and to aid in identifying the ruffians. This, *policy* would have suggested. He had been seen with the girl. He had crossed the river with her in an open ferry-boat. The denouncing of the assassins would have appeared, even to an idiot, the surest and sole means of relieving himself from suspicion. We cannot suppose him, on the night of the fatal Sunday, both innocent himself and incognizant of an outrage committed. Yet only under such circumstances is it possible to imagine that he would have failed, if alive, in the denouncement of the assassins.

"And what means are ours, of attaining the truth? We shall find

---

d *After this* We are not forced to suppose a premeditated design of murder or of violation. But there was the friendly shelter of the thicket, and the approach of rain – there was opportunity and strong temptation – and then a sudden and violent wrong, to be concealed only by one of darker dye. *(A)*

e *why (A)*

f *the gang? (A)*

g the dark *(A)*

these means multiplying and gathering distinctness as we proceed.[h] Let us sift to the bottom this affair of the first elopement. Let us know the full history of 'the officer,' with his present circumstances, and his whereabouts at the precise period of the murder. Let us carefully compare with each other the various communications sent to the evening paper, in which the object was to inculpate *a gang*. This done, let us compare these communications, both as regards style and MS., with those sent to the morning paper, at a previous period, and insisting so vehemently upon the guilt of Mennais. And, all this done, let us again compare these various communications with the known MSS. of the officer.[114] Let us endeavor to ascertain, by repeated questionings of Madame Deluc and her boys, as well as of the omnibus-driver, Valence, something more of the personal appearance and bearing of the 'man of dark complexion.' Queries, skilfully directed, will not fail to elicit, from some of these parties, information on this particular point [i](or upon others)[i] — information which the parties themselves may not even be aware of possessing.[115] And let us now trace *the boat* picked up by the bargeman on the morning of Monday the twenty-third of June, and which was removed from the barge-office, without the cognizance of the officer in attendance, and *without the rudder,* at some period prior to the discovery of the corpse.[116] With a proper caution and perseverance we shall infallibly trace this boat; for not only can the bargeman who picked it up identify it, but the *rudder is at hand*. The rudder *of a sail-boat* would not have been abandoned, without inquiry, by one altogether at ease in heart. And here let me pause to insinuate a question. There was no *advertisement* of the picking up of this boat. It was silently taken to the barge-office, and as silently removed. But its owner or employer — how *happened* he, at so early a period as Tuesday morning, to be informed, without the agency of advertisement, of the locality of the boat taken up on Monday, unless we imagine some connexion with the *navy* — some personal permanent connexion leading to cognizance of its minute interests — its petty local news?

h proceed — provided that our preparatory analysis of the subject has not greatly diverged from the principles of truth. *(A)*

i . . . i *Omitted (A)*

"In speaking of the lonely assassin dragging his burden to the shore, I have already suggested the probability of his availing himself *of a boat*.[117] Now we are to understand that Marie Rogêt *was* precipitated from a boat. This would naturally have been the case. The corpse could not have been trusted to the shallow waters of the shore. The peculiar marks on the back and shoulders of the victim tell of the bottom ribs of a boat.[118] That the body was found without weight is also corroborative of the idea.[119] If thrown from the shore a weight would have been attached. We can only account for its absence by supposing the murderer to have neglected the precaution of supplying himself with it before pushing off. In the act of consigning the corpse to the water, he would unquestionably have noticed his oversight; but then no remedy would have been at hand. Any risk would have been preferred to a return to that accursed shore. Having rid himself of his ghastly charge, the murderer would have hastened to the city. There, at some obscure wharf, he would have leaped on land. But the boat — would he have secured it? He would have been in too great haste for such things as securing a boat. Moreover, in fastening it to the wharf, he would have felt as if securing evidence against himself. His natural thought would have been[j] to cast from him, as far as possible, all that had held connection with his crime. He would not only have fled from the wharf, but he would not have permitted *the boat* to remain. Assuredly he would have cast it adrift. Let us pursue our fancies. — In the morning, the wretch is stricken with unutterable horror at finding that the boat has been picked up and detained at a locality which he is in the daily habit of frequenting — at a locality, perhaps, which his duty compels him to frequent. The next night, [k]*without daring to ask for the rudder,*[k] he removes it. Now *where* is that rudderless boat? Let it be one of our first purposes to discover. With the first glimpse we obtain of it, the dawn of our success shall begin. This boat shall guide us, with a rapidity which will surprise even ourselves, to him who employed it in the midnight of the fatal Sabbath. Corroboration will rise upon [l]corroboration, and the murderer[l] will be traced."

---

j have been/be *(A)*
k . . . k *Not italicized (A)*
l . . . l corroboration. *The murderer (A)*

[For reasons which we shall not specify, but which to many readers will appear obvious, we have taken the liberty of here omitting, from the MSS. placed in our hands, such portion as details the *following up* of the apparently slight clew obtained by Dupin. We feel it advisable only to state, in brief, that the result desired was brought to pass; and[m] that the Prefect fulfilled punctually, although with reluctance, the terms of his compact with the Chevalier. Mr. Poe's article concludes with the following words. — *Eds.**[n]][120]

It will be understood that I speak of coincidences *and no more.* What I have said above upon this topic must suffice. In my own heart there dwells no faith in præter-nature. That Nature and its God are two, no man who thinks, will deny. That the latter, creating the former, can, at will, control or modify it, is also unquestionable. I say "at will;" for the question is of will,[o] and not, as the insanity of logic has assumed, of power.[p] It is not that the Deity *cannot* modify his laws, but that we insult him in imagining a possible necessity for modification. In their origin these laws were fashioned to embrace *all* contingencies which *could* lie in the Future. With God all is *Now.*[121]

I repeat, then, that I speak of these[q] things only as of coincidences. And farther: in what I relate it will be seen that between the fate of the unhappy Mary Cecilia Rogers, [r]so far as that fate is known,[r] and the fate of one Marie Rogêt [s]up to a certain epoch in her history,[s] there has existed a parallel in the contemplation of whose wonderful exactitude the reason becomes embarrassed. I say all this will be seen. But let it not for a moment be supposed that, in proceeding with the sad narrative of Marie from the epoch just mentioned, and in tracing to its *dénouement* the mystery which

* Of the Magazine in which the article was originally published.

m that an individual assassin was convicted, upon his own confession, of the murder of Marie Rogêt, and *(A)*

n *The starred footnote is omitted in A. The reader is reminded that Poe added this and all other footnotes, except that on the motto, and the one referring to "The Murders in the Rue Morgue," in his second printing of the story,* Tales *(1845). See note 120.*

o *will, (A)*

p *power. (A)*

q certain *(A)*

r ... r *so far as that fate is known, (A)*

s ... s *up to a certain epoch in her history, (A)*

enshrouded her, it is my covert design to hint [t]at an extension of the parallel,[t] or even to suggest that the measures adopted in Paris for the discovery of the assassin of a grisette, or measures founded in any similar ratiocination, would produce any similar result.

For, in respect to the latter branch of the supposition, it should be considered that the most trifling variation in the facts of the two cases might give rise to the most important miscalculations, by diverting thoroughly the two courses of events; very much as, in arithmetic, an error which, in its own individuality, may be inappreciable, produces, at length, by dint of multiplication at all points of the process, a result enormously at variance with truth. And, in regard to the former branch, we must not fail to hold in view that the very Calculus of Probabilities to which I have referred, forbids all idea of the extension of the parallel: — forbids it with a positiveness strong and decided just in proportion as this parallel has already been long-drawn and exact. This is one of those anomalous propositions which, seemingly appealing to thought altogether apart from the mathematical, is yet one which only the mathematician can fully entertain. Nothing, for example, is more difficult than to convince the merely general reader that the fact of sixes having been thrown twice in succession by a player at dice, is sufficient cause for betting the largest odds that sixes will not be thrown in the third attempt.[122] A suggestion to this effect is usually rejected by the intellect at once. It does not appear that the two throws which have been completed, and which lie now absolutely in the Past, can have influence upon the throw which exists only in the Future. The chance for throwing sixes seems to be precisely as it was at any ordinary time — that is to say, subject only to the influence of the various other throws which may be made by the dice. And this is a reflection which appears so exceedingly[u] obvious that attempts to controvert it are received more frequently with a derisive smile than with anything like respectful attention. The error here involved — a gross error redolent of mischief — I cannot pretend to expose within the limits assigned me at present; and with the philosophical it needs no exposure. It may be sufficient here to say that it forms one of an infinite series of

t . . . t *an extension of the parallel, (A)*　　u *exceedingly (A)* mistakes which arise in the path of Reason through her propensity for seeking truth *in detail.*

NOTES

Title: Throughout the texts of the tale and in the manuscript table of contents for PHANTASY-PIECES Poe used the circumflex in "Rogêt," but none of the printed texts collated carried the accent in the title, which in each case is printed in large capitals. Practice among scholars in referring to the tale differs; some follow the title literally as printed; others adopt the circumflex, which seems to be the form intended by Poe.

Motto: The English translation Poe found in a book he reviewed in *Graham's* for December 1841, Sarah Austin's *Fragments from German Prose Writers* (London, reprinted in New York, 1841), p. 97. He improved the translator's style slightly. In "Poe's Knowledge of German," *Modern Philology,* June 1904, Gustav Gruener traced the original to "Moralische Ansichten," in *Novalis Schriften* edited by Ludwig Tieck and Friedrich Schlegel (first edition, Berlin, 1802, II, 532). Other fragments from Novalis – correctly, Friedrich von Hardenberg, 1772–1801 – in Mrs. Austin's book are used in "A Tale of the Ragged Mountains" and "Marginalia," no. 164 (*Democratic Review,* April 7, 1846, p. 270).

1. "The facts of the case as given by Poe are in the main correct," says Wimsatt; "that is, he reproduces rather faithfully what he read in the widely published documents I have listed" (*PMLA,* March 1941, p. 233). Poe did indeed follow "in minute detail" many of the "essential" facts, but more than once he deliberately altered them and proceeded to develop his arguments on the fictitious basis; see, for example, n. 12 below. His repeated references to a second confession are not substantiated by the evidence found.

2. Poe refers again to the Calculus of Probabilities at the end of his story, and dallies with mathematical probability several times between. Wimsatt (n. 32) says that "French writers of Poe's time hailed him with delight as a *pupil* of Laplace," but I think it unlikely that he went directly to the works of that mathematical philosopher.

3. Avowedly writing fiction, Poe gave his characters French (or French-sounding) names and helped himself, with fiction-writer's license, to actual Parisian streets and landmarks, inventing others. The liberties he took disturbed some French readers; see n. 17 below. The "essential" facts of Mary Rogers' background here used – widowed mother, boarding house, offer of employment – along with other interesting details quoted from the *Sunday News* are mentioned in the New York *Brother Jonathan,* August 14, 1841. *Brother Jonathan* was published weekly, on Saturday, but it had a daily edition, the *Tattler,* from which – as well as from many unrelated papers – it printed excerpts, often explicitly credited.

4. *Brother Jonathan,* August 14, 1841, refers to this first disappearance of

Mary Rogers. Walsh (*Poe the Detective,* pp. 11–13) quotes passages dealing with it from New York papers of October 5 and 6, 1838.

5. At the beginning of this paragraph Poe made a very significant manuscript change in the Lorimer Graham copy of his *Tales* – from "five months" to "three years." For the Barrière du Roule, see n. 17 below.

6. The French word *émeutes* – tumults or uprisings – Poe quoted from Mrs. Trollope in his review of her *Paris and the Parisians* (*SLM,* May 1836). He used it again in a review of Isabella F. Romer's *Sturmer* in *Graham's* for March 1842 and in the "Literati" sketch of N. P. Willis in 1846.

7. The New York *Evening Post,* August 12, 1841, reported that a meeting of citizens on August 11 had subscribed the sum of $445 to "be paid on the conviction of the murderer, aside from any reward which the civil authorities may offer." On August 31, Governor Seward issued a proclamation offering a reward of $750 and enjoining "all . . . ministers of justice that they be diligent in their efforts to bring the offender or offenders to condign punishment." Seward's proclamation was printed in *Brother Jonathan* for September 4 from the *Albany Journal* of September 1, with the remark that the total reward now amounted to $1350. Seward later "offered a pardon to any accomplice in the crime who should turn state's evidence, so that the others might be ferreted out and convicted" (*Autobiography of William H. Seward,* 1877, edited by F. W. Seward, p. 566).

8. One of the men the police suspected was William Koekkoek of the *U.S.S. North Carolina.* He was thrice questioned by the police. He had boarded with Mrs. Rogers in 1840, and called on Mary on July 3, 1841, but he had an alibi to show he was not in Mary's company on the fatal Sunday of July 25. His testimony was printed in the *Evening Post,* August 13, 1841. The surname (meaning cuckoo) is not rare in Holland. Its pronunciation involves a sound unknown in English (save that of some New Yorkers). The newspapers spelled it in half a dozen ways, never correctly. My informant is Professor Byron Koekkoek, no relation of Mary's sailor.

9. In this connection it may (or may not) be significant that Peterson's article in the *Saturday Evening Post* of August 14 calling for an *analysis* of the case appeared at the end of the third week following Mary Rogers' death.

10. Here, in his translation of Poe's story, Baudelaire identified the Prefect, Gisquet, in a footnote; see "The Murders in the Rue Morgue," n. 31. With the Prefect's visit Poe begins his fictional dating, without, however, specifying the day of the week.

11. Green spectacles are mentioned also in "Bon-Bon" and "The Purloined Letter."

12. Poe substitutes "June the twenty-second, 18–" for July 25, 1841, and – with several exceptions – cites later dates accordingly. He may have found it convenient to follow the readily available calendar of August 1841 – in which the twenty-second fell on Sunday – and thus may have been trapped into giving a date of Wednesday, June 31, to a newspaper article. He deliberately departs, however, from the scheme announced in his introductory footnote, of following

"in minute detail the essential facts . . . of the real murder of Mary Rogers," and gives the hour of the girl's setting forth as nine o'clock instead of ten – here and in every subsequent reference to the time of her leaving home. See n. 1 above. The account otherwise follows with only minor changes the testimony of Mary's fiancé, Daniel Payne, reported in the New York *Evening Post* of August 12 and in *Brother Jonathan* of August 14, 1841. See n. 14 below.

13. The Rue des Drômes is a made-up name for Jane Street.

14. From the *Evening Post* of August 12, 1841:

> Daniel C. Payne, of No. 47 John street, cork cutter, went yesterday to the Police office, at the request of Justice Parker, to give any information he might possess or which might lead to throw any light upon the disappearance of Miss Mary C. Rogers, said to have been murdered at Hoboken, and made the following statements: –
>
> "I have known Mary C. Rogers since October or November last, at which time I went to board at her mother's, at No. 126 Nassau street. During my stay there, (which was until within a few days of the time Mrs. Rogers gave up keeping boarders,) myself and Miss Rogers formed an attachment for each other, the result of which was that we were engaged to be married. The last time I saw her was on Sunday morning, the 25th July last.
>
> "About the hour of ten o'clock on that morning, I was busy shaving myself in my room, when she came and knocked on my door; upon which I opened the same, when she told me she was going to Mrs. Downing's; when I replied, very well, Mary, I shall look out for you in the evening. At this time she appeared cheerful and lively as usual. – During the time that I had been acquainted with her she had been to Mrs. Downing's some three or four times to my knowledge; and [on] two occasions as she returned from there, I had waited for her about dark, at the corner of Broadway and Ann street, until she alighted from an omnibus, and then walked home with her.
>
> "Mrs. Downing lives in Jane street, No. 68. I did not go to the corner of Ann street and Broadway on this occasion to wait for her, as I had done before, on account of a very heavy storm coming on about dusk, and I feeling in my own mind that she would not leave Mrs. Downing's that night, but remain there, as she had done on another occasion."

15. The remark of Mrs. Rogers was made to a colored servant woman who recounted it to Officer Cockefair, according to the *Evening Post* of August 16, 1841, following the *Democratic Republican New Era* of the same day. *Brother Jonathan,* August 28, p. 2, col. 8, repeated this information.

16. Payne further testified (*Evening Post,* August 12): "[On Monday] I returned home for my dinner, and then heard that she had not been either at Mrs. Downing's or Mrs. Hayes' at which the family were much alarmed. I then commenced searching for her . . . at Harlem . . . and Williamsburg . . . and next day proceeded to Hoboken and also to Staten Island, and also . . . to South Ferry and enquired of different persons at all those places if they had seen any person of her description . . . On the evening of the same day, [Tuesday] I carried an advertisement to the Sun newspaper reporting her absence . . . On the following day

Wednesday I made further enquiry and searched for her... but obtained no trace of her whatever... and returned home again about seven o'clock."

17. This is one of the juxtapositions that upset the critic E. D. Forgues, who in his discussion of Poe's *Tales* (1845) in the *Revue des deux mondes,* October 1846, remarked: "French readers would be greatly astonished to find... the Barrière du Roule on the shore of the Seine 'on the bank opposite the rue Pavée-Saint-André.'" Actually, the rue Pavée-Saint-André is an old Parisian street dating from the thirteenth century, and the Barrière du Roule, erected in the eighteenth century, is one of the impressive structures marking the places where taxes were collected on merchandise coming into the city. They are *not* geographically related as Poe has them. See *Dictionnaire administratif et historique des rues de Paris et de ses monuments* by Felix and Louis Lazare (Paris, 1844).

18. The substance of this account of the finding of the body appeared in the *Evening Post* of August 13, which reported the depositions of Mary's former suitor, Alfred Crommelin, and his friend Archibald Padley, both of 19 John Street and both former boarders with Mrs. Rogers. The paper also reported the depositions of Henry Mallin and James Boullard, who testified that they had brought the body ashore. Poe omitted many of the details in the testimony, probably because they were unnecessary for the development of his narrative but also, perhaps, as Wimsatt (*PMLA,* n. 19) suggests, he had not seen this issue of the *Evening Post;* see n. 68 below. *Brother Jonathan,* in its issues of August 14, 21, and 28, covers, piecemeal, the items used by Poe. The reference to Beauvais's hesitation comes from *Brother Jonathan* of August 28; see nn. 60 and 62 below.

19. The foregoing description follows very closely the answers of Dr. Richard F. Cook, who performed the coroner's autopsy, when he was questioned on August 16 by the Mayor of New York. Originally reported in the *New York Herald* of August 17, the Mayor's examination of Dr. Cook was reprinted in *Brother Jonathan* of August 21. See p. 730 above.

20. This paragraph also closely follows Dr. Cook's testimony – with some omissions – as reported in *Brother Jonathan,* August 21.

21. Deposition of Crommelin, *Evening Post,* August 13: "[Deponent] remained with the body all afternoon until the coroner had taken an inquest which was at nearly nine o'clock at night. Deponent took a part of the skirt of her dress, and a piece from off the sleeve. Dr. Cook who was associated with the coroner gave him the flowers from inside and outside of Mary's hat, a garter, the bottom of her pantalette, a shoe, and a curl of her hair, which deponent brought over to Mary's mother, and all of which was recognized by her and the family... Deponent further says that when he first saw the body he cut her sleeve open and rubbed her arm for the purpose of identifying her... Deponent also says that at the meeting between the coroner, Dr. Cook and himself at Hoboken, on the morning after the inquest was held on Mary's body it was deemed necessary, in consequence of the great heat of the weather to temporarily inter the body which was done, at two feet from the surface of the earth and in a double coffin."

22. *Brother Jonathan,* on September 4, averred: "It is true as has been as-

serted that the attention of the police was first called to the matter by the paragraph of the Sunday Mercury of August 1."

23. From the *Evening Post,* August 13, 1841 (p. 2, col. 7), crediting the *Express:* "Phoebe Rogers, of No. 126 Nassau street, deposed that she has this day [August 12] seen the dress, now in the police office, taken from the person of a drowned female at Hoboken, and that it is the clothing of her daughter, Mary Cecilia Rogers, who had the same on her person when she left her house on Sunday morning, the 25th of July last."

24. *Brother Jonathan,* August 21, 1841: "Payne has procured a string of affidavits setting forth where he was at every hour of the day."

25. *Brother Jonathan,* August 28: "From our Daily Paper of Monday [August 23]: IS MARY ROGERS MURDERED? . . . we have had strong doubts . . . never entirely satisfied of her death. . ."

26. The three passages "translated" from *L'Etoile* at nn. 27, 29, and 31 are virtually literal *transcriptions* from the weekly *Brother Jonathan,* August 28, 1841, reprinting excerpts from its daily sheet, the *Tattler.* Except for substituting fictional for actual names and dates, and asterisks for omitted material, the quoted passages follow their sources almost verbatim. Much of the history of the Rogers' case is to be found in this one issue of the weekly.

27. This first quoted passage (pp. 731–732) comes from *Brother Jonathan* of Saturday, August 28, reprinting an excerpt from the *Tattler* of Monday, August 23. It provides material (including the altered time – see n. 12 above) for much of Dupin's later discussion.

28. Report of Crommelin's deposition (*Evening Post,* August 13, 1841): "On looking at the person deponent recognized the body to be that of Miss Mary C. Rogers . . . Archibald W. Padley of 19 John Street corroborated the statements of Mr. Crommelin."

Examination of Dr. Cook by the Mayor of New York, Monday, August 16, reported by the *New York Herald,* August 17, and copied by *Brother Jonathan* August 21:

> Mayor – Was the body in such a state when you first saw it that there could be no difficulty about the recognizing of it?
>
> Dr. Cook – It was; and Mr. Crommelin appeared to recognize it immediately.

29. This second "translation" (p. 732) also comes from *Brother Jonathan* of August 28, again quoting the *Tattler* of August 23, which reports an apparent indifference toward Mary's fate on the part of those closest to her.

30. The accusations of "apathy" on the part of Mary's family were "disproved" in the same issue of *Brother Jonathan* in which they were made – that of August 28, 1841, this time quoting from the *Tattler* of August 25 an interview with Mary's kinsman, Edward B. Hayes.

31. This third quoted passage (p. 733), from "a subsequent number of the

paper," is from the *Tattler* of Wednesday, August 25, reprinted, like the excerpts from the issue of August 23, in *Brother Jonathan* of August 28.

32. Archibald Padley, who "corroborated the statements of Mr. Crommelin" – see n. 28 – also deposed that "On Saturday the 24th of July last he saw the name of Miss Rogers written on Mr. Crommelin's slate, and also a rose put into his keyhole at the same time" (*Evening Post,* August 13, and *Brother Jonathan,* September 4, which identified the visitor as Padley).

33. Gangs of ruffians were plaguing the metropolitan area at the time; there were frequent reports of the molestation of women and other cases of violence, and the papers were full of indignation and demands for solutions to the problem. On the day of Mary Rogers' disappearance a young girl had been abducted and assaulted at Hoboken by a group of young men in a boat. See Wimsatt, *PMLA,* p. 237.

34. The extract on p. 734 from *Le Commerciel* is actually from the New York *Journal of Commerce,* August 23, 1841, p. 2, col. 2. Poe reproduces the passage almost verbatim, substituting his fictional names for Weehawken and Jane Street and asterisks for material omitted. His source made "pocket handkerchief" plural.

35. Here Poe again takes liberties with the timing of events. The information referred to, according to the narrator on p. 728, was in the hands of the police less than three weeks after the death of Marie; the parallel "discovery" of Mary Rogers' possessions was dated August 25, a month after her death. See Wimsatt, *PMLA,* nn. 20 and 40, pp. 234 and 237. See also Walsh's account (pp. 29–33) of how the *Herald* hinted, September 6 and 7, at the disclosure to come and on September 17 broke the sensational news. The "essential" details all appear in the *Herald's* report, which was the basis of *Brother Jonathan's* on September 25. The factual original of Madame Deluc was Mrs. Frederica Loss, alias Kellenbarack, keeper of the tavern known as Nick Moore's House at Weehawken. Later evidence shows that she had three sons but that only "her little boy Oscar" – mentioned by the *Herald* and by *Brother Jonathan* – could be called a small boy.

36. Except for the asterisks indicating Poe's omissions, the passage (p. 735) on the things found in the thicket is verbatim from the *Saturday Evening Post,* September 25, 1841, p. 2, col. 3. *Brother Jonathan* published the same material the same day; both papers copied it from the *New York Herald* of September 17.

37. The stories of the fatal Sunday told by Mrs. Loss (p. 735) were the first indication that Mary Rogers had been seen alive as late as three o'clock in the afternoon on July 25. The material here presented by the narrator is to be found in *Brother Jonathan,* September 18 and 25. Poe left out some bits that indicated suspicion of Mrs. Loss.

38. The *New York Herald,* September 17, p. 2, reported that Mary Rogers "was seen to arrive at Hoboken about 3 o'clock by the ferry boat. Adam – the stage driver for Mr. Van Buskirk, and another young man saw her and recognized her as she left the boat." *Brother Jonathan,* September 18, gave the name

of the stage driver as Adam Wall. For the identification of the clothing, see n. 23 above.

39. Here again Poe tampered with chronology. Payne died on October 8, not immediately after but more than six weeks after Mary Rogers' clothes turned up at Weehawken. He was found, breathing but unconscious, on a roadside bench near the place where Mary's body had been discovered and a mile or so from the thicket supposed to be the site of the murder. His hat was found soon afterward in the thicket, and a bottle that had contained laudanum just outside. The *Herald* of October 9 under the heading "More Mystery – Extraordinary Circumstance – Suicide of the lover of Mary Rogers" carried a short article, noting the calling of a coroner's inquest. On Monday, October 11, the *Herald* and the *New-York Tribune* gave considerable space to the story. *Brother Jonathan* published a shorter account on October 16. According to the *Tribune,* "From the evidence deduced before the coroner's jury it appeared that Payne had not committed suicide as was at first reported, but had fallen victim to his own melancholy and insane wanderings while brooding over the memory of her he loved." A note found with his body read: "To the World. Here I am on the spot. God forgive me for my misfortune, or for my misspent time." The verdict of the coroner's jury was "dead with congestion of the brain, supposed to be brought about by exposure and irregularity of living incident to aberration of mind."

The empty bottle found near Payne's hat, according to the *Tribune* article, was "marked laudanum, Souillard & Delluc." Walsh, pp. 37 and 87, suggests that the marking on the bottle may have been Poe's source for Madame Deluc's name.

40. Myrmidons were the followers of Achilles, hence, jocularly, the term means "brave fellows," in an uncomplimentary way.

41. Dupin begins his analysis with a restatement of one of his basic tenets. Compare his discussion in "The Murders in the Rue Morgue," pp. 547–548, at n. 33.

42. *Brother Jonathan,* August 28, quoting the *Tattler* of August 24 commenting on the *Tattler* of Monday, August 23 – the "conclusive" article. See excerpts from the latter at notes 27 and 29 above. Wimsatt observes, "True, the papers spoke of the article, but not as 'conclusive' " (*PMLA,* p. 235), and points out that the editorial arguments and the material used in refuting them come principally from the same source, the August 28 issue of *Brother Jonathan.*

43. "The mingled epigram and melodrame" is a light-hearted phrase not included among the instances of rhymes in serious prose given in Appendix I to the Poems (Mabbott I, 484). Melodrame for melodrama is nearly obsolete today but was used with some frequency in the first half of the nineteenth century. The *OED* cites its use by (among others) Lady Morgan in 1817 and 1818, Byron in 1822, the *Gentleman's Magazine* in 1825, J. P. Kennedy in 1835, and the *Quarterly Review* in 1845.

44. Dupin quotes the first "translation" from *L'Etoile,* at n. 27 above.

45. Here Poe repeats his alteration of the evidence, substituting 9 o'clock for 10. See notes 1, 12, and 27, above.

46. Quoted from the remarks about drowned bodies in the first passage from *L'Etoile,* at n. 27 above.

47. Wimsatt (*PMLA,* p. 235) says: "The papers, far from 'tacitly agreeing,' united in a chorus of dissent," and in his note 28 cites five papers besides the *Commercial Advertiser,* which Poe himself cites.

48. The first installment of the tale ends as it began, with an allusion to the mathematics of probability. See n. 2. The text of the second installment begins with the next paragraph; the motto is repeated.

49. Dupin's long discussion of corpses in water opens the second installment of the story (December 1841) in Snowden's *Ladies' Companion.* It is "closely in accord with medico-legal authorities," says Wimsatt (*PMLA,* p. 235), who failed to find Poe's specific source but found "almost point for point agreement with Poe in a later authority" – Alfred S. Taylor's *Principles and Practice of Medical Jurisprudence* (1873).

50. Second repetition (first at n. 46) from the passage about drowned bodies at n. 27.

51. Another quotation from the *L'Etoile* excerpt at n. 27.

52. This quotation about the body without a weight is also from the excerpt at n. 27.

53. The concluding sentence of this paragraph does not appear in any of the "translated" extracts from *L'Etoile* furnished by the narrator. It does appear in the first paragraph of the "conclusive" article in the *Tattler* of August 23 as reprinted in *Brother Jonathan* of August 28 (see n. 42, above). Poe used it where it would best further his effect.

54. Still quoting the first passage from *L'Etoile,* at n. 27, Dupin repeats the altered time – nine o'clock – to which he will refer again in later reasoning.

55. See the second quoted passage from *L'Etoile,* p. 732 at n. 29, and compare Crommelin's deposition as reported in the *Evening Post,* August 13: "Deponent further says that when he first saw the body he cut her sleeve open and rubbed her arm for the purpose of identifying her and also made use of every proper means for the same purpose."

56. This discussion, not included in the excerpts, is from *Brother Jonathan,* August 28, p. 3.

57. There are similar arguments on the increasing weight of multiple facts in the "Longfellow War" papers in 1845. For a brief description of the "Longfellow War, see Quinn, *Poe,* pp. 453–455.

58. A writ issued under common-law rules, on petition to the chancery court, calling for a jury trial of the fact of insanity. On January 12, 1842, the *New-York Tribune* carried the announcement: "'The Commissioner, or De Lunatico Inquirendo,' is the title of a new satirical romance, now publishing in monthly numbers by Carey and Hart, Philadelphia, and Wiley & Putnam, New-York."

59. The footnote is quoted from *Stanley* (Philadelphia, 1838), II, 78. This anonymous novel, written by Horace Binney Wallace, whom Poe knew under the pseudonym "William Landor," Poe often quoted, with and without credit.

60. Editorial comment in *Brother Jonathan's* issues of September 4, 18, and 25 indicates that the editorial staff had several interviews with Crommelin, whose statements were frequently confusing or conflicting.

61. Most of the material in this paragraph comes from *Brother Jonathan,* August 28. Dupin's designation of Beauvais as a *busybody* is justified by the accounts of Crommelin's manifold activities.

62. For the background of Dupin's dismissal of Beauvais as a suspect, see nn. 29–32.

63. See the passage from *Le Commerciel* quoted at n. 34.

64. See nn. 12, 27, 45, and 54 above for Poe's change of the time.

65. The passage from *Le Commerciel* as quoted at n. 34 makes pocket-handkerchief singular, whereas Dupin, here and on p. 766 at n. 103, makes it plural (as the sense requires).

66. The passage from *Le Soleil* is quoted at n. 36.

67. Wimsatt (*PMLA,* n. 17) points out that although Dupin, commenting on the passage from *Le Soleil,* says that the articles were gathered up "from this paper and from that," the whole thing was from the account in the *New York Herald,* September 17.

68. Dupin's question about jewelry supports Wimsatt's suggestion (his note 19) that Poe may never have seen the testimony of Mallin and Boullard (*Evening Post,* August 13, 1841), who deposed that when the body of Mary Rogers was found, "There were no rings, breastpin or any other jewelry on her person." See n. 18 above.

69. Walsh (p. 43) says this passage "anticipated the tone of a good deal of the detective fiction that followed." An elaborated version of Dupin's exposition in this paragraph and the next appears in Poe's sixth letter to *The Columbia Spy,* June 18, 1844, where he mentions the Mary Rogers case in a discussion of magisterial justice with reference to the impending trial of Polly Bodine. See *Doings of Gotham,* pp. 66–67. See also Dupin on the effectiveness of indirect vision in "The Murders in the Rue Morgue," pp. 545–546, at n. 30.

70. For the spirit and the letter see Romans 7:6 – "But now we are delivered from the law, that being dead wherein we were held: that we should serve in newness of spirit, and not in the oldness of the letter." See also II Corinthians 3:6 – "Who also hath made us able ministers of the new testament; not of the letter, but of the spirit: for the letter killeth, but the spirit giveth life."

71. The "scrupulous examination" is part of the fiction. Payne's affidavits had been accepted by the authorities (n. 24 above), but the circumstances of his death, as revealed by the official inquest, served to wipe out lingering skepticism

and exonerate him of all guilt in regard to Mary's death. *Brother Jonathan,* August 16, recorded the change of attitude in two articles, one critical, the other an apology to Payne for past suspicion. Compare Wimsatt, p. 233.

72. Dupin's six "extracts" on pp. 753 and 754 are not as clearly traceable to their sources as are most of those collected by the narrator. Wimsatt, p. 239, n. 48, commented, "Since the [foot]notes in which Poe supplies the names of the papers would seem to have been prepared especially for the 1845 version, and very likely from memory, the remarkable thing is not that some of the references cannot be found but that so many can be." Dupin, *alias* Poe, seems to have used the process he ascribed to the editor of *Le Soleil* (see n. 67 above), putting together items collected "with laudable industry from this paper and from that." Note the change from the first printing that Poe made at the beginning of the first passage, and watch the variants for significant deletions and insertions modifying the direction of Dupin's argument.

73. Two newspaper articles, widely spaced in time, may have contributed to the first two "extracts." Walsh, p. 13, reproduces from the *New York Times and Commercial Intelligencer* of October 5, 1838, a paragraph on the first disappearance of Mary Rogers that mentions "a gallant gay Lothario whose name did not transpire," and Wimsatt (see his note 50) found in the *New York Herald,* August 3, 1841, a piece on the murder recalling that "this young girl, Mary Rogers, was missing from Anderson's cigar store three years ago, for two weeks. It is asserted that she was then seduced by an officer of the United States Navy and kept at Hoboken for two weeks. His name is well known on board his ship."

74. Dupin's third extract was probably derived from a report in the *Courier and Enquirer,* August 16, 1841 (obtained through the courtesy of Mildred M. Ledden, Associate Librarian of the University of the State of New York):

> On Thursday evening last, a gentleman accompanied by his wife and daughter, the latter aged about 18 years, engaged a small boat, in which were four men, in the upper part of the city, to take them to a spot near Williamsburg – on landing the party left the boat, but after they had proceeded a short distance, the daughter discovering she had left her parasol in the boat, went back to get it, her parents continuing on their walk. When she reached the boat she saw the parasol in the stern sheets, where she had been sitting, and stepped in to get it, when the ruffians in charge of the boat pushed from the shore and pulled into the middle of the stream, where they accomplished their hellish designs – they then rowed to the New York side, and left the poor girl on the dock, more dead than alive. We believe that this case has not been made known to the authorities here, but surely if it were it could not be difficult to detect these scoundrels. We hope that no motives of delicacy will prevent the making of the complaint. [The above case we have from a gentleman in Brooklyn].

The same story in different words appeared on August 16 in the *Commercial Advertiser* and the *Evening Post,* which credited the *Brooklyn Daily News* of August 13. The article in the Brooklyn paper, however, recounted the outrage as something not fully authenticated; the file of the paper used is at the Long

Island Historical Society. Poe again disregards the actual chronology. The episode described in Dupin's extract is reported as occurring on the day of Marie's disappearance; that in the newspapers was said to have taken place nearly two weeks after the disappearance of Mary Rogers. See n. 83.

75. Mennais, in the fourth of Dupin's excerpts, is named for a French philosopher, Père Felicité-Robin de Lamennais (1782–1854). In Poe's story he represents Joseph W. Morse, a wood-engraver of 120 Nassau Street, an acquaintance of Mary Rogers. On the fatal Sunday he went with a girl to Staten Island, quarreled with her, returned alone, and fearing the anger of his wife, fled to Worcester, Massachusetts. Suspicion fell upon him, and he was arrested and brought back to New York, but the girl who had gone to Staten Island came forward to provide the alibi that cleared him. There is much about this in the newspapers, including the *Courier and Enquirer,* August 16–23, 1841, but this passage has not been located and was probably composed by Poe.

76. Note the impossible date assigned to the fifth extract. It is true that the papers received numbers of letters in support of the gang theory, but this passage itself has not been found. See Wimsatt, *PMLA,* p. 237, n. 40. He calls attention again to Poe's inconsistent chronology of events.

77. Poe documents this sixth extract as from the *Standard,* but search of the unique file of that paper in the New York Society Library did not reveal it. Wimsatt, who examined eight papers, found no more than a reference to the supposed carrying of Mary from shore to deep water in a boat. See *New York Herald,* September 24, 1841. I believe this incident to be Poe's invention.

78. See the narrator's account, at n. 15, p. 729, saying that the remark was made by Mrs. Rogers toward nightfall. Wimsatt points out (p. 244, n. 73) that Poe refers twice to this remark by Mary's mother but makes no inference from it. The inference is not explicit, but Dupin's further argument certainly suggests that the inference was made in Poe's mind.

79. The hour comes from the testimony of Madame Deluc and the omnibus driver, at nn. 37 and 38 above. Observe Poe's significant insertion, t . . . t, for the second printing.

80. See variants w . . . w and b . . . b in this paragraph, indicating important changes for the second printing.

81. See the narrator's report on gang activities at n. 33.

82. See Dupin's third extract, at n. 74.

83. Dupin summarizes and comments on the episode recounted in his third extract as understandably influencing popular opinion. He goes on, however, to argue that, "the one atrocity, known to be so committed, is, if any thing, evidence that the other, committed at a time nearly coincident, was *not* so committed." Of this statement Wimsatt (p. 236) says, "Here as again, flagrantly, at the end of his story, Poe has asserted the contrary of one of the principles of *a priori* probability." Wimsatt further (p. 237) indicates that there actually were two such episodes: the one on the East River, August 12, which seems to be the genesis of Dupin's third extract, and one on the Hudson at Hoboken on July 25 (see n.

33), "widely discussed and widely confused with the case of Mary Rogers." The incident on the Hudson was referred to in *Brother Jonathan* as late as September 4 (p. 3, col. 4): *"The Hoboken Villainy.* We learn that the young woman so badly treated on July 25 was a mere child of fifteen. . ."

84. The delayed third installment of the tale in Snowden's *Ladies' Companion* for February 1843 begins with the next paragraph, first repeating the motto.

85. See the narrator's account of the thicket, at n. 35, pp. 734 and 735.

86. The variants here reveal another significant change for the second printing.

87. See the passage quoted from *Le Commerciel* at n. 34.

88. Dupin here refers to the passage from *Le Soleil* quoted at n. 36.

89. According to the testimony of Mrs. Loss, the boys found Mary Rogers' belongings on August 25 (*New York Herald,* September 17, and *Brother Jonathan,* September 25), one month after her disappearance. See n. 35 above.

90. Only one of the boys was small (see n. 35), but Dupin makes a point here that is sometimes overlooked, the dubious reliability of the testimony. In this connection Walsh (p. 34) points out that the newspaper accounts failed to note that the description of the clothes in the thicket rested solely on the account of Mrs. Loss. *"No one else saw the clothes in place,* not even the police."

91. Rolland McKee, of the United States Department of Agriculture, wrote me that timothy grass grew ten inches in a week in Ohio, and that crabgrass might grow faster in more southern latitudes, in a part of the country Poe knew better than he knew Hoboken. I observed an extraordinary growth of grass between cobblestones on Fifth Avenue beside Central Park in Manhattan on July 20, 1942.

92. For information concerning the date of the discovery of the articles, see n. 89. See Dupin's fifth extract, at n. 76, for a date that does not exist. The rest of this paragraph is probably intentionally confusing, but it does further Dupin's argument fostering doubts of the validity of the evidence discussed. See also Wimsatt, pp. 237–238 and his notes 40 and 41. He cites the long article in *Brother Jonathan,* September 25, p. 2, col. 8, "based on a visit to the spot," that casts further doubt on the evidence concerning the thicket. The *Brother Jonathan* article undoubtedly provided both arguments and information supplementing the material included in the "extracts."

93. The next few pages are based on the passage quoted at n. 36 as from *Le Soleil;* see also the narrator's description at n. 35.

94. Here (g . . . g) Poe made a significant addition for the second printing.

95. See the narrator's summary of the medical testimony, at n. 19 above. *Brother Jonathan,* August 21, reproducing the report of Dr. Cook's examination by the Mayor of New York, concluded with the following statements (p. 2, col. 7):

> The rest of Dr. Cook's examination is of such a nature that it cannot be

> given in detail. It related, however, to the appearance of the body, which enabled the Doctor to state positively that the poor girl had been brutally violated. The following, however, is the substance of what he did say on this subject. He said that previous to the shocking outrage, she had evidently been a person of chastity and correct habits; that her person was horribly violated *by more than two or three persons;* he gave sufficient reasons for coming to this conclusion. He also stated distinctly, that he examined fully on that point, and found that there was not the slightest trace of pregnancy.

On September 4, however, having altered its view of the case, *Brother Jonathan* characterized the doctor's inferences as "disgustingly ridiculous." For further details in other papers see Wimsatt's notes 43 and 72.

At the end of the paragraph Poe added a significant sentence for the second printing.

96. Dupin continues to discuss the material in the quotation from *Le Soleil* reproduced at n. 36 above. For mention of "traces of a struggle," see also the narrator's description of the thicket on p. 734 and another mention on p. 758. See the variants here for a sentence in the first printing significantly deleted for the second.

97. Dupin mentioned "ground for suspicion" on p. 761 at n. 93.

98. The handkerchief with the victim's name is mentioned in the narrator's account at n. 35.

99. Dupin's hypothetical description of the individual murderer alone with the dead may have been influenced by a flight of imagination in the *New York Herald,* September 24, 1841, found by Wimsatt, who quotes it on his p. 239 as follows: "[The murderer] stayed by the dead and mangled body of his victim, in that dark thicket, with no eye but that of God upon the murderer and the murdered maid, until all was still – perhaps till near midnight. Then, tying the frock around her to form a handle, he carried her to the river, and hurled her in, and fled, too horror stricken to think of returning to the scene of the murder, to remove the articles found by the boys."

100. For fleeing from "the wrath to come," see St. Matthew 3:7 and St. Luke 3:7: "O generation of vipers, who hath warned you of the wrath to come?"

101. The "slip . . . torn upward from the bottom hem" and the "hitch in the back" are from Dr. Cook's testimony (*Brother Jonathan,* August 21) and are mentioned by the narrator at n. 20.

102. For the fences taken down, see the narrator's account at n. 35.

103. Dupin quotes *Le Commerciel* here from the excerpt at n. 34.

104. He first made this suggestion at n. 65 when commenting on the extract from *Le Commerciel.*

105. The strip of muslin fitting loosely around the neck is mentioned by the narrator at n. 20. Compare the account Dr. Cook gave the Mayor of New York, reported in *Brother Jonathan,* August 21, p. 3, cols. 6 and 7: "The dress immediately beneath the frock, and between the frock and the upper petticoat, was made of fine muslin; a piece was torn clean out of this garment, about a foot or

eighteen inches in width; this piece was torn very evenly, and with great care, commencing at the bottom of the garment. This same piece was afterwards tied round her mouth, with a hard knot at the back part of the neck; I think this was done to smother her cries, and that it was probably held tight round her mouth by one of her ravishers: This same piece of muslin was found by me around her neck, fitting loosely to the neck with the knot remaining. – Over these were tied the hat and hat strings."

106. The "bandage *hitched* around its middle" – "the bandage about the loins" – is described, from Dr. Cook's testimony, at n. 101.

107. See the variants for the record of three insertions in this paragraph made for the second printing in an endeavor to suggest distrust of Madame Deluc's testimony. Poe's Latin phrase means "And hence this anger?" He used it again in an editorial in the *Broadway Journal,* November 1, 1845. It is a mixture of *tantaene animis caelestibus irae* from the *Æneid,* I, 11; and *hinc illae lacrimae* quoted by Horace, *Epistolae,* I, xix, 41, from Terence's *Andria.*

108. For Madame Deluc's testimony concerning the fatal day, discussed in this paragraph and the next two, see the narrator's summary at n. 37.

109. For "cakes and ale" see *Twelfth Night,* II, iii, 124; Poe used this commonplace in his exordium in "Review of New Books," *Graham's,* January 1842, p. 69.

110. Compare the skepticism indicated by the addition here with that at n. 107.

111. See the narrator's account of the rewards offered for the apprehension of the murderer or murderers, at n. 7. Two significant insertions for the second printing were made in the last sentence of this paragraph; see the variants.

112. The insertion c . . . c here is very important.

113. In this paragraph Dupin has brought together a series of clues leading toward the identification of the murderer. The dark (sunburned?) complexion comes from the testimony of Madame Deluc and the omnibus driver Valence (at nn. 37 and 38); the hitch in the carrying bandage and the "sailor's knot," from the testimony of Dr. Cook relayed by the narrator at n. 20. The murderer's status is deduced from his companionship with a young, beautiful, and popular girl and from the evidence of intelligence and education Dupin sees in the letters to the papers he almost ascribes to the culprit himself (Dupin's fourth and fifth extracts, at nn. 75 and 76), and finally, the mention of the naval officer of the first disappearance (in Dupin's second extract, at n. 73). Note in the variants the deletion from the end of the paragraph that appeared in the first printing.

114. Dupin apparently feels that it would be possible to find, for comparison, authentic specimens of the handwriting of a man "well known on board his ship." See n. 73 above.

115. This sentence includes another face-saving insertion in parentheses.

116. For the boat picked up by the bargeman, see the last of Dupin's extracts, at n. 77.

117. For the suggestion that the lonely assassin might use a boat, see pp. 764 and 765 above.

118. The marks on the victim's back and shoulders are mentioned by the narrator (at note 19) and in the report of Dr. Cook's testimony before the Mayor of New York (*Brother Jonathan,* August 21, p. 3, col. 6):

> Dr. Cook – There was considerable excoriation upon the top of the back and both shoulder bones, and excoriation at the bottom of the back.
>
> Mayor – How, in your opinion, was this produced?
>
> Dr. C. – I think, by the young girl struggling to get free, while being brutally held down on her back, to effect her violation; and therefore, that this outrage was a hard board floor, the bottom of a boat, or something similar.

119. Dupin comments on the body without a weight at n. 52; it is mentioned in the first "translation" from *L'Etoile* at n. 27. Henry Mallin, one of the men who brought Mary Rogers' body to the shore, deposed that when the body was found "it was perfectly free, without rope, cord or anything attached" (*Evening Post,* August 13, 1841).

120. Poe of course invented this entire bracketed explanation (in which he found it necessary to make some changes for the second printing). Compare a similar maneuver in "Von Kempelen and His Discovery." In reply to a question from George Eveleth he wrote, January 4, 1848: "Nothing was omitted in 'Marie Roget' but what I omitted myself: – all *that* is mystification. The story was originally published in Snowden's 'Lady's Companion.' The 'naval officer' who committed the murder (or rather the accidental death arising from an attempt at abortion) *confessed* it; and the whole matter is now well understood – but, for the sake of relatives, this is a topic on which I must not speak further."

I am convinced that the second confession – that of the "naval officer" referred to here – was also mystification. Sarah Helen Whitman, on March 2, 1867, wrote Eveleth that the officer's name was Spencer (her letter is number 103 in the Ingram List), and Ingram mentioned this in his *Life* (1880), p. 190. Wimsatt could find no naval man of the name who could have had any connection with the Rogers case; but reminds us that Philip Spencer was the wild young midshipman of prominent family who was hanged at sea for mutiny in December 1842. I find no reason to think that he ever injured a woman.

121. Compare "The Landscape Garden" at n. 14: "Art is made to assume the air of an intermediate or secondary Nature – a Nature which is not God, nor any emanation of God, but which still is Nature, in the sense that it is the handiwork of the angels that hover between man and God." Walsh (p. 66) thought this was the final paragraph of Poe's first draft of the story, and that the next two paragraphs were tacked on in order "to forestall any too-serious linking of the story with the Rogers case."

122. "Poe states a principle which he could have read in Laplace's *Essai Philosophique sur les Probabilities*... that equally probable independent events (e.g. throws of a given number with dice) remain equally probable at any point in any series" (Wimsatt, n. 32). Then, quoting the penultimate sentence of this paragraph, "The error here involved..." Wimsatt (*ibid.*) remarks, wryly, "It is hardly necessary to say that Poe stands almost alone among the 'philosophical'."

THE TELL-TALE HEART

This story is a supreme artistic achievement. Since it is an uninterrupted speech of the protagonist, it preserves the unities completely, and is often read as a dramatic monologue.

It is one of the series of Poe's tales founded on popular superstitions. In this case it is the Evil Eye — something feared in so many parts of the world that it seems fruitless to seek an exact source for Poe. He probably heard of the Eye at first hand while he was stationed at Fort Moultrie in Charleston Harbor, since Negroes in South Carolina (as I was reminded by my student, Harriet Holman) sometimes carry a horse chestnut (a "buckeye") as a protection. It should be remembered that a man who possesses the Evil Eye need not be wicked, for many people (for example, in Hungary and Sicily) think it may be unwillingly acquired, and some kindly men avoid looking at other people intently. In the story, the veiling of the eye is probably symbolic, although any deformation of an eye is widely regarded with apprehension.

Although Poe's narrator tells a plain and simple story, which leaves no doubt that he is mad, the author carefully leaves unanswered the question of how much is hallucination. Did the protagonist go mad before he fancied the old man had the Evil Eye — or did a real Evil Eye drive the young man mad? Most readers suppose that the killer hears his own heart.*

If Poe needed no special source for his main idea, he based his plot on two literary sources that can be pointed out with confidence, for there is evidence that Poe saw them. The chief inspiration was a description by Daniel Webster of a real crime committed in Massachusetts, when John Francis Knapp employed Richard Crowninshield, Jr., of Danvers, to rob and kill Joseph White of Salem on the night of April 6, 1830. The criminals were apprehended and Crowninshield committed suicide, but Knapp

* See Edward Wagenknecht, *Edgar Allan Poe* (1963), p. 60, for references to clinical books, including *Sixteen Introductory Lectures* (1811) by Dr. Benjamin Rush, who described the "remorseful criminal type" of madmen. At least one of my students suggested that everything was the diseased imagining of the speaker, who had really killed nobody, and mistook for policemen the guards from an asylum. See also reference in n. 3 below.

was brought to trial July 20 to August 20, 1830. Webster was employed as a special prosecutor, and Knapp was convicted. Webster's *Argument on the Trial* . . . was published as a pamphlet at Salem during the year. The following are pertinent extracts from his speech:

An aged man, without an enemy in the world, in his own house, and in his own bed, is made the victim of a butcherly murder, for mere pay. Truly, here is a new lesson for painters and poets. Whoever shall hereafter draw the portrait of murder, if he will show it . . . where . . . last to be looked for . . . let him not give it the grim visage of Moloch . . . Let him draw, rather, a decorous, smooth-faced, bloodless demon; a picture in repose, rather than in action; not so much an example of human nature in its depravity, and in its paroxysms of crime, as an infernal being, a fiend, in the ordinary display and development of his character.

The deed was executed with a degree of self-possession and steadiness equal to the wickedness with which it was planned. The circumstances now clearly in evidence spread out the whole scene before us. Deep sleep had fallen on the destined victim . . . A healthful old man . . . The assassin enters . . . With noiseless foot he paces the lonely hall . . . and reaches the door of the chamber. Of this, he moves the lock, by soft and continued pressure, till it turns on its hinges without noise; and he enters, and beholds his victim before him . . . The face of the innocent sleeper . . . show[s] him where to strike. The fated blow is given! . . . It is the assassin's purpose to make sure work . . . To finish the picture, he explores the wrist for the pulse! He feels for it and ascertains that it beats no longer! The deed is done. He retreats, retraces his steps to the window . . . and escapes. He has done the murder. No eye has seen him, no ear has heard him. The secret is his own, and it is safe!

Ah! Gentlemen, that was a dreadful mistake. Such a secret can be safe nowhere . . . True it is, generally speaking, that "murder will out" . . . the guilty soul cannot keep its own secret. It is false to itself; or rather it feels an irresistible impulse to be true to itself. It labors under its guilty possession and knows not what to do with it. The human heart was not made for the residence of such an inhabitant . . . The secret which the murderer possesses soon comes to possess him; and like the evil spirits of which we read, it overcomes him, and leads him withersoever it will. He feels it beating at his heart, rising to his throat, and demanding disclosure. He thinks the whole world sees it in his face, reads it in his eyes, and almost hears its workings in the very silence of his thoughts. It has become his master . . . It must be confessed, it will be confessed.†

† A copy of the original pamphlet has been examined at the New-York Historical Society. The passages here quoted may be more conveniently seen in the National Edition of Daniel Webster's *Writings and Speeches* (1903), XI, 52–54. The pertinent material was found by Gunnar Bjurman; see his *Edgar Allan Poe* (Lund, 1916), pp. 220f. Poe's attention may have been called to Webster's speech by quotations from it in an article on the case of Mary Rogers in *Brother Jonathan*, August 21, 1841, where it was called "the most thrilling speech ever made in this country." Poe quoted directly from that paper of the following week in "The Mystery of Marie Rogêt."

THE TELL-TALE HEART

Webster's remark on the "lesson for painters and poets" was the kind of challenge Poe sometimes took up.

A contributory source of the action was pointed out by Edith S. Krappe in *American Literature,* March 1940. This is "A Confession Found in a Prison in the Time of Charles the Second," by Dickens. In the "Confession" a murderer tells how he killed his little nephew for his fortune, and placed his chair over the child's secret grave in the presence of two visitors. Bloodhounds drove him away, and the body was discovered.‡ It may be noted that Dickens' criminal disliked his nephew partly because he could not look the child in the eye.

Poe had his tale ready late in 1842 and sent it off to Bradbury & Soden, publishers of the *Boston Miscellany,* which he supposed was edited by Nathan Hale Jr. Hale had been succeeded, however, by Henry T. Tuckerman, who had the publishers send word of rejection with the comment, "If Mr. Poe would condescend to furnish more quiet articles, he would be a most desirable correspondent." Poe had the manuscript sent to Lowell, who, on December 17, 1842, accepted the story for the first number of *The Pioneer,* which appeared early in 1843.§

TEXTS

(A) Boston *Pioneer,* January 1843 (1: 29–31); *(B) Broadway Journal,* August 23, 1855 (2: 97–99); *(C) Works* (1850), I, 382–387.

Griswold's text *(C),* showing auctorial revisions, is followed.

Reprints

The Dollar Newspaper (Philadelphia), January 25, 1843, from the *Pioneer.* This was the first issue of *The Dollar Newspaper* and the reprint was noted by Killis Campbell (*MLN,* May 1917). [Dwight Thomas in a recent letter points out that the Philadelphia *Spirit of the Times* (January 26, 1843) and other papers

‡ This tale is an early number of *Master Humphrey's Clock,* begun by Dickens in April 1840 as a weekly vehicle for "essays, tales, adventures, letters from imaginary correspondents, and so forth," but soon monopolized by *The Old Curiosity Shop* and then by *Barnaby Rudge.* As with many periodicals of the time, the separate numbers were brought together in one large volume; in this form Poe reviewed — and praised — *Master Humphrey's Clock* in *Graham's* for May 1841. (See *Master Humphrey's Clock and Other Early Stories and Sketches, by Charles Dickens,* edited by Frank T. Marzials, London, 1891.)

§ Both Lowell's letter to Poe of December 17 and Poe's to Lowell, December 25, are printed by Woodberry (*Life,* I, 346–348).

carried advertisements of the new weekly which announced "Three Excellent Stories. One by Willis, one by Poe, and a third entitled 'Precious Minutes.' "]

Spirit of the Times (Philadelphia), August 27, 1845, probably from the *Broadway Journal.*

THE TELL-TALE HEART. [*C*]

TRUE! — nervous — very, very dreadfully nervous I had been and am; but why *will* you say that I am mad? The disease had sharpened my senses — not destroyed — not dulled them. Above all was the sense of hearing acute. I heard all things in the heaven and in the earth.[1] I heard many things in hell. How, then, am I mad? Hearken! and observe how healthily — how calmly I can tell you the whole story.

It is impossible to say how first the idea entered my brain; but,[a] once conceived, it haunted me day and night. Object there was none. Passion there was none. I loved the old man. He had never wronged me. He had never given me insult. For his gold I had no desire. I think it was his eye! yes, it was this! [b]One of his eyes resembled that[b] of a vulture — a pale blue eye, with a film over it. Whenever it fell upon me, my blood ran cold; and so by degrees — very gradually — I made up my mind to take the life of the old man, and thus rid myself of the eye forever.[2]

Now this is the point. You fancy me mad. Madmen know nothing. But you should have seen *me*. You should have seen how wisely I proceeded — with what caution — with what foresight — with what dissimulation I went to work! I was never kinder to the old man than during the whole week before I killed him. And every night, about midnight, I turned the latch of his door and opened it — oh, so gently! And then, when I had made an opening sufficient for my head, I[c] put in a dark lantern, all closed, closed,

---

Motto: Art is long and Time is fleeting,
And our hearts, though stout and brave,
Still, like muffled drums, are beating
Funeral marches to the grave.
Longfellow. (A)

a but *(B, C) comma added from A*

b . . . b He had the eye *(A, B)*

c I first *(A)*

so that no light shone out, and then I thrust in my head. Oh, you would have laughed to see how cunningly I thrust it in! I moved it slowly — very, very slowly, so that I might not disturb the old man's sleep. It took me an hour to place my whole head within the opening so far that I could see him[d] as he lay upon his bed. Ha! — would a madman have been so wise as this?[3] And then, when my head was well in the room, I undid the lantern cautiously — oh, so cautiously — cautiously[e] (for the hinges creaked) — I undid it just so much that a single thin ray fell upon the vulture eye. And this I did for seven long nights — every night just at midnight — but I found the eye always closed; and so it was impossible to do the work; for it was not the old man who vexed me, but his Evil Eye. And every morning, when the day broke, I went boldly into the[f] chamber, and spoke courageously to him, calling him by name in a hearty tone, and inquiring how he had passed the night.[4] So you see he would have been a very profound old man, indeed, to suspect that every night, just at twelve, I looked in upon him while he slept.

Upon the eighth night I was more than usually cautious in opening the door. A watch's minute hand moves more quickly than did mine. Never,[g] before that night, had I *felt* the extent of my own powers — of my sagacity. I could scarcely contain my feelings of triumph. To think that there I was, opening the door, little by little, and he[h] not even to dream of my secret deeds or thoughts. I fairly chuckled at the idea; and perhaps he[i] heard me; for he moved on[j] the bed suddenly, as if startled. Now you may think that I drew back — but no. His room was as black as pitch with the thick darkness,[5] (for the shutters were close fastened, through fear of robbers,) and so I knew that he could not see the opening of the door, and I kept [k]pushing it on[k] steadily, steadily.

I had[l] my head in, and was about to open the lantern, when my thumb slipped upon the tin fastening, and the old man sprang up in the bed, crying out — "Who's there?"

---

d the old man *(A)*
e — cautiously *omitted (A)*
f his *(A)*
g Never *(B, C) comma added from A*
h the old man *(A)*
i the old man *(A)*
j in *(A)*
k . . . k on pushing it *(A)*
l had got *(A)*

I kept quite still and said nothing. For a whole[m] hour I did not move a muscle, and in the meantime I did not hear him[n] lie down. He was still sitting up in the bed, listening; — just as I have done, night after night, hearkening to the death-watches[o] in the wall.[6]

Presently I heard a slight groan, and I knew[p] it was the groan of mortal terror. It was not a groan of pain or of grief — oh, no! — it was the low stifled sound that arises from the bottom of the soul when overcharged with awe.[q] I knew the sound well. Many a night, just at midnight, when all the world slept, it has welled up from my own bosom, deepening, with its dreadful echo, the terrors that distracted me. I say I knew it well. I knew what the old man felt, and pitied him, although I chuckled at heart. I knew that he had been lying awake ever since the first slight noise, when he had turned in the bed. His fears had been ever since growing upon him. He had been trying to fancy them causeless, but could not. He had been saying to himself — "It is nothing but the wind in the chimney — it is only a mouse crossing the floor,"[7] or "it is merely a cricket which has made a single chirp." Yes, he has[r] been trying to comfort himself with these suppositions: but he had found all in vain. *All in vain;* because Death, in approaching him,[s] had stalked with his black shadow before him, and[t] enveloped the victim.[8] And it was the mournful influence of the unperceived shadow that caused him to feel — although he neither saw nor heard[u] — to *feel* the presence of my head within the room.

When I had waited a long time, very patiently, without hearing him[v] lie down, I resolved to open a little — a very, very little crevice in the lantern. So I opened it — you cannot imagine how stealthily, stealthily — until, at length, a single dim ray, like the thread of the spider, shot from out the crevice and fell[w] upon the vulture eye.

---

m a whole/another *(A)*
n the old man *(A)*
o death watches *(B, C) hyphen added from A*
p knew that *(A)*
q *awe. (A)*
r had *(A)*
s the old man, *(A)*
t and the shadow had now reached and *(A)*
u heard me *(A)*
v the old man *(A)*
w fell full *(A, B)*

It was open — wide, wide open — and I grew furious as I gazed upon it. I saw it with perfect distinctness — all a dull blue, with a hideous veil over it that chilled the very marrow in my bones; but I could see nothing else of the old man's face or person: for I had directed the ray as if by instinct, precisely upon the damned spot.[9]

And now — [x] have I not told you that what you mistake foɪ madness is but over acuteness of the senses?[10] — now, I say, there came to my ears [y]a low, dull, quick sound, such as a watch makes when enveloped in cotton.[y] I knew *that* sound well, too. It was the beating of the old man's heart. It increased my fury, as the beating of a drum stimulates the soldier into courage.[11]

But even yet I refrained and kept still. I scarcely breathed. I held the lantern motionless. I tried how steadily I could maintain the ray upon the eye. Meantime the hellish tattoo of the heart increased. It grew [z]quicker and[z] quicker, and louder and louder every instant. The old man's terror *must* have been extreme! It grew louder, I say, louder every moment! — do you mark me well? I have told you that I am nervous: so I am. And now at the dead hour of the night, amid[a] the dreadful silence of that old house, so strange a noise as this excited me to uncontrollable terror.[b] Yet, for some minutes longer I refrained and stood[c] still. But the beating grew louder, louder![d] I thought the heart must burst. And now a new anxiety seized me — the sound would be heard by a neighbor! The old man's hour had come! With a loud yell, I threw open the lantern and leaped into the room. He shrieked once — once only. In an instant I dragged him to the floor, and pulled the heavy bed over him. I then[e] smiled gaily, to find the deed so far done. But, for many minutes, the heart beat on with a muffled sound. This, however, did not vex me; it would not be heard through the wall.[f] At length it ceased. The old man was dead. I removed the bed and ex-

---

x And now — /And *(B);* And now *(C); reading adopted from A*
y . . . y *a low, dull, quick sound — much such a sound as a watch makes when enveloped in cotton. (A)*
z . . . z *Omitted (A)*
a and amid *(A)*
b wrath. *(A)*
c kept *(A)*
d *louder! (A)*
e then sat upon the bed and *(A)*
f walls. *(A)*

amined the corpse. Yes, he was stone, stone dead. I placed my hand upon the heart and held it there many minutes. There was no pulsation. He[g] was stone dead. His eye would trouble me[h] no more.

If still you think me mad, you will think so no longer when I describe the wise precautions I took for the concealment of the body. The night waned, and I worked hastily, but in silence. First of all I dismembered the corpse. I cut off the head and the arms and the legs.

I then took up three planks from the flooring of the chamber, and deposited all between the scantlings.[12] I then replaced the boards so cleverly, so cunningly, that no human eye — not even *his* — could have detected anything wrong. There was nothing to wash out — no stain of any kind — no blood-spot whatever. I had been too wary for that. A tub had caught all — ha! ha!

When I had made an end of these labors, it was four o'clock — still dark as midnight. As the bell sounded the hour, there came a knocking at the street door. I went down to open it with a light heart, — for what had I *now* to fear? There entered three men, who introduced themselves, with perfect suavity, as officers of the police. A shriek had been heard by a neighbor during the night; suspicion of foul play had been aroused; information had been lodged at the police office, and they (the officers) had been deputed to search the premises.

I smiled, — for *what* had I to fear? I bade the gentlemen welcome. The shriek, I said, was my own in a dream. The old man, I mentioned, was absent in the country. I took my visiters all over the house. I bade them search — search *well*. I led them, at length, to *his* chamber. I showed them his treasures, secure, undisturbed. In the enthusiasm of my confidence, I brought chairs into the room, and desired them *here* to rest from their fatigues, while I myself, in the wild audacity of my perfect triumph, placed my own seat upon the very spot beneath which reposed the corpse of the victim.

The officers were satisfied. My *manner* had convinced them. I was singularly at ease. They sat, and while I answered cheerily, they chatted of familiar things. But, ere long, I felt myself getting pale

g The old man *(A)* h *me (A)*

and wished them gone. My head ached, and I fancied a ringing in my ears: but still they sat and still chatted. The ringing became more [i]distinct: — it continued and became more[i] distinct: I talked more freely to get rid of the feeling: but it continued and gained definitiveness — until, at length, I found that the noise was *not* within my ears.

No doubt I now grew *very* pale; — but I talked more fluently, and with a heightened voice. Yet the sound increased — and what could I do? It was *a low, dull, quick sound — much such a sound as a watch makes when enveloped in cotton.* I gasped for breath — and yet the officers heard it not. I talked more quickly — more vehemently; but the noise steadily increased. I arose and argued about trifles, in a high key and with violent gesticulations; but the noise steadily increased. Why *would* they not be gone? I paced the floor to and fro with heavy strides, as if excited to fury by the observations of the men — but the noise steadily increased. Oh God! what *could* I do? I foamed — I raved — I swore! I swung the chair upon which I had been sitting,[j] and grated it upon the boards, but the noise arose over all and continually increased. It grew louder —louder — *louder!* And still the men chatted pleasantly, and smiled. Was it possible they heard not? Almighty God! — no, no! They heard! — they suspected! — they *knew!* — they were making a mockery of my horror! — this I thought, and this I think. But anything was[k] better than this agony! Anything was more tolerable than this derision! I could bear those hypocritical smiles no longer! I felt that I must scream or die! — and now — again! — hark! louder! louder! louder! *louder!* —[13]

"Villains!" I shrieked, "dissemble no more! I admit the deed! — tear up the planks! — here, here! — it is the beating of his hideous heart!"

NOTES

Motto: The Longfellow quotation in the first version is the fourth stanza of "A Psalm of Life," a poem published in the *Knickerbocker Magazine,* September 1838. Poe omitted the quotation in later versions, probably as only tangentially related to his tale.

---

i . . . i *Omitted (A)* j been sitting,/sat, *(A)* k *Omitted (A)*

1. Compare Philippians 2:10, "... things in heaven, and things in earth, and things under the earth."

2. The eye is a powerful and fearful instrument in a number of Poe's tales – "the young Metzengerstein turned pale and shrunk away from the rapid and searching expression of his [horse's] earnest and human-looking eye"; Egaeus "shrunk involuntarily" from the "lifeless, lustreless and seemingly pupilless" eyes of Berenicë. The beautiful eyes of Ligeia at once delighted and appalled the narrator. The most fearful eye of all is the accusatorial "solitary eye of fire" of "The Black Cat."

3. In "The Trial of James Wood," *Alexander's Weekly Messenger,* April 1, 1840, Poe stated that the extreme calmness of that murderer, when buying pistols to shoot his daughter, argued that the man was insane, as the jury found him.

4. Since Poe's narrator mentions calling the old man by name, the crime was not parricide, as some have suspected. A century ago, children did not address parents by name.

5. See Job 38:9, for "thick darkness."

6. Wyatt's *Synopsis of Natural History,* with which Poe was familiar – he probably assisted Wyatt in preparing it, and he reviewed it in *Burton's Gentleman's Magazine* for July 1839 – on p. 128, under *Coleoptera, Serricornes,* reads: "*Anobium* ... these Insects gnaw the wood of old furniture, and in the nuptial season call each other by striking the head upon the surface of solid bodies, after fixing themselves there firmly with their claws; the noise thus produced has procured them the vulgar appellation of Death-watch." The phrase with its suggestion of superstitious implications has often been used in literature, referring to the sound usually ascribed either to the serricorn beetle or to a much smaller insect, *Atropus pulsatorius.* In his mention of the death-watch here Poe again unobtrusively provides, as he frequently does, the possibility of a natural explanation for hypercritical readers. [Recent discussions of the death-watch in this tale have been published by John E. Reilly, in *American Transcendental Quarterly,* No. 2 (II Quarter 1969), 3–9, and E. Arthur Robinson in *Poe Studies,* June 1971.]

7. Compare "The Raven," line 36, " 'Tis the wind and nothing more."

8. Compare Thomas Campbell, "Lochiel's Warning," line 56, "... coming events cast their shadows before."

9. See *Macbeth,* V, i, 39, for "damned spot."

10. In "The Fall of the House of Usher," Roderick Usher "suffered much from a morbid acuteness of the senses."

11. Compare the lines from Longfellow's "Psalm of Life" used as motto to the first version of the story, and also what, in "Reply to Outis" (*Broadway Journal,* March 29, 1845), Poe pointed out as Longfellow's probable source, the lines

> But hark! my pulse, like a soft drum,
> Beats my approach, tells thee I come!

by Bishop Henry King, in his "Exequy," from which Poe himself quoted the motto for the later versions of "The Assignation."

12. Scantlings are small timbers used to support a floor.

13. Daniel Webster's words, quoted in the introductory note above, are reflected here.

THE GOLD-BUG

This story is one of the most popular in the world. Less than a year after its first publication Poe wrote to J. R. Lowell on May 28, 1844: "Of the 'Gold-Bug' (my most successful tale) more than 300,000 copies have been circulated."* Obviously after a discussion with Poe himself, Thomas Dunn English wrote in the *Aristidean* for October 1845: "The intent of the author was evidently to write a popular tale: money, and the finding of money being chosen as the most popular thesis. In this he endeavoured to carry out his idea of the perfection of the plot, which he defines as — that, in which nothing can be disarranged, or from which nothing can be removed, without ruin to the mass — as that, in which we are never able to determine whether any one point depends upon or sustains any one other . . . The bug, which gives title to the story, is used only in the way of mystification, having throughout a seeming and no real connection with the subject. Its purpose is to seduce the reader into the idea of supernatural machinery and keeping him so mystified until the last moment."

For the foundation of his tale Poe chose the most popular of all pirates, the notorious Captain William Kidd (*c.* 1645–1701). Commissioned to suppress buccaneers, Kidd turned pirate himself. He was seized in Boston and taken to London, where he was tried and condemned. At Execution Dock in 1701 he was dropped twice, for the first rope broke. The circumstances of his trial and execu-

* Later, in the *Broadway Journal* of October 11, 1845, he wrote: "Should we ever think of such a thing [republishing in England], we should undoubtedly give The 'Bug' a more prominent position than it even occupies at present. We should call the book 'The Gold-Bug and Other Tales' — instead of 'Tales,' as its title now stands."

tion served to popularize him in song and story.† Some of Kidd's booty was found on Gardiner's Island, but it was (and is) widely believed that more is still hidden somewhere.

Those who know Poe's methods of composition look also for literary sources. Some are striking, in particular Irving's story "Wolfert Webber." This tale concerns a stolid Dutchman, who clings to his cabbage farm on Manhattan Island, because he has dreamt of a treasure hidden there. He enlists the aid, in his search for the treasure, of the "High German Doctor," Knipperhausen, who dabbles in astrology, divination and spells; and of an aged, free, "black fisherman," Mud Sam. Here, of course, are the prototypes of Poe's narrator, of Legrand, and of Jupiter, as I pointed out in 1951.‡

Another probable source is in Robert M. Bird's novel, *Sheppard Lee.* There Jim Jumble, an old Negro who has declined manumission, gets a notion that money buried by Captain Kidd is in a certain swamp. This causes Lee, his master, to dream three nights in succession of finding it at the foot of a beech tree. He sets out at midnight at the full of the moon, sees what he supposes to be demons dancing among tombstones, digs a hole at the foot of the beech, but does not find the treasure. Since Jim speaks in dialect, and is a crotchety old fellow, who is always sure he is right, the resemblance to Poe's tale seems to me considerable.§

† It was said that Kidd had made a compact with the Devil by burying a Bible, and the story was disseminated and perpetuated by lines in varying versions of a "Ballad of Captain Kidd," traceable to a London broadside of 1701:

> I'd a Bible in my hand when I sailed, when I sailed,
> I'd a Bible in my hand when I sailed;
> I'd a Bible in my hand by my father's great command,
> And I sunk it in the sand when I sailed, when I sailed;
> I sunk it in the sand when I sailed.

See *Ballads and Sea Songs from Nova Scotia,* collected by W. Roy Mackenzie (Cambridge, Massachusetts, 1928), pp. 278–282, presenting a text and many references, among them Joanna C. Colcord, *Roll and Go, Songs of American Sailormen* (Indianapolis, 1924) and Louise Pound, *American Ballads and Songs* (New York, 1922). See also a six-stanza version that Poe might have seen, in J. G. Watson's *Annals of Philadelphia* (1830), p. 462. For a concise factual account of Kidd's career, see the article by Frank Monaghan in the *DAB.*

‡ *Selected Poetry and Prose of Edgar Allan Poe,* p. 423. Irving's story is in his *Tales of a Traveller* (1824), a book which Poe mentioned familiarly when reviewing Hawthorne's *Twice-Told Tales* in *Graham's Magazine,* April 1842.

§ Poe reviewed Bird's book in the *Southern Literary Messenger,* September 1836. A. H. Quinn, however (*Poe,* p. 394), dismissed this suggestion as "remote."

THE GOLD-BUG

It has been suggested that Poe's source was *The Journal of Llewellin Penrose, A Seaman,* edited by John Eagles (London 1815 and 1825). In this semi-autobiographical novel there is a short episode about finding treasure. Near the skeleton of a pirate, sacrificed so that his ghost would guard the gold, the hero finds in a bottle three papers: "what the seamen term a round robin," an "oath of most horrid import," and a diagram with "some very odd characters mixed with words . . . intended as a direction to their booty." In company with his young Indian servant-companion and a Dutchman who talks in dialect, Penrose finds the treasure — "seven large candlesticks, silver gilt, about four feet long, and very massive — ten more of smaller size . . . a large vessel . . . nearly full of gold coin." Although there was no Negro — and no dog — in the company of diggers, there may be something in the suggestion that Poe was indebted to this book. He seems never to have mentioned Penrose.*

Poe may have heard of a wreck off the South Carolina coast of the Spanish brigantine *Cid Campeador* in 1745; but that he searched records of the Probate Court of Charleston on the subject is improbable.† Some have seen an "analogue" in "The Money Diggers" by Seba Smith (*Burton's Gentleman's Magazine,* August 1840). There the searchers are driven *away* from a treasure by a *supernatural* dog.

One more "source" is still somewhat controversial. Soon after Poe's story appeared, Colonel Du Solle, in the Philadelphia *Spirit of the Times,* July 1, 1843, pointed out similarities in *Imogine,*‡ a little book by George Ann Humphreys Sherburne (a schoolgirl

* See the Bristol *Times and Mirror,* January 2, 1909 (Ingram List no. 942); and views of R. M. Hogg outlined by Miss Phillips (*Poe the Man,* I, 787–793), where a man named Williams is presented as telling his own story under the name of Penrose. Some of the details there are incorrect. For a clearer picture of *The Journal of Llewellin Penrose, A Seaman* and its author, who was William Williams — a Philadelphia painter known to Benjamin West — see James Thomas Flexner, "The Amazing William Williams: Painter, Author, Teacher, Musician, Stage Designer, Castaway," *American Magazine of Art,* November 1944. The novel, leaning heavily on *Robinson Crusoe* for inspiration, was admired by Lord Byron, and possibly read by Poe. The copy at the Columbia University Libraries has been consulted.

† Woodberry, *Life* (1909), II, 421, quotes undated anonymous newspaper clippings on this suggestion.

‡ *Imogine* was printed in Baltimore but published at Washington. Copies of this uncommon book are in the Berg Collection, the Library Company of Philadelphia, and the Mabbott Poe Collection at the University of Iowa Libraries.

of "thirteen summers," as stated in the Preface). A reply in the *Dollar Newspaper* of the nineteenth, ostensibly by the editor, Joseph Sailer, is given in full, since Poe probably helped in composing it.

THE GOLD-BUG.

About a fortnight ago, there appeared an article in the "Philadelphia Spirit of the Times," pointing out an imagined similarity between Mr. Poe's Prize Tale, "The Gold-Bug," and a story entitled, "Imogene, or The Pirate's Treasure," the composition of Miss Sherburne, a young lady of this city. "The Gold-Bug" has been so universally read that we need not recur to its plot. Miss Sherburne's tale runs thus: – A young girl has a lover, but refuses to marry him on the ground that her wealth is not equal to his. Near her residence stands an oak tree upon which the date 1712 is inscribed, with a hand pointing to the roots. Not far from the tree is a stone-shed. A storm occurs; the tree is blown down; it falls upon the shed, and knocks therefrom a MS. endorsed "The Pirate's Journal," of which nothing farther is said. From the hole caused by the uprooting of the tree, two pots containing money are abstracted – and by means of this money the girl marries her lover. This is all. There is not a word about Kidd – not a word about secret writing – not a syllable about a Gold-Bug – not a syllable about anything that is found in Mr. Poe's story; the only point of coincidence being *the finding of money* – a subject which has been handled not only by Miss Sherburne, but by some fifty, if not by some five hundred talewriters; Mr. P. himself, in "The Gold-Bug," alluding to the multiplicity of stories current upon this topic. The man who should write a tale upon the subject of finding money, and propose, at the same time, to be original in his *theme,* must be a fool. But every one knows that the truest and surest test of *originality* is the manner of handling a hackneyed subject. The more hackneyed the theme, indeed, the better chance for the display of originality in its conduct.

The article published by "The Times," was, no doubt, hurriedly written, before a full perusal of both tales – or rather, upon a hasty glance at each. There was, evidently, no design to do injustice – and this fact is made apparent by the annexed disclaimer; which appeared in "The Times" of the 15th, and in which the *amende honorable* is magnanimously made.

"The Gold-Bug. – We have read this prize tale by Mr. Poe carefully, and also the 'Pirate's Treasure' by Miss Sherburne, and while we confess that the Gold-Bug pleases us much, is exceedingly well written and ingenious, we are constrained to add that it bears no further resemblance to Miss Sherburne's tale, than it must necessarily bear from the fact of touching upon the same general grounds. Mr. Poe well deserved the prize of $100."

We are not aware that any paper has alluded to the charge of plagiarism, (unless to deny it,) with the exception of the "New York Herald," and we have no doubt that this journal will now, in justice, copy the correction, as above.

We have only to add that Miss Sherburne's story is now in our possession, and will be cheerfully loaned to any one who may feel an interest in the subject.

This piece disposes of any idea of real plagiarism.§ Yet there are peculiarities that may have influenced Poe. Imogine Belmont's home was called "Beacon Oak or The Pirate's Look Out," a dead branch is instrumental in locating the treasure, a skeleton is found with it, and "The Pirate's Journal" is wrapped in leather.

To the principal theme of finding money Poe added two more from interests of his own. His articles on cryptography (1839–1841) in *Alexander's Weekly Messenger* and *Graham's Magazine* had excited wide popular interest, but "The Gold-Bug" is the only story in which he made important literary use of this — to him — expensive hobby.* His own considerable knowledge of natural history he had acquired from collaborating with Professor Thomas Wyatt in 1839.†

"The Gold-Bug" probably began to take shape soon after Poe wrote, in *Graham's* for November 1841, of Samuel Warren's *Ten Thousand a Year:* "A main source of the interest which this book possesses for the mass, is to be referred to the *pecuniary* nature of its theme . . . it is an affair of pounds, shillings, and pence — a topic which comes at least *as* immediately to the bosoms . . . of mankind, as any which could be selected."

Poe had "The Gold-Bug" ready sometime in 1842 and sold it to George R. Graham, at space rates, for fifty-two dollars, but Graham later returned it at the author's request, according to Poe himself, in exchange for "some critical papers."‡

The story is planned in two parts. Poe now expected to use it

§ No retraction of the charge made in the *New York Herald,* July 4, 1843 (p. 2, col. 1) has been found in that paper. In the New York *Rover,* June 28, 1845, Lawrence Labree mentioned the supposed plagiarism in reviewing Poe's *Tales.*

* In a letter to John Tomlin, August 28, 1843, he said, "You will hardly believe me when I tell you that I have lost, in time, which to me is money, more than a thousand dollars in solving ciphers." In *PMLA,* September 1943, pp. 754–779, Professor William K. Wimsatt Jr. published an exhaustive discussion of "What Poe Knew about Cryptography."

† For Wyatt, see "Murders in the Rue Morgue," note 35. Quinn (*Poe,* p. 130) suggests that Poe learned something from a conchologist, Dr. Edmund Ravenel, who lived on Sullivan's Island in 1826, but this is pure conjecture. Poe evinced no special interest in natural history before meeting Wyatt, and never mentioned Ravenel.

‡ See Poe's undated letter to Graham printed first in Graham's sympathetic article on Poe in *Graham's Magazine,* March 1850; and see also Poe's letter of January 4, 1848 to G. W. Eveleth.

as a serial in *The Stylus,* which he hoped to bring out in partnership with Thomas Cottrell Clarke. In January 1843 they arranged for Felix O. C. Darley to prepare woodcut illustrations, which were designed after discussion with the author.§ Poe's projected magazine came to nothing, but another channel for publication soon opened.

A new weekly, the *Dollar Newspaper,* had been begun in Philadelphia, January 25, 1843. In the issue of April 5, the publishers, A. H. Simmons & Co., announced a prize contest for a story, to be judged by Robert T. Conrad, H. S. Patterson, M.D., and W. L. Lane. Poe submitted "The Gold-Bug," which won the first prize of a hundred dollars. Second place, with a premium of sixty dollars, was awarded for "The Banker's Daughter" by Robert Morris. The first part of the winning tale was published in the issue of June 21 and the second (together with a reprint of the first) in that of June 28; and the entire tale was reprinted again in a supplement dated July 12, 1843.* Darley's two illustrations were used. The publishers took out a copyright — an unusual action — on June 23,† and the reprint in the Philadelphia *Saturday Courier,* June 24, July 1, and July 8, 1843, which includes the two woodcuts, was presumably by permission. Many country newspapers paid no attention to the copyright and reprinted the story.

There is an interesting English piracy, a pamphlet of 36 pages, *The Gold Bug,* printed in London in 1846 or 1847.‡ The story was

§ See quotation from Darley's letter, February 26, 1884 in Woodberry's *Poe* (1885), p. 181, and *Life* (1909), II, 2. The original sketch for the illustration showing the open chest at the foot of a tree is now in the Prints Division of the New York Public Library.

* There was a canard that there had been no real contest. In the *Daily Forum* of June 27, 1843, was a communication headed "The 'Gold-Bug' A Decided Humbug" alleging that Poe had been hired to write the story for fifteen dollars. In the *Spirit of the Times* of June 29, Colonel Du Solle recorded that an action for damages was "brought against Mr. F. H. Duffee, No. 3 South Third street" for the communication. That worthy saw fit to withdraw his "opinion" in the *Spirit* of July 1, and the matter was dropped. A notice of the action, based on Du Solle's item in the *Spirit,* was given in the *New York Herald* on June 30, but that paper ignored Duffee's retraction. This affair was discussed in some detail by William H. Gravely (*MLN,* May 1945).

† Eastern District of Pennsylvania, No. 154 — the entry was kindly verified by Joseph P. Auslander.

‡ See Heartman and Canny, *A Bibliography* (1943), pp. 114, 115, with a note by Clarence S. Brigham. The only known specimen is now at the University of Texas.

translated into French as "Le Scarabée d'or," with Poe acknowledged as the original author, in the *Revue britannique,* November 1845,§ and with the same title by Isabelle Meunier in *La Démocratie pacifique,* May 23, 25, 27, 1848.

Reprints and translations were not the only form of tribute. The *Public Ledger* of August 5, 1843 carried an advertisement: "Walnut Street Theatre . . . S. S. Steele's Farewell Benefit . . . Tuesday Evening, August 8 . . . will conclude with an entire new piece, entitled The Gold-Bug, or, The Pirate's Treasure. Dramatized from the Prize Story of Edgar A. Poe, Esq. . . ." The advertisement was repeated August 7 and 8, when the following cast was listed:

Friendling	Mr. [J. S.] Charles
Legrand	Mr. Thompson
Jupiter	Mr. J. H. White
Old Martha of the Isle	Mrs. Knight

The piece, the only dramatization of Poe produced during his lifetime, was probably very short, since Steele's "popular drama *Clandare*" preceded it on the bill.*

§ This translation, by A. B. (for Alphonse Borghers, a pseudonym) has been identified as the first actual translation of Poe into French, and since the author was specifically named, as the first reference to him in print outside English-speaking countries. The translator was really the prolific *littérateur* Amédée Pichot, chief editor of the *Revue britannique.* See W. T. Bandy, "Poe's Secret Translator," in *MLN,* May 1964.

* In the Play List of Arthur H. Wilson's *History of the Philadelphia Theatre, 1835–1855* (Philadelphia, 1935), The Gold Bug (without hyphen) is listed as "by S. S. Steele." See also my article in *MLN,* June 1920, and Quinn, *Poe,* p. 392. [We are grateful to Dwight Thomas for sharing his recent checking of the material from the Philadelphia *Public Ledger,* obtained in the course of the preparation of his forthcoming "Poe in Philadelphia, 1838–1844: A Documentary Record." The files of the *Dollar Newspaper* of 1843 are not available for checking (See "The Oblong Box" under Reprints), but Mr. Thomas has been able from other newspapers of the time to fill out the details of the first publication of Poe's most popular story. The *Spirit of the Times* on March 30 and the Baltimore *Sun* on March 31 reported that the *Dollar Newspaper* carried details of the contest on March 29, and the *Pennsylvania Inquirer* of June 15 reprinted the *Dollar Newspaper* June 14 notice that "The Gold-Bug" had won first prize. The *Public Ledger,* whose firm also published the *Dollar Newspaper,* had further information about that paper's extra printings of the story "in order to supply the demand": On June 30 there was a "second edition," on July 12 "an additional supply of extra sheets" (the "Supplement" noted in our *A* text description), and on July 14 all the prize stories were printed together, making, as the *Ledger* says, "the fourth edition of 'The Gold-Bug' " published by the *Dollar Newspaper.*]

TALES: 1843–1844

TEXTS

(A) The *Dollar Newspaper* (Philadelphia), June 21, 1843 (first half of the story), and June 28, 1843 (complete), reprinted in "Supplement," July 12, 1843; *(B) Tales* (1845), pp. 1–36; *(C)* J. Lorimer Graham copy of the last with manuscript revisions about 1849; *(D) Works* (1850), I, 52–87.

The best text is certainly that of the J. Lorimer Graham copy of *Tales (C)*. This volume did not reach Griswold soon enough for use in preparing the first volume of the *Works (D)*, where an ordinary copy of the *Tales (B)* was reprinted without intentional change. Unhappily, in his extensive revision, Poe changed the text of the cipher and the table of secret characters inconsistently. Editorial revision of the errors would involve changes of Poe's phraseology, which do not seem to me justified.

Reprints

From the *Dollar Newspaper: Saturday Courier* (Philadelphia), June 24, July 1, July 8, 1843; *Volunteer* (Montrose, Pa.), August 3, 10, and 17, 1843; *Boston Museum,* July 22, 1848; *Maine Farmer* (Augusta, Me.), September 7, 1848.

Separate printing from *Tales* (1845): *The Gold Bug* by Edgar A. Poe. London [1846–1847], 36 pp.

Translations

Revue britannique, November 1845, signed A.B.; *La Démocratie pacifique,* May 23, 25, and 27, 1848, trans. by Isabelle Meunier, reprinted in *Le Journal du Loiret,* June 17, 20, 22, and 24, 1848.

THE GOLD-BUG. [*C*]

What ho! what ho! this fellow is dancing mad!
He hath been bitten by the Tarantula.

All in the Wrong.

Many years ago, I contracted an intimacy with a Mr. William Legrand.[1] He was of an ancient Huguenot family, and had once been wealthy; but a series of misfortunes had reduced him to want. To avoid the mortification consequent upon his disasters, he left New Orleans, the city of his forefathers, and took up his residence at Sullivan's Island, near Charleston, South Carolina.[2]

This Island is a very singular one. It consists of little else than the sea sand, and is about three miles long. Its breadth at no point

Title: The Gold-Bug. A Prize Story. Written expressly for "The Dollar Newspaper," by Edgar A. Poe, Esq.; *And for which the First Premium of One Hundred Dollars was paid (A).*

exceeds a quarter of a mile. It is separated from the main land by a scarcely perceptible creek, oozing its way through a wilderness of reeds and slime, a favorite resort of the marsh-hen. The vegetation, as might be supposed, is scant, or at least dwarfish. No trees of any magnitude are to be seen. Near the western extremity, where Fort Moultrie stands, and where are some miserable frame buildings, tenanted, during summer, by the fugitives from Charleston dust and fever, may be found, indeed, the bristly palmetto; but the whole island, with the exception of this western point, and a line of hard, white beach on the seacoast, is covered with a dense undergrowth of the sweet myrtle, so much prized by the horticulturists of England. The shrub here often attains the height of fifteen or twenty feet, and forms an almost impenetrable coppice, burthening the air with its fragrance.[3]

In the inmost recesses of this coppice, not far from the eastern or more remote end of the island, Legrand had built himself a small hut, which he occupied when I first, by mere accident, made his acquaintance. This soon ripened into friendship — for there was much in the recluse to excite interest and esteem. I found him well educated, with unusual powers of mind, but infected with misanthropy, and subject to perverse moods of alternate enthusiasm and melancholy. He had with him many books, but rarely employed them. His chief amusements were gunning and fishing, or sauntering along the beach[a] and through the myrtles, in quest of shells or entomological specimens; — his collection of the latter might have been envied by a Swammerdamm.[4] In these excursions he was usually accompanied by an old negro, called Jupiter,[5] who had been manumitted before the reverses of the family, but who could be induced, neither by threats nor by promises, to abandon what he considered his right of attendance upon the footsteps of his young "Massa Will." It is not improbable that the relatives of Legrand, conceiving him to be somewhat unsettled in intellect, had contrived to instil this obstinacy into Jupiter, with a view to the supervision and guardianship of the wanderer.

The winters in the latitude of Sullivan's Island are seldom very severe, and in the fall of the year it is a rare event indeed when a

a bank *(A)*

fire is considered necessary. About the middle of October, 18–, there occurred, however, a day of remarkable chilliness. Just before sunset I scrambled my way through the evergreens to the hut of my friend, whom I had not visited for several weeks – my residence being, at that time, in Charleston, a distance of nine miles from the Island, while the facilities of passage and re-passage were very far behind those of the present day. Upon reaching the hut I rapped, as was my custom, and getting no reply, sought for the key where I knew it was secreted, unlocked the door and went in. A fine fire was blazing upon the hearth. It was a novelty, and by no means an ungrateful[b] one. I threw off an overcoat, took an arm-chair by the crackling logs, and awaited[c] patiently the arrival of my hosts.

Soon after dark they arrived, and gave me a most cordial welcome. Jupiter, grinning from ear to ear, bustled about to prepare some marsh-hens for supper.[6] Legrand was in one of his fits – how else shall I term them? – of enthusiasm. He had found an unknown bivalve, forming a new genus, and, more than this, he had hunted down and secured, with Jupiter's assistance, a *scarabæus*[7] which he believed to be totally new, but in respect to which he wished to have my opinion on the morrow.

"And why not to-night?" I asked, rubbing my hands over the blaze, and wishing the whole tribe of *scarabæi* at the devil.

"Ah, if I had only known you were here!" said Legrand, "but it's so long since I saw you; and how could I foresee that you would pay me a visit this very night of all others? As I was coming home I met Lieutenant G––,[8] from the fort, and, very foolishly, I lent him the bug; so it will be impossible for you to see it until the morning. Stay here to-night, and I will send Jup down for it at sunrise. It is the loveliest thing in creation!"

"What? – sunrise?"

"Nonsense! no! – the bug. It is of a brilliant gold color – about the size of a large hickory-nut – with two jet black spots near one extremity of the back, and another, somewhat longer, at the other. The *antennæ* are – "

b unwelcome *(A)* c waited *(A)*

"Dey aint *no* tin in him, Massa Will, I keep a tellin on you," here interrupted Jupiter;[9] "de bug is a goole bug, solid, ebery bit of him, inside and all, sep him wing – neber feel half so hebby a bug in my life."

"Well, suppose it is, Jup," replied Legrand, somewhat more earnestly, it seemed to me, than the case[d] demanded, "is that any reason for your letting the birds burn? The color" – here he turned to me – "is really almost enough to warrant Jupiter's idea. You never saw a more brilliant metallic lustre than the scales emit – but of this you cannot judge till to-morrow. In the mean time I can give you some idea of the shape." Saying this, he seated himself at a small table, on which were a pen and ink, but no paper. He looked for some in a drawer, but found none.

"Never mind," said he at length, "this will answer;" and he drew from his waistcoat pocket a scrap of what I took to be very dirty foolscap, and made upon it a rough drawing with the pen. While he did this, I retained my seat by the fire, for I was still chilly. When the design was complete, he handed it to me without rising. As I received it, a loud growl was heard, succeeded by a scratching at the door. Jupiter opened it, and a large Newfoundland, belonging to Legrand, rushed in, leaped upon my shoulders, and loaded me with caresses; for I had shown him much attention during previous visits. When his gambols were over, I looked at the paper, and, to speak the truth, found myself not a little puzzled at what my friend had depicted.

"Well!" I said, after contemplating it for some minutes, "this *is* a strange *scarabæus,* I must confess: new to me: never saw anything like it before – unless it was a skull, or a death's-head – which it more nearly resembles than anything else that has come under *my* observation."

"A death's-head!" echoed Legrand – "Oh – yes – well, it has something of that appearance upon paper, no doubt. The two upper black spots look like eyes, eh? and the longer one at the bottom like a mouth – and then the shape of the whole is oval."

"Perhaps so," said I; "but, Legrand, I fear you are no artist. I

d occasion *(A)*

must wait until I see the beetle itself, if I am to form any idea of its personal appearance."

"Well, I don't know," said he, a little nettled, "I draw tolerably — *should* do it at least — have had good masters, and flatter myself that I am not quite a blockhead."

"But, my dear fellow, you are joking then," said I, "this is a very passable *skull* — indeed, I may say that it is a very *excellent* skull, according to the vulgar notions about such specimens of physiology — and your *scarabæus* must be the queerest *scarabæus* in the world if it resembles it. Why, we may get up a very thrilling bit of superstition upon this hint. I presume you will call the bug *scarabæus caput hominis,* or something of that kind — there are many similar titles in the Natural Histories. But where are the *antennæ* you spoke of?"

"The *antennæ!*" said Legrand, who seemed to be getting unaccountably warm upon the subject; "I am sure you must see the *antennæ.* I made them as distinct as they are in the original insect, and I presume that is sufficient."

"Well, well," I said, "perhaps you have — still I don't see them;" and I handed him the paper without additional remark, not wishing to ruffle his temper; but I was much surprised at the turn affairs had taken; his ill humor puzzled me — and, as for the drawing of the beetle, there were positively *no antennæ* visible, and the whole *did* bear a very close resemblance to the ordinary cut of a death's-head.

He received the paper very peevishly, and was about to crumple it, apparently to throw it in the fire, when a casual glance at the design seemed suddenly to rivet his attention. In an instant his face grew violently red — in another as excessively pale. For some minutes he continued to scrutinize the drawing minutely where he sat. At length he arose, took a candle from the table, and proceeded to seat himself upon a sea-chest in the farthest corner of the room. Here again he made an anxious examination of the paper; turning it in all directions. He said nothing, however, and his conduct greatly astonished me; yet I thought it prudent not to exacerbate the growing moodiness of his temper by any comment. Presently he took from his coat pocket a wallet, placed the paper carefully in it, and deposited both in a writing-desk, which he locked. He now grew more composed in his demeanor; but his original air of enthusiasm had quite disappeared. Yet he seemed not so much sulky as abstracted. As the evening wore away he became more and more absorbed in reverie, from which no sallies of mine could arouse him. It had been my intention to pass the night at the hut, as I had frequently done before, but, seeing my host in this mood, I deemed it proper to take leave. He did not press me to remain, but, as I departed, he shook my hand with even more than his usual cordiality.

It was about a month after this (and during the interval I had seen nothing of Legrand) when I received a visit, at Charleston, from his man, Jupiter. I had never seen the good old negro look so dispirited, and I feared that some serious disaster had befallen my friend.

"Well, Jup," said I, "what is the matter now? — how is your master?"

"Why, to speak de troof, massa, him not so berry well as mought be."

"Not well! I am truly sorry to hear it. What does he complain of?"

"Dar! dat's it! — him neber plain of[e] notin — but him berry sick for all dat."

"*Very* sick, Jupiter! — why didn't you say so at once? Is he confined to bed?"

"No, dat he aint! — he aint find nowhar — dat's just whar de shoe pinch — my mind is got to be berry hebby bout poor Massa Will."

"Jupiter, I should like to understand what it is you are talking about. You say your master is sick. Hasn't he told you what ails him?"

"Why, massa, taint worf while for to git mad bout[f] de matter — Massa Will say noffin at all aint de matter wid him — but den what make him go about[g] looking dis here way, wid he head

e ob *(A)*
f about *(B, D)*
g bout *(A)*

down and he soldiers up, and as white as a gose?[10] And den he keep a syphon all de time – "

"Keeps a what, Jupiter?"

"Keeps a syphon wid de figgurs on de slate – de queerest figgurs[h] I ebber did see. Ise gitting to be skeered, I tell you. Hab for to keep mighty tight eye pon him noovers. Todder day he gib me slip fore de sun up and was gone de whole ob de blessed day. I had a big stick ready cut for to gib him d – d[i] good beating[j] when he did come – but Ise sich a fool dat I hadn't de heart arter all – he look so berry poorly."[11]

"Eh? – what? – ah yes! – upon the whole I think you had better not be too severe with the poor fellow – don't flog him, Jupiter – he can't very well stand it – but can you form no idea of what has occasioned this illness, or rather this change of conduct? Has anything unpleasant happened since I saw you?"

"No, massa, dey aint bin noffin onpleasant *since* den – 'twas *fore* den I'm feared – 'twas de[k] berry day you was dare."

"How? what do you mean?"

"Why, massa, I mean de bug – dare now."

"The what?"

"De bug – I'm berry sartain dat Massa Will bin bit somewhere bout de[l] head by dat[m] goole-bug."

"And what cause have you, Jupiter, for such a supposition?"

"Claws enuff, massa, and mouff too. I nebber did see sich a d – d[n] bug – he kick and he bite ebery ting what cum near him. Massa Will cotch him fuss, but had for to let him go gin mighty quick, I tell you – den was de time he must ha got de bite. I didn't like de look ob de bug mouff, myself, no how, so I wouldn't take hold ob him wid my finger, but I[o] cotch him wid a piece ob paper dat I found. I rap him up in de paper and stuff piece ob it in he mouff – dat was de way."

"And you think, then, that your master was really bitten by the beetle, and that the bite made him sick?"

---

h figures *(A)*
i d – n *(A)*; deuced *(B, D)*
j beatin *(A)*
k the *(A)*
l the *(A)*
m dat d – n *(A)*
n d – n *(A)*; deuced *(B, D)*
o *Omitted (A)*

"I don't tink noffin about[p] it — I nose it. What make him dream bout de goole so much, if taint cause he bit by de goole-bug?[12] Ise heerd bout dem goole-bugs fore dis."

"But how do you know he dreams about gold?"

"How I know? why cause he talk about it in he sleep — dat's how I nose."

"Well, Jup, perhaps you are right; but to what fortunate circumstance am I to attribute the honor of a visit from you to-day?"

"What de matter, massa?"

"Did you bring any message from Mr. Legrand?"

"No, massa, I bring dis here pissel;" and here Jupiter handed me a note which ran thus:

MY DEAR ——

Why have I not seen you for so long a time? I hope you have not been so foolish as to take offence at any little *brusquerie* of mine; but no, that is improbable.

Since I saw you I have had great cause for anxiety. I have something to tell you, yet scarcely know how to tell it, or whether I should tell it at all.

I have not been quite well for some days past, and poor old Jup annoys me, almost beyond endurance, by his well-meant attentions. Would you believe it? — he had prepared a huge stick, the other day, with which to chastise me for giving him the slip, and spending the day, *solus,* among the hills on the main land. I verily believe that my ill looks alone saved me a flogging.

I have made no addition to my cabinet since we met.

If you can, in any way, make it convenient, come over with Jupiter. *Do* come. I wish to see you *to-night,* upon business of importance. I assure you that it is of the *highest* importance.

Ever yours, WILLIAM LEGRAND.

There was something in the tone of this note which gave me great uneasiness. Its whole style differed materially from that of Legrand. What could he be dreaming of? What new crotchet pos-

---

p bout *(A)*

sessed his excitable brain? What "business of the highest importance" could *he* possibly have to transact? Jupiter's account of him boded no good. I dreaded lest the continued pressure of misfortune had, at length, fairly unsettled the reason of my friend. Without a moment's hesitation, therefore, I prepared to accompany the negro.

Upon reaching the wharf, I noticed a scythe and three spades, all apparently new, lying in the bottom of the boat in which we were to embark.

"What is the meaning of all this, Jup?" I inquired.

"Him syfe, massa, and spade."

"Very true; but what are they doing here?"

"Him de syfe and de spade what[q] Massa Will sis pon my buying for him in de town, and de debbil's[r] own lot of money I had to gib for em."

"But what, in the name of all that is mysterious, is your 'Massa Will' going to do with scythes and spades?"

"Dat's more dan *I* know, and debbil take me if I don't blieve 'tis more dan he know, too. But it's all cum ob de bug."

Finding that no satisfaction was to be obtained of Jupiter, whose whole intellect seemed to be absorbed by "de bug," I now stepped into the boat and made sail. With a fair and strong breeze we soon ran into the little cove to the northward of Fort Moultrie, and a walk of some two miles brought us to the hut. It was about three in the afternoon when we arrived. Legrand had been awaiting us in eager expectation. He grasped my hand with a nervous *empressement* which alarmed me and strengthened the suspicions already entertained. His countenance was pale even to ghastliness, and his deep-set eyes glared with unnatural lustre. After some inquiries respecting his health, I asked him, not knowing what better to say, if he had yet obtained the *scarabæus* from Lieutenant G——.

"Oh, yes," he replied, coloring violently, "I got it from him the next morning. Nothing should tempt me to part with that *scarabæus*. Do you know that Jupiter is quite right about it?"

"In what way?" I asked, with a sad foreboding at heart.

---

q which *(A)* *from A*

r debbils *(B, C, D) apostrophe added*

"In supposing it to be a bug of *real gold.*" He said this with an air of profound seriousness, and I felt inexpressibly shocked.

"This bug is to make my fortune," he continued, with a triumphant smile, "to reinstate me in my family possessions. Is it any wonder, then, that I prize it? Since Fortune has thought fit to bestow it upon me, I have only to use it properly and I shall arrive at the gold of which it is the index. Jupiter, bring me that *scarabæus!*"

"What! de bug, massa? I'd rudder not go fer[s] trubble dat bug — you mus git him for your own self." Hereupon Legrand arose, with a grave and stately air, and brought me the beetle from a glass case in which it was enclosed. It was a beautiful *scarabæus,* and, at that time, unknown to naturalists — of course a great prize in a scientific point of view. There were two round, black spots near one extremity of the back, and a long[t] one near the other. The scales were exceedingly hard and glossy, with all the appearance of burnished gold.[13] The weight of the insect was very remarkable, and, taking all things into consideration, I could hardly blame Jupiter for his opinion respecting it; but what to make of Legrand's agreement[u] with that opinion, I could not, for the life of me, tell.

"I sent for you," said he, in a grandiloquent tone, when I had completed my examination of the beetle, "I sent for you, that I might have your counsel and assistance in furthering the views of Fate and of the bug" —

"My dear Legrand," I cried, interrupting him, "you are certainly unwell, and had better use some little precautions. You shall go to bed, and I will remain with you a few days, until you get over this. You are feverish and" —

"Feel my pulse," said he.

I felt it, and, to say the truth, found not the slightest indication of fever.

"But you may be ill and yet have no fever. Allow me this once to prescribe for you. In the first place, go to bed. In the next" —

---

s fer to *(A)*
t longer *(A)*
u concordance *(A, B, D)*

"You are mistaken," he interposed, "I am as well as I can expect to be under the excitement which I suffer. If you really wish me well, you will relieve this excitement."

"And how is this to be done?"

"Very easily. Jupiter and myself are going upon an expedition into the hills, upon the main land, and, in this expedition, we shall need the aid of some person in whom we can confide. You are the only one we can trust. Whether we succeed or fail, the excitement which you now perceive in me will be equally allayed."

"I am anxious to oblige you in any way," I replied; "but do you mean to say that this infernal beetle has any connection with your expedition into the hills?"

"It has."

"Then, Legrand, I can become a party to no such absurd proceeding."

"I am sorry — very sorry — for we shall have to try it by ourselves."

"Try it by yourselves! The man is surely mad! — but stay! — how long do you propose to be absent?"

"Probably all night. We shall start immediately, and be back, at all events, by sunrise."

"And will you promise me, upon your honor, that when this freak of yours is over, and the bug business (good God!) settled to your satisfaction, you will then return home and follow my advice implicitly, as that of your physician?"

"Yes; I promise; and now let us be off, for we have no time to lose."

With a heavy heart I accompanied my friend. We started about four o'clock — Legrand, Jupiter, the dog, and myself. Jupiter had with him the scythe and spades — the whole of which he insisted upon carrying — more through fear, it seemed to me, of trusting either of the implements within reach of his master, than from any excess of industry or complaisance. His demeanor was dogged in the extreme, and "dat d — d[v] bug" were the sole words which escaped his lips during the journey. For my own part, I had charge

---

v d — n *(A)*; deuced *(B, D)*

of a couple of dark lanterns, while Legrand contented himself with the *scarabæus,* which he carried attached to the end of a bit of whip-cord; twirling it to and fro, with the air of a conjuror, as he went. When I observed this last, plain evidence of my friend's aberration of mind, I could scarcely refrain from tears. I thought it best, however, to humor his fancy, at least for the present, or until I could adopt some more energetic measures with a chance of success. In the mean time I endeavored, but all in vain, to sound him in regard to the object of the expedition. Having succeeded in inducing me to accompany him, he seemed unwilling to hold conversation upon any topic of minor importance, and to all my questions vouchsafed no other reply than "we shall see!"

We crossed the creek at the head of the island by means of a skiff, and, ascending the high grounds on the shore of the main land, proceeded in a northwesterly[w] direction, through a tract of country excessively wild and desolate, where no trace of a human footstep was to be seen. Legrand led the way with decision; pausing only for an instant, here and there, to consult what appeared to be certain landmarks of his own contrivance upon a former occasion.

In this manner we journeyed for about two hours, and the sun was just setting when we entered a region infinitely more dreary than any yet seen. It was a species of table land, near the summit of an almost inaccessible hill, densely wooded from base to pinnacle, and interspersed with huge crags[14] that appeared to lie loosely upon the soil, and in many cases were prevented from precipitating themselves into the valleys below, merely by the support of the trees against which they reclined. Deep ravines, in various directions, gave an air of still sterner solemnity to the scene.

The natural platform to which we had clambered was thickly overgrown with brambles, through which we soon discovered that it would have been impossible to force our way but for the scythe; and Jupiter, by direction of his master, proceeded to clear for us a path to the foot of an enormously tall tulip-tree, which stood, with some eight or ten oaks, upon the level, and far surpassed them all,

w northwesternly *(A)*

and all other trees which I had then ever seen, in the beauty of its foliage and form, in the wide spread of its branches, and in the general majesty of its appearance. When we reached this tree, Legrand turned to Jupiter, and asked him if he thought he could climb it. The old man seemed a little staggered by the question, and for some moments made no reply. At length he approached the huge trunk,[x] walked slowly [y]around it,[y] and examined it with minute attention. When he had completed his scrutiny, he merely said,

"Yes, massa, Jup climb any tree he ebber see in he life."

"Then up with you as soon as possible, for it will soon be too dark to see what we are about."

"How far mus go up, massa?" inquired Jupiter.

"Get up the main trunk first, and then I will tell you which way to go – and here – stop! take this beetle[z] with you."

"De bug, Massa Will! – de goole bug!" cried the negro, drawing back in dismay – "what for mus tote de bug way up de tree? – d – n if I do!"

"If you are afraid, Jup, a great big negro like you, to take hold of a harmless little dead beetle, why you can carry it up by this string – but, if you do not take it up with you in some way, I shall be under the necessity of breaking your head with this shovel."

"What de matter now, massa?" said Jup, evidently shamed into compliance; "always want for to raise fuss wid old nigger. Was only funnin any how. *Me* feered de bug! what I keer for de bug?" Here he took cautiously hold of the extreme end of the string, and, maintaining the insect as far from his person as circumstances would permit, prepared to ascend the tree.

In youth, the tulip-tree, or *Liriodendron Tulipiferum,* the most magnificent of American foresters,[15] has a trunk peculiarly smooth, and often rises to a great height without lateral branches; but, in its riper age, the bark becomes gnarled and uneven, while many short limbs make their appearance on the stem. Thus the difficulty of ascension, in the present case, lay more in semblance than in reality. Embracing the huge cylinder, as closely as possible, with his arms and knees, seizing with his hands some projections, and

---

x huge trunk,/tree, *(A)*

y . . . y round its huge trunk, *(A)*

z beetle up *(A)*

resting his naked toes upon others, Jupiter, after one or two narrow escapes from falling, at length wriggled himself into the first great fork, and seemed to consider the whole business as virtually accomplished. The *risk* of the achievement was, in fact, now over, although the climber was some sixty or seventy feet from the ground.

"Which way mus go now, Massa Will?" he asked.

"Keep up the largest branch – the one on this side," said Legrand. The negro obeyed him promptly, and apparently with but little trouble; ascending higher and higher, until no glimpse of his squat figure could be obtained through the dense foliage which enveloped it. Presently his voice was heard in a sort of halloo.

"How much fudder is got for go?"

"How high up are you?" asked Legrand.

"Ebber so fur," replied the negro; "can see de sky fru de top of de tree."

"Never mind the sky, but attend to what I say. Look down the trunk and count the limbs below you on this side. How many limbs have you passed?"

"One, two, tree,[a] four, fibe – I done pass fibe big limb, massa, pon dis side."

"Then go one limb higher."

In a few minutes the voice was heard again, announcing that the seventh limb was attained.

"Now, Jup," cried Legrand, evidently much excited, "I want you to work your way out upon that limb as far as you can. If you see anything strange, let me know."

By this time what little doubt I might have entertained of my poor friend's insanity, was put finally at rest. I had no alternative but to conclude him stricken with lunacy, and I became seriously anxious about getting him home. While I was pondering upon what was best to be done, Jupiter's voice was again heard.

"Mos feerd for to ventur pon dis limb berry far – tis dead limb putty much all de way."

"Did you say it was a *dead* limb, Jupiter?" cried Legrand in a quavering voice.

---

a three, *(A)*

"Yes, massa, him dead as de door-nail – done up for sartain – done departed dis here life."

"What in the name of heaven shall I do?" asked Legrand, seemingly in the greatest distress.

"Do!" said I, glad of an opportunity to interpose a word, "why come home and go to bed. Come now![b] – that's a fine fellow. It's getting late, and, besides, you remember your promise."

"Jupiter," cried he, without heeding me in the least, "do you hear me?"

"Yes, Massa Will, hear you ebber so plain."

"Try the wood well, then, with your knife, and see if you think it *very* rotten."

"Him rotten, massa, sure nuff," replied the negro in a few moments, "but not so berry rotten as mought be. Mought ventur out leetle way pon de limb by myself, dat's true."

"By yourself! – what do you mean?"

"Why I mean de bug. 'Tis *berry* hebby bug. Spose I drop him down fuss, and den de limb won't break wid just de weight ob one nigger."

"You infernal scoundrel!" cried Legrand, apparently much relieved, "what do you mean by telling me such nonsense as that? As sure as you let[c] that beetle fall[d] I'll break your neck. Look here, Jupiter! – [e] do you hear me?"

"Yes, massa, needn't hollo at poor nigger dat style."

"Well! now listen! – if you will venture out on the limb as far as you think safe, and not let go[f] the beetle, I'll make you a present of a silver dollar as soon as you get down."

"I'm gwine, Massa Will – deed I is," replied the negro very promptly – "mos out to the[g] eend now."

"Out to the end!" here fairly screamed Legrand, "do you say you are out to the end of that limb?"

"Soon be to de eend, massa, – o-o-o-o-oh! Lor-gol-a-marcy! what *is* dis here pon de tree?"

"Well!" cried Legrand, highly delighted, "what is it?"

---

b Come now!/Do *(A)*
c drop *(A, B, D)*
d *Omitted (A)*
e Jupiter, *(A, B, D)*
f go of *(A)*
g de *(A)*

"Why taint noffin but a skull — somebody bin lef him head up de tree, and de crows done gobble ebery bit ob de meat off."

"A skull, you say! — very well! — how is it fastened to the limb? — what holds it on?"

"Sure nuff, massa; mus look. Why dis berry curous sarcumstance, pon my word — dare's a great big nail in de skull, what fastens ob it on to de tree."[16]

"Well now, Jupiter, do exactly as I tell you — do you hear?"

"Yes, massa."

"Pay attention, then! — find the left eye of the skull."

"Hum! hoo! dat's good! why dar[h] aint no eye lef at all."

"Curse your stupidity! do you know your right hand from your left?"[17]

"Yes, I nose dat — nose all bout dat — tis my lef hand what I chops de wood wid."

"To be sure! you are left-handed; and your left eye is on the same side as your left hand. Now, I suppose, you can find the left eye of the skull, or the place where the left eye has been. Have you found it?"

Here was a long pause. At length the negro asked,

"Is de lef eye of de skull pon de same side as de lef hand of de skull, too? — cause de skull aint got not a bit ob a hand at all — nebber mind! I got de lef eye now — here de lef eye! what mus do wid it?"

"Let the beetle drop through it, as far as the string will reach — but be careful and not let go your hold of the string."

"All dat done, Massa Will; mighty easy ting for to put de bug fru de hole — look out for him dar[i] below!"[j]

During this colloquy no portion of Jupiter's person could be seen; but the beetle, which he had suffered to descend, was now visible at the end of the string, and glistened, like a globe of burnished gold, in the last rays of the setting sun, some of which still faintly illumined the eminence upon which we stood. The *scarabæus* hung quite clear of any branches, and, if allowed to fall,

h dare *(A, B, D)*
i dare *(A, B, D)*
j *A adds a paragraph* "Very well! — now just keep as you are for a few minutes."

would have fallen at our feet. Legrand immediately took the scythe, and cleared with it a circular space, three or four yards in diameter, just beneath the insect, and, having accomplished this, ordered Jupiter to let go the string and come down from the tree.

Driving a peg, with great nicety, into the ground, at the precise spot where thc beetle fell,[k] my friend now produced from his pocket a tape-measure. Fastening one end of this at that point of the trunk of the tree which was nearest the peg, he unrolled it till it reached the peg, and thence farther unrolled it, in the direction already established by the two points of the tree and the peg, for the distance of fifty feet — Jupiter clearing away the brambles with the scythe. At the spot thus attained a second peg was driven, and about this, as a centre, a rude circle, about four feet in diameter, described. Taking now a spade himself, and giving one to Jupiter and one to me, Legrand begged us to set about digging as quickly as possible.

To speak the truth, I had no especial relish for such amusement at any time, and, at that particular moment,[l] would most willingly have declined it; for the night was coming on, and I felt much fatigued with the exercise already taken; but I saw no mode of escape, and was fearful of disturbing my poor friend's equanimity by a refusal. Could I have depended, indeed, upon Jupiter's aid, I would have had no hesitation in attempting to get the lunatic home by force; but I was too well assured of the old negro's disposition, to hope that he would assist me, under any circumstances, in a personal contest with his master. I made no doubt that the latter had been infected with some of the innumerable Southern superstitions about money buried, and that his phantasy had received confirmation by the finding of the *scarabæus,* or, perhaps, by Jupiter's obstinacy in maintaining it to be "a bug of real gold." A mind disposed to lunacy would readily be led away by such suggestions — especially if chiming in with favorite preconceived ideas — and then I called to mind the poor fellow's speech about the beetle's being "the index of his fortune."[18] Upon the whole, I was sadly vexed and puzzled, but, at length, I concluded to make a virtue of neces-

k lay, *(A)*

l moment, I *(A)*

sity[19] — to dig with a good will, and thus the sooner to convince the visionary,[m] by ocular demonstration, of the fallacy of the opinions he entertained.

The lanterns having been lit, we all fell to work with a zeal worthy a more rational cause; and, as the glare fell upon our persons and implements, I could not help thinking how picturesque a group we composed, and how strange and suspicious our labors must have appeared to any interloper who, by chance, might have stumbled upon our whereabouts.

We dug very steadily for two hours. Little was said; and our chief embarrassment lay in the yelpings of the dog, who took exceeding interest in our proceedings. He, at length, became so obstreperous that we grew fearful of his giving the alarm to some stragglers in the vicinity; — or, rather, this was the apprehension of Legrand; — for myself, I should have rejoiced at any interruption which might have enabled me to get the wanderer home. The noise was, at length, very effectually silenced by Jupiter, who, getting out of the hole with a dogged air of deliberation, tied the brute's mouth up with one of his suspenders, and then returned, with a grave chuckle, to his task.

When the time mentioned had expired, we had reached a depth of five feet, and yet no signs of any treasure became manifest. A general pause ensued, and I began to hope that the farce was at an end. Legrand, however, although evidently much disconcerted, wiped his brow thoughtfully and recommenced. We had excavated the entire circle of four feet diameter, and now we slightly enlarged the limit, and went to the farther depth of two feet. Still nothing appeared. The gold-seeker, whom I sincerely pitied, at length clambered from the pit, with the bitterest disappointment imprinted upon every feature, and proceeded, slowly and reluctantly, to put on his coat, which he had thrown off at the beginning of his labor. In the mean time I made no remark. Jupiter, at a signal from his master, began to gather up his tools. This done, and the dog having been unmuzzled, we turned in[n] profound silence towards home.

---

m the visionary,/him, *(A)* n in a *(A)*

We had taken, perhaps, a dozen steps in this direction, when, with a loud oath, Legrand strode up to Jupiter, and seized him by the collar. The astonished negro opened his eyes and mouth to the fullest extent, let fall the spades, and fell upon his knees.

"You scoundrel," said Legrand, hissing out the syllables from between his clenched teeth – "you infernal black villain! – speak, I tell you! – answer me this instant, without prevarication! – which – which is your left eye?"

"Oh, my golly, Massa Will! aint dis here my lef eye for sartain?" roared the terrified Jupiter, placing his hand upon his *right* organ of vision, and holding it there with a desperate pertinacity, as if in immediate dread of his master's attempt at a gouge.[20]

"I thought so! – I knew it! –[o] hurrah!" vociferated Legrand, letting the negro go, and executing a series of curvets and caracols,[21] much to the astonishment of his valet, who, arising from his knees, looked, mutely, from his master to myself, and then from myself to his master.

"Come! we must go back," said the latter, "the game's not up yet;" and he again led the way to the tulip-tree.

"Jupiter," said he, when we reached its foot, "come here! was the skull nailed to the limb with the face outward,[p] or with the face to the limb?"

"De face was out, massa, so dat de crows could get at de eyes good, widout any trouble."[q]

"Well, then, was it this eye or that through which you let fall[r] the beetle?" – here Legrand touched each of Jupiter's eyes.

"Twas dis eye, massa – de lef eye – jis as you tell me," and here it was his right eye that the negro indicated.

"That will do – we must try it again."

Here my friend, about whose madness I now saw, or fancied that I saw, certain indications of method, removed the peg [s]which marked the spot where the beetle fell,[s] to a spot about three inches to the westward of its former position. Taking, now, the tape-measure from the nearest point of the [t]trunk to the peg,[t] as before,

---

o *Dash omitted (B, D)*
p outwards, *(A, B, D)*
q trubble." *(A)*
r let fall/dropped *(A, B, D)*
s . . . s nearest the tree, *(A)*
t . . . t trunk, *(A)*

and continuing the extension in a straight line to the distance of fifty feet, a spot was indicated, removed, by several yards, from the point at which we had been digging.[22]

Around the new position a circle, somewhat larger than in the former instance, was now described, and we again set to work with the spades. I was dreadfully weary, but, scarcely understanding what had occasioned the change in my thoughts, I felt no longer any great aversion from the labor imposed. I had become most unaccountably interested – nay, even excited. Perhaps there was something, amid all the extravagant demeanor of Legrand – some air of forethought, or of deliberation, which impressed me. I dug eagerly, and now and then caught myself actually looking, with something that very much resembled expectation, for the fancied treasure, the vision of which had demented my unfortunate companion. At a period when such vagaries of thought most fully possessed me, and when we had been at work perhaps an hour and a half, we were again interrupted by the violent howlings of the dog. His uneasiness, in the first instance, had been, evidently, but the result of playfulness or caprice, but he now assumed a bitter and serious tone. Upon Jupiter's again attempting to muzzle him, he made furious resistance, and, leaping into the hole, tore up the mould frantically with his claws. In a few seconds he had uncovered a mass of human bones, forming two complete skeletons,[u] intermingled with several buttons of metal, and what appeared to be the dust of decayed woollen. One or two strokes of a spade upturned the blade of a large Spanish knife, and, as we dug farther, three or four loose pieces of gold and silver coin came to light.

At sight of these the joy of Jupiter could scarcely be restrained, but the countenance of his master wore an air of extreme disappointment. He urged us, however, to continue our exertions, and the words were hardly uttered when I stumbled and fell forward, having caught the toe of my boot in a large ring of iron that lay half buried in the loose earth.

We now worked in[v] earnest, and never did I pass ten minutes of more intense excitement. During this interval we had fairly un-

u skeletons, and *(A)*

v in good *(A)*

earthed an oblong chest of wood, which, from its perfect preservation and wonderful hardness, had plainly been subjected to some mineralizing process — perhaps that of the Bi-chloride of Mercury.[23] This box was three feet and a half long, three feet broad, and two and a half feet deep. It was firmly secured by bands of wrought iron, riveted, and forming a kind of[w] trellis-work over the whole. On each side of the chest, near the top, were three rings of iron — six in all — by means of which a firm hold could be obtained by six persons. Our utmost united endeavors served only to disturb the coffer very slightly in its bed. We at once saw the impossibility of removing so great a weight. Luckily, the sole fastenings of the lid consisted of two sliding bolts. These we drew back — trembling and panting with anxiety. In an instant, a treasure of incalculable value lay gleaming before us. As the rays of the lanterns fell within the pit, there flashed upwards [x]from a confused heap of gold and of jewels, a glow and a glare[x] that absolutely dazzled our eyes.

I shall not pretend to describe the feelings with which I gazed. Amazement was, of course, predominant. Legrand appeared exhausted with excitement, and spoke very few words. Jupiter's countenance wore, for some minutes, as deadly a pallor as it is possible, in the nature of things, for any negro's visage to assume. He seemed stupified — thunderstricken. Presently he fell upon his knees in the pit, and, burying his naked arms up to the elbows in gold, let them there remain, as if enjoying the luxury of a bath. At length, with a deep sigh, he exclaimed, as if in a soliloquy,

"And dis all cum ob de goole-bug! de putty goole-bug! de poor little goole-bug, what I boosed in dat sabage kind ob style! Aint you shamed ob yourself, nigger? — answer me dat!"

It became necessary, at last, that I should arouse both master and valet to the expediency of removing the treasure. It was growing late, and it behooved us to make exertion, that we might get every thing housed before daylight. It was difficult to say what should be done;[y] and much time was spent in deliberation — so confused were the ideas of all. We, finally, lightened the box by removing two thirds of its contents, when we were enabled, with some

---

w of open *(A, B, D)*

x . . . x a glow and a glare, from a confused heap of gold and of jewels, *(A, B, D)*

y done;/done *(A, B, D)*

trouble, to raise it from the hole. The articles taken out were deposited among the brambles, and the dog left to guard them, with strict orders from Jupiter neither, upon any pretence, to stir from the spot, nor to open his mouth until our return. We then hurriedly made for home with the chest; reaching the hut in safety, but after excessive toil, at one o'clock in the morning. Worn out as we were, it was not in human nature to do more just then.[z] We rested until two, and had supper; starting for the hills immediately afterwards, armed with three stout sacks, which, by good luck, were upon the premises. A little before four we arrived at the pit, divided the remainder of the booty, as equally as might be, among us, and, leaving the holes unfilled, again set out for the hut, at which, for the second time, we deposited our golden burthens, just as the first[a] streaks of the dawn gleamed from over the tree-tops in the East.

We were now thoroughly broken down; but the intense excitement of the time denied us repose. After an unquiet slumber of some three or four hours' duration, we arose, as if by preconcert, to make examination of our treasure.

The chest had been full to the brim, and we spent the whole day, and the greater part of the next night, in a scrutiny of its contents. There had been nothing like order or arrangement. Every thing had been heaped in promiscuously. Having assorted all with care, we found ourselves possessed of even vaster wealth than we had at first supposed. In coin there was rather more than four hundred and fifty thousand dollars — estimating the value of the pieces, as accurately as we could, by the tables of the period. There was not a particle of silver. All was gold of antique date and of great variety — French, Spanish, and German money, with a few English guineas, and some counters,[24] of which we had never seen specimens before. There were several very large and heavy coins, so worn that we could make nothing of their inscriptions. There was no American money. The value of the jewels we found more difficulty in estimating. There were diamonds — some of them exceedingly large and fine — a hundred and ten in all, and not one of them small; eighteen rubies of remarkable brilliancy; — three hundred and ten emeralds, all very beautiful; and twenty-one sapphires, with an

z just then./immediately. *(A, B, D)* a first faint *(A, B, D)*

opal. These stones had all been broken from their settings and thrown loose in the chest. The settings themselves, which we picked out from among the other gold, appeared to have been beaten up with hammers, as if to prevent identification. Besides all this, there was a vast quantity of solid gold ornaments; — nearly two hundred massive finger and ear rings; — rich chains — thirty of these, if I remember; — eighty-three very large and heavy crucifixes; — five[b] gold censers of great value; — a prodigious golden punch-bowl, ornamented with richly chased vine-leaves and Bacchanalian figures; with two sword-handles exquisitely embossed, and many other smaller articles which I cannot recollect. The weight of these valuables exceeded three hundred and fifty pounds avoirdupois; and in this estimate I have not included one hundred and ninety-seven superb gold watches; three of the number being worth each five hundred dollars, if one. Many of them were very old, and as time keepers valueless; the works having suffered, more or less, from corrosion — but all were richly jewelled and in cases of great worth. We estimated the entire contents of the chest, that night, at a million and a half of dollars; and, upon the subsequent disposal of the trinkets and jewels (a few being retained for our own use), it was found that we had greatly undervalued the treasure.

When, at length, we had concluded our examination, and the intense excitement of the time had, in some measure, subsided, Legrand, who saw that I was dying with impatience for a solution of this most extraordinary riddle, entered into a full detail of all the circumstances connected with it.[25]

"You remember," said he, "the night when I handed you the rough sketch I had made of the *scarabæus*. You recollect also, that I became quite vexed at you for insisting that my drawing resembled a death's-head. When you first made this assertion I thought you were jesting; but afterwards I called to mind the peculiar spots on the back of the insect, and admitted to myself that your remark had some little foundation in fact. Still, the sneer at my graphic powers irritated me — for I am considered a good artist — and, therefore, when you handed me the scrap of parchment, I was about to crumple it up and throw it angrily into[c] the fire."

---

b fine *(A)* c in *(A)*

"The scrap of paper, you mean," said I.

"No; it had much of the appearance of paper, and at first I supposed it to be such, but when I came to draw upon it, I discovered it, at once, to be a piece of very thin parchment. It was quite dirty, you remember. Well, as I was in the very act of crumpling it up, my glance fell upon the sketch at which you had been looking, and you may imagine my astonishment when I perceived, in fact, the figure of a death's-head just where, it seemed to me, I had made the drawing of the beetle. For a moment I was too much amazed to think with accuracy. I knew that my design was very different in detail from this — although there was a certain similarity in general outline. Presently I took a candle, and seating myself at the other end of the room, proceeded to scrutinize the parchment more closely. Upon turning it over, I saw my own sketch upon the reverse, just as I had made it. My first idea, now, was mere surprise at the really remarkable similarity of outline — at the singular coincidence involved in the fact, that unknown to me, there should have been a skull upon the other side of the parchment, immediately beneath my figure of the *scarabæus,* and that this skull, not only in outline, but in size, should so closely resemble my drawing. I say the singularity of this coincidence absolutely stupified me for a time. This is the usual effect of such coincidences. The mind struggles to establish a connexion — a sequence of cause and effect — and, being unable to do so, suffers a species of temporary paralysis. But, when I recovered from this stupor, there dawned upon me gradually a conviction which startled me even far more than the coincidence. I began distinctly, positively, to remember that there had been *no* drawing on[d] the parchment when I made my sketch of the *scarabæus.* I became perfectly certain of this; for I recollected turning up first one side and then the other, in search of the cleanest spot. Had the skull been then there, of course I could not have failed to notice it. Here was indeed a mystery which I felt it impossible to explain; but, even at that early moment, there seemed to glimmer, faintly, within the most remote and secret chambers of my intellect, a glow-worm-like conception of that truth which last night's adventure brought to so magnificent a demonstration.

d upon *(A, B, D)*

I arose at once, [e]and putting the parchment securely away,[e] dismissed[f] all farther reflection until I should be alone.

"When you had gone, and when Jupiter was fast asleep, I betook myself to a more methodical investigation of the affair. In the first place I considered the manner in which the parchment had come into my possession. The spot where we discovered the *scarabæus* was on the coast of the main land, about a mile eastward of the island, and but a short distance above high water mark. Upon my taking hold of[g] it, it gave me a sharp bite, which caused me to let it drop. Jupiter, with his accustomed caution, before seizing the insect, which had flown towards him, looked about him for a leaf, or something of that nature, by which to take hold of it. It was at this moment that his eyes, and mine also, fell upon the scrap of parchment, which I then supposed to be paper. It was lying half buried in the sand, a corner sticking up. Near the spot where we found it, I observed the remnants of the hull of what appeared to have been a ship's long boat. The wreck seemed to have been there for a very great while; for the resemblance to boat timbers could scarcely be traced.

"Well, Jupiter picked up the parchment, wrapped the beetle in it, and gave it to me. Soon afterwards we turned to go home, and on the way met Lieutenant G——. I showed him the insect, and he begged me to let him take it to the fort. On[h] my consenting, he thrust it forthwith into his waistcoat pocket, without the parchment in which it had been wrapped, and which I had continued to hold in my hand during his inspection. Perhaps he dreaded my changing my mind, and thought it best to make sure of the prize at once – you know how enthusiastic he is on all subjects connected with Natural History. At the same time, without being conscious of it, I must have deposited the parchment in my own pocket.

"You remember that when I went to the table, for the purpose of making a sketch of the beetle, I found no paper where it was usually kept. I looked in the drawer, and found none there. I searched my pockets, hoping to find an old [i]letter – and then[i] my hand fell upon the parchment. I thus detail the precise mode in

e . . . e *Omitted (A)*
f dismissing *(A)*
g taking hold of/seizing *(A)*
h Upon *(A, B, D)*
i . . . i letter, when *(A, B, D)*

which it came into my possession; for the circumstances impressed me with peculiar force.

"No doubt you will think me fanciful – but I had already established a kind of *connexion*. I had put together two links of a great chain. There was a boat lying on[j] a sea-coast, and not far from the boat was a parchment – *not a paper* – with a skull depicted on[k] it. You will, of course, ask 'where is the connection?' I reply that the skull, or death's-head, is the well-known emblem of the pirate.[26] The flag of the death's-head is hoisted in all engagements.

"I have said that the scrap was parchment, and not paper. Parchment is durable – almost imperishable. Matters of little moment are rarely consigned to parchment; since, for the mere ordinary purposes of drawing or writing, it is not nearly so well adapted as paper. This reflection suggested some meaning —some relevancy —[27] in the death's-head. I did not fail to observe, also, the *form* of the parchment. Although one of its corners had been, by some accident, destroyed, it could be seen that the original form was oblong. It was just such a slip, indeed, as might have been chosen for a memorandum – for a record of something to be long remembered and carefully preserved."

"But," I interposed, "you say that the skull was *not* upon the parchment when you made the drawing of the beetle. How then do you trace any connexion between the boat and the skull – since this latter, according to your own admission, must have been designed (God only knows how or by whom) at some period subsequent to your sketching the *scarabæus?*"

"Ah, hereupon turns the whole mystery; although the secret, at this point, I had comparatively little difficulty in solving. My steps were sure, and could afford but a single result. I reasoned, for example, thus: When I drew the *scarabæus,* there was no skull apparent on[l] the parchment. When I had completed the drawing,[m] I gave it to you, and observed you narrowly until you returned it. *You,* therefore, did not design the skull, and no one else was present to do it. Then it was not done by human agency. And nevertheless it was done.

j upon *(A, B, D)*
k upon *(A, B, D)*
l upon *(A, B, D)*
m drawing,/drawing *(A, B, D)*

"At this stage of my reflections I endeavored to remember, and *did* remember, with entire distinctness, every incident which occurred about the period in question. The weather was chilly (oh rare and happy accident!), and a fire was blazing on[n] the hearth. I was heated with exercise and sat near the table. You, however, had drawn a chair close to the chimney. Just as I placed the parchment in your hand, and as you were in the act of inspecting it, Wolf, the Newfoundland, entered, and leaped upon your shoulders. With your left hand you caressed him and kept him off, while your right, holding the parchment, was permitted to fall listlessly between your knees, and in close proximity to the fire. At one moment I thought the blaze had caught it, and was about to caution you, but, before I could speak, you had withdrawn it, and were engaged in its examination. When I considered all these particulars, I doubted not for a moment that *heat* had been the agent in bringing to light, on[o] the parchment, the skull which I saw designed on[p] it. You are well aware that chemical preparations exist, and have existed time out of mind, by means of which it is possible to write on[q] either paper or vellum, so that the characters shall become visible only when subjected to the action of fire. [r]Zaffre, digested in *aqua regia,* and diluted with four times its weight of water, is sometimes employed; a green tint results. The regulus of cobalt, dissolved in spirit of nitre, gives a red.[28] These colors disappear at longer or shorter intervals after the material written on[s] cools, but again become apparent upon the reapplication of heat.[r]

"I now scrutinized the death's-head with care. Its outer edges – the edges of the drawing nearest the edge of the vellum – were far more *distinct* than the others. It was clear that the action of the caloric had been imperfect or unequal. I immediately kindled a fire, and subjected every portion of the parchment to a glowing heat. At first, the only effect was the strengthening of the faint lines in the skull; but, on[t] persevering in the experiment, there became visible, at the corner of the slip, diagonally opposite to the spot in

n upon *(A, B, D)*
o upon *(A, B, D)*
p upon *(A, B, D)*
q upon *(A, B, D)*
r . . . r *Omitted (A)*
s upon *(A, B, D)*
t upon *(A, B, D)*

which the death's-head was delineated, the figure of what I at first supposed to be a goat. A closer scrutiny, however, satisfied me that it was intended for a kid."

"Ha! ha!" said I, "to be sure I have no right to laugh at you – a million and a half of money is too serious a matter for mirth – but you are not about to establish a third link in your chain – you will not find any especial connexion between your pirates and a goat – pirates, you know, have nothing to do with goats; they appertain to the farming interest."

"But I have just said that the figure was *not* that of a goat."

"Well, a kid then – pretty much the same thing."

"Pretty much, but not altogether," said Legrand. "You may have heard of one *Captain* Kidd. I at once looked on[u] the figure of the animal as a kind of punning or hieroglyphical signature. I say signature; because its position on[v] the vellum suggested this idea. The death's-head at the corner diagonally opposite, had, in the same manner, the air of a stamp, or seal. But I was sorely put out by the absence of all else – of the body to my imagined instrument – of the text for my context."

"I presume you expected to find a letter between the stamp and the signature."

"Something of that kind. The fact is, I felt irresistibly impressed with a presentiment of some vast good fortune impending. I can scarcely say why. Perhaps, after all, it was rather a desire than an actual belief; – but do you know that Jupiter's silly words, about the bug being of solid gold, had a remarkable effect on[w] my fancy? And then the series of accidents and coincidences – these were so *very* extraordinary. Do you observe how mere an accident it was that these events should have occurred on[x] the *sole* day of all the year in which it has been, or may be, sufficiently cool for fire, and that without the fire, or without the intervention of the dog at the precise moment in which he appeared, I should never have become aware of the death's-head, and so never the possessor of the treasure?"

"But proceed – I am all impatience."

---

u upon *(A, B, D)*
v upon *(A, B, D)*
w upon *(A, B, D)*
x upon *(A, B, D)*

"Well; you have heard, of course, the many stories current — the thousand vague rumors afloat about money buried, somewhere on[y] the Atlantic coast, by Kidd and his associates. These rumors must have had some foundation in fact. And that the rumors have existed so long and so continuously,[z] could have resulted, it appeared to me, only from the circumstance of the buried treasure still *remaining* entombed. Had Kidd concealed his plunder for a time, and afterwards reclaimed it, the rumors would scarcely have reached us in their present unvarying form. You will observe that the stories told are all about money-seekers, not about money-finders. Had the pirate recovered his money, there the affair would have dropped. It seemed to me that some accident — say the loss of a memorandum indicating its locality — had deprived him of the means of recovering it, and that this accident had become known to his followers, who otherwise might never have heard that treasure had been concealed at all, and who, busying themselves in vain, because unguided attempts, to regain it, had given first birth, and then universal currency, to the reports which are now so common. Have you ever heard of any important treasure [a]being unearthed[a] along the coast?"

"Never."

"But that Kidd's accumulations were immense, is well known. I took it for granted, therefore, that the earth still held them; and you will scarcely be surprised when I tell you that I felt a hope, nearly amounting to certainty, that the parchment so strangely found, involved a lost record of the place of deposit."

"But how did you proceed?"

"I held the vellum again to the fire, after increasing the heat; but nothing appeared. I now thought it possible that the coating of dirt might have something to do with the failure; so I carefully rinsed the parchment by pouring warm water over it, and, having done this, I placed it in a tin pan, with the skull downwards, and put the pan upon a furnace of lighted charcoal. In a few minutes, the pan having become thoroughly heated, I removed the slip, and, to my inexpressible joy, found it spotted, in several places, with what appeared to be figures arranged in lines. Again I placed it in

y upon *(A, B, D)*
z continuous, *(B, D)*
a . . . a having been unearthed by the diggers for money *(A)*

the pan, and suffered it to remain another minute. On[b] taking it off, the whole was just as you see it now."

Here [c]Legrand, having re-heated the parchment,[c] submitted it[d] to my inspection. The following characters[29] were rudely [e]traced, in a red tint,[e] between the death's-head and the goat:

53‡‡†305))6*;4826)4‡.)4‡);806*;48†8¶60))85;;]8*[f];:‡*8†83 (88)
5*†;46(;88*96*?;8)*‡(;485);5*†2:*‡(;4956*2(5* — 4)8¶8*;40692
85);)6†8)4‡‡;1(‡9;48081;8:8‡1;48†85;4)485†528806*81(‡9;48;
(88;4 (‡?34;48)4‡;161;:188;‡?;

"But," said I, returning him the slip, "I am as much in the dark as ever. Were all the jewels of Golconda[30] awaiting me on[g] my solution of this enigma, I am quite sure that I should be unable to earn them."

"And yet," said Legrand, "the solution is by no means so difficult as you might be led[h] to imagine from the first hasty inspection of the characters. These characters, as any one might readily guess, form a cipher — that is to say, they convey a meaning; but then, from what is known of Kidd, I could not suppose him capable of constructing any of the more abstruse cryptographs. I made up my mind, at once, that this was of a simple species — such, however, as would appear, to the crude intellect of the sailor, absolutely insoluble without the key."

"And you really solved it?"

"Readily; I have solved others of an abstruseness ten thousand times greater. Circumstances, and a certain bias of mind, have led me to take interest in such riddles, and it may well be doubted whether human ingenuity can construct an enigma of the kind which human ingenuity may not, by proper application, resolve.[31] In fact, having once established connected and legible characters, I scarcely gave a thought to the mere difficulty of developing their import.

"In the present case — indeed in all cases of secret writing — the first question regards the *language* of the cipher; for the prin-

b Upon *(A, B, D)*
c . . . c Legrand *(A)*
d the parchment *(A)*
e . . . e traced *(A)*
f *For* ;]8* *A, B and D have* 1‡(
g upon *(A, B, D)*
h lead *(B, D)*

ciples of solution, so far, especially, as the more simple ciphers are concerned, depend upon, and are varied by, the genius of the particular idiom. In general, there is no alternative but experiment (directed by probabilities) of every tongue known to him who attempts the solution, until the true one be[i] attained. But, with the cipher now before us, all difficulty is[j] removed by the signature. The pun on[k] the word 'Kidd' is appreciable in no other language than the English. But for this consideration I should have begun my attempts with the Spanish and French, as the tongues in which a secret of this kind would most naturally have been written by a pirate of the Spanish main. As it was, I assumed the cryptograph to be English.

"You observe there are no divisions between the words. Had there been divisions, the task would have been comparatively easy. In such case I should have commenced with a collation and analysis of the shorter words, and, had a word of a single letter occurred, as is most likely, (*a* or *I*, for example,) I should have considered the[l] solution as assured. But, there being no division, my first step was to ascertain the predominant letters, as well as the least frequent. Counting all, I constructed a table,[32] thus:

Of the character	8	there are	33.
	;	"	26.
	4	"	19.
	‡)	"	16.
	*	"	13.
	5	"	12.
	6	"	11.
	† 1	"	8.
	0	"	6.
	9 2	"	5.
	: 3	"	4.
	?	"	3.
	¶	"	2.
	][m] — .	"	1.

i is *(A)*
j was *(A, B, D)*
k upon *(A, B, D)*
l this *(A)*
m] *omitted (A, B, D)*

"Now, in English, the letter which most frequently occurs is *e*. Afterwards, the succession runs thus: *a o i d h n r s t u y c f g l m w b k p q x z*. [n]E, however,[n] predominates so remarkably that an individual sentence of any length is rarely seen, in which it is not the prevailing character.[33]

"Here, then, we have, in the very beginning, the groundwork for something more than a mere guess. The general use which may be made of the table is obvious – but, in this particular cipher, we shall only very partially require its aid. As our predominant character is 8, we will commence by assuming it as the *e* of the natural alphabet. To verify the supposition, let us observe if the 8 be seen often in couples – for *e* is doubled with great frequency in English – in which words, for example, as 'meet,' 'fleet,' 'speed,' 'seen,' 'been,'[o] 'agree,' &c. In the present instance we see it doubled no less than five times, although the cryptograph is brief.

"Let us assume 8, then, as *e*. Now, of all *words* in the language, 'the' is most usual; let us see, therefore, whether there are not repetitions of any three characters, in the same order of collocation, the last of them being 8. If we discover repetitions of such letters, so arranged, they will most probably represent the word 'the.' On[p] inspection, we find no less than seven such arrangements, the characters being ;48. We may, therefore, assume that the semicolon[q] represents *t*, that[r] 4 represents *h*, and that[s] 8 represents *e* – the last being now well confirmed. Thus a great step has been taken.

"But, having established a single word, we are enabled to establish a vastly important point; that is to say, several commencements and terminations of other words. Let us refer, for example, to the last instance but one, in which the combination ;48 occurs – not far from the end of the cipher. We know that the semicolon[t] immediately ensuing is the commencement of a word, and, of the six characters succeeding this 'the,' we are cognizant of no less than five. Let us set these characters down, thus, by the letters we know them to represent, leaving a space for the[u] unknown –

t eeth.

n . . . n E *(A, B, D)*
o 'been,'/been,' *(B, C, D) corrected from A*
p Upon *(A, B, D)*
q the semicolon/ ; *(A, B, D)*
r *Omitted (A, B, D)*
s *Omitted (A, B, D)*
t semicolon/ ; *(A, B, D)*
u the one *(A)*

"Here we are enabled, at once, to discard the *'th,'* as forming no portion of the word commencing with the first *t;* since, by experiment of the entire alphabet for a letter adapted to the vacancy, we perceive that no word can be formed of which this *th* can be a part. We are thus narrowed into

t ee,

and, going through the alphabet, if necessary, as before, we arrive at the word 'tree,' as the sole possible reading. We thus gain another letter, *r,* represented by (, with the words 'the tree' in juxtaposition.

"Looking beyond these words, for a short distance, we again see the combination ;48, and employ it by way of *termination* to what immediately precedes. We have thus this arrangement:

the tree ;4(‡?34 the,

or, substituting the natural letters, where known, it reads thus:

the tree thr‡?3h the.

"Now, if, in place of the unknown characters, we leave blank spaces, or substitute dots, we read thus:

the tree thr...h the,

when the word *'through'* makes itself evident at once. But this discovery gives us three new letters, *o, u* and *g,* represented by ‡ ? and 3.

"Looking now, narrowly, through the cipher for combinations of known characters, we find, not very far from the beginning, this arrangement,

83(88, or egree,

which, plainly, is the conclusion of the word 'degree,' and gives us another letter, *d,* represented by †.

"Four letters beyond the word 'degree,' we perceive the combination

;46(;88*[v]

"Translating the known characters, and representing the unknown by dots, as before, we read thus:

th . rtee.[w]

an arrangement immediately suggestive of the word 'thirteen,' and

v ;46(;88. *(A);* ;48(;88. *(B, D)* w th rtee *(B, C, D) corrected from A* again furnishing us with two new characters, *i* and *n,* represented by 6 and *.

"Referring, now, to the beginning of the cryptograph, we find the combination,

53‡‡†.

"Translating, as before, we obtain

. good,

which assures us that the first letter is *A,* and that the first two words are 'A good.'

[x]"To avoid confusion, it[x] is now time that we arrange our key, as far as discovered, in a tabular form.[y] It will stand thus:

5	represents	a
†	"	d
8	"	e
3	"	g
4	"	h
6	"	i
*	"	n
‡	"	o
(	"	r
;	"	t

"We have, therefore, no less than ten of the most important letters represented, and it will be unnecessary to proceed with the details of the solution. I have said enough to convince you that ciphers of this nature are readily soluble, and give you some insight into the *rationale* of their development. But be assured that the specimen before us appertains to the very simplest species of cryptograph. It now only remains to give you the full translation of the characters upon the parchment, as unriddled. Here it is:

'A good glass in the bishop's hostel in the devil's seat twenty-one[z] degrees and thirteen minutes northeast and by north main branch seventh limb east side shoot from the left eye of the death's-head a bee line from the tree through the shot fifty feet out.' "

---

x . . . x "It *(A, B, D)*

y form, to avoid confusion. *(A, B, D)*

z forty-one *(A, B, D)*

"But," said I, "the enigma seems still in as bad a condition as ever. How it is possible to extort a meaning from all this jargon about 'devil's seats,' 'death's-heads,' and 'bishop's hotels?' "

"I confess," replied Legrand, "that the matter still wears a serious aspect, when regarded with a casual glance. My first endeavor was to divide the sentence into the natural division intended by the cryptographist."

"You mean, to punctuate it?"

"Something of that kind."

"But how was it possible to effect this?"

"I reflected that it had been a *point* with the writer to run his words together without division, so as to increase the difficulty of solution. Now, a not over-acute man, in pursuing such an object, would be nearly certain to overdo the matter. When, in the course of his composition, he arrived at a break in his subject which would naturally require a pause, or a point, he would be exceedingly apt to run his characters, at this place, more than usually close together. If you will observe the MS., in the present instance, you will easily detect five such cases of unusual crowding. Acting on[a] this hint, I made the division thus:

'A good glass in the Bishop's hostel in the Devil's seat — twenty-one[b] *degrees and thirteen minutes — northeast and by north — main branch seventh limb east side — shoot from the left eye of the death's-head — a bee-line from the tree through the shot fifty feet out.'* "

"Even this division," said I, "leaves me still in the dark."

"It left me also in the dark," replied Legrand, "for a few days; during which I made diligent inquiry, in the neighborhood of Sullivan's Island, for any building which went by the name of the 'Bishop's Hotel;' for, of course, I dropped the obsolete word 'hostel.' Gaining no information on the subject, I was on the point of extending my sphere of search, and proceeding in a more systematic manner, when, one morning, it entered into my head, quite suddenly, that this 'Bishop's Hostel' might have some reference to an old family, of the name of Bessop, which, time out of mind, had

a upon *(A, B, D)* b forty-one *(A, B, D)*

held possession of an ancient manor-house, about four miles to the northward of the Island.[34] I accordingly went over to the plantation, and re-instituted my inquiries among the older negroes of the place. At length one of the most aged of the women said that she had heard of such a place as *Bessop's Castle,* and thought that she could guide me to it, but that it was not a castle, nor a tavern, but a high rock.

"I offered to pay her well for her trouble, and, after some demur, she consented to accompany me to the spot. We found it without much difficulty, when, dismissing her, I proceeded to examine the place. The 'castle' consisted of an irregular assemblage of cliffs and rocks — one of the latter being quite remarkable for its height as well as for its insulated and artificial appearance. I clambered to its apex, and then felt much at a loss as to what should be next done.

"While I was busied in reflection, my eyes fell upon a narrow ledge in the eastern face of the rock, perhaps a yard below the summit on[c] which I stood. This ledge projected about eighteen inches, and was not more than a foot wide, while a niche in the cliff just above it, gave it a rude resemblance to one of the hollow-backed chairs used by our ancestors. I made no doubt that here was the 'devil's-seat' alluded to in the MS., and now I seemed to grasp the full secret of the riddle.

"The 'good glass,' I knew, could have reference to nothing but a telescope; for the word 'glass' is rarely employed in any other sense by seamen. Now here, I at once saw, was a telescope to be used, and a definite point of view, *admitting no variation,* from which to use it. Nor did I hesitate to believe that the phrases, "twenty-one[d] degrees and thirteen minutes,' and 'northeast and by north,' were intended as directions for the levelling of the glass. Greatly excited by these discoveries, I hurried home, procured a telescope, and returned to the rock.

"I let myself down to the ledge, and found that it was impossible to retain a seat on[e] it unless[f] in one particular position. This

c upon *(A, B, D)*
d "forty-one *(A, B, D)*
e upon *(A, B, D)*
f except *(A, B, D)*

fact confirmed my preconceived idea. I proceeded to use the glass. Of course, the 'twenty-one[g] degrees and thirteen minutes' could allude to nothing but elevation above the visible horizon, since the horizontal direction was clearly indicated by the words, 'northeast and by north.' This latter direction I at once established by means of a pocket-compass; then, pointing the glass as nearly at an angle of twenty-one[h] degrees of elevation as I could do it by guess, I moved it cautiously up or down, until my attention was arrested by a circular rift or opening in the foliage of a large tree that overtopped its fellows in the distance. In the centre of this rift I perceived a white spot, but could not, at first, distinguish what it was. Adjusting the focus of the telescope, I again looked, and now made it out to be a human skull.

"On[i] this discovery I was so sanguine as to consider the enigma solved; for the phrase 'main branch, seventh limb, east side,' could refer only to the position of the skull on[j] the tree, while 'shoot from the left eye of the death's-head' admitted, also, of but one interpretation, in regard to a search for buried treasure. I perceived that the design was to drop a bullet from the left eye of the skull, and that a bee-line, or, in other words, a straight line, drawn from the nearest point of the trunk through 'the shot,' (or the spot where the bullet fell,) and thence extended to a distance of fifty feet, would indicate a definite point – and beneath this point I thought it at least *possible* that a deposit of value lay concealed."

"All this," I said, "is exceedingly clear, and, although ingenious, still simple and explicit. When you left the Bishop's Hotel, what then?"

"Why, having carefully taken the bearings of the tree, I turned homewards. The instant that I left 'the devil's seat,' however, the circular rift vanished; nor could I get a glimpse of it afterwards, turn as I would. What seems to me the chief ingenuity in this whole business, is the fact (for repeated experiment has convinced me it *is* a fact) that the circular opening in question is visible from

g 'forty-one *(A, B, D)*
h forty-one *(A, B, D)*
i Upon *(A, B, D)*
j upon *(A, B, D)*

no other attainable point of view than that afforded by the narrow ledge on[k] the face of the rock.

"In this expedition to the 'Bishop's Hotel' I had been attended by Jupiter, who had, no doubt, observed, for some weeks past, the abstraction of my demeanor, and took especial care not to leave me alone. But, on the next day, getting up very early, I contrived to give him the slip, and went into the hills in search of the tree. After much toil I found it. When I came home at night my valet proposed to give me a flogging. With the rest of the adventure I believe you are as well acquainted as myself."

"I suppose," said I, "you missed the spot, in the first attempt at digging, through Jupiter's stupidity in letting the bug fall through the right instead of through the left eye of the skull."

"Precisely. This mistake made a difference of about two inches and a half in the 'shot' — that is to say, in the position of the peg nearest the tree; and had the treasure been *beneath* the 'shot,' the error would have been of little moment; but 'the shot,' together with the nearest point of the tree, were merely two points for the establishment of a line of direction; of course the error, however trivial in the beginning, increased as we proceeded with the line, and by the time we had gone fifty feet, threw us quite off the scent. But for my deep-seated conviction[l] that treasure was here somewhere actually buried, we might have had all our labor in vain."

[m]"I presume the fancy of *the skull* — of letting fall a bullet through the skull's-eye — was suggested to Kidd by the piratical flag. No doubt he felt a kind of poetical consistency in recovering his money through this ominous insignium."

"Perhaps so; still I cannot help thinking that common-sense had quite as much to do with the matter as poetical consistency. To be visible from the Devil's seat, it was necessary that the object, if small, should be *white;* and there is nothing like your human skull for retaining and even increasing its whiteness under exposure to all vicissitudes of weather."[m]

"But your grandiloquence, and your conduct in swinging the

k upon *(A, B, D)*
l impressions *(A, B, D)*
m . . . m *Two paragraphs omitted (A, B, D)*

beetle — how excessively odd! I was sure you were mad. And why did you insist on[n] letting fall[o] the bug, instead of a bullet, from the skull?"

"Why, to be frank, I felt somewhat annoyed by your evident suspicions touching my sanity, and so resolved to punish you quietly, in my own way, by a little bit of sober mystification. For this reason I swung the beetle, and for this reason I [p]let it fall[p] from the tree. An observation of yours about its great weight suggested the latter idea."

"Yes, I perceive; and now there is only one point which puzzles me. What are we to make of the skeletons found in the hole?"

"That[q] is a question I am no more able to answer than yourself. There seems, however, only one plausible way of accounting for them — and yet it is dreadful to believe in such atrocity as my suggestion would imply. It is clear that Kidd — if Kidd indeed secreted this treasure, which I doubt not — it is clear that he must have had assistance in the labor. [r]But, the worst of[r] this labor concluded, he may have thought it expedient to remove all participants in his secret. Perhaps a couple of blows with a mattock were sufficient, while his coadjutors were busy in the pit; perhaps it required a dozen — who shall tell?"

NOTES

Title: The word bug in America is used for almost any beetle, but in England has long meant only a bedbug. N. P. Willis in a "Letter from London" in an Extra of the New York *Weekly Mirror,* October 4, 1845, said he thought this might interfere with sales of Poe's *Tales* in England. Thomas Dunn English in the *Aristidean* for October 1845 said, "Willis . . . talks about . . . the word 'bug.' This is mere affectation . . . the junction with 'gold' saves it." However, in a London collection of works by Poe, *Tales of Mystery, Imagination, & Humour; and Poems,* the story is called "The Gold-Beetle." This volume is described in the British Museum Catalogue as No. 1 in a series called Readable Books, published by Henry Vizetelly, London, 1852 [53]. My copy was issued by Clarke, Beeton, and Co., without date.

Motto: These lines are fully discussed (as Poe's own composition, "Motto for 'The Gold-Bug' ") in the first volume of this edition, p. 329. They are not from Arthur Murphy's comedy *All in the Wrong* (1761). The bite of the tarantula

n upon *(A, B, D)*
o letting fall/dropping *(A)*
p . . . p dropped it *(A);* let it fall it it *(B, C) misprint*
q This *(A)*
r . . . r But *(A, B, D)*

spider was held responsible for a wild hysterical impulse to dance – tarantism – that affected great numbers of people, especially in Italy, during the latter Middle Ages. In Frederick Reynolds' play *The Dramatist* (1789), IV, ii, a character named Floriville says, "I'm afraid you have been bitten by a tarantula – you'll excuse me, but the symptoms are wonderfully alarming. There is a blazing fury in your eye – a wild emotion in your countenance." Poe quoted loosely from speeches of Vapid, another character in *The Dramatist,* in a review of Theodore S. Fay's *Norman Leslie,* in the *Southern Literary Messenger,* December 1835; and in a review of Defoe's *Robinson Crusoe* in that magazine, January 1836.

1. Le Grand is the name of a Huguenot family once represented in Charleston. Poe may have known of a Baltimore orator, John C. Legrand, who became a judge, and there was a seventeenth-century French natural historian named Antoine Legrand.

2. Poe was stationed at Fort Moultrie from November 1827 to December 1828, hence knew Sullivan's Island and the vicinity of Charleston at first hand; but he took liberties with fact in his description. Basil L. Gildersleeve (who came from Charleston) later remarked on how this annoyed him and his friends when they were boys. See Harrison, *Complete Works,* I, 315, and the article by Ellison A. Smyth mentioned in note 13, below.

3. There are myrtles on the eastern end of Sullivan's Island, which Quinn (*Poe,* p. 130) says are of a local species.

4. Jan Swammerdamm (1637–1680), a Dutch naturalist and collector, wrote *Biblia naturae, sive Historia insectorum,* posthumously published in 1737–1738, and translated in 1758 as *A General History of Insects.*

5. Jupiter, like many Negroes in the old South, bore a grandiloquent Roman name.

6. Poe himself sometimes hunted game birds for his larder. When he lived on Coates Street in Philadelphia, he asked Benjamin Detwiler, the young son of his next door neighbor, to go with him for reed birds and they brought home a big bag. See Phillips, *Poe the Man,* I, 745–749, where credit is given to a manuscript by Dr. Ellis P. Oberholtzer.

7. *Scarabaeus* is the name of an Old World genus of beetle of which certain species were held sacred by the ancient Egyptians. A discussion of the insect appears on p. 128 of Wyatt's *Synopsis of Natural History.* Small images of the sacred beetles were the most popular of amulets, and thousands of these scarabs survive, usually of soapstone or faïence, but specimens made of gold have been found. Poe undoubtedly knew of them as symbols of life. (Compare "Some Words with a Mummy.")

8. One of Poe's officers at Fort Moultrie was Captain Henry Griswold, who wrote a letter of recommendation when Poe was discharged from the army. This Griswold died in 1834; it is not known if he was interested in natural history.

9. Harry Warfel reminded me that in Legrand's Southern speech *antennae* is pronounced "Ann-tinny."

10. Baudelaire, finding no equivalent in his language for Jupiter's dialect, translated his remarks into standard French. Misunderstanding "gose" (ghost) as

goose, he wrote *comme une oie* – an unintentional improvement that one thinks Poe might have liked himself.

11. The question is sometimes asked if a Negro's threat to beat a white man would have been accepted in the old South. It should be observed that if not malicious it could have been approved. A beating was popularly regarded as excellent treatment for incipient madness.

12. Jupiter seems to have some ideas of sympathetic magic, an affinity of gold bugs for gold.

13. Poe's bug is imaginary, but combines features of real insects found on Sullivan's Island. One is *Callichroma splendidum* (LeConte), iridescent golden yellow with green forewings. Another is a click beetle, *Alaus oculatus* (called by local boys a jumping jack), having on its prothorax two oval black spots edged with white, reminding one of a pirate flag. They were first discussed as the basis for Poe's gold bug in the *Sewanee Review,* January 1910, by Professor Ellison A. Smyth Jr., who is quoted in Hervey Allen's *Israfel* (1926), I, 216, where illustrations are given. My information was checked by Professor William J. Clench at the Agassiz Museum. Carroll D. Laverty in *American Literature,* March 1940, calls attention to the markings of the death's head moth, the Death's Head Sphinx, *Anobium,* pictured in the *Saturday Magazine,* August 25, 1832. This creature is the subject of Poe's later story "The Sphinx," and it may be pointed out that *Scarabaeus* and *Anobium* are both discussed on page 128 of Thomas Wyatt's *Synopsis of Natural History* (1839), which Poe helped to compile.

14. Compare Lowell's "Pictures from Appledore" (1854): "A heap of bare and splintery crags/Tumbled about by lightning and frost."

15. Poe was fond of the huge tulip trees, which he mentions in "The Elk" and "Landor's Cottage." The name used by botanists is *Liriodendron tulipifera,* but Poe changed the adjective to agree with *dendron,* which is neuter. There are no specimens on or near Sullivan's Island.

16. A metallurgist consulted assured me that an iron nail embedded as Poe describes would not rust and break.

17. See Jonah 4:11 on people who did not know their left from their right hands, and compare the old custom of drilling recruits "hayfoot, strawfoot!"

18. The index of his fortune *pointed* to it.

19. "Virtue of necessity" is from *Two Gentlemen of Verona,* IV, i, 62.

20. Gouging (the eyes) was part of the savage rough-and-tumble fighting of the backwoods. Poe quotes a burlesque of such a fight in reviewing *Georgia Scenes* by A. B. Longstreet in the *Southern Literary Messenger,* March 1836. He mentions it in "The Man that Was Used Up" at note 28.

21. Curvets and caracoles are leaps and half-turns, terms commonly used only of horses.

22. The mathematical calculations here are said to be incorrect. See Dana C. Hill, "Poe's Error," *Northwestern Magazine,* January 1916. See also Edward Wagenknecht, *Edgar Allan Poe,* p. 241, for a listing of articles on Poe's errors.

I agree with Wagenknecht when he says (p. 103), "Poe was less concerned with accuracy than with the appearance of accuracy."

23. Poe refers again to bichloride of mercury as an agent for preserving wood in "Street Paving," *Broadway Journal*, April 19, 1845.

24. The description is vague; by "counters" Poe probably merely meant old coins not current.

25. The *Dollar Newspaper's* first installment, June 21, 1843, ended here.

26. The white skull on a black field is called the Jolly Roger.

27. Compare "The Raven," line 50, "little meaning, little relevancy bore."

28. The information about an invisible writing fluid comes from the article "Ink" in *Rees's Cyclopaedia*. Zaffre is a blue pigment made by roasting cobalt ore with silica. Aqua regia, a mixture of nitric and hydrochloric acids, dissolves gold. A regulus is a reduced or metallic mass obtained in treating ore.

29. The cipher was correct in the first printing, but when Poe revised it, he treated the cipher, the transliteration, and the list of code characters inconsistently. As Professor Wimsatt pointed out in *PMLA*, September 1943, Poe certainly used William Blair's article on "Cipher" in Abraham Rees's *Cyclopaedia* (1819); one of like title in the *Encyclopaedia Britannica* (third to sixth editions, 1798–1836); and "Cryptography" in the *Encyclopaedia Americana* (1836).

30. Golconda, an ancient city of India, was famous for its treasures, especially diamonds. Its ruins are seven miles north of Hyderabad.

31. Poe had already printed the substance of this sentence on a number of occasions in connection with ciphers, twice equating his own ingenuity with "human ingenuity," but in *Graham's*, August 1841, in "Secret Writing," he said that he did not propose to make himself "the test of 'human ingenuity' in general." See Wimsatt, cited above, p. 776.

32. The table is somewhat incorrect, but I have forborne emendation.

33. Wimsatt, pp. 771–772, shows how Poe derived his order of frequency from Rees.

34. Considerable investigation has failed to locate anyone named Bessop in South Carolina, or indeed in Baltimore, Boston, New York, Philadelphia, or Richmond.

THE BLACK CAT

Unsurpassed of its kind, "The Black Cat" combines several themes that fascinated Poe — reincarnation, perversity, and retribution. The author treated perversity more philosophically later in "The Imp of the Perverse," a piece less famous because it is not quite so good a story.

Poe had actually owned a black cat, and in 1840 published a little article about her called "Instinct vs Reason" which is collected above. In it there is a significant remark, "Black cats are all of them witches." This is said playfully — but the author obviously came to see that there might be a story for a writer who would treat the superstition as if there was something in it. "The Black Cat" is a story of "orthodox" witchcraft; the sudden appearance of the second cat from nowhere, the slow growth of the white marking, and the murder of the wife after the animal brushes against the protagonist on the stairs are touches of the supernatural.* It may also be recalled that many people consider the semiprecious stones called cat's eyes unlucky.

Poe put much of himself into the story. Every student of his life knows instances of his tendency to do the wrong thing when he should have known better. But there was an instance in Poe's boyhood rarely mentioned that may be pertinent here. On one occasion he wantonly killed a pet fawn belonging to his foster-mother, the first Mrs. Allan,† something for which he very likely later felt remorse.

I have mentioned retribution. Poe was from his earliest youth very fond of cats (see Quinn, *Poe,* p. 58). In 1840 he seems to conclude that they think. The killing of a cat was for him the slaughter of a reasonable creature. The protagonist of "The Black Cat" was already morally a murderer when his ultimate act of cruelty made him one legally.‡

"The Black Cat" was written late in 1842. Felix O. C. Darley recalled that early in the next year Poe read it to him from a roll manuscript and discussed a possible illustration for it.§ No such illustration has been found.

* It is unlikely that Poe read the play, but one may compare *The Witch of Edmonton* (1621) by Rowley, Dekker, and Ford, Act III, where a man murders his wife after the possessed familiar (a dog) rubs against his leg.

† Father John B. Tabb, to J. H. Ingram, November 4, 1880 (Ingram List, no. 361), who had the story from one of the Poitiaux family in Richmond.

‡ Commenting on the "minor" character of the first killing in "The Black Cat" (*The Fall of the House of Usher and Other Tales,* 1960, p. 383), R. P. Blackmur does not take into account Poe's affection — like Dr. Johnson's — for cats.

§ Darley to Woodberry, February 26, 1884, quoted in Woodberry's *Edgar Allan Poe* (1885), p. 181.

THE BLACK CAT

Poe finally sold the story to the *Saturday Evening Post,* during a brief period when the paper bore a different title. The piece was selected by E. A. Duyckinck for inclusion in the *Tales* of 1845. It was reprinted again in the *Pictorial National Library,* November 1848. This was a Boston magazine, published by William Simonds, that used few original articles. None of the four verbal variants seems to be an author's change, but I am not absolutely sure the printing was unauthorized.

"The Black Cat" was parodied by Thomas Dunn English sometime before February 1844, in "The Ghost of a Grey Tadpole" (see Phillips, *Poe the Man,* pp. 851–854).

TEXTS

(A) United States Saturday Post (Philadelphia), August 19, 1843; *(B) Tales* (1845), pp. 37–46; *(C) Pictorial National Library* (Boston), November 1848 (1:255–259); *(D) Works* (1850), I, 281–290.

The first publication *(A)* was in a Philadelphia weekly known as the *Saturday Evening Post* during most of its long career. It bore the title given above for only a short time in 1843.

The text of *Tales (B)* is followed; Griswold's text *(D)* shows no verbal changes. The Boston publication *(C)* shows changes that seem to me definitely unauthorized; but since I am just short of absolute certainty, I record the four verbal variants.

Translation

La Démocratie pacifique, January 27, 1847, by Isabelle Meunier.

THE BLACK CAT. [*B*]

For the most wild, yet most homely narrative which I am about to pen, I neither expect nor solicit belief. Mad indeed would I be to expect it, in a case where my very senses reject their own evidence. Yet, mad am I not — and very surely do I not dream. But to-morrow I die, and to-day I would unburthen my soul. My immediate purpose is to place before the world, plainly, succinctly, and without comment, a series of mere household events. In their consequences, these events have terrified — have tortured — have destroyed me. Yet I will not attempt to expound them. To me, they have presented little but Horror — to many they will seem less terrible[a] than *barroques.*[1] Hereafter, perhaps, some intellect may be found which will reduce my phantasm to the common-place — some intellect more calm, more logical, and far less excitable than my own, which will perceive, in the circumstances I detail with awe, nothing more than an ordinary succession of very natural causes and effects.

From my infancy I was noted for the docility and humanity of my disposition. My tenderness of heart was even so conspicuous as to make me the jest of my companions. I was especially fond of animals, and was indulged by my parents with a great variety of pets. With these I spent most of my time, and never was so happy as when feeding and caressing them. This peculiarity of character grew with my growth,[2] and, in my manhood, I derived from it one of my principal sources of pleasure. To those who have cherished an affection for a faithful and sagacious dog, I need hardly be at the trouble of explaining the nature or the intensity of the gratification thus derivable. There is something in the unselfish and self-sacrificing love of a brute, which goes directly to the heart of him who has had frequent occasion to test the paltry friendship and gossamer fidelity of mere *Man.*

I married early, and was happy to find in my wife a disposition not uncongenial with my own. Observing my partiality for domestic pets, she lost no opportunity of procuring those of the most agreeable kind. We had birds, gold-fish, a fine dog, rabbits, a small monkey, and *a cat.*

This latter was a remarkably large and beautiful animal, entirely black, and sagacious to an astonishing degree. In speaking of his[b] intelligence, my wife, who at heart was not a little tinctured with superstition, made frequent allusion to the ancient popular notion, which regarded all black cats as witches in disguise. Not that she was ever *serious* upon this point — and I mention the matter at all for no better reason than that it happens, just now, to be remembered.

Pluto[3] — this was the cat's name — was my favorite pet and play-

a horrible *(C)* b her *(A)*

mate. I alone fed him, and he attended me wherever I went about the house. It was even with difficulty that I could prevent him from following me through the streets.

Our friendship lasted, in this manner, for several years, during which my general temperament and character — through the instrumentality of the Fiend Intemperance — had (I blush to confess it) experienced a radical alteration for the worse. I grew, day by day, more moody, more irritable, more regardless of the feelings of others. I suffered myself to use intemperate language to my wife. At length, I even offered her personal violence. My pets, of course, were made to feel the change in my disposition. I not only neglected, but ill-used them. For Pluto, however, I still retained sufficient regard to restrain me from maltreating him, as I made no scruple of maltreating the rabbits, the monkey, or even the dog, when by accident, or through affection, they came in my way. But my disease grew upon me — for what disease is like Alcohol! — and at length even Pluto, who was now becoming old, and consequently somewhat peevish — even Pluto began to experience the effects of my ill temper.

One night, returning home, much intoxicated, from one of my haunts about town, I fancied that the cat avoided my presence. I seized him; when, in his fright at my violence, he inflicted a slight wound upon my hand with his teeth. The fury of a demon instantly possessed me.[4] I knew myself no longer. My original soul seemed, at once, to take its flight from my body; and a more than fiendish malevolence, gin-nurtured, thrilled every fibre of my frame. I took from my waistcoat-pocket a pen-knife, opened it, grasped the poor beast by the throat, and deliberately cut one of its eyes from the socket! I blush, I burn, I shudder, while I pen the damnable atrocity.

When reason returned with the morning — when I had slept off the fumes of the night's debauch — I experienced a sentiment half of horror, half of remorse, for the crime of which I had been guilty; but it was, at best, a feeble and equivocal feeling, and the soul remained untouched. I again plunged into excess, and soon drowned in wine all memory of the deed.

In the meantime the cat slowly recovered. The socket of the lost eye presented, it is true, a frightful appearance, but he no longer appeared to suffer any pain. He went about the house as usual, but, as might be expected, fled in extreme terror at my approach. I had so much of my old heart left, as to be at first grieved by this evident dislike on the part of a creature which had once so loved me. But this feeling soon gave place to irritation. And then came, as if to my final and irrevocable overthrow, the spirit of PERVERSENESS. Of this spirit philosophy takes no account.[c] Yet I am not more sure that my soul lives, than I am that perverseness is one of the primitive impulses of the human heart – one of the indivisible primary faculties, or sentiments, which give direction to the character of Man.[5] Who has not, a hundred times, found himself committing a vile or a silly action, for no other reason than because he knows he should *not?* Have we not a perpetual inclination, in the teeth of our best judgment, to violate that which is *Law,* merely because we understand it to be such? This spirit of perverseness, I say, came to my final overthrow. It was this unfathomable longing of the soul *to vex itself* – to offer violence to its own nature – to do wrong for the wrong's sake only – that urged me to continue and finally to consummate the injury I had inflicted upon the unoffending[d] brute. One morning, in cool blood, I slipped a noose about its neck and hung it to the limb of a tree; – hung it with the tears streaming from my eyes, and with the bitterest remorse at my heart; – hung it *because* I knew that it had loved me, and *because* I felt it had given me no reason of offence; – hung it *because* I knew that in so doing I was committing a sin – a deadly sin that would so jeopardize my immortal soul as to place it – if such a thing were possible – even beyond the reach of the infinite mercy of the Most Merciful and Most Terrible God.

On the night of the day on which this cruel deed was done, I was aroused from sleep by the cry of fire. The curtains of my bed were in flames. The whole house was blazing. It was with great difficulty that my wife, a servant, and myself, made our escape from the conflagration. The destruction was complete. My entire worldly wealth was swallowed up, and I resigned myself thenceforward to despair.

c *After this:* Phrenology finds no place for it among its organs. *(A)*

d offending *(C)*

I am above the weakness of seeking to establish a sequence of cause and effect, between the disaster and the atrocity. But I am detailing a chain of facts — and wish not to leave even a possible link imperfect. On the day succeeding the fire, I visited the ruins. The walls, with one exception, had fallen in. This exception was found in a compartment wall, not very thick, which stood about the middle of the house, and against which had rested the head of my bed. The plastering had here, in great measure, resisted the action of the fire — a fact which I attributed to its having been recently spread. About this wall a dense crowd were collected, and many persons seemed to be examining a particular portion of it with very minute and eager attention. The words "strange!" "singular!" and other similar expressions, excited my curiosity. I approached and saw, as if graven in *bas relief* upon the white surface, the figure of a gigantic *cat*. The impression was given with an accuracy truly marvellous. There was[e] a rope about the animal's neck.

When I first beheld this apparition — for I could scarcely regard it as less — my wonder and my terror were extreme. But at length reflection came to my aid. The cat, I remembered, had been hung in a garden adjacent to the house. Upon the alarm of fire, this garden had been immediately filled by the crowd — by some one of whom the animal must have been cut from the tree and thrown, through an open window, into my chamber. This had probably been done with the view of arousing me from sleep. The falling of other walls had compressed the victim of my cruelty into the substance of the freshly-spread plaster; the lime of which, with the flames, and the *ammonia* from the carcass, had then accomplished the portraiture as I saw it.

Although I thus readily accounted to my reason, if not altogether to my conscience, for the startling fact just detailed, it did not the less fail to make a deep impression upon my fancy. For months I could not rid myself of the phantasm of the cat; and, during this period, there came back into my spirit a half-sentiment that seemed, but was not, remorse. I went so far as to regret the loss of the animal, and to look about me, among the vile haunts which I now habitually frequented, for another pet of the same species, and of some-

e had been *(A)*

what similar appearance, with which to supply its place.

One night as I sat, half stupified, in a den of more than infamy, my attention was suddenly drawn to some black object, reposing upon the head of one of the immense hogsheads of Gin, or of Rum, which constituted the chief furniture of the apartment.[6] I had been looking steadily at the top of this hogshead for some minutes, and what now caused me surprise was the fact that I had not sooner perceived the object thereupon.[7] I approached it, and touched it with my hand. It was a black cat — a very large one — fully as large as Pluto, and closely resembling him in every respect but one. Pluto had not a white hair upon any portion of his body; but this cat had a large, although indefinite splotch of white, covering nearly the whole region of the breast.

Upon my touching him, he immediately arose, purred loudly, rubbed against my hand, and appeared delighted with my notice. This, then, was the very creature of which I was in search. I at once offered to purchase it of the landlord; but this person made no claim to it — knew nothing of it — had never seen it before.

I continued my caresses, and, when I prepared to go home, the animal evinced a disposition to accompany me. I permitted it to do so; occasionally stooping and patting it as I proceeded. When it reached the house it domesticated itself at once, and became immediately a great favorite with my wife.

For my own part, I soon found a dislike to it arising within me. This was just the reverse of what I had anticipated; but — I know not how or why it was — its evident fondness for myself rather disgusted and[f] annoyed. By slow degrees, these feelings of disgust and annoyance rose into the bitterness of hatred. I avoided the creature; a certain sense of shame, and the remembrance of my former deed of cruelty, preventing me from physically abusing it. I did not, for some weeks, strike, or otherwise violently ill use it; but gradually — very gradually — I came to look upon it with unutterable loathing, and to flee silently from its odious presence, as from the breath of a pestilence.

What added, no doubt, to my hatred of the beast, was the dis-

---

f then *(C)*

covery, on the morning after I brought it home, that, like Pluto, it also had been deprived of one of its eyes. This circumstance, however, only endeared it to my wife, who, as I have already said, possessed, in a high degree, that humanity of feeling which had once been my distinguishing trait, and the source of many of my simplest and purest pleasures.

With my aversion to this cat, however, its partiality for myself seemed to increase. It followed my footsteps with a pertinacity which it would be difficult to make the reader comprehend. Whenever I sat, it would crouch beneath my chair, or spring upon my knees, covering me with its loathsome caresses. If I arose to walk it would get between my feet and thus nearly throw me down, or, fastening its long and sharp claws in my dress, clamber, in this manner, to my breast. At such times, although I longed to destroy it with a blow, I was yet withheld from so doing, partly by a memory of my former crime, but chiefly — let me confess it at once — by absolute *dread* of the beast.

This dread was not exactly a dread of physical evil — and yet I should be at a loss how otherwise to define it. I am almost ashamed to own — yes, even in this felon's cell, I am almost ashamed to own — that the terror and horror with which the animal inspired me, had been heightened by one of the merest chimæras it would be possible to conceive. My wife had called my attention, more than once, to the character of the mark of white hair, of which I have spoken, and which constituted the sole visible difference between the strange beast and the one I had destroyed. The reader will remember that this mark, although large, had been originally very indefinite; but, by slow degrees — degrees nearly imperceptible, and which for a long time my Reason struggled to reject as fanciful — it had, at length, assumed a rigorous distinctness of outline. It was now the representation of an object that I shudder to name — and for this, above all, I loathed, and dreaded, and would have rid myself of the monster *had I dared* — it was now, I say, the image of a hideous — of a ghastly thing — of the GALLOWS! — oh, mournful and terrible engine of Horror and of Crime — of Agony and of Death!

And now was I indeed wretched beyond the wretchedness of mere Humanity. And *a brute beast* — whose fellow I had contemptuously destroyed — *a brute beast* to work out for *me* — for me a man, fashioned in the image of the High God[8] — so much of insufferable wo! Alas! neither by day nor by night knew I the blessing of Rest any more! During the former the creature left me no moment alone; and, in the latter, I started, hourly, from dreams of unutterable fear, to find the hot breath of *the thing* upon my face, and its vast weight — an incarnate Night-Mare that I had no power to shake off — incumbent eternally upon my *heart!*

Beneath the pressure of torments such as these, the feeble remnant of the good within me succumbed. Evil thoughts became my sole intimates — the darkest and most evil of thoughts. The moodiness of my usual temper increased to hatred of all things and of all mankind; while, from the sudden, frequent, and ungovernable outbursts of a fury to which I now blindly abandoned myself, my uncomplaining wife, alas! was the most usual and the most patient of sufferers.

One day she accompanied me, upon some household errand, into the cellar of the old building which our poverty compelled us to inhabit. The cat followed me down the steep stairs, and, nearly throwing me headlong, exasperated me to madness. Uplifting an axe, and forgetting, in my wrath, the childish dread which had hitherto stayed my hand, I aimed a blow at the animal which, of course, would have proved instantly fatal had it descended as I wished. But this blow was arrested by the hand of my wife. Goaded, by the interference, into a rage more than demoniacal, I withdrew my arm from her grasp and buried the axe in her brain. She fell dead upon the spot, without a groan.

This hideous murder accomplished, I set myself forthwith, and with entire deliberation, to the task of concealing the body. I knew that I could not remove it from the house, either by day or by night, without the risk of being observed by the neighbors. Many projects entered my mind. At one period I thought of cutting the corpse into minute fragments, and destroying them by fire. At another, I resolved to dig a grave for it in the floor of the cellar. Again, I deliberated about casting it in the well in the yard — about packing it in a box, as if merchandize, with the usual arrangements, and so getting a porter to take it from the house. Finally I hit upon what

I considered a far better expedient than either of these. I determined to wall it up in the cellar — as the monks of the middle ages are recorded to have walled up their victims.[9]

For a purpose such as this the cellar was well[g] adapted. Its walls were loosely constructed, and had lately been plastered throughout with a rough plaster, which the dampness of the atmosphere had prevented from hardening. Moreover, in one of the walls was a projection, caused by a false chimney, or fireplace, that had been filled[h] up, and made to resemble the rest of the cellar. I made no doubt that I could readily displace the bricks at this point, insert the corpse, and wall the whole up as before, so that no eye could detect any thing suspicious.

And in this calculation I was not deceived. By means of a crow-bar I easily dislodged the bricks, and, having carefully deposited the body against the inner wall, I propped it in that position, while, with little trouble, I re-laid the whole structure as it originally stood. Having procured mortar, sand, and hair, with every possible precaution, I prepared a plaster which could not be distinguished from the old, and with this I very carefully went over the new brick-work.[10] When I had finished, I felt satisfied that all was right. The wall did not present the slightest appearance of having been disturbed. The rubbish on the floor was picked up with the minutest care. I looked around triumphantly, and said to myself — "Here at least, then, my labor has not been in vain."

My next step was to look for the beast which had been the cause of so much wretchedness; for I had, at length, firmly resolved to put it to death. Had I been able to meet with it, at the moment, there could have been no doubt of its fate; but it appeared that the crafty animal had been alarmed at the violence of my previous anger, and forebore to present itself in my present mood. It is impossible to describe, or to imagine, the deep, the blissful sense of relief which the absence of the detested creature occasioned in my bosom. It did not make its appearance during the night — and thus for one night at least, since its introduction into the house, I soundly and tranquilly slept; aye, *slept* even with the burden of murder upon my soul!

---

g admirably *(A)* h filled, or walled *(A)*

The second and the third day passed, and still my tormentor came not. Once again I breathed as a freeman. The monster, in terror, had fled the premises forever! I should behold it no more! My happiness was supreme! The guilt of my dark deed disturbed me but little. Some few inquiries had been made, but these had been readily answered. Even a search had been instituted — but of course nothing was to be discovered. I looked upon my future felicity as secured.

Upon the fourth day of the[i] assassination, a party of the police came, very unexpectedly, into the house, and proceeded again to make rigorous investigation of the premises. Secure, however, in the inscrutability of my place of concealment, I felt no embarrassment whatever. The officers bade me accompany them in their search. They left no nook or corner unexplored. At length, for the third or fourth time, they descended into the cellar. I quivered not in a muscle. My heart beat calmly as that of one who slumbers in innocence. I walked the cellar from end to end. I folded my arms upon my bosom, and roamed easily to and fro. The police were thoroughly satisfied and prepared to depart. The glee at my heart was too strong to be restrained. I burned to say if but one word, by way of triumph, and to render doubly sure their assurance of my guiltlessness.[11]

"Gentlemen," I said at last, as the party ascended the steps, "I delight to have allayed your suspicions. I wish you all health, and a little more courtesy. By the bye, gentlemen, this — this is a very well constructed house." [In the rabid desire to say something easily, I scarcely knew what I uttered at all.] — "I may say an *excellently* well constructed house. These walls — are you going, gentlemen? — these walls are solidly put together;" and here, through the mere phrenzy of bravado, I rapped heavily, with a cane which I held in my hand, upon that very portion of the brick-work behind which stood the[j] corpse of the wife of my bosom.

But may God shield and deliver me from the fangs of the Arch-Fiend! No sooner had the reverberation of my blows sunk into silence, than I was answered by a voice from within the tomb! — by

i my *(C)*

j the ghastly *(A)*

a cry, at first muffled and broken, like the sobbing of a child, and then quickly swelling into one long, loud, and continuous scream, utterly anomalous and inhuman – a howl – a wailing shriek, half of horror and half of triumph, such as might have arisen only out of hell, conjointly from the throats of the damned in their agony and of the demons that exult in the damnation.[13]

Of my own thoughts it is folly to speak. Swooning, I staggered to the opposite wall. For one instant the party upon the stairs remained motionless, through extremity of terror and of awe. In the next, a dozen stout arms were toiling at the wall. It fell bodily. The corpse, already greatly decayed and clotted with gore, stood erect before the eyes of the spectators. Upon its head, with red extended mouth and solitary eye of fire, sat the hideous beast whose craft had seduced me into murder, and whose informing voice had consigned me to the hangman. I had walled the monster up within the tomb!

NOTES

1. *Barroques* here means bizarre. Poe's spelling of French words is undependable.

2. Compare Pope's *Essay on Man,* II, 136: "Grows with his growth, and strengthens with his strength" – used also in "The Colloquy of Monos and Una" and "Never Bet the Devil Your Head."

3. The cat's name, Pluto, from the ruler of Hades, is symbolic; so is the gallows marking of the second cat.

4. Note the hint of the supernatural.

5. For an elaboration of this theme see "The Imp of the Perverse." Note that Poe retained a reference to phrenology in "The Imp," but canceled that made in the earliest version of "The Black Cat."

6. See "Gin-Shops" in Dickens' *Sketches by Boz* for a description of hogsheads of liquor decorating drinking places in London.

7. Sir Walter Scott in the first chapter of his *Letters on Demonology* (1830) tells of a lawyer who told his physician: "I found myself . . . embarrassed by the presence of a large cat, which came and disappeared I could not exactly tell how . . . I was compelled to regard it . . . [as having] no existence save in my deranged visual organs, or depraved imagination." The cat in Poe's tale, whatever his origin, has a real body.

8. See Genesis 1:27, "God created man in his own image," and Poe's "Model Verses": "Deity . . . /Made in his image a mannikin." In "Al Aaraaf," I, 104–105 and his note there Poe rejects literal anthropomorphism. See Mabbott I, 103, and comment on p. 118.

9. See Scott's *Marmion,* note 33; Scott thought that in the Middle Ages offenders in monastic orders were sometimes walled up, but that practice was very rare. Compare Poe's tale "The Cask of Amontillado."

10. Poe shows a curious and perhaps "professional" interest in bricks here as well as in "The Cask of Amontillado," in *Doings of Gotham,* Letter V, and in the essay on "Street Paving." In *Scribner's Magazine* for November 1875, R. T. P. A[llen] of the West Point Class of 1834 and superintendent of the Military Institute at Farmdale, Kentucky, gave an account of once seeing Poe working in a brickyard in Baltimore. See *American Notes & Queries,* June 1943.

11. Compare a similar bravado where the protagonist sits over the very place where his victim is hidden, in "The Tell-Tale Heart."

12. "Wife of my bosom" appears also in "Ligeia." The phrase echoes Deuteronomy 13:6 and 28:54.

13. Compare *Arthur Gordon Pym,* Chapter I, "a loud and long scream or yell, as if from the throats of a thousand demons."

MORNING ON THE WISSAHICCON ("THE ELK")

This "quiet landscape sketch of the environs of Philadelphia" was contributed to a New York annual, *The Opal for 1844,* edited by N. P. Willis and illustrated by J. G. Chapman. The tale was a plate article, or letterpress, to accompany one of Chapman's pictures called "Morning" and showing an elk in romantic scenery. It was first pointed out by Woodberry (1885, p. 189, quoted above), and is Poe's only signed and completed story that Griswold overlooked.*

There have been numerous literary treatments of the Wissahickon, which has been known to nature lovers for its distinctive charm since the early eighteenth century (see J. Bennett Nolan, *The Schuylkill,* 1951, ch. 17). In addition to Fanny Kemble's notice, mentioned by Poe in his story, he must have seen an unsigned article, "The Wissahiccon,"† in the *Southern Literary Messenger* for December 1835, which said the deer were gone.

* In his letter of May 28, 1844 to James Russell Lowell, Poe called this piece "The Elk," and several editors have adopted the latter title. The illustrator, John Gadsby Chapman, is referred to in "Philosophy of Furniture" at note 13.)

† Unsigned, but dated "Philadelphia, October 1835", this article was ascribed to B[enjamin] Matthias when it appeared in *The Philadelphia Book* (1836).

Poe himself undoubtedly visited the sylvan spot he described, probably a number of times. Horace Wemyss Smith said "Poe was very fond of visiting my grandmother, Mrs. William Moore Smith, at her place at the Falls of the Schuylkill" – within a stone's throw of the Ridge Road, mentioned in the story. It may be added that "his favorite seat was in the doorway of the family Mausoleum."‡ A. H. Quinn, a lifelong Philadelphian, says (*Poe,* p. 397) that the narrator floated "down from the northwest" and saw the rock called Mom Rinker's in memory of a lady spy, who is said to have dropped from it balls of yarn concealing messages that found their way to General Washington at Valley Forge.

Since annuals were usually prepared several months in advance, Poe's tale was presumably composed in the late spring or summer of 1843.

TEXTS

(A) The Opal: A Pure Gift for the Holy Days. New York, 1844, pages 249–256; *(B) Works,* ed. Stedman and Woodberry (1895), II, 77–83.

The original publication *(A)* is followed.

MORNING ON THE WISSAHICCON. [*A*]

The natural scenery of America has often been contrasted, in its general features as well as in detail, with the landscape of the Old World – more especially of Europe – and not deeper has been the enthusiasm, than wide the dissension, of the supporters of each region. The discussion is one not likely to be soon closed, for, although much has been said on both sides, a world more yet remains to be said.

The most conspicuous of the British tourists who have at-

‡ The statement appears in Smith's reminiscences of Poe printed by Hyman Polock Rosenbach in the Philadelphia *American* of February 26, 1887 and reprinted by Edwin Wolf 2nd in *The Library Chronicle* of the University of Pennsylvania, Spring–Summer 1951. Smith was the eldest son of Richard Penn Smith who was a leading member of the Philadelphia literary clique and a close associate of William E. Burton.

tempted a comparison, seem to regard our northern and eastern seaboard, comparatively speaking, as all of America, at least as all of the United States, worthy consideration. They say little, because they have seen less, of the gorgeous interior scenery of some of our western and southern districts — of the vast valley of Louisiana, for example, — a realization of the wildest dreams of paradise. For the most part, these travellers content themselves with a hasty inspection of the natural *lions* of the land — the Hudson, Niagara, the Catskills, Harper's Ferry, the lakes of New York, the Ohio, the prairies, and the Mississippi. These, indeed, are objects well worthy the contemplation even of him who has just clambered by the castellated Rhine, or roamed

By the blue rushing of the arrowy Rhone;[1]

but these are not *all* of which we can boast; and, indeed, I will be so hardy as to assert that there are innumerable quiet, obscure, and scarcely explored nooks, within the limits of the United States, that, by the true artist, or cultivated lover of the grand and beautiful amid the works of God, will be perfected to each *and to all* of the chronicled and better accredited scenes to which I have referred.

In fact, the real Edens of the land lie far away from the track of our own most deliberate tourists — how very far, then, beyond the reach of the foreigner, who, having made with his publisher at home arrangements for a certain amount of comment upon America, to be furnished in a stipulated period, can hope to fulfil his agreement in no other manner than by steaming it, memorandum-book in hand, through only the most beaten thoroughfares of the country!

I mentioned, just above, the valley of Louisiana.[2] Of all extensive areas of natural loveliness, this is perhaps the most lovely. No fiction has approached it. The most gorgeous imagination might derive suggestions from its exuberant beauty. And *beauty* is, indeed, its sole character. It has little, or rather nothing, of the sublime. Gentle undulations of soil, interwreathed with fantastic crystallic streams, banked by flowery slopes, and backed by a forest vegetation, gigantic, glossy, multicoloured, sparkling with gay birds and burthened with perfume — these features make up, in the vale of Louisiana, the most voluptuous natural scenery upon earth.

But, even of this delicious region, the sweeter portions are reached only by bypaths. Indeed, in America generally, the traveller who would behold the finest landscapes, must seek them not by the railroad, nor by the steamboat, nor by the stage-coach, nor in his private carriage, nor yet even on horseback — but on foot. He must *walk,* he must leap ravines, he must risk his neck among precipices, or he must leave unseen the truest, the richest, and most unspeakable glories of the land.[3]

Now in the greater portion of Europe no such necessity exists. In England it exists not at all. The merest dandy of a tourist may there visit every nook worth visiting without detriment to his silk stockings; so thoroughly known are all points of interest, and so well-arranged are the means of attaining them. This consideration has never been allowed its due weight, in comparisons of the natural scenery of the Old and New Worlds. The entire loveliness of the former is collated with only the most noted, and with by no means the most eminent items in the general loveliness of the latter.

River scenery has, unquestionably, within itself, all the main elements of beauty, and, time out of mind, has been the favourite theme of the poet. But much of this fame is attributable to the predominance of travel in fluvial over that in mountainous districts. In the same way, large rivers, because usually highways, have, in all countries, absorbed an undue share of admiration. They are more observed, and, consequently, made more the subject of discourse, than less important, but often more interesting streams.

A singular exemplification of my remarks upon this head may be found in the Wissahiccon, a brook, (for more it can scarcely be called,) which empties itself into the Schuylkill, about six miles westward of Philadelphia.[4] Now the Wissahiccon is of so remarkable a loveliness that, were it flowing in England, it would be the theme of every bard, and the common topic of every tongue, if, indeed, its banks were not parcelled off in lots, at an exorbitant price, as building-sites for the villas of the opulent. Yet it is only within a very few years that any one has more than heard of the Wissahiccon, while the broader and more navigable water into which it flows, has been long celebrated as one of the finest specimens of American river scenery. The Schuylkill, whose beauties have been much exaggerated, and whose banks, at least in the neighbourhood of Philadelphia, are marshy like those of the Delaware, is not at all comparable, as an object of picturesque interest, with the more humble and less notorious rivulet of which we speak.

It was not until Fanny Kemble, in her droll book about the United States, pointed out to the Philadelphians the rare loveliness of a stream which lay at their own doors, that this loveliness was more than suspected by a few adventurous pedestrians of the vicinity.[5] But, the "Journal" having opened all eyes, the Wissahiccon, to a certain extent, rolled at once into notoriety. I say "to a certain extent," for, in fact, the true beauty of the stream lies far above the *route* of the Philadelphian picturesque-hunters, who rarely proceed farther than a mile or two above the mouth of the rivulet — for the very excellent reason that here the carriage-road stops. I would advise the adventurer who would behold its finest points to take the Ridge Road, running westwardly from the city, and, having reached the second lane beyond the sixth mile-stone, to follow this lane to its termination. He will thus strike the Wissahiccon, at one of its best reaches, and, in a skiff, or by clambering along its banks, he can go up or down the stream, as best suits his fancy, and in either direction will meet his reward.

I have already said, or should have said, that the brook is narrow. Its banks are generally, indeed almost universally, precipitous, and consist of high hills, clothed with noble shrubbery near the water, and crowned at a greater elevation, with some of the most magnificent forest trees of America, among which stands conspicuous the *liriodendron tulipiferum*.[6] The immediate shores, however, are of granite, sharply-defined or moss-covered, against which the pellucid water lolls in its gentle flow, as the blue waves of the Mediterranean upon the steps of her palaces of marble. Occasionally in front of the cliffs, extends a small definite *plateau* of richly herbaged land, affording the most picturesque position for a cottage and garden which the richest imagination could conceive. The windings of the stream are many and abrupt, as is usually the case where banks are precipitous, and thus the impression conveyed to the voyager's eye, as he proceeds, is that of an endless succession of infinitely varied small lakes, or, more properly speaking, tarns. The Wissahiccon, however, should be visited, not like "fair Melrose," by moonlight, or even in cloudy weather,[7] but amid the brightest glare of a noonday sun; for the narrowness of the gorge through which it flows, the height of the hills on either hand, and the density of the foliage, conspire to produce a gloominess, if not an absolute dreariness of effect, which, unless relieved by a bright general light, detracts from the mere beauty of the scene.

Not long ago I visited the stream by the route described, and spent the better part of a sultry day in floating in a skiff upon its bosom. The heat gradually overcame me, and, resigning myself to the influence of the scenes and of the weather, and of the gently moving current, I sank into a half slumber, during which my imagination revelled in visions of the Wissahiccon of ancient days — of the "good old days" when the Demon of the Engine was not, when pic-nics were undreamed of, when "water privileges" were neither bought nor sold, and when the red man trod alone, with the elk, upon the ridges that now towered above. And, while gradually these conceits took possession of my mind, the lazy brook had borne me, inch by inch, around one promontory and within full view of another that bounded the prospect at the distance of forty or fifty yards. It was a steep rocky cliff, abutting far into the stream, and presenting much more of the Salvator character than any portion of the shore hitherto passed.[8] What I saw upon this cliff, although surely an object of very extraordinary nature, the place and season considered, at first neither startled nor amazed me — so thoroughly and appropriately did it chime in with the half-slumberous fancies that enwrapped me. I saw, or dreamed that I saw, standing upon the extreme verge of the precipice, with neck outstretched, with ears erect, and the whole attitude indicative of profound and melancholy inquisitiveness, one of the oldest and boldest of those identical elks which had been coupled with the red men of my vision.

I say that, for a few moments, this apparition neither startled nor amazed me. During this interval my whole soul was bound up in intense sympathy alone. I fancied the elk repining, not less than wondering, at the manifest alterations for the worse, wrought upon the brook and its vicinage, even within the last few years, by the stern hand of the utilitarian. But a slight movement of the animal's head at once dispelled the dreaminess which invested me, and aroused me to a full sense of the novelty of the adventure. I arose upon one knee within the skiff, and, while I hesitated whether to stop my career, or let myself float nearer to the object of my wonder, I heard the words "hist! hist!" ejaculated quickly but cautiously, from the shrubbery overhead. In an instant afterwords, a negro emerged from the thicket, putting aside the bushes with care, and treading stealthily. He bore in one hand a quantity of salt, and, holding it towards the elk, gently yet steadily approached. The noble animal, although a little fluttered, made no attempt at escape. The negro advanced; offered the salt; and spoke a few words of encouragement or conciliation. Presently, the elk bowed and stamped, and then lay quietly down and was secured with a halter.

Thus ended my romance of the elk. It was a *pet* of great age and very domestic habits, and belonged to an English family occupying a villa in the vicinity.[9]

NOTES

1. Byron's *Childe Harold,* III, lxxi, 3.

2. Poe's description of "the valley of Louisiana" is probably from a book, since he had not visited the place.

3. "Unspeakable" with favorable connotation was rare even in Poe's day, but is used in the King James Bible; see I Peter 1:8, and II Corinthians 9:15.

4. Thomas Moore's "Lines . . . on Leaving Philadelphia" begin, "Alone by the Schuylkill a wanderer roved/And bright were its flowery banks to his eye." The name is pronounced "skoolkill."

5. Fanny Kemble's description is in her *Journal* under date of October 18, 1832 (2 vols., London, 1835, II, 92): "I stopped for a long time opposite the Wissihiccon creek. The stone bridge . . . the sheet of foaming water falling like a curtain of gold over the dam among the dark stones below, on whose brown sides the ruddy sunlight and glittering water fell like splinters of light . . . the smooth

open field, along whose side the river waters, after receiving this child of the mountains into their bosom, wound deep, and bright, and still, the whole radiant with the softest light I ever beheld, formed a most enchanting and serene object of contemplation." The review of the work in the *Southern Literary Messenger,* May 1835, reprinted by Harrison (VIII, 19–31), is definitely not Poe's work.

6. Poe gives the scientific name of the tulip tree not as in books on natural history (*Liriodendron tulipifera*), but in more correct Latin since "dendron" is neuter. He liked these huge trees; wrote of one in "Landor's Cottage"; and even placed one, quite incorrectly, near Sullivan's Island in "The Gold-Bug."

7. See Scott's *Lay of the Last Minstrel,* II. i, 1–2, "If thou would'st view fair Melrose aright,/Go visit it by the pale moonlight."

8. Salvator Rosa (1615–1673) of the Neapolitan school was famed for painting scenes in wild parts of the Apennines. He is mentioned again in "Landor's Cottage," and was more highly regarded a century ago than now.

9. There was a real elk resident in the vicinity, according to Quinn (*Poe,* p. 397). It belonged to the proprietor of a sanitorium at a villa called Spring Bank who kept a number of pet animals for the pleasure of his patients.

RAISING THE WIND (DIDDLING)

The close resemblance of this series of anecdotes to those of "The Business Man" will be noticed at once. But in "Diddling" the tricks are all in the realm of the possible.* Indeed most of them had already been played. Hence Poe was not really repeating himself. Some of his sources in contemporary papers have been found; the others are pretty surely in periodicals that have not been examined.†

Responding characteristically to popular interest, Poe seems to have put the pieces together in a hurry for immediate sale. It was published in the *Saturday Courier,* October 14, 1843. Its theme, and in its first version its primary title, came from James

* R. P. Blackmur, in his edition of *The Fall of the House of Usher and Other Tales* (1960), p. 382, says, "In that story ["Diddling"] the possible edges into the impossible; in most others it is the impossible that trespasses."

† The late Professor Carl Shreiber told me he thought accounts of several of the tricks were in the columns of the *Saturday Courier;* a search by Richard P. Benton of the files for 1842 and 1843 revealed several reports of diddles, though not of any Poe used. Mr. Benton wrote to me, however, that he found the phrase "raising the wind" — obtaining a supply of ready money through some shift or other — current at the time, and, specifically, in the *Courier* of February 18, 1843, he had found "a trick of defraudment" referred to as a "New Way to Raise the Wind."

Kenney's durable farce, *Raising the Wind,* which deals with the efforts of one Jeremy Diddler to live by means of petty swindles. First produced in London on November 5, 1803, it became extremely popular. There was a New York edition in 1804, Poe's father appeared in it at least three times (Quinn, *Poe,* pp. 710–712), and it was played repeatedly in both England and America for decades.‡

Poe's story enjoyed surprising popularity. There was a pirated reprint in *Lloyd's Entertaining Journal* (London) for Saturday, January 4, 1845, which, however, carried Poe's name as author. Twenty-three years later a small book, *The Diddler,* By A. E. Senter (New York: Doolady, 1868), reproduced nearly all of Poe's material.§

In the 1940's there was also offered, in advertisements in in magazines lacking respectability, a separate pamphlet of Poe's story for two dollars. This was itself a diddle.*

TEXTS

(A) Philadelphia *Saturday Courier,* October 14, 1843; *(B) Broadway Journal,* September 13, 1845 (2:145–148); *(C) Works* (1856), IV, 267–277.

The version of the *Broadway Journal (B)* is used. Griswold's version *(C)* shows no auctorial change and introduces a new misprint. The earliest text *(A)* was facsimiled by John Grier Varner, *Edgar Allan Poe and the Philadelphia Saturday Courier* (1933), pages 67–85.

Reprint

Lloyd's Entertaining Journal (London), January 4, 1845, as "Raising the Wind; or, Diddling Considered as One of the Exact Sciences," from the *Saturday Courier.*

‡ [Burton Pollin, in the *Southern Literary Journal,* Fall 1969, points out that the play was produced in Philadelphia on September 9 and October 11, 1843.]

§ Its so-called "preface" consists of Poe's first fourteen paragraphs and all but the last sentence of the fifteenth. All ten of Poe's "diddles" are used, with the omission of some transitional phrasing, but they are scattered among many bits from other sources. The "Preface" is footnoted: "We are indebted to the unknown author of this preface and other articles from his pen. May his shadow never grow less and never be diddled worse." Senter's small volume concludes with a reprint (authorship acknowledged) of Kenney's *Raising the Wind.*

* As a last word one may note that in some parts of America "diddling" like "cheating" is slang for irregular lovemaking.

DIDDLING

DIDDLING CONSIDERED AS ONE OF THE EXACT SCIENCES. [*B*]

Hey, diddle diddle,
The cat and the fiddle.

Since the world began there have been two Jeremys. The one wrote a Jeremiad about usury, and was called Jeremy Bentham. He has been much admired by Mr. John Neal,[1] and was a great man in a small way. The other gave name to the most important of the Exact Sciences,[2] and was[a] a great man in a *great* way – I may say, indeed, in the very greatest of ways.

Diddling – or the abstract idea conveyed by the verb to diddle – is sufficiently well understood.[3] Yet the fact, the deed, the thing *diddling,* is somewhat difficult to define. We may get, however, at a tolerably distinct conception of the matter in hand, by defining – not the thing, diddling, in itself – but man, as an animal that diddles. Had Plato but hit upon this, he would have been spared the affront of the picked chicken.

Very pertinently it was demanded of Plato, why a picked chicken, which was clearly a "biped without feathers,"[4] was not, according to his own definition, a man? But I am not to be bothered by any similar query. Man is an animal that diddles, and there is *no* animal that diddles *but* man. It will take an entire hen-coop of picked chickens[b] to get over that.

What constitutes the essence, the nare,[c] [5] the principle of diddling is, in fact, peculiar to the class of creatures that wear coats and pantaloons. A crow thieves;[d] a fox cheats; a weasel outwits; a man diddles. To diddle is his destiny. "Man was made to mourn," says the poet.[6] But not so: – he was made to diddle. This is his aim – his object – his *end.* And for this reason when a man's diddled we say[e] he's *"done."*

Diddling, rightly considered, is a compound, of which the in-

---

Title Raising the Wind; or, Diddling Considered as One of the Exact Sciences. *(A)*

Motto Ascribed in A From an Epic by "Flaccus."

a was entitled Jeremy Diddler. He was *(A)*

b chickeus *(A) misprint*

c ware, *(A) misprint*

d theives; *(B) misprint*

e say that *(A)*

gredients are minuteness, interest, perseverance, ingenuity, audacity, *nonchalance,* originality, impertinence, and *grin.*

Minuteness: — Your diddler is minute. His operations are upon a small scale. His business is retail, for cash, or approved paper at sight. Should he ever be tempted into magnificent speculation, he then, at once, loses his distinctive features, and becomes what we term "financier." This latter word conveys the diddling idea in every respect except that of magnitude. A diddler may thus be regarded as a banker *in petto* — a "financial operation," as a diddle at Brobdingnag.[f] [7] The one is to the other, as [g]Homer to "Flaccus"[8] — as a Mastodon to a mouse — as the tail of a comet to that of a pig.[g] [9]

Interest: — Your diddler is guided by self-interest. He scorns to diddle for the mere *sake* of the diddle. He has an object in view — his pocket — and yours. He regards always the main chance. He looks to Number One. You are Number Two, and must look to yourself.

Perseverance: — Your diddler perseveres. He is not readily discouraged. Should even the banks break, he cares nothing about it. He steadily pursues his end, and

Ut canis[h] *a corio nunquam absterrebitur uncto,*[10]

so he never lets go of his game.

Ingenuity: — Your diddler is ingenious. He has constructiveness large. He understands plot. He invents and circumvents. Were he not Alexander he would be Diogenes.[11] Were he not a diddler,[i] he would be a maker of patent rat-traps or an angler for trout.

Audacity: — Your diddler is audacious. — He is a bold man. He carries the war into Africa. He conquers all by assault. He would not fear the daggers of the Frey Herren.[j] With a little more prudence Dick Turpin would have made a good diddler; with a trifle less blarney, Daniel O'Connell; with a pound or two more brains, Charles the Twelfth.[12]

Nonchalance: — Your diddler is nonchalant. He is not at all

f Brobdignag. *(A, B, C)*

g . . . g a Mastodon to a mouse — as a tail of a comet to that of a pig — as Homer to Flaccus — as the "Iliad" to "Sam Patch." *(A)*

h *camis (A) misprint*

i a diddler,/what he is, *(A)*

j Harren. *(A) misprint*

nervous. He never *had* any nerves. He is never seduced into a flurry. He is never put out – unless put out of doors. He is cool – cool as a cucumber. He is calm – "calm as a smile from Lady Bury." He is easy – easy as an old glove, or the damsels of ancient Baiæ.[13]

Originality: – Your diddler is original – conscientiously so. His thoughts are his own. He would scorn to employ those of another. A stale trick is his aversion. He would return a purse, I am sure, upon discovering that he had obtained it by an unoriginal diddle.

Impertinence: – Your diddler is impertinent. He swaggers. He sets his arms a-kimbo. He thrusts his hands in his trowsers' pockets. He sneers in your face. He treads on your corns. He eats your dinner,[k] he drinks[l] your wine, he borrows your money, he pulls your nose, he kicks your poodle, and he kisses your wife.[14]

Grin: – Your *true* diddler winds up all with a grin. But this nobody sees but himself. He grins when his daily work is done – when[m] his allotted labors are accomplished – at night in his own closet, and altogether for his own private entertainment. He goes home. He locks his door. He divests himself of his clothes. He puts out his candle. He gets into bed. He places his head upon the pillow. All this done, and your diddler *grins.* This is no hypothesis. It is a matter of course. I reason *à priori,* and a diddle would be *no* diddle without a grin.

The origin of the diddle is referrible to the infancy of the Human Race. Perhaps the first diddler was Adam. At all events, we can trace the science back to a very remote period of antiquity. The moderns, however, have brought it to a[n] perfection never dreamed of by our thick-headed progenitors. Without pausing to speak of the "old saws," therefore, I shall content myself with a compendious account of some of the more "modern instances."[15]

A very good diddle is this. A housekeeper in want of a sofa, for instance, is seen to go in and out of several cabinet warehouses. At length she arrives at one offering an excellent variety. She is accosted, and invited to enter, by a polite and voluble individual at the door. She finds a sofa well adapted to her views, and, upon

k dinners, *(A)*
l dinks *(C) misprint*
m wken *(B) misprint*
n a point of *(A)*

inquiring the price, is surprised and delighted to hear a sum named at least twenty per cent. lower than her expectations. She hastens to make the purchase, gets a bill and receipt, leaves her address, with a request that the article be sent home as speedily as possible, and retires amid a profusion of bows from the shop-keeper. The night arrives and no sofa. The next day passes, and still none. A servant is sent to make inquiry about the delay. The whole transaction is denied. No sofa has been sold — no money received — except by the diddler who played shop-keeper for the nonce.

Our cabinet warehouses are left entirely unattended, and thus afford every facility for a trick of this kind. Visiters enter, look at furniture, and depart unheeded and unseen. Should any one wish to purchase, or to inquire the price of an article, a bell is at hand, and this is considered amply sufficient.

Again, quite a respectable diddle is this. A well-dressed individual enters a shop; makes a purchase to the value of a dollar; finds, much to his vexation, that he has left his pocket-book in another coat pocket: and so says to the shop-keeper —

"My dear sir, never mind! — just oblige me, will you, by sending the bundle[o] home? But stay! I really believe that I have nothing less than a five dollar bill, even *there*. However, you can send four dollars in change *with* the bundle, you know."

"Very good, sir," replies the shop-keeper, who entertains, at once, a lofty opinion of the high-mindedness of his customer. "I know fellows," he says to himself, "who would just have put the goods under their arm, and walked off with a promise to call and pay the dollar as they came by in the afternoon."

A boy is sent with the parcel and change. On the route, quite accidentally, he is met by the purchaser, who exclaims:

"Ah! this is my bundle, I see — I thought you had been home with it, long ago. Well, go on! My wife, Mrs. Trotter, will give you the five dollars — I left instructions with her to that effect. The change you might as well give to *me* — I shall want some silver for the Post Office. Very good! One, two, — is this a good quarter?

o parcel *(A)*

— three, four — quite right! Say to Mrs. Trotter that you met me, and be sure now and *do* not loiter on the way."

The boy doesn't[p] loiter at all — but he is a very long time in getting back from his errand — for no lady of the precise name of Mrs. Trotter is to be discovered. He consoles himself, however, that he has not been such a fool as to leave the goods without the money, and re-entering his shop with a self-satisfied[q] air, feels sensibly hurt and indignant when his master asks him what has become of the change.

A very simple diddle, indeed, is this. The captain of a ship which is about to sail, is presented by an official looking person,[r] with an unusually moderate bill of city charges. Glad to get off so easily, and confused by a hundred duties pressing upon him all at once, he discharges the claim forthwith. In about fifteen minutes, another and less reasonable bill is handed him by one who soon makes it evident that the first collector was a diddler, and the original collection a diddle.

And here, too, is a somewhat similar thing. A steamboat is casting loose from the wharf. A traveller, portmanteau in hand, is discovered running towards the wharf at full speed. Suddenly, he makes a dead halt, stoops, and picks up something from the ground in a very agitated manner. It is a pocket book, and — "Has any gentleman lost a pocket book?" he cries. No one can say that he has exactly lost a pocket-book; but a great excitement ensues, when the treasure trove is found to be of value. The boat however, must not be detained.

"Time and tide wait for no man," says the captain.[16]

"For God's sake, stay only a few minutes," says the finder of the book — "the true claimant will presently appear."

"Can't wait!" replies the man in authority; "cast off there, d'ye hear?"

"What *am* I to do?" asks the finder, in great tribulation. "I am about to leave the country for some years, and I cannot conscientiously retain this large amount in my possession. I *beg* your pardon, sir," [here he addresses a gentleman on shore,] "but you have

p does'nt *(A);* does n't *(B);* does't *(C)*

q self satisfied *(B) hyphen added as in A and C*

r personage, *(A)*

the air of an honest man. *Will* you confer upon me the[s] favor of taking charge of this pocket-book — I *know* I can trust you — and of advertising it? The notes,[t] you see, amount[u] to a very considerable sum. The owner will, no doubt, insist upon rewarding you for your trouble —"

"*Me!* — no, *you!* — it was *you* who found the book."

"Well, if you *must* have it so — *I* will take a small reward — just to satisfy your scruples. Let me see — why these[v] notes are all hundreds — bless my soul! a hundred is too much to take — fifty would be quite enough, I am sure —"

"Cast off there!" says the captain.

"But then I have no change for a hundred, and upon the whole, *you* had better" —

"Cast off there!" says the captain.

"Never mind!" cries the gentleman[w] on shore, who has been examining his own pocket-book for the last minute or so — "never mind! *I* can fix it — here is a fifty on the Bank of North America — throw me the book."[17]

And the over-conscientious finder takes the fifty with marked reluctance, and throws the gentleman the book, as desired, while the steamboat fumes and fizzes on her way. In about[x] half an hour after her departure, the "large amount" is seen to be "a counterfeit presentment," and the whole thing a capital diddle.[18]

A bold diddle is this. A camp-meeting, or something similar, is to be held at a certain spot which is accessible only by means of a free bridge. A diddler stations himself upon this bridge, respectfully informs all passers by of the new county law, which establishes a toll of one cent for foot passengers, two for horses and donkeys, and so forth, and so forth. Some grumble but all submit, and the diddler goes home a wealthier man by some fifty or sixty dollars well earned. This taking a toll from a great crowd of people is an excessively troublesome thing.[19]

A neat diddle is this. A friend holds one of the diddler's promises to pay, filled up and signed in due form, upon the ordi-

s the great *(A)*
t note, *(A)*
u amounts *(A)*
v them *(A)*
w gentlemen *(C) misprint*
x about an *(A)*

nary blanks printed in red ink. The diddler purchases one or two dozen of these blanks, and every day[y] dips one of them in his soup, makes his dog jump for it, and finally gives it to him as a *bonne bouche.* The note arriving at maturity, the diddler, with the diddler's dog, calls upon the friend, and the promise to pay is made the topic[z] of discussion. The friend produces it from his *escritoire,* and is in the act of reaching it to the diddler, when up jumps the diddler's dog and devours it forthwith. The diddler is not only surprised but vexed and incensed at the absurd behavior of his dog, and expresses his entire readiness to cancel the obligation at any moment when the evidence of the obligation shall be forthcoming.

A very minute diddle is this. A lady is insulted in the street by a diddler's accomplice. The diddler himself flies to her assistance, and, giving his friend a comfortable thrashing, insists upon attending the lady to her own door. He bows, with his hand upon his heart, and most respectfully bids[a] her adieu. She entreats him, as her deliverer, to walk in and be introduced to her big brother and her papa. With a sigh, he declines to do so. "Is there *no* way, then, sir," she murmurs, "in which I may be permitted to testify my gratitude?"

"Why, yes, madam, there is. Will you be kind enough to lend me a couple of shillings?"[20]

In the first excitement of the moment the lady decides upon fainting outright. Upon second thought, however, she opens her purse-strings and delivers the specie. Now this, I say, is a diddle minute — for one entire moiety of the sum borrowed has to be paid to the gentleman who had the trouble of performing the insult, and who had then to stand still and be thrashed for performing it.

Rather a small, but still a scientific diddle is this. The diddler approaches the bar of a tavern, and demands a couple of twists of tobacco. These are handed to him, when, having slightly examined them, he says:

"I don't much like this tobacco. Here, take it back, and give me

y day, at dinner, *(A)*
z subject *(A)*
a bidding *(A)*

a glass of brandy and water in its place."

The brandy and water is furnished and imbibed, and the diddler makes his way to the door. But the voice of the tavern-keeper arrests him.

"I believe, sir, you have forgotten to pay for your brandy and water."

"Pay for my brandy and water! — didn't I give you the tobacco for the brandy and water? What more would you have?"

"But, sir, if you please, I don't remember that you paid for the tobacco."

"What do you mean by that, you scoundrel? — Didn't I give you back your tobacco? Isn't *that* your tobacco lying *there?* Do you expect me to pay for what I did not take?"

"But, sir," says the publican, now rather at a loss what to say, "but, sir —"

"But me no buts, sir," interrupts the diddler, apparently in very high dudgeon, and slamming the door after him, as he makes his escape. — "But me no buts, sir, and none of your tricks upon travellers."[21]

Here again is a very clever diddle, of which the simplicity is not its least recommendation. A purse, or pocket-book, being really lost, the loser inserts in *one* of the daily papers of a large city a fully descriptive advertisement.

Whereupon our diddler copies the *facts* of this advertisement, with a change of heading, of general phraseology, and *address*. The original, for instance, is long, and verbose, is headed "A Pocket-Book Lost!" and requires the treasure, when found, to be left at No. 1 Tom[b] street. The copy is brief, and being headed with "Lost" only, indicates No. 2 Dick,[c] or No. 3 Harry street, as the locality at which the owner may be seen. Moreover, it is inserted in at least five or six of the daily[d] papers of the day, while in point of time, it makes its[e] appearance only a few hours after the original. Should it be read by the loser of the purse, he would hardly suspect it to have any reference to his own misfortune. But, of course, the chances are five or six to one, that the finder will

b Dick *(A)*
c Tom, *(A)*
d *Omitted (A)*
e it *(B) misprint*

repair to the address given by the diddler, rather than to that pointed out by the rightful proprietor. The former pays the reward, pockets the treasure and decamps.

Quite an analogous diddle is this. A lady of ton has dropped, somewhere in the street, a diamond ring of very unusual value. For its recovery, she offers some forty or fifty dollars reward — giving, in her advertisement, a very minute description of the gem, and of its settings, and declaring that, upon its restoration to No. so and so, in such and such Avenue, the reward will be paid *instanter*, without a single question being asked. During the lady's absence from home, a day or two afterwards, a ring is heard at the door of No. so and so, in such and such Avenue; a servant appears; the lady of the house is asked for and is declared to be out, at which astounding information, the visitor expresses the most poignant regret. His business is of importance and concerns the lady herself. In fact, he had the good fortune to find her diamond ring. But, perhaps it would be as well that he should call again. "By no means!" says the servant; and "By no means!" says the lady's sister and the lady's sister-in-law, who are summoned forthwith. The ring is clamorously identified, the reward is paid, and the finder[f] nearly thrust out of doors. The lady returns, and expresses some little dissatisfaction with her sister and sister-in-law, because they happen to have paid forty or fifty dollars for a *fac-simile* of her diamond ring — a *fac-simile* made out of real pinchbeck and unquestionable[g] paste.

But as there is really no end to diddling, so there would be none to this essay, were I even to hint at half the variations, or inflections, of which this science is susceptible. I must bring this paper, perforce, to a conclusion, and this I cannot do better than by a summary notice of a very decent, but rather elaborate diddle, of which our own city was made the theatre, not very long ago, and which was subsequently repeated with success, in other still more verdant localities of the Union. A middle-aged gentleman arrives in town from parts unknown. He is remarkably precise, cautious, staid, and deliberate in his demeanor. His dress is scrupulously neat, but plain, unostentatious. He wears a white cravat,

f finder very *(A)*　　g *Omitted (A)*

an ample waistcoat, made with an eye to comfort alone; thick-soled cosy-looking shoes, and pantaloons without straps. He has the whole air, in fact, of your well-to-do, sober-sided, exact, and respectable "man of business," *par excellence* — one of the stern and outwardly hard, internally soft, sort of people that we see in the crack high comedies — fellows whose words are so many bonds, and who are noted for giving away guineas, in charity, with the one hand, while, in the way of mere bargain, they exact the uttermost fraction of a farthing, with the other.

He makes much ado before he can get suited with a boarding house. He dislikes children. He has been accustomed to quiet. His habits are methodical — and then he would prefer getting into a private and respectable small family, piously inclined. Terms, however, are no object — only he *must*[h] insist upon settling his bill on the first of every month, (it is now the second) and begs his landlady, when he finally obtains one to his mind, *not* on any account, to forget his instructions upon this point — but to send in a bill, *and* receipt, precisely at ten o'clock, on the *first* day of every month, and under *no* circumstances to put it off to the second.

These arrangements made, our man of business rents an office in a reputable rather than in a fashionable quarter of the town. There is nothing he more despises than pretence. "Where there is much show," he says, "there is seldom anything very solid behind" — an observation which so profoundly impresses his landlady's fancy, that she makes a pencil memorandum of it forthwith, in her great family Bible, on the broad margin of the Proverbs of Solomon.

The next step is to advertise, after some such fashion as this, in the principal business sixpennies of this[i] city — the pennies are eschewed as not "respectable" — and as demanding payment for all advertisements in advance.[22] Our man of business holds it as a point of his faith that work should never be paid for until done.

WANTED. — The advertisers, being about to commence extensive business operations in this city, will require the services of

h must *(C)* i the *(A)*

three or four intelligent and competent clerks, to whom a liberal salary will be paid. The very best recommendations, not so much for capacity, as for integrity, will be expected. Indeed, as the duties to be performed, involve high responsibilities, and large amounts of money must necessarily pass through the hands of those engaged, it is deemed advisable to demand a deposit of fifty dollars from each clerk employed. No person need apply, therefore, who is not prepared to leave this sum in the possession of the advertisers, and who cannot furnish the most satisfactory testimonials of morality. Young gentlemen piously inclined will be preferred. Application should be made between the hours of ten[j] and eleven,[k] A.M., and four[l] and five,[m] P.M., of Messrs.

BOGGS,[n] HOGS,[o] LOGS, FROGS, & CO.
No. 110 Dog Street.[23]

By the thirty-first day of the month, this advertisement has brought to the office of Messrs. Boggs,[p] Hogs,[q] Logs, Frogs and Company, some fifteen or twenty young gentlemen piously inclined. But our man of business is in no hurry to conclude a contract with any — no man of business is *ever* precipitate — and it is not until the most rigid catechism in respect to the piety of each young gentleman's inclination, that his services are engaged and his fifty dollars receipted for, *just* by way of proper precaution, on the part of the respectable firm of Boggs,[r] Hogs,[s] Logs, Frogs, and Company. On the morning of the first day of the next month, the landlady does *not* present her bill according to promise — a piece of neglect for which the comfortable head of the house endings in *ogs,* would no doubt have chided her severely, could he have been prevailed upon to remain in town a day or two for that purpose.

As it is, the constables have had[t] a sad time of it, running

j 10 *(A)*
k 11 *(A)*
l 4 *(A)*
m 5 *(A)*
n Bogs, *(C)*
o Hoggs, *(A)*
p *Bogs, (C)*
q Hoggs, *(A)*
r Bogs, *(C)*
s Hoggs, *(A)*
t *Omitted (A)*

hither and thither, and all they can do is to declare the man of business most emphatically, a "hen knee high" – by which some persons imagine them to imply that, in fact, he is n. e. i. – by which again the very classical phrase *non est inventus,* is supposed to be understood.[24] In the meantime the young gentlemen, one and all, are somewhat less piously inclined than before, while the landlady purchases a shilling's worth of the best Indian rubber, and very carefully obliterates the pencil memorandum that some fool has made in her great family Bible, on the broad margin of the Proverbs of Solomon.

NOTES

Title: The title – the subtitle in the first version – is probably a parody on the title of Thomas De Quincey's essay "On Murder Considered as One of the Fine Arts," first published in two parts, separated by more than twelve years, in *Blackwood's,* for February 1827 and November 1839.

Motto: This is from Mother Goose.

1. In England (1824–1827) Poe's correspondent John Neal became a friend of the utilitarian Jeremy Bentham (1748–1832), and was for some months a member of his household.

2. In the first version Poe named Jeremy Diddler, who was the leading character in James Kenney's *Raising the Wind.*

3. The *OED* describes the verb to diddle, in the sense used by Poe, as colloquial – "a recent word, of obscure origin," suggests that it may be a back-formation from the name Diddler, and gives 1806 as the date of the earliest example cited. The *Century Dictionary* calls it slang and cites B. Disraeli, *The Young Duke,* II, 3: "I should absolutely have diddled Hounslow if it had not been for her pretty face flitting about my stupid brain."

4. The phrase is not now considered to be Plato's, but see Diogenes Laertius VI, vi, 40:

> Plato had defined man as an animal, biped and featherless, and was applauded. Diogenes plucked a fowl and brought it into the lecture room with the words, "Here is Plato's man." In consequence of which there was added to the definition, "having broad nails." – Loeb ed., vol. II, p. 43

5. This archaic word appears in the lines from Butler's *Hudibras* adopted as motto for "The Folio Club." Poe used it himself "with a figurative twist for which the dictionaries record no parallel" in the earlier versions of "King Pest," here, and in "Byron and Miss Chaworth." (See Killis Campbell in *MLN,* Decem-

ber 1927, pp. 519–520.) Poe's metonymy uses the obsolete word for nostril to represent that which the nostril detects. It may be added that the word was accurately transcribed from *Hudibras* in the manuscript of "The Folio Club," but Harrison (II, xxxvi) printed it "hare." Poe used "nare" in all the earlier versions of "King Pest," but our text (Griswold's) has "nature" – presumably an auctorial change. In the first version of the present tale the word was misprinted "ware." In "Byron and Miss Chaworth" it is given correctly in both the texts collated. Poe's use of nare is probably another of his borrowings from *Vivian Grey*. See Ruth Hudson, "Poe and Disraeli" (*AL,* January 1937).

6. The poet is Robert Burns.

7. Without the regulating influence of the Second Bank of the United States, lost in 1836 when President Jackson vetoed the renewal of its charter, there were years of bank failures and bankers came to be suspected (sometimes justly) of fraudulent practices. Brobdingnag (frequently spelled Brobdignag; see *OED* for instances from Pope, Southey, and Carlyle) is the land of giants in Swift's *Gulliver's Travels.*

8. "Flaccus" was the pen-name of Thomas Ward, M.D. (1807–1873), whose volume *Passaic* (1842) was unfavorably reviewed by Poe in *Graham's* for March 1843. Ward wrote regularly for the *Knickerbocker,* which did not endear him to Poe. In the first version Poe mentioned the poem by "Flaccus" as "Sam Patch." By this he meant "The Great Descender," an account of the eccentric Sam Patch, who went about the country accompanied by a pet bear, diving down waterfalls. He was killed at the falls of the Genesee, Rochester, New York, on November 13, 1829. I heard an old-fashioned saying, "As queer as Sam Patch," in New York as late as 1920.

9. Poe elsewhere compares great things to small. See a review of Horne's *Orion* in *Graham's* for March 1844, comparing "an anthill with the Andes"; "The Spectacles," comparing "a rushlight to the evening star – a glow-worm to Antares"; and "Editorial Miscellany" in the *Broadway Journal,* October 11, 1845, where Poe says "Putting the author of 'Norman Leslie' by the side of the author of the 'Sketch-Book' is like speaking of 'The King and I' – of Pop Emmons and Homer – of a mastodon and a mouse."

10. "As a dog is never driven from a greasy hide" is from Horace, *Satires,* II, v, 83.

11. Edward Hungerford, in "Poe and Phrenology" (p. 219) says: *"Constructiveness* is the organ which lies just below *Ideality,"* and quotes George Combe's *Lectures on Phrenology* (3rd ed., New York, 1841, p. 172) on that organ: "It does not invent; but merely fashions or configurates, though when large it stimulates the understanding to invent what will employ it agreeably in constructing."

Diogenes the Cynic's independence caused Alexander the Great to say, according to Diogenes Laertius, VI, vi, 32: "Had I not been Alexander, I should like to be Diogenes." Compare "The Duc De L'Omelette," n. 32.

12. Scipio defeated Hannibal (202 B.C.) by carrying the war into Africa; see Livy, XXIX, 26. The Frey Herren means literally "The Free Gentlemen," a term used obviously for desperadoes, but its source has not been traced. Dick Turpin (1706–1739), English highwayman executed for stealing horses, is the hero of various legendary romances. Daniel O'Connell (1775–1847), Irish patriot, had recently declared himself an abolitionist, and hence was unpopular with Americans of another opinion. Charles XII, King of Sweden from 1697 to 1718, was a reckless fighter.

13. "Cold as cowcumbers" is in the first scene of Beaumont and Fletcher's *Cupid's Revenge.* The word was formerly pronounced coo-cumber, and the vegetable was thought to be of a cold nature (and hence indigestible). The source of the quotation about Lady Charlotte Susan Maria Bury (1775–1861), English novelist and diarist, is not yet found. "Easy as an old glove," is perhaps slightly misquoted from *All's Well,* V, iii, 278, "This woman's an easy glove." Baiæ, near Naples, was a watering place, noted in ancient times for licentiousness.

14. Some of these offenses may have been suggested by the doings of Jeremy Diddler in Kenney's farce.

15. Compare *As You Like It,* II, vii, 156; "Full of wise saws and modern instances."

16. "Time and tide wait for no man" is an old proverb.

17. The Bank of North America, founded in Philadelphia in 1781, had, through years of nationwide financial uncertainty, the proud record of redeeming its currency in specie on demand.

18. See *Hamlet,* III, iv, 54, "counterfeit presentment of two brothers," also quoted in *Graham's* for February 1842 in "A Few Words about Brainard" by Poe.

19. For another account of the toll gate trick see *The Rover,* New York, September 14, 1844, which says it was played on the National Road, near Wheeling (now in West Virginia).

20. Two shillings means two bits, a quarter of a dollar.

21. This widespread story is told in *Atkinson's Casket* (Philadelphia, May 1831), p. 237, as "Tricks upon Travellers." Some of Poe's poems were reprinted in that number of the magazine. "But me no buts" is traced to Fielding's *Rape upon Rape,* II, xi.

22. Note the distinction in price and character of newspapers; penny (one cent) newspapers had only been established since 1833.

23. There is a firm of similar rhyming name in "Thou Art the Man."

24. *Non est inventus* means "He is not to be found." The Latin phrase is very frequently used in the second part (November 1839) of De Quincey's satire on murder.

THE SPECTACLES

This is the longest of Poe's purely comic tales, and one of the least meritorious. Few will disagree with Woodberry's description of it as "an extremely weak piece of humor,"* but Dr. Thomas Holley Chivers read it to some ladies who "shouted" with laughter at the joke about the "universe of bustle."†

The central idea of "The Spectacles" is that of mistaken identity. A close analogue to Poe's tale was found by Burton Pollin in an unsigned story called "The Mysterious Portrait" in a London periodical, *The New Monthly Belle Assemblée, a Magazine of Literature and Fashion,* of July 1836.‡ In this tale young Frederic de Forlanges lives with his grandmother and her ward Amelia. The two young people have been in love since early youth, but when Frederic is twenty-two his ardor cools because he thinks he has fallen in love with a young lady whose miniature portrait he has found in the Champs Elysées. He confides in the family servant, who shows the miniature to the grandmother. Recognizing it, she devises a plan to remedy the state of affairs. Accordingly, the servant reports that he has found the original of the portrait, the ward of a jealous older man who wishes to marry her and keeps her confined in a nearby house and its garden. With the servant's help, Frederic plans an elopement. They obtain a key to the garden and after various interruptions find the lady awaiting them there. She turns out to be Frederic's grandmother, who explains that the miniature is her portrait at the age of twenty, which she had dropped by accident in the park, and that the costume in the picture seems to be contemporary because its style is again in fashion after fifty years. She reconciles Amelia and Frederic, but among their friends a "theme of mirth . . . was the Young Man's passion for his Grandmother."

Another probable source for Poe's tale is a story called "The Blunderer" in the *Knickerbocker Magazine* for February 1837,

* *Poe* (1885), p. 246.

† Chivers to Poe, February 21, 1847, in *The Complete Works of Thomas Holley Chivers,* edited by E. L. Chase and L. F. Parks, I (1957), 70.

‡ See *American Literature,* May 1965.

reprinted in the *New-Yorker,* February 11 of that year. This tells of a New York gentleman, near-sighted from infancy, whose brothers and sisters in childhood stole his food and hid his spectacles. In maturity, when he fails to wear them he suffers a number of unhappy adventures including two of which seem to be used by Poe. The hero embarrasses ladies by speaking to some whom he has never met, and, on kicking a dog that is not, as he supposes, his own, but the property of a polite Frenchman, is reproached in a dialect resembling that of the old lady in "The Spectacles."

Poe's tale may owe something to *You Can't Marry Your Grandmother,* a farce by Thomas Haynes Bayly, first performed in London on March 1, 1838, which in the following year was "a farcical success on May 15th" at the Olympic Theater in New York. There, during the rest of the month, it "was presented almost nightly."§ Bayly's plot concerns a grandfather who, through a mock wedding with his charming ward (he fancies he himself would like to marry her), convinces his frivolous grandson that among his many lady friends the ward is his one true love. When the distraught young man declares himself, the lady mockingly protests, "You can't marry your grandmother!" — but the grandfather's hoax is revealed and the union of the two young people is accomplished.

Apparently Poe came to realize that his tale is too long. When he reprinted it in the *Broadway Journal,* November 22, 1845, he wrote in his Editorial Miscellany: "We have to apologize for the insufficient variety of the present number. We were not aware of the great length of 'The Spectacles' until too late to remedy the evil."

Although Poe published the story in the Philadelphia *Dollar Newspaper* late in March 1844, he, at about the same time, sent a manuscript of it to a new British correspondent, Richard Henry ("Hengist") Horne,* for possible sale in England. Horne men-

§ See George C. D. Odell, *Annals of the New York Stage,* IV (1928), 314. Bayly's farce was performed in several American cities in 1839 and subsequent years, and copies of many London issues during the next few decades are to be found in American libraries.

*See Poe's letter to Cornelius Mathews, March 15, 1844. Poe had reviewed Horne's epic *Orion* enthusiastically in *Graham's* for that month.

tioned it specifically in a letter of April 27, 1844 to Poe (printed in Woodberry's *Life,* II, 52–55), and the manuscript itself survives, although Horne did not preserve Poe's letters to him. Long afterwards, Horne stated that his efforts to sell the tale failed because of the "false modesty, and . . . hypocrisy" of the editors he approached.† It may be that this was a polite way of declining to pay for so long and poor a story. Prudery did not prevent the editor of *Lloyd's Entertaining Journal,* London, May 3, 1845, from copying it from the *Dollar Newspaper* version.‡

A so-called earliest version of "The Spectacles," quite different in plot, was published in the popular American magazine *Liberty* for September 24, 1938 as from an "old periodical," which was not named; I cannot believe it authentic.§

† Horne's reminiscences of Poe, in a letter of April 8, 1876, were published by Sara Sigourney Rice in *Edgar Allan Poe: A Memorial Volume* (1877), pp. 81–84. Poe's manuscript came into the hands of Horne's literary executor, H. Buxton Forman; I saw it at the auction of his collection in New York, March 16, 1920 (item 551). It was sold again in the Frank J. Hogan sale, January 24, 1945 (lot 562). It is now at the University of Texas. A complete photostat of the manuscript (which is not in roll form) was sent me by William H. Koester.

‡ My attention was called to this reprinting by Miss Harriet MacPherson, who told me the item was discovered by R. M. Hogg. The copy of the magazine in the Yale University Library shows that Poe's name as author is carried under the title.

§ The article in *Liberty* introducing the tale is credited to one Edward Doherty. It ascribes the discovery of the text to the noted collector Richard Gimbel who found it, unsigned, in "a bound volume of an American magazine" and "has convinced himself and the editors of Liberty that it is a genuine Poe story." The article concludes with the statement that "The name of the magazine in which the story was found is being withheld for a short time to permit of additional research and of copyright protection." [Mr. Howell J. Heaney, Rare Book Librarian of the Free Library of Philadelphia where the Richard Gimbel Collection now is, in a letter of March 25, 1976, states: "We have no evidence that Colonel Gimbel ever said where he found the story, or left a note citing its publication in any of the magazines in his very large collection of those of the period at which the story was supposed to have been published."]

The text of the tale as given in *Liberty* is the same as that "Uncovered and Published by Richard Gimbel, Philadelphia, July 1938" in an edition limited to 100 copies of a tiny sixteen-page brochure with stiff purple paper covers. Heartman and Canny (*A Bibliography of . . . Poe,* 1943, pp. 30–31) describe the little brochure and quote Mr. Gimbel as saying that he published the text "in three forms besides that in *Liberty,* all using the same printing of the text" — 100 copies in the stiff purple paper covers, a later issue of 1000 copies in thin pink paper covers, then a number of copies "bound up for presentation purposes in heavy white paper with a rough edge in purple."

The same text as that in Mr. Gimbel's pamphlet appears on the second, third, and fourth pages — two columns to a page — of a square (12 mo) four-page pamphlet entitled "THE SPECTACLES/Short Story By/EDGAR ALLEN [*sic*] POE" with

TEXTS

(*A*) Philadelphia *Dollar Newspaper,* March 27, 1844; (*B*) Manuscript sent to R. H. Horne, March or April 1844, now in the Koester Collection at the University of Texas; (*C*) *Broadway Journal,* November 22, 1845 (2:299–307); (*D*) *Works* (1850), II, 322–346.

Griswold's version (*D*) is followed.

[The manuscript is described by Professor Joseph J. Moldenhauer in *A Descriptive Catalog of Edgar Allan Poe Manuscripts in The Humanities Research Center Library, The University of Texas at Austin* (1973) and the following is quoted by his permission: "Black ink on 10 sheets of white paper, folded and gathered into a booklet of 40 pp., each page measuring 4½ x 7". Pages 1 through 38 are numbered in Poe's hand, while the last leaf is blank on both sides. The booklet is sewn into a marbled paper cover and its first and last leaves are stained with the marbling."]

The manuscript (*B*) is an entirely rewritten version, showing very numerous abortive readings, which in some cases might be regarded as improvements. On this occasion it can be argued that the latest text is not the best, but in view of the unimportance of the story, it does not seem necessary to print the manuscript version in full, or to use it in place of the form long known to the world. Eugénie, incorrectly accented in the *Broadway Journal* (*C*) and in *Works* (*D*) except on one occasion, has been corrected in our text throughout.

Reprint

Lloyd's Entertaining Journal (London), May 3, 1845, from the *Dollar Newspaper.*

THE SPECTACLES. [*D*]

[a]Many years ago, it was the fashion to[a] ridicule the idea of "love at first sight;"[1] but those who think,[b] not less than those who feel deeply, have always advocated its existence. Modern discoveries, indeed, in what may be termed ethical magnetism or

the imprint "CAREY & LEA/Philadelphia/1830." This item, in the collection of the American Antiquarian Society, is described and discussed by Heartman and Canny (pp. 29–32), and firmly rejected as a "wretched piece of printing, apparently done in the last couple of years." It is obviously a fraud. [Professor J. J. Moldenhauer writes us that at the University of Texas there is a pamphlet imprinted "CAREY & LEA/Philadelphia/1842" which presents on seven pages 3 5/16 by 4 5/8 inches a text identical with that in *Liberty.* This item is noted as a "Printed Pamphlet, THE SPECTACLES . . . text unrelated to the manuscript and authentic published forms, and apparently a forgery" on page 7 of Professor Moldenhauer's *Descriptive Catalog* cited below.]

In printed letters beneath the title: By Edgar Allan Poe *(B)*

a . . . a Some persons *(B)*

b think clearly, *(B)*

magnetœsthetics, render it probable that the most natural, and, consequently, the [c]truest and[c] most intense of the human affections, are those which arise in the heart as if by electric sympathy — in a word, that the brightest and most enduring of the psychal fetters are those which are riveted by[d] a glance. The confession I am about to make, will add another to the already [e]almost innumerable[e] instances of the truth of the[f] position.

[g]My story requires[g] that I should[h] be somewhat minute. I am still a very[i] young man — not yet [j]twenty-two years of age.[j] My name, at present, is a very usual and rather plebeian one — Simpson. I say "at present;" for it is only lately that I have been so called — having legislatively adopted this surname within the last year, in order to receive a large[k] inheritance left me by a distant male relative, Adolphus Simpson, Esq.[l] The bequest was conditioned upon my taking the name of the testator; — the family, not the Christian name; my Christian [m]name is Napoleon Buonaparte — or, more properly, these are my first and middle appellations.[m] [2]

[n]I assumed the [o]name, Simpson, with some reluctance, as[o] in my true patronym, Froissart, I felt a very pardonable pride — believing that I could trace a descent from the immortal author of the "Chronicles." While on the subject of names, by the by, I may[p] mention a singular coincidence of sound attending the names of some of my immediate predecessors. My father was a [q]Monsieur Froissart,[q] of Paris. His wife — my mother, whom he married at fifteen — was a Mademoiselle Croissart,[r] eldest daughter of Croissart the [s]banker; whose[s] wife, again, being[t] only sixteen when married, was the eldest daughter of one [u]Victor Voissart. Monsieur Voissart,[u] very singularly, had married[v] a lady of similar name — a

c . . . c most real and the *(B)*
d at *(B)*
e . . . e numerous *(B)*
f this *(B)*
g . . . g It is necessary *(B)*
h *Omitted (B)*
i *Omitted (B)*
j . . . j twenty-two. *(B)*
k a large/an *(B)*
l Esquire. *(A)*
m . . . m or baptismal names are Napoleon Buonaparte. I am now Napoleon Buonaparte Simpson. *(B)*
n *Not a paragraph (B)*
o . . . o "Simpson" with much reluctance; for *(B)*
p may as well *(B)*
q . . . q Monsieur George *Froissart, (B)*
r *Croissart, (B)*
s . . . s banker. *His (B)*
t *Omitted (B)*
u . . . u Monsieur *Voissart;* and this gentleman, *(B)*
v wedded *(A, B)*

Mademoiselle Moissart.[w] She, too, was quite a child when married; and her mother, also, Madame Moissart, was only fourteen when led to the altar. These early marriages are usual in France. [x]Here, however, are Moissart, Voissart, Croissart, and Froissart, all[x] in the direct line of descent.[3] My own name, though, as I say, became Simpson, by [y]act of Legislature, and[y] with so much repugnance on my part, that, at one period, I actually hesitated about accepting the legacy with the [z]useless and annoying[z] *proviso* attached.

As to personal endowments I am [a]by no means deficient. On the contrary,[a] I believe that I am well made, and[b] possess what nine-tenths of the world would call a handsome face. [c]In height[c] I am five feet eleven. My hair is black and curling. My nose is sufficiently good. My eyes are large and gray; and although, in fact, they are weak to a very inconvenient degree, still no defect in this regard would be suspected from their appearance. The weakness itself, however, has always much annoyed me, and I have resorted to every remedy — [d]short of wearing glasses.[d] Being youthful and good-looking, I naturally dislike these, and have resolutely refused to employ them. I know nothing, indeed, which so disfigures the countenance of a young person, or[e] so impresses every feature with an air of demureness, if not altogether[f] of [g]sanctimoniousness and of age.[g] An eye-glass, on the other hand, has a savor of downright foppery and affectation. I have hitherto managed as well as I could without either. But something too much of these merely personal details, which, after all, are of little importance. I will content myself with saying, in addition, that my temperament is sanguine, rash, ardent, enthusiastic — and that all my life I have been a devoted[h] admirer of the women.[i]

One night last winter, I entered a box at the P——[j] Theatre,[4]

w *Moissart. (B)*
x . . . x But what I speak of now is the coincidence. Observe! Here are *Moissart, Voissart, Croissart,* and *Froissart* — all *(B)*
y . . . y Act of the Pennsylvania Legislature; but *(B)*
z . . . z annoying and useless *(B)*
a . . . a so, so. *(B)*
b and that I *(B)*
c . . . c *Omitted (B)*
d . . . d *short of wearing spectacles. (B)*
e or which *(B)*
f exactly *(B)*
g . . . g sanctimoniousness. *(B)*
h devout *(B)*
i gentle sex. *(B)*
j C—*(A);* — *(B)*

in company with a friend, Mr. Talbot. It was an opera [k]night, and the[k] bills presented a very rare [l]attraction, so that[l] the house was excessively crowded. We were in time, however, to obtain the front seats which had been reserved[m] for us, and into which, with some little difficulty, we elbowed our way.

For two hours, my companion, who was a musical *fanatico,* gave his undivided attention to the stage; and, in the meantime, I amused myself by observing the audience, which consisted, in chief part, of the very *élite* of the city. Having satisfied myself upon this point, I was about turning my eyes to the *prima donna,* when they were arrested and riveted by a figure in one of the private boxes which had escaped my observation.

If I live a thousand years, I can never forget the intense emotion with which I regarded[n] this figure. It was that of a female, the most exquisite [o]I had ever beheld.[o] The face was so far turned towards the stage[p] that, for some minutes, I could not obtain a view of it — but the form was *divine;* no other word can sufficiently express its magnificent proportion — and even the term "divine"[q] seems ridiculously feeble as I write it.

The magic of a lovely form in woman — the necromancy of female gracefulness — was always a power which I had found it impossible to resist; but here was grace personified, incarnate, the *beau idéal* of my wildest and most enthusiastic visions. The [r]figure, almost[s] all of[t] which the construction of the box permitted to be seen, was[r] somewhat above the medium height, and nearly approached, without positively reaching, the majestic. Its perfect fulness and *tournure* were delicious. The head, of which only the back was visible, rivalled in outline that of the Greek Psyche,[5] and was rather displayed than concealed by an elegant cap of *gaze aérienne,*[u] which put me in mind of the *ventum textilem* of

k . . . k night; the *(B)*
l . . . l attraction; and thus *(B)*
m preserved *(A, B)*
n gazed at *(B)*
o . . . o imaginable. *(B)*
p stage, *(D) comma deleted to follow A, B, C*
q "divine," *(D) comma deleted to follow A, B, C*
r . . . r construction of the box permitted nearly all of the person to be seen. It was *(B)*
s nearly *(A)*
t *Omitted (A)*
u *äerienne, (A, B, C, D)*

Apuleius.[6] The right arm hung over the balustrade of the box, and thrilled every nerve of my frame with its exquisite[v] symmetry. Its upper portion was draperied by one of the loose open sleeves now in fashion. This extended but little below the elbow. Beneath it was worn an under one of some frail[w] material, close-fitting, and terminated by a cuff of rich lace which fell gracefully over the top of the hand, revealing only the delicate fingers, upon one of which sparkled a diamond ring, which I at once saw was of extraordinary value. The admirable roundness of the wrist was well set off by a bracelet which encircled it, and which also was ornamented and clasped by a magnificent *aigrette* of jewels — telling, in words [x]that could not be mistaken,[x] at once of the wealth and[y] fastidious taste of the wearer.

I gazed at this queenly apparition for at least half an hour, as if I had been suddenly converted to stone; and, during this period, I felt the full force and truth[z] of all that has been said or sung concerning[a] "love at first sight." My feelings were totally different from any which I had hitherto experienced, in the presence of even the most celebrated specimens of female loveliness. An unaccountable, and what I am compelled to consider a *magnetic* sympathy of soul for soul, seemed to rivet, not only my vision, but my whole powers of thought and feeling upon the admirable object before me. I saw — I felt — I knew that I was deeply, madly, irrevocably[b] in love — and this even before seeing the face of the person[c] beloved. So intense, indeed, was the passion that consumed me, that I really believe it would have received little if any abatement had the features, yet unseen, proved of merely ordinary character; so anomalous is the nature of the only true love — of the love at first sight — and so little really dependent is it upon the external conditions which only seem[d] to create and control it.

While I was thus[e] wrapped in admiration of this lovely[f] vision, a sudden disturbance among the audience caused her to turn her

v delicious *(B)*
w gossamer *(B)*
x . . . x not to be misunderstood, *(B)*
y and of the *(B)*
z and truth *omitted (B)*
a about *(B)*
b irrecoverably *(A, B)*
c one *(B)*
d *seem (B)*
e *Omitted (A, B)*
f enchanting *(B)*

head partially towards me, so that I beheld the entire profile of the face. Its beauty even exceeded my anticipations — and yet there was something about it which disappointed me without my being able to tell exactly what it was. [g]I said "disappointed," but this is not altogether the word. My sentiments were at once quieted[h] and exalted.[i] They partook less of transport and more of[j] calm enthusiasm — of[k] enthusiastic repose. This state of feeling arose, perhaps, from the Madonna-like and[l] matronly air of the face; and yet I at once understood that it could not have arisen entirely[m] from this. There was something else[n] — some mystery which[o] I could not develope — some expression about the countenance which slightly disturbed me while it greatly[p] heightened my interest. In fact, I was just in that condition of mind which prepares a young and susceptible man for any act of extravagance. Had the lady been alone, I should undoubtedly have entered her box and accosted her at all hazards; but, fortunately, she was attended by two companions — a gentleman, and a strikingly beautiful woman, to all appearance a few years younger than herself.

I revolved in my[q] mind a thousand schemes by which I might obtain, hereafter, an introduction to the elder lady, or, for the present, at all events, a more distinct view of her beauty. I would have removed my position to one nearer her[r] own, but the crowded state of the theatre rendered this impossible; and the stern decrees of Fashion had, of late, imperatively prohibited the use of the opera-glass, in a case such as [s]this,[7] even had I been so fortunate as to have one with me — but I had not — [s]and was thus in despair.

At length I bethought me of applying to my companion.[t]

"Talbot," I said, "*you* have [u]an opera-glass. Let[u] me have it."

[v]"An opera-glass![v] — no! — what do you suppose *I*[w] would be

g *New paragraph (B)*
h exalted *(B)*
i subdued. *(B)*
j of a *(B)*
k of an *(B)*
l — from the *(B)*
m *entirely (B)*
n behind *(B)*
o *Omitted (B)*
p *Omitted (B)*
q *Omitted (A, B)*
r my *(B) Poe's error*
s . . . s this. But even if this had not been so, I had no glass with me, *(B)*
t companion, whose very existence I had for some time forgotten. *(B)*
u . . . u a *lorgnette* — let *(B)*
v . . . v "A *lorgnette! (B)*
w I *(A, B, C)*

doing with [x]an opera-glass?"[x] Here he turned impatiently towards the stage.

"But, Talbot," I continued,[y] pulling him by the shoulder, "listen to me, will you? Do you see the stage-box? — there! — no, the next — Did you ever behold as[z] lovely a woman?"

[a]"She is very beautiful, no doubt,"[a] he said.

"I wonder who she can be?"[b]

"Why, in the name of all that is angelic, don't you *know* who she is? 'Not to know her, argues yourself unknown.'[8] She is the celebrated Madame Lalande[9] — the beauty of the day *par excellence,* and the talk of the whole town. Immensely wealthy, too — a widow — and a great match — has just arrived from Paris."

"Do you know her?"

"Yes — [c]I have the honor."

"Will you introduce[d] me?"

[e]"Assuredly — with the greatest pleasure; when[e] shall it be?"

"To-morrow, at one, I will call upon you at B——'s."

"Very good; and now [f]*do* hold[f] your tongue, *if* you can."

In this latter respect I was forced to [g]take Talbot's advice;[g] for he remained obstinately deaf to every further question or suggestion, and occupied himself exclusively for the rest of the evening with what was transacting upon the stage.

In the meantime I kept my eyes riveted on[h] Madame Lalande, and at length had the good fortune to obtain a full front view of her face. It was exquisitely[i] lovely: this, of course, my heart had told me before, even had not Talbot fully satisfied me upon the point — but still[j] the unintelligible something[k] disturbed me. I finally concluded that my [l]senses were[l] impressed by a certain air of gravity, sadness,[m] or, still more properly, of weariness, which

---

x . . . x opera-glass? — low! — very." *(A)*; a *lorgnette?" (B)*
y resumed, *(B)*
z so *(B)*
a . . . a "No doubt she is very beautiful," *(B)*
b be!" *(A, C)*; be." *(B)*
c Yes — *omitted (B)*
d present *(B)*
e . . . e "Assuredly. When *(B)*
f . . . f oblige me by just holding *(B)*
g . . . g put Talbot under the obligation desired; *(B)*
h upon *(A, B)*
i supremely *(B)*
j still there was *(B)*
k something which *(B)*
l . . . l imagination was *(B)*
m of sadness, *(B)*

took something from the youth and freshness of the countenance, only to endow it with a seraphic tenderness and majesty, and thus, of course,[n] to my enthusiastic and romantic temperament, with an interest tenfold.

While I thus feasted my eyes, I perceived, at last, to my great trepidation, by an almost imperceptible start on the part of the lady, that she had become suddenly[o] aware of the intensity of my gaze. Still,[p] I was absolutely fascinated, and could not withdraw it, even for an instant. She [q]turned aside[q] her face, and again I saw only the chiselled contour of the back portion of the head. After some minutes, as if urged by curiosity to see if I was still looking, she gradually brought her face again around[r] and again encountered my burning gaze. Her large dark eyes fell instantly, and a deep blush mantled her cheek. But what was my astonishment at perceiving that she not only did not a second time avert[s] her head, but that she actually took from her girdle a double [t]eye-glass — elevated it — adjusted it — and then[t] regarded me through it, intently and deliberately, for the space of several minutes.

Had a thunderbolt fallen at my feet I could not have been more thoroughly astounded — astounded *only* — not offended or disgusted in the slightest degree; although an action so bold in any other woman, would have been likely[u] to offend or[v] disgust. But the whole thing was done with so much quietude — so much *nonchalance* — so much repose — with[w] so evident an air of the highest [x]breeding, in short[x] — that nothing of mere effrontery was perceptible, and my sole sentiments were[y] those of admiration and surprise.

I observed that, upon her first elevation of the glass, she had seemed satisfied with a momentary inspection of my person, and was withdrawing the instrument, when, as if struck by a second thought, she resumed it, and so continued to regard me with fixed

n of course, *omitted (B)*
o *Omitted (B)*
p Nevertheless, *(B)*
q . . . q averted *(B)*
r round, *(A, B)*
s turn aside *(B)*
t . . . t eye-glass, elevated it, and *(B)*
u sure *(B)*
v or to *(B)*
w in short, with *(B)*
x . . . x breeding *(B)*
y was *(A) misprint*

attention for [z]the space of[z] several minutes — for five minutes, at the very least, I am sure.

This[a] action, so remarkable in an American theatre, attracted [b]very general[b] observation, and gave rise to an indefinite movement, or *buzz,* among the audience, which for a moment filled me with confusion, but produced no visible effect upon the countenance of Madame Lalande.

Having satisfied her curiosity — if such it was — she dropped the glass, and quietly gave her attention again to the stage; her profile now being[c] turned toward[d] myself, as before. I continued to watch her unremittingly, although I was fully conscious of my rudeness in so doing. Presently I saw the head slowly and slightly change its position; and soon I became convinced that the lady, while pretending to look at the stage was, in fact, attentively regarding myself. It is needless to say what effect this conduct, on the part of so fascinating a woman, had upon my excitable mind.

[e]Having thus scrutinized me[e] for perhaps a quarter of an hour, [f]the fair object of my passion[f] addressed the gentleman who attended [g]her, and, while[g] she spoke, I saw distinctly, by the glances of both, that the conversation had reference to myself.

[h]Upon its conclusion, [i]Madame Lalande[i] again turned towards the stage, and, for a few minutes, seemed absorbed in the performances. At the expiration of this period, however, I was thrown into an extremity of agitation by seeing her unfold, for the second time, the eye-glass which hung at her side, fully confront me as before, and, disregarding the renewed buzz of the audience, survey me, from head to foot, with the same miraculous composure which had previously so delighted and confounded my soul.

This extraordinary behavior, by throwing me into a perfect fever of excitement — into an absolute delirium of love — served rather to embolden than to disconcert me. In the mad intensity of my devotion, I forgot everything but the presence and the majestic loveliness of the vision which confronted my gaze. Watch-

---

z . . . z *Omitted (B)*
a The *(A, B)*
b . . . b universal *(B)*
c now being/being now *(B)*
d towards *(A, B)*
e . . . e She scrutinized me thus *(B)*
f . . . f and then suddenly *(B)*
g . . . g her. While *(B)*
h *Not a new paragraph (B)*
i . . . i she *(B)*

ing my opportunity, when I thought the audience were fully engaged with the opera, I at length caught the eyes of Madame Lalande, and, upon the instant, made a slight but unmistakeable bow.[j]

She blushed very deeply — then averted her eyes — then slowly and cautiously looked around, apparently to see if my rash action had been noticed — then leaned over towards[k] the gentleman who sat by her side.

I now felt a burning sense of the impropriety I had committed, and expected nothing less than instant exposure; while a vision of pistols upon the morrow floated[l] rapidly and uncomfortably through my brain. I was [m]greatly and[m] immediately relieved, however, when I saw the lady merely hand the gentleman a play-bill, without speaking; but the reader may form some feeble conception of my astonishment — of my *profound*[n] amazement — my[o] delirious bewilderment of heart and soul — when, instantly afterwards, having again glanced furtively around, she allowed her bright eyes to settle fully and steadily upon my own, and then, with a faint smile, disclosing a bright line of her pearly teeth, made two distinct, pointed and unequivocal [p]affirmative inclinations of the head.[p]

It is useless, of course, to dwell upon my joy — upon my transport — upon my illimitable ecstasy of heart.[q] If ever man was mad with excess of happiness, it was myself at that moment. [r]I loved. This was my *first*[s] love — so I felt it to be. It was love supreme — indescribable. It was [t]"love at first sight;" and at[t] first sight too, it had been appreciated and[u] *returned*.

Yes, returned. How and why should I doubt it for an instant? What other construction could I possibly put upon such conduct, on the part of a lady so beautiful — so wealthy — evidently so accomplished — of so high breeding[v] — of so lofty a position in

---

j *bow. (B)*
k to *(B)*
l flitted *(B)*
m . . . m *Omitted (B)*
n profound *(A, B, C)*
o of my *(B)*
p . . . p *nods. (B)*
q of heart *omitted (B)*
r *New paragraph (B)*
s first *(B)*
t . . . t *"love at first sight."* At *(B)*
u and was *(B)*
v breeding — so refined *(B)*

society — in every regard so entirely respectable as I felt assured was Madame Lalande? Yes, she loved me — she returned the enthusiasm of my love, with an enthusiasm as blind — as [w]uncompromising — as uncalculating — as[w] abandoned — and as utterly unbounded as my own! [x]These delicious fancies and reflections, however, were now interrupted by the falling of the drop-curtain. The audience arose; and the usual tumult immediately[y] supervened. Quitting Talbot abruptly, I made every effort[z] to force my way into closer[a] proximity with Madame Lalande. Having failed in this,[b] on account of the crowd, I at length gave up the chase, and bent my steps homewards; consoling myself for [c]my disappointment in[c] not having been able to touch even the hem of her robe,[10] by[d] the reflection that I should be introduced by Talbot, in due form upon the morrow.

This morrow at last came; that is to say, a day finally dawned upon a long and weary night of impatience; and then the hours until "one," were [e]snail-paced, dreary[e] and innumerable. But [f]even Stamboul,[f] it is said, [g]shall have an end,[g] [11] and there came an end to this long delay. The clock struck. As the[h] last echo ceased, I stepped into B——'s and inquired for Talbot.

"Out," said the[i] footman — Talbot's own.

"Out!" I replied, staggering back half a dozen [j]paces — "let[j] me tell you, my fine fellow, that this thing is thoroughly impossible and impracticable; Mr. Talbot is *not* out. What do you mean?"

"Nothing, sir: only Mr. Talbot is not in. That's all. He rode over to S——, immediately after breakfast, and left word that he would[k] not be in town again for a week."

I stood petrified with horror and rage. I endeavored to reply,[l] but my tongue refused its office. At length I turned on my heel,

---

w . . . w uncalculating, as uncompromising, as *(B)*
x *New paragraph (B)*
y *Omitted (B)*
z endeavor *(A)*; endeavour *(B)*
a *Omitted (B)*
b this attempt, *(B)*
c . . . c *Omitted (B)*
d with *(B)*
e . . . e dreary, snail-paced, *(B)*
f . . . f "even Stamboul," *(B)*
g . . . g "shall have an end," *(B)*
h its *(B)*
i a *(B)*
j . . . j paces, "out! — let *(B)*
k should *(A, B)*
l say something, *(B)*

livid with wrath, and inwardly consigning the whole tribe of the Talbots to the innermost regions of Erebus.[12] It was evident that my considerate friend, *il fanatico,* had quite forgotten his appointment with [m]myself — had[m] forgotten it as soon as it was made. At no time was he[n] a very scrupulous man of his word. There was no help for it; so smothering my vexation as well as I could, I strolled moodily up the street, propounding futile inquiries about Madame Lalande to every male[o] acquaintance I met. By report [p]she was known, I found,[p] to all — [q]to many by sight[q] — but she had been in town only a few [r]weeks, and there were very few, therefore, who claimed her personal acquaintance.[r] These few,[s] being still comparatively strangers, could not, or would not, take the liberty of introducing me through[t] the formality of a morning call. While I stood thus,[u] in despair, conversing with a trio of friends upon the all absorbing subject of my heart, it so happened that the subject itself passed by.

"As I live, there she is!" cried one.

"Surpassingly[v] beautiful!" exclaimed a[w] second.

"An angel upon earth!" ejaculated a[x] third.

I looked; and, in an open carriage which approached us, passing[y] slowly down the street, sat[z] the enchanting vision of the opera, accompanied by the younger lady who had occupied a portion of her box.

"Her companion also wears remarkably well," said the one of my trio who had spoken first.

"Astonishingly," said the second; "still[a] quite a brilliant air; but art will do wonders. Upon my word, she looks better than she did at Paris five years ago. A beautiful[b] woman still; — don't you think so, Froissart? — Simpson, I mean."

---

m . . . m myself; perhaps, indeed, he had *(B)*
n was he/had he been *(B)*
o *Omitted (B)*
p . . . p I found, she was known *(B)*
q . . . q by sight to many *(B)*
r . . . r days, and thus there were not more than one or two who professed a personal knowledge. *(B)*
s few, *omitted (B)*
t with *(B)*
u stood thus,/stood, however, *(B)*
v surpassingly *(B)*
w the *(B)*
x the *(A, B)*
y as it passed *(B)*
z sate *(A, B)*
a "has still *(B)*
b lovely *(B)*

[c]"*Still!*" said I, "and why shouldn't she be?[c] But compared with her friend she is as[d] a rushlight to the evening star — a glowworm to Antares."[e] [13]

"Ha! ha! [f]ha! — why,[f] Simpson, you have an astonishing tact at making discoveries — original ones, I mean." And here[g] we separated, [h]while one of the trio began[h] humming a gay *vaudeville,* of which I caught only the lines —

Ninon, Ninon, Ninon à bas — [14]
A bas Ninon De L'Enclos![i]

During this little scene, however, one thing had served greatly to console me, although it fed the passion by which I was consumed. As the carriage of Madame Lalande rolled by our group, I had observed that she recognised me; and more than this, she had blessed me, by the most seraphic of [j]all imaginable[j] smiles, with no equivocal mark of the recognition.

As for an introduction, I was obliged[k] to abandon all hope of it, until such time as Talbot should think proper to return from the country. In the meantime I perseveringly frequented every reputable place of public amusement; and, at length, at the theatre, where I first saw her, I had the supreme bliss of meeting her, and of exchanging glances with her once again. [l]This did not occur, however, until[m] the lapse of a fortnight. Every day, in the *interim,* I had inquired for Talbot at his hotel, and every day had been thrown into a spasm of wrath by the everlasting "Not come home yet" of his footman.

Upon the evening in question, therefore, I was in a condition little short of madness. Madame Lalande, I had been told, was a Parisian — had lately arrived from Paris — might she not suddenly return? — return before Talbot came back — and might she not be thus[n] lost to me forever? The thought was too terrible to bear. Since my future happiness was at issue, I resolved to act

c . . . c "Still!" said I, "and why not?" *(B)*
d *Omitted (A, B)*
e Here the whole trio laughed. *added as a new paragraph (B)*
f . . . f ha!" said the third, "why, *(B)*
g here, as *(B)*
h . . . h he commenced *(B)*
i *Couplet italicized (B)*
j . . . j *Omitted (B)*
k forced *(B)*
l *New paragraph (B)*
m until after *(A, B)*
n be thus/thus be *(B)*

with a manly decision. In a word, upon the breaking up of the play, I traced the lady to her residence, noted the[o] address, and the[p] next morning sent her a full and elaborate letter, in which I poured out my whole heart.

I spoke boldly, freely — in a word, I spoke with passion. I concealed nothing — nothing even of my weakness.[q] I alluded to the romantic circumstances of our first meeting — even to the glances which had passed between us. I went so far as to say that I felt assured of her love; while I offered this assurance, and my own intensity of devotion, as two excuses for my otherwise unpardonable conduct. As a third, I spoke of my fear that she might quit[r] the city before I could have the opportunity of a formal introduction.[s] I concluded the most wildly enthusiastic epistle ever penned, with a frank declaration of my worldly circumstances — of my affluence — and with an offer of my [t]heart and of my hand.[t]

In an agony of expectation I awaited the reply. After what seemed the lapse of[u] century it came.

[v]Yes, *actually came.*[v] Romantic as all this may appear, I really received a letter from Madame Lalande — the[w] beautiful, the wealthy, the idolised Madame Lalande. — Her eyes — her magnificent eyes — had not belied her noble[x] heart. Like a true Frenchwoman, as she was, she had obeyed the frank dictates of her reason — the generous impulses of her nature — despising the conventional pruderies of the world. She had *not* scorned my proposals.[y] She had *not* sheltered herself in silence. She had *not* returned my letter unopened. She had even sent me, in reply, one penned by her own exquisite fingers. It ran thus:

> Monsieur Simpson vill[z] pardonne me for not compose de butefulle tong of his contrée so vell[a] as might. It is only[b] de late dat I am arrive, and not yet ave[c] de opportunité[d] for to — l'étudier.[e]

---

o her *(B)*
p *Omitted (B)*
q folly. *(B)*
r leave *(B)*
s presentation. *(B)*
t . . . t hand, as of my heart. *(B)*
u of a *(A, B)*
v . . . v Yes; — came. *(B)*
w from the *(B)*
x *Omitted (B)*
y proposal. *(B)*
z will *(A)*
a well *(A)*
b only of *(B)*
c have *(A)*
d opportunite *(A)*
e to — l'etudier. *(A)*; to learn. *(B)*

Vid[f] dis apologie for the manière,[g] I vill now say dat, hélas! – Monsieur Simpson ave guess but de too true. Need[h] I say de more? Hélas![i] am I not ready speak de too moshe? EUGENIE[j] LALANDE.

This noble-spirited note[k] I kissed a million times, and committed, no doubt, on its account, a thousand other extravagances that[l] have now escaped my memory. Still[m] Talbot *would* not return. Alas! could he have formed even the vaguest idea of the suffering his absence occasioned his friend, would not his sympathising nature have flown immediately[n] to my relief? Still, however, he came *not*.[o] I wrote. He replied. He was detained by urgent business – but would[p] shortly return. He begged me not to be impatient – to moderate my transports – to read soothing books – to drink nothing stronger than Hock – [15]and to bring the consolations of philosophy to my aid. The fool![q] if he could not come himself, why, in the name of everything rational, could he not [r]have enclosed me a letter of presentation?[r] I wrote again, entreating him to forward one forthwith. My letter was returned by *that* footman, with the following endorsement in [s]pencil. The scoundrel had joined his master in the country:[s]

Left[t] S—— yesterday, for parts [u]unknown – did not[u] say where – or when be back – so thought best to return letter, knowing your handwriting, and as how you is always, more or less, in a hurry.

Yours, sincerely, STUBBS.

After this, it is needless to say, that I devoted to the infernal deities both master and valet; – but there was little use in anger, and no consolation at all in complaint.

But[v] I had yet a resource left,[w] in my constitutional audacity. Hitherto it had served me well, and I now[x] resolved to make it

f Wid *(A)*
g the manière,/de maniere, *(A)*; de maniére of dis leettle note, *(B)*; de manière, *(C)*
h Vat is need *(B)*
i Hélas? *(D) changed to follow A, B, C*
j EUGÉNIE *(B) unaccented in A, C, D*
k letter *(B)*
l which *(B)*
m *New paragraph* And still *(B)*
n instantly *(B)*
o not. *(B)*
p would now *(A, B)*
q fool! I had acquainted him with the exigencies of the case, and, *(B)*
r . . . r enclose me an introduction? *(B)*
s . . . s pencil: *(B)*
t Mr Talbot left *(B)*
u . . . u unknown. Didn't *(B)*
v *Omitted (B)*
w left me, however, *(B)*
x *Omitted (B)*

avail me to the end. Besides, after the correspondence which had passed between us, what act of mere informality *could* I commit, within bounds, that ought to be regarded as indecorous by Madame Lalande? Since the affair of the letter, I had been in the habit[y] of watching her house, and thus discovered that, about twilight,[z] it was her custom[a] to promenade, attended only by a negro in livery, in a [b]public square[b] overlooked by [c]her windows.[c] Here, amid the luxuriant and [d]shadowing groves,[d] in the gray gloom[e] of a [f]sweet midsummer evening, I observed my opportunity and[f] accosted her.

The better to deceive the servant in attendance, I did this with the assured air of an old and familiar acquaintance. With a presence of mind truly Parisian, she took the cue at once, and, to greet[g] me, held out the most bewitchingly little[h] of hands. The valet[i] at once fell into the rear; and now, with hearts full to overflowing, we discoursed long and unreservedly of our love.

As Madame Lalande spoke English even[j] less fluently than she wrote it, our conversation was necessarily in French. In this sweet tongue, so adapted to passion, I gave loose to[k] the impetuous enthusiasm of my nature, and with all the eloquence I could command, besought her consent to an immediate marriage.[l]

At this impatience she smiled. She urged the old story of decorum — that bug-bear which deters so many from bliss until the opportunity for bliss has forever gone by.[m] I had most imprudently made it known among my friends, she observed, that I desired her acquaintance — thus[n] that I did not possess it — thus, again, there was no possibility of concealing the date[o] of our first knowledge of each other. And then she adverted, with a blush, to the extreme recency of this date. To wed immediately would be

---

y custom *(B)*
z twilight every fine evening, *(B)*
a practice *(B)*
b . . . b certain one of our public squares *(B)*
c . . . c the windows of her residence. *(B)*
d . . . d overshadowing grove, *(B)*
e uncertainty *(B)*
f . . . f Midsum-[*sic*] gloaming — here, at length, watching my opportunity, I *(B)*
g welcome *(B)*
h diminutive *(B)*
i valêt *(C)*
j even much *(B)*
k to all *(A, B)*
l union. *(B)*
m gone by./departed. What would the world say? *(B)*
n thus, of course, *(B)*
o *date (B)*

improper — would be indecorous — would be *outré*. All this she said with a charming[p] air of *naïveté*[q] which enraptured while it grieved and convinced me. She went even so far as to accuse me, laughingly, of rashness — of imprudence. She bade me remember that I really even knew not who she was — what were her prospects, her connections, her standing in society. She begged me, but with a sigh, to reconsider my proposal, and termed my love an infatuation — a will 'o the wisp — a [r]fancy or fantasy[r] of the moment — a baseless and unstable creation rather of the imagination than of the heart. These things she uttered as the shadows of the sweet twilight gathered darkly and more darkly around us — and then, with a gentle pressure of her fairy-like hand, overthrew, in a single sweet instant, all the [s]argumentative fabric[s] she had reared.

I replied as best I[t] could — as only a true lover can. I spoke at length, and perseveringly of my [u]devotion, of my passion[u] — of her exceeding beauty, and of my own enthusiastic admiration.[v] In conclusion, I dwelt, with a convincing energy, upon the perils that encompass the course of[w] love — that course of true love that never did run smooth, and thus deduced the manifest[x] danger of rendering that course unnecessarily long.[16]

This latter argument seemed finally to soften the rigor of her determination.[y] She relented; but there was yet an obstacle, she said, which she felt assured I had not properly[z] considered. This was a delicate point — for a woman to urge, especially [a]so; in mentioning[a] it, she saw that she must make a sacrifice of her [b]feelings; still,[b] for *me*, every sacrifice should be[c] made. She alluded to the topic of *age*. Was I aware — was I fully aware of the discrepancy between us? That the age of the husband should surpass by a few years — even by fifteen or twenty — the age of the wife, was regarded by the world as admissible, and, indeed, as even[d] proper; but she had always entertained the belief that the years of the wife

p a charming/an *(B)*
q *näiveté (A, B, C, D)*
r . . . r phantasy *(B)*
s . . . s fabric of argumentation *(B)*
t . . . t best I/I best *(A, B)*
u . . . u passion — of my devotion *(B)*
v adoration. *(B)*
w of true *(B)*
x *Omitted (B)*
y resistance. *(B)*
z sufficiently *(B)*
a . . . a delicate. In touching upon *(B)*
b . . . b feelings — of the finest sensibilities of her nature; — still, *(B)*
c and would be willingly *(B)*
d very *(B)*

[e]should *never*[e] exceed in number those of the husband. A discrepancy of this unnatural kind gave rise, too frequently, alas! to a life of unhappiness. Now she was aware that my own age did not exceed two and twenty; and I, on the contrary, perhaps, was *not* aware that the years of my Eugénie[f] extended very considerably beyond that sum.

About all this there was a nobility of soul — a dignity of[g] candor — which delighted — which enchanted me — which eternally riveted my chains. I could scarcely restrain the excessive transport which possessed me.

[h]"My sweetest Eugénie,"[h] I cried, "what is all this about which you are discoursing? Your [i]years surpass[i] in some measure my own. But what[j] then? The customs of the world [k]are so many conventional follies.[k] To those who love as ourselves,[l] in what respect differs a year from an hour? I am twenty-two, you say; granted: indeed you may as well call me, at once, twenty-three. Now you yourself, my dearest[m] Eugénie, can have numbered no more than — can have numbered no more than — no more than — than — than — [n]than —"

Here I paused for an[o] instant, in the expectation that Madame Lalande would interrupt me by supplying her true age. But a French woman is seldom direct, and has always, by way of answer to an embarrassing query,[p] some little practical reply of her own. In the present instance, Eugénie, who, for a few moments past, had seemed to be searching for something in her bosom, at length let fall upon the grass a miniature, which I immediately picked up and presented to her.[q]

"Keep it!" she said, with one of her most ravishing smiles. "Keep it for my sake — for the sake of her whom it too flatteringly represents. Besides, upon the back of the trinket, you may discover,

e . . . e should, under *no* circumstances, *(B)*
f Eugénie *(A, B)*; Eugènie *(C, D)* *throughout*
g and *(B)*
h . . . h "Dearest," *(B)*
i . . . i age surpasses, *(B)*
j But what/What *(B)*
k . . . k — what are they, after all, but so many conventional impertinences? *(B)*
l we do, *(B)*
m sweetest *(B)*
n than — *omitted* *(B)*
o a brief *(A)*
p question, *(B)*
q presented to her./presented. *(A, B)*

perhaps, the very[r] information you seem[s] to desire. It is [t]now, to be sure, growing rather dark[t] — but you can examine it at your leisure in the morning. In the meantime, you shall be my escort home to-night. My friends[u] are about holding a little musical *levée*. I can promise you, too,[v] some good singing. We French are not nearly so punctilious as you Americans, and I shall have no difficulty in smuggling you in, in the character of an old acquaintance."

With this, she took my arm, and I attended her home. The mansion[w] was quite a fine one, and, I believe, furnished in good taste. Of this latter point, however, I am scarcely qualified to judge; for it was just dark as we arrived; and in American mansions of the better sort, lights seldom, during the heat of summer, make their appearance at this, the most pleasant period of the day.[x] [y]In about an hour[y] after my arrival, to be sure, a single shaded solar lamp[17] was lit in the principal drawing-room; and this apartment, I could thus see, was arranged with unusual good taste and even splendor; but two other rooms of the suite,[z] and in which the company chiefly assembled, remained, during the whole evening, in a very agreeable shadow. This is a well conceived custom, giving the[a] party at least a choice of light or shade, and one[b] which our friends over the water could not do better than immediately adopt.

The evening thus spent was unquestionably the most delicious of my life. Madame Lalande had not overrated the musical abilities of her friends; and the singing I here heard I had never heard excelled in any private circle out of Vienna. The instrumental performers were many and of superior talents. The vocalists were chiefly ladies, and no individual sang less than well. At length, upon a peremptory call for "Madame Lalande," she arose at once, without affectation or[c] demur, from the *chaise longue* upon which

r *Omitted (B)*
s seem just now *(B)*
t . . . t growing rather dark, to be sure, *(B)*
u friends here *(A, B)*
v you, too,/you *(B)*
w mansion, which belonged to one of her relatives, *(B)*
x twenty-four hours. *(B)*
y . . . y Not long *(B)*
z *suite, (B)*
a the individual members of a *(B)*
b and one/ — a custom *(B)*
c of *(A, B)*

she had sate[d] by my side, and, accompanied by one or two gentlemen and her female friend of[e] the opera, repaired to the piano in the main drawing-room. I would have escorted her[f] myself; but felt that, under the[g] circumstances of my introduction to the house, [h]I had better[h] remain unobserved where I was. I was thus deprived of the pleasure of seeing, although not of hearing her, sing.

The impression she produced upon the company seemed[i] electrical — but the effect upon myself was something[j] even more. I know not how adequately to describe it.[18] It arose in part, no doubt, from the sentiment of love with which I was imbued; but chiefly from my conviction of the extreme sensibility of the singer. It is beyond the reach of art to endow either air or recitative with more impassioned *expression* than was hers. Her utterance of the romance in Otello — the tone with which she gave the words *"Sul mio sasso,"* in the Capuletti — is[k] ringing in my memory yet.[19] Her lower tones were absolutely miraculous. Her voice embraced three complete octaves, extending from the contralto D to the D upper soprano, and, though sufficiently powerful to have filled the San Carlos,[l] [20] executed, with the minutest precision, every difficulty of vocal composition — ascending and descending scales, cadences, or *fioriture.*[m] In the finale[n] of the Sonnambula, she brought about[o] a most remarkable effect at the words —

Ah! non giunge[p] uman pensiero
Al contento ond 'io son piena.[q]

Here, in imitation of Malibran, she modified the original phrase of Bellini,[21] so as to let her voice descend to the tenor G, when by a rapid transition, she struck the G above the treble stave, springing over an interval of two octaves.

Upon rising from the piano after these miracles of vocal execution, she resumed her seat by my side; when I expressed to her, in terms of the deepest enthusiasm, my delight at her performance.

d been sitting *(B)*
e friend of/companion at *(B)*
f her thither *(B)*
g the peculiar *(A, B)*
h . . . h it might be more agreeable to Madame Lalande that I should *(B)*
i was *(B)*
j *Omitted (B)*
k are *(A, B)*
l Carlos, it *(B)*
m *fiorituri (A, B, C, D)*
n *finale (B)*
o brought about/wrought *(B)*
p *guinge (A, B, C, D)*
q *Couplet italicized (B)*

Of my surprise I said nothing, and yet was I most unfeignedly surprised; for a certain feebleness, or rather a certain tremulous indecision of voice in ordinary conversation, had prepared me to anticipate[r] that, in singing, she would not acquit herself with any remarkable ability.

Our conversation was now long, earnest, uninterrupted, and totally unreserved. She made me relate many of the earlier passages of my life, and[s] listened with breathless attention, to every word of the narrative. I concealed nothing — I felt that I had a right to conceal nothing from her confiding affection. Encouraged by her candor upon the delicate point of her age, I entered, with perfect frankness, not only into a detail of my many minor vices, but made full confession of those moral and even of those physical infirmities, the disclosure of which, in demanding so much higher a degree of courage, is so much surer[t] an evidence of love. [u]I touched upon my college indiscretions — upon my extravagances — upon my carousals — upon my [v]debts — upon my flirtations.[v] I even[w] went so far as to speak of a slightly hectic cough with which, at one time, I had been troubled — of a chronic rheumatism — of a twinge of hereditary gout — and, in conclusion, of the disagreeable and inconvenient, but hitherto carefully concealed, weakness of my eyes.

"Upon this latter point," said Madame Lalande, laughingly, "you have been surely[x] injudicious in coming to confession; for, [y]without the confession, I take it for granted that no one would have accused you[y] of the crime. By the by," she continued, "have you any recollection"[z] — and here I fancied that a blush, even through the gloom of the apartment, became distinctly visible upon her cheek — "have you any recollection, *mon cher ami,* of this little ocular assistant[a] which now depends from my neck?"

As she spoke she twirled in her fingers the identical double eye-

r imagine *(B)*

s while she *(B)*

t more acceptable *(B)*

u *New paragraph (B)*

v . . . v flirtations — even upon my personal defects. *(B)*

w *Omitted (B)*

x been surely/surely been *(B)*

y . . . y I take it for granted that, without the confession, you would never have been suspected *(B)*

z remembrance" *(B)*

a assistant — of this little aid to vision, *(B)*

glass, which had so overwhelmed me with confusion at the opera.[b]

"Full well — alas! do[c] I remember it," I exclaimed, pressing passionately the delicate hand which offered the glasses[d] for my inspection. They formed a [e]complex and magnificent[e] toy, richly chased and filagreed, and gleaming with jewels, which, even in the deficient light, I could not help perceiving were of high value.

"Eh bien! mon ami," she resumed with a certain *empressement* of manner that rather[f] surprised me — *"Eh bien, mon ami,* you have earnestly besought of me a favor which you have been pleased to denominate priceless. You have demanded of me my hand upon the morrow. Should I yield to your entreaties — and, I may add, to the pleadings of my own bosom — would I not be entitled to demand of you a very[g] — a very[h] little boon in return?"

"Name it!" I exclaimed with an energy that had nearly drawn upon us the observation of the company, and restrained by their presence alone from throwing myself impetuously at her feet. "Name it, my beloved, my Eugénie, my own! — name it! — but alas, it is already yielded ere named."

"You shall conquer then, [i]*mon ami,*[i]" said she,[j] "for the sake of the Eugénie whom you love, this little weakness which you have last confessed — this weakness more[k] moral than physical — [l]and which, let me assure you, is[l] so unbecoming the nobility of your real nature — so inconsistent with the candor of your usual character — and which, if permitted farther control, will assuredly involve you, sooner or later, in some very disagreeable scrape. You shall conquer, for my sake, this[m] affectation which leads you, as you yourself acknowledge, to the tacit or implied denial of your infirmity of vision. For, this infirmity you virtually deny, in refusing to employ the customary means for its relief. You will understand me to say, then, that I wish you [n]to wear spectacles:[n] — ah, hush! — you have already consented to wear them, *for my*

---

b opera, while she had employed it with so magnificent a *nonchalance. (B)*
c too well do *(A, B)*
d glass, or rather glasses, *(B)*
e . . . e gorgeous and complex *(B)*
f somewhat *(B)*
g little *(B)*
h *very (B)*
i . . . i *Omitted (B); mon amie, (D) misprint*
j said she,/she said, *(A, B, C)*
k rather *(B)*
l . . . l this weakness *(B)*
m this paltry *(B)*
n . . . n *to wear spectacles: (B)*

sake. You shall accept the little toy which I now hold in my hand, and which, though[o] admirable as an aid to vision, is really of no very immense[p] value [q]as a gem.[q] You perceive that, by a trifling modification [r]thus — or thus[r] — [s]it can be adapted to the eyes in the form of spectacles, or worn in the waistcoat pocket as an eye-glass.[s] It is in the former mode,[t] however, and habitually, that you have already[u] consented to wear it *for my sake*."

This request — must I confess it? — confused[v] me in no little[w] degree. But the condition with which it was coupled rendered hesitation, of course, a matter altogether out of the question.

"It is done!" I cried, with all the enthusiasm that[x] I could muster at the moment. "It is done — it is most cheerfully agreed. I sacrifice[y] every feeling for your sake. To-night I wear this dear eye-glass, *as* an eye-glass,[z] and upon my heart; but with the earliest dawn of that morning which gives me the pleasure[a] of calling you wife, I will place it upon my — upon my nose — and there wear it ever afterwards, in the less romantic, and less fashionable, but certainly in the more serviceable form which you desire."

Our[b] conversation now turned upon the details of our arrangements[c] for the morrow. Talbot, I learned from my betrothed, had just arrived in town. I was to see him at once, and procure a carriage. The *soirée*[d] would scarcely break up before two; and by this hour the vehicle was to be at the door; when, in the confusion occasioned by the departure of the company, Madame L. could easily enter it unobserved. We were then to call at the house of a clergyman who would be in waiting; there be married, drop Talbot, and proceed on a short tour to the East; leaving the fashionable world at home to make whatever comments upon the matter it thought best.

---

o although *(A, B)*
p great *(B)*
q . . . q intrinsically. *(B)*
r . . . r — thus *(B)*
s . . . s the jewels with which it is set, disappear, and it assumes the form of ordinary *spectacles;* by sliding it thus, again, it re-appears in the more gaudy dress, and the more tonnish shape, of an eye-glass. *(B)*
t arrangement, *(B)*
u *Omitted (B)*
v confused and annoyed *(B)*
w small *(B)*
x *Omitted (A, B)*
y sacrifise *(C)*
z eye-glass, in my waist-coat pocket, *(B)*
a privilege *(A, B)*
b The *(B)*
c arrangement *(A, B)*
d *soirèe (C, D)*

Having planned all this, I immediately took leave, and went in search of Talbot, but, on the way, I could not refrain from stepping into a hotel,[e] for the purpose of inspecting the miniature; and this I did by the powerful aid of the glasses. [f]The countenance was a surpassingly beautiful one! Those large luminous eyes![g] — that proud Grecian nose! — those dark luxuriant curls! — "Ah!" said I exultingly to myself, "this is indeed the speaking image of my beloved!"[22] I turned the reverse, and discovered the words — "[h]Eugénie Lalande — aged twenty-seven years and seven months."[h]

I found Talbot at home, and proceeded at once to acquaint him with my good fortune. He professed excessive astonishment, of course, but congratulated me most cordially, and proffered every assistance in his power. In a word, we carried out our arrangement[i] to the letter; and, at two in the morning, just ten minutes after the ceremony, I found myself in a close carriage with Madame Lalande — with Mrs. Simpson, I should say — and driving at a great rate out of town, in a direction North-east by[j] North, half-North.

It had been determined for us by Talbot, that, as we were to be up all night, we should make our first stop at C——, a village about twenty miles from the city, and there[k] get an early breakfast and some repose, before proceeding upon our route. At four precisely, therefore, the carriage drew up at the door of the principal inn. I handed my adored wife out, and ordered breakfast forthwith. In the mean time we were shown into a small parlor, and sat[l] down.

It was now nearly if not altogether daylight; and, as I gazed, enraptured, at the angel by my side, the singular idea came, all at once, into my head, that this was really the very first moment since my acquaintance with the celebrated loveliness of Madame Lalande, that I had enjoyed a near inspection of that loveliness by daylight at all.[m]

"And now, *mon ami,*" said she, taking my hand, and so[n] inter-

---

e a hotel,/an Hotel, *(B)*
f *New paragraph (B)*
g eyes! — those resplendent teeth! *(B)*
h . . . h *Italicized (B)*
i arrangements *(B)*
j and by *(A, B)*
k and there/there to *(B)*
l sate *(A, B, C)*
m daylight at all./daylight. *(B)*
n thus *(B)*

rupting [o]this train of reflection,[o] "and now, *mon cher ami,* since we are[p] indissolubly one – since I have yielded to your passionate [q]entreaties, and[q] performed my portion of our agreement – I presume you have not forgotten that you[r] also have a little favor to bestow – a little promise which it is your intention to keep. Ah! – let me see! Let me remember! Yes; full easily do I call to mind the precise words of the dear promise you made to Eugénie last night. Listen! You spoke thus: [s]'It is done![t] – it is most cheerfully agreed! I sacrifice[u] every feeling for your sake. Tonight I wear this dear eye-glass [v]*as* an eye-glass,[v] and upon my heart; but with the earliest dawn of that morning which gives me the privilege[23] of calling you wife, I will place it upon my — upon my nose — and there wear it ever afterwards, in the less romantic, and less fashionable, but certainly in the more serviceable form which you desire.' These were the exact words, my beloved husband, were they not?"

"They were," I [w]said; "you[w] have an excellent[x] memory; and assuredly, my beautiful Eugénie, there is no disposition on my part to evade the performance of the trivial promise they[y] imply. See! Behold! They are becoming – rather[z] – are they not?" [a]And here, having arranged the glasses[a] in the ordinary form of spectacles, I applied them gingerly in their proper position; while Madame[b] Simpson, adjusting her cap, and folding her arms, sat bolt upright in her chair, in a somewhat stiff and prim, and indeed,[c] in a somewhat[d] undignified position.[e]

"Goodness gracious me!" I exclaimed almost at the very instant that the rim of the spectacles had[f] settled upon my nose – *"My!*[g] goodness gracious me! – why what *can* be the matter with

o . . . o my reflections, *(B)*
p are, at length, *(B)*
q . . . q entreaties – since I have *(B)*
r *you (B)*
s *New paragraph (B)*
t done,' you said, *(B)*
u sacrifise *(C)*
v . . . v in my waist coat-pocket, *(B)*
w . . . w replied – "by the bye, you *(B)*
x an excellent/a capital *(B)*
y these words *(B)*
z *rather (B)*
a . . . a *In a new paragraph* Here, taking the glasses from my waistcoat-pocket, and arranging them *(B)*
b Mrs *(B)*
c indeed, I am sorry to say, *(B)*
d rather *(B)*
e posture. *(B)*
f *Omitted (B)*
g "My! *(B)*

these glasses? and taking them quickly[h] off, I wiped them carefully with a silk handkerchief, and adjusted them again.[i]

But[j] if, in the first instance, there had occurred something which occasioned me surprise, in the second, this surprise became elevated into astonishment; and this astonishment was[k] profound — was extreme — indeed I [l]may say it was horrific.[l] What, in the name of everything hideous, did this mean? Could I believe my eyes? — *could* I? — that was the question. Was that — was that — was that *rouge?* And were those — and[m] were those — were those *wrinkles* upon the visage of Eugénie Lalande? And oh, Jupiter! and every one of the gods and goddesses, little and big! — what — what — what — *what* had become of her teeth? I dashed the spectacles violently[n] to the ground, and, leaping to my feet, stood erect in the middle of the floor, confronting Mrs. Simpson, [o]with my arms set a-kimbo,[o] and grinning and foaming, but, at the same time utterly speechless and helpless with terror and with rage.

Now I have already said that Madame Eugénie Lalande — that is to say, Simpson — spoke the English language but very little better[p] than she wrote it: and for this [q]reason she very properly[q] never attempted to speak it upon ordinary occasions. But rage will carry a lady to any extreme; and in the present case it carried Mrs. Simpson to the very extraordinary extreme of attempting to hold a conversation in a tongue [r]that she did not altogether understand.[r]

"Vell, Monsieur," said she, after surveying [s]me, in great apparent astonishment,[s] for some moments — "Vell, Monsieur! — and vat den? — vat de matter now? Is it de dance of de Saint Vitusse dat you ave? If not like me, vat for vy buy de pig in de poke?"

"You wretch!" said I, catching my breath — "you — you — you villainous old hag!"

---

h hurriedly *(B)*
i While I was doing all this, Mrs Simpson said not a word, and moved not a muscle, but looked very serious and very solemn, and continued to sit bolt upright, as before. *added (B)*
j Well, I adjusted the glasses and put them on again; but *(B)*
k was immense — was *(B)*
l . . . l may as well say, at once, it was *horrific. (B)*
m *Omitted (A, B, C)*
n *Omitted (B)*
o . . . o *Omitted (B)*
p better, if not a great deal worse, *(B)*
q . . . q reason, very properly, she *(B)*
r . . . r she knew nothing about. *(B)*
s . . . s me, with great disdain, *(B)*

"Ag? — ole? — me not so *ver* ole, after all! me not one single[t] day more dan de eighty-doo."

"Eighty-two!"[u] I ejaculated, staggering to the wall — "eighty-two hundred thousand[v] baboons! The miniature said twenty-seven years and seven months!"

"To be sure! — dat is so! — ver true! but den de portraite has been take for dese[w] fifty-five year. Ven I go marry my segonde usbande, Monsieur Lalande, at dat time I had de portraite take for my daughter by my first usbande, Monsieur Moissart."[x]

"Moissart!" said I.

"Yes, Moissart;"[y] said she, mimicking my pronunciation, which, to speak the truth, was none of the best; "and vat den? Vat *you* know bout de Moissart?"

"Nothing, you old fright! — I know nothing about him at all; only I had an ancestor of that name, once upon a time."

"Dat name! and vat you ave for say to dat name? 'Tis ver *goot* name; and so is Voissart — *dat* is ver goot name too. My daughter, Mademoiselle[z] Moissart, she marry von Monsieur Voissart; and de name[a] is bote *ver* respectaable[b] name."

"Moissart?" I exclaimed, "and Voissart! why what is it you mean?"

"Vat I [c]mean? — I[c] mean Moissart and Voissart; and for de matter of dat, I mean Croissart and Froissart, too, if I only tink proper[d] to mean it. My daughter's daughter, Mademoiselle[e] Voissart, she marry von Monsieur Croissart, and den agin, my daughter's grande daughter, Mademoiselle[f] Croissart, she marry von Monsieur Froissart; and I suppose you say dat *dat* is not von *ver* respectaable name."

"Froissart!" said I, beginning to faint, "why surely you don't say Moissart, and Voissart, and Croissart, and Froissart?"

---

t one single/von *(B)*
u *"Eighty-two!" (B)*
v thousand of she *(A, B)*
w dis *(B)*
x Moissart?" *(D) changed to period as in A, B, C*
y Moissart, Moissart," *(A, B, C)*
z Ma'mselle *(B)*; Madamoiselle *(C, D)*
a names *(A)*
b respectable *(A)*
c . . . c mean?" said she, putting her arms akimbo — "vy, I *(B)*
d proper for *(B)*
e Ma'mselle *(B)*; Madamoiselle *(C)*
f Ma'mselle *(B)*

"Yes," she replied, [g]leaning fully back in her chair, and stretching out her lower limbs at great length; "yes, Moissart,[g] and Voissart, and Croissart, and Froissart. But Monsieur [h]Froissart, he vas[h] von *ver* big vat you call[i] fool — he vas von ver[j] great big donce like yourself[k] — for he lef *la belle France* for come to dis [l]stupide Amérique[l] — and ven he get here he vent and ave von *ver* stupide,[m] von *ver, ver* stupide[n] sonn, so I hear, dough[o] I not yet av[p] ad de plaisir to meet vid him — neither[q] me nor my companion, de Madame Stéphanie[r] Lalande. He is name[s] de Napoleon Bonaparte[t] Froissart, and I suppose[u] you say dat *dat,* too is not[v] von *ver* respectaable name."

Either the length or the nature of this speech, had the effect of working up Mrs. Simpson into a very [w]extraordinary passion[w] indeed: and [x]as she made an end of it, with great labor,[x] she jumped up from her chair like somebody bewitched, dropping upon the floor an entire universe of bustle as she jumped.[24] Once upon her feet, she gnashed her gums, brandished her arms, rolled up her sleeves, shook her fist in my face, and concluded the performance by tearing the cap from her head, and with it an immense wig of [y]the most valuable and beautiful[y] black hair, the whole of which she dashed upon the ground[z] with a [a]yell, and there trampled and danced[a] a fandango upon it, in an absolute ecstasy and agony of rage.

Meantime I sank aghast into the chair, which she had[b] vacated. "Moissart and Voissart!" I repeated, thoughtfully,[c] as she cut one of her pigeon-wings, and "Croissart and Froissart!" as she completed another — "Moissart and Voissart and Croissart and Napo-

---

g . . . g shaking her head up and down, as some people do when very much in a passion, — "Yes! Yes! — Moissart, *(B)*
h . . . h Froissart, who married my grande-daughter, he was *(B)*
i call de *(B)*
j *ver (B)*
k youself *(B)*
l . . . l stoopide *Amerique (B)*
m stoopide, *(B)*
n stoopide *(B)*
o for *(B)*
p *Omitted (B)*
q neider *(B)*
r *Accent omitted (A, C, D)*
s name, dough, *(B)*
t Buonaparte *(B)*
u sooppose *(B)*
v not de *(B)*
w . . . w stupendous excitement, *(B)*
x . . . x as, with great labor, she made an end of it, *(B)*
y . . . y valuable *(B)*
z floor *(B)*
a . . . a yell — there trampling and dancing *(B)*
b *Omitted (A)*
c musingly, *(B)*

leon[d] Bonaparte[e] Froissart! — why, you ineffable old serpent,[f] that's [g]*me* — that's *me* — d'ye[g] hear? — that [h]*me*" — here I screamed at the top of my voice — "that's *me e e!*[h] *I* am Napoleon Bonaparte[i] Froissart! and if I haven't[j] married my great, great, grandmother, I wish I may be everlastingly confounded!"[25]

Madame Eugénie Lalande, *quasi* Simpson — formerly Moissart — was, in sober fact, my great, great, grandmother. In her youth she had been beautiful, and even at eighty-two, retained the majestic height, the sculptural contour of head, the fine eyes and the Grecian nose of her girlhood. By the aid of [k]these, of pearl-powder, of rouge,[k] of false hair, false teeth, and false *tournure,* as well as of the most skilful modistes[l] of Paris, she[m] contrived to hold a respectable footing among the beauties *un*[m'] *peu passées* of the French metropolis. In this respect, indeed, she might have been regarded as little less than the equal of the celebrated Ninon De L'Enclos.

She was immensely wealthy, and being left, for the second time, a [n]widow without[n] children, she bethought herself of my existence in America, [o]and, for the purpose of making[o] me her heir,[p] paid a visit to the United States, in company with a [q]distant and exceedingly lovely[q] relative of her second husband's[r] — a Madame Stéphanie[s] Lalande.

At the opera, my great, great, grandmother's attention was arrested by my notice; and, upon surveying me through her eye-glass, she was struck with a certain family resemblance to herself. Thus interested and knowing that the heir she sought was actually in the city, she made inquiries of her party respecting me. The gentleman who attended her knew my person, and told her who I was. The information thus obtained induced her to renew her

d Napolean *(D) misprint*
e Buonaparte *(B)*
f wretch, *(B)*
g . . . g *me.* D'ye *(B)*
h . . . h *me* — that's *mee*" [Here I shouted at the top of my voice] — "that's me-e-e-e! *(B)*
i Buonaparte *(B)*
j havn't *(A, B, C);* hav'nt. *(D)*
k . . . k these — of rouge, of pearl-powder, *(B)*
l *modistes (B)*
m she easily *(A, B)*
m' *en (D) misprint*
n . . . n I widow, with no surviving *(B)*
o . . . o and resolved, in a freak of fancy, to make *(B)*
p heir. For this purpose she *(B)*
q . . . q very lovely and accomplished friend — a distant *(B)*
r husband *(B)*
s *Stéphanie (B);* Stephanie *(A, C, D)*

scrutiny; and [t]this scrutiny it was which so emboldened me that I behaved[t] in the absurd manner already detailed. She returned my bow, however, under the impression that, by some odd accident, I had discovered her identity. When, deceived by my weakness of vision, and the arts of the toilet, in respect to the age and charms of the strange lady, I demanded so enthusiastically of Talbot who she was, he [u]concluded that I meant the younger beauty, as a matter of course, and so informed me, with perfect truth,[u] that she was "the celebrated widow, Madame Lalande."

In the street, next morning, my great, great, grandmother encountered Talbot, an old Parisian acquaintance; and[v] the conversation, very naturally, turned upon myself. My deficiencies of vision were then explained; for these were notorious, although I was entirely ignorant of their [w]notoriety; and my[w] good old relative[x] discovered much to her chagrin, that she had been deceived in supposing me aware of her identity, and that I had been merely making a fool of myself, in making open love, in a theatre, to an old woman unknown. [y]By way of punishing me for this imprudence, she concocted with Talbot a plot.[z] He purposely kept out of my way, to avoid giving me the introduction. My street inquiries about "the lovely widow, Madame Lalande," were supposed to refer to the younger lady, of course; and thus the[a] conversation with the three gentlemen whom I encountered shortly after[b] leaving Talbot's [c]hotel, will be easily explained, as also their allusion[c] to Ninon De L'Enclos. [d]I had no opportunity of seeing Madame Lalande closely during daylight and, at her[e] musical *soirée,* my silly weakness in refusing the aid of glasses, effectually prevented me from making a discovery of her age. When "Madame Lalande" was called upon to sing, [f]the younger lady[f] was intended; and it was she who arose to obey the call; my

---

t . . . t it was this scrutiny which emboldened me to behave *(B)*
u . . . u concluded, as a matter of course, that it was the younger beauty whom I meant. He therefore told me, with perfect sincerity, *(B)*
v when *(B)*
w . . . w notoriety. My *(B)*
x relative thus *(B)*
y *New paragraph (B)*
z *Clauses transposed (B)*
a will be understood my *(B)*
b shortly after/upon *(B)*
c . . . c Hotel. Thus, also, is explained the allusion of one of them *(B)*
d *New paragraph (B)*
e the *(B)*
f . . . f Madame *Stéphanie* Lalande (B)

great, great, grandmother, to further the deception, arising at the same moment, and accompanying her to the piano in the main drawing-room. Had I decided upon escorting her thither, it had been her design to suggest the propriety of my remaining where I was; but[g] my own prudential views[h] rendered this unnecessary. The songs which I so much admired, and which so confirmed my impression[i] of the youth of my mistress, were executed[j] by Madame Stéphanie[k] Lalande. [l]The eye-glass was presented by way of adding a reproof to the hoax — a sting to the epigram of the deception. Its presentation afforded an opportunity for the lecture upon affectation with which I was so especially edified. It is almost superfluous to add that the glasses[m] of the instrument, as worn by the old lady, had been exchanged by her for a pair better adapted to my years. They suited me, in fact to a T.

The clergyman,[n] who merely pretended to tie the fatal knot, was a boon companion of Talbot's, and no priest. He was an excellent "whip,"[26] however; and having doffed[o] his cassock to put on a great coat, he drove the hack which conveyed the "happy couple" out of town. Talbot took a seat at his side. The two scoundrels were thus "in at the death," and through a half open window of the back parlor of the inn, amused themselves in grinning at the *dénouement* of the drama. I believe I shall be forced[p] to call them both out.

Nevertheless, I am *not* the husband of my great, great, grandmother; and this is a reflection which affords me infinite relief; — but I *am* the husband of Madame Lalande — of Madame Stéphanie[q] Lalande — with whom my good old relative, besides making me her sole heir when she dies — if she ever does — has been at the trouble of concocting me a match. [r]In conclusion: I am done forever[s] with *billets doux,* and am never to be met[t] without SPECTACLES.

g *Omitted (B)*
h views, however, *(B)*
i impressions *(A, B)*
j executed, of course, *(B)*
k *Stéphanie (B);* Stephanie *(A, C, D)*
l *New paragraph (B)*
m *glasses (B)*
n "clergyman," *(B)*
o donned *(A, B)*
p be forced/have *(B)*
q *Stéphanie (B);* Stephanie *(A, C, D)*
r *New paragraph (B)*
s *Omitted (B)*
t seen *(B)*

THE SPECTACLES

NOTES

1. "Love at first sight" seems to be first recorded from Marlowe's *Hero and Leander* (1598), I, 176.

2. The absurdity of the term "Christian" for a name like Buonaparte is obvious; Napoleon is, however, as the Emperor remarked, the name of a Corsican saint. In reviewing Ellery Channing's poems in *Graham's* for August 1843, Poe has a concluding paragraph making humorous comparison of Socrates Smith and Napoleon Bonaparte Jones with their famous namesakes.

It may be noted that Alexander Slidell, whose signature Poe had reproduced with letter 31 of "Autography," added MacKenzie to his name by authority of the New York legislature. The name was much in the news in 1843 and 1844 while he was being tried and vindicated for his action as commander of the brig *Somers* in ordering the execution at sea of young Philip Spencer, son of the Secretary of War, and another member of the crew for attempted mutiny in December 1842.

3. Poe may have had in mind his later friend Richard Adams Locke's collateral descent from John Locke. There also may be a subtle joke in that Jean Froissart (1338–1410) almost certainly never married.

Compare other lists of rhyming names in "Diddling" at n. 23 and "Thou Art the Man," paragraph 23. Haldeen Braddy (in *Glorious Incense,* p. 44) contrasts the set of rhyming names here with an anagrammatic series in Voltaire's *Zadig:* Nabussan, Nussanab, Nabassun, and Sanbusna.

4. The Park Theatre was the leading playhouse of New York.

5. The Psyche *par excellence* is the head and torso at Naples.

6. *Ventum textilem* is really from Petronius, *Satyricon,* 55, but the ascription to Apuleius is in *Ménagiana* (2nd ed., Paris, 1694), p. 265; Poe might have found it also under "Some Ingenious Thoughts" in D'Israeli's *Curiosities of Literature:* "Apuleius calls these neck-kerchiefs so glassy fine, (may I so express myself?) which in veiling, discover the beautiful bosom of a woman, *ventum textilem;* which may be translated, *woven air.* It is an expression beautifully fanciful." Poe alluded to *ventum textilem* also in the review of Drake and Halleck in the *Southern Literary Messenger,* April 1836; in a review of Moore's *Alciphron* in *Burton's,* January 1840; and again in "Marginalia," number 44 (*Democratic Review,* December 1844, p. 580). See also "aerial silk" in the first version of "The Duc De L'Omelette" (variants, at n. 18).

7. The hero of "The Business Man," in his Day-Book, under January 3, recounts how he rudely quizzed a theater party through an opera glass hoping to provoke assault and battery as grounds for a suit.

8. *Paradise Lost,* IV, 830, "Not to know me argues yourselves unknown," is slightly misquoted.

9. The name Lalande is from the celebrated opera singer, Mme. Henriette Clementine Lalande (1797–1867) who married M. Méric (but used her maiden name). She is mentioned in the Countess de Merlin's *Memoirs and Letters of*

Madame Malibran (Philadelphia, 1840). Poe reviewed the book in *Burton's,* May 1840. See n. 18 below for another use of this book in the present tale.

10. See St. Matthew 14:36 for touching the hem of a garment.

11. Poe used the proverbial expression about "Stamboul" (Constantinople) also in "Letter to Mr.———" in 1831.

12. Erebus is Hades.

13. Antares, alpha of the southern constellation Scorpio, is a red star of the first magnitude. For other comparisons of great and small things see "Diddling" at n. 9, and that note.

14. Ninon de Lenclos, or l'Enclos, a seventeenth century French "woman of pleasure" celebrated for her wit and charm, was famous also for her beauty even in old age; she is said to have had lovers mad about her in her ninth decade.

15. Hock is a common term for Rhine wine and is the Anglicized form of Hochheimer, the label under which most Rhine wine was shipped to England in the eighteenth century.

16. Compare Poe's dedication of *The Raven and Other Poems* (1845): "... To Miss Elizabeth Barrett Barrett ... with the most enthusiastic admiration." (See Mabbott I, 578.) "The course of true love never did run smooth" is from *Midsummer Night's Dream,* I, i, 134.

17. This is the Argand lamp, of which in "Philosophy of Furniture" at n. 10 the author says, "Never was a more lovely thought than that of the astral lamp."

18. The description of Madame Lalande's singing comes from the account given of Malibran's practice in the Countess de Merlin's *Memoirs and Letters of Madame Malibran* (cited in n. 9 above), II, 110, "Notes, Anecdotes – Style of Singing."

19. The references must be to the canzone sung by Desdemona in Gioachino Antonio Rossini's *Otello* (1816), Act III, Scene 1; and to Vincenzo Bellini, *Montecchi e Capuletti* (1830), Act IV, Scene 1 (information by courtesy of H. Mott Brennan).

20. San Carlo is the opera house at Naples.

21. See Bellini's *Sonnambula* (1831), Act III, Scene x.

22. "Speaking image" is a commonplace; compare note on the motto of "Life in Death," the earliest version of "The Oval Portrait," p. 666.

23. Evidence of Poe's haste in revising the *Broadway Journal* text of the story is his failure to make the repeated speech conform to its first occurrence.

24. Poe also ridiculed bustles in "The Thousand-and-Second Tale" and in "Mellonta Tauta."

25. Compare Poe's letter to his friends F. W. Thomas and Jesse E. Dow, March 16, 1843: "I never saw a man ... more surprised to see another. He ... would as soon have thought of seeing his great-great-great-grandmother."

26. The *OED* quotes *Pickwick Papers* in illustration of the word "whip" used as Poe uses it here: "You're a wery good whip, and can do what you like with your horses."

THE OBLONG BOX

This story is generally regarded as one of Poe's less successful tales of horror. Woodberry (*Poe,* 1885, p. 220) called it an "inferior grotesque." A. H. Quinn (*Poe,* p. 422) found it "singularly uninteresting," and meant no compliment when he said it was "suited quite well to *Godey's.*" It had some timeliness, for it must have recalled to its first readers a recent sensational murder case. The popular superstition involved was more prevalent in Poe's day than in ours, and thus better known.

When he wrote the story, voyages from Charleston to New York may have been in Poe's mind, for he used one in his "Balloon Hoax," printed in April 1844, as Hervey Allen pointed out in *Israfel* (1926), II, 590.

There is probably a small element of autobiography in the work, which according to Poe's letter of May 28, 1844 to J. R. Lowell had been written but not yet published. Poe's letter was dated only a few weeks after he had moved to New York with his ailing wife, leaving her mother to come later from Philadelphia to join them. This is the reverse of a situation in which a husband tries to take his dead wife to her mother, but Poe's state of mind at the time may be the reason the story somehow manages to be more sad than grotesque.*

The main incidents have all been traced to sources in print. The sensational climax comes from a poor Byronic poem called "Geraldine" by Rufus Dawes, which Poe discussed in a review. In this poem, Geraldine falls in love with Waldron who, having killed another suitor for her hand, runs away to become a pirate. Geraldine takes a sea voyage; her ship encounters the pirate ship,

* See David M. Rein, *Edgar A. Poe, the Inner Pattern* (1960), pp. 5–8. Rein tends to overplay his hand, but in this case, since the date is right, I accept his views, as slightly modified above.

and in a battle both vessels are destroyed. Waldron escapes in a boat and Geraldine, wounded, is taken on board another, but she dies before the two boats come together. Poe quotes the final stanza (cccv) of the poem:

> And round her neck the miniature was hung
>   Of him who gazed with Hell's unmingled wo;
> He saw her, kissed her cheek, and wildly flung
>   His arms around her with a mad'ning throw –
> Then plunged within the cold unfathomed deep
> While sirens sang their victim to his sleep.

Poe thought this "preposterous" – but saw that something might be made of it, if artistically treated.†

The celebrated crime Poe obviously had in mind when he wrote "The Oblong Box" would have been familiar to most contemporary readers, many of whom must have been following the Mary Rogers case through the summer of 1841. On the night of September 17, 1841, John C. Colt (older brother of Samuel Colt, who at this time was beginning to get backing for his revolver) quarreled with a printer named Samuel Adams over the payment for some books. Adams visited Colt in his apartment in a building at Chambers Street and Broadway in New York City. There Colt slew his creditor. Colt packed the body in a wooden box, addressed it to be sent by way of New Orleans to St. Louis, and had it put aboard the ship *Kalamazoo,* then at Maiden Lane Pier. Adams was missed by friends, suspicious circumstances were reported to the police, Colt was arrested, and on September 25 the box was found aboard the ship. The mayor of New York the next day ordered the box opened. "On opening it the body of Mr. Adams with only his shirt on, was found therein, packed round with salt," and wrapped about with sail cloth. (I quote *Brother Jonathan* of December 11, 1841.) Colt was brought to trial on January 21, 1842. A claim of self-defense was not believed and Colt

† The poem is included in Dawes's volume *Geraldine, Athenia of Damascus, and Miscellaneous Poems* (1839), which Poe criticized so harshly that he could not get his review published before its appearance in *Graham's* for October 1842. Poe's quotation does not make it clear that the heroine was dead before her lover leaped into the sea with her.

was convicted and sentenced to hang. But on the afternoon of the day set for his execution, November 18, 1842, he contrived to kill himself.‡

Another leading element in the tale comes from a story that Poe must have read in proof when it was published in *Burton's Gentleman's Magazine,* June 1840. This is "The Picture" by Professor John Frost, a Philadelphia teacher and editor. The hero in Jerry Godowny, a dilettante who, while visiting Spain, had bought for five dollars a picture of the Madonna. Cleaning it, he felt convinced that it was a great work of art and became much attached to it. Frost says of his hero:

> His next voyage was to London, and the picture hung up in his cabin. Unfortunately the ship was wrecked on the coast of England, and the officers and crew were barely able to save their lives and their lightest valuables, by taking to the boats. Jerry had learnt to love his picture; and when they refused to let him take his portable desk, on account of its bulk and weight, he hastily seized the Madonna, saying, "Surely you will not object to my taking this." The sailors laughed at his odd fancy, and permitted him to convey it on board the boat.

According to Frost's story, the picture was ultimately authenticated as by Raphael, and sold for ten thousand pounds.

To some extent Poe wrote whereof he knew. He had been to Charleston, and he located his shipwreck at a place where such disasters were not uncommon.

Poe offered the story to N. P. Willis for the *New Mirror* in a letter of May 21, 1844, and again, on May 29, to Mrs. Sarah J. Hale for *The Opal for 1845*. Both declined it — Willis because he could not afford to pay at the time. Godey proved more favorable, and the tale was noticed as accepted in his *Lady's Book* for August 1844 (29:96) along with "Thou Art the Man."

‡See Clifford Vierra Carley in *American Literature,* November 1957, and *Modern Language Notes,* December 1959 (under pen name of Clifford Carley Vierra). Mr. Carley referred chiefly to secondary sources. I have read the *New-York Tribune* and the *New York Herald* for September 27 and following issues, the New York weekly *Brother Jonathan* (its first notice of the murder — four columns — was in the issue of October 2, 1841, although it had noted Adams' disappearance in the issue of September 25), and pamphlets about the crime in the New-York Historical Society. There is also an account of the trial in *American State Trials* (St. Louis, 1914), volume I. It is an interesting coincidence that on the day of Colt's suicide, Friday, November 18, 1842, the daily *New-York Tribune* carried "The Mystery of Mary Rogers Explained"; see my introduction to "The Mystery of Marie Rogêt," p. 719 above.

TEXTS

(A) Godey's Lady's Book for September 1844 (29:132–136); *(B) Broadway Journal,* December 13, 1845 (2:349–352); *(C) Works* (1850), II, 351–362.

Griswold's version *(C)* is followed. The hyphen, omitted in the first three uses of state-room, has been reintroduced to conform to the usage throughout.

Reprint

The Philadelphia *Dollar Newspaper,* August 28, 1844, with the subtitle, "A Capital Story." See Killis Campbell, "Gleanings in the Bibliography of Poe," *Modern Language Notes,* May 1917. [The files of the *Dollar Newspaper* used by Campbell are not available for checking. In a letter of April 3, 1975, Hester Rich, Librarian at the Maryland Historical Society, states that their 1843–45 files of the *Dollar Newspaper* "have been missing for several years."]

THE OBLONG BOX. [*C*]

Some years ago, I engaged passage from Charleston, S. C., to the city of New York, in the fine packet-ship "Independence," Captain Hardy.[1] We were to sail on the fifteenth of the month (June,) weather permitting; and, on the fourteenth, I went on board to arrange some matters in my state-room.

I found that we were to have a great many passengers, including a more than usual number of ladies. On the list were several of my acquaintances; and among other names, I was rejoiced to see that of Mr. Cornelius Wyatt, a young artist, for whom I entertained feelings of warm friendship. He had been with me a fellow student at C—— University,[2] where we were very much together. He had the ordinary temperament of genius, and was a compound of misanthropy, sensibility, and enthusiasm. To these qualities he united the warmest and truest heart which ever beat in a human bosom.

I observed that his name was carded upon *three* state-rooms; and, upon again referring to the list of passengers, I found that he had engaged passage for himself, wife, and two sisters – his own. The state-rooms were sufficiently roomy, and each had two berths, one above the other. These berths, to be sure, were so exceedingly narrow as to be insufficient for more than one person; still, I could not comprehend why there were *three* state-rooms for these four persons. I was, just at that epoch, in one of those moody frames of mind which make a man abnormally inquisitive about trifles: and I confess, with shame, that I busied myself in a variety of ill-bred and preposterous conjectures about this matter of the supernumerary state-room. It was no business of mine, to be sure; but with none the less pertinacity did I occupy myself in attempts to resolve the enigma. At last I reached a conclusion which wrought in me great wonder why I had not arrived at it before. "It is a servant, of course," I said; "what a fool I am, not sooner to have thought of so obvious a solution!" And then I again repaired to the list – but here I saw distinctly that *no* servant was to come with the party; although, in fact, it had been the original design to bring one – for the words "and servant" had been first written and then overscored. "Oh, extra baggage to be sure," I now said to myself – "something he wishes not to be put in the hold – something to be kept under his own eye – ah, I have it – a painting or so – and this is what he has been bargaining about with Nicolino, the Italian Jew.[3] This idea satisfied me, and I dismissed my curiosity for the nonce.

Wyatt's two sisters I knew very well, and most amiable and clever girls they were. His wife he had newly married, and I had never yet seen her. He had often talked about her in my presence, however, and in his usual style of enthusiasm. He described her as of surpassing beauty, wit, and accomplishment. I was, therefore, quite anxious to make her acquaintance.

On the day in which I visited the ship, (the fourteenth,) Wyatt and party were also to visit it – so the captain informed me – and I waited on board an hour longer than I had designed, in hope of being presented to the bride; but then an apology came. "Mrs. W. was a little indisposed, and would decline coming on board until to-morrow, at the hour of sailing."

The morrow having arrived, I was going from my hotel to the wharf, when Captain Hardy met me and said that, "owing to circumstances," (a stupid but convenient phrase,) "he rather thought the 'Independence' would not sail for a day or two, and that when all was ready, he would send up and let me know." This I thought strange, for there was a stiff southerly breeze; but as "the circumstances" were not forthcoming, although I pumped for them with much perseverance, I had nothing to do but to return home and digest my impatience at leisure.

I did not receive the expected message from the captain for nearly a week. It came at length, however, and I immediately went on board. The ship was crowded with passengers, and everything was in the bustle attendant upon making sail. Wyatt's party arrived in about ten minutes after myself. There were the two sisters, the bride, and the artist — the latter in one of his customary fits of moody misanthropy. I was too well used to these however, to pay them any special[a] attention. He did not even introduce me to his wife; — this courtesy devolving, per force, upon his sister Marian — a very sweet and intelligent girl, who, in a few hurried words, made us acquainted.

Mrs. Wyatt had been closely veiled; and when she raised her veil, in acknowledging my bow, I confess that I was very profoundly astonished. I should have been much more so, however, had not long experience advised me not to trust, with too implicit[b] a reliance, the enthusiastic descriptions of my friend, the artist, when indulging in comments upon the loveliness of woman. When beauty was the theme, I well knew with what facility he soared into the regions of the purely ideal.

The truth is, I could not help regarding Mrs. Wyatt as a decidedly plain-looking woman. If not positively ugly, she was not, I think, very far from it. She was dressed, however, in exquisite taste — and then I had no doubt that she had captivated my friend's heart by the more enduring graces of the intellect and soul She said very few words, and passed at once into her state-room with Mr. W.

My old inquisitiveness now returned. There was *no* servant — *that* was a settled point. I looked, therefore, for the extra baggage. After some delay, a cart arrived at the wharf, with an oblong pine box, which was everything that seemed[c] to be expected. Immediately upon its arrival we made sail, and in a short time were safely over the bar and standing out to sea.

The box in question was, as I say, oblong. It was about six

a especial *(A)*
b inplicit *(B)* ***misprint***
c seeemed *(B)* ***misprint***

feet in length by two and a half in breadth; — I observed it attentively, and like to be precise. Now this shape was *peculiar;* and no sooner had I seen it, than I took credit to myself for the accuracy of my guessing. I had reached the conclusion, it will be remembered, that the extra baggage of my friend, the artist, would prove to be pictures, or at least a picture; for I knew he had been for several weeks in conference with Nicolino: — and now here was a box which, from its shape, *could* possibly contain nothing in the world but a copy of Leonardo's "Last Supper;" and a copy of this very "Last Supper," done by Rubini the younger,[4] at Florence, I had known, for some time, to be in the possession of Nicolino. This point, therefore, I considered as sufficiently settled. I chuckled excessively when I thought of my acumen. It was the first time I had ever known Wyatt to keep from me any of his artistical secrets; but here he evidently intended to steal a march upon me, and smuggle a fine picture to New York, under my very nose; expecting me to know nothing of the matter. I resolved to quiz him *well,* now and hereafter.

One thing, however, annoyed me not a[d] little. The box did *not* go into the extra state-room. It was deposited in Wyatt's own; and there, too, it remained, occupying very nearly the whole of the floor — no doubt to the exceeding discomfort of the artist and his wife; — this the more especially as the tar or paint with which it was lettered in sprawling capitals, emitted a strong, disagreeable, and, to *my* fancy, a peculiarly disgusting odor. On the lid were painted the words — *"Mrs. Adelaide Curtis, Albany, New York. Charge of Cornelius Wyatt, Esq. This side up. To be handled with care."*

Now, I was aware that Mrs. Adelaide Curtis, of Albany,[5] was the artist's wife's mother; — but then I looked upon the whole address as a mystification, intended especially for myself. I made up my mind, of course, that the box and contents would never get farther north than the studio of my misanthropic friend, in Chambers Street, New York.[6]

For the first three or four days we had fine weather, although the wind was dead ahead; having chopped round to the north-

d not a/no *(A)*

ward, immediately upon our losing sight of the coast. The passengers were, consequently, in high spirits, and disposed to be social. I *must* except, however, Wyatt and his sisters, who behaved stiffly, and, I could not help thinking, uncourteously to the rest of the party. *Wyatt's* conduct I did not so much regard. He was gloomy, even beyond his usual habit – in fact he was *morose* – but in[e] him I was prepared for eccentricity. For the sisters, however, I could make no excuse. They secluded themselves in their state-rooms during the greater part of the passage, and absolutely refused, although I repeatedly urged them, to hold communication with any person on board.

Mrs. Wyatt herself was far more agreeable. That is to say, she was *chatty;* and to be chatty is no slight recommendation at sea. She became *excessively* intimate with most of the ladies; and, to my profound astonishment, evinced no equivocal disposition to coquet with the men. She amused us all very much. I say *"amused"* – and scarcely know how to explain myself. The truth is, I soon found that Mrs. W. was far oftener laughed *at* than *with.*[7] The gentlemen said little about her; but the ladies, in a little while, pronounced her "a good-hearted thing, rather indifferent-looking, totally uneducated, and decidedly vulgar." The great wonder was, how Wyatt had been entrapped into such a match. Wealth was the general solution – but this I knew to be no solution at all; for Wyatt had told me that she neither brought him a dollar nor had any expectations from any source whatever. "He had married," he said, "for love, and for love only; and his bride was far more than worthy of his love." When I thought of these expressions, on the part of my friend, I confess that I felt indescribably puzzled. Could it be possible that he was taking leave of his senses? What else could I think? *He,* so refined, so intellectual, so fastidious, with so exquisite a perception of the faulty, and so keen an appreciation of the beautiful! To be sure, the lady seemed especially fond of *him* – particularly so in his absence – when she made herself ridiculous by frequent quotations of what had been said by her "beloved husband, Mr. Wyatt." The word "husband" seemed forever – to use one of her own delicate expressions –

---

e with *(A)*

forever "on the tip of her tongue." In the meantime, it was observed by all on board, that he avoided *her* in the most pointed manner, and, for the most part, shut himself up alone in his stateroom, where, in fact, he might have been said to live altogether, leaving his wife at full liberty to amuse herself as she thought best, in the public society of the main cabin.

My conclusion, from what I saw and heard, was, that the artist, by some unaccountable freak of fate, or perhaps in some fit of enthusiastic and fanciful passion, had been induced to unite himself with a person altogether beneath him, and that the natural result, entire and speedy disgust, had ensued. I pitied him from the bottom of my heart — but[f] could not, for that reason, quite forgive his incommunicativeness in the matter of the "Last Supper." For this I resolved to have my revenge.

One day he came upon deck, and, taking his arm as had been my wont, I sauntered with him backwards and forwards. His gloom, however, (which I considered quite natural under the circumstances,) seemed entirely unabated. He said little, and that[g] moodily, and with evident effort. I ventured a jest or two, and he made a sickening attempt at a smile. Poor fellow! — as I thought of *his wife,* I wondered that he could have heart [h]to put on even[h] the semblance of mirth. At last I ventured a home thrust. I determined to commence a series of covert insinuations, or inuendoes,[h'] about the oblong box — just to let[i] him perceive, gradually, that I was *not* altogether the butt, or victim, of his little bit of pleasant mystification. My first observation was by way of opening a masked battery.[8] I said something about the "peculiar shape of *that* box;" and, as I spoke the words, I smiled knowingly, winked, and touched him gently with my fore-finger in the ribs.

The manner in which Wyatt received this harmless pleasantry, convinced me, at once, that he was mad. At first he stared at me as if he found it impossible to comprehend the witticism of my remark; but as its point seemed slowly to make its way into his brain, his eyes in the same proportion, seemed protruding from their

f but I *(A)*
g tha *(B) misprint*
h . . . h ever to put on *(A)*
h′ inuendos, *(A)*
i to let/by way of letting *(A)*

sockets. Then he grew very red — then hideously pale — then, as if highly amused with what I had insinuated, he began a loud and boisterous laugh, which, to my astonishment, he kept up, with gradually increasing vigor, for ten minutes or more. In conclusion, he fell flat and heavily upon the deck. When I ran to uplift him, to all appearance he was[j] *dead.*

I called assistance, and, with much difficulty, we brought him to himself. Upon reviving he spoke incoherently for some time. At length we bled him and put him to bed. The next morning he was quite recovered, so far as regarded his mere bodily health. Of his mind I say nothing, of course. I avoided him during the rest of the passage, by advice of the captain, who seemed to coincide with me altogether in my views of his insanity, but cautioned me to say nothing on this head to any person on board.

Several circumstances occurred immediately after this fit of Wyatt's, which contributed to heighten the curiosity with which I was already possessed. Among other things, this: I had been nervous — drank too much strong green tea, and slept ill at night — in fact, for two nights I could not be properly said to sleep at all. Now, my state-room opened into the main cabin, or dining-room, as did those of all the single men on board. Wyatt's three rooms were in the after-cabin, which was separated from the main one by a slight sliding door, never locked even at night. As we were almost constantly on a wind, and the breeze was not a little[k] stiff, the ship[l] heeled to leeward very considerably; and whenever her[m] starboard side[n] was to leeward, the sliding door between the cabins slid open, and so remained, nobody taking the trouble to get up and shut it. But my berth was in such a position, that when my own state-room door was open, as well as the sliding door in question, (and my own door was *always* open on account of the heat,) I could see into the after cabin quite distinctly, and just at that portion of it, too, where were situated the state-rooms of Mr. Wyatt. Well, during two nights (*not* consecutive) while I lay awake, I clearly saw Mrs. W., about eleven o'clock upon each

j was utterly *(A)*
k not a little *omitted (A)*
l vessel *(A)*
m the *(A)*
n side of the ship *(A)*

night, steal cautiously from the state-room of Mr. W., and enter the extra room, where she remained until day break, when she was called by her husband and went back. That they were virtually separated was clear. They had separate apartments — no doubt in contemplation of a more permanent divorce; and here, after all, I thought, was the mystery of the extra state-room.

There was another circumstance, too, which interested me much. During the two wakeful nights in question, and immediately after the disappearance of Mrs. Wyatt into the extra state-room, I was attracted by certain singular, cautious, subdued noises in that of her husband. After listening to them for some time, with thoughtful attention, I at length succeeded perfectly in translating their import. They were sounds occasioned by the artist in prying open the oblong box, by means of a chisel and mallet — the latter being apparently muffled, or deadened, by some soft woollen or cotton substance in which its head was enveloped.

In this manner I fancied[o] I could distinguish the precise moment when he fairly disengaged the lid — also, that I could determine when he removed it altogether, and when he deposited it upon the lower berth in his room; this latter point I knew, for example, by certain slight taps which the lid made in striking against the wooden edges of the berth, as he endeavored to lay it down *very* gently — there being no room for it on the floor. After this there was a dead stillness, and I heard nothing more, upon either occasion, until nearly daybreak; unless, perhaps, I may mention a low sobbing, or murmuring sound, so very much suppressed as to be nearly inaudible — if, indeed, the whole of this latter noise were not rather produced by my own imagination. I say it seemed to *resemble* sobbing or sighing — but, of course, it could not have been either. I rather think it was a ringing in my own ears. Mr. Wyatt, no doubt, according to custom, was merely giving the rein to one of his hobbies — indulging in one of his fits of artistic enthusiasm. He had opened his oblong box, in order to feast his eyes on[p] the pictorial treasure within. There was nothing in this however, to make him *sob*. I repeat therefore, that it must have been simply a freak of my own fancy, distempered by

---

o fancied that *(A)*

p upon *(A)*

good Captain Hardy's green tea. Just before dawn, on each of the two nights of which I speak, I distinctly heard Mr. Wyatt replace the lid upon the oblong box, and force the nails into their old places, by means of the muffled mallet. Having done this, he issued from his state-room, fully dressed, and proceeded to call Mrs. W. from hers.

We had been at sea seven days, and were now off Cape Hatteras, when there came[q] a tremendously heavy blow from the southwest.[9] We were, in a measure, prepared for it, however, as the weather had been holding out threats for some time. Everything was made snug, alow and aloft; and as the wind steadily freshened, we lay to, at length, under spanker and foretopsail, both double-reefed.

In this trim, we rode safely enough for forty-eight hours — the ship proving herself an excellent sea boat, in many respects, and shipping no water of any consequence. At the end of this period, however, the gale had freshened into a hurricane, and our aftersail split into ribbons, bringing us so much in the trough of the water that we shipped several prodigious seas, one immediately after the other. By this accident we lost three men overboard, with the caboose, and nearly the whole of the larboard bulwarks. Scarcely had we recovered our senses, before the foretopsail went into shreds, when we got up a storm stay-sail, and with this did pretty well for some hours, the ship heading the sea[r] much more steadily than before.

The gale still held on, however, and we saw no signs of its abating. The rigging was found to be ill-fitted, and greatly strained; and on the third day of the blow, about five in the afternoon, our mizzen-mast, in a heavy lurch to windward, went by the board. For an hour or more, we tried in vain to get rid of it, on account of the prodigious rolling of the ship; and, before we had succeeded, the carpenter came aft and announced four feet water in the hold. To add to our dilemma, we found the pumps choked and nearly useless.

All was now confusion and despair — but an effort was made to lighten the ship by throwing overboard as much of her cargo

q came on *(A, B)* r seas *(A, B)*

as could be reached, and by cutting away the two masts that remained. This we at last accomplished — but we were still unable to do anything at the pumps; and, in the meantime, the leak gained on us very fast.

At sundown, the gale had sensibly diminished in violence, and, as the sea went down with it, we still entertained faint hopes of saving ourselves in the boats. At eight, P. M., the clouds broke away to windward, and we had the advantage of a full moon — a piece of good fortune which served wonderfully to cheer our drooping spirits.

After incredible labor we succeeded, at length, in getting the long-boat over the side without material accident, and into this we crowded the whole of the crew and most of the passengers. This party made off immediately, and, after undergoing much suffering, finally arrived, in safety, at Ocracoke Inlet,[10] on the third day after the wreck.

Fourteen passengers, with the Captain, remained on board, resolving to trust their fortunes to the jolly-boat at the stern. We lowered it without difficulty, although it was only by a miracle that we prevented it from swamping as it touched the water. It contained, when afloat, the captain and his wife, Mr. Wyatt and party, a Mexican officer, wife, four children, and myself, with a negro valet.

We had no room, of course, for anything except a few positively necessary instruments, some provision, and the clothes upon our backs. No one had thought of even attempting to save anything more. What must have been the astonishment of all then, when, having proceeded a few fathoms from the ship, Mr. Wyatt stood up in the stern-sheets, and coolly demanded of Captain Hardy that the boat should be put back for the purpose of taking in his oblong box!

"Sit down, Mr. Wyatt," replied the Captain, somewhat sternly; "you will capsize us if you do not sit quite still. Our gunwale is almost in the water now."

"The box!" vociferated Mr. Wyatt, still standing — "the box, I say! Captain Hardy, you cannot, you *will* not refuse me. Its weight will be but a trifle — it is nothing — mere nothing. By the mother who bore you — for the love of Heaven — by your hope of salvation, I *implore* you to put back for the box!"[11]

The Captain, for a moment, seemed touched by the earnest appeal of the artist, but he regained his stern composure, and merely said —

"Mr. Wyatt, you are *mad.* I cannot listen to you. Sit down, I say, or you will swamp the boat. Stay — hold him — seize him! — he is about to spring overboard! There — I knew it — he is over!"

As the Captain said this, Mr. Wyatt, in fact, sprang from the boat, and, as we were yet in the lee of the wreck, succeeded, by almost superhuman exertion, in getting hold of a rope which hung from the fore-chains. In another moment he was on board, and rushing frantically down into the cabin.

In the meantime, we had been swept astern of the ship, and being quite out of her lee, were at the mercy of the tremendous sea which was still running. We made a determined effort to put back, but our little boat was like a feather in the breath of the tempest.[s] We saw at a glance that the doom of the unfortunate artist was sealed.

As our distance from the wreck rapidly increased, the madman (for as such only could we regard him) was seen to emerge from the companion-way, up which, by dint of a strength that appeared gigantic,[t] he dragged, bodily, the oblong box. While we gazed in the[u] extremity of astonishment, he passed, rapidly, several turns of a three-inch rope, first around the box and then around his body. In another instant both body and box were in the sea — disappearing suddenly, at once and forever.[12]

We lingered awhile sadly upon our oars, with our eyes riveted upon the spot. At length we pulled[v] away. The silence remained unbroken for an hour.[w] Finally, I hazarded a remark.

"Did you observe, Captain, how suddenly they sank? Was not that an exceedingly singular thing? I confess that I entertained some feeble hope of his final deliverance, when I saw him lash himself to the box, and commit himself to the sea."

"They sank as a matter of course," replied the Captain, "and

s simoom. *(A)*
t superhuman, *(A)*
u *Omitted (A)*
v pulled steadily *(A)*
w hour, so heavy were all our hearts. *(A)*

that like a shot. They will soon rise again, however — *but not till the salt melts.*"

"The salt!" I ejaculated.

"Hush!" said the Captain, pointing to the wife and sisters of the deceased. "We must talk of these things at some more appropriate time."

We suffered much, and made a narrow escape; but fortune befriended *us,* as well as our mates in the long boat. We landed, in fine, more dead than alive, after four days of intense distress, upon the beach opposite Roanoke Island. We remained here a week, were not ill-treated by the wreckers, and at length obtained a passage to New York.[13]

About a month after the loss of the "Independence," I happened to meet Captain Hardy in Broadway. Our conversation turned, naturally, upon the disaster, and especially upon the sad fate of poor Wyatt. I thus learned the following particulars.

The artist had engaged passage for himself, wife, two sisters, and a[x] servant. His wife was, indeed, as she had been represented, a most lovely, and[y] most accomplished woman. On the morning of the fourteenth of June, (the day in which I first visited the ship,) the lady suddenly sickened and died. The young husband was frantic with grief — but circumstances imperatively forbade the deferring his voyage to New York. It was necessary to take to her mother the corpse of his adored wife, and on the other hand, the universal prejudice which would prevent his doing so openly, was well known. Nine-tenths of the passengers would have abandoned the ship rather than take passage with a dead body.

In this dilemma, Captain Hardy arranged that the corpse, being first partially embalmed, and packed, with a large quantity of salt, in a box of suitable dimensions, should be conveyed on board as merchandise. Nothing was to be said of the lady's decease; and, as it was well understood that Mr. Wyatt had engaged passage for his wife, it became necessary that some person should personate her during the voyage. This the deceased's lady's-maid was easily prevailed on to do. The extra state-room, originally en-

---

x *Omitted (A)* y and a *(A)*

gaged for this girl, during her mistress'[z] life, was now merely retained. In this state-room the pseudo wife slept, of course, every night. In the day-time she performed, to the best of her ability, the part of her mistress — whose person, it had been carefully ascertained, was unknown to any of the passengers on board.

My own mistakes arose, naturally enough, through too careless, too inquisitive, and too impulsive a temperament. But of late, it is a rare thing that I sleep soundly at night. There is a countenance which haunts me, turn as I will. There is an hysterical laugh which will forever ring within my ears.

NOTES

Title: See the following from "A Tale of a Nose" by "Pertinax Placid" (Edward Vernon Sparhawk) in the *Southern Literary Messenger,* April 1835:

> Those persons who have not travelled in a "night-boat" . . . are probably not aware of the kind of lodgings it affords when the number of passengers is large . . . The berths are . . . limited in number . . . Settees, cots, and a kind of oblong box, having thin mattresses spread over them, with a sheet and blanket perhaps, are wedged together, each calculated to hold the body of a human being by the most scanty and economical measurement.

(This note is by courtesy of David K. Jackson.)

1. There was a noted packet ship named *Independence,* launched in 1834, but it belonged to the Blue Swallowtail Line, and plied between New York and Liverpool. Hardy is an appropriate name for a sea-captain; it was borne by the officer in whose arms Lord Nelson died.

2. C—— may be for Charlottesville University; Poe's own alma mater was sometimes so called; but the hero of John Frost's story "The Picture" went to "Cambridge" – meaning Harvard.

3. The art dealer's name may have come from Jose Nicolini (1788–1855), an Italian poet who translated Byron, and whom Poe mentions in a review of Mrs. Ellet in the *Southern Literary Messenger,* January 1836.

4. Rubini's name may suggest a follower of Rubens, but Giovanni Battista Rubini (1794–1854) was a great Italian tenor whose name Poe undoubtedly encountered when reviewing the *Memoirs . . . of . . . Malibran* (see "The Spectacles," nn. 9 and 18). Rubini supported Malibran at the Paris Opera in 1832; and with "his starry troupe" appeared later in London. See N. P. Willis, *Prose Works* (1845), reprinting contributions to the *Mirror* and other periodicals, pp. 14 and 721.

5. Adelaide Curtis sounds like a New Yorker of good family.

---

z mistress'/mistress's *(A)*

6. Chambers Street is grimly appropriate for Wyatt's studio. Colt's box began its journey there.

7. Compare "Hop-Frog" for "a jester to laugh *with,* and a dwarf to laugh *at,*" and a similar locution in a review of *Madrid in 1835* in the *Southern Literary Messenger,* October 1836, which mentions "readers who, in laughing over a book, care not overmuch whether the laugh be at the author or with him."

8. Military terminology – a masked battery is a cannon emplacement concealed from the enemy.

9. Cape Hatteras, the southeastern point of an island east of Pamlico Sound, North Carolina, is noted for bad storms, usually from the southwest.

10. Ocracoke Inlet is a passage from Pamlico Sound to the Atlantic, twenty-five miles southwest of Hatteras. There, on October 9, 1837, occurred the wreck of the *Home,* bound from New York to Charleston, one of the worst disasters in the history of the Carolina coast.

11. Compare "The Raven," lines 89–92, " – tell me – tell me, I implore!'/ . . . By that Heaven that bends above us – by that God we both adore – "

12. In "MS. Found in a Bottle" we read: "It appears to me a miracle of miracles that our enormous bulk is not swallowed up at once and forever."

13. Roanoke Island on the coast of North Carolina was the site of Sir Walter Raleigh's colony. Many of the dwellers on the coast lived in part by salvaging wreckage from vessels demolished by ocean storms.

A TALE OF THE RAGGED MOUNTAINS

In "A Tale of the Ragged Mountains" Poe took up again the theme of reincarnation, and for the first time the theme of mesmerism, which was currently the subject of much discussion. Woodberry *(Life,* 1909, II, 109) said little about the tale, which he called "a picturesque story of metempsychosis ascribed to the influence of Hoffmann." A. H. Quinn, however *(Poe,* pp. 400–401), gave it most of a thoughtful paragraph, saying, "The realistic treatment of the supernatural was rarely better done by Poe." He noted that Bedloe's background of therapy "leaves a possible natural explanation for what follows," praised Poe's skill in dealing with Bedloe's dream – "quite in keeping with the normal dream state," and commended Poe's success in "preserving an atmosphere of the supernatural." But notions of the close mental relations between mesmerists and their subjects were common in Poe's time, and in "Poe and Mesmerism" *(PMLA,* December

1947) Sidney Lind argued that " 'A Tale of the Ragged Mountains' is a case study in mesmerism . . . There is no metempsychotic basis in this tale as there is, for example, in 'Morella' and 'Ligeia.' Rather, *it is* [neither the narrator nor the reader necessarily, but] *Dr. Templeton who believes in metempsychosis.*"

Whatever its basis, this tale is another demonstration of Poe's extraordinary ability to put together images and ideas from a number of different recognizable sources to make a coherent fabric distinctively his own. He succeeded so well in verisimilar presentation that my predecessors have not noticed the element that was a pure invention of the author for his plot. Neither in fact, nor in fable (before Poe's), can a poisonous sangsue (or leech) be found!

The title and the setting came from Poe's own experience. The Ragged Mountains are a group of hills, none probably more than a thousand feet high, occupying about eighty square miles southwest of Charlottesville on the highway to Lynchburg. They are shown on some but not all maps of Virginia.

One major influence on Poe's story was pointed out by Boyd Carter in Charles Brockden Brown's *Edgar Huntly,* which had already contributed some details to "The Pit and the Pendulum."* Poe uses so many "paralleling characters, motives, situations and incidents" that the resemblances between the two stories can hardly be merely coincidental. "There is even," says Carter, "a reticent implication of metempsychosis and of thought transference in *Edgar Huntly.*" In Brown's novel, Mrs. Lorimer believed (wrongly) that her own life was linked with that of her rascally twin brother, Wiatte, and that when he died she would die. Her protégé, Clithero, killed Wiatte in self-defense, and, in horror after recognizing the identity of his victim, wondered whether Mrs. Lorimer could possibly "arrive at a knowledge of his miserable end by other than verbal means? . . . Were they linked together by a sympathy whose influence was independent of sensible communication . . . instantaneous intercourse among

* *Prairie Schooner,* Summer 1953. Poe thought highly of Brown and planned to write a study of Brown's novels in 1839, although he probably did not complete the article. He announced the project at the end of his unsigned paper, "American Novel Writing," in the Pittsburgh *Literary Examiner,* August 1839.

beings locally distant." The parallel of this idea of telepathy and communication in the hypnotic state in Poe's story is patent.

The scenery of the two stories shows marked similarity, for Brown's protagonist, describing "a desolate and solitary grandeur in the scene," continues:

A sort of sanctity and awe environed it, owing to the consciousness of absolute and utter loneliness. It was probable that human feet had never before gained this recess, that human eye had never been fixed upon these gushing waters... Since the birth of this continent, I was probably the first who had deviated thus remotely from the customary paths of men.

Dr. Templeton and Dr. Sarsefield (of *Huntly*) both had visited Benares, and had narrow escapes there. Sarsefield had a gun of extraordinary workmanship, "the legacy of an English officer who died in Bengal." Huntly armed himself with a gun he took from a fallen officer – as did Oldeb with the weapons of a fallen officer; and engaged in unequal combat with five Indians whom he slew – as did Oldeb with the Bengalese.†

The second source of great importance is in T. B. Macaulay's essay on Warren Hastings.‡ The four passages chiefly used by Poe are given here from the first publication of Macaulay's famous essay, in the *Edinburgh Review,* October 1841 (74:160–255), where it appeared as a review of G. R. Gleig's *Memoirs of the Life of the Right Hon. Warren Hastings* (3v., London, 1841):

His [Hastings'] first design was on Benares, a city which in wealth, population, dignity, and sanctity, was among the foremost of Asia. It was commonly believed that half a million of human beings was crowded into that labyrinth of lofty alleys, rich with shrines, and minarets, and balconies, and carved oriels, to which the sacred apes clung by hundreds. The traveller could scarcely make his way through the press of holy mendicants, and not less holy bulls. The broad and stately flights of steps which descended from these swarming haunts to the bathing-places along the Ganges, were worn every day by the footsteps of an innumerable multitude of worshippers. The schools and temples drew crowds of pious Hindoos from every province... Hundreds of devotees came thither every month to die – for it was believed that a peculiarly happy fate awaited the man

† Some other parallels are mentioned in the endnotes.

‡ This source has been independently noticed on several occasions. See especially Henry Austin in *Literature,* August 4, 1899, and Jesse Turner in *The Case of Macaulay v. Poe,* a paper read at a meeting of the Arkansas State Bar Association at Little Rock, May 27–28, 1902, and subsequently issued by the association as a pamphlet. Poe reviewed in *Graham's* for June 1841 the first two volumes of the (unauthorized) Philadelphia edition of Macaulay's *Critical and Miscellaneous Essays.*

who could pass from the sacred city into the sacred river . . . Commerce had as many pilgrims as religion. All along the shores of the venerable stream, lay great fleets of vessels laden with rich merchandize . . . (p. 208).

The handful of sepoys who attended Hastings, would probably have been sufficient to overawe . . . the Black Town of Calcutta. But they were unequal to a conflict with the hardy rabble of Benares. The streets surrounding the palace were filled by an immense multitude; of whom a large proportion . . . wore arms. The tumult became a fight, and the fight a massacre. The English officers defended themselves with desperate courage against overwhelming numbers, and fell . . . sword in hand. The sepoys were butchered. The gates were forced. The captive prince, neglected by his jailers during the confusion, discovered an outlet which opened on the precipitous bank of the Ganges, let himself down to the water by a string made of the turbans of his attendants, found a boat, and escaped to the opposite shore . . . (p. 213).

An English officer of more spirit than judgment, eager to distinguish himself, made a premature attack on the insurgents beyond the river. His troops were entangled in narrow streets, and assailed by a furious population. He fell, with many of his men; and the survivors were forced to retire . . . (p. 214).

[*On Burke, prime mover of Hastings' impeachment*]: India and its inhabitants were . . . to him . . . a real country and a real people. The burning sun; the strange vegetation of the palm and the cocoa-tree; the rice-field and the tank; the huge trees, older than the Mogul empire . . . the thatched roof of the peasant's hut, and the rich tracery of the mosque . . . the drums, and banners, and gaudy idols . . . the graceful maiden, with the pitcher on her head, descending the steps to the river-side; the black faces, the long beards, the yellow streaks of sect; the turbans and the flowing robes; the spears and the silver maces; the elephants with their canopies of state; the gorgeous palankin of the prince, and the close litter of the noble lady . . . All India was present . . . from the halls where suitors laid gold and perfumes at the feet of sovereigns, to the wild moor where the gipsy-camp was pitched – from the bazars, humming like bee-hives with the crowd of buyers and sellers, to the jungle where the lonely courier shakes his bunch of iron rings to scare away the hyaenas (pp. 232–233).

It has been suggested that Poe's story owes something also to Robert Montgomery Bird's *Sheppard Lee,* which Poe reviewed elaborately in 1836.§

Poe probably wrote his story in 1843, since that year is mentioned in the first versions.

TEXTS

(A) Original manuscript in the Pierpont Morgan Library; *(B) Godey's Magazine and Lady's Book* for April 1844 (28 : 177–181); *(C) Broadway Journal,* November 29, 1845 (2 : 315–318); *(D) Works* (1850), II, 311–321.

The *Broadway Journal (C)* is our basic text, but the six "printer's dashes"

§ See note 16 below.

used by that journal to fill out lines have been eliminated. See Introduction to the Tales, under Variants. Griswold's text shows no revisions, but introduces two misprints.

The manuscript *(A)* is that from which the story was first printed. It was obtained for the Pierpont Morgan Library in 1909, through the dealer George H. Richmond, from the family of the Philadelphia collector George C. Thomas, in whose privately printed catalogue (1907) it is first known to have been described. It is still in a roll, measuring approximately 3 3/4 inches wide. Most of the segments are 12 to 13 inches long, but several are shorter; they have been connected with red sealing wax. The paper is light tan, the ink medium to dark brown. The first segment has been silk-lined for strengthening. [We are indebted to J. Rigbie Turner, Assistant Curator of Autograph Manuscripts at the Pierpont Morgan Library, for a recent survey of this manuscript.]

Godey's printers did not follow Poe's punctuation in all instances. They disregarded the capitalization of Darkness, Nonentity, Consciousness, Death, Galvanic Battery, Past, Real, Soul, and Man in paragraphs 22 and 23, and eliminated semicolons, for which many times they substituted commas. One might argue that Poe's manuscripts, coming from his own hand, revealed his pointing preferences, but I do not believe so. In the *Broadway Journal,* which reproduced rather faithfully Godey's punctuation and added some commas (but no semicolons), Poe made a number of verbal changes. If he had wanted his manuscript pointings preserved, I think he would have reinstated them, since he was the editor. There are several instances in PHANTASY-PIECES where he did just this.

Reprints

The Columbia Spy, Columbia, Pennsylvania, April 27, 1844, from *Godey's Magazine and Lady's Book.* [This copy of *The Columbia Spy* is not available for checking. See *Doings of Gotham* (Spannuth and Mabbott, 1929), p. 121, as the authority for this listing.]

The Brooklyn Daily Eagle and King's County Democrat, Brooklyn, New York, October 9 and 10, 1846, from the *Lady's Book* or the *Broadway Journal.* Walt Whitman was editor of the *Eagle* from March 1846 through January 1848, as noted in *The Gathering of the Forces . . . and Other Material Written by Walt Whitman,* ed. by Cleveland Rogers and John Black, 2 v. (1920), p. xiv.

A TALE OF THE RAGGED MOUNTAINS. [C]

During the fall of the year 1827, while residing near Charlottesville, Virginia,[a] I casually made the acquaintance of[b] Mr. Augustus Bedloe.[1] This young gentleman was remarkable in every respect, and excited in me a profound interest and curiosity. I found it impossible to comprehend him either in his[c] moral or his

Title By Edgar A. Poe. *beneath the title in same script (A)*
a in Virginia, *(A, B)*
b of a *(A, B)*
c his mental, his *(A, B)*

physical relations. Of his family I could[d] obtain no[e] satisfactory account. Whence[f] he came,[g] I never ascertained. Even about his age — although I call him a young gentleman — there was something which perplexed me in no little degree. He certainly *seemed* young — and he made a[h] point of speaking about his youth — yet[i] there were moments when I should have had little trouble in imagining him a hundred years of age. But in no regard was he more peculiar than in his personal appearance. He was singularly tall and thin. He stooped much. His limbs were exceedingly long and emaciated. His forehead was broad and low.[j] His complexion was absolutely bloodless. His mouth was large and flexible, and his teeth were more wildly uneven, although sound, than I had ever before seen teeth in a human head. The expression of his smile, however, was by no means unpleasing, as might be supposed; but it[k] had no variation whatever. It was one of profound melancholy — of a phaseless and unceasing gloom. His eyes were abnormally large, and round like those of a cat. The pupils, too, upon any accession or diminution of light, underwent contraction or dilation,[l] just such as is observed in the feline tribe. In moments of excitement the orbs grew bright to a degree almost inconceivable; seeming to emit luminous rays, not of a reflected, but of an intrinsic lustre, as does a candle or the sun; yet their ordinary condition was so totally vapid, filmy and dull, as to convey the idea of the eyes[m] of a long-interred corpse.

These peculiarities of person appeared to cause him much annoyance, and he was continually alluding to them in a sort of half explanatory, half apologetic strain, which, when I first heard it, impressed me very painfully. I soon, however, grew accustomed to it, and[n] my uneasiness wore off. It seemed to be his design rather to insinuate than directly to assert that, physically, he had not always been what he was — that a long series of neuralgic attacks had reduced him from a condition of more than usual personal

d could <never> *(A)*
e <any> ↑no↓ *(A)*
f Where *(A, B)*
g came from *(A, B)*
h a frequent *(A, B)*
i but *(A, B)*
j low. His hair resembled the web of the spider in its tenuity, and levity. *(A, B) comma omitted in B*
k ↑it↓ *(A)*
l dilatation, *(A, B)*
m eyes of a vulture, or even *(A, B)*
n when *(A, B)*

beauty, to that which I saw. For many years past he had been attended by a physician, named Templeton – an old gentleman, perhaps seventy years of age – whom he had first encountered at Saratoga,[2] and from whose attention,[o] while there, he either received, or fancied that he received, great benefit. The result was that Bedloe, who was wealthy, had made an arrangement with Doctor Templeton, by which the latter, in consideration of a liberal annual allowance, had consented to devote his time and medical experience exclusively to the care of the invalid.

Doctor Templeton had been a traveller in his younger days, and, at Paris, had become a convert, in great measure, to the doctrines of Mesmer.[3] It was altogether by means of magnetic remedies that he had succeeded in alleviating the acute pains of his patient; and this success had very naturally inspired the latter with a certain degree of confidence in the opinions from which the remedies had been educed. The Doctor, however, like all enthusiasts, had struggled hard to make a thorough convert of his pupil, and finally so far gained his point as to induce the sufferer to submit to numerous experiments. By a[p] frequent repetition of these, a result had arisen, which of late days has become so common as to attract little or no attention, but which, at the period of which I write, had very rarely been known in America. I mean to say, that between Doctor Templeton and Bedloe there had grown up, little by little, a very distinct and strongly marked *rapport,* or magnetic relation. I am not prepared to assert, however, that this *rapport* extended beyond the limits of the simple sleep-producing power; but this power itself had attained great intensity. At the first attempt to induce the magnetic somnolency, the mesmerist entirely failed. In the fifth or sixth he succeeded very partially, and after long continued effort. Only at the twelfth was the triumph complete. After this the will of the patient succumbed rapidly to that of the physician, so that, when I first became acquainted with the two, sleep was brought about almost instantaneously, by the mere volition of the operator, even when the invalid was unaware of his presence. It is only now, in the year

o attentions, *(A, B)*

p the *(A, B)*

1845,[q] when similar miracles are witnessed daily by thousands, that I dare venture to record this apparent impossibility as a matter of serious fact.[4]

The temperament[r] of Bedloe was, in the highest degree, sensitive, excitable, enthusiastic. His imagination was singularly vigorous and creative; and no doubt it derived additional force from the habitual use of morphine, which he swallowed in great quantity, and without which he would have found it impossible to exist.[5] It was his practice to take a very large dose of it immediately after breakfast, each morning — or rather immediately after a cup of strong coffee, for he ate nothing in the forenoon — and then[s] set forth alone, or attended only by a dog, upon a long ramble among the chain of wild and dreary hills that lie westward and southward of Charlottesville, and are there dignified by the title of the Ragged Mountains.

Upon a dim, warm, misty day, towards the close of November, and during the strange *interregnum* of the seasons which in America is termed the Indian Summer, Mr. Bedloe departed, as usual, for the hills. The day passed, and still he did not return.

About eight o'clock at night, having become seriously alarmed at[t] his protracted absence, we were about setting out in search of him, when he unexpectedly made his appearance, in health no worse than usual, and in rather more than ordinary spirits. The account which he gave of his expedition, and of the events which had detained him, was a singular one indeed.

"You will remember," said he, "that it was about nine in the morning when I left Charlottesville. I bent my steps immediately to the mountains, and, about ten, entered a gorge which was entirely new to me. I followed the windings of this pass with much interest. The scenery which presented itself on all sides, although scarcely entitled to be called grand, had about it an indescribable, and to me, a delicious aspect of dreary desolation. The solitude seemed absolutely virgin. I could not help believing that the green sods and the gray rocks upon which I trod, had been trodden

q 1843, *(A, B)*
r temperature *(C, D) misprint, corrected from A, B*
s then to *(A, B)*
t as *(D) misprint*

never before by the foot of a human being. So entirely secluded, and in fact inaccessible, except through a series of accidents, is the entrance of the ravine, that it is by no means impossible that I was indeed the first adventurer — the very first and sole adventurer who had ever penetrated its[u] recesses.[6]

"The thick and peculiar mist, or smoke, which distinguishes the Indian Summer, and which now hung heavily over all objects, served, no doubt, to deepen the vague impressions which these objects created.[7] So dense was this pleasant fog, that I could at no time see more than a dozen yards of the path before me. This path was excessively sinuous, and as the sun could not be seen, I soon lost all idea of the direction in which I journeyed. In the meantime the morphine had its customary effect — that of enduing all the external world with an intensity of interest. In the quivering of a leaf — in the hue of a blade of grass — in the shape of a trefoil — in the humming of a bee — in the gleaming of a dew-drop — in the breathing of the wind — in the faint odors that came from the forest — there came a whole universe of suggestion — a gay and motley[u'] train of rhapsodical and immethodical thought.

"Busied in this, I walked on for several hours, during which the mist deepened around me to so great an extent, that at length I was reduced to an absolute groping of the way. And now an indescribable uneasiness possessed me — a species of nervous hesitation and tremor. I feared to tread, lest I should be precipitated into some abyss. I remembered, too, strange stories told about these Ragged Hills, and of the uncouth and fierce races of men who tenanted their groves and caverns.[8] A thousand vague fancies oppressed and disconcerted me — fancies the more distressing because vague. Very suddenly my attention was arrested by the loud beating of a drum.

"My amazement was, of course, extreme. A drum in these hills was a thing unknown. I could not have been more surprised at the sound of the trump of the Archangel.[9] But a new and still more astounding source of interest and perplexity arose. There came a wild rattling or jingling sound, as if of a bunch of large keys — and upon the instant a dusky-visaged and half-naked man

---

u its wierd *(A);* its weird *(B)* ú motly *(C, D) corrected from A, B*

rushed past me with a shriek. He came so close to my person that I felt his hot breath upon my face. He bore in one hand an instrument composed of an assemblage of steel rings, and shook them vigorously as he ran. Scarcely had he disappeared in the mist, before, panting after him, with open mouth and glaring eyes, there darted a huge beast. I could not be mistaken in its character. It was a hyena.[10]

"The sight of this monster rather relieved than heightened my terrors – for I now made sure that I dreamed, and endeavored to arouse myself to waking consciousness. I stepped boldly and briskly forward. I rubbed my eyes. I called aloud. I pinched my limbs. A small spring of water presented itself to my view, and here, stooping, I bathed my hands and my head and neck.[11] This seemed to dissipate the equivocal sensations which had hitherto annoyed me. I [v]arose, as I thought,[v] a new man, and proceeded steadily and complacently on my unknown way.

"At length, quite overcome by[w] exertion, and by[x] a certain oppressive closeness of the atmosphere, I seated myself beneath a tree. Presently there came a feeble gleam of sunshine, and the shadow of the leaves of the tree fell faintly but definitely[y] upon the grass. At this shadow I gazed wonderingly for many minutes. Its character stupified me with astonishment. [z]I looked upward.[z] The tree was a palm.

"I now arose hurriedly, and in a state of fearful agitation – for the fancy that I dreamed would serve me no longer. I saw – I felt that I had perfect command of my senses – and these senses now brought to my soul a world of novel and singular sensation. The heat became all at once intolerable. A strange odor loaded the breeze. A low continuous murmur, like that arising from a full, but gently-flowing river, came to my ears, intermingled with the peculiar hum of multitudinous human voices.

"While I listened in an extremity of astonishment which I need not attempt to describe, a strong and brief gust of wind bore off the incumbent fog as if by the wand of an enchanter.

"I found myself at the foot of a high mountain, and looking

v . . . v arose *(A, B)*
w with *(A, B)*
x with *(A, B)*
y definitively *(A, B)*
z . . . z *Omitted (A, B)*

down into a vast plain, through which wound a majestic river. On the margin of this river stood an Eastern-looking city, such as we read of in the Arabian Tales, but of a character even more singular than any there described. From my position, which was far above the level of the town, I could perceive its every nook and corner, as if delineated on[a] a map. The streets seemed innumerable, and crossed each other irregularly in all directions, but were rather long winding alleys than streets, and absolutely swarmed with inhabitants. The houses were wildly picturesque. On every hand was a wilderness of balconies, of verandahs, of minarets, of shrines, and fantastically carved oriels. Bazaars abounded; and in these were displayed rich wares in infinite variety and profusion — silks, muslins, the most dazzling cutlery, the most magnificent jewels and gems. Besides these things, were seen, on all sides, banners and palanquins, litters with stately dames close veiled,[b] elephants gorgeously caparisoned, idols grotesquely hewn, drums, banners and gongs, spears, silver and gilded[c] maces. And amid the crowd, and the clamor, and the general intricacy and confusion — amid the million of black and yellow men, turbaned and robed, and of flowing beard, there roamed a countless multitude of holy filleted bulls, [d]while vast legions of the filthy but sacred ape clambered, chattering and shrieking, about the cornices of the mosques,[12] or clung to the minarets and oriels.[d] From the swarming streets to the banks of the river, there descended innumerable flights of steps leading to bathing places,[e] while the river itself seemed to force a passage with difficulty through the vast fleets of deeply-burthened ships that far and wide encumbered[f] its surface. Beyond the limits of the city arose, in frequent majestic groups, the palm and the cocoa, with other gigantic and weird[g] trees of vast age; and here and there might be seen a field of rice, the thatched hut of a peasant, a tank, a stray temple, a gypsy camp, or a solitary graceful maiden taking her way, with a pitcher upon her head, to the banks of the magnificent river.

a upon *(A, B)*
b close-veiled, *(A)*
c gilden *(A, B)*
d . . . d and clambered, chattering and shrieking about the cornices of the mosques, and clinging to the oriels and minarets, vast legions of the filthy but sacred ape. *(A, B)*
e bathing-places, *(A, B)*
f encountered *(D)*
g wierd *(A, C, D)*

"You will say [h]now, of course, that[h] I dreamed; but not so. What I saw — what I heard — what I felt — what I thought — had about it nothing of the unmistakeable idiosyncrasy of the dream. All was rigorously self-consistent. At first, doubting that I was really awake, I entered into a series of tests, which soon convinced me that I really was. Now, when one dreams, and, in the dream, suspects that he dreams, the suspicion *never fails to confirm itself,* and the sleeper is almost immediately aroused. Thus Novalis errs not in saying that 'we are near waking when we dream that we dream.'[13] Had the vision occurred[i] to me as I describe it, without my suspecting it as a dream, then a dream it might absolutely have been, but, occurring as it did, and suspected and tested as it was, I am forced to class it among other phenomena."

"In this I am not sure that you are wrong," observed Dr. Templeton, "but proceed. You arose and descended into the city."

"I arose," continued Bedloe, regarding the Doctor with an air of profound astonishment, "I arose, as you say, and descended into the city. On my way, I fell in with an immense populace, crowding, through every avenue, all[j] in the same direction, and exhibiting in every action the wildest excitement.[k] Very suddenly, and by some inconceivable impulse, I became intensely imbued with personal interest in what was going on. I seemed to feel that I had an important part to play, without exactly understanding what it was. Against the crowd which environed me, however, I experienced a deep sentiment of animosity. I shrank[l] from amid them, and, swiftly, by a circuitous path, reached and entered the city. Here all was the wildest tumult and contention. A small party of men, clad in garments half Indian,[m] half European, and officered by gentlemen in a uniform partly British, were engaged, at great odds, with the swarming rabble of the alleys. I joined the weaker party, arming myself with the weapons of a fallen officer, and fighting I knew not whom with the nervous ferocity of despair. We were soon overpowered by numbers, and driven to seek refuge in a species of kiosk.[14] Here we barricaded ourselves, and, for the

h . . . h that now, of course, *(A, B)*
i occured *(C) misprint*
j *Omitted (A, B)*
k excitements. *(B)* [*Godey's error*]
l shrunk *(A, B)*
m half-Indian *(C) hyphen deleted to follow all other texts. Comma added*

present, were secure. From a loop-hole near the summit of the kiosk, I perceived a vast crowd, in furious agitation, surrounding and assaulting a gay palace that overhung the river. Presently, from an upper window of this palace, there descended an effeminate-looking person, by means of a string made of the turbans of his attendants. A boat was at hand, in which he escaped to the opposite bank of the river.

"And now a new object[n] took possession of my soul. I spoke a few hurried but energetic words to my companions, and, having succeeded in gaining over a few of them to my purpose, made a frantic sally from the kiosk. We rushed amid the crowd that surrounded it. They retreated, at first, before us. They rallied, fought madly, and retreated again. In the meantime we were borne far from the kiosk, and became bewildered and entangled among the narrow streets of tall overhanging houses, into the recesses of which the sun had never been able to shine. The rabble pressed impetuously upon us, harassing us with their spears, and overwhelming us with flights of arrows. These latter were very remarkable, and resembled in some respects the writhing creese of the Malay.[15] They were made to imitate the body of a creeping serpent, and were long and black, with a poisoned barb. One of them struck me upon the right temple. I reeled and fell. An instantaneous and deadly sickness seized me. I struggled – I gasped – I died."

"You will hardly persist *now*," said I, smiling, "that the whole of your adventure was not a dream. You are not prepared to maintain that you are dead?"

When I said these words, I of course expected some lively sally from Bedloe in reply; but, to my astonishment, he hesitated, trembled, became fearfully pallid, and remained silent. I looked towards Templeton. He sat erect and rigid in his chair – his teeth chattered, and his eyes were starting from their sockets. "Proceed!" he at length said hoarsely to Bedloe.

"For many minutes," continued the latter, "my sole sentiment – my sole feeling – was that of darkness and nonentity, with the

---

n and altogether objectless impulse *(A, B); Quotation marks are added editorially at the beginning of the paragraph, omitted in A, B, C*

consciousness of death. At length, there seemed to pass a violent and sudden shock through my soul, as if of electricity. With it came the sense of elasticity and of light. This latter I felt — not saw. In an instant I seemed to rise from the ground. But I had no bodily, no visible, audible, or palpable presence. The crowd had departed. The tumult had ceased. The city was in comparative repose. Beneath me lay my corpse, with the arrow in my[o] temple, the whole head greatly swollen and disfigured. But all these things I felt — not saw. I took interest in nothing. Even the corpse seemed a matter in which I had no concern. Volition I had [p]none, but[p] appeared to be impelled into motion, and flitted buoyantly out of the city, retracing the circuitous path by which I had entered it.[16] When I had attained that point of the ravine in the mountains, at which I had encountered the hyena, I again experienced a shock as of a galvanic battery;[17] the sense of weight, of [q]volition, of substance,[q] returned. I became my original self, and bent my steps eagerly homewards — but the past had not lost the vividness of the real — and not now, even for an instant, can I compel my understanding to regard it as a dream."

"Nor was it," said Templeton, with an air of deep solemnity, "yet it would be difficult to say how otherwise it should be termed. Let us suppose only, that the soul of the man of to-day is upon the verge of some stupendous psychal discoveries.[18] Let us content ourselves with this supposition. For the rest I have some explanation to make. Here is a water-colour drawing, which I should have shown you before, but which an unaccountable sentiment of horror has hitherto prevented me from showing."

We looked at the picture which he presented. I saw nothing in it of an extraordinary character; but its effect upon Bedloe was prodigious. He nearly fainted as he gazed. And yet it was but a miniature portrait — a miraculously accurate one, to be sure — of his own very remarkable features. At least this was my thought as I regarded it.

"You will perceive," said Templeton, "the date of this picture — it is here, scarcely visible, in this corner — 1780. In this year was

o the *(A, B)*
p . . . p none. But I *(A)*; none, but I *(B)*
q . . . q substance and of volition *(A, B)*

the portrait taken. It is the likeness of a dead friend — a Mr. Oldeb[19] — to whom I became much attached at Calcutta, during the administration of Warren Hastings. I was then only twenty years old. When I first saw you, Mr. Bedloe, at Saratoga, it was the miraculous similarity which existed between yourself and the painting, which induced me to accost you, to seek your friendship, and to bring about those arrangements which resulted in my becoming your constant companion. In accomplishing this point, I was urged partly, and perhaps principally, by a regretful memory of the deceased, but also, in part, by an uneasy, and not altogether horrorless curiosity respecting yourself.

"In your detail of the vision which presented itself to you amid the hills, you have described, with the minutest accuracy, the Indian city of Benares, upon the Holy River. The riots, the combats, the massacre, were the actual events of the insurrection of Cheyte Sing, which took place in 1780, when Hastings was put in imminent peril of his life.[20] The man escaping by the string of turbans, was Cheyte Sing himself. The party in the kiosk were sepoys and British officers, headed by Hastings. Of this party I was one, and did all I could to prevent the rash and fatal sally of the officer who fell, in the crowded alleys, by the poisoned arrow of a Bengalee.[21] That officer was my dearest friend. It was Oldeb. You will perceive by these manuscripts," (here the speaker produced a note-book in which several pages appeared to have been freshly written) "that at the very period in which you fancied these things amid the hills, I was engaged in detailing them upon paper here at home."[22]

In about a week after this conversation, the following paragraphs appeared in a Charlottesville paper.

"We have the painful duty of announcing the death of Mr. Augustus Bedlo, a gentleman whose amiable manners and[r] many virtues have long endeared him to the citizens of Charlottesville.

"Mr. B., for some years past, has been subject to neuralgia, which has often threatened to terminate fatally; but this can be regarded only as the mediate cause of his decease. The proximate cause was one of especial singularity. In an excursion to the

r *Omitted (D) misprint*

Ragged Mountains, a few days since, a slight cold and fever were[s] contracted, attended with great determination of blood to the head. To relieve this, Dr. Templeton resorted to topical bleeding. Leeches were applied to the temples. In a fearfully brief period the patient died, when it appeared that, in the jar containing the leeches, had been introduced, by accident, one of the venomous vermicular sangsues which are now and then found in the neighboring ponds. This creature fastened itself upon a small artery in the right temple. Its close resemblance to the medicinal leech caused the mistake to be overlooked until too late.

"N.B. The poisonous sangsue of Charlottesville may always be distinguished from the medicinal leech by its blackness, and especially by its writhing or vermicular motions, which very nearly resemble those of a snake."[23]

I was speaking with the editor of the paper in question, upon the topic of this remarkable accident, when it occurred to me to ask how it happened that the name of the deceased had been given as Bedlo.

"I presume," said I, "you have authority for this spelling, but I have always supposed the name to be written with an *e* at the end."

"Authority? — no," he replied. "It is a mere typographical error. The name is Bedloe[t] with an *e*, all the world over, and I never knew it to be spelt otherwise in my life."

"Then," said I mutteringly, as I turned upon my heel, "then indeed has it come to pass that one truth is[u] stranger than any fiction[24] — for Bedlo, without the *e*, what is it but Oldeb conversed? And this man tells me it is a typographical error."

NOTES

1. Poe was actually at Charlottesville a year earlier than that mentioned, and of course walked among the nearby Ragged Mountains. The Bedloe family gave its name to Bedloe's Island, upon which the Statue of Liberty now stands, in New York Harbor near Manhattan Island. Another Bedloe, William, the seventeenth century English informer against Papists, is mentioned in Macaulay's essay on Warren Hastings.

---

s was *(B)*
t Bedlo *(C, D) emended from A, B*
u is far *(A, B)*

2. Saratoga Springs, New York, noted from colonial times for the therapeutic value of its mineral waters, had become a popular resort by 1820. Poe visited the place in the summer of 1843 and is traditionally believed there to have composed "The Raven." See Mabbott I, 358, and Marjorie Peabody Waite, *Yaddo* (Saratoga Springs, 1933), pp. 16–23.

3. Franz Anton Mesmer (1733–1815), a Swiss-German physician, was the inventor of a therapy the effectiveness of which he ascribed to a force he called "animal magnetism." His theories, enormously popular in Europe and America, were early discredited, but responsible investigation of the phenomena produced by his method led eventually to the development of modern hypnotism.

4. When Poe wrote his story, serious research into the phenomena of mesmerism had not proceeded very far, but there was much discussion and popular awareness of some of the terms (*rapport,* for example) and some of the results. As Sidney Lind observed, mesmerism "was in the air, and it was logical that Poe, as a journalist sensitive to popular interest, should have exploited it." He used its theories again in "Mesmeric Revelation" and "The Facts in the Case of M. Valdemar."

Poe here updates his story; the year was given as 1843 in the first versions.

5. Morphine, mentioned frequently in Poe's stories, helps provide a natural explanation of some of the happenings recounted.

6. Compare the passage from *Edgar Huntly* (chapter X) quoted in the introduction above. On delight in virgin wilderness, compare "Julius Rodman," chapter V: "... that deep and most intense excitement with which I surveyed the wonders and majestic beauties of the wilderness ... As yet, however, I felt as if in too close proximity to the settlements for the full enjoyment of my burning love of Nature, and of *the unknown.*"

7. Compare "Landor's Cottage": "A smoky mist, resembling that of Indian Summer, enveloped all things and, of course, added to my uncertainty."

8. Compare *Edgar Huntly,* chapter X: "The aboriginal inhabitants had no motives to lead them into caves like this and ponder on the verge of such a precipice. Their successors were still less likely to have wandered hither."

9. For the trump of the Archangel, see I Thessalonians 4:16, "For the Lord ... shall descend from heaven with a shout, with the voice of the archangel, and with the trump."

10. See the last passage from Macaulay's essay quoted in my introduction above. Other bits from all the passages quoted are skillfully intermingled throughout the next six paragraphs.

11. Compare *Edgar Huntly,* end of chapter XVI: "I approached the torrent, and not only drank copiously, but laved my head, neck, and arms, in this delicious element."

12. The great mosque at Benares was built by the Mogul Emperor Aurungzebe, to insult the Hindus in their most sacred city. The name of the Emperor (son of Shah Jehan, who built the Taj Mahal) means "ornament of the throne";

he was enthroned in 1678, and reigned until 1707, the most powerful of the Moguls.

13. The quotation from Novalis (Friedrich Leopold von Hardenberg, 1772–1801) Poe found with an English translation in a book he reviewed in *Graham's* for December 1841, Sarah T. Austin's *Fragments from German Prose Writers* (New York, 1841), p. 21. See *Novalis Schriften* (Jena, 1907), II, p. 141, where it is number 121 of the "Fragmente, Paralipomena zum Blütenstaub, I" from the second part of *Athenaeum.* See the motto of "The Mystery of Marie Rogêt" for another Novalis fragment from Mrs. Austin's book.

14. [For Poe's accurate use of this word as an indication that he went beyond Macaulay and Gleig to Hastings' own account and other sources, see Muktar Ali Isani in *Poe Studies,* December 1972.]

15. The creese, or kris, is defined as a short sword or heavy dagger with a wavy blade. The serpentine arrowheads are probably Poe's invention. See n. 23, below.

16. With this may be compared a passage in R. M. Bird's *Sheppard Lee,* as synopsized in Poe's review in the *Southern Literary Messenger,* September 1836: "He feels exceedingly light and buoyant, with the power of moving without exertion. He sweeps along without putting his feet to the ground . . . Mr. Lee . . . flies, instinctively to the nearest hut for assistance."

17. Poe mentioned the galvanic battery in several tales. See "A Decided Loss," n. 21, and canceled references noted in the variants in "MS. Found in a Bottle" and "The Oval Portrait."

18. Whereas the narrator's earlier mention of "miracles" (at n. 4) referred to the accomplishments of mesmerism, Dr. Templeton here, as Sidney Lind pointed out, is referring to the mysteries of metempsychosis. [Poe uses the rare word "psychal" a number of times; see Pollin, *Poe: Creator of Words* (1974), p. 35.]

19. Boyd Carter, cited in the introduction, thought it significant that "Old Deb" is the name of an American Indian woman who gave the solution of Waldegrave's murder in Charles Brockden Brown's *Edgar Huntly.* [See also Pollin, *Discoveries in Poe,* p. 26, for Macaulay's essay as a source for Oldeb's name.]

20. Cheyte Sing or Chait Singh was the Rajah of Benares, driven to revolt by Hastings' larger and larger demands for money to support the English power in India. The events described took place in 1781, rather than 1780. See Warren Hastings, *A Narrative of the Insurrection which happened in the Zemeedary of Banaris, in the Month of August 1781* (Calcutta, Printed by order of the Governor-General, 1782), widely reprinted.

21. Compare the third quotation from Macaulay, in the introduction above.

22. Here, Sidney Lind remarks, "Bedloe's strange experience is revealed in its true light as a mesmeric trance, transmitted from Templeton's mind, and not the workings of metempsychosis."

23. As stated in the introduction, poisonous "sangsues" (leeches) are unknown

to natural historians. Poe may have picked up the French term from Victor Hugo's *Notre Dame* [see Pollin, *Discoveries in Poe,* pp. 24–25], or he may have taken it directly from Cuvier's *Le Règne Animal* (1817, II, 531–532) while he was working with Thomas Wyatt on the *Synopsis of Natural History* (see n. 35 to "The Murders in the Rue Morgue"). Wyatt's text on leeches is derived from Cuvier. The serpentine shape may have been suggested by the illustration of "AMPHITRITE, Cuv." on Wyatt's plate 31 (lithographed by P. S. Duval), which also depicts medicinal leeches. Poe had reason to associate a leech unpleasantly with Charlottesville, for Samuel Leitch, Jr. was a merchant of that place who dunned John Allan for a debt of $68.46, incurred by "Edgar A. Powe," while at the University, according to Quinn, *Poe* (1941), p. 112. This was suggested to me by Mr. Glen M. Pound of Indianapolis, and I think Poe was quite capable of such a punning invention.

24. "Truth is stranger than fiction" is from Byron's *Don Juan,* XIV, ci, 1–2, a passage often quoted or alluded to by Poe. It is the cardinal idea of "The Thousand-and-Second Tale of Scheherazade."

THE PREMATURE BURIAL

The subject of this tale was one that had long fascinated, even haunted, Poe.* A tradition has reached us from Virginia that early in the nineteenth century a lady of one of the first families apparently died, and was entombed above ground. The head servant of the family visited the vault, heard her move, and rescued her. She later became the mother of a famous Southern hero. Whether this story has been authenticated I do not know, but it was surely talked about above and below stairs, and little Edgar may have heard it in the kitchen.

Poe was himself troubled by fear of the dark. A Richmond friend of his last few years, Susan Archer Talley Weiss, in her *Home Life of Poe,* 1907, page 29, says:

> Mr. John Mackenzie, in speaking of Edgar, bore witness to his high spirit and pluckiness in occasional schoolboy encounters, and also to his timidity in regard to being alone at night, and his belief in and fear of the supernatural. He had heard Poe say, when grown, that the most horrible thing he could imagine as a boy was to feel an ice-cold hand laid upon his face in a pitch-dark room when alone at night; or to awaken in semi-darkness and see an evil face gazing close into his own; and that these fancies had so haunted him that he would often keep his head under the bed-covering until nearly suffocated.

* Hints of this fascination may be seen in a number of his earlier stories: "Loss of Breath," "Berenicë," "Morella," "Ligeia," "The Fall of the House of Usher," "King Pest," and "The Colloquy of Monos and Una."

TALES: 1843–1844

The impulse to write "The Premature Burial" presumably came from the publicity attendant on the "life preserving coffin" exhibited at the annual fair of the American Institute, New York City, in 1843. In the tale Poe recounts (with his own additions) several stories of premature burial culled from his reading (as A. H. Quinn remarked, *Poe,* p. 417) to prepare the reader for the final episode, which was probably drawn from his own imagination or from a dream of his own, since no specific literary source for it has yet been pointed out. The tale was listed as completed but not yet published in Poe's letter to James Russell Lowell, May 28, 1844. It was printed in the *Dollar Newspaper* of July 31, which it is known (from the *Public Ledger* of the morning of that day) was sold at three o'clock in the afternoon on Tuesday, July 30, 1844.

Extracts from paragraphs 4–7 and 14–19 were reprinted some two weeks later — surely without authorization — in an article called "Burying Alive" in the New York *Rover* (3:380–381), giving evidence of popular interest in this topic.†

TEXTS

(A) Philadelphia *Dollar Newspaper,* July 31, 1844; *(B) Broadway Journal,* June 14, 1845 (1:369–373); *(C) Works* (1850), I, 325–338; (*D*) *Southern Literary Messenger,* June 1849 (15:338), in "Marginalia," number 251 (last paragraph).

Griswold's version *(C)* is followed, as it shows slight auctorial changes.

A fragment of manuscript, detached from the roll of which it must have been a part, I collated in the auction room of the Anderson Galleries many years ago. It was clearly that from which the final paragraph was printed as part of "Marginalia" in the *Southern Literary Messenger.* The variants from our text were the same in both.

Reprint

The Rover (New York weekly), August 1844 (3:380–381), as "Burying Alive," an article incorporating paragraphs 4–7 and 14–19 from the *Dollar Newspaper.*

THE PREMATURE BURIAL. [*C*]

There are certain themes of which the interest is all-absorbing, but which are too entirely horrible for the purposes of legitimate

† This form was known to Woodberry (1909, II, 405) long before Killis Campbell (*MLN,* May 1917) recovered the first printing. *The Rover* contains the earliest collectible form of Poe's tale.

fiction. These the mere romanticist must eschew, if he do not wish to offend, or to disgust. They are with propriety handled, only when the severity and majesty of truth sanctify and sustain them. We thrill, for example, with the most intense of "pleasurable pain,"[1] over the accounts of the Passage of the Beresina, of the Earthquake at Lisbon, of the Plague at London, of the Massacre of St. Bartholomew, or of the stifling of the hundred and twenty-three prisoners in the Black Hole at Calcutta.[2] But, in these accounts, it is the fact — it is the reality — it is the history which excites. As inventions, we should regard them with simple abhorrence.

I have mentioned some few of the more prominent and august calamities on[a] record; but, in these, it is the extent, not less than the character of the calamity, which so vividly impresses the fancy. I need not remind the reader that, from the long and weird[b] catalogue of human miseries, I might have selected many individual instances more replete with essential suffering than any of these vast generalities of disaster. The true wretchedness, indeed — the ultimate wo — is particular, not diffuse. That the ghastly extremes of agony are endured by man the unit, and never by man the mass — for this let us thank a merciful God!

To be buried while alive, is, beyond question, the most terrific of these extremes which has ever fallen to the lot of mere mortality. That it has frequently, very frequently, so fallen will scarcely be denied by those who think. The boundaries which divide Life from Death, are at best shadowy and vague. Who shall say where the one ends, and where the other begins? We know that there are diseases in which occur total cessations of all the apparent functions of vitality, and yet in which these cessations are merely suspensions, properly so called. They are only temporary pauses in the incomprehensible mechanism. A certain period elapses, and some unseen mysterious principle again sets in motion the magic pinions and the wizard wheels. The silver cord was not for ever loosed, nor the golden bowl irreparably broken.[3] But where, meantime, was the soul?

Apart, however, from the inevitable conclusion, *à*[c] *priori,* that

a upon *(A)*
b wierd *(A, B)*
c *a (C) accent added from A, B*

such causes must produce such effects — that the well known occurrence of such cases of suspended animation must naturally give rise, now and then, to premature interments — apart from this consideration, we have the direct testimony of medical and[d] ordinary experience, to prove that a vast number of such interments have actually taken place. I might refer at once, if necessary, to a hundred well authenticated instances. One of very remarkable character, and of which the circumstances may be fresh in the memory of some of my readers, occurred, not very long ago, in the neighboring city of Baltimore, where it occasioned a painful, intense, and widely extended excitement. The wife of one of the most respectable citizens — a lawyer of eminence and a member of Congress — was seized with a sudden and unaccountable illness, which completely baffled the skill of her physicians. After much suffering, she died, or was supposed to die. No one suspected, indeed, or had reason to suspect, that she was not actually dead. She presented all the ordinary appearances of death. The face assumed the usual pinched and sunken outline. The lips were of the usual marble pallor. The eyes were lustreless. There was no warmth. Pulsation had ceased. For three days the body was preserved unburied, during which it had acquired a stony[e] rigidity. The funeral, in short, was hastened, on account of the rapid advance of what was supposed to be decomposition.

The lady was deposited in her family vault, which, for three subsequent years, was undisturbed. At the expiration of this term, it was opened for the reception of a sarcophagus; — but, alas! how fearful a shock awaited the husband, who, personally, threw open the door. As its portals swung outwardly back, some white-apparelled[f] object fell rattling within his arms. It was the skeleton of his wife in her yet unmouldered shroud.

A careful investigation rendered it evident that she had revived within two days after her entombment — that her struggles within the coffin had caused it to fall from a ledge, or shelf, to the floor, where it was so broken as to permit her escape. A lamp which had been accidentally left, full of oil, within the tomb, was found

---

d and of *(A)*
e strong *(A)*
f white-apparrelled *(A, B)*

empty; it might have been exhausted, however, by evaporation. On the uppermost of the steps which led down into the dread chamber, was a large fragment of the coffin, with which it seemed that she had endeavored to arrest attention, by striking the iron door. While thus occupied, she probably swooned, or possibly died, through sheer terror; and, in falling, her shroud became entangled in some iron-work which projected interiorly. Thus she remained, and thus she rotted, erect.[4]

In the year 1810, a case of living inhumation happened in France, attended with circumstances which go far to warrant the assertion that truth is, indeed, stranger than fiction.[5] The heroine of the story was a Mademoiselle Victorine Lafourcade, a young girl of illustrious family, of wealth, and of great personal beauty. Among her numerous suitors was Julien Bossuet, a poor *littérateur,*[g] or journalist, of Paris. His talents and general amiability had recommended him to the notice of the heiress, by whom he seems to have been truly beloved; but her pride of birth decided her, finally, to reject him, and to wed a Monsieur Rénelle,[h] a banker, and a diplomatist of some eminence. After marriage, however, this gentleman neglected, and, perhaps, even more positively ill-treated her. Having passed with him some wretched years, she died, — at least her condition so closely resembled death as to deceive every one who saw her. She was buried — not in a vault — but in an ordinary grave in the village of her nativity. Filled with despair, and still inflamed by the memory of a profound attachment, the lover journeys from the capital to the remote province in which the village lies, with the romantic purpose of disinterring the corpse, and possessing himself of its luxuriant tresses. He reaches the grave. At midnight he unearths the coffin, opens it, and is in the act of detaching the hair, when he is arrested by the unclosing of the beloved eyes. In fact, the lady had been buried alive. Vitality had not altogether departed; and she was aroused, by the caresses of her lover, from the lethargy which had been mistaken for death. He bore her frantically to his lodgings in the village. He employed certain powerful restoratives suggested by no

---

g *litterateur, (C) accent added from A, B*

h Renelle, *(C) accented to follow A and B*

little medical learning. In fine, she revived. She recognised her preserver. She remained with him until, by slow degrees, she fully recovered her original health. Her woman's heart was not adamant, and this last lesson of love sufficed to soften it. She bestowed it upon Bossuet. She returned no more to her husband, but concealing from him her resurrection, fled with her lover to America. Twenty years afterwards, the two returned to France, in the persuasion that time had so greatly altered the lady's appearance, that her friends would be unable to recognise her. They were mistaken, however; for, at the first meeting, Monsieur Rénelle[i] did actually recognise and make claim to his wife. This claim she resisted; and a judicial tribunal sustained her in her resistance; deciding that the peculiar circumstances, with the long lapse of years, had extingushed, not only equitably, but legally, the authority of the husband.

The "Chirurgical Journal," of Leipsic — a periodical, of high authority and merit, which some American bookseller would do well to translate and republish — records, in a late number, a very distressing event of the character in question.[6]

An officer of artillery, a man of gigantic stature and of robust health, being thrown from an unmanageable horse, received a very severe contusion upon the head, which rendered him insensible at once; the skull was slightly fractured; but no immediate danger was apprehended. Trepanning was accomplished successfully. He was bled, and many other of the ordinary means of relief were adopted. Gradually, however, he fell into a more and more hopeless state of stupor, and, finally, it was thought that he died.

The weather was warm; and he was buried, with indecent haste, in one of the public cemeteries. His funeral took place on Thursday. On the Sunday following, the grounds of the cemetery were, as usual, much thronged with visiters; and, about noon, an intense excitement was created by the declaration of a peasant, that, while sitting upon the grave of the officer, he had distinctly felt a commotion of the earth, as if occasioned by some one struggling beneath. At first, little attention was paid to the man's asseveration; but his evident terror, and the dogged obstinacy with which he persisted in his story, had at length their natural effect

i Renelle *(C)*

upon the crowd. Spades were hurriedly procured, and the grave, which was shamefully shallow, was, in a few minutes, so far thrown open that the head of its occupant appeared. He was then, seemingly, dead; but he sat nearly erect within his[j] coffin, the lid of which, in his furious struggles, he had partially uplifted.

He was forthwith conveyed to the nearest hospital, and there pronounced to be still living, although in an asphyctic[k] condition.[7] After some hours he revived, recognised individuals of his acquaintance, and, in broken sentences, spoke of his agonies in the grave.

From what he related, it was clear that he must have been conscious of life for more than an hour, while inhumed, before lasping into insensibility. The grave was carelessly and loosely filled with an exceedingly porous soil; and thus some air was necessarily admitted. He heard the footsteps of the crowd overhead, and endeavored to make himself heard in turn. It was the tumult within the grounds of the cemetery, he said, which appeared to awaken him from a deep sleep — but no sooner was he awake than he became fully aware of the awful horrors of his position.

This patient, it is recorded, was doing well, and seemed to be in a fair way of ultimate recovery, but fell a victim to the quackeries of medical experiment. The galvanic battery was applied; and he suddenly expired in one of those ecstatic paroxysms which, occasionally, it superinduces.[8]

The mention of the galvanic battery, nevertheless, recalls to my memory a well known and very extraordinary case in point, where its action proved the means of restoring to animation a young attorney in London, who had been interred for two days. This occurred in 1831,[l] and created, at the time, a very profound sensation wherever it was made the subject of converse.[9]

The patient, Mr. Edward Stapleton, had died, apparently, of typhus fever, accompanied with some anomalous symptoms which had excited the curiosity of his medical attendants. Upon his seeming decease, his friends were requested to sanction a *post*

j the *(A)* *from A*
k asphytic *(B, C) misprint, corrected*
l 1821, *(A)*

mortem examination, but declined to permit it. As often happens, when such refusals are made, the practitioners resolved to disinter the body and dissect it at leisure, in private. Arrangements were easily effected with some of the numerous corps of body-snatchers with which London abounds; and, upon the third night after the funeral, the supposed corpse was unearthed from a grave eight feet deep, and deposited in the operating chamber of one of the private hospitals.

An incision of some extent had been actually made in the abdomen, when the fresh and undecayed appearance of the subject suggested an application of the battery. One experiment succeeded another, and the customary effects supervened, with nothing to characterize them in any respect, except, upon one or two occasions, a more than ordinary degree of life-likeness[m] in the convulsive action.

It grew late. The day was about to dawn; and it was thought expedient, at length, to proceed at once to the dissection. A student, however, was especially desirous of testing a theory of his own, and insisted upon applying the battery to one of the pectoral muscles. A rough gash was made, and a wire hastily brought in contact; when the patient, with a hurried, but quite unconvulsive movement, arose from the table, stepped into the middle of the floor, gazed about him uneasily for a few seconds, and then — spoke. What he said was unintelligible; but words were uttered; the syllabification was distinct. Having spoken, he fell heavily to the floor.

For some moments all were paralyzed with awe — but the urgency of the case soon restored them their presence of mind. It was seen that Mr. Stapleton was alive, although in a swoon. Upon exhibition of ether he revived and was rapidly restored to health, and to the society of his friends — from whom, however, all knowledge of his resuscitation was withheld, until a relapse was no longer to be apprehended. Their wonder — their rapturous astonishment — may be conceived.

The most thrilling peculiarity of this incident, nevertheless, is involved in what Mr. S. himself asserts. He declares that at no

---

m life-likliness *(A, B)*

period was he altogether insensible — that, dully and confusedly he was aware of every thing which happened to him, from the moment in which he was pronounced *dead* by his physicians, to that in which he fell swooning to the floor of the hospital. "I am alive," were the uncomprehended words which, upon recognising the locality of the dissecting-room, he had endeavored, in his extremity, to utter.

It were an easy matter to multiply such histories as these — but I forbear — for, indeed, we have no need of such to establish the fact that premature interments occur. When we reflect how very rarely, from the nature of the case, we have it in our power to detect them, we must admit that they may *frequently* occur without our cognizance. Scarcely, in truth, is a graveyard ever encroached upon, for any purpose, to any great extent, that skeletons are not found in postures which suggest the most fearful of suspicions.[10]

Fearful indeed the suspicion — but more fearful the doom! It may be asserted, without hesitation, that *no* event is so terribly well adapted to inspire the supremeness of bodily and of mental distress, as is burial before death. The unendurable oppression of the lungs — the stifling fumes of[n] the damp earth — the clinging to[o] the death garments — the rigid embrace of the narrow house — the blackness of the absolute Night — the silence like a sea that overwhelms — the unseen but palpable presence of the Conqueror Worm[11] — these things, with thoughts of the air and grass above, with memory of dear friends who would fly to save us if but informed of our fate, and with consciousness that of this fate they can *never* be informed — that our hopeless portion is that of the really dead — these considerations, I say, carry into the heart, which still palpitates, a degree of appalling and intolerable horror from which the most daring imagination must recoil. We know of nothing so agonizing upon Earth — we can dream of nothing half so hideous in the realms of the nethermost Hell. And thus all narratives upon this topic have an interest profound; an interest, nevertheless, which, through the sacred awe of the topic itself, very properly and very peculiarly depends upon our convic-

n from *(A, B)* o of *(A, B)*

tion of the *truth* of the matter narrated. What I have now to tell, is of my own actual knowledge — of my own positive and personal experience.

For several years I had been subject to attacks of the singular disorder which physicians have agreed to term catalepsy, in default of a more definitive title. Although both the immediate and the predisposing causes, and even the actual diagnosis of this disease, are still mysterious,[p] its obvious and apparent character is sufficiently well understood. Its variations seem to be chiefly of degree. Sometimes the patient lies, for a day only, or even for a shorter period, in a species of exaggerated lethargy. He is senseless and externally motionless; but the pulsation of the heart is still faintly perceptible; some traces of warmth remain; a slight color lingers within the centre of the cheek; and, upon application of a mirror to the lips, we can detect a torpid, unequal, and vacillating action of the lungs. Then again the duration of the trance is for weeks — even for months; while the closest scrutiny, and the most rigorous medical tests, fail to establish any material distinction between the state of the sufferer and what we conceive of absolute death. Very usually, he is saved from premature interment solely by the knowledge of his friends that he has been previously subject to catalepsy, by the consequent suspicion excited, and, above all, by the non-appearance of decay. The advances of the malady are, luckily, gradual. The first manifestations, although marked, are unequivocal. The fits grow successively more and more distinctive, and endure each for a longer term than the preceding. In this lies the principal security from inhumation. The unfortunate whose *first* attack should be of the extreme character which is occasionally seen, would almost inevitably be consigned alive to the tomb.

My own case differed in no important particular from those mentioned in medical books. Sometimes, without any apparent cause, I sank, little by little, into a condition of semi-syncope,[q] or half swoon; and, in this condition, without pain, without ability to stir, or, strictly speaking, to think, but with a dull lethargic consciousness of life and of the presence of those who surrounded

p mysteries, *(A, B)* q hemi-syncope, *(A, B)*

my bed, I remained, until the crisis of the disease restored me, suddenly, to perfect sensation. At other times I was quickly and impetuously smitten. I grew sick, and numb, and chilly, and dizzy, and so fell prostrate at once. Then, for weeks, all was void, and black, and silent, and Nothing became the universe. Total annihilation could be no more. From these latter attacks I awoke, however, with a gradation slow in proportion to the suddenness of the seizure.[r] Just as the day dawns to the friendless and houseless beggar who roams the streets throughout the long desolate winter night — just so tardily — just so wearily — just so cheerily came back the light of the Soul to me.

Apart from the tendency to trance, however, my general health appeared to be good; nor could I perceive that it was at all affected by the one prevalent malady — unless, indeed, an idiosyncrasy in my ordinary *sleep* may be looked upon as superinduced. Upon awaking from slumber, I could never gain, at once, thorough possession of my senses, and always remained, for many minutes, in much bewilderment and perplexity; — the mental faculties in general, but the memory in especial, being in a condition of absolute abeyance.

In all that I endured there was no physical suffering, but of moral distress an infinitude. My fancy grew charnal. I talked "of worms, of tombs and epitaphs."[12] I was lost in reveries of death, and the idea of premature burial held continual possession of my brain. The ghastly Danger to which I was subjected, haunted me day and night. In the former, the torture of meditation was excessive — in the latter, supreme. When the grim Darkness overspread the Earth, then, with very horror of thought, I shook — shook as[s] the quivering plumes upon the hearse. When Nature could endure wakefulness no longer, it was with a struggle that I consented to sleep — for I shuddered to reflect that, upon awaking, I might find myself the tenant of a grave. And when, finally, I sank into slumber, it was only to rush at once into a world of phantasms, above which, with vast, sable, overshadowing wings, hovered, predominant, the one sepulchral Idea.[13]

From the innumerable images of gloom which thus oppressed

---

r seisure. *(B, C) emended from A* s like *(A)*

me in dreams, I select for record but a solitary vision. Methought I was immersed in a cataleptic trance of more than usual duration and profundity. Suddenly there came an icy hand upon my forehead, and an impatient, gibbering voice whispered the word "Arise!" within my ear.

I sat erect. The darkness was total. I could not see the figure of him who had aroused me. I could call to mind neither the period at which I had fallen into the trance, nor the locality in which I then lay. While I remained motionless, and busied in endeavors to collect my thoughts, the cold hand grasped me fiercely by the wrist, shaking it petulantly, while the gibbering voice said again:

"Arise! did I not bid thee arise?"

"And who," I demanded, "art thou?"

[t]"I have no name[t] in the regions which I inhabit," replied the voice, mournfully; "I was mortal, but am fiend. I was merciless, but am pitiful. Thou dost feel that I shudder. My teeth chatter as I speak, yet it is not with the chilliness of the night — of the night without end. But this hideousness is insufferable. How canst *thou* tranquilly sleep? I cannot rest for the cry of these great agonies. These sights are more than I can bear. Get thee up! Come with me into the outer Night, and let me unfold to thee the graves.[14] Is not this a spectacle of wo? — Behold!"

I looked; and the unseen figure, which still grasped me by the wrist, had caused to be thrown open the graves of all mankind; and from each issued the faint phosphoric radiance of decay; so that I could see into the innermost recesses, and there view the shrouded bodies in their sad and solemn slumbers with the worm. But, alas! the real sleepers were fewer, by many millions, than those who slumbered not at all; and there was a feeble struggling; and there was a general sad unrest; and from out the depths of the countless pits there came a melancholy rustling from the garments of the buried. And, of those who seemed tranquilly to repose, I saw that a vast number had changed, in a greater or less degree, the rigid and uneasy position in which they had originally been entombed. And the voice again said to me, as I gazed:

t . . . t "I am called *Shadow (A)*

"Is it not — oh, is it *not* a pitiful sight?" But, before I could find words to reply, the figure had ceased to grasp my wrist, the phosphoric lights expired, and the graves were closed with a sudden violence, while from out them arose a tumult of despairing cries, saying again, "Is it not — oh, God! is it *not* a very pitiful sight?"

Phantasies such as these, presenting themselves at night, extended their terrific influence far into my waking hours. My nerves became thoroughly unstrung, and I fell a prey to perpetual horror. I hesitated to ride, or to walk, or to indulge in any exercise that would carry me from home. In fact, I no longer dared trust myself out of the immediate presence of those who were aware of my proneness to catalepsy, lest, falling into one of my usual fits, I should be buried before my real condition could be ascertained. I doubted the care, the fidelity of my dearest friends. I dreaded that, in some trance of more than customary duration, they might be prevailed upon to regard me as irrecoverable. I even went so far as to fear that, as I occasioned much trouble, they might be glad to consider any very protracted attack as sufficient excuse for getting rid of me altogether. It was in vain they endeavored to reassure me by the most solemn promises. I exacted the most sacred oaths, that under no circumstances they would bury me until decomposition had so materially advanced as to render farther[u] preservation impossible. And, even then, my mortal terrors would listen to no reason — would accept no consolation. I entered into a series of elaborate precautions. Among other things, I had the family vault so remodelled as to admit of being readily opened from within. The slightest pressure upon a long lever that extended far into the tomb would cause the iron portals to fly back. There were arrangements also for the free admission of air and light, and convenient receptacles for food and water, within immediate reach of the coffin intended for my reception. This coffin was warmly and softly padded, and was provided with a lid, fashioned upon the principle of the vault-door, with the addition of springs so contrived that the feeblest movement of the body would be sufficient to set it at liberty. Besides all this, there was suspended from the roof of the tomb, a large bell, the rope of

u further *(A)*

which, it was designed, should extend through a hole in the coffin, and so be fastened to one of the hands of the corpse.[15] But, alas! what avails the vigilance against the Destiny of man? Not even these well contrived[v] securities sufficed[w] to save from the uttermost agonies of living inhumation, a wretch to these agonies foredoomed!

There arrived an epoch — as often before there had arrived — in which I found myself emerging from total unconsciousness into the first feeble and indefinite sense of existence. Slowly — with a tortoise gradation — approached the faint gray dawn of the psychal day. A torpid uneasiness. An apathetic endurance of dull pain. No care — no hope — no effort. Then, after long interval, a ringing in the ears; then, after a lapse still longer, a pricking or tingling sensation in the extremities; then a seemingly eternal period of pleasurable quiescence,[x] during which the awakening feelings are struggling into thought; then a brief re-sinking into nonentity; then a sudden recovery. At length the slight quivering of an eyelid, and immediately thereupon, an electric shock of a terror, deadly and indefinite, which sends the blood in torrents from the temples to the heart. And now the first positive effort to think. And now the first endeavor to remember. And now a partial and evanescent success. And now the memory has so far regained its dominion, that, in some measure, I am cognizant of my state. I feel that I am not awaking from ordinary sleep. I recollect that I have been subject to catalepsy. And now, at last, as if by the rush of an ocean, my shuddering spirit is overwhelmed by the one grim Danger — by the one spectral and ever-prevalent Idea.

For some minutes after this fancy possessed me, I remained without motion. And why? I could not summon courage to move. I dared not make the effort which was to satisfy me of my fate — and yet there was something at my heart which whispered me *it was sure.* Despair — such as no other species of wretchedness ever calls into being — despair alone urged me, after long irresolution, to uplift the heavy lids of my eyes. I uplifted them. It was dark — all dark. I knew that the fit was over. I knew that the crisis of my

v conceived *(A)*
w suffice *(A)*
x acquiescence, *(A)*

disorder had long passed. I knew that I had now fully recovered the use of my visual faculties — and yet it was dark — all dark — the intense and utter raylessness of the Night that endureth for evermore.[16]

I endeavored to shriek; and my lips and my parched tongue moved convulsively together in the attempt — but no voice issued from the cavernous lungs, which, oppressed as if by the weight of some incumbent mountain, gasped and palpitated, with the heart, at every elaborate and struggling inspiration.

The movement of the jaws, in this effort to cry aloud, showed me that they were bound up, as is usual with the dead. I felt, too, that I lay upon some hard substance; and by something similar my sides were, also, closely compressed. So far, I had not ventured to stir any of my limbs — but now I violently threw up my arms, which had been lying at length, with the wrists crossed. They struck a solid wooden substance, which extended above my person at an elevation of not more than six inches from my face. I could no longer doubt that I reposed within a coffin at last.

And now, amid all my infinite miseries, came sweetly the cherub Hope[17] — for I thought of my precautions. I writhed, and made spasmodic exertions to force open the lid: it would not move. I felt my wrists for the bell-rope: it was not to be found. And now the Comforter fled for ever, and a still sterner Despair reigned triumphant; for I could not help perceiving the absence of the paddings which I had so carefully prepared — and then, too, there came suddenly to my nostrils the strong peculiar odor of moist earth. The conclusion was irresistible. It was *not* within the vault. I had fallen into a trance while absent from home — while among strangers — when, or how, I could not remember — and it was they who had buried me as a dog — nailed up in some common coffin — and thrust, deep, deep, and for ever, into some ordinary and nameless *grave*.

As this awful conviction forced itself, thus, into the innermost chambers of my soul, I once again struggled to cry aloud. And in this second endeavor I succeeded. A long, wild, and continuous shriek, or yell, of agony, resounded through the realms of the subterrene Night.

"Hillo! hillo, there!" said a gruff voice, in reply.

"What the devil's the matter now?" said a second.

"Get out o' that!" said a third.

"What do you mean by yowling[y] in that ere kind of style, like a cattymount?" said a fourth; and hereupon I was seized and shaken without ceremony, for several minutes, by a junto of very rough-looking individuals. They did not arouse me from my[z] slumber — for I was wide awake when I screamed — but they restored me to the full possession of my memory.[a]

This adventure occurred near Richmond, in Virginia. Accompanied by a friend, I had proceeded, upon a gunning expedition, some miles down the banks of James River. Night approached, and we were overtaken by a storm. The cabin of a small sloop lying at anchor in the stream, and laden with garden mould, afforded us the only available shelter. We made the best of it, and passed the night on board. I slept in one of the only two berths in the vessel — and the berths of a sloop of sixty or seventy tons, need scarcely be described. That which I occupied had no bedding of any kind. Its extreme width was eighteen inches. The distance of its bottom from the deck overhead, was precisely the same. I found it a matter of exceeding difficulty to squeeze myself in. Nevertheless, I slept soundly; and the whole of my vision — for it was no dream, and no nightmare — arose naturally from the circumstances of my position — from my ordinary bias of thought — and from the difficulty, to which I have alluded, of collecting my senses, and especially of regaining my memory, for a long time after awaking from slumber. The men who shook me were the crew of the sloop, and some laborers engaged to unload it. From the load itself came the earthy smell. The bandage about the jaws was a silk handkerchief in which I had bound up my head, in default of my customary nightcap.

The tortures endured, however, were undubitably quite[b] equal, for the time, to those of actual sepulture. They were fearfully — they were inconceivably hideous; but out of Evil proceeded Good;

---

y yawling *(A)*
z *Omitted (A)*
a memery *(C) misprint, corrected from A, B*
b fully *(A)*

for their very excess wrought in my spirit an inevitable revulsion. My soul acquired tone — acquired temper. I went abroad. I took vigorous exercise. I breathed the free air of Heaven. I thought upon other subjects than Death. I discarded my medical books. "Buchan" I burned.[18] I read no "Night Thoughts"[19] — no fustian about church-yards — no bugaboo tales — *such as this.* In short, I became a new man, and lived a man's life. From that memorable night, I dismissed forever my charnal apprehensions, and with them vanished the cataleptic disorder, of which, perhaps, they had been less the consequence than the cause.

There are moments when, even to the sober eye of Reason, the world of our sad Humanity may[c] assume the semblance of a[d] Hell — but the imagination[e] of man is no Carathis, to explore with impunity its every cavern. Alas! the grim legion of sepulchral terrors cannot[f] be regarded as altogether fanciful — but, like the Demons in whose company Afrasiab made his voyage down the Oxus, they must sleep, or they will devour us — they must be suffered to slumber, or we perish.[20]

NOTES

1. Pleasurable pain is mentioned in E. K.'s Introduction to Spenser's *Shepheardes Calender* (1579).

2. Napoleon lost 20,000 men crossing the river Beresina in Minsk Government, Russia, November 26–29, 1812. The Lisbon Earthquake, November 1, 1755, cost more than 30,000 lives. The great Plague at London was that of 1665; Defoe wrote a famous, although partly fictitious, account of it called *A Journal of the Plague Year* (1722). The Massacre of St. Bartholomew, August 24, 1572, was the slaughter of the Huguenot French Protestants ordered by Charles IX under the influence of his mother, Catherine de Médicis. Suraj-ud-Dowlah, Nawab of Bengal, murdered more than a hundred English prisoners at Calcutta in 1756.

3. Ecclesiastes 12:6, "Or ever the silver cord be loosed, or the golden bowl be broken," is also echoed in the first line of Poe's poem "Lenore": "Ah, broken is the golden bowl . . ."

4. Poe's source for this account of the Baltimore lady has not been pointed out, but I found the story with slight variations (implying a source other than

c must *(D)*
d *Omitted (D)*
e intellect *(A)*
f can*not (D)*

Poe's tale) printed as told by "the Baltimore correspondent of a New York paper" in the *Democrat* of Lancaster, Pennsylvania, December 5, 1845.

5. Killis Campbell (*MLN,* May 1917) found Poe's source for the following narrative in the Philadelphia *Casket* (forerunner of *Graham's Magazine*) for September 1827. The article, headed "The Lady Buried Alive," presents two versions of a very old story, ascribing one to "the *Causes Célèbres*" (see Gayot de Pitavol, *Causes Celebres et interessantes,* vol. VII, 1737, pp. 434–437) and the other to Domenico Maria Manni (1690–1788, author of *Istoria del Decamerone di Giovanni Boccaccio,* Firenze, 1742), who gave his version as an account of a real happening during the plague of 1460 in Florence. Poe made use of both versions, taking most of his narrative from the first and the happy ending from the second. The only proper name in Pitavol's version is that of the *rue Saint Honoré;* Manni as quoted in the *Casket* calls the heroine Ginevra de Bmiera; her lover, Antonio Rondinelli; but he does not name the husband. M. Rénelle may be indebted to Mr. Rennell, father of the heroine in "The Dead Alive" (*Fraser's,* August 1834) – the title was mentioned by Mr. Blackwood in his conversation with the Psyche Zenobia (see n. 9 below) – but the story is of the safe return of a lover believed to have been lost at sea, and has nothing to do with premature burial. Poe apparently invented most of the names as well as the date he supplied for verisimilitude.

6. Poe's exact source for the following story of the artillery officer has not been located. It probably was a newspaper article crediting a German medical journal, as was suggested by Gustav Gruener in *Modern Philology,* June 1904, but Palmer Cobb (*Influence of Hoffmann,* p. 28) reported that "a search of all the medical periodicals in the libraries of Berlin for the period 1834–44 . . . failed to result in a discovery of the case cited by Poe." The *Union List of Serials* includes a *Zeitschrift für Chirurgen,* Osterode [Poland], 1841–46, in the National Medical Library; it has not been consulted.

7. Asphyctic is an adjective derived from asphyxia. N. P. Willis (cited in n. 15 below) noted that "asphyxia, or a suspension of life, with all the appearance of death, is certified to in many instances, and carefully provided for in some countries" (p. 640).

8. On uses of the galvanic battery compare "Loss of Breath" and "Some Words with a Mummy."

9. This "extraordinary case" is clearly adapted from an anonymous first-person narrative, "The Buried Alive" (*Blackwood's Magazine* for October 1821, pp. 262–264) – an article pointed out by Margaret Alterton (*Origins,* 1925, pp. 11, 18–20, 23) and quoted in connection with the life-in-death theme in a number of Poe's stories. It was outlined in "How to Write a Blackwood Article," at n. 11, where it is assigned to the wrong title (see n. 5 above). The date of occurrence (given as 1821 in the first version of Poe's tale), the name of the hero (possibly suggested by "The Adventures of Tom Stapleton," which ran for many weeks in *Brother Jonathan* in the autumn of 1841 while news of the Mary Rogers case was still appearing and the sensational story of J. C. Colt's murder of Samuel Adams was filling columns), the amplification of some details following the exhumation, and the effective concluding paragraph were added by Poe.

10. N. P. Willis (cited in n. 15, below) records the finding of a young lady's body turned over, but an undertaker reassured him that it resulted from rough handling of the coffin (p. 639).

11. The phrase "Conqueror Worm" is from Spencer Wallace Cone's *Proud Ladye* (New York, 1840); Poe used it as the title of his powerful poem first published in *Graham's* for January 1843, and inserted in "Ligeia" in 1845.

12. Misquoted from *Richard II,* III, ii, 145, "Let's talk of graves, of worms and epitaphs."

13. Compare *Paradise Lost,* II, 962, "sable vested night," and lines 13–16 of "The Conqueror Worm."

14. Compare the early prose bit "A Dream," especially the final paragraph and n. 7.

15. Compare N. P. Willis, in the *New Mirror,* November 18, 1843, p. 111, reprinted among the "Ephemera" in *Prose Works* (1845), pp. 639, 640:

> The "life-preserving coffin," lately exhibited at the fair of the Institute, is so constructed as to fly open with the least stir of the occupant, and made as comfortable within as if intended for a temporary lodging. The proprietor recommends . . . a corresponding facility of exit from the vault, and arrangements for privacy, light and fresh air – in short all that would be agreeable to the *revenant* on first waking . . . In Frankfort, Germany, the dead man is laid in a well-aired room, and his hand fastened for three days to a bell-pull.

The same article includes Willis's remarks referred to in notes 7 and 10 above.
The Rover (I, 249), June 1843, reprinted an article by Thomas Hood, "The Death Watch," reporting that at Frankfurt-am-Main one "corpse" did come to life and pull the bell – and the aged caretaker died of a heart attack. A poem on the coffin by Seba Smith is in the New York *Columbian Lady's and Gentleman's Magazine* for January 1844, with a note naming the inventor as a Mr. Eisenbrant of Baltimore.

16. Compare similar passages in the early versions of "Loss of Breath"; in *Arthur Gordon Pym,* chapter 21, and in "The Pit and the Pendulum."

17. Compare *Politian,* IV, 66, "The Seraph Hope," and VII, 81, "the angel Hope."

18. William Buchan (1729–1805) wrote *Domestic Medicine; or The Family Physician,* first published in 1769 and long highly regarded. The 21st edition was brought out by Buchan's son, Alexander, in 1813; the 29th American edition appeared in 1854.

19. Dr. Edward Young's *Night Thoughts, of Death, Time and Immortality* (1742), the foremost poem of the Graveyard School with its emphasis on details about death, was still immensely popular in America in Poe's day.

20. In this paragraph Poe combined and rewrote two widely separated sentences in Horace Binney Wallace's *Stanley* (1838): ". . . with all the ardor of desperation; he sounded passion to its depths, and raked the bottom of the gulf of sin; he explored, with the indomitable spirit of Carathis, every chamber and

cavern of the earthly hell of bad delights" (II, 83–84), and "The passions are like those demons with whom Afrasiab sailed down the river Oxus, our safety consists in keeping them asleep; if they wake we are lost" (I, 124). Wallace refers to the wicked old witch in William Beckford's *Vathek* (1786) who, granted a day to command the treasures of Hell before her damnation, boldly enjoys them. (Beckford's book, with which Poe himself was directly acquainted, is fantastic fiction but uses historical names of the debauched Caliph Haroun Vathek Billah [842–847 A.D.] and of his mother Carathis, who was a Greek). Afrasiab was the legendary bad King of Turân, leading enemy of Rustam in Firdusi's *Shah Nameh,* but Wallace used a story I do not find in the Persian epic.

THE PURLOINED LETTER

Poe wrote J. R. Lowell on July 2, 1844 that " 'The Purloined Letter,' forthcoming in 'The Gift' is perhaps the best of my tales of ratiocination." Many judicious critics have agreed, some even considering it the best of all Poe's stories. Its great merit lies in the fascination of the purely intellectual plot, and in the absence of the sensational.

No exact source for Poe's plot has been pointed out, but Poe remarked on *not* seeking truth in a well in his prefatory "Letter to Mr. ——" in *Poems* (1831); in a review of Alexander Slidell's *An American in England* in the *Southern Literary Messenger,* February 1836; and in "The Murders in the Rue Morgue," at n. 29.

The story was apparently hastily completed for the annual in which it was first printed. On May 31, 1844, Poe wrote Edward L. Carey, the publisher, requesting a proof, because "the MS had many interlineations and erasures" – whereas most of his printer's copy was carefully prepared and unusually clean.* The revision for the publication of "The Purloined Letter" in the *Tales* of 1845 was moderate but skillful, and the story was hardly changed at all in the J. Lorimer Graham copy.

The tale was reprinted in *Chambers' Edinburgh Journal* of November 30, 1844, with the following introduction:

* The untidy condition referred to is paralleled in the case of "The Murders in the Rue Morgue," but in no other surviving manuscript of a Poe story. The May 31st letter was printed in the first supplement of Ostrom's *Letters of Edgar Allan Poe* (see *AL,* November 1952).

THE PURLOINED LETTER

> *The Gift* is an American annual of great typographical elegance, and embellished with many beautiful engravings. It contains an article, which, for several reasons, appears to us so remarkable, that we leave aside several effusions of our ordinary contributors in order to make room for an abridgment of it. The writer, Mr. Edgar A. Poe, is evidently an acute observer of mental phenomena; and we have to thank him for one of the aptest illustrations which could well be conceived, of that curious play of two minds, in which one person, let us call him A, guesses what another, B, will do, judging that B will adopt a particular line of policy to circumvent A.

Some students have believed that the abridgment, which is well done, was by the author, but Poe's failure to adopt the version in 1845 argues that the changes were unauthorized.†

Poe knew of the immediate success of his story abroad. In reviewing Poe's *Tales* in his *Aristidean* for October 1845, Dr. English, who had certainly discussed them with the author, wrote:

> There is much made of nothing in "The Purloined Letter," – the story of which is simple; but the reasoning is remarkably clear, and directed solely to the required end. It first appeared in the "Gift," and was thence copied into Chambers' "Edinburgh Journal," as a most notable production.

An unsigned translation, "Une Lettre volée," was published in the Paris *Magasin pittoresque* of August 1845, and the story became popular in France.‡ Although some of the ideas are from books in which Poe was interested, and some of the characters are based on real people, it goes without saying that the real Queen of France, Marie Amélie, was not portrayed.

TEXTS

(A) The Gift: a Christmas, New Year, and Birthday Present, MDCCCXLV. (issued in September 1844), pages 41–61; *(B) Tales* (1845), pages 200–218; *(C)*

† A separate pamphlet reprint of the abridged text was issued in London in an edition of 325 copies in 1931, with an introduction by Dr. Jacob Schwarz, who wished to regard the Edinburgh version as the earliest — and omitted Chambers' introduction! Actually, *The Gift* was published in the fall of 1844 — Wiley and Putnam advertised it for sale in the *New-York Daily Tribune* for September 24 – and two or three weeks was ample time for copies to reach Edinburgh.

‡ Later on, a play founded on Poe's story by Victorien Sardou, *Les Pattes de Mouche* (1860), translated as *A Scrap of Paper* (1861), gave rise to the sinister phrase used contemptuously to describe the treaty broken in 1914 by the invasion of Belgium that began the First World War. See C. P. Cambiaire, *The Influence of . . . Poe in France* (1927), p. 286, for a synopsis of the literature on this curious subject.

J. Lorimer Graham copy of *Tales,* with manuscript changes of 1849; *(D) Works* (1850), I, 262–280.

The J. Lorimer Graham copy of the *Tales (C)* is followed. Griswold's version *(D)* is merely a reprint of an unrevised copy of the *Tales (B)* and has no independent authority; it introduces three typographical errors.

Reprints

Chambers' Edinburgh Journal, November 30, 1844, abridged from *The Gift.* The abridgment was copied by: *Littell's Living Age* (Boston), January 18, 1845; the *Spirit of the Times* (Philadelphia), January 20 and 22, 1845; and the *New York Weekly News,* January 25, 1845, labeled *"Chambers' Journal via Littell's Living Age"* (for the last, see G. Thomas Tanselle, *Publications of the Bibliographical Society of America,* Second Quarter 1962).

Translation

Magasin pittoresque, August 1845, as "Une Lettre volée," and reprinted in *L'Echo de la Presse,* August 25, 1845.

THE PURLOINED LETTER. [*C*]

Nil sapientiae odiosius acumine nimio.

Seneca.

At Paris, just after dark one gusty evening in the autumn of 18—, I was enjoying the twofold luxury of meditation and a meerschaum,[1] in company with my friend C. Auguste Dupin, in his little back library, or book-closet, *au troisième,*[a] *No.* 33, *Rue Dunôt, Faubourg St. Germain.*[2] For one hour at least we had maintained a profound silence; while each, to any casual observer, might have seemed intently and exclusively occupied with the curling eddies of smoke that oppressed the atmosphere of the chamber. For myself, however, I was mentally discussing certain topics which had formed matter for conversation between us at an earlier period of the evening; I mean the affair of the Rue Morgue, and the mystery attending the murder of Marie Rogêt.[b] I looked upon it, therefore, as something of a coincidence, when the door of our apartment was thrown open and admitted our old acquaintance, Monsieur G——, the Prefect of the Parisian police.[3]

We gave him a hearty welcome; for there was nearly half as

Motto omitted in A

a *troisiême, (A, B, C, D)*

b Roget. *(A)*

much of the entertaining as of the contemptible about the man, and we had not seen him for several years. We had been sitting in the dark, and Dupin now arose for the purpose of lighting a lamp, but sat down again, without doing so, upon G.'s saying that he had called to consult us, or rather to ask the opinion of my friend, about some official business which had occasioned a great deal of trouble.

"If it is any point requiring reflection," observed Dupin, as he forebore to enkindle the wick, "we shall examine it to better purpose in the dark."

"That is another of your odd notions," said the Prefect, who had a fashion of calling every thing "odd" that was beyond his comprehension, and thus lived amid an absolute legion of "oddities."

"Very true," said Dupin, as he supplied his visiter with a pipe, and rolled towards him a[c] comfortable chair.

"And what is the difficulty now?" I asked. "Nothing more in the assassination way, I hope?"

"Oh no; nothing of that nature. The fact is, the business is *very* simple indeed, and I make no doubt that we can manage it sufficiently well ourselves; but then I thought Dupin would like to hear the details of it, because it is so excessively *odd.*"

"Simple and odd," said Dupin.

"Why, yes; and not exactly that, either. The fact is, we have all been a good deal puzzled because the affair *is* so simple, and yet baffles us altogether."

"Perhaps it is the very simplicity of the thing which puts you at fault," said my friend.

"What nonsense you *do* talk!" replied the Prefect, laughing heartily.

"Perhaps the mystery is a[d] little *too* plain," said Dupin.

"Oh, good heavens! who ever heard of such an idea?"

"A little *too* self-evident."

"Ha! ha! ha! — ha! ha! ha! — ho! ho! ho!" roared[e] our visiter, profoundly amused, "oh, Dupin, you will be the death of me yet!"[4]

---

c a very *(A)*
d *Omitted (D)*
e roared out *(A)*

"And what, after all, *is* the matter on hand?" I asked.

"Why, I will tell you," replied the Prefect, as he gave a long, steady, and contemplative puff, and settled himself in his chair. "I will tell you in a few words; but, before I begin, let me caution you that this is[f] an affair demanding the greatest secrecy, and that I should most probably lose the position I now hold, were it known that I confided it to any one."

"Proceed," said I.

"Or not," said Dupin.

"Well, then; I have received personal information, from a very high quarter, that a certain document of the last importance, has been purloined from the royal apartments. The individual who purloined it is known; this beyond a doubt; he was seen to take it. It is known, also, that it still remains in his possession."

"How is this known?" asked Dupin.

"It is clearly inferred," replied the Prefect, "from the nature of the document, and from the non-appearance of certain results which would at once arise from its passing *out* of the robber's possession; – that is to say, from his employing it as he must design in the end to employ it."

"Be a little more explicit," I said.

"Well, I may venture so far as to say that the paper gives its holder a certain power in a certain quarter where such power is immensely valuable." The Prefect was fond of the cant of diplomacy.

"Still I do not quite understand," said Dupin.

"No? Well; the disclosure of the document to a third person, who shall be nameless, would bring in question the honor of a personage of most exalted station; and this fact gives the holder of the document an ascendancy over the illustrious personage whose honor and peace are so jeopardized."

"But this ascendancy," I interposed, "would depend upon the robber's knowledge of the loser's knowledge of the robber. Who would dare—"

"The thief," said G., "is the Minister D——, who dares all things, those unbecoming as well as those becoming a man. The

f *Omitted (D)*

method of the theft was not less ingenious than bold. The document in question — a letter, to be frank — had been received by the personage robbed while alone in the royal *boudoir*. During its perusal she was suddenly interrupted by the entrance of the other exalted personage from whom especially it was her wish to conceal it. After a hurried and vain endeavor to thrust it in a drawer, she was forced to place it, open as it was, upon a table. The address, however, was uppermost, and, the contents thus unexposed, the letter escaped notice. At this juncture enters the Minister D——. His lynx eye immediately perceives the paper, recognises the handwriting of the address, observes the confusion of the personage addressed, and fathoms her secret. After some business transactions, hurried through in his ordinary manner, he produces a letter somewhat similar to the one in question, opens it, pretends to read it, and then places it in close juxtaposition to the other. Again he converses, for some fifteen minutes, upon the public affairs. At length, in taking leave, he takes also from the table the letter to which he had no claim. Its rightful owner saw, but, of course, dared not call attention to the act, in the presence of the third personage who stood at her elbow. The minister decamped; leaving his own letter — one of no importance — upon the table."

"Here, then," said Dupin to me, "you have precisely what you demand to make the ascendancy complete — the robber's knowledge of the loser's knowledge of the robber."

"Yes," replied the Prefect; "and the power thus attained has, for some months past, been wielded, for political purposes, to a very dangerous extent. The personage robbed is more thoroughly convinced, every day, of the necessity of reclaiming her letter. But this, of course, cannot be done openly. In fine, driven to despair, she has committed the matter to me."

"Than whom," said Dupin, amid a perfect whirlwind of smoke, " no more sagacious agent could, I suppose, be desired, or even imagined."

"You flatter me," replied the Prefect; "but it is possible that some such opinion may have been entertained."

"It is clear," said I, "as you observe, that the letter is still in possession of the minister; since it is this possession, and not any employment of the letter, which bestows the power. With the employment the power departs."

"True," said G.; "and upon this conviction I proceeded. My first care was to make thorough search of the minister's hotel;[5] and here my chief embarrassment lay in the necessity of searching without his knowledge. Beyond all things, I have been warned of the danger which would result from giving him reason to suspect our design."

"But," said I, "you are quite *au fait* in these investigations. The Parisian police have done this thing often before."

"O yes; and for this reason I did not despair. The habits of the minister gave me, too, a great advantage. He is frequently absent from home all night. His servants are by no means numerous. They sleep at a distance from their master's apartment,[g] and, being chiefly Neapolitans, are readily made drunk.[6] I have keys, as you know, with which I can open any chamber or cabinet in Paris. For three months a night has not passed, during the greater part of which I have not been engaged, personally, in ransacking the D—— Hotel. My honor is interested, and, to mention a great secret, the reward is enormous. So I did not abandon the search until I had become fully satisfied that the thief is a more astute man than myself. I fancy that I have investigated every nook and corner of the premises in which it is possible that the paper can be concealed."

"But is it not possible," I suggested, "that although the letter may be in possession of the minister, as it unquestionably is, he may have concealed it elsewhere than upon his own premises?"

"This is barely possible," said Dupin. "The present peculiar condition of affairs at court, and especially of those intrigues in which D—— is known to be involved, would render the instant availability of the document – its susceptibility of being produced at a moment's notice – a point of nearly equal importance with its possession."

"Its susceptibility of being produced?" said I.

"That is to say, of being *destroyed*," said Dupin.

"True," I observed; "the paper is clearly then upon the

---

g apartments, *(A)*

premises. As for its being upon the person of the minister, we may consider that as out of the question."

"Entirely," said the Prefect. "He has been twice waylaid, as if by footpads, and his person rigorously searched under my own inspection."

"You might have spared yourself this trouble," said Dupin. "D——, I presume, is not altogether a fool, and, if not, must have anticipated these waylayings, as a matter of course."

"Not *altogether* a fool," said G., "but then he's a poet, which I take to be only one remove from a fool."[7]

"True," said Dupin, after a long and thoughtful whiff from his meerschaum, "although I have been guilty of certain doggrel myself."

"Suppose you detail," said I, "the particulars of your search."[8]

"Why the fact is, we took our time, and we searched *every where*. I have had long experience in these affairs. I took the entire building, room by room; devoting the nights of a whole week to each. We examined, first, the furniture of each apartment. We opened every possible drawer; and I presume you know that, to a properly trained police agent, such a thing as a *secret* drawer is impossible. Any man is a dolt who permits a 'secret' drawer to escape him in a search of this kind. The thing is *so* plain. There is a certain amount of bulk – of space – to be accounted for in every cabinet. Then we have accurate rules. The fiftieth part of a line could not escape us. After the cabinets we took the chairs. The cushions we probed with the fine long needles you have seen me employ. From the tables we removed the tops."

"Why so?"

"Sometimes the top of a table, or other similarly arranged piece of furniture, is removed by the person wishing to conceal an article; then the leg is excavated, the article deposited within the cavity, and the top replaced. The bottoms and tops of bedposts are employed in the same way."

"But could not the cavity be detected by sounding?" I asked.

"By no means, if, when the article is deposited, a sufficient wadding of cotton be placed around it. Besides, in our case, we were obliged to proceed without noise."

"But you could not have removed – you could not have taken

to pieces *all* articles of furniture in which it would have been possible to make a deposit in the manner you mention. A letter may be compressed into a thin spiral roll, not differing much in shape or bulk from a large knitting-needle, and in this form it might be inserted into the rung of a chair, for example. You did not take to pieces all the chairs?"

"Certainly not; but we did better — we examined the rungs of every chair in the hotel, and, indeed, the jointings of every description of furniture, by the aid of a most powerful microscope. Had there been any traces of recent disturbance we should not have failed to detect it instantly.[h] A single grain of gimlet-dust,[i] for example, would have been as obvious as an apple. Any disorder in the glueing — any unusual gaping in the joints — would have sufficed to insure detection."

"I presume[j] you looked to the mirrors, between the boards and the plates, and you probed the beds and the bed-clothes, as well as the curtains and carpets."

"That of course; and when we had absolutely completed every particle of the furniture in this way, then we examined the house itself. We divided its entire surface into compartments, which we numbered, so that none might be missed; then we scrutinized each individual square inch throughout the premises, including the two houses immediately adjoining, with the microscope, as before."

"The two houses adjoining!" I exclaimed; "you must have had a great deal of trouble."

"We had; but the reward offered is prodigious."

"You include the *grounds* about the houses?"

"All the grounds are paved with brick. They gave us comparatively little trouble. We examined the moss between the bricks, and found it undisturbed."[k]

"You looked among D——'s papers, of course, and into the books of the library?"

---

h *instanter. (A)*
i gimlet-dust, or saw-dust, *(A)*
j "I presume/"Of course *(A)*
k *After this are two additional paragraphs:*

"And the roofs?"

"We surveyed every inch of the external surface, and probed carefully beneath every tile." *(A)*

"Certainly; we opened every package and parcel; we not only opened every book, but we turned over every leaf in each volume, not contenting ourselves with a mere shake, according to the fashion of some of our police officers.[9] We also measured the thickness of every book-*cover,* with the most accurate admeasurement, and applied to each[l] the most jealous scrutiny of the microscope. Had any of the bindings been recently meddled with, it would have been utterly impossible that the fact should have escaped observation. Some five or six volumes, just from the hands of the binder, we carefully probed, longitudinally, with the needles."

"You explored the floors beneath the carpets?"

"Beyond doubt. We removed every carpet, and examined the boards with the microscope."

"And the paper on the walls?"

"Yes."

"You looked into the cellars?"

"We did."[m]

"Then," I said, "you have been making a miscalculation, and the letter is *not* upon the premises, as you suppose."

"I fear you are right there," said the Prefect. "And now, Dupin, what would you advise me to do?"

"To make a thorough re-search of the premises."

"That is absolutely needless," replied G——. "I am not more sure that I breathe than I am that the letter is not at the Hotel."

"I have no better advice to give you," said Dupin. "You have, of course, an accurate description of the letter?"

"Oh yes!" — And here the Prefect, producing a memorandum-book, proceeded to read aloud a minute account of the internal, and especially of the external appearance of the missing document. Soon after finishing the perusal of this description, he took his departure, more entirely depressed in spirits than I had ever known the good gentleman before.

In about a month afterwards he paid us another visit, and found us occupied very nearly as before. He took a pipe and a chair and entered into some ordinary conversation. At length I said, —

---

l them *(A)*
m "We did."/"We did; and, as time and labour were no objects, we dug up every one of them to the depth of four feet." *(A)*

"Well, but G——, what of the purloined letter? I presume you have at last made up your mind that there is no such thing as overreaching the Minister?"

"Confound him, say I — yes; I made the re-examination, however, as Dupin suggested — but it was all labor lost, as I knew it would be."

"How much was the reward offered, did you say?" asked Dupin.

"Why, a very great deal — a *very* liberal reward — I don't like to say how much, precisely; but one thing I *will* say, that I wouldn't mind giving my individual check for fifty thousand francs to any one who could obtain me that letter. The fact is, it is becoming of more and more importance every day; and the reward has been lately doubled. If it were trebled, however, I could do no more than I have done."

"Why, yes," said Dupin, drawlingly, between the whiffs[n] of his meerschaum, "I really — think, G——, you have not exerted yourself — to the utmost in this matter. You might — do a little more, I think, eh?"

"How? — in what way?"

"Why — puff, puff — you might — puff, puff — employ counsel in the matter, eh? — puff, puff, puff. Do you remember the story they tell of Abernethy?"

"No; hang Abernethy!"

"To be sure! hang him and welcome. But, once upon a time, a certain rich miser conceived the design of spunging upon this Abernethy for a medical opinion.[10] Getting up, for this purpose, an ordinary conversation in a private company, he insinuated his case to the physician, as that of an imaginary individual.

" 'We will suppose,' said the miser, 'that his symptoms are such and such; now, doctor, what would *you* have directed him to take?'

" 'Take!' said Abernethy, 'why, take *advice,* to be sure.' "

"But," said the Prefect, a little discomposed, "*I* am *perfectly* willing to take advice, and to pay for it. I would *really* give fifty thousand francs[o] to any one who would aid me in the matter."

---

n which *(D) misprint*

o francs, every *centime* of it, *(A)*

"In that case," replied Dupin, opening a drawer, and producing a check-book, "you may as well fill me up a check for the amount mentioned. When you have signed it, I will hand you the letter."

I was astounded. The Prefect appeared absolutely thunderstricken. For some minutes he remained speechless and motionless, looking incredulously at my friend with open mouth, and eyes that seemed starting from their sockets; then, apparently recovering himself in some measure, he seized a pen, and after several pauses and vacant stares, finally filled up and signed a check for fifty thousand francs, and handed it across the table to Dupin. The latter examined it carefully and deposited it in his pocket-book; then, unlocking an *escritoire,* took thence a letter and gave it to the Prefect. This functionary grasped it in a perfect agony of joy, opened it with a trembling hand, cast a rapid glance at its contents, and then, scrambling and struggling to the door, rushed at length unceremoniously from the room and from the house, without having uttered a[p] syllable since Dupin had requested him to fill up the check.

When he had gone, my friend entered into some explanations.

"The Parisian police," he said, "are exceedingly able in their way. They are persevering, ingenious, cunning, and thoroughly versed in the knowledge which their duties seem chiefly to demand. Thus, when G—— detailed to us his mode of searching the premises at the Hotel D——, I felt entire confidence in his having made a satisfactory investigation — so far as his labors extended."

"So far as his labors extended?" said I.

"Yes," said Dupin. "The measures adopted were not only the best of their kind, but carried out to absolute perfection. Had the letter been deposited within the range of their search, these fellows would, beyond a question, have found it."

I merely laughed — but he seemed quite serious in all that he said.

"The measures, then," he continued, "were good in their kind, and well executed; their defect lay in their being inapplicable to

p a solitary *(A)*

the case, and to the man. A certain set of highly ingenious resources are, with the Prefect, a sort of Procrustean bed,[11] to which he forcibly adapts his designs. But he perpetually errs by being too deep or too shallow, for the matter in hand; and many a schoolboy is a better reasoner than he. I knew one about eight years of age, whose success at guessing in the game of 'even and odd' attracted universal admiration. This game is simple, and is played with marbles. One player holds in his hand a number of these toys, and demands of another whether that number is even or odd. If the guess is right, the guesser wins one; if wrong, he loses one. The boy to whom I allude won all the marbles of the school. Of course he had some principle of guessing; and this lay in mere observation and admeasurement of the astuteness of his opponents. For example, an arrant simpleton is his opponent, and, holding up his closed hand, asks, 'are they even or odd?' Our schoolboy replies, 'odd,' and loses; but upon the second trial he wins, for he then says to himself, "the simpleton had them even upon the first trial, and his amount of cunning is just sufficient to make him have them odd upon the second; I will therefore guess odd; — he guesses odd, and wins. Now, with a simpleton a degree above the first, he would have reasoned thus: 'This fellow finds that in the first instance I guessed odd, and, in the second, he will propose to himself, upon the first impulse, a simple variation from even to odd, as did the first simpleton; but then a second thought will suggest that this is too simple a variation, and finally he will decide upon putting it even as before. I will therefore guess even;' — he guesses even, and wins. Now this mode of reasoning in the schoolboy, whom his fellows termed 'lucky,' — what, in its last analysis, is it?"

"It is merely," I said, "an identification of the reasoner's intellect with that of his opponent."

"It is," said Dupin; "and, upon inquiring of the boy by what means he effected the *thorough* identification in which his success consisted, I received answer as follows: 'When I wish to find out how wise, or how stupid, or how good, or how wicked is any one, or what are his thoughts at the moment, I fashion the expression of my face, as accurately as possible, in accordance with the expression of his, and then wait to see what thoughts or sentiments arise in my mind or heart, as if to match or correspond with the expression.'[12] This response of the schoolboy lies at the bottom of all the spurious profundity which has been attributed to Rochefoucault,[q] to La Bruyère,[r] to Machiavelli, and to Campanella."[13]

"And the identification," I said, "of the reasoner's intellect with that of his opponent, depends, if I understand you aright, upon the accuracy with which the opponent's intellect is admeasured."

"For its practical value it depends upon this," replied Dupin; "and the Prefect and his cohort fail so frequently, first, by default of this identification, and, secondly, by ill-admeasurement, or rather through non-admeasurement, of the intellect with which they are engaged. They consider only their *own* ideas of ingenuity; and, in searching for anything hidden, advert only to the modes in which *they* would have hidden it. They are right in this much — that their own ingenuity is a faithful representative of that of *the mass;* but when the cunning of the individual felon is diverse in character from their own, the felon foils them, of course. This always happens when it is above their own, and very usually when it is below. They have no variation of principle in their investigations; at best, when urged by some unusual emergency — by some extraordinary reward — they extend or exaggerate their old modes of *practice,* without touching their principles. What, for example, in this case of D——, has been done to vary the principle of action? What is all this boring, and probing, and sounding, and scrutinizing with the microscope, and dividing the surface of the building into registered square inches — what is it all but an exaggeration *of the application* of the one principle or set of principles of search, which are based upon the one set of notions regarding human ingenuity, to which the Prefect, in the long routine of his duty, has been accustomed? Do you not see he has taken it for granted that *all* men proceed to conceal a letter, — not exactly in a gimlet-hole bored in a chair-leg — but, at least, in *some* out-of-the-way hole or corner suggested by the same tenor of thought which would urge a man to secrete a letter in a gimlet-hole bored in a chair-leg? And do you not see also, that such *recherchés*[s]

q *In all texts* *editorially*
r Bougive, *(A, B, C, D) corrected*
s *recherches (A)*

nooks for concealment are adapted only for ordinary occasions, and would be adopted only by ordinary intellects; for, in all cases of concealment, a disposal of the article concealed — a disposal of it in this *recherché* manner, — is, in the very first instance, [t]presumable and presumed;[t] and thus its discovery depends, not at all upon the acumen, but altogether upon the mere care, patience, and determination of the seekers; and where the case is of importance — or, what amounts to the same thing in the policial eyes, when the reward is of magnitude, — the qualities in question have *never* been known to fail. You will now understand what I meant in suggesting that, had the purloined letter been hidden any where within the limits of the Prefect's examination — in other words, had the principle of its concealment been comprehended within the principles of the Prefect — its discovery would have been a matter altogether beyond question. This functionary, however, has been thoroughly mystified; and the remote source of his defeat lies in the supposition that the Minister is a fool, because he has acquired renown as a poet. All fools are poets; this the Prefect *feels;*[14] and he is merely guilty of a *non distributio medii*[15] in thence inferring that all poets are fools."

"But is this really the poet?" I asked. "There are two brothers, I know; and both have attained reputation in letters. The Minister I believe has written learnedly on the Differential Calculus. He is a mathematician, and no poet."

"You are mistaken; I know him well; he is both. As poet *and* mathematician, he would reason well;[u] as mere mathematician, he could not have reasoned at all, and thus would have been at the mercy of the Prefect."

"You surprise me," I said, "by these opinions, which have been contradicted by the voice of the world. You do not mean to set at naught the well-digested idea of centuries. The mathematical reason has long been[v] regarded as *the* reason *par excellence*."

"'*Il y a à parier*,'[w]" replied Dupin, quoting from Chamfort, "'*que toute idée publique, toute convention reçue, est une sottise,*

t . . . t presumed and presumable; *(A)*
u well; as poet, profoundly; *(A)*
v long been/been long *(A)*
w *pariër,' (A, B, C, D) accent deleted editorially*

car elle a convenu[x] *au plus grand nombre.*[y]'[16] The mathematicians, I grant you, have done their best to promulgate the popular error to which you allude, and which is none the less an error for its promulgation as truth. With an art worthy a better cause, for example, they have insinuated the term 'analysis' into application to algebra. The French are the originators of this particular deception; but if a term is of any importance — if words derive any value from applicability — then 'analysis' conveys 'algebra' about as much as, in Latin, *'ambitus'* implies 'ambition,' *'religio'* 'religion,' or *'homines honesti,'* a set of *honorable* men."[17]

"You have a quarrel on hand, I see," said I, "with some of the algebraists of Paris; but proceed."[18]

"I dispute the availability, and thus the value, of that reason which is cultivated in any especial form other than the abstractly logical. I dispute, in particular, the reason educed by mathematical study. The mathematics are the science of form and quantity; mathematical reasoning is merely logic applied to observation upon form and quantity. The great error lies in supposing that even the truths of what is called *pure* algebra, are abstract or general truths. And this error is so egregious that I am confounded at the universality with which it has been received. Mathematical axioms are *not* axioms of general truth. What is true of *relation* — of form and quantity — is often grossly false in regard to morals, for example. In this latter science it is very usually *un*true that the aggregated parts are equal to the whole. In chemistry also the axiom fails. In the consideration of motive it fails; for two motives, each of a given value, have not, necessarily, a value when united, equal to the sum of their values apart. There are numerous other mathematical truths which are only truths within the limits of *relation*. But the mathematician argues, from his *finite truths*, through habit, as if they were of an absolutely general applicability — as the world indeed imagines them to be. Bryant, in his very learned 'Mythology,' mentions an analogous source of error, when he says that 'although the Pagan fables are not believed, yet we forget ourselves continually, and make inferences from them

x *convenue (A, B, C, D) corrected editorially*

y *This sentence not italicized (A)*

as existing realities.'[19] With the algebraists,[z] however, who are Pagans themselves, the 'Pagan fables' *are* believed, and the inferences are made, not so much through lapse of memory, as through an unaccountable addling of the brains. In short, I never yet encountered the mere mathematician who could be trusted out of equal roots, or one who did not clandestinely hold it as a point of his faith that x^2+px was absolutely and unconditionally equal to q. Say to one of these gentlemen, by way of experiment, if you please, that you believe occasions may occur where x^2+px is *not* altogether equal to q, and, having made him understand what you mean, get out of his reach as speedily as convenient, for, beyond doubt, he will endeavor to knock you down.

"I mean to say," continued Dupin, while I merely laughed at his last observations, "that if the Minister had been no more than a mathematician, the Prefect would have been under no necessity of giving me this check.[a] I knew him, however, as both mathematician and poet, and my measures were adapted to his capacity, with reference to the circumstances by which he was surrounded. I knew him as a courtier, too, and as a bold *intriguant*. Such a man, I considered, could not fail to be aware of the ordinary policial modes of action. He could not have failed to anticipate — and events have proved that he did not fail to anticipate — the waylayings to which he was subjected. He must have foreseen, I reflected, the secret investigations of his premises. His frequent absences from home at night, which were hailed by the Prefect as certain aids to his success, I regarded only as *ruses*, to afford opportunity for thorough search to the police, and thus the sooner to impress them with the conviction to which G——, in fact, did finally arrive — the conviction that the letter was not upon the premises. I felt, also, that the whole train of thought, which I was at some pains in detailing to you just now, concerning the invariable principle of policial action in searches for articles concealed — I felt that this whole train of thought would necessarily pass through the mind of the Minister. It would imperatively lead him to despise all the ordinary *nooks* of concealment. *He* could not, I

z algebraist, *(A)*
a *After this* Had he been no more than a poet, I think it probable that he would have foiled us all. *(A)*

reflected, be so weak as not to see that the most intricate and remote recess of his hotel would be as open as his commonest closets to the eyes, to the probes, to the gimlets, and to the microscopes of the Prefect. I saw, in fine, that he would be driven, as a matter of course, to *simplicity,* if not deliberately induced to it as a matter of choice. You will remember, perhaps, how desperately the Prefect laughed when I suggested, upon our first interview, that it was just possible this mystery troubled him so much on account of its being so *very* self-evident."

"Yes," said I, "I remember his merriment well. I really thought he would have fallen into convulsions."

"The material world," continued Dupin, "abounds with very strict analogies to the immaterial; and thus some color of truth has been given to the rhetorical dogma, that metaphor, or simile, may be made to strengthen an argument, as well as to embellish a description. The principle of the *vis inertiæ,*[20] for example,[b] seems to be identical in physics and metaphysics. It is not more true in the former, that a large body is with more difficulty set in motion than a smaller one, and that its subsequent *momentum*[c] is commensurate with this difficulty, than it is, in the latter, that intellects of the vaster capacity, while more forcible, more constant, and more eventful in their movements than those of inferior grade, are yet the less readily moved, and more embarrassed and full of hesitation in the first few steps of their progress. Again: have you ever noticed which of the street signs, over the shop-doors, are the most attractive of attention?"

"I have never given the matter a thought," I said.

"There is a game of puzzles," he resumed, "which is played upon a map. One party playing requires another to find a given word — the name of town, river, state or empire — any word, in short, upon the motley and perplexed surface of the chart. A novice in the game generally seeks to embarrass his opponents by giving them the most minutely lettered names; but the adept selects such words as stretch, in large characters, from one end of the chart to the other. These, like the over-largely lettered signs

b example, with the amount of *momentum* proportionate with it and consequent upon it, *(A)*
c *impetus (A)*

and placards of the street, escape observation by dint of being excessively obvious; and here the physical oversight is precisely analogous with the moral inapprehension by which the intellect suffers to pass unnoticed those considerations which are too obtrusively and too palpably self-evident. But this is a point, it appears, somewhat above or beneath the understanding of the Prefect. He never once thought it probable, or possible, that the Minister had deposited the letter immediately beneath the nose of the whole world, by way of best preventing any portion of that world from perceiving it.[21]

"But the more I reflected upon the daring, dashing, and discriminating ingenuity of D——; upon the fact that the document must always have been *at hand,* if he intended to use it to good purpose; and upon the decisive evidence, obtained by the Prefect, that it was not hidden within the limits of that dignitary's ordinary search – the more satisfied I became that, to conceal this letter, the Minister had resorted to the comprehensive and sagacious expedient of not attempting to conceal it at all.

"Full of these ideas, I prepared myself with a pair of green spectacles,[22] and called one fine morning, quite by accident, at the Ministerial hotel. I found D—— at home, yawning, lounging, and dawdling, as usual, and pretending to be in the last extremity of *ennui.* He is, perhaps, the most really energetic human being now alive – but that is only when nobody sees him.

"To be even with him, I complained of my weak eyes, and lamented the necessity of the spectacles, under cover of which I cautiously and thoroughly surveyed the[d] apartment, while seemingly intent only upon the conversation of my host.

"I paid especial attention to a large writing-table near which he sat, and upon which lay confusedly, some miscellaneous letters and other papers, with one or two musical instruments and a few books. Here, however, after a long and very deliberate scrutiny, I saw nothing to excite particular suspicion.

"At length my eyes, in going the circuit of the room, fell upon a trumpery fillagree card-rack of pasteboard, that hung dangling by a dirty blue ribbon[e] from a little brass knob just beneath the

d the whole *(A, B, D)*   e riband, *(A)*

middle of the mantel-piece. In this rack, which had three or four compartments, were five or six visiting cards and a solitary letter. This last was much soiled and crumpled. It was torn nearly in two, across the middle — as if a design, in the first instance, to tear it entirely up as worthless, had been altered, or stayed, in the second. It had a large black seal, bearing the D—— cipher *very* conspicuously, and was addressed, in a diminutive female hand, to D——, the minister, himself. It was thrust carelessly, and even, as it seemed, contemptuously, into one of the upper[f] divisions of the rack.

"No sooner had I glanced at this letter, than I concluded it to be that of which I was in search. To be sure, it was, to all appearance, radically different from the one of which the Prefect had read us so minute a description. Here the seal was large and black, with the D—— cipher; there it was small and red, with the ducal arms of the S—— family. Here, the address, to the Minister, was diminutive and feminine; there the superscription, to a certain royal personage, was markedly bold and decided; the size alone formed a point of correspondence. But, then, the *radicalness* of these differences, which was excessive; the dirt; the soiled and torn condition of the paper, so inconsistent with the *true* methodical habits of D——, and so suggestive of a design to delude the beholder into an idea of the worthlessness of the document; these things, together with the hyperobtrusive situation of this document, full in the view of every visiter, and thus exactly in accordance with the conclusions to which I had previously arrived; these things, I say, were strongly corroborative of suspicion, in one who came with the intention to suspect.

"I protracted my visit as long as possible, and, while I maintained a most animated discussion with the Minister, on[g] a topic which I knew well had never failed to interest and excite him, I kept my attention really riveted upon the letter. In this examination, I committed to memory its external appearance and arrangement in the rack; and also fell, at length, upon a discovery which set at rest whatever trivial doubt I might have entertained. In scrutinizing the edges of the paper, I observed them to be more

f uppermost *(A, B, D)* g upon *(A, B, D)*

chafed than seemed necessary. They presented the *broken* appearance which is manifested when a stiff paper, having been once folded and pressed with a folder, is refolded in a reversed direction, in the same creases or edges which had formed the original fold. This discovery was sufficient. It was clear to me that the letter had been turned, as a glove, inside out, re-directed, and re-sealed.[23] I bade the Minister good morning, and took my departure at once, leaving a gold snuff-box upon the table.

"The next morning I called for the snuff-box, when we resumed, quite eagerly, the conversation of the preceding day. While thus engaged, however, a loud report, as if of a pistol, was heard immediately beneath the windows of the hotel, and was succeeded by a series of fearful screams, and the shoutings of a[h] mob. D—— rushed to a casement, threw it open, and looked out. In the meantime, I stepped to the card-rack, took the letter, put it in my pocket, and replaced it by a *fac-simile,* [i](so far as regards externals,)[i] which I had carefully prepared at my lodgings;[j] imitating the D—— cipher, very readily, by means of a seal formed of bread.

"The disturbance in the street had been occasioned by the frantic behavior of a man with a musket. He had fired it among a crowd of women and children. It proved, however, to have been without ball, and the fellow was suffered to go his way as a lunatic or a drunkard. When he had gone, D—— came from the window, whither I had followed him immediately upon securing the object in view. Soon afterwards I bade him farewell. The pretended lunatic was a man in my own pay."

"But what purpose had you," I asked, "in replacing the letter by a *fac-simile?* Would it not have been better, at the first visit, to have seized it openly, and departed?"

"D——," replied Dupin, "is a desperate man, and a man of nerve. His hotel, too, is not without attendants devoted to his interests. Had I made the wild attempt you suggest, I might[k] never have left the Ministerial presence alive. The good people of Paris might[l] have heard of me no more. But I had an object apart from

h a terrified *(A, B, D)*
i . . . i *Omitted (A)*
j lodgings;/lodgings – *(A, B, D)*
k should *(A)*
l would *(A)*

these considerations. You know my political prepossessions. In this matter, I act as a partisan of the lady concerned. For eighteen months the Minister has had her in his power. She has now him in hers;[m] since, being unaware that the letter is not in his possession, he will proceed with his exactions as if it was. Thus will he inevitably commit himself, at once, to his political destruction. His downfall, too, will not be more precipitate than awkward. It is all very well to talk about the *facilis descensus Averni;*[24] but in all kinds of climbing, as Catalani[n] said of singing, it is far more easy to get up than to come down.[25] In the present instance I have no sympathy — at least no pity — for him who descends. He is that *monstrum horrendum,*[26] an unprincipled man of genius. I confess, however, that I should like very well to know the precise character of his thoughts, when, being defied by her whom the Prefect terms 'a certain personage,' he is reduced to opening the letter which I left for him in the card-rack."

"How? did you put any thing particular in it?"

"Why — it did not seem altogether right to leave the interior blank — that would have been insulting. D——,[o] at Vienna once, did me an evil turn, which I told him, quite good-humoredly, that I should remember. So, as I knew he would feel some curiosity in regard to the identity of the person who had outwitted him, I thought it a pity not to give him a clue. He is well acquainted with my MS., and I just copied into the middle of the blank sheet the words —

> —— Un[p] dessein si funeste,
> S'il n'est digne d'Atrée, est digne de Thyeste.

They are to be found in Crébillon's 'Atrée.' "[27]

NOTES

Motto: The Latin quotation ascribed to Seneca has not been located. Poe used it first in the 1843 version of "The Murders in the Rue Morgue," near the end of the tale (see variants on p. 568), but omitted it in later texts. It means "Nothing is more hateful to wisdom than too much cunning." Compare Dupin's

m hers;/hers — *(A, B, D)*
n Catalini *(A) misprint*
o To be sure, D———, *(A)*
p —— Un/" '—— ——Un *(B, D)*

comment: "The Parisian police, so much extolled for *acumen,* are cunning but no more" ("Murders," p. 545).

1. A meerschaum pipe is also mentioned in "The Light-House."

2. Dupin lived up three flights of stairs, on what we call the fourth floor. The name of the street is imaginary, as are a number of the street names in Poe's other Dupin stories.

3. The chief of police in Paris from 1831 to 1836 was Henri-Joseph Gisquet, who died in February 1866. See note 31 to "Murders."

4. Compare *Politian,* II, 3–4, "I shall die, Castiglione, I shall die... of laughing!"

5. Hôtel means mansion or town residence; the word is capitalized later, when used in connection with the owner's name.

6. Compare getting rid of the servants in "The Cask of Amontillado," at n. 7.

7. See *Midsummer Night's Dream,* V, i, 7–8, "The lunatic, the lover, and the poet/Are of imagination all compact."

8. The method of search described may come from some account of Napoleon's detective Vidocq. See "Murders," n. 28.

9. In a letter of August 28, 1849, Poe instructed Mrs. Clemm how to excuse the loss of a drawing of Elmira Shelton: "Just copy the following words in your letter: I... cannot find it anywhere. I took down all the books and shook them one by one."

10. The great British surgeon, John Abernethy (1764–1831) was very gruff, but Dupin's story is told about another surgeon, Sir Isaac Pennington (1745–1817), at p. 31 of *Nuts to Crack* (Philadelphia, 1835), a jest book Poe reviewed in the *Southern Literary Messenger,* December 1835.

11. Procrustean bed – rigorous, ruthless, and arbitrary limits – derived from Procrustes, a legendary Attic robber, slain by Theseus, who fitted his victims to a bed by stretching the short and cutting the feet off the tall.

12. The system of mind reading used by the schoolboy has long been attributed to Tommaso Campanella. An account of how he uncovered his inquisitor's thoughts appears in the *Voyage to the Moon* of Cyrano de Bergerac (1619–1655), a work referred to in Poe's "Hans Phaall." [S. L. Varnado, in *Poe Newsletter,* October 1968, quotes a description by Edmund Burke of Campanella's system.] Horace Binney Wallace, in *Stanley* (1838), a book Poe drew on frequently, said (II, 242):

> It was remarked by the ingenious Campanella that when he wished to discover the leading characteristics of any one whom he saw, he arranged his features into a similitude with theirs and then observed what emotions rose within his heart to *play up,* as it were, to that expression of countenance; in the same manner, if we dispose our interests, and wishes, which may be

called the features of feeling, into a conformity with those of others, we shall find that their thoughts and counsels start naturally up in our mind.

"The Duc de L'Omelette" contains references to its hero's use of physiognomy; see notes 2 and 27 on that tale.

13. Poe's spelling (Rochefoucault) for François de la Rochefoucauld (1630–1680) is found in the first edition of his maxims listed in the British Museum Catalogue as carrying the author's name on the title page: *Reflexiones ou Sentences et Maximes morales de Monsieur de la Rochefoucault* ... (Amsterdam, 1705); in Isaac D'Israeli's *Curiosities of Literature,* so frequently used by Poe; and in *The Duke de la Rochefoucault's Maxims and Moral Reflections* (New York: G. & C. Carvill, 1835), which was apparently based on an "improved edition" (with the same spelling) issued in Edinburgh in 1796. "La Bougive," which I have emended to La Bruyère, is undoubtedly a printer's error, from a misreading of Poe's manuscript. Poe spelled the name correctly in crediting the motto for "The Man of the Crowd" and in his review of Longstreet's *Georgia Scenes* (*SLM,* March 1836), where he also mentioned Rochefoucault. Machiavelli was mentioned in Satanic company in "Bon-Bon," along with Rochefoucault and Seneca in the introduction to "Pinakidia" (*SLM,* August 1836, reworked in "Marginalia," number 46, *Democratic Review,* December 1844, p. 581); with Campanella was represented on the bookshelves of the House of Usher (*Burton's Magazine,* September 1839); and with Rochefoucault was mentioned in a review of *The Canons of Good Breeding* (*Burton's,* November 1839).

14. In "Lionizing" we read that "Sir Positive Paradox ... observed that all fools were philosophers, and that all philosophers were fools."

15. *Non distributio medii* – the fallacy of the undistributed middle – is ignoring the fact that if all A's are B's, all B's may not necessarily be A's.

16. Poe quotes from the French cynic Sébastien-Roch Nicolas, called Chamfort (1740–1794), *Maximes et Pensées,* II, 42: "It is safe to wager that every idea that is public property, every accepted convention, is a bit of stupidity, for it has suited the majority." Poe had already used the French quotation in reviewing J. P. Robertson's *Solomon Seesaw* in *Burton's,* September 1839, *Writings of Charles Sprague* in *Graham's,* May 1841, and Longfellow's *Ballads and Other Poems* in *Graham's,* March 1842; he used it again later in "Marginalia," number 250 (*SLM,* June 1849, p. 338).

17. In Classical Latin *ambitus* means seeking office, *religio* is superstition, and *homines honesti* is Cicero's term for men of his party. Poe also referred to *religio* in the first version of "Metzengerstein" and in "Marginalia," number 176 (*Graham's,* November 1846, p. 246).

18. J. J. Cohane, in his book list, April 1959 (Item 86, Catalogue 30), pointed out that Poe's source for Dupin's argument in the following paragraph is Horace Binney Wallace's novel *Stanley* (cited in n. 12 above), I, 206–208:

> As a means ... of cultivating the intellect ... I consider mathematics as a study of little value as compared with moral logic ... The axioms of mathematics are not axioms of general truth; they are derived from the consideration

> of form and quantity, and it does not follow that what is true of form and quantity is true of moral principles or of human motives... In morals, things are considered and compared by their categories or qualities, whereof each thing has many, according to the view and purpose in reference to which the thing is looked at; what is affirmed of a thing in contemplation of one category is not true of it in respect of another, nor true in respect of that category in reference to all considerations... Thus, the position, that two things being equal to a third are equal to one another, may be true universally if we define 'equal' with absolute strictness, but, in use, will constantly lead to the logical fallacy of an undistributed middle term; and if you will examine the logic of a mathematician you will find the error of a non-distributed medii very often committed. Another mathematical axiom which is not true in the scope of general reason is, that all the parts taken together are equal to the whole. This is not always true of physical science, and is generally false in morals. It is not true in chymical combination, and the instinct of a chymist's mind would be to deny the axiom; it is not necessarily true that if two motives separately have given values, these motives united will have a value equal to their sum... I might name to you many other principles of mathematical science which are not true beyond the boundaries of that science. In truth, mathematics is a composite science... and not a fundamental exhibition of reason; it is *logic applied to the sciences of form and quantity*... There is danger that the mathematician will mistake the axioms of his science for the principles of reason, and will apply universally what is true only of a particular system.

19. The remark of Jacob Bryant comes from *A New System of Antient Mythology* (Third Edition, 1807), II, 173. Poe referred to it in "Pinakidia," number 70 (SLM, August 1836, p. 577), and used it again in *Eureka*.

20. *Vis inertiae* is the force of inertia.

21. Compare "Just as the moderately-sized shop-signs are better adapted to their object than those which are Brobdignagian, so, in at least three cases out of five, is a fact or a reason overlooked solely on account of being excessively obvious. It is almost impossible to see a thing that is immediately beneath one's nose." ("Does the Drama of the Day Deserve Support?" in *Evening Mirror,* January 9, and *Weekly Mirror,* January 18, 1845.)

22. Green spectacles are mentioned also in "The Folio Club," "Bon-Bon," and "The Mystery of Marie Rogêt."

23. The letter was on an old-fashioned four-page sheet, with text on the first and address on the last page, and so could be turned inside out. The Minister erred in using his own seal.

24. *Facilis descensus Averno* – "The descent to Hades is easy" – comes from Vergil's *Æneid,* VI, 126. Poe used the Latin words earlier in a criticism of Miss Sedgwick's *Tales and Sketches* in the *Southern Literary Messenger,* January 1836.

25. Where the remark of Angelica Catalani (1779–1849), Italian opera star and teacher, is recorded is not known. Poe used her name punningly in "A Decided Loss," p. 57.

26. "A terrifying monster" is from the *Æneid,* III, 658, and is also quoted in "The System of Doctor Tarr and Professor Fether."

27. The quotation, "So baleful a plan, if unworthy of Atreus, is worthy of Thyestes," comes from *Atrée et Thyeste* (1707), V, iv, 13–15, by Prosper-Jolyot de Crébillon (1674–1762). Poe had used it previously in a review of Thomas Campbell's *Life of Petrarch* in *Graham's Magazine,* September 1841, and earlier had quoted Crébillon's *Xerxes* in the motto to "Epimanes," and referred to the play in "Murders in the Rue Morgue." A brief comment on Crébillon is quoted in "Pinakidia," number 129 (*SLM* August 1836, p. 580) and repeated in "Marginalia," number 24 (*Democratic Review,* November 1844, p. 488).

THE SYSTEM OF DOCTOR TARR AND PROFESSOR FETHER

This story seems to me one of Poe's best humorous pieces. Many people still find it laughable. There is not a great deal of printed discussion, and that by no means all favorable. Woodberry called it an "absurd madhouse grotesque"; A. H. Quinn thought it clever but "not important," and Wagenknecht felt that Poe's "comic use of lunacy . . . comes pretty close to eighteenth-century brutality."* But it has found enthusiastic admirers, one of whom remarked:

> Half a dozen . . . sketches . . . give Poe a real claim as an American humorist . . . "The System of Dr. Tarr and Professor Fether" is so unique in conception that it will live as long as "The Jumping Frog" [of Mark Twain]. On that one story alone Poe's reputation as a humorist must stand secure.†

The originality lies chiefly in having the head of an insane asylum losing his *reason* but not his *wits,* and leading his patients into mischief. These patients are not wretched or really pitiable — but amiable folk whose harmless fantasies make them happier than many normal people. There is obviously (as in most of Poe's stories) an undercurrent of serious thought, but it is not clinical. One of my students, Carole Yasner, compared the remark in "Eleonora" that "the question is not yet settled whether madness

* Woodberry, *Life,* II, 162; Quinn, *Poe,* p. 470; Wagenknecht, *Edgar Allan Poe,* p. 57. The story was dramatized for the famous Grand Guignol Theatre in Paris as one of pure horror by André de Lorde, in 1903.

† From an anonymous essay, "Poe as a Humorist," reprinted from the *Denver Republican* in the *Philadelphia Evening Telegraph,* July 6, 1911, and referred to in Phillips, *Poe the Man,* II, 1067.

is or is not the loftiest intelligence." In "Marginalia," number 247 (*SLM*, June 1849, p. 337), Poe records a fancy that "any individual gifted, or rather accursed, with an intellect *very* far superior to that of his race . . . would be considered a madman." The narrator is more of a fool than the madmen he encounters at the asylum.

Among Poe's sources for his tale are two articles by N. P. Willis, based on his visit to an asylum in Palermo, Sicily, on June 28, 1832. Immediately after the visit he described it in a letter to the *New-York Mirror*, and later wrote a rather touching story called "The Madhouse of Palermo" based on his earlier account.‡ In his letter Willis wrote:

> PALERMO. June 28. – Two of the best-conducted lunatic asylums in the world are in the kingdom of Naples – one at Aversa, near Capua, and the other at Palermo. The latter is managed by a whimsical Sicilian baron, who has devoted his time and fortune to it, and with the assistance of the government, has carried it to great extent and perfection . . . [This] hospital stands in an airy situation in the lovely neighborhood of Palermo. We were received by a porter in a respectable livery, who introduced us immediately to the old baron – a kind-looking man, rather advanced beyond middle life, of manners singularly genteel and prepossessing. *"Je suis le premier fou,"* said he, throwing his arms out, as he bowed on our entrance. We stood in an open court, surrounded with porticoes lined with stone seats. On one of them lay a fat, indolent-looking man, in clean gray clothes, talking to himself with great apparent satisfaction. He smiled at the baron as he passed . . . (*Prose Works*, p. 103.)

Taken on a tour of the establishment, Willis saw

> the kitchen . . . occupied by eight or ten people all at work, and all, the baron assured us, *mad*. One man, of about forty, was broiling a steak with the gravest attention. Another, who had been furious till employment was given him, was chopping meat with violent industry in a large wooden bowl. Two or three girls were about, obeying the little orders of a middle-aged man, occupied with several messes cooking on a patent stove . . . We passed from the kitchen into an open court, curiously paved, and ornamented with Chinese grottoes, artificial rocks, trees, cottages, and fountains . . . Everything about us . . . he assured us, was the work of his patients. They had paved the court, built the grottoes and cottages, and painted the walls, under his direction . . . The secret of his whole system, he said, was employment and constant kindness. He had usually about one hundred

‡ The letter was first printed in the *New-York Mirror*, November 23, 1833, as number LXIX of "First Impressions of Europe," and was collected in *Pencillings by the Way* (1835) as Letter LXIX. The story (of which I have found no prior periodical publication) was published in *Inklings of Adventure* (1836), a book Poe reviewed in the *Southern Literary Messenger* of August 1836, naming the story. The texts of the letter and story are available in Willis's *Prose Works* (1845), pp. 103 and 457.

and fifty patients, and he dismissed upon an average two thirds of them quite recovered.

We went into the apartment of the women. These, he said, were his worst subjects. In the first room sat eight or ten employed in spinning, while one infuriated creature, not more than thirty, but quite gray, was walking up and down the floor, talking and gesticulating with the greatest violence. A young girl of sixteen, an attendant, had entered into her humor, and with her arm put affectionately round her waist, assented to everything she said, and called her by every name of endearment while endeavoring to silence her.

We . . . went out into the court, where eight or ten women in gray gowns of the establishment were walking up and down, or sitting under the trees, lost in thought. (*Prose Works,* p. 104.)

[Another apartment] opened upon a pretty court, in which a fountain was playing, and against the columns of the portico sat some half dozen patients. A young man of eighteen, with a very pale, scholar-like face, was reading Ariosto. Near him, under the direction of an attendant, a fair, delicate girl, with a sadness in her soft blue eyes that might have been a study for a *mater dolorosa,* was cutting paste upon a board laid across her lap. She seemed scarcely conscious of what she was about . . . I bowed to her as we took our leave, and she returned it gracefully but coldly. The young man looked up from his book and smiled, the old man lying on the stone seat in the outer court rose up and followed us to the door, and we were bowed out by the baron and his gentle madmen as politely and kindly as if we were concluding a visit with a company of friends (p. 105).

The soothing system in the treatment of the mentally deranged was still something of a novelty, and must have been much discussed when Poe composed his story. Dickens took an interest in it, both in England and in America, where he visited and described asylums at South Boston, Massachusetts, and at Hartford, Connecticut.§ He tells us that at the South Boston establishment (opened for patients in 1839) the resident physician explained that his custom was to "evince a desire to show some confidence, and repose some trust, even in mad people." The distinguished visitor saw "an elderly female, in as many scraps of finery as Madge Wildfire herself . . . radiant with imaginary jewels," to whom the doctor introduced him as "the hostess of this mansion [which] . . . requires a great many attendants." He met other inmates in

§ *American Notes for General Circulation* (1842), chapters 3 and 5 in vol. I. Dickens' book as a source for Poe's tale was pointed out by Maxwell V. Z. W. Morton in *A Builder of the Beautiful* (1928), and independently noticed. For instance, Professor William Whipple, in *Nineteenth Century Fiction,* September 1954, referred to it, and suggested that Dickens himself is satirized in Poe's narrator — something Wagenknecht (*Edgar Allan Poe,* p. 244) mildly calls "far from proved," and I think absurd. Nor can I believe, like at least one academic commentator, that Poe's story satirizes phrenology!

similar fashion. "The rest . . . seemed to understand the joke perfectly (not only in this case, but in all the others, except their own), and to be highly amused by it . . . We left each of them in high good humor." Dickens tells how "Every patient sits down to dinner every day with a knife and fork . . . moral influence alone restrains the more violent among them from cutting the throats of the rest . . . For amusement, they walk, run, fish, paint, read, and ride out . . . in carriages." The visitor tells of the patients working on the farm and in the garden, and of the ladies' sewing circle. There was a weekly ball, in which "the doctor and his family, with all the nurses and attendants take . . . part. Dances and marches are performed . . . and . . . some gentleman or lady . . . obliges with a song; nor does it ever degenerate . . . into a screech or howl; wherein, I must confess, I should have thought the danger lay."

When Dickens visited Hartford, he met a patient, a "little prim old lady," who asked him questions about long past things as if contemporary, and explained, "*I* am an antediluvian, sir." This lady, however, acted oddly, occasionally giving a "skip, smirked and sidled down the gallery in a most extraordinary manner." He also met a man who had a scheme for recapturing New York for Queen Victoria; a love-sick musician who assured him he merely stayed in the asylum "for a whim"; and a lady who "heard voices in the air" but requested and obtained Dickens' autograph. "I very much questioned within myself," Dickens wrote (I, 176), "as I walked through the Insane Asylum, whether I should have known the attendants from the patients."

Maxwell Morton found something highly similar to part of Poe's plot in *Charles O'Malley,* by Charles Lever, a work Poe reviewed in *Graham's* for March 1842. This is "Mr. Sparks' Story," which is the thirty-second chapter of Lever's book.* Young Sparks, while visiting Wales, becomes infatuated with a beautiful young lady named Isabella, whom he sees at the Goat Inn in Barmouth, but of whom he can learn nothing after her departure. Three weeks later he encounters her in a sylvan spot, in a company of

* Poe does not allude to this story in his review, but quotes another from the eighty-fourth chapter, which Morton points out is utilized for one incident in "The System of Doctor Tarr and Professor Fether"; see n. 19, below.

ladies and gentlemen preparing for a picnic. They are presided over by one called "The General," who invites Sparks to join the party, but takes him aside, and explains it "is a kind of club, . . . where everyone assumes a certain character, and is bound to sustain it." (It is explained later that The General is "the famous Doctor Andrew Moorville, that had the great madhouse at Bangor," who gave "his patients every now and then a . . . country party" with numerous "servants" to watch over them.) As in Poe's story, there is a magnificent feast. But the guests are puzzling to the stupid Mr. Sparks. One man thinks himself a red Indian; a lady thinks she is an hourglass; Isabella, "driven mad by a card playing aunt," thinks her lover should be the ace of spades; and, when Sparks does not fall in with her fantasy, pulls his whiskers. Immediately:

> "Cuckoo, cuckoo," shouted one; "bow, wow, wow," roared another; "phiz," went a third; and in an instant, such a scene of commotion and riot ensued; plates, dishes . . . flew right and left; every one pitched into his neighbour with the most fearful cries, and hell itself seemed broke loose.

Sparks is rescued (by the guards, apparently), but not before one man, who thinks himself a tiger, bites his ear.

Poe has a few types of madmen not mentioned in the sources described, but all are conventional in literature; two come from Pope's *Rape of the Lock.* Although in October 1840 he corresponded with the celebrated alienist Dr. Pliny Earle (1809–1892), who was also a poet, no visit to an asylum by Poe can be assumed.† The names of his characters are typically French, and some of them are certainly amusingly appropriate.

Poe mentioned the tale as written but not yet published when writing to James Russell Lowell, May 28, 1844, and publication was further delayed for more than a year. The manuscript fortu-

† From Franklin B. Sanborn's *Memoirs of Pliny Earle, M.D.* (1898), pp. 147–149, I judge that Poe did not call on Earle at Frankford, Pennsylvania, where his patients were gently treated. The correspondence in October 1840 concerned some verses for the projected *Penn Magazine.* A review of Earle's *Visit to Thirteen Asylums* (1841) is described in *Graham's Magazine* for May 1841 as "crowded out" of its columns, but Poe had a kindly notice of his *Marathon and Other Poems* in the June issue, as well as in "A Chapter on Autography" in the issue of December 1841, and retrospectively mentioned his "very beautiful poetry" in a letter of June 28, 1849.

nately survives, and reveals that someone on the staff of *Graham's Magazine* canceled more than one hundred words. The deletions have all now been recorded — they were probably made by Charles J. Peterson, whose Victorian delicacy must amaze modern readers — and are included in the variants by permission of the Trustees of the Pierpont Morgan Library.

TEXTS

(A) Manuscript, before May 28, 1844; (A2) Changes made by an editor in the manuscript; *(B) Graham's Magazine* for November 1845 (27 [incorrectly numbered 28]: 193–200); *(C) Works* (1850), IV, 191–209.

The text used is Griswold's *(C)* with three obviously auctorial changes. The fairly extensive changes made by Graham's editor in the manuscript are designated by A2. They are distinguishable, even when mere cancellations, by the color of the ink. Only the *B* text accents château; in this respect it is followed in our text.

The roll manuscript is traced to the Stephen H. Wakeman Collection, acquired *en bloc* in 1909 by the first J. Pierpont Morgan. The original roll was about 270 inches long; it has been cut into 64 leaves, averaging 4 or 5 inches each. It is 3 13/16 inches wide. Paper and ink are faded. The manuscript is now bound in full red morocco binding. The original segments of the roll were probably approximately the same length as those in the other roll manuscripts. [We are indebted to J. Rigbie Turner, Assistant Curator of Autograph Manuscripts at the Pierpont Morgan Library, for a recent description of this manuscript.]

THE SYSTEM OF DOCTOR TARR AND PROFESSOR FETHER. [*C*]

During the autumn of 18—, while on a tour through the extreme Southern provinces of France, my route led me within a few miles of a certain *Maison de Santé,* or private Mad House, about which I had heard much, in Paris, from my medical friends. As I had never visited a place of the kind, I thought the opportunity too good to be lost; and so proposed to my travelling companion, (a gentleman with whom I had made casual acquaintance a few days before,) that we should turn aside, for an hour or so, and look through the establishment. To this he objected — pleading haste, in the first place, and, in the second, a very usual horror

---

Title: By Edgar A. Poe *in small print beneath the title (A);* The System of Dr. Tarr and Prof. Fether. *(B)*

at the sight of a lunatic. He begged me, however, not to let any mere courtesy towards[a] himself interfere with the gratification of my curiosity, and said that he would ride on leisurely, so that I might overtake him during the day, or, at all events, during the next. As he bade me good-by, I bethought me that there might be some difficulty in obtaining access to the premises, and mentioned my fears on this point. He replied that, in fact, unless I had personal knowledge of the superintendent, Monsieur Maillard,[1] or some credential in the way of a letter, a difficulty might be found to exist, as the regulations of these private mad-houses were more rigid than the public hospital laws. For himself, he added, he had, some years since, made the acquaintance of Maillard, and would so far assist me as to ride up to the door and introduce me; although his feelings on the subject of lunacy would not permit of his entering the house.

I thanked him, and, turning from the main-road, we entered a grass-grown by-path, which, in half an hour, nearly lost itself in a dense forest, clothing the base of a mountain. Through this dank and gloomy wood we rode some two miles, when the *Maison de Santé* came in view. It was a fantastic *château,* much dilapidated, and indeed scarcely tenantable through age and neglect. Its aspect inspired me with absolute dread, and, checking my horse, I half resolved to turn back. I soon, however, grew ashamed of my weakness, and proceeded.

As we rode up to the gate-way, I perceived it slightly open, and the visage of a man peering through. In an instant afterward,[b] this man came forth, accosted my companion by name, shook him cordially by the hand, and begged him to alight. It was Monsieur Maillard himself. He was a portly, fine-looking gentleman of the old school, with a polished manner, and a certain air of gravity, dignity, and authority which was very impressive.

My friend, having presented me, mentioned my desire to inspect the establishment, and received Monsieur Maillard's assurance that he would show me all attention, now took leave, and I saw him no more.

---

a toward<s> *(A)*; toward *(B)*   b afterwards *(A)*

When he had gone, the superintendent ushered me into a small and exceedingly[c] neat parlor, containing among other indications of refined taste, many books, drawings, pots of flowers, and musical instruments. A cheerful fire blazed upon the hearth. At a piano, singing an aria from Bellini,[2] sat a young and very beautiful woman, who, at my entrance, paused in her song, and received me with graceful courtesy. Her voice was low, and her whole manner subdued. I thought, too, that I perceived the traces of sorrow in her countenance, which was excessively, although to my taste, not unpleasingly pale. She was attired in deep mourning, and excited in my bosom a feeling of mingled respect, interest, and admiration.

I had heard, at Paris, that the institution of Monsieur Maillard was managed upon what is vulgarly termed the "system of soothing" — that all punishments were avoided — that even confinement was seldom resorted to — that the patients, while secretly watched, were left much apparent liberty, and that most of them were permitted to roam about the house and grounds, in the ordinary apparel of persons in right mind.

Keeping these impressions in view, I was cautious in what I said before the young lady; for I could not be sure that she was sane; and, in fact, there was a[d] certain restless brilliancy about her eyes which half led me to imagine she was not. I confined my remarks, therefore, to general topics, and to such as I thought would not be displeasing or exciting even to a lunatic. She replied in a perfectly rational manner to all that I said; and even her original observations were marked with the soundest good sense; but a long acquaintance with the metaphysics of *mania,* had taught me to put no faith in such evidence of sanity, and I continued to practice, throughout the interview, the caution with which I commenced it.

Presently a smart footman in livery brought in a tray with fruit, wine, and other refreshments, of which I partook, the lady soon afterwards leaving the room. As she departed I turned my eyes in an inquiring manner towards[e] my host.

---

c *excedingly (A)*
d ↑a↓ *(A)*
e toward<s> *(A);* toward *(B)*

"No," he said, "oh, no — a member of my family — my niece, and a most accomplished woman."

"I beg a thousand pardons for the suspicion," I replied, "but of course you will know how to excuse[f] me. The excellent administration of your affairs here is well understood in Paris, and I thought it just possible, you know —"

"Yes, yes — say no more — or rather it is myself who should thank you for the commendable prudence you have displayed. We seldom find so much of forethought in young men; and, more than once, some unhappy *contre-temps* has occurred in consequence of thoughtlessness on the part of our visitors. While my former system was in operation, and my patients were permitted the privilege of roaming to and fro at will, they were often aroused to a dangerous frenzy[g] by injudicious persons who called to inspect the house. Hence I was obliged to enforce a rigid system of exclusion; and none obtained access to the premises upon whose discretion I could not rely."

"While your *former* system was in operation!" I said, repeating his words — "do I understand you, then, to say that the 'soothing system' of which I have heard so much, is no longer in force?"

"It is now," he replied, "several weeks since we have concluded to renounce it forever."

"Indeed! you astonish me!"

"We found it, sir," he said, with a sigh, "absolutely necessary to return to the old usages. The *danger* of the soothing system was, at all times, appalling; and its advantages have been much over-rated. I believe, sir, that in this house it has been given a fair trial, if ever in any. We did every thing that rational humanity could suggest. I am sorry that you could not have paid us a visit at an earlier period, that you might have judged for yourself. But I presume you are conversant with the soothing practice — with its details."

"Not altogether. What I have heard has been at third or fourth hand."

"I may state the system then, in general terms, as one in which

---

f <pardon> ↑excuse↓ *(A)* g *phrenzy (A)*

the patients were[h] *ménagés*,[h′] humored. We contradicted *no* fancies which entered the brains of the mad. On the contrary, we not only indulged but encouraged them; and many of our most permanent cures have been thus effected. There is no argument which so touches the feeble reason of the madman as the *reductio*[i] *ad absurdum*. We have had men, for example, who fancied themselves chickens. The cure was, to insist upon the thing as a fact — to accuse the patient of stupidity in not sufficiently perceiving it to be a fact — and thus to refuse him any other diet for a week than that which properly appertains to a chicken. In this manner a little corn and gravel were made to perform wonders."

"But was this species of acquiescence[j] all?"

"By no means. We put much faith in amusements of a simple kind, such as music, dancing, gymnastic exercises generally, cards, certain classes of books, and so forth. We affected to treat each individual as if for some ordinary physical disorder; and the word 'lunacy' was never employed. A great point was to set each lunatic to guard the actions of all the others. To repose confidence in the understanding or discretion of a madman, is to gain him body and soul. In this way we were enabled to dispense with an expensive body of keepers."

"And you had no punishments of any kind?"

"None."

"And you never confined your patients?"

"Very rarely. Now and then, the malady of some individual growing to a crisis, or taking a sudden turn of fury, we conveyed him to a secret cell, lest his disorder should infect the rest, and there kept him until we could dismiss him to his friends — for with the raging maniac we have nothing to do. He is usually removed to the public hospitals."

"And you have now changed all this — and you think for the better?"

"Decidedly. The system had its disadvantages, and even its dangers. It is now, happily, exploded throughout all the *Maisons de Santé* of France."

---

h <are> ↑were↓ *(A)*
h′ *menagés (A, B, C)*
i *argumentum (A, B)*
j acquiesence *(B) misprint*

"I am very much surprised," I said, "at what you tell me; for I made sure that, at this moment, no other method of treatment for mania existed in any portion of the country."

"You are young yet, my friend," replied my host, "but the time will arrive when you will learn to judge for yourself of what is going on in the world, without trusting to the gossip of others. Believe nothing you hear, and only one half that you see. Now, about our *Maisons de Santé,* it is clear that some ignoramus has misled you. After dinner, however, when you have sufficiently recovered from the fatigue of your ride, I will be happy to take you over the house, and introduce to you a system which, in my opinion, and in that of every one who has witnessed its operation, is incomparably the most effectual as yet devised."

"Your own?" I inquired — "one of your own invention?"

"I am proud," he replied, "to acknowledge that it is — at least in some measure."

In this manner I conversed with Monsieur Maillard for an hour or two, during which he showed me the gardens and conservatories of the place.

[k]"I cannot let you see my patients," he said, "just at present. To a sensitive mind there is always more or less of the shocking in such exhibitions; and I do not wish to spoil your appetite for dinner. We will dine. I can give you some veal *à la St.*[l] *Menehoult,* with cauliflowers in *velouté* sauce — after that a glass of[m] *Clos de Vougeôt* — then your nerves will be sufficiently steadied."[3]

At six, dinner was announced; and my host conducted me into a large *salle à manger,* where a very numerous company were assembled — twenty-five or thirty in all. They were, apparently, people of rank — certainly of high breeding — although their habiliments, I thought, were extravagantly rich, partaking somewhat too much of the ostentatious finery of the *vieille*[n] *cour.*[4] I noticed that at least two-thirds of these guests were ladies; and some of the latter were by no means accoutred in what a Parisian would consider good taste at the present day. Many females, for example, whose age could not have been less than seventy, were

k *Not a new paragraph (A)*

l *Omitted (C) restored from A, B*

m *Omitted (B)*

n *vielle (A, B, C)*

bedecked with a profusion of jewelry, such as rings, bracelets, and ear-rings, and wore their bosoms and arms shamefully bare. I observed, too, that very few of the dresses were well made — or, at least, that very few of them fitted the wearers. In looking about, I discovered the interesting girl to whom Monsieur Maillard had presented me in the little parlor; but my surprise was great to see her wearing a hoop and farthingale, with high-heeled shoes, and a dirty cap of Brussels lace, so much too large for her that it gave her face a ridiculously diminutive expression. When I had first seen her, she was attired, most becomingly, in deep mourning. There was an air of oddity, in short, about the dress of the whole party, which, at first, caused me to recur to my original idea of the "soothing system," and to fancy that Monsieur Maillard had been willing to deceive me until after dinner, that I might experience no uncomfortable feelings during the repast, at finding myself dining with lunatics; but I remembered having been informed, in Paris, that the southern provincialists were a peculiarly eccentric people, with a vast number of antiquated notions; and then, too, upon conversing with several members of the company, my apprehensions were immediately and fully dispelled.

The dining-room, itself, although perhaps sufficiently comfortable, and of good dimensions, had nothing too much of elegance about it. For example, the floor was uncarpeted; in France however a carpet is frequently dispensed with. The windows, too, were without curtains; the shutters, being shut, were securely fastened with iron bars, applied diagonally, after the fashion of our ordinary shop-shutters. The apartment, I observed, formed, in itself, a wing of the *château,* and thus the windows were on three sides of the parallelogram;[o] the door being at the other. There were no less than ten windows in all.

The table was superbly set out. It was loaded with plate, and more than loaded with delicacies. The profusion was absolutely barbaric. There were meats enough to have feasted the Anakim.[5] Never, in all my life, had I witnessed so lavish, so wasteful an expenditure of the good things of life. There seemed very little taste, however, in the arrangements; and my eyes, accustomed to quiet

o parrallelogram; *(A)*

lights, were sadly offended by the prodigious glare of a multitude of wax candles, which, in silver *candelabra,* were deposited upon the table, and all about the room, wherever it was possible to find a place. There were several active servants in attendance; and, upon a large table, at the farther end of the apartment, were seated seven or eight people with fiddles, fifes, trombones, and a drum. These fellows annoyed me very much, at intervals, during the repast, by an infinite variety of noises, which were intended for music, and which appeared to afford much entertainment to all present, with the exception of myself.

Upon the whole, I could not help thinking that there was much of the *bizarre* about every thing I saw — but then the world is made up of all kinds of persons, with all modes of thought, and all sorts of conventional customs. I had [p]travelled, too, so[p] much as to be quite an adept in the *nil admirari;*[6] so I took my seat very coolly[q] at the right hand of my host, and, having an excellent appetite, did justice to the good cheer set before me.

The conversation, in the meantime, was spirited and general. The ladies, as usual, talked a great deal. I soon found that nearly all the company were well educated; and my host was a world of good-humored anecdote in himself. He seemed quite willing to speak of his position as superintendent of a *Maison de Santé;* and, indeed, the topic of lunacy was, much to my surprise, a favorite one with all present. A great many amusing stories were told, having reference to the *whims* of the patients.

"We had a fellow here once," said a fat little gentleman, who sat at my right — "a fellow that fancied himself a tea-pot; and, by the way, it is not especially singular how often this particular crotchet has entered the brain of the lunatic? There is scarcely an insane asylum in France which cannot supply a human tea-pot. *Our* gentleman was a Britannia-ware[r] tea-pot,[7] and was careful to polish himself every morning with buckskin and whiting."[s]

"And then," said a tall man, just opposite, "we had here, not long ago, a person who had taken it into his head that he was a

---

p . . . p travelled so *(A, B)*
q cooly *(A)*
r Britania-ware *(A)*
s whiting./whiting. <He held his left arm, generally, extended thus, at right angles from his body; this was the spout. His right rested a-kimbo upon the hip; this was the handle."> *(A2)*

donkey — which, allegorically speaking, you will say, was quite true. He was a troublesome patient; and we had much ado to keep him within bounds. For a long time he would eat nothing but thistles; but of this idea we soon cured him by insisting upon his eating nothing else. Then he was perpetually kicking out his heels — so — so —"

"Mr. De Kock![8] I will thank you to behave yourself!" here interrupted an old lady, who sat next to the speaker. "Please keep your feet to yourself! You have spoiled[t] my brocade![u] Is it necessary, pray, to illustrate a remark in so practical a style? Our friend, here, can surely comprehend you without all this. Upon my word, you are nearly as great a donkey as the poor unfortunate imagined himself. Your acting is very natural, as I live."

"Mille pardons! Mam'selle!"[v] replied Monsieur De Kock, thus addressed — "a thousand pardons! I had no intention of offending.[w] [x]Ma'mselle Laplace[9] — Monsieur De Kock will do himself the honor of taking wine with you."

[y]Here Monsieur De Kock bowed low, kissed his hand with much ceremony, and took wine with Ma'mselle Laplace.

"Allow me, *mon ami,*" now said Monsieur Maillard, addressing myself, "allow me to send you a morsel of this veal *à*[z] *la St. Menehoult* — you will find it particularly fine."

[a]At this instant three sturdy waiters had just succeeded in depositing safely upon the table an enormous dish, or trencher, containing what I supposed to be the *"monstrum, horrendum, informe, ingens, cui lumen ademptum."*[10] A closer scrutiny assured me, however, that it was only a small calf roasted whole, and set upon its knees, with an apple in its mouth, as is the English fashion of dressing a hare.

"Thank you, no," I replied; "to say the truth, I am not particularly partial to veal *à*[b] *la St.* — what is it? — for I do not find

---

t spoilt *(A)*

u brocade! <and broken my shins!> *(A2)*

v *Ma'mselle," (A);* ma'mselle!" *(B)*

w offending./<breaking your shins> ↑offending↓. *(A2)*

x *Before this sentence a new paragraph has:* <"Of this I am sure", cried our host, who seemed a man of much amiability. "Monsieur De Kock would never willingly have broken the shins of Ma'mselle Laplace.> *(A2)*

y *Not a new paragraph (A)*

z *a (C) accent added from A, B*

a *Not a new paragraph (A)*

b *a (C)*

that it altogether agrees with me. I will change my plate, however, and try some of the rabbit."

[c]There were several side-dishes on the table, containing what appeared to be the ordinary French rabbit – a very delicious *morceau,* which I can recommend.

"Pierre," cried the host, "change this gentleman's plate, and give him a side-piece of this rabbit *au-chât.*"[d] [11]

"This what?" said I.

"This rabbit *au-chât.*"[e]

"Why, thank you – upon second thoughts, no. I will just help myself to some of the ham."

[f]There is no knowing what one eats, thought I to myself, at the tables of these people of the province. I will have none of their rabbit *au-chât*[g] – and, for the matter of that, none of their *cat-au-rabbit*[h] either.

"And then," said a cadaverous-looking personage, near the foot of the table, taking up the thread of the conversation where it had been broken off – "and then, among other oddities, we had a patient, once upon a time, who very pertinaciously maintained himself to be a Cordova cheese,[12] and went about, with a knife in his hand, soliciting his friends to try a small slice from the middle of his leg."

"He was a great fool, beyond doubt," interposed some one, "but not to be compared with a certain individual whom we all know, with the exception of this strange gentleman. I mean the man who took himself for a bottle of champagne, and always went off with a pop and a fizz, in this fashion."

[i]Here the speaker, very rudely, as I thought, put his right thumb in his left cheek, withdrew it with a sound resembling the popping of a cork, and then, by a dexterous movement of the tongue upon the teeth, created a sharp hissing and fizzing, which lasted for several minutes, in imitation of the frothing of champagne.[13] This behavior, I saw plainly, was not very pleasing to

c *Not a new paragraph (A)*
d *au-chât." (A, B)*
e *au-chât." (A, B)*
f *Not a new paragraph (A)*
g *au-chât (A, B)*
h cat-*au*-rabbit *(A)*
i *Not a new paragraph (A)*

Monsieur Maillard; but that gentleman said nothing, and the conversation was resumed by a very lean little man in a big wig.

"And then there was an ignoramus," said he, "who mistook himself for a frog; which, by the way, he resembled in no little degree. I wish you could have seen him, sir," — here the speaker addressed myself — "it would have done your heart good to see the natural airs that he put on. Sir, if that man was *not* a frog, I can only observe that it is a pity he was not. His croak thus — [j]o-o-o-o-gh — o-o-o-o-gh![j] was the finest note in the world — B flat; and when he put his elbows upon the table thus — after taking a glass or two of wine — and distended his mouth, thus, and rolled up his eyes, thus, and winked them with excessive rapidity, thus, why then, sir, I take it upon myself to say, positively, that you would have been lost in admiration of the genius of the man."

"I have no doubt of it," I said.

"And then," said somebody else, "then there was Petit Gaillard,[14] who thought himself a pinch of snuff, and was truly distressed because he could not take himself between his own finger and thumb."

"And then[k] there was Jules Desoulières,[l] who was a very singular genius, indeed, and went mad with the idea that he was a pumpkin. He persecuted the cook to make him up into pies — a thing which the cook indignantly refused to do.[15] For my part, I am by no means sure that a pumpkin pie *à la Desoulières*[m] would not have been very capital eating, indeed!"[n]

"You astonish me!" said I; and I looked inquisitively at Monsieur Maillard.

"Ha! ha! ha!" said that gentleman — "he! he! he! — hi! hi! hi! — ho! ho! ho! — hu! hu! hu! — very good indeed! You must not be astonished, *mon ami;* our friend here is a wit — a *drôle* — you must not understand him to the letter."

"And then," said some other one of the party, "then there was Bouffon Le Grand — another extraordinary personage in his way.[16] He grew deranged through love, and fancied himself pos-

j . . . j ooough – oooogh! *(A)*
k then/then, <"said somebody else, "then> *(A)*
l Desoulieres, *(C)*
m *a la Desouléries. (C) accent and spelling from A, B*
n indeed." *(A)*

sessed of two heads. One of these he maintained to be the head of Cicero; the other he imagined a composite one, being Demosthenes' from the top of the forehead to the mouth, and Lord Brougham from the mouth to the chin.[17] It is not impossible that he was wrong; but he would have convinced you of his being in the right; for he was a man of great eloquence. He had an absolute passion for oratory, and could not refrain from display. For example, he used to leap upon the dinner-table thus, and — and —"

[o]Here a friend, at the side of the speaker, put a hand upon his shoulder, and whispered a few words in his ear; upon which he ceased talking with great suddenness, and sank back within his chair.

"And then," said the friend, who had whispered, "there[p] was Boullard, the tee-totum.[18] I call him the tee-totum, because, in fact, he was seized with the droll, but not altogether irrational crotchet, that he had been converted into a tee-totum. You would have roared wih laughter to see him spin. He would turn round upon one heel by the hour, in this manner — so —"

[q]Here the friend whom he had just interrupted by a whisper, performed an exactly similar office for himself.

"But then," cried an old lady, at the top of her voice, "your Monsieur Boullard was a madman, and a very silly madman at best; for who, allow me to ask you, ever heard of a human tee-totum? The thing is absurd. Madame Joyeuse was a more sensible person, as you know. She had a crotchet, but it was instinct with common sense, and gave pleasure to all who had the honor of her acquaintance. She found, upon mature deliberation, that, by some accident, she had been turned into a chicken-cock; but, as such, she behaved with propriety. She flapped her wings with prodigious effect — so — so — so — and, as for her crow, it[r] was delicious! Cock-a-doodle-doo! — cock-a-doodle-doo — cock-a-doodle-de-doo-[s]doo-dooo[s]-do-o-o-o-o-o-o-!"

"Madame Joyeuse, I will thank you to behave yourself!" here

---

o *Not a new paragraph (A)*
p <and then> ↑there↓ *(A)*
q *Not a new paragraph (A)*
r <my God,> it *(A2)*
s . . . s dooo — doooo *(A)*

interrupted our host, very angrily. "You can either conduct yourself as a lady should do, or you can quit the table forthwith — take your choice."

The lady, (whom I was much astonished to hear addressed as Madame Joyeuse, after the description of Madame Joyeuse she had just given,) blushed up to the eye-brows, and seemed exceedingly abashed at the reproof.[19] She hung down her head, and said not a syllable[t] in reply. But another and younger lady resumed the theme. It was my beautiful girl of the little parlor!

"Oh, Madame Joyeuse *was* a fool!"[u] she exclaimed; "but there was really much sound sense, after all, in the opinion of Eugénie Salsafette. She was a very beautiful and painfully modest young lady, who thought the ordinary mode of habiliment indecent, and wished to dress herself, always, by getting outside, instead of inside of her clothes. It is a thing very easily done, after all. You have only to do so — and then so — so — so — and then so — so — so — and then —"

"Mon dieu! Mam'selle Salsafette!"[v] here cried a dozen voices at once. "What *are* you about? — forbear! — that is sufficient! — we see, very plainly, how it is done! —hold! hold!"[20] and several persons were already leaping from their seats to withhold[w] Mam'selle Salsafette from putting herself upon a par with the Medicean Venus,[21] when the point was very effectually and suddenly accomplished by a series of loud screams, or yells, from some portion of the main body of the château.

My nerves were very much affected, indeed, by these yells; but the rest of the company I really pitied. I never saw any set of reasonable people so thoroughly frightened in my life. They all grew as pale as so many corpses, and, shrinking within their seats, sat quivering and gibbering with terror, and listening for a repetition of the sound. It came again — louder and seemingly nearer — and then a third time *very* loud, and then a fourth time with a vigor evidently diminished. At this apparent dying away of the noise, the spirits of the company were immediately regained, and all was life and anecdote as before. I now ventured to inquire the cause of the disturbance.

---

t sylable *(A)*
u fool," *(A)*
v Salsafette," *(A)*
w withold *(A, C) corrected from B*

"A mere *bagatelle,*" said Monsieur Maillard. "We are used to these things, and care really very little about them. The lunatics, every now and then, get up a howl in concert; one starting another, as is sometimes the case with a bevy of dogs at night. It occasionally happens, however, that the *concerto* yells are succeeded by a simultaneous effort at breaking loose; when, of course, some little danger is to be apprehended."

"And how many have you in charge?"

"At present, we have not more than ten, altogether."

"Principally females, I presume?"[x]

"Oh, no – every one of them men, and stout fellows, too, I can tell you."

"Indeed! I have always understood that the majority of lunatics were of the gentler sex."

"It is generally so, but not always. Some time ago, there were about twenty-seven patients here; and, of that number, no less than eighteen were women; but, lately, matters have changed very much, as you see."

"Yes – have changed very much, as you see," here interrupted the gentleman who had broken the shins of Ma'mselle Laplace.[22]

"Yes – have changed very much as you [y]see!" chimed in the whole company at once.[y]

[z]"Hold your tongues, every one of you!" said my host, in a great rage. Whereupon the whole company maintained a dead silence for nearly a minute. As for one[a] lady, she obeyed Monsieur Maillard to the letter, and thrusting out her tongue, which was an excessively long one, held it very resignedly, with both hands, until the end of the entertainment.

"And this gentlewoman," said I, to Monsieur Maillard, bending over and addressing him in a whisper – "this good lady who

---

x presume." *(A)*

y . . . y see," <repeated the gentleman who had tried to get upon the table.> ↑chimed in the whole company at once.↓ *(A2)*

z *Before this are four paragraphs crossed out by Graham's editor:*

"Yes; have changed very much as you see," said also the one who had wished to display his capacities as a tee-totum.

"Yes; have changed very much, as you see," said likewise the person who imitated the bottle of champagne.

"Yes; have changed very much, as you see," said the man who had played the frog.

"Yes; have changed very much, as you see," said the old lady who had set up the cock-a-doodle-de-doo. *(A2)*

a <the old cock-a-doodle> ↑one↓ *(A2)*

has just spoken, and who gives us the cock-a-doodle-de-doo – she, I presume, is harmless – quite harmless, eh?"

"Harmless!" ejaculated he, in unfeigned surprise, "why – why what *can* you mean?"

"Only slightly touched?" said I, touching my head. "I take it for granted that she is not particularly – not dangerously affected, eh?"

"*Mon Dieu!* what *is* it you imagine? This lady, my particular old friend, Madame Joyeuse, is as absolutely sane as myself. She has her little eccentricities, to be sure – but then, you know, all old women – all *very* old women are more or less eccentric!"[b]

"To be sure," said I – "to be sure – and then the rest of these ladies and gentlemen –"

"Are my friends and keepers," interrupted Monsieur Maillard, drawing himself up with *hauteur* – "my very good friends and assistants."

"What! all of them?" I asked – "the women and all?"

"Assuredly," he said – "we could not do at all without the women; they are the best lunatic nurses in the world; they have a way of their own, you know; their bright eyes have a marvellous effect; – something like the fascination of the snake, you know."

"To be sure," said I – "to be sure![c] They behave a little odd, eh? – they are a little *queer*, eh? – don't you think so?"

"Odd! – queer! – why, do you *really* think so? We are not very prudish, to be sure, here in the South – do pretty much as we please – enjoy life, and all that sort of thing, you know –"

"To be sure," said I – "to be sure."

"And then, perhaps, this *Clos de Vougeôt* is a little heady, you know – a little *strong* – you understand, eh?"

"To be sure," said I – "to be sure. By-the-by, monsieur, did I understand you to say that the system you have adopted, in place of the celebrated soothing system, was one of very rigorous[d] severity?"

"By no means. Our confinement is necessarily close; but the treatment – the medical treatment, I mean – is rather agreeable to the patients than otherwise."

---

b eccentric." *(A)*
c sure; *(A)*
d vigorous *(B)*

"And the new system is one of your own invention?"

"Not altogether. Some portions of it are referable[e] to Professor Tarr, of whom you have, necessarily, heard; and, again, there are modifications in my plan which I am happy to acknowledge as belonging of right to the celebrated Fether, with whom, if I mistake not, you have the honor of an intimate acquaintance."

"I am quite ashamed to confess," I replied, "that I have never even heard the name of either gentleman before."

"Good Heavens!" ejaculated my host, drawing back his chair abruptly, and uplifting his hands. "I surely do not hear you aright! You did not intend to say, eh? that you had never *heard* either of the learned Doctor Tarr, or of the celebrated Professor Fether?"

"I am forced to acknowledge my ignorance," I replied; "but the truth should be held inviolate above all things. Nevertheless, I feel humbled to the dust, not to be acquainted with the works of these, no doubt, extraordinary men. I will seek out their writings forthwith, and peruse them[f] with deliberate care. Monsieur Maillard, you have really — I must confess it — you have *really* — made me ashamed of myself!"[g]

[h]And this was the fact.[h]

"Say no more, my good young friend," he said kindly, pressing my hand — "join me now in a glass of Sauterne."

We drank. The company followed our example, without stint. They chatted — they jested — they laughed — they perpetrated a thousand absurdities — the fiddles shrieked — the drum row-de-dowed — the trombones bellowed like so many brazen bulls of Phalaris[23] — and the whole scene, growing gradually worse and worse, as the wines gained the ascendancy, became at length a sort of Pandemonium *in petto*. In the meantime, Monsieur Maillard and myself, with some bottles of Sauterne and Vougeôt between us, continued our conversation at the top of the voice. A word spoken in an ordinary key stood no more chance of being heard than the voice of a fish from the bottom of Niagara Falls.

"And, sir," said I, screaming in his ear, "you mentioned something before dinner, about the danger incurred in the old system of soothing. How is that?"

---

e referrible *(A)*
f ↑them↓ *(A)*
g myself." *(A)*
h . . . h *Part of the preceding paragraph (A)*

"Yes," he replied, "there was, occasionally, very great danger, indeed. There is no accounting for the caprices of madmen; and, in my opinion, as well as in that of Doctor Tarr and[i] Professor Fether, it is *never* safe to permit them to run at large unattended. A lunatic may be 'soothed,' as it is called, for a time, but, in the end, he is very apt to become obstreperous. His cunning, too, is proverbial, and great. If he has a project in view, he conceals his design with a marvellous wisdom; and the dexterity with which he counterfeits sanity, presents, to the metaphysician, one of the most singular problems in the study of mind. When a madman appears *thoroughly* sane, indeed, it is high time to put him in a straight jacket."

"But the *danger,* my dear sir, of which you were speaking – in your own experience – during your control of this house – have you had practical reason to think liberty hazardous, in the case of a lunatic?"

"Here? – in my own experience? – why, I may say, yes. For example: – no *very* long while ago, a singular circumstance occurred in this very house. The 'soothing system,' you know, was then in operation, and the patients were at large. They behaved remarkably well – especially so – any one of sense might have known that some devilish scheme was brewing from that particular fact, that the fellows behaved so *remarkably* well. And, sure enough, one fine morning the keepers found themselves pinioned hand and foot, and thrown into the cells, where they were attended, as if *they* were the lunatics, by the lunatics themselves, who had usurped the offices of the keepers."

"You don't tell me so! I never heard of anything so absurd in my life!"[j]

"Fact – it all came to pass by means of a stupid fellow – a lunatic – who, by some means, had taken it into his head that he had invented a better system of government than any ever heard of before – of lunatic government, I mean. He wished to give his invention a trial, I suppose – and so he persuaded the rest of the patients to join him in a conspiracy for the overthrow of the reigning powers."

---

i and of *(A)*

j life." *(A)*; life?" *(B)*

"And he really succeeded?"

"No doubt of it. The keepers and kept were soon made to exchange[k] places. Not that exactly either — for the madmen had been free, but the keepers were shut up in cells forthwith, and treated, I am sorry to say, in a very cavalier manner."

"But I presume a counter revolution was soon effected. This condition of things could not have long existed. The country people in the neighborhood — visitors coming to see the establishment — would have given the alarm."

"There you are out. The head rebel was too cunning for that. He admitted no visitors at all — with the exception, one day, of a very stupid-looking young gentleman of whom he had no reason to be afraid. He let him in to see the place — just by way of variety — to have a little fun with him. As soon as he had gammoned him sufficiently, he let him out, and sent him about his business."

"And *how* long, then, did the madmen reign?"

"Oh, a very long time, indeed — a month certainly — how much longer I can't precisely say. In the meantime, the lunatics had a jolly season of it — that you may swear. They doffed their own shabby clothes, and made free with the family wardrobe and jewels. The cellars of the *château* were well stocked with wine; and these madmen are just the devils that know how to drink it. They lived well, I can tell you."

"And the treatment — what was the particular species of treatment which the leader of the rebels put into operation?"

"Why, as for that, a madman is not necessarily a fool, as I have already observed; and it is my honest opinion that his treatment was a much better treatment than that which it superseded. It was a very capital system indeed — simple — neat — no trouble at all — in fact it was delicious — it was —"

Here my host's observations were cut short by another series of yells, of the same character as those which had previously disconcerted us. This time, however, they seemed to proceed from persons rapidly approaching.

"Gracious Heavens!" I ejaculated — "the lunatics have most undoubtedly broken loose."[l]

---

k ↑ex↓ change *(A)*　　l loose!" *(A)*

"I very much fear it is so," replied Monsieur Maillard, now becoming excessively pale. He had scarcely finished the sentence, before loud shouts and imprecations were heard beneath the windows; and, immediately afterward,[m] it became evident that some persons outside were endeavoring to gain entrance into the room. The door was beaten with what appeared to be a sledgehammer, and the shutters were wrenched and shaken with prodigious violence.

A scene of the most terrible confusion ensued. Monsieur Maillard, to my excessive astonishment, threw himself under the sideboard.[n] I had expected more resolution at his hands.[24] The members of the orchestra, who, for the last fifteen minutes, had been seemingly too much intoxicated to do duty, now sprang all at once to their feet and to their instruments, and, scrambling upon their table, broke out, with one accord, into "Yankee Doodle," which they performed, if not exactly in tune, at least with an energy superhuman, during the whole of the uproar.[25]

Meantime, upon the main dining-table, among the bottles and glasses, leaped the gentleman, who, with such difficulty, had been restrained from leaping there before. As soon as he fairly settled himself, he commenced an oration, which, no doubt, was a very capital one, if it could only have been heard. At the same moment, the man with the tee-totum predilections, set himself to spinning around the apartment, with immense energy, and with arms outstretched at right angles with his body; so that he had all the air of a tee-totum in fact, and knocked every body down that happened to get in his way. And now, too, hearing an incredible popping and fizzing of champagne, I discovered at length, that it proceeded from the person who performed the bottle of that delicate drink during dinner. And then, again, the frog-man croaked away as if the salvation of his soul depended upon every note that he uttered. And, in the midst of all[o] this, the continuous braying of a donkey arose over all. As for my old friend, Madame Joyeuse, I really could have wept for the poor lady, she appeared so terribly perplexed. All she did, however, was to stand up in a corner, by

m afterwards, *(A)*
n <table> ↑side-board↓ *(A)*
o <all> *(A)*

the fire-place, and sing out incessantly, at the top of her [p]voice, "Cock[p]-a-doodle-de-dooooooh!"

And now came the climax — the catastrophe of the drama. As no resistance, beyond whooping and yelling and cock-a-doodleing, was offered to the encroachments of the party without, the ten windows were very speedily, and almost simultaneously, broken in. But I shall never forget the emotions of wonder and horror with which I gazed, when, leaping through these windows, and down among us *pêle-mêle,*[q] fighting, stamping, scratching, and howling, there rushed [r]a perfect[r] army of what I took to be Chimpanzees, Ourang-Outangs,[26] or big black baboons of the Cape of Good Hope.[s]

I received a terrible beating — after which I rolled under a sofa and lay still. After lying there some fifteen minutes, however, during which time I listened with all my ears to what was going on in the room, I came to some satisfactory *dénouement* of this tragedy. Monsieur Maillard, it appeared, in giving me the account of the lunatic who had excited[t] his fellows to rebellion, had been merely relating his own exploits. This gentleman had, indeed, some two or three years before, been the superintendent of the establishment; but grew crazy himself, and so became a patient. This fact was unknown to the travelling companion who introduced me. The keepers, [u]ten in number,[u] having been suddenly overpowered, were first well tarred, then carefully feathered, and then shut up in underground cells. They had been so imprisoned for more than a month, during which period Monsieur Maillard had generously allowed them not only the tar and feathers (which constituted his "system"), but some bread and abundance of water. The latter was pumped on them daily. At length, one escaping through a sewer, gave freedom to all the rest.

The "soothing system," with important modifications, has been resumed at the *château;* yet I cannot help agreeing with Monsieur Maillard, that his own "treatment" was a very capital

p . . . p voice, "Cock-a-doodle! — Cock *(A)*

q *pele-mêle, (A)*

r . . . r a<n> ↑perfect↓ *(A)*

s Hope! *(A, B)*

t incited *(A)*

u . . . u ↑ten in number,↓ *(A)*

one of its kind. As he justly observed, it was "simple — neat — and gave no trouble at all — not the least."

I have only to add that, although I have searched every library in Europe for the works of Doctor *Tarr* and Professor *Fether,* I have, up to the present day, utterly failed in my endeavors at procuring an edition.

NOTES

Title: In a letter of May 28, 1844, to James R. Lowell, Poe called the story "The System of Doctors Tar and Fether"; and to E. A. Duyckinck on January 8, 1846, "Tarr and Fether."

1. The name Maillard is borne by one of the three captains in George Chapman's play, *The Revenge of Bussy D'Ambois.* Poe quoted from "the vigorous words" of Chapman in "The Assignation" at n. 30. The superintendent's name is appropriate, for Stanislas-Marie Maillard (1763–1794) was a leader of the captors of the Bastille.

2. Vincenzo Bellini (1801–1835) is best known for his operas *La Sonnambula* and *Norma* both of 1831. For other references to Bellini, see "The Spectacles," nn. 19 and 21.

3. Veal à la St. Menehoult is coated with butter and fine bread crumbs, braised and grilled, and a specialty of the province of Champagne. Velouté sauce is a white sauce made with butter, flour, parsley, and white stock; the seasoning should include nutmeg. Clos de Vougeot is a fine red wine of Burgundy. All are mentioned in Poe's "Lionizing" at n. 18.

4. *Salle à manger* — dining room; *vieille cour* — old court.

5. See Numbers 13:33: "And there we saw the giants, the sons of Anak."

6. The Latin commonplace from Horace, *Epistle,* I, vi, 1, means "be astonished at nothing."

7. The madman resembled one in Pope's *Rape of the Lock,* IV, 49–50, "Here living Teapots stand, one arm held out,/One bent; the handle this, and that the spout."

8. Paul de Kock (1794–1871) was a popular and sensational French novelist of Parisian life.

9. Poe borrows the name of Pierre-Simon, Marquis de Laplace (1749–1827), the great French mathematician and astronomer. He is referred to particularly in *Eureka.*

10. The Latin phrase, from *Æneid,* III, 658, means "a horrible malformed huge monster, deprived of light," and describes the Cyclops blinded by Ulysses. Poe quoted it also in "The Purloined Letter."

11. Poe's French.

12. Cordova is not famous for its cheese today, although Poe wrote of it also in "Hans Pfaall."

13. Compare Pope's *Rape of the Lock,* IV, 54: "And maids, turn'd bottles, called aloud for corks."

14. Petit Gaillard may mean, appropriately, jolly little fellow.

15. Jules Desoulières has a name derived from *soulier,* shoe, an absurd ingredient for a pie.

16. Georges-Louis Leclerc de Buffon (1707–1788) was a great naturalist; but *bouffon* means clown.

17. The combination of Henry Lord Brougham with Demosthenes is not inappropriate. In *Burton's,* July 1839, Poe reviewed a collection of *Sketches* by Brougham, in which some of his translations from Demosthenes were included. Poe remarked on Brougham's "intellect, essentially Demosthenic in the almost rude strength, directness, and impetuosity of its operations." In *Burton's,* December 1839, reviewing *An Address* by Joseph R. Chandler, Poe called Lord Brougham an orator who would please a modern audience more than Demosthenes and Cicero, were they alive again; this remark was later quoted in "Marginalia," number 112 (*Democratic Review,* December 1844). Poe referred to Brougham with some frequency; perhaps the first reference in the tales appears in "How to Write a Blackwood Article," n. 5.

18. Boullard suggests a connection with *boule,* a ball, or *bouler,* to swell – which may be suitable for a spinning top.

19. Madame Joyeuse is obviously happy in her assumed character. Maxwell Morton (p. 35) points out that the description of her performance is modeled on an incident involving sane characters in the eighty-fourth chapter of Lever's *Charles O'Malley* – an incident Poe copied out and discussed as not very well told in reviewing the book in *Graham's* for March 1842, where it appears thus:

"Ah, by-the-by, how's the Major?"

"Charmingly: only a little bit in a scrape just now. Sir Arthur – Lord Wellington, I mean – had him up for his fellows being caught pillaging, and gave him a devil of a rowing a few days ago.

" 'Very disorderly corps yours, Major O'Shaugnessy,' said the general; 'more men up for punishment than any regiment in the service.'

"Shaugh muttered something, but his voice was lost in a loud cock-a-doo-doo-doo, that some bold chanticleer set up at the moment.

" 'If the officers do their duty Major O'Shaugnessy, these acts of insubordination do not occur.'

"Cock-a-doo-doo-doo, was the reply. Some of the staff found it hard not to laugh; but the general went on –

" 'If, therefore, the practice does not cease, I'll draft the men into West India regiments.'

" 'Cock-a-doo-doo-doo!'

" 'And if any articles pillaged from the inhabitants are detected in the quarters, or about the persons of the troops – '

" 'Cock-a-doo-doo-*doo!*' screamed louder here than ever.

" 'Damn that cock – where is it?'

"There was a general look around on all sides, which seemed in vain; when a tremendous repetition of the cry resounded from O'Shaughnessy's coat-pocket; thus detecting the valiant Major himself in the very practice of his corps. There was no standing this: every one burst out into a peal of laughter; and Lord Wellington himself could not resist, but turned away, muttering to himself as he went — 'Damned robbers every man of them,' while a final war-note from the Major's pocket closed the interview."

20. Nothing significant has been noticed about the name of Eugénie Salsafette, perhaps related to *salsifis* (salsify, or oyster plant). Her aberration is extremely common among deranged people, and no special source for Poe's use of it need be sought.

21. The Venus de Medici was the most celebrated nude statue of the goddess at the time Poe wrote. Poe mentions it in "The Assignation."

22. For the broken shins of Mademoiselle Laplace, see the variants on page 1010. The *Graham's* editor missed this indelicate reference.

23. For the bull of Phalaris, see "A Decided Loss," n. 14.

24. Maillard's conduct resembles that of a character in "Some Words with a Mummy."

25. In Poe's day "Yankee Doodle" was our most popular national air, but its selection by a French orchestra, even if mad, was certainly extraordinary!

26. For other references to orangutans see "The Murders in the Rue Morgue" and "Hop-Frog."

MESMERIC REVELATION

This is the second of Poe's three tales involving mesmerism.* That Poe was, for a time at least, seriously interested in the subject is indicated by his praise of Chauncey Hare Townshend's *Facts in Mesmerism* (London, 1840).† Lectures, demonstrations, and publications, both responsible and irresponsible, had intensified general interest in mesmerism; sensationalism and quackery were concur-

* For "animal magnetism" and the background of mesmerism in the United States, see the introduction and notes 3 and 4 to "A Tale of the Ragged Mountains," and Sidney E. Lind's important paper, "Poe and Mesmerism," *PMLA,* December 1947.

† See note 1 below. Poe's enthusiastic comment, calling Townshend's book "one of the most truly profound and philosophical works of the day — a work to be valued properly only in a day to come," appeared near the end of a carping review of William Newnham's *Human Magnetism* in the *Broadway Journal,* April 5, 1845. The last part was repeated in "Marginalia," number 180 (*Graham's Magazine,* November 1846, p. 248).

rent with serious scientific investigation. The notion that mesmerized persons might be clairvoyant was widespread. The following is copied from the New York *Brother Jonathan* of November 18, 1843:

> ANIMAL MAGNETISM! – A series of experiments are now going forward in different parts of this Country, with *different subjects,* by *different magnetisers – wholly ignorant of what others are doing* – and by people who have not direct communication with one another; all of which go to *prove* that the Moon *is* inhabited – that the people have a written language – and make war. The most miraculous *coincidences* have happened. We are quite serious.

This series of experiments gave Poe the setting for his story, and he seized the opportunity to establish "a framework of mesmeric experimentation as the basis for his venture into metaphysical speculation" (Lind, p. 1087). He called the piece an "Essay" in a letter of February 24, 1845 to Griswold, and referred to it several times as an article. Apparently he thought of it primarily as a piece of exposition, and undoubtedly saw its principal significance not in the fictitious account of mesmerism but in the discussion of ideas that A. H. Quinn (*Poe,* p. 419) called "a prelude to *Eureka.*"

The tale is entirely fictional, but some of the ideas propounded by the principal speaker were hypothetical opinions of the author. He expounds the idea, going back to Democritus and to the Epicureans, that spirit is a rarified kind of matter. Poe seems to have believed in it himself. The technical term for it is Materialism, but the notion is not incompatible with orthodox Christian ideas, in the form used by Poe.‡

"Mesmeric Revelation" was listed as completed but not yet published in Poe's letter to Lowell dated May 28, 1844, and mentioned in his letter of July 10 to Chivers, as forthcoming in the *Columbian Magazine,* where it appeared before the end of the month. On August 18 Poe wrote to Lowell again, sending a copy of the first publication with "many corrections and alterations." He lamented

‡ See Poe's letters of July 2, 1844 to Lowell and July 10, 1844 to Chivers for the ideas of particled and unparticled matter. See also his letter of January 4, 1845 to the Reverend George Bush, professor of Hebrew at New York University, enclosing a copy of the tale and saying, "You will, of course, understand that the article is purely a fiction; but I have embodied in it some thoughts which are original with myself and I am exceedingly anxious to learn if they have claim to absolute originality, and also how far they will strike you as well based."

that "the article was wofully misprinted," and begged Lowell to have it "copied (with corrections) in the . . . Boston Notion — or any other paper where you have interest." Lowell did not arrange for any reprint or preserve the revised copy of the story.

There were reprints, however. In the climate of belief in the wonders of animal magnetism, the credulous were many. The editor of the New York *New World* reprinted the "marvellous article" in the number for August 3, 1844, remarking:

> Mr. Poe cannot, on so serious a subject, trifle with his readers: yet more extraordinary statements can hardly be conceived. We *do* believe in the facts of mesmerism, although we have not yet been able to arrive at any theory sufficient to explain them. Here, however, we are almost staggered.

This was duly copied in the Philadelphia *Saturday Museum* of August 31, 1844.

Other editors and reviewers, especially in the newer fields of thought, were inclined to take it as a factual report. In "Marginal Notes" in *Godey's,* August 1845, p. 50 ("Marginalia," number 130), Poe said:

> The Swedenborgians inform me that they have discovered all that I said in a magazine article entitled "Mesmeric Revelation," to be absolutely true, although at first they were very strongly inclined to doubt my veracity — a thing which, in this particular instance, I never dreamed of not doing myself. The story is a pure fiction from beginning to end.§

One John S. Clackner of Rochester, New York, wrote to the *Regenerator* of Fruit Hills, Ohio, on July 18, 1845: "I feel inclined to make a few remarks on the subject of Mesmerism — or rather on a piece entitled, 'A Mesmeric Revelation,' which I saw in the 'Western Luminary,' May 31st, '45, also in the Regenerator, May 14th do., by 'Edgar A. Poe.' " He summarized the first part of the narrative, apparently accepting it as a true account of a mesmeric experiment "entered into with faith and alacrity by both sides," but expressed doubts concerning the validity of the revelation. "I am not yet so great a novice, or so credulous, as to believe that Deity condescended

§ The reviewer of Poe's *Tales* in the *Aristidean* for October 1845 was led to remark on the story, "A large number of the mesmerists, . . . take it all for gospel. Some of the Swedenborgians, at Philadelphia, wrote word to Poe, that at first they doubted, but in the end became convinced, of its truth. This was excruciatingly . . . funny . . . It is evidently meant to be nothing more than the vehicle of the author's views concerning the Deity, immateriality, spirit, etc., which he apparently believes to be true, in which belief he is joined by Professor Bush." The writer was Dr. English, but his remarks obviously are based on a discussion with Poe.

to reveal such astounding mysteries to a clairvoyant, which have hitherto been withheld from the intelligent mass of mankind." He went on to argue that the "revelations" might well be the product of the clairvoyant's illness and imagination.

Clackner's letter was published in the *Regenerator* of September 1,* and Poe remarked on it in the *Broadway Journal,* September 20: "The Mesmeric journals, and some others, are still making a to-do about the tenability of Mr. Vankirk's doctrines as broached in a late Magazine paper of our own, entitled 'Mesmeric Revelation.' 'The Regenerator' has some very curious comments indeed." His response fizzled out, however; after quoting a part of Clackner's summary of the discussion over "What is God?" he took issue only with Clackner's charge of "incoherent language," and concluded: "These things, however, are of little consequence. We wait with great patience for the end of the argumentation."

The piece was sensibly received by some, like Eli Ballou, the editor who reprinted it in the *Universalist Watchman* of Montpelier, Vermont, August 30 and September 6, 1845, with an introduction saying: "We do not take the following article as an historical account, nor, as a burlesque on mesmerism; but, as a presentation of the writer's philosophical theory which he wished to commend to the attention of his readers." But credulity continued. The *American Phrenological Journal* of Philadelphia published "Mesmeric Revelation" in its issue for September 1845 with introductory remarks carrying enthusiastic support:

> As chroniclers of magnetic occurrences, we cannot well refuse admission to our pages of an article as important as the subject matter of the following "Magnetic Revelation" ... claims to be ... [It] was written by Edgar A. Poe, a man favorably known in the literary world; so that it may be relied on as authentic. Its mere literary merit, the reader will perceive, is by no means inconsiderable. Read and re-read.†

* I consulted the copy of this issue at Cornell University.

† In the next issue, however, having learned that Poe himself had declared the tale to be fiction, the editor of the *Phrenological Journal* issued a retraction, saying: "The article in his last number, quoted from Mr. Poe, proves not to be that 'magnetic revelation' it claims for itself, but simply the production of its author's own brain ... The Editor ... gave it the insertion it really merited, provided it had been genuine ... [but] *takes back* all responsibility concerning it, and regrets its occupancy of his pages." For both quoted passages see Madeline B. Stern in "Poe: 'The Mental Temperament for Phrenologists,'" *American Literature,* May 1968, pp. 162–163.

Some spiritualists were a bit more guarded. Clarence S. Brigham found in the Lowell, Massachusetts, *Star of Bethlehem,* October 4, 1845, a reprint with an introduction saying:

> The following extraordinary article was, we believe, originally published in the "Columbian Magazine." Whether it is a statement of facts, or merely a development of the writer's system of mental philosophy we know not. Be that as it may it is worthy of a careful perusal. The reader can draw his own conclusions. – We give it as it is, without farther comments.

In its issue for November 29, 1845, the London *Popular Record of Modern Science* printed Poe's story with the heading "The Last Conversation of a Somnambule" – a change of title that Poe criticized severely in "Marginalia," number 200 (*Graham's Magazine,* March 1848); see note 1 below.

Poe was obviously amused by the reception accorded his story, and made the most of it in society. A common acquaintance wrote Mrs. Sarah Helen Whitman of meeting Mr. Poe "very often at the receptions" (of Miss Anne Lynch) where "People seem to think there is something uncanny about him, and the strangest stories are told, what is more, *believed,* about his mesmeric experiences, at the mention of which he always smiles."‡

By the middle of 1848, Poe's story was known in Paris, where Charles Baudelaire published in *La Liberté de Penser* for July 15, 1848, "Révélation magnétique." As Wagenknecht notes, "It is eloquent testimony to the interests of the time that 'Mesmeric Revelation' should have been the very first piece Baudelaire selected for translation."§

TEXTS

(A) Columbian Magazine for August 1844 (2:67–70); *(B) Tales* (1845), pages 47–57; *(C)* J. Lorimer Graham copy of *Tales,* with a manuscript correction; *(D) Works* (1850), I, 110–120.

The J. Lorimer Graham copy of *Tales (C)* is followed. Its only change is the correction of a misprinted word. Griswold *(D)* followed an uncorrected copy of *Tales (B).* The copy of the magazine text with changes sent to J. R. Lowell on August 18, 1844, is not preserved.

‡ The letter, dated January 7, 1846, presumably by Mrs. Mary E. Hewitt, was quoted by E. L. Didier, *Life and Poems of . . . Poe* (1877), p. 13.

§ *Edgar Allan Poe, The Man Behind the Legend* (1963), p. 240, n. 8.

MESMERIC REVELATION

Reprints

All derived from the *Columbian Magazine* text: *The New World* (New York), August 3, 1844; *The Philadelphia Saturday Museum* (copied from the *New World*), August 31, 1844; *The Universalist Watchman and Christian Repository* (Montpelier, Vermont), August 30 (first installment) and September 6 (second installment), 1845; *The American Phrenological Journal* (Philadelphia), September 1845; *The Star of Bethlehem* (Lowell, Mass.), October 4, 1845 (Poe not named but the *Columbian Magazine* credited); *Popular Record of Modern Science* (London), November 29, 1845, as "The Last Conversation of a Somnambule."

Reprints Not Located

Poe, in his letter to George Bush, January 4, 1845, says: "With this I take the liberty of sending you a newspaper – 'The Dollar Weekly' – in which there is an article by myself, entitled 'Mesmeric Revelation.' It has been copied into the paper from a Monthly Magazine – 'The Columbian' in which it originally appeared in July last." The paper referred to was not the *Dollar Newspaper* which was searched for me in 1961 by John D. Kilbourne, Librarian of the Maryland Historical Society, but was probably the *Dollar Weekly*, published by Herrick and Ropes, listed in the New York City Directory for 1844–1845, of which only a very few copies are extant. See Louis H. Fox, "New York City Newspapers, 1820–1850, A Bibliography," *Papers of the Bibliographical Society of America* for 1927 (v. 21, parts I and II), published in December 1928. The issue containing Poe's story has not been found.

The reprints cited by John S. Clackner (see the introduction to this tale) as appearing in the *Regenerator* and in the *Western Luminary* have not been located.

Separate Printing

The Conversation of a Somnambule. Held just before Death with his Magnetiser Edgar A. Poe. London: V. Torras [n.d. 1845 or 1846?] from the *Popular Record.*

Translation

In *La Liberté de Penser,* July 15, 1848, as "Révélation magnétique," from *Tales* (1845).

MESMERIC REVELATION. [*C*]

WHATEVER doubt may still envelop the *rationale* of mesmerism, its startling *facts* are now almost universally admitted. Of these latter, those who doubt, are your mere doubters by profession – an unprofitable and disreputable tribe. There can be no more absolute waste of time than the attempt to *prove,* at the present day, that man, by mere exercise of will, can so impress his fellow, as to cast him into an abnormal condition, of which the[a] phenomena resemble very closely those of *death,* or at least resemble them more nearly than they do the phenomena of any other normal condition within our cognizance; that, while in this state, the person so impressed employs only with effort, and then feebly, the external organs of sense, yet perceives, with keenly refined perception, and through channels supposed unknown, matters beyond the scope of the physical organs; that, moreover, his intellectual faculties are wonderfully exalted and invigorated; that his sympathies with the person so impressing him are profound; and, finally, that his susceptibility to the impression increases with its frequency, while, in the same proportion, the peculiar phenomena elicited are more extended and more *pronounced.*

I say that these — which are the laws of mesmerism in its general features — it would be supererogation to demonstate; nor shall I inflict upon my readers so needless a demonstration to-day. My purpose at present is a very different one indeed. I am impelled, even in the teeth of a world of prejudice, to detail without comment the very remarkable substance of a colloquy, occurring[b] between a sleep-waker[1] and myself.

I had been long in the habit of mesmerizing the person in question, (Mr. Vankirk,)[2] and the usual acute susceptibility and exaltation of the mesmeric perception had supervened. For many months he had been laboring under confirmed phthisis, the more distressing effects of which had been relieved by my manipulations; and on the night of Wednesday, the fifteenth instant, I was summoned to his bedside.

The invalid was suffering with acute pain in the region of the heart, and breathed with great difficulty, having all the ordinary symptoms of asthma. In spasms such as these he had usually found relief from the application of mustard to the nervous centres, but to-night this had been attempted in vain.

As I entered his room he greeted me with a cheerful smile, and although evidently in much bodily pain, appeared to be, mentally, quite at ease.

---

a of which the/whose *(A)*

b occurring not many days ago *(A)*

"I sent for you to-night," he said, "not so much to administer to my bodily ailment, as to satisfy me concerning certain psychal[3] impressions which, of late, have occasioned me much anxiety and surprise. I need not tell you how sceptical I have hitherto been on the topic of the soul's immortality. I cannot deny that there has always existed, as if in that very soul which I have been denying, a vague half-sentiment of its own existence. But this half-sentiment at no time amounted to conviction. With it my reason had nothing to do. All attempts at logical inquiry resulted, indeed, in leaving me more sceptical than before. I had been advised to study Cousin.[4] I studied him in his own works as well as in those of his European and American echoes. The 'Charles Elwood' of Mr. Brownson, for example, was placed in my hands.[5] I read it with profound attention. Throughout I found it logical, but the portions which were not *merely* logical were unhappily the initial arguments of the disbelieving hero of the book. In his summing up it seemed evident to me that the reasoner had not even succeeded in convincing himself. His end had plainly forgotten his beginning, like the government of Trinculo.[6] In short, I was not long in perceiving that if man is to be intellectually convinced of his own immortality, he will never be so convinced by the mere abstractions[c] which have been so long the fashion of the moralists of England, of France, and of Germany. Abstractions may amuse and exercise, but take no hold on[d] the mind. Here upon earth, at least, philosophy, I am persuaded, will always in vain call upon us to look upon qualities as things. The will may assent — the soul — the intellect, never.

[e]"I repeat, then, that I only half felt, and never intellectually believed. But latterly there has been a certain deepening of the feeling, until it has come so nearly to resemble the acquiescence of reason, that I find it difficult to distinguish between the two. I am enabled, too, plainly to trace this effect to the mesmeric influence. I cannot better explain my meaning than by the hypothesis that the mesmeric exaltation[7] enables me to perceive a train [f]of ratiocination[f] which, in my abnormal existence, convinces, but which, in full

c *abstractions (A)*
d upon *(A)*
e *No quotation marks here or in next paragraph (A)*
f . . . f of convincing ratiocination — a train *(A)*

accordance with the mesmeric phenomena, does not extend, except through its *effect,* into my normal condition. In sleep-waking, the reasoning and its conclusion — the cause and its effect — are present together. In my natural state, the cause vanishing, the effect only, and perhaps only partially, remains.

"These considerations have led me to think that some good results might ensue from a series of well-directed questions propounded to me while mesmerized. You have often observed the profound self-cognizance evinced by the sleep-waker — the extensive knowledge he displays upon all points relating to the mesmeric condition itself; and from this self-cognizance may be deduced hints for the proper conduct of a catechism."

I consented of course to make this experiment. A few passes threw Mr. Vankirk into the mesmeric sleep. His breathing became immediately more easy, and he seemed to suffer no physical uneasiness. The following conversation then ensued: — V. in the dialogue representing the patient,[g] and P. myself.

P. Are you asleep?

V. Yes — no; I would rather sleep more soundly.

P. [*After a few more passes.*][h] Do you sleep now?

V. Yes.[i]

P. How do you think your present illness will result?

V. [*After a*[j] *long hesitation and speaking as if with effort.*] I must die.

P. Does the idea of death afflict you?

V. [*Very quickly.*] No — no!

P. Are you pleased with the prospect?

V. If I were awake I should like to die, but now it is no matter. The mesmeric condition is so near death as to content me.

P. I wish you would explain yourself, Mr. Vankirk.

V. I am willing to do so, but it requires more effort than I feel able to make. You do not question me properly.

P. What then shall I ask?

---

g the patient,/Mr. Vankirk, *(A)*

h *pauses.*] *(A)*

i *Followed by two paragraphs in A:*
P. Do you still feel the pain in your heart?
V. No.

j *Omitted (A)*

V. You must begin at the beginning.

P. The beginning! but where is the beginning?[k]

V. You know that the beginning is GOD.[8] [*This was said in a low, fluctuating tone, and with every sign of the most profound veneration.*][l]

P. What then is God?

V. [*Hesitating for many minutes.*] I cannot tell.

P. Is not God spirit?[9]

V. While I was awake I knew what you meant by "spirit," but now it seems only a word — such for instance as truth, beauty — a quality, I mean.

P. Is not God immaterial?

V. There is no immateriality — it is a mere word. That which is not matter, is not at all — unless qualities are things.

P. Is God, then, material?

V. No. [*This reply startled me very much.*]

P. What then is he?

V. [*After a long pause, and mutteringly.*] I see — but it is a thing difficult to tell. [*Another long pause.*][m] He is not spirit, for he exists. Nor is he matter, *as you understand it.* But there are *gradations* of matter of which man knows nothing; the grosser impelling the finer, the finer pervading the grosser. The atmosphere, for example, impels[n] the electric principle, while the electric principle permeates the atmosphere. These gradations of matter increase in rarity or fineness, until we arrive at a matter *unparticled* — without particles — indivisible — *one;* and here the law of impulsion and permeation is modified. The ultimate, or unparticled matter, not only permeates all things but impels all things — and thus *is* all things within itself. This matter is God. What men[o] attempt to embody in the word "thought," is this matter in motion.[10]

P. The metaphysicians maintain that all action is reducible to motion and thinking, and that the latter is the origin of the former.

V. Yes; and I now see the confusion of idea. Motion is the action of *mind* — not of *thinking.* The unparticled matter, or God, in

k beginning. *(A)*
l *This sentence not italicized (A)*
m *Not italicized (A)*
n impels or modifies *(A)*
o men vaguely *(A)*

quiescence, is (as nearly as we can conceive it) what men call mind. And the power of self-movement (equivalent in effect to human volition) is, in the unparticled matter, the result of its unity and omniprevalence; *how* I know not, and now clearly see that I shall never know. But the unparticled matter, set in motion by a law, or quality, existing within itself, is thinking.

P. Can you give me no more precise idea of what you term the unparticled matter?

V. The matters of which man is cognizant, escape the senses in gradation. We have, for example, a metal, a piece of wood, a drop of water, the atmosphere, a gas, caloric,[p] electricity, the luminiferous ether. Now we call all these things matter, and embrace all matter in one general definition; but in spite of this, there can be no two ideas more essentially distinct than that which we attach to a metal, and that which we attach to the luminiferous ether. When we reach the latter, we feel an almost irresistible inclination to class it with spirit, or with nihility. The only consideration which restrains us is our conception of its atomic constitution; and here, even, we have to seek aid from our notion of an atom, as something[q] possessing in infinite minuteness, solidity, palpability, weight. Destroy the idea of the atomic constitution and we should no longer be able to regard the ether as an entity, or at least as matter. For want of a better word we might term it spirit. Take, now, a step beyond the luminiferous ether — conceive a matter as much more rare than the ether, as this ether is more rare than the metal, and we arrive at once (in spite of all the school dogmas) at a [r]unique mass — an[r] unparticled matter. For although we may admit infinite littleness in the atoms themselves, the infinitude of littleness in the spaces between them is an absurdity. There will be a point — there will be a degree of rarity, at which, if the atoms are sufficiently numerous, the interspaces must vanish, and the mass absolutely coalesce. But the consideration of the atomic constitution[s] being now taken away, the nature of the mass inevitably glides into what we conceive of spirit.[t] It is clear, however, that it is as fully matter[u] as before. The truth is, it is im-

p caloric, light, *(A)*
q as something *omitted (A)*
r . . . r *unique* mass — at *(A)*
s construction *(A)*
t *spirit. (A)*
u *matter (A)*

possible to conceive spirit, since it is impossible to imagine what is not. When we flatter ourselves that we have formed its conception, we have merely deceived our understanding by the consideration of infinitely rarified matter.

[v]*P.* There seems to me an insurmountable objection to the idea of absolute coalescence; — and that is the very slight resistance experienced by the heavenly bodies in their revolutions through space — a resistance now ascertained, it is true, to exist in *some* degree, but which is, nevertheless, so slight as to have been quite overlooked by the sagacity even of Newton. We know that the resistance of bodies is, chiefly, in proportion to their density. Absolute coalescence is absolute density. Where there are no interspaces, there can be no yielding. An ether, absolutely dense, would put an infinitely more effectual stop to the progress of a star than would an ether of adamant or of iron.[11]

V. Your objection is answered with an ease which is nearly in the ratio of its apparent unanswerability. — As regards the progress of the star, it can make no difference whether the star passes through the ether *or the ether through it.* There is no astronomical error more unaccountable than that which reconciles the known retardation of the comets with the idea of their passage through an ether: for, however rare this ether be supposed, it would put a stop to all sidereal revolution in a very far briefer period than has been admitted by those astronomers who have endeavored to slur over a point which they found it impossible to comprehend. The retardation actually experienced is, on the other hand, about that which might be expected from the *friction* of the ether in the instantaneous passage through the orb. In the one case, the retarding force is momentary and complete within itself — in the other it is endlessly accumulative.[v]

P. But in all [w]this — in this identification of mere matter with God — is[w] there nothing of irreverence? [*I was forced to repeat this question before the sleep-waker fully comprehended my meaning.*][x]

V. Can you say *why* matter should be less reverenced than

v . . . v *Omitted (A)*
w . . . w this, is *(A)*
x *Sentence not italicized (A)*

mind? But you forget that the matter of which I speak is, in all respects,[y] the very "mind" or "spirit" of the schools, so far as regards its high capacities, and is, moreover, the "matter" of these schools at the same time. God, with all the powers attributed to spirit, is but the perfection of matter.

P. You assert, then, that the unparticled matter, in motion, is thought?

V. In general, this motion is the universal thought of the universal mind. This thought creates. All created things are but the thoughts of God.

P. You say, "in general."

V. Yes. The universal mind is God. For new individualities, *matter* is necessary.

P. But you now speak of "mind" and "matter" as do the metaphysicians.

V. Yes — to avoid confusion. When I say "mind," I mean the unparticled or ultimate matter; by "matter," I intend all else.

P. You were saying that "for new individualities matter is necessary."

V. Yes; for mind, existing unincorporate, is merely God. To create individual, thinking beings, it was necessary to incarnate portions of the divine mind. Thus man is individualized. Divested of corporate investiture, he were God. Now, the particular motion of the incarnated portions of the unparticled matter is the thought of man; as the motion of the whole is that of God.

P. You say that divested of the body man will be God?

V. [*After much hesitation.*] I could not have said this; it is an absurdity.

P. [*Referring to my notes.*] You *did* say that "divested of corporate investiture man were God."

V. And this is true. Man thus divested *would be* God — would be unindividualized. But he can never be thus divested — at least never *will be* — else we must imagine an action of God returning upon itself — a purposeless and futile action. Man is a creature. Creatures are thoughts of God. It is the nature of thought to be irrevocable.

---

y respcets *(B, D) corrected in C*

P. I do not comprehend. You say that man will never put off the body?

V. I say that he will never be bodiless.

P. Explain.

V. There are two bodies — the rudimental and the complete; corresponding with the two conditions of the worm and the butterfly.[12] What we call "death," is but the painful metamorphosis. Our present incarnation is progressive, preparatory, temporary. Our future is perfected, ultimate, immortal. The ultimate life is the full design.

P. But of the worm's metamorphosis we are palpably cognizant.

V. *We,* certainly — but not the worm. The matter of which our rudimental body is composed, is within the ken of the organs of that body; or, more distinctly, our rudimental organs are adapted to the matter of which is formed the rudimental body; but not to that of which the ultimate is composed. The ultimate body thus escapes our rudimental senses, and we perceive only the shell which falls, in decaying, from the inner form; not that inner form itself; but this inner form, as well as the shell, is appreciable by those who have already acquired the ultimate life.

P. You have often said that the mesmeric state very nearly resembles death. How is this?

V. When I say that it resembles death, I mean that it resembles the ultimate life; [z]for when I am entranced[z] the senses of my rudimental life are in abeyance, and I perceive external things directly, without organs, through a medium which I shall employ in the ultimate, unorganized life.

P. Unorganized?

V. Yes; organs are contrivances by which the individual is brought into sensible relation with particular classes and forms of matter, to the exclusion of other classes and forms. The organs of man are adapted to his rudimental condition, and to that only; his ultimate condition, being unorganized, is of unlimited comprehension in all points but one — the nature of the [a]volition of God — that is to say, the motion[a] of the unparticled matter. You will have a distinct idea of the ultimate body by conceiving it to be entire brain.

---

z . . . z for *(A)* a . . . a volition, or motion, *(A)*

This it is *not;* but a conception of this nature will bring you near a comprehension of what it *is*. A luminous body imparts vibration to the luminiferous ether. The vibrations generate similar ones within the [b]retina; these[b] again communicate similar ones to the optic nerve. The nerve conveys similar ones to the brain; the brain, also, similar ones to the unparticled matter which permeates it. The motion of this latter is thought, of which perception is the first undulation. This is the mode by which the mind of the rudimental life communicates with the external world; and this external world [c]is, to the rudimental life,[c] limited, through the idiosyncrasy of its[d] organs. But in the ultimate, unorganized life, the external world reaches the whole body, (which is of a substance having affinity to brain, as I have said,) with no other intervention than that of an infinitely rarer ether than even the luminiferous; and to this ether — in unison with it — the whole body vibrates, setting in motion the unparticled matter which permeates it. It is to the absence of idiosyncratic organs, therefore, that we must attribute the nearly unlimited perception of the ultimate life. To rudimental beings, organs are the cages necessary to confine them until fledged.

P. You speak of rudimental "beings." Are there other rudimental thinking beings than man?

V. The multitudinous conglomeration of rare matter into nebulæ, planets, suns, and other bodies which are neither nebulæ, suns, nor planets, is for the sole purpose of supplying *pabulum* for the idiosyncrasy of the organs of an infinity of rudimental beings. But for the necessity of the rudimental, prior to the ultimate life, there would have been no bodies such as these. Each of these is tenanted by a distinct variety of organic, rudimental, thinking creatures. In all, the organs vary with the features of the place tenanted. At death, or metamorphosis, these creatures, enjoying the ultimate [e]life — immortality — and[e] cognizant of all secrets but *the one,* [f]act all things and pass everywhere by mere volition: — indwelling, not the stars, which to us seem the sole palpabilities, and for the accommodation of which we blindly deem space created — but that SPACE itself — that infinity of which the truly substantive

b . . . b retina, which *(A)*
c . . . c is *(A)*
d the *(A)*
e . . . e life, and *(A)*

vastness swallows up the star-shadows — blotting them out as non-entities from the perception of the angels.[f]

[g]*P.* You say that "but for the *necessity* of the rudimental life" there would have been no stars. But why this necessity?[13]

V. In the inorganic life, as well as in the inorganic matter generally, there is nothing to impede the action of one simple *unique* law — the Divine Volition. With the view of producing impediment, the organic life and matter, (complex, substantial, and law-encumbered,) were contrived.

P. But again — why need this impediment have been produced?

V. The result of law inviolate is perfection — right — negative happiness. The result of law violate is imperfection, wrong, positive pain. Through the impediments afforded by the number, complexity, and substantiality of the laws of organic life and matter, the violation of law is rendered, to a certain extent, practicable. Thus pain, which in the inorganic life is impossible, is possible in the organic.

P. But to what good end is pain thus rendered possible?

V. All things are either good or bad by comparison. A sufficient analysis will show that pleasure, in all cases, is but the contrast of pain. *Positive* pleasure is a mere idea. To be happy at any one point we must have suffered at the same. Never to suffer would have been never to have been blessed. But it has been shown that, in the inorganic life, pain cannot be; thus the necessity for the organic. The pain of the primitive life of Earth, is the sole basis of the bliss of the ultimate life in Heaven.

P. Still, there is one of your expressions which I find it impossible to comprehend — "the truly *substantive* vastness of infinity."

V. This, probably, is because you have no sufficiently generic conception of the term *"substance"* itself. We must not regard it as a quality, but as a sentiment: — it is the perception, in thinking beings, of the adaptation of matter to their organization. There are many things on the Earth, which would be nihility to the inhabitants of Venus — many things visible and tangible in Venus, which we could not be brought to appreciate as existing at all. But to the

---

f...f pervade at pleasure the weird dominions of the infinite. *(A)*

g...g *Eight paragraphs omitted (A)*

inorganic beings — to the angels — the whole of the unparticled matter is substance; that is to say, the whole of what we term "space" is to them the truest substantiality; — the stars, meantime, through what we consider their materiality, escaping the angelic sense, just in proportion as the unparticled matter, through what we consider its immateriality, eludes the organic.[g]

As the sleep-waker pronounced these latter words, in a feeble tone, I observed on[h] his countenance a singular expression, which somewhat alarmed me, and induced me to awake him at once. No sooner had I done this, than, with a bright smile irradiating all his features, he fell back upon his pillow and expired. I noticed that in less than a minute afterward his corpse had all the stern rigidity of stone.[14] [i]His brow was of the coldness of ice. Thus, ordinarily, should it have appeared, only after long pressure from Azrael's hand.[15] Had the sleep-waker, indeed, during the latter portion of his discourse, been addressing me from out the region of the shadows?[i]

NOTES

1. A sleep-waker here means a person in a mesmeric trance. Chauncey Hare Townshend, undoubtedly one of Poe's sources on mesmerism, used the term "sleepwaking" throughout his book, "on the ground that Somnambulism, strictly speaking, was not always, nor necessarily, an adjunct of the condition I wished to describe" (*Facts in Mesmerism,* Harper edition, New York, 1841, p. vi). Poe followed Townshend, insisting upon the distinction between the old term and the new; see "Marginalia," number 200 (*Graham's Magazine,* March 1848, p. 178).

2. Vankirk means "of a church"; all authorized texts spell the name thus, although most New York Dutch names with the "van" prefix retain the two-word form: Van Cortlandt, Van Rensselaer — and Van Buskirk, employer of the stage driver who recognized Mary Rogers (see n. 38 to "The Mystery of Marie Rogêt").

3. "Psychal" is listed as rare, in both the *Century Dictionary* and the *OED.*

4. Victor Cousin (1792–1867), French eclectic philosopher, editor of Proclus and Descartes, brilliant translator of Plato, liberal, active in educational reform, exerted a wide influence through both his lectures and his writings, notably, perhaps, from Poe's point of view, his important *Fragments philosophiques* (1826) and his *Cours de philosophie professé ... pendant l'année 1818 ... sur le fonde-*

h upon *(A)* i ... i *Omitted (A)*

ment des idées absolues du vrai, du beau, et du bien (1836; many subsequent editions). Though Poe made few mentions of Cousin in his writings, the significance of his mention here may be suggested by his nearly contemporary reference (in reviewing Horne's "Orion" – *Graham's,* March 1844) to "that divine sixth sense which is yet so faintly understood – that sense which phrenology has attempted to embody in its organ of *ideality* – that sense which is the basis of all Cousin's dreams – that sense which speaks of God through his purest, if not his *sole* attribute – which proves, and which alone proves his existence."

5. Orestes A. Brownson (1803–1876), "eloquent and irascible" New England liberal, was "one of the most attractive and commanding figures in the periodical history of the times," according to Mott, *History of American Magazines,* I, 367–368. His *Charles Elwood, or the Infidel Converted* (1840) is "a semi-autobiographical romance, in which the infidel hero is converted, through Cousin's philosophy, to a rather tepid unitarianism" (E. S. Bates, in *DAB*). Poe included an appreciative and discerning paragraph on Brownson in "A Chapter on Autography," *Graham's Magazine,* November 1841. He is also mentioned in "X-ing a Paragrab."

6. The "government of Trinculo" is a confused allusion to *The Tempest,* II, i, 158: "The latter end of his commonwealth forgets the beginning." Antonio says this, not of Trinculo but of Gonzalo's description of his ideal commonwealth (II, i, 148–169), a description that is Shakespeare's echo of Montaigne's praise of primitive American society. The "Literati" sketch of Miss Sedgwick (*Godey's,* September 1846) and "Marginalia," number 273 (*SLM,* July 1849, p. 415) repeat the same confused reference.

7. Compare a statement from the account by Signor Ranieri regarding his mesmerization by Townshend (*Facts,* p. 387): "All my conceptions were more rapid; I experienced nervous startings to which I am not accustomed; in short, my whole nervous system was in a state of exaltation, and appeared to have acquired all the super abundance of power which the muscular system had lost."

8. Compare Genesis 1:1: "In the beginning God created the heaven and the earth."

9. See St. John 4:24: "God is a Spirit . . ."

10. The "philosophical lucubrations" (Woodberry, 1885, p. 214) that follow concerning the nature of God, immateriality, and particled and unparticled matter were discussed briefly in Poe's letters of July 2 to Lowell and July 10 to Chivers, and were to be elaborated in 1848, in *Eureka.*

11. This paragraph and the next one were added for *Tales* in 1845.

12. See St. Paul's first letter to the Corinthians, 15:44, "There is a natural body, and there is a spiritual body" – words especially familiar as part of the funeral service in the Book of Common Prayer. The analogy of the worm and the butterfly appears in the letters of July 2 and 10 to Lowell and Chivers, mentioned above. It is undoubtedly a familiar figure: Townshend, p. 355, says: "Everywhere we behold that one state includes the embryo of the next, not metaphysically, but materially; and entering on a new scene of existence is not so much a change as a continuation of what went before . . .

'The wings that form
The butterfly lie folded in the worm.' "

In Greek the word *psyche* means both "butterfly" and "soul"; compare "Ulalume," line 12 (and, in another mood, the first paragraph of "How to Write a Blackwood Article").

13. This and the next seven paragraphs were added for *Tales* in 1845.

14. The original version of the story ended here. The next three sentences may have been added as another of Poe's concessions to the incredulous reader.

15. Poe also referred to Azrael, the Mahometan angel of death, in the first version of "Metzengerstein"; in *Politian,* IX, 4; and in "Ligeia."

THOU ART THE MAN

"Thou Art the Man" is outstandingly important in literary history, for it is ancestral to so much later entertaining fiction. It is generally recognized as the first comic detective story, and it is "a trail blazing tour de force" in its first use of the least-likely-person theme, of the "scattering of false clues by the real criminal," and of "the psychological third degree."* As Vincent Buranelli remarks (*Poe,* pp. 80, 85): "It represents one critical step forward in the handling of the psychology of the detective story," making the villain not a "glowering thug" but a friend of the victim, thus leading the way to stories "which conceal the criminal because he is indiscernible among the group of ordinary people." A. H. Quinn (*Poe,* p. 422) found most significant Poe's "use of moral contrast in which Dickens was so adept." He commented, "Poe's story is not great in itself; but we might think better of it had we not come to expect so much from the author of 'The Purloined Letter.' "

Poe's sources have received some attention from students. His use of what is now called ballistics is early, but not the first in fact or fiction. In an American story by William Leggett, "The Rifle," an innocent man is cleared of a charge of murder by a demonstration that the fatal bullet did not fit his gun.† In 1835 Henry God-

* Howard Haycraft, *Murder for Pleasure: The Life and Times of the Detective Story* (1941), pp. 9–11. A complaint that Poe conceals essential evidence is not quite fair. A careful reading of the sixth paragraph reveals enough.

† This story first appeared in *The Atlantic Souvenir for 1828,* and was collected in *Tales and Sketches of a Country Schoolmaster* (1829), from which Jacques Barzun

dard, a Bow Street runner in London, traced an irregularly shaped bullet found in a man's body to a correspondingly misshapen mold owned by his assassin.‡ Ventriloquism was popular with writers after its use in Charles Brockden Brown's novel *Wieland* (1798) — and there is a scene in the eighth chapter of *Arthur Gordon Pym* in which a murderer is literally scared to death by the supposed ghost of his victim.

Poe's story is mentioned in his letter of May 28, 1844 to J. R. Lowell as finished but not yet published, and is noticed as accepted in *Godey's Lady's Book* for August 1844, although it was not published until three months later. Louis A. Godey preserved the roll manuscript, and his son, Frank Godey, gave it to the New York Public Library in 1924. It shows that Poe twice wrote the name of one character when he meant another. (See notes following the list of texts, below.)

TEXTS

(A) Manuscript prior to May 28, 1844; *(B) Godey's Lady's Book* for November 1844 (29:219–224); *(C) Works* (1850), II, 418–432.

Griswold's version *(C)* is the best and is followed.

The manuscript, which is still in the roll, consists of 39 pieces of paper fastened together with wax seals. The roll is 3 and 15/16 inches wide and 321 inches long. Most of the pieces of paper run about 10 inches, but many are shorter. The paper itself was probably near white and is now a light tan color with age. The ink is brown/black, typical of inks of the period. Aside from the first sheet or two, which have been backed for strength, the manuscript is in remarkably fine condition. [We are indebted to Mr. Paul R. Rugen, Keeper of Manuscripts, the New York Public Library, for a recent examination and description of this manuscript.]

The manuscript was long in the possession of the Godey family. See my article "A Poe Manuscript" in the *Bulletin of the New York Public Library,* February 1924. It shows that someone in Godey's office made two changes for elegance. Poe accepted these when he made a few clearly auctorial revisions which were adopted by Griswold. Godey's printers did not follow Poe's manuscript punctuation, even in the title, perhaps because of his really excessive pointing, especially in the use of semicolons. Two accidental substitutions of the name

---

reprinted it in *Delights of Detection* (1961). Leggett's story was mentioned as famous in Duyckinck's *Cyclopaedia of American Literature* (1856), II, 343; but was unknown to historians of the detective story until Vincent Starrett announced in the Chicago *Sunday Tribune,* June 20, 1948, the discovery by Arthur Lovell, a bookseller. See Jacques Barzun, *Energies of Art* (1956), p. 309.

‡ See George D. Murphy in *American Notes & Queries,* March 1966. Fictional use of ballistics may have preceded its actual use by several years.

"Goodfellow" for "Shuttleworthy" were overlooked by Godey's editor, Poe, Griswold, and Ingram. They are emended below as they were by Stedman and Woodberry, and by Harrison. Hyphens are used inconsistently in the manuscript, as will be seen in the variants. None of Poe's texts accents "Chateau."

"THOU ART THE MAN." [*C*]

I will now play the Œdipus to the Rattleborough enigma.[1] I will expound to you — as I alone can — the secret of the enginery that effected the Rattleborough miracle — the one, the true, the admitted, the undisputed, the indisputable miracle, which put a definite end to infidelity among the Rattleburghers, and converted to the orthodoxy of the grandames all the carnal-minded[2] who had ventured to be skeptical before.

This event — which I should be sorry to discuss in a tone of unsuitable levity — occurred in the summer of 18—. Mr. Barnabas Shuttleworthy — one of the wealthiest and most respectable citizens of the borough — had been missing for several days under circumstances which gave rise to suspicion of foul play. Mr. Shuttleworthy had set out from Rattleborough very early one Saturday morning, on horseback, with the avowed intention of proceeding to the city of ——, about fifteen miles distant, and of returning the night of the same day. Two hours after his departure, however, his horse returned without him, and without the saddle-bags which had been strapped on his back at starting. [a]The animal was wounded, too, and covered with mud.[a] These circumstances naturally gave rise to much alarm among the friends of the missing man; and when it was found, on Sunday morning, that he[b] had not yet made his appearance, the whole borough arose *en masse* to go and look for his body.

The foremost and most energetic in instituting this search, was the bosom friend of Mr. Shuttleworthy — a Mr. Charles Goodfellow or, as he was universally called, "Charley Goodfellow," or "Old Charley Goodfellow."[3] Now, whether it is a marvellous coincidence, or whether it is that the name itself has an imperceptible effect upon the character, I have never yet been able to ascertain; but the fact is

Title "Thou art the Man" By Edgar A. Poe *in script beneath the title (A);* "THOU ART THE MAN!" *(B)*

a . . . a *Inserted (A)*

b <the missing man> ↑he↓ *(A)*

unquestionable, that there never yet was any person named Charles who was not an open, manly, honest, good-natured, and frank-hearted fellow, with a rich, clear voice, that did you good to hear it, and an eye that looked you always straight in the face, as much as to say, "I have a clear conscience myself; am afraid of no man, and am altogether above doing a mean action." And thus all the hearty, careless, "walking gentlemen" of the stage[4] are very certain to be called Charles.

Now, "Old Charley Goodfellow," although he had been in Rattleborough not longer than six months or thereabouts, and although nobody knew anything about him before he came to settle in the neighborhood, had experienced no difficulty in the world in making the acquaintance of all the respectable people in the borough. Not a man of them but would have taken his bare word for a thousand at any moment; and as for the women, there is no saying what they would not have done to oblige him. And all this came of his having been christened Charles, and of his possessing, in consequence, that ingenuous face which is proverbially the very "best letter of recommendation."[5]

I have already said[c] that Mr. Shuttleworthy was one of the most respectable, and, undoubtedly, he was the most wealthy man in Rattleborough, while "Old Charley Goodfellow" was upon as intimate terms with him as if he had been his own brother. The two old gentlemen were next-door neighbors, and, although Mr. Shuttleworthy seldom, if ever, visited "Old Charley," and never was known to take a meal in his house, still this did not prevent the two friends from being exceedingly intimate, as I have just observed; for "Old Charley" never let a day pass without stepping in three or four times to see how his neighbor came on, and very often he would stay to breakfast or tea, and almost always to dinner; and then the amount of wine that was made way with by the two cronies at a sitting, it would really be[d] a difficult thing to ascertain. Old Charley's favorite beverage was *Château Margaux,*[6] and it appeared to do Mr. Shuttleworthy's heart good to see the old fellow swallow it, as he did, quart after quart; so that, one day, when the wine was *in* and the wit, as a

---

c said, *(C) comma deleted to follow A, B* d ↑be↓ *(A)*

natural consequence, somewhat *out,* he said to his crony, as he slapped him upon the back — "I tell you what it is, Old Charley, you are, by all odds, the heartiest old fellow[e] I ever came across in all my born days; and, since you love to guzzle the wine at that fashion, I'll be darned if I don't have to make thee a present of a big box of the Château Margaux. Od rot me," — (Mr. Shuttleworthy[f] had a sad habit of swearing, although he seldom went beyond "Od rot me," or "By gosh," or "By the jolly golly,") [7] — "Od rot me," says he, "if I don't send an order to town this very afternoon for a double box of the best that can be got, and I'll make ye a present of it, I will! — ye needn't say a word now — I *will,* I tell ye, and there's an end of it; so look out for it — it will come to hand some of these fine days, precisely[g] when ye are looking for it the least!" I mention this little bit of liberality on the part of Mr. Shuttleworthy, just by way of showing you how *very* intimate an understanding existed between the two friends.

Well, on the Sunday morning in question, when it came to be fairly understood that Mr. Shuttleworthy had met with foul play, I never saw anyone so profoundly affected as "Old Charley Goodfellow." When he first heard that the horse had come home without his master, and without his master's saddle-bags, and all bloody from a pistol-shot,[h] that had gone clean through and through the poor animal's chest without quite killing him — when he heard all this, he turned as pale as if the missing man had been his own dear brother or father, and shivered and shook all over as if he had had a fit of the ague.

At first, he was too much overpowered with grief to be able to do anything at all, or to decide[i] upon any plan of action; so that for a long time he endeavored to dissuade Mr. Shuttleworthy's other friends from making a stir about the matter, thinking it best to wait awhile — say for a week or two, or a month or two — to see if something wouldn't turn up, or if Mr. Shuttleworthy wouldn't come in the natural way, and explain his reasons for sending his horse on before. I dare say you have often observed this disposition to

e <cock> ↑fellow↓ *(A) change not in Poe's hand*
f Shuttleworth *(A)*
g <just> ↑precisely↓ *(A)*
h pistol shot *(A, B)*
i concert *(A, B)*

temporize, or to procrastinate, in people who are laboring under any very poignant sorrow. Their powers of mind seem to be rendered torpid, so that they have a horror of anything like action, and like nothing in the world so well as to lie quietly in bed and "nurse their grief," as the old ladies[j] express it – that is to say, ruminate over their trouble.

The people of Rattleborough had, indeed, so high an opinion of the wisdom and discretion of "Old Charley"[k] that the greater part of them felt disposed to agree with him, and not make a stir in the business "until something should turn up," as the honest old gentleman worded it; and I believe that, after all, this would have been the general determination, but for the very suspicious interference of Mr. Shuttleworthy's nephew, a young man of very dissipated habits, and otherwise of rather bad character. This nephew, whose name was Pennifeather, would listen to nothing like reason in the matter of "lying quiet," but insisted upon making immediate search for the "corpse of the murdered man." This was the expression he employed; and Mr. Goodfellow acutely remarked,[l] at the time, that it was "a *singular* expression, to say no more." This remark of Old Charley's, too, had great effect upon the crowd; and one of the party was heard to ask, very impressively, "how it happened that young Mr. Pennifeather was so intimately cognizant of all the circumstances connected with his wealthy uncle's disappearance, as to feel authorized to assert, distinctly and unequivocally, that his uncle *was* 'a murdered man.' " Hereupon some little squibbing and bickering occurred among various members of the crowd, and especially between "Old Charley" and Mr. Pennifeather – although this latter occurrence was, indeed, by no means a novelty, for little[m] good will had subsisted between the parties for the last three or four months; and matters had even gone so far[n] that Mr. Pennifeather had actually knocked down his uncle's friend for some alleged excess of liberty that the latter had taken in the uncle's house, of which the nephew was an inmate. Upon this occasion,

j <women> ↑ladies↓ *(A) change not in Poe's hand*

k Charley," *(B, C) comma deleted to follow A*

l remarked *(B, C) comma added from A*

m no *(A, B)*

n far, *(C) comma deleted to follow A, B*

"Old Charley" is said to have behaved with exemplary moderation and Christian charity. He arose from the blow, adjusted his clothes, and made no attempt at retaliation at all — merely muttering a few words about "taking summary vengeance at the first convenient opportunity," — a natural and very justifiable ebullition of anger, which meant nothing, however, and, beyond doubt, was no sooner given vent to than forgotten.

However these matters may[o] be, (which have no reference to the point now at issue,) it is quite certain that the people of Rattleborough, principally through the persuasion of Mr. Pennifeather, came at length to the determination of dispersing over the adjacent country in search of the missing Mr. Shuttleworthy. I say they came to this determination in the first instance. After it had been fully resolved that a search should be made, it was considered almost a matter of course that the seekers should disperse — that is to say, distribute themselves in parties — for the more thorough examination of the region round about. I forget, however, by what ingenious train of reasoning it was that "Old Charley" finally convinced the assembly that this was the most injudicious plan that could be pursued. Convince them, however, he did — all except Mr. Pennifeather; and, in the end, it was arranged that a search should be instituted, carefully and very thoroughly, by the burghers *en masse,* "Old Charley" himself leading the way.

As for the matter of that, there could have been no better pioneer than "Old Charley," whom everybody[p] knew to have the eye of a lynx; but, although he led them into all manner of out-of-the-way holes and corners, by routes that nobody had ever suspected of existing in the neighborhood, and although the search was incessantly kept up day and night for nearly a week, still no trace of Mr. Shuttleworthy could be discovered. When I say no trace, however, I must not be understood to speak literally; for trace, to some extent, there certainly was. The poor gentleman had been tracked, by his horse's shoes, (which were peculiar,) to a spot about three miles to the east of the borough, on the main road leading to the city. Here the track made off into a by-path[q] through a piece of woodland — the[r] path

---

o ↑may↓ *(A)*
p every body *(A, B)*
q by path *(A)*
r this *(A, B)*

coming out again into the main road, and cutting off about half a mile of the regular distance. Following the shoe-marks down this lane, the party came at length to a pool of stagnant water, half hidden by the brambles to the right of the lane, and opposite this pool all vestige of the track was lost sight of. It appeared, however, that a struggle of some nature had here taken place, and it seemed as if some large and heavy body, much larger and heavier than a man, had been drawn[s] from the by-path to the pool. This latter was carefully dragged twice, but nothing was found; and the party were upon the point of going away, in despair of coming to any result, when Providence suggested to Mr. Goodfellow the expediency of draining the water off altogether. This project was received with cheers, and many high compliments to "Old Charley" upon his sagacity and consideration. As many of the burghers had brought spades with them, supposing that they might possibly be called upon to disinter a corpse, the drain was easily and speedily effected; and no sooner was the bottom visible, than right in the middle of the mud that remained was discovered a black silk velvet waistcoat, which nearly every one present immediately recognised as the property of Mr. Pennifeather. This waistcoat was much torn and stained with blood, and there were several persons among the party who had a distinct remembrance of its having been worn by its owner on the very morning of Mr. Shuttleworthy's departure for the city; while there were others, again, ready to testify upon oath, if required, that Mr. P. did *not* wear the garment in question at any period during the *remainder* of that memorable day; nor could any one be found to say that he had seen it upon Mr. P.'s person at any period at all subsequent to Mr. Shuttleworthy's disappearance.

Matters now wore a very serious aspect for Mr. Pennifeather, and it was observed, as an indubitable confirmation of the suspicions which were excited against him, that he grew exceedingly pale, and when asked what he had to say for himself, was utterly incapable of saying a word. Hereupon, the few friends his riotous mode of living had left him deserted him at once to a man,[8] and were even more clamorous than his ancient and avowed enemies for his instantaneous arrest. But, on the other hand, the magnanimity

s dragged *(A, B)*

of Mr. Goodfellow shone forth with only the more brilliant lustre through contrast. He made a warm and intensely eloquent defence of Mr. Pennifeather, in which he alluded more than once to his own sincere forgiveness of that wild young gentleman — "the heir of the worthy Mr. Shuttleworthy"[t] — for the insult which he (the young gentleman) had, no doubt in the heat of passion, thought proper to put upon him (Mr. Goodfellow.) "He forgave him for[u] it," he said, "from the very bottom of his heart; and for himself (Mr. Goodfellow,) so far from pushing the suspicious circumstances to extremity, which, he was sorry to say, really *had* arisen against Mr. Pennifeather, he (Mr. Goodfellow) would make every exertion in his power, would employ all the little eloquence in his possession to — to — to — soften down, as much as he could conscientiously do so, the worst features of this really exceedingly perplexing piece of business."

Mr. Goodfellow went on for some half hour longer in this strain, very much to the credit both of his head and of his heart; but your warm-hearted people are seldom apposite in their observations — they run into all sorts of blunders, *contre-temps* and *mal àpropos-isms,* in the hot-headedness of their zeal to serve a friend — thus, often with the kindest intentions in the world, doing infinitely more to prejudice his cause than to advance it.

So, in the present instance, it turned out with all the eloquence of "Old Charley;" for, although he labored earnestly in behalf of the suspected, yet it so happened, somehow or other, that every syllable he uttered of which the direct but unwitting tendency was not to exalt the speaker in the good opinion of his audience, had the effect [v]of deepening[v] the suspicion already attached to the individual whose cause he pleaded,[w] and [x]of arousing[x] against[y] him the fury of the mob.

One of the most unaccountable errors committed by the orator was his allusion to the suspected as "the heir of the worthy old gentleman Mr. Shuttleworthy."[z] The people had really never

t Goodfellow," *(A, B, C) emended for sense*

u for <t> *(A)*

v . . . v to deepen *(A, B)*

w plead, *(C) emended to follow A, B*

x . . . x to arouse *(A, B)*

y *Written over erasure (A)*

z Goodfellow." *(A, B, C) emended for sense*

thought of this before. They had only remembered certain threats of disinheritance [a]uttered a year or two previously[a] by the uncle, (who had no living relative except the nephew;) and they had, therefore, always looked upon this disinheritance as a matter that was settled — so single-minded a race of beings were the Rattleburghers; but the remark of "Old Charley" brought them at once to a consideration of this point, and thus gave them to see the possibility of the threats having been nothing *more* than a threat. And straightway, hereupon, arose the natural question of *cui bono?*[9] — a question that tended even more than the waistcoat to fasten the terrible crime upon the young man. And here, lest I be misunderstood, permit me to digress for one moment merely to observe that the exceedingly brief and simple Latin phrase which I have employed, is invariably mistranslated and misconceived. "*Cui bono,*" in all the crack novels and elsewhere, — in those of Mrs. Gore, for example, (the author of "Cecil,") a lady who quotes all tongues from the Chaldæan to Chickasaw, and is helped to her learning, "as needed," upon a systematic plan, by Mr. Beckford,[10] — in *all* the crack novels, I say, from those of Bulwer and Dickens to those of Turnapenny and Ainsworth,[11] the two little Latin words *cui bono* are rendered "to what purpose," or, (as if *quo bono,*) "to what good." Their true meaning, nevertheless, is "for whose advantage." *Cui,* to whom; *bono,* is it for a benefit. It is a purely legal phrase, and applicable precisely in cases such as we have now under consideration, where the probability of the doer of a deed hinges upon the probability of the benefit accruing to this individual or to that from the deed's accomplishment. Now, in the present instance, the question *cui bono* very pointedly implicated Mr. Pennifeather. His uncle had threatened him, after making a will in his favor, with disinheritance. But the threat had not been actually kept; the original will, it appeared, had not been altered. *Had* it been altered, the only supposable motive for murder on the part of the suspected would have been the ordinary one of revenge; and even this would have been counteracted by the hope of reinstation into the good graces of the uncle. But the will being unaltered, while the threat to alter remained suspended over the nephew's head, there appears

a . . . a uttered, a year or two previous <ly>, *(A)*

at once the very strongest possible inducement for the atrocity: and so concluded, very sagaciously, the worthy citizens of the borough of Rattle.

Mr. Pennifeather was, accordingly, arrested upon the spot, and the crowd, after some farther search, proceeded homewards, having him in custody. On the route, however, another circumstance occurred tending to confirm the suspicion entertained. Mr. Goodfellow, whose zeal led him to be always a little in advance of the party, was seen suddenly to run forward a few paces, stoop, and then apparently to pick up some small object from the grass. Having quickly examined it, he was observed, too, to make a sort of[b] half attempt at concealing it in his coat pocket;[c] but this action was noticed, as I say, and consequently prevented, when the object picked up was found to be a Spanish knife which a dozen persons at once recognised as belonging to Mr. Pennifeather. Moreover, his initials were engraved upon the handle. The blade of this knife was open and bloody.

No doubt now remained of the guilt of the nephew, and immediately upon reaching Rattleborough he was taken before a magistrate for examination.

Here matters again took a most unfavorable turn. The prisoner, being questioned as to his whereabouts on the morning of Mr. Shuttleworthy's disappearance, had absolutely the audacity to acknowledge that on that very morning he had been out with his rifle deer-stalking, in the immediate neighborhood of the pool where the blood-stained waistcoat had been discovered through the sagacity of Mr. Goodfellow.

This latter now came forward, and, with tears in his eyes, asked permission to be examined. He said that a[d] stern sense of the duty he owed[e] his Maker, not less than[f] his fellow-men,[g] would permit him no longer to remain silent. Hitherto, the sincerest affection for the young man (notwithstanding the latter's ill treatment of himself, Mr. Goodfellow,) had induced him to make every hypothesis which imagination could suggest, by way of endeavoring to account

b of/of <a> *(A)*; of a *(B)*
c coat-pocket; *(A)*
d <a> *(A)*
e owed to *(A, B)*
f than to *(A, B)*
g fellow men, *(A, B)*

for what appeared suspicious in the circumstances that told so seriously against Mr. Pennifeather; but these circumstances were now altogether *too* convincing — *too* damning; he would hesitate no longer — he would tell all he knew, although his heart (Mr. Goodfellow's) should absolutely burst asunder in the effort. He then went on to state that, on the afternoon of the day previous to Mr. Shuttleworthy's departure for the city, that worthy old gentleman had mentioned to his nephew, in *his* hearing, (Mr. Goodfellow's,) that his object in going to town on the morrow was to make a deposit of an unusually large sum of money in the "Farmers'[h] and Mechanics' Bank,"[12] and that, then and there the said Mr. Shuttleworthy had distinctly avowed to the said nephew his irrevocable determination of rescinding the will originally made and of cutting him off with a shilling. He (the witness) now solemnly called upon the accused to state whether what he (the witness) had just stated was or was not the truth in every substantial particular. Much to the astonishment of every one present,[i] Mr. Pennifeather frankly admitted that *it was.*

The magistrate now considered it his duty to send a couple of constables to search the chamber of the accused in the house of his uncle. From this search they almost immediately returned with the well known[j] steel-bound, russet leather[k] pocket-book which the old gentleman had been in the habit of carrying for years. Its valuable contents, however, had been abstracted, and the magistrate in vain endeavored to extort from the prisoner the use which had been made of them, or the place of their concealment. Indeed, he obstinately denied all knowledge of the matter. The [l]constables also[l] discovered, between the bed and sacking of the unhappy man, a shirt and neck-handkerchief both marked with the initials of his name, and both hideously besmeared with the blood of the victim.

At this juncture, it was announced that the horse of the murdered man had just expired in the stable from the effects of the wound he had received, and it was proposed by Mr. Goodfellow that a *post mortem* examination of the beast should be immediately

h Farmer's *(A)*; Farmers *(B)*
i one ↑present↓, *(A)*
j well-known, *(A)*
k russet-leather *(A)*
l . . . l constables, also, *(B, C) emended from A*

made, with the view, if possible, of discovering the ball. This was accordingly done; and, as if to demonstrate beyond a question the guilt of the accused, Mr. Goodfellow, after considerable searching in the cavity of the chest, was enabled to detect and to pull forth a bullet of very extraordinary size, which, upon trial, was found to be exactly adapted to the bore of Mr. Pennifeather's rifle, while it was far too large for that of any other person in the borough or its vicinity. To render the matter even surer yet, however, this bullet was discovered to have a flaw or seam at right angles to the usual suture; and upon examination, this seam corresponded precisely with an accidental ridge or elevation in a pair of moulds acknowledged by the accused himself to be his own property. Upon the finding of this bullet, the examining magistrate refused to listen to any farther testimony, and immediately committed the prisoner for trial — declining resolutely to take any bail in the case, although against this severity Mr. Goodfellow very warmly remonstrated, and offered to become surety in whatever amount might be required. This generosity on the part of "Old Charley" was only in accordance with the whole tenor of his amiable and chivalrous conduct during the entire period of his sojourn in the borough of Rattle. In the present[m] instance, the worthy man was so entirely carried away by the excessive warmth of his sympathy, that he seemed to have quite forgotten, when he offered to go bail for his young friend, that he himself (Mr. Goodfellow) did not possess a single dollar's worth of property upon the face of the earth.

The result of the committal may be readily foreseen. Mr. Pennifeather, amid the loud execrations of all Rattleborough, was brought to trial at the next criminal sessions, when the chain of circumstantial evidence (strengthened as it was by some additional damning facts, which Mr. Goodfellow's sensitive conscientiousness forbade him to withhold from the court,) was considered so unbroken and so thoroughly conclusive, that the jury, without leaving their seats, returned an immediate verdict of *"Guilty of murder in the first degree."* Soon afterwards the unhappy wretch received sentence of death, and was remanded to the county jail to await the inexorable vengeance of the law.

---

m presence *(A)*

In the mean time,[n] the noble behavior of "Old Charley Goodfellow" had doubly endeared him to the honest citizens of the borough. He became ten times a greater favorite than ever; and, as a natural result of the hospitality with which he was treated, he relaxed, as it were, perforce, the extremely parsimonious habits which his poverty had hitherto impelled him to observe, and very frequently had little *réunions* at his own house, when wit and jollity reigned supreme — dampened a little, *of course,* by the occasional remembrance of the untoward and melancholy fate which impended over the nephew of the late lamented bosom friend of the generous host.

One fine day, this magnanimous old gentleman was agreeably surprised at the receipt of the following letter: —

From H. F. B. & Co.
Charles Goodfellow, Esq., Rattleborough.
Chat. Mar. A — No. 1. — 6 doz. bottles (½ Gross).

"Charles Goodfellow, Esquire —

"Dear Sir — In conformity with an order transmitted to our firm about two months since, by our esteemed correspondent, Mr. Barnabas Shuttleworthy, we have the honor of forwarding this morning, to your address, a double box of Château-Margaux, of the antelope brand, violet seal. Box numbered and marked as per margin.

"We remain, sir,

"Your most ob'nt ser'ts,

HOGGS, FROGS, BOGS & CO.[13]

"City of ——, *June 21st, 18*—.

"P. S. — *The box will reach you, by wagon, on the day after your receipt of this letter. Our respects to Mr. Shuttleworthy.*

H. F. B. & Co."[o]

The fact is, that Mr. Goodfellow had, since the death of Mr. Shuttleworthy, given over all expectation of ever receiving the promised Château Margaux;[p] and he, therefore, looked upon it *now* as a sort of especial dispensation of Providence in his behalf. He

n meantime *(A)*

o *The letter is not quoted in the manuscript (A) and has* Dear Sir—/Dr. Sir,; "Your most ob'nt ser'ts, /Yr. mo. ob. sts,

In A the address reads from the bottom to the top of the sheet: Chat: Mar: A — No 1 — 6 Doz. Bottles (½ Gross). from/H. F. B & Co./Charles Goodfellow, Esq: Rattleborough.

The address in B is the same as in A except that the punctuation is like C

p *Chateau-Margaux; (C)*

was highly delighted, of course, and in the exuberance of his joy, invited a large party of friends to a *petit souper* on the morrow, for the purpose of broaching the good old Mr. Shuttleworthy's present. Not that he *said* any thing[q] about "the good old Mr. Shuttleworthy" when he issued the invitations. The fact is, he thought much and concluded to say nothing at all. He did *not* mention to any one — if I remember aright — that he had received a *present* of Château Margaux.[r] He merely asked his friends to come and help him[s] drink some of a remarkably fine quality and rich flavor, that he had ordered up from the city a couple of months ago, and of which he would be in the receipt upon the morrow. I have often puzzled myself to imagine *why* it was that "Old Charley" came to the conclusion to say nothing about having received the wine from his old friend, but I could never precisely understand his reason for the silence, although he had *some* excellent and very magnanimous reason, no doubt.

The morrow at length arrived, and with it a very large and highly respectable company at Mr. Goodfellow's house. Indeed, half the borough was there — I myself among the number — but, much to the vexation of the host, the Château Margaux[t] did not arrive until a late hour, and when the sumptuous supper supplied by "Old Charley" had been done very ample justice by the guests. It came at length, however, — a monstrously big box of it there was, too, — and as the whole party were in excessively good humor, it was decided, *nem. con.*,[14] that it should be lifted upon the table and its contents disemboweled forthwith.

No sooner said than done. I lent a helping hand; and, in a trice, we had the box upon the table, in the midst of all the bottles and glasses, not a few of which were demolished in the scuffle. "Old Charley," who was pretty much intoxicated, and excessively red in the face, now took a seat, with an air of mock dignity, at the head of the board, and thumped furiously upon it with a decanter, calling upon the company to keep order "during the ceremony of disinterring the treasure."

After some vociferation, quiet was at length fully restored, and,

q anything *(A)*
r Chateau-Margaux. *(A, B, C)*
s him to *(A, B)*
t Chateau-Margaux *(B, C)*

as very often happens in similar cases, a profound and remarkable silence ensued. Being then requested to force open the lid, I complied, of course, "with an infinite deal of pleasure."[15] I inserted a chisel, and giving it a few slight taps with a hammer, the top of the box flew suddenly and violently off, and, at the same instant, there sprang up into a sitting position, directly facing the host, the bruised, bloody and nearly putrid corpse of the murdered Mr. Shuttleworthy himself. It gazed for a few moments, fixedly and sorrowfully, with its decaying and lack-lustre eyes, full into the countenance of Mr. Goodfellow; uttered slowly, but clearly and impressively, the words – "Thou art the man!" and then, falling over the side of the chest as if thoroughly satisfied, stretched out its limbs quiveringly upon the table.

The scene that ensued is altogether beyond description. The rush for the doors and windows was terrific, and many of the most robust men in the room fainted outright through sheer horror. But after the first wild, shrieking burst of affright, all eyes were directed to Mr. Goodfellow. If I live a thousand years, I can never forget the more than mortal agony which was depicted in that ghastly face of his, so lately rubicund with triumph and wine. For several minutes, he sat rigidly as a statue of marble; his eyes seeming, in the intense vacancy of their gaze, to be turned inwards and absorbed in the contemplation of his own miserable, murderous soul. At length, their expression appeared to flash suddenly out into the external world, when with a quick leap, he sprang from his chair, and falling heavily with his head and shoulders upon the table, and in contact with the corpse, poured out rapidly and vehemently a detailed confession of the hideous crime for which Mr. Pennifeather was then imprisoned and doomed to die.

What he recounted was in substance this: – He followed his victim to the vicinity of the pool; there shot his horse with a pistol; despatched the rider with its butt end;[u] possessed himself of the pocket-book;[v] and, supposing the horse dead, dragged it with great labor to the brambles by the pond. Upon his own beast he slung the corpse of Mr. Shuttleworthy, and thus bore it to a secure place of concealment a long distance off through the woods.

u butt-end; *(A)* v pocket book; *(A)*

The waistcoat, the knife, the pocket-book and[w] bullet, had been placed by himself where found, with the view of avenging himself upon Mr. Pennifeather. He had also contrived the discovery of the stained handkerchief and shirt.

Towards the end of the blood-chilling recital, the words of the guilty wretch faltered and grew hollow. When the record was finally exhausted, he arose, staggered backwards from the table, and fell — *dead.*

The means by which this happily-timed confession was extorted, although efficient, were simple indeed. Mr. Goodfellow's excess of frankness had disgusted me, and excited my suspicions[x] from the first. I was present when Mr. Pennifeather had struck him, and the fiendish expression which then arose upon his countenance, although momentary, assured me that his threat of vengeance would, if possible, be rigidly fulfilled. I was thus prepared to view the *manœuvring* of "Old Charley" in a very different light from that in which it was regarded by the good citizens of Rattleborough. I saw at once that all the criminating discoveries arose, either directly, or indirectly, from himself. But the fact which clearly opened my eyes to the true state of the case, was the affair of the bullet, *found* by Mr. G. in the carcass of the horse. *I* had not forgotten, although the Rattleburghers *had,* that there was a hole where the ball had entered the horse, and another where it *went out.* If it were found in the animal then, after having made its exit, I saw clearly that it must have been deposited by the person who found it.[16] The bloody shirt and handkerchief confirmed the idea suggested by the bullet; for the blood upon examination proved to be capital claret, and no more. When I came to think of these things, and also of the late increase of liberality and expenditure on the part of Mr. Goodfellow, I entertained a suspicion which was none the less strong because I kept it altogether to myself.

In the mean time,[y] I instituted a rigorous private search for the corpse of Mr. Shuttleworthy, and, for good reasons, searched in

---

w and the *(A, B)*

x suspicion *(A, B)*

y meantime *(A)*

quarters as divergent as possible from those to which Mr. Goodfellow conducted his party. The result was that, after some days, I came across an old dry well, the mouth of which was nearly hidden by brambles; and here, at the bottom, I discovered what I sought.

Now it so happened that I had overheard the colloquy between the two cronies, when Mr. Goodfellow had contrived to cajole his host into the promise of a box of Château Margaux.[z] Upon this hint I acted. I procured a stiff piece of whalebone, thrust it down the throat of the corpse, and deposited the latter in an old wine box[a] — taking care so to double the body up as to double the whalebone with it. In this manner I had to press forcibly upon the lid to keep it down while I secured it with nails; and I anticipated, of course, that as soon as these latter were removed, the top would fly *off* and the body[b] *up*.

Having thus arranged the box, I marked, numbered and addressed it as already told; and then writing a letter in the name of the wine merchants with whom Mr. Shuttleworthy dealt, I gave instructions to my servant to wheel the box to Mr. Goodfellow's door, in a barrow, at a given signal from myself. For the words which I intended the corpse to speak, I confidently depended upon my ventriloquial abilities; for their effect, I counted upon the conscience of the murderous wretch.

I believe there is nothing more to be explained. Mr. Pennifeather was released upon the spot, inherited the fortune of his uncle, profited by the lessons of experience, turned over a new leaf, and led happily ever afterwards a new life.

NOTES

Title: See II Samuel 12:7. These are the words of Nathan the prophet to King David, who brought about the death of Uriah the Hittite to obtain his wife Bathsheba.

1. Oedipus solved the riddle of the Sphinx; Poe has a similar locution in "Eleonora," at n. 5.

2. Compare Romans 8:6, "For to be carnally minded is death."

---

z Chateau-Margaux. *(B, C)*

a wine-box *(A)*

b body ↑fly↓ *(A)*; body fly *(B)*

3. We may recall that Robin Goodfellow is a sprite who sometimes misleads travelers.

4. A "walking gentleman of the stage" is an actor who plays "well-dressed parts of small importance" according to the *Century Dictionary,* which cites an example from Dickens' *Sketches by Boz.* In 1823 Thomas Colley Grattan (1792–1864), who served as British consul in Boston, 1839–46, published the first series of his *High-ways and By-ways, or Tales of the Roadside, Picked up in the French Province by a Walking Gentleman.* A new American edition of the work was reviewed in *Burton's,* June 1840. This unsigned piece was obviously written by Poe, who repeated much the same phraseology in his comments on Grattan in "Marginalia," no. 114 (*Democratic Review,* December 1844, p. 503) and in no. 203 (*SLM,* April 1849, p. 219).

5. See Francis Bacon, *Apophthegms,* number 99 (74): "Queen Isabella of Spain used to say 'Whosoever hath a good presence and a good fashion, carries continually letters of recommendation.' " Dickens has Gabriel Varden say in the second chapter of *Barnaby Rudge,* "You don't carry in your countenance a letter of recommendation."

6. Châteaux Margaux is a fine claret mentioned also in the earlier versions of "Bon-Bon." It was one of the three most expensive wines, commanding $2.50 a bottle at Delmonico's in 1838 for the 1825 vintage.

7. Compare the mild oaths of Toby Dammit in "Never Bet the Devil Your Head."

8. In St. Luke 15:13, we read that the prodigal son had "wasted his substance in riotous living."

9. *Cui bono* is from Cicero's oration *Pro Roscio Amerino,* xxx, 84, and is correctly explained by Poe. Examples of its misuse, including one by Bulwer, were collected in the London *Notes and Queries,* February 15, 1941 (180:116).

10. Mrs. Catherine Gore (1799–1861) published *Cecil* in 1841. That she cribbed from William Beckford, author of *Vathek,* was suggested in the seventh chapter of *A New Spirit of the Age* (1843), by R. H. Horne, with whom Poe had lately corresponded. I use, as Poe probably did, the New York reprint of 1844, pp. 138–139.

11. Poe complained of Harrison Ainsworth's use of "his own Latin" in "Marginalia," no. 12 (*Democratic Review,* November 1844, p. 486) and made Ainsworth one of the narrators of "The Balloon Hoax." Turn-a-penny, of course, is a made-up name, for one who writes for money.

12. Poe uses a real name here. The Farmers' and Mechanics' Bank, founded in 1824, was on Chestnut Street, west of Fourth Street, Philadelphia.

13. In "Diddling," there is a firm of like rhyming names – "Bogs, Hogs, Logs, Frogs, & Co."

14. *Nem. con.* (*nemine contradicente*) means "without opposition"; see n. 16 in "The Business Man."

15. The phrase echoes "Gratiano speaks an infinite deal of nothing" in the *Merchant of Venice, I,* i, 114.

16. See the note in the introduction on ballistics in detection.

TALES: 1844–1845

THE BALLOON HOAX

This is one of the most famous of Poe's compositions, and is an entertaining adventure story. It is a hoax in that it is an account of a fictional aeronautic crossing of the Atlantic, told as if it had really occurred. Published on April 13, 1844, it was less a flight of the imagination than many have supposed. There were serious plans both here and in England, by respectable flyers, to cross the ocean by air. These plans did not come to fruition for many years, but that they did not was due to circumstances which probably need not have been insurmountable in 1844. The idea was in the air. Poe and his earliest readers knew it.* Subsequently, interest in transatlantic flying waned to such a degree that in the later decades of the last century the average man thought of it as incredible.†

In 1910 Walter B. Norris‡ recalled for twentieth-century readers that "in 1836 and thereabouts there was a great interest in aeronautics, and several aeronauts, especially Charles Green and John Wise, the prominent balloonists in England and America, respectively, had proposed to try crossing the Atlantic." Norris also pointed out that Poe in "The Balloon Hoax" had depended chiefly on the story of an actual balloon trip, Monck Mason's *Account of the Late Aeronautical Expedition from London to Weilburg, accomplished by Robert Hollond, Esq., Monck Mason, Esq., and*

*See John Edmund Hodgson, *The History of Aeronautics in Great Britain from the Earliest Times to the Latter Part of the Nineteenth Century* (London, 1924), for the progress of experiments in "aerial transit" and the attendant publicity during Poe's time.

† A. R. Leslie Melville, himself a pilot, published an article in London *N & Q*, November 11, 1933, on W. S. Henson and other early experimenters with aerial transit. Among other things he said, "As the value of their work was not realised in 1900, the D.N.B. does not include Henson . . . or Sir George Cayley (1774–1857), the Father of British Aeronautics."

‡ "Poe's Balloon Hoax," in the New York *Nation*, October 27, 1910.

Charles Green, Aeronaut, published in London in 1836 and in New York in 1837. Norris's material was greatly amplified by Harold H. Scudder and by Ronald Sterne Wilkinson.§

Poe certainly was long aware of plans to cross the ocean in a balloon, for he must have seen references in *Burton's Gentleman's Magazine* for March and May 1840* to Charles Green's belief in the possibility of going by that means from New York to Europe. Another probable inspiration was a plan of the American, John Wise, described in an article headed "Aerial Voyage" in the *Dollar Newspaper,* June 21, 1843, the issue containing the first installment of "The Gold-Bug." Wise planned a spherical balloon using hydrogen gas, designed to take advantage of west-to-east current. He estimated the trip would take three days. One Pennington, inventor of a flying machine, was willing to accompany him.†

§ Their articles in *American Literature,* May 1949 and November 1960, respectively, will be referred to in more detail later.

* In parts of a series headed "A Chapter on Science and Art," sometimes ascribed to Poe's pen — it now seems to me, on unsatisfactory evidence. Parts of it are quoted in note 9 below.

† The article in the *Dollar Newspaper* began, "Wise the aeronaut announces through the columns of the Lancaster Intelligencer that he intends to make an aerial trip across the Atlantic in a balloon in 1844," and quoted from the announcement the following paragraph:

"The balloon is to be one hundred feet in diameter, which will give a nett ascending power of twenty-five thousand pounds — being amply sufficient to make everything safe and comfortable. A sea-worthy boat is to be used for the car, which is to be depended on, in case the balloon should happen to fail in accomplishing the voyage. The boat would also be calculated upon in case the regular current of wind should be diverted from the course by the influence of the ocean, or through other causes. The crew to consist of three persons, viz: an aeronaut, a navigator and a scientific landsman."

No file of the Lancaster (Pennsylvania) paper for the right period has been located.

[On June 15, 1843, however, in an article headed "Crossing the Ocean in Balloons" (discovered by Dwight Thomas in his research on "Poe in Philadelphia, 1838–1844" and generously shared with us), the Philadelphia *Spirit of the Times,* p. 2 col. 3, had discussed Wise's proposed adventure and said, "Our pleasant friend of the Lancaster Intelligencer from whose paper we cut Mr. Wise's letter, remarks that 'though the scheme may look Quixotic, we have no doubt that Mr. W. possesses the nerve to attempt and, we believe, the ability to carry it out!' " The *Spirit of the Times* then permitted Mr. Wise to speak for himself and copied his letter in full.

Little more than a month after the statement by John Wise the *Spirit of the Times* (July 20, 21, 22, 24, 25, 1843) published a story in five installments called "A Flight in the Aerial." This is wildly fictional account of what can only be called an aerial binge over Europe and Africa on the part of some well-known characters, including Henson and Ainsworth who later reappeared in Poe's story. The author,

An even more immediate inspiration appeared in *Alexander's Express Messenger,* February 21, 1844, in an article entitled "Another Aerial Machine," describing Monck Mason's model, on exhibition in London, which had just been moved from Willis's Rooms to the Adelaide Gallery, and giving "an engraving illustrative of its construction." With very slight variations, the article in the *Express Messenger* was taken from an unsigned pamphlet, written by Mason (see Hodgson, *History of Aeronautics,* p. 411), *Remarks on the Ellipsoidal Balloon propelled by the Archimedean Screw, described as the New Aerial Machine* (London, 1843). The pamphlet was undoubtedly the ultimate source of some paragraphs in Poe's story, as Wilkinson, cited above, pointed out, but small details indicate that Poe actually used, as he did so often, the article immediately at hand, paraphrasing this material freely, as Wilkinson says, "to add realism to his description of the construction of the 'Victoria,' much as he used Mason's *Account* to give the required verisimilitude to the transatlantic voyage."‡ The parallel passages from Mason's two pieces, collected by Scudder and Wilkinson, are given in the notes following Poe's text, below.

Shortly before the article in the *Express Messenger* appeared, there occurred an event that provided the means for having the pretended report of the voyage received by only one newspaper. The *New York American for the Country,* February 15, 1844,§ printed the following note:

> *Ahead of the Mail.* – The Charleston papers of last Monday acknowledge the receipt of papers from this city three days in advance of the mail. They were carried by the brig Moon, Capt. Hayes, who made a very short run.

---

who used the pen name of Bon Gaultier, was William Edmonstoune Aytoun, shortly to become one of the editors of *Blackwood's* and son-in-law of its "Christopher North," John Wilson. This amusing piece, recently brought to our attention by Professor Pollin, was no doubt known by Poe, and an important part of the ballooning balloon climate he was living in during the summer before he concocted "The Balloon Hoax."]

‡ Unlike the pamphlet, *Alexander's Express Messenger* (see notes 5 and 7 below) names the gallery, the Adelaide, where Mason's model was exhibited, does not capitalize the words "balloon" and "screw," and has "15 degrees" instead of "15°," all followed by Poe. [We are indebted to Ruth M. Doyle in the Reference Department of the Carnegie Library of Pittsburgh for recent access to the February 21, 1844 issue of *Alexander's Express Messenger.*]

§ The American Antiquarian Society's copy of the issue cited was consulted.

In the first paragraph of his story Poe says, "By the energy of an agent at Charleston, S.C., we are enabled to be the first to furnish the public with a detailed account of this most extraordinary voyage."

Poe's tale was presumably written or at least begun before the Poes left Philadelphia, early in April 1844, for New York, where Poe soon sold his production to Richard Adams Locke of the *Sun*, author of the celebrated Moon Hoax.* In the regular issue of the *Sun* for April 13, 1844, an announcement (possibly written by Poe) was printed. It reads:

Postscript / By Express

Astounding Intelligence by Private Express from Charleston via Norfolk! – The Atlantic Ocean crossed in three days!! – Arrival at Sullivan's Island of a Steering Balloon invented by Mr. Monck Mason.

We stop the press at a late hour to announce that by a Private Express from Charleston, S.C., we are just put in possession of full details of the most extraordinary adventure ever accomplished by man. *The Atlantic Ocean has been actually traversed in a balloon and in the incredibly brief period of Three Days!* Eight persons have crossed in the machine – among others Sir Everard Bringhurst and Mr. Monck Mason. We have barely time now to announce this most novel and unexpected intelligence; but we hope by 10 this morning to have ready an Extra with a detailed account of the voyage.

P.S. The Extra will be positively ready and for sale at our counter by 10 o'clock this morning. It will embrace all the particulars yet known. We have also placed in the hands of an excellent artist a representation of the "Steering Balloon," which will accompany the particulars of the voyage.

The actual reception of the "Balloon Hoax" was less enthusiastic than its author had hoped. His own description of what happened, published less than six weeks after the event,† tells us that the "Extra" announced for ten o'clock was not delivered until nearly noon, that there was a great crowd about the *Sun* building (corner of Nassau and Fulton streets) from soon after sunrise, that it was hard to get possession of a paper, that some newsboys re-

* Locke's paper, written for the *Sun* in 1835, "purported to reveal the discovery, by Sir John Herschel with his new telescope at the Cape of Good Hope, of men and animals on the moon . . . the hoax increased the *Sun's* circulation to more than nineteen thousand, the largest of any daily of that time" (F. M. O'Brien in *DAB*). Poe mentioned Locke frequently, and published an (inaccurate) account of him as the last of the "Literati" papers, in *Godey's* for September 1846.

† Dated May 21 and published in the *Columbia Spy*, May 25, 1844, as Letter II in the *Doings of Gotham* series.

ceived twelve and a half cents for each copy, and that one sold for fifty cents.‡ Poe claimed, "The more intelligent believed, while the rabble . . . rejected the whole with disdain." He admitted that good grounds for doubt were the difficulty of running an express ahead of the mail from Charleston and "publication . . . in the suspected 'Sun' (the organ of the Moon-Hoax)" – but said that he would not be surprised to learn in the course of a month or two that a balloon had made the voyage.

Major Mordecai M. Noah, who republished the hoax in his *Sunday Times* of April 14, also printed a humorous comment: "If it be true that the ballooning experiment has succeeded, there will probably be a demand for the material whereof gas is formed. We would recommend any company to engage Mr. - - - - -, he being the greatest condensation of gas that we know of."

Another New York Sunday paper – the *Mercury* – of the same day printed a story headed:

> By Express/Astounding Intelligence from the Man in the/Moon/Boundless space travelled in the/Twinkling of a Bed Post/Arrival, in New York, of a/ Moon-Beam,/With extraordinary and exclusive intelligence/for the Sunday Mercury./

Monday's papers were in general unimpressed. The elder James Gordon Bennett, calling the piece "Beach's Last Hoax" (Moses Y. Beach was editor of the *Sun*), said in the *New York Herald* that a better writer should have been employed. The New York *American* of April 15, 1844 said, "The *Sun* has issued an *Extra* with a poor imitation of the Moon Hoax." In Philadelphia, the *Native American* referred to the story as brought by "jackass express" in almost a column of jocular comment entitled "Extraordinary Arrival. The New Era Commenced."

The *Sun* itself, of course, carried a retraction on April 15 that reads:

> BALLOON – The mails from the South last Saturday night not having brought a confirmation of the arrival of the Balloon from England, the particulars of which from our correspondent we detailed in our Extra, we are inclined to believe that the intelligence is erroneous. The description of the Balloon and the voyage was written with a minuteness and scientific ability calculated to

‡ *The Extra Sun* bore no marked price.

obtain credit everywhere, and was read with great pleasure and satisfaction. We by no means think such a project impossible.

Whether Poe or Locke wrote the retraction is uncertain, but it sums up the case nicely.

Poe took little pains to conceal his authorship.§ James Russell Lowell was allowed to publish the firm ascription in his sketch of Poe (which had the subject's approval) in *Graham's Magazine* for February 1845, issued about January 15.

TEXTS

(A) The Extra Sun, April 13, 1844; *(B) Works* (1850), I, 88–101. The immediate reprint of *A* in the New York *Sunday Times*, April 14, 1844, is regarded as permitted by the author but shows no deliberate revisions.

Griswold's text *(B)* which shows a few slight auctorial revisions is followed.

The only known copy of *A* is at the American Antiquarian Society. Clarence S. Brigham's *Poe's "Balloon Hoax"* (Metuchen, New Jersey, 1932) is a little pamphlet with a much reduced reproduction of the broadside, a separate from *American Book Collector*, February 1932.

THE BALLOON-HOAX. [*B*]

[a][Astounding News by Express, *via* Norfolk! – The Atlantic crossed in Three Days! Signal Triumph of Mr. Monck Mason's Flying Machine! – Arrival at Sullivan's Island, near Charleston, S.C., of Mr. Mason, Mr. Robert Holland, Mr. Henson, Mr. Harrison Ainsworth, and four others, in the Steering Balloon, "Victoria," after a passage of Seventy-five Hours from Land to Land! Full Particulars of the Voyage![a] [1]

[b]The subjoined *jeu d'esprit* with the preceding heading in magnificent capitals, well interspersed with notes of admiration, was originally published, as matter of fact, in the "New-York Sun," a daily newspaper, and therein fully subserved the purpose of creating indigestible aliment for the *quidnuncs* during the few hours intervening between a couple of the Charleston mails. The

§ There was a tradition, given me by a member of the staff of the *Sun* as long told by newspapermen, that on the day the hoax was published Poe, inebriated, stood outside the office telling people not to buy it, as he had written it! See Heartman and Canny, p. 85.

Title: *Added in B* a . . . a *Printed in headline form (A)*

rush for the "sole paper which had the news," was something beyond even the prodigious; and, in fact, if (as some assert) the "Victoria" *did* not absolutely accomplish the voyage recorded, it will be difficult to assign a reason why she *should* not have accomplished it.][b]

The great problem is at length solved![c] The air, as well as the earth and the ocean, has been subdued by science, and will become a common and convenient highway for mankind. *The Atlantic has been actually crossed in a Balloon!*[d] and this too without difficulty — without any great apparent danger — with thorough control of the machine — and in the inconceivably brief period of seventy-five hours from shore to shore! By the energy of an agent at Charleston, S.C., we are enabled to be the first to furnish the public with a detailed account of this most extraordinary voyage, which was performed between Saturday, the 6th instant, at 11, A.M., and 2, P.M., on Tuesday, the[e] 9th instant, by Sir Everard Bringhurst; Mr. Osborne, a nephew of Lord Bentinck's;[2] Mr. Monck Mason and Mr. Robert Holland, the well-known æronauts; Mr. Harrison Ainsworth, author of "Jack Sheppard," &c.; and Mr. Henson, the projector of the late unsuccessful flying machine — with two seamen from Woolwich — in all, eight persons. The particulars furnished below may be relied on as authentic and accurate in every respect, as, with a slight[f] exception, they are copied *verbatim* from the joint diaries of Mr. Monck Mason and Mr. Harrison Ainsworth, to whose politeness our agent is also indebted for much verbal information respecting the balloon itself, its construction, and other matters of interest. The only alteration in the MS. received, has been made for the purpose of throwing the hurried account of our agent, Mr. Forsyth,[3] in a connected and intelligible form.

THE BALLOON.

Two very decided failures, of late — those of Mr. Henson and Sir George Cayley — had much weakened the public interest in the

b . . . b *Added in B*
c solved. *(A)*
d *Balloon; (A)*
e *Omitted (A)*
f a slight/slight *(A)*

subject of aerial navigation.[4] Mr. Henson's scheme (which at first was considered very feasible even by men of science,) was founded upon the principle of an inclined plane, started from an eminence by an extrinsic force, applied and continued by the revolution of impinging vanes, in form and number resembling the vanes of a windmill. But, in all the experiments made with models at the Adelaide Gallery, it was found that the operation of these fans not only did not propel the machine, but actually impeded its flight. The only propelling force it ever exhibited, was the mere *impetus* acquired from the descent of the inclined plane; and this *impetus* carried the machine farther when the vanes were at rest, than when they were in motion — a fact which sufficiently demonstrates their inutility; and in the absence of the propelling, which was also the *sustaining* power, the whole fabric would necessarily descend. This consideration led Sir George Cayley to think only of adapting a propeller to some machine having of itself an independent power of support — in a word, to a balloon; the idea, however, being novel, or original, with Sir George, only so far as regards the mode of its application to practice. He exhibited a model of his invention at the Polytechnic Institution. The propelling principle, or power, was here, also, applied to interrupted surfaces, or vanes, put in revolution. These vanes were four in number, but were found entirely ineffectual in moving the balloon, or in aiding its ascending power. The whole project was thus a complete failure.[5]

It was at this juncture that Mr. Monck Mason (whose voyage from Dover to Weilburg in the balloon, "Nassau," occasioned so much excitement in 1837,) conceived the idea of employing the principle of the Archimedean screw for the purpose of propulsion through the air — rightly attributing the failure of Mr. Henson's scheme, and of Sir George Cayley's, to the interruption of surface in the independent vanes. He made the first public experiment at Willis's Rooms, but afterwards removed his model to the Adelaide Gallery.[6]

Like Sir George Cayley's balloon, his own was an ellipsoid.[7] Its length was[g] thirteen feet six inches — height, six feet eight inches.[g]

g . . . g   13 feet 6 inches — height 6 feet   8 inches *(A)*

It contained about [h]three hundred and twenty[h] cubic feet of gas, which, if pure hydrogen, would support twenty-one[i] pounds upon its first inflation, before the gas has time to deteriorate or escape. The weight of the whole machine and apparatus was seventeen[j] pounds — leaving about four[k] pounds to spare. Beneath the centre of the balloon, was a frame of light wood, about nine[l] feet long, and rigged on to the balloon itself with a network in the customary manner. From this framework was suspended a wicker basket or car.[m]

The screw consists of an axis of hollow brass tube, eighteen[n] inches in length, through which, upon a semi-spiral inclined at fifteen[o] degrees, pass a series of a steel wire radii, two[p] feet long, and thus projecting a foot on either side. These radii are connected at the outer extremities by two[q] bands of flattened wire — the whole in this manner forming the framework of the screw, which is completed by a covering of oiled silk cut into gores, and tightened[r] so as to present a tolerably uniform surface. At each end of its axis this screw is supported by pillars of hollow brass tube descending from the hoop. In the lower ends of these tubes are holes in which the pivots of the axis revolve. From the end of the axis which is next the car, proceeds a shaft of steel, connecting the screw with the pinion of a piece of spring machinery fixed in the car. By the operation of this spring, the screw is made to revolve with great rapidity, communicating a progressive motion to the whole. By means of the rudder, the machine was readily turned in any direction. The spring was of great power, compared with its dimensions, being capable of raising forty-five[s] pounds upon a barrel of four[t] inches diameter, after the first turn, and gradually increasing as it was wound up. It weighed, altogether, eight pounds six ounces. The rudder was a light frame of cane covered with silk,

h . . . h 320 *(A)*
i 21 *(A)*
j 17*(A)*
k 4 *(A)*
l 9 *(A)*
m car. The mode of arrangement of the rudder and of the Archimedean screw, will be best shown in the annexed engraving, which we have kindly been permitted to use. *(A)*
n 18 *(A)*
o 15 *(A)*
p 2 *(A)*
q 2 *(A)*
r lightened *(A) misprint*
s 45 *(A)*
t 4 *(A)*

shaped somewhat like a battledoor, and was about three[u] feet long, and at the widest, one foot. Its weight was about two[v] ounces. It could be turned *flat,* and directed upwards or downwards, as well as to the right or left; and thus enabled the æronaut to transfer the resistance of the air which in an inclined position it must generate in its passage, to any side upon which he might desire to act; thus determining the balloon in the opposite direction.

This model (which, through want of time, we have necessarily described in an imperfect manner,) was put in action at the Adelaide Gallery, where it accomplished a velocity of five[w] miles per hour; although, strange to say, it excited very little interest in comparison with the previous complex machine of Mr. Henson — so resolute is the world to despise anything which carries with it an air of simplicity. To accomplish the great desideratum of ærial navigation, it was very generally supposed that some exceedingly complicated application must be made of some unusually profound principle in dynamics.

So well satisfied, however, was Mr. Mason of the ultimate success of his invention, that he determined to construct immediately, if possible, a balloon of sufficient capacity to test the question by a voyage of some extent — the original design being to cross the British Channel, as before, in the Nassau balloon. To carry out his views, he solicited and obtained the patronage of Sir Everard Bringhurst and Mr. Osborne, two gentlemen well known for scientific acquirement, and especially for the interest they have exhibited in the progress of ærostation. The project, at the desire of Mr. Osborne, was kept a profound secret from the public — the only persons entrusted with the design being those actually engaged in the construction of the machine, which was built (under the superintendence of Mr. Mason, Mr. Holland, Sir Everard Bringhurst, and Mr. Osborne,) at the seat of the latter gentleman near Penstruthal in Wales.[8] Mr. Henson, accompanied by his friend Mr. Ainsworth, was admitted to a private view of the balloon, on Saturday last — when the two gentlemen made final arrangements to be included in the adventure. We are not informed for what reason the two seamen were also included in the party — but, in the course

u 3 *(A)*
v 2 *(A)*
w 5 *(A)*

of a day or two, we shall put our readers in possession of the minutest particulars respecting this extraordinary voyage.

The balloon[x] is composed of silk, varnished with the liquid gum caoutchouc.[y] It is of vast dimensions, containing more than 40,000 cubic feet of gas; but as coal gas was employed in place of the more expensive and inconvenient hydrogen; the supporting power of the machine, when fully inflated, and immediately after inflation, is not more than about 2500 pounds. The coal gas is not only much less costly, but is easily procured and managed.

For its introduction into common use for purposes of aerostation, we are indebted to Mr. Charles Green. Up to his discovery, the process of inflation was not only exceedingly expensive, but uncertain. Two, and even three days, have frequently been wasted in futile attempts to procure a sufficiency of hydrogen to fill a balloon, from which it had great tendency to escape owing to its extreme subtlety, and its affinity for the surrounding atmosphere. In a balloon sufficiently perfect to retain its contents of coal-gas unaltered, in quality or amount, for six months, an equal quantity of hydrogen could not be maintained in equal purity for six weeks.[9]

The supporting power being estimated at 2500 pounds, and the united weights of the party amounting only to about 1200, there was left a surplus of 1300, of which again 1200 was exhausted by ballast, arranged in bags of different sizes, with their respective weights marked upon them — by cordage, barometers, telescopes, barrels containing provision for a fortnight, water-casks, cloaks, carpet-bags, and various other indispensable matters, including a coffee-warmer, contrived for warming coffee by means of slack-lime, so as to dispense altogether with fire, if it should be judged prudent to do so. All these articles, with the exception of the ballast, and a few trifles, were suspended from the hoop overhead.[10] The car is much smaller and lighter, in proportion, than the one appended to the model. It is formed of a light wicker, and is wonderfully strong, for so frail looking a machine. Its rim is about four[z] feet deep. The rudder is also very much larger, in proportion, than that of the model; and the screw is considerably smaller. The balloon is furnished besides, with a grapnel, and a guide-rope;

x balloon (an ellipsoid as represented in our engraving of the model) *(A)*

y chauchonc *(A) misprint*

z 4 *(A)*

which latter is of the most indispensable importance. A few words, in explanation, will here be necessary for such of our readers as are not conversant with the details of aerostation.

As soon as the balloon quits the earth, it is subjected to the influence of many circumstances tending to create a difference in its weight; augmenting or diminishing its ascending power. For example, there may be a disposition of dew upon the silk, to the extent, even, of several hundred pounds; ballast has then to be thrown out, or the machine may descend. This ballast being discarded, and a clear sunshine evaporating the dew, and at the same time expanding the gas in the silk, the whole will again rapidly ascend. To check this ascent, the only resource is, (or rather *was*, until Mr. Green's invention of the guide-rope), the permission of the escape of gas from the valve; but, in the loss of gas, is a proportionate general loss of ascending power; so that, in a comparatively brief period, the best constructed balloon must necessarily exhaust all its resources, and come to the earth. This was the great obstacle to voyages of length.[11]

The guide-rope remedies the difficulty in the simplest manner conceivable. It is merely a very long rope which is suffered to trail from the car, and the effect of which is to prevent the balloon from changing its level in any material degree. If, for example, there should be a deposition of moisture upon the silk, and the machine begins to descend in consequence, there will be no necessity for discharging ballast to remedy the increase of weight, for it is remedied, or counteracted, in an exactly just proportion, by the deposit on the ground of just so much of the end of the rope as is necessary. If, on the other hand, any circumstances should cause undue levity, and consequent ascent, this levity is immediately counteracted by the additional weight of rope upraised from the earth. Thus, the balloon can neither ascend or descend, except within very narrow limits, and its resources, either in gas or ballast, remain comparatively unimpaired. When passing over an expanse of water, it becomes necessary to employ small kegs of copper or wood, filled with liquid ballast of a lighter nature than water. These float, and serve all the purposes of a[a] mere rope on land.[12]

a the *(A)*

Another most important office of the guide-rope, is to point out the *direction* of the balloon. The rope *drags,* either on land or sea, while the balloon is free; the latter, consequently, is always in advance, when any progress whatever is made: a comparison, therefore, by means of the compass, of the relative positions of the[b] two objects, will always indicate the *course.* In the same way, the angle formed by the rope with the vertical axis of the machine, indicates the *velocity.* When there is *no* angle – in other words, when the rope hangs perpendicularly, the whole apparatus is stationary; but the larger the angle, that is to say, the farther the balloon precedes the end of the rope, the greater the velocity; and the converse.[13]

As the original design was to cross the British Channel,[14] and alight as near Paris as possible, the voyagers had taken the precaution to prepare themselves with passports directed to all parts of the Continent, specifying the nature of the expedition, as in the case of the Nassau voyage, and entitling the adventurers to exemption from the usual formalities of office: unexpected events, however, rendered these passports superfluous.

The inflation was commenced very quietly at daybreak, on Saturday morning, the 6th instant, in the Court-Yard of Weal-Vor House,[15] Mr. Osborne's seat, about a mile from Penstruthal, in North Wales; and at 7 minutes past 11, every thing being ready for departure, the balloon was set free, rising gently but steadily, in a direction nearly South; no use being made, for the first half hour, of either the screw or the rudder. We proceed now with the journal, as transcribed by Mr. Forsyth from the joint MSS. of Mr. Monck Mason, and Mr. Ainsworth. The body of the journal, as given, is in the hand-writing of Mr. Mason, and a P. S. is appended, each day, by Mr. Ainsworth, who has in preparation, and will shortly give the public a more minute, and no doubt, a thrillingly interesting account of the voyage.

THE JOURNAL.

Saturday, April the 6th. – Every preparation likely to embarrass us, having been made over night, we commenced the inflation

b *Omitted (A)*

this morning at daybreak; but owing to a thick fog, which encumbered the folds of the silk and rendered it unmanageable, we did not get through before nearly eleven o'clock. Cut loose, then, in high spirits, and rose gently but steadily, with a light breeze at North, which bore us in the direction of the Bristol[c] Channel.[16] Found the ascending force greater than we had expected; and as we arose higher and so got clear of the cliffs, and more in the sun's rays, our ascent became very rapid. I did not wish, however, to lose gas at so early a period of the adventure, and so concluded to ascend for the present. We soon ran out our guide-rope; but even when we had raised it clear of the earth, we still went up very rapidly. The balloon was unusually steady, and looked beautifully. In about ten[d] minutes after starting, the barometer indicated an altitude of 15,000 feet. The weather was remarkably fine, and the view of the subjacent country — a most romantic one when seen from any point, — was now especially sublime. The numerous deep gorges presented the appearance of lakes, on account of the dense vapors with which they were filled, and the pinnacles and crags to the South East, piled in inextricable confusion, resembled nothing so much as the giant cities of eastern fable. We were rapidly approaching the mountains in the South; but our elevation was more than sufficient to enable us to pass them in safety. In a few minutes we soared over them in fine style; and Mr. Ainsworth, with the seamen, were surprised at their apparent want of altitude when viewed from the car, the tendency of great elevation in a balloon being to reduce inequalities of the surface below, to nearly a dead level. At half-past eleven still proceeding nearly South, we obtained our first view of the Bristol Channel; and, in fifteen minutes afterwards, the line of breakers on the coast appeared immediately beneath us, and we were fairly out at sea. We now resolved to let off enough gas to bring our guide-rope, with the buoys affixed, into the water. This was immediately done, and we commenced a gradual descent. In about twenty[e] minutes our first buoy dipped, and at the touch of the second soon afterwards, we remained stationary as to elevation.[17] We were all now anxious to test the

c British *(B) misprint corrected from A* e 20 *(A)*
d 10 *(A)*

efficiency of the rudder and screw, and we put them both into requisition forthwith, for the purpose of altering our direction more to the eastward, and in a line for Paris. By means of the rudder we instantly effected the necessary change of direction, and our course was brought nearly at right angles to that of the wind; when we set in motion the spring of the screw, and were rejoiced to find it propel us readily as desired. Upon this we gave nine hearty cheers, and dropped in the sea a bottle, enclosing a slip of parchment with a brief account of the principle of the invention.[18] Hardly, however, had we done with our rejoicings, when an unforeseen accident occurred which discouraged us in no little degree.[19] The steel rod connecting the spring with the propeller was suddenly jerked out of place, at the car end, (by a swaying of the car through some movement of one of the two seamen we had taken up,) and in an instant hung dangling out of reach, from the pivot of the axis of the screw. While we were endeavoring to regain it, our attention being completely absorbed, we became involved in a strong current of wind from the East, which bore us, with rapidly increasing force, towards the Atlantic. We soon found ourselves driving out to sea at the rate of not less, certainly, than fifty[f] or sixty[g] miles an hour, so that we came up with Cape Clear, at some forty[h] miles to our North, before we had secured the rod, and had time to think what we were about. It was now that Mr. Ainsworth made an extraordinary, but to my fancy, a by no means unreasonable or chimerical proposition, in which he was instantly seconded by Mr. Holland — viz.: that we should take advantage of the strong gale which bore us on, and in place of beating back to Paris, make an attempt to reach the coast of North America. After slight reflection I gave a willing assent to this bold proposition, which (strange to say) met with objection from the two seamen only. As the stronger party, however, we overruled their fears, and kept resolutely upon our course. We steered due West; but as the trailing of the buoys materially impeded our progress, and we had the balloon abundantly at command, either for ascent or descent, we first threw out fifty pounds of ballast, and then wound up (by

---

f 50 *(A)*
g 60 *(A)*
h 40 *(A)*

means of a windlass) so much of a rope as brought it quite clear of the sea. We perceived the effect of this manœuvre immediately, in a vastly increased rate of progress; and, as the gale freshened, we flew with a velocity nearly inconceivable; the guide-rope flying out behind the car like a streamer from a vessel. It is needless to say that a very short time sufficed us to lose sight of the coast. We passed over innumerable vessels of all kinds, a few of which were endeavoring to beat up, but the most of them lying to. We occasioned the greatest excitement on board all — an excitement greatly relished by ourselves, and especially by our two men, who, now under the influence of a dram of Geneva, seemed resolved to give all scruple, or fear, to the wind. Many of the vessels fired signal guns;[i] and in all we were saluted with loud cheers (which we heard with surprising distinctness) and the waving of caps and handkerchiefs.[20] We kept on in this manner throughout the day, with no material incident, and, as the shades of night closed around us, we made a rough estimate of the distance traversed. It could not have been less than five hundred[j] miles, and was probably much more. The propeller was kept in constant operation, and, no doubt, aided our progress materially. As the sun went down, the gale freshened into an absolute hurricane, and the ocean beneath was clearly visible on account of its phosphorescence. The wind was from the East all night, and gave us the brightest omen of success. We suffered no little from cold, and the dampness of the atmosphere was most unpleasant; but the ample space in the car enabled us to lie down, and by means of cloaks and a few blankets, we did sufficiently well.[21]

P. S. (by Mr. Ainsworth). The last nine hours have been unquestionably the most exciting of my life. I can conceive nothing more sublimating than the strange peril and novelty of an adventure such as this. May God grant that we succeed! I ask not success for mere safety to my insignificant person, but for the sake of human knowledge and — for the vastness of the triumph. And yet the feat is only so evidently feasible that the sole wonder is why men have scrupled to attempt it before. One single gale such as now befriends us — let such a tempest whirl forward a balloon for

i guns; some displayed flags *(A)*   j 500 *(A)*

four or five[k] days (these gales often last longer) and the voyager will be easily borne, in that period, from coast to coast. In view of such a gale the broad Atlantic becomes a mere lake. I am more struck, just now, with the supreme silence which reigns in the sea beneath us, notwithstanding its agitation, than with any other phenomenon presenting itself. The waters give up no voice to the heavens. The immense flaming ocean writhes and is tortured uncomplainingly.[22] The mountainous surges suggest the idea of innumerable dumb gigantic fiends struggling in impotent agony. In a night such as is this to me, a man *lives* — lives a whole century of ordinary life — nor would I forego this rapturous delight for that of a whole century of ordinary existence.[23]

Sunday, the seventh. [Mr. Mason's MS.] This morning the gale, by 10, had subsided to an eight or nine knot breeze, (for a vessel at sea,) and bears us, perhaps, thirty[l] miles per hour, or more. It has veered however, very considerably to the north; and now, at sundown, we are holding our course due west, principally by the screw and rudder, which answer their purposes to admiration. I regard the project as thoroughly successful, and the easy navigation of the air in any direction (not exactly in the teeth of a gale) as no longer problematical. We could not have made head against the strong wind of yesterday; but, by ascending, we might have got out of its influence, if requisite. Against a pretty stiff breeze, I feel convinced, we can make our way with the propeller. At noon, to-day, ascended to an elevation of nearly 25,000 feet,[m] by discharging ballast. Did this to search for a more direct current, but found none so favorable as the one we are now in. We have an abundance of gas to take us across this small pond, even should the voyage last three[n] weeks. I have not the slightest fear for the result. The difficulty has been strangely exaggerated and misapprehended. I can choose my current, and should I find *all* currents against me, I can make very tolerable headway with the propeller. We have had no incidents worth recording. The night promises fair.

P. S. [By Mr. Ainsworth.] I have little to record, except the fact

k 4 or 5 *(A)*
l 30 *(A)*
m feet (about the height of Cotopaxi) *(A)*
n 3 *(A)*

(to me quite a surprising one) that, at an elevation equal to that of Cotopaxi, I experienced neither very intense cold, nor headache, nor difficulty of breathing; neither, I find, did Mr. Mason, nor Mr. Holland, nor Sir Everard. Mr. Osborne complained of constriction of the chest — but this soon wore off.[24] We have flown at a great rate during the day, and we must be more than half way across the Atlantic. We have passed over some twenty[o] or thirty[p] vessels of various kinds, and all seem to be delightfully astonished. Crossing the ocean in a balloon is not so difficult a feat after all. *Omne ignotum pro magnifico.*[25] *Mem:* at 25,000 feet elevation the sky appears nearly black, and the stars are distinctly visible;[26] while the sea does not seem convex (as one might suppose) but absolutely and most unequivocally *concave.**

Monday, the 8th. [Mr. Mason's MS.] This morning we had again some little trouble with the rod of the propeller, which must be entirely remodelled, for fear of serious accident — I mean the steel rod not the vanes. The latter could not be improved. The wind has been blowing steadily and strongly from the northeast all day; and so far fortune seems bent upon favoring us. Just before day, we were all somewhat alarmed at some odd noises and concussions in the balloon, accompanied with the apparent rapid subsidence of the whole machine. These phenomena were occasioned by the expansion of the gas, through increase of heat in the

* *Note.* — Mr. Ainsworth has not attempted to account for this phenomena,[q] which, however, is quite susceptible of explanation. A line dropped from an elevation of 25,000 feet, perpendicularly to the surface of the earth (or sea), would form the perpendicular of a right-angled triangle, of which the base would extend from the right angle to the horizon, and the hypothenuse from the horizon to the balloon. But the 25,000 feet of altitude is little or nothing, in comparison with the extent of the[r] prospect. In other words, the base[s] and hypothenuse of the supposed triangle would be so long when compared with the perpendicular, that the two former may be regarded as nearly parallel. In this manner the horizon of the æronaut[t] would appear to be *on a level* with the car. But, as the point immediately beneath him seems, and is, at a great distance below him, it seems, of course, also, at a great distance below the horizon. Hence the impression of *concavity;* and this impression must remain, until the elevation shall bear so great a proportion to the extent of prospect, that the apparent parallelism of the base and hypothenuse disappears — when the earth's real convexity must become apparent.[u]

---

o 20 *(A)*
p 30 *(A)*
q phenomenon *(A)*
r *Omitted (A)*
s case *(A) misprint*
t aronaut *(A) misprint*
u become apparent./appear. *(A)*

atmosphere, and the consequent disruption of the minute particles of ice with which the network had become encrusted during the night.[27] Threw down several bottles to the vessels below. Saw one of them picked up by a large ship — seemingly one of the New York line packets. Endeavored to make out her name, but could not be sure of it. Mr. Osborne's telescope made it out something like "Atalanta."[28] It is now 12, at night, and we are still going nearly west, at a rapid pace. The sea is peculiarly phosphorescent.

P. S. [By Mr. Ainsworth.] It is now 2, A.M., and nearly calm, as well as I can judge — but it is very difficult to determine this point, since we move *with* the air so completely.[v] I have not slept since quitting Wheal-Vor, but can stand it no longer, and must take a nap. We cannot be far from the American coast.

Tuesday, the 9th. [Mr. Ainsworth's MS.] *One, P.M. We are in full view of the low coast of South Carolina.* The great problem is accomplished. We have crossed the Atlantic — fairly and *easily* crossed it in a balloon! God be praised! Who shall say that anything is impossible hereafter?

—

The Journal here ceases. Some particulars of the descent were communicated, however, by Mr. Ainsworth to Mr. Forsyth. It was nearly dead calm when the voyagers first came in view of the coast, which was immediately recognised by both the seamen, and by Mr. Osborne. The latter gentleman having acquaintances at Fort Moultrie,[29] it was immediately resolved to descend in its vicinity. The balloon was brought over the beach (the tide being out and the sand hard, smooth, and admirably adapted for a descent,) and the grapnel let go, which took firm hold at once. The inhabitants of the island, and of the fort, thronged out, of course, to see the balloon; but it was with the greatest difficulty that any one could be made to credit the actual voyage — *the crossing of the Atlantic.* The grapnel caught at 2, P. M., precisely; and thus the whole voyage was completed in seventy-five[w] hours;[30] or rather less, counting from shore to shore. No serious accident occurred. No real

v completely. The vanes are working admirably. *(A)*

w 75 *(A)*

danger was at any time apprehended. The balloon was exhausted and secured without trouble; and when the MS. from which this narrative is compiled was despatched from Charleston, the party were still at Fort Moultrie. Their farther intentions were not ascertained; but we can safely promise our readers some additional information either on Monday or in the course of the next day, at farthest.

This is unquestionably the most stupendous, the most interesting, and the most important undertaking, ever accomplished or even attempted by man. What magnificent events may ensue, it would be useless now to think of determining.

NOTES

1. This paragraph repeats verbatim the screaming newspaper headlines of the *Extra Sun.* The first six words were omitted when the *Sunday Times* reprinted the piece. The four men named were real Englishmen. Thomas Monck Mason had accompanied Charles Green (1785–1870) on the famous flight of the *Great Nassau* balloon from Vauxhall Gardens, London, to Weilburg in Nassau, Germany, November 7–8, 1836. Green considered making regular flights, but also planned an "Atlantic Balloon," to be operated by clockwork-driven propellers and steered by a rudder. There is an account of his experiments in the London *Mirror,* April 4, 1840; his invention, the dragrope or guide rope, is mentioned in "Mellonta Tauta" at n. 5. Mason wrote an account of the Nassau Voyage, and built a model balloon in 1843; both are referred to in the story. The man is curiously obscure; no date of birth is known. J. E. Hodgson, in his *History of Aeronautics in Great Britain* (1924), p. 249, says Mason was prominent in the operatic world, at one time a lessee of Her Majesty's Theatre in London, and lived until 1889. Robert Hollond M.P. backed Green financially, made the trip to Nassau, represented Hastings in Parliament, 1837–1851, and lived until 1870. Poe (or the printer) misspelled his name consistently, as "Holland." William Samuel Henson was born in 1805, and in 1842 organized the Aerial Steam Transportation Company. His experiments ended in failure and in 1849 he emigrated to the United States. He lived first near Philadelphia, and died in Newark, New Jersey, March 22, 1888. William Harrison Ainsworth (1805–1882) was an English novelist, whose *Guy Fawkes* Poe reviewed unfavorably in *Graham's Magazine* for November 1841. I find no evidence of any interest in flying on the part of Ainsworth, but he was an extremely popular writer, and his name gives an excuse for literary touches in his part of the narrative. He is even made to quote Latin – and in "Marginalia," number 12 *(Democratic Review,* November 1844, p. 486), Poe remarked on Ainsworth's love of phrases in that language.

2. Sir Everard Bringhurst is imaginary; no knight or baronet of the name is listed by British authorities. Mr. Osborne is also made up. Lord William George Bentinck (1802–1848), son of the fourth Duke of Portland, had nephews through

his sister, the wife of Lord Howard de Walden, but their family name was Scott-Ellis.

3. Nobody named Forsyth[e] is in the Charleston directories for 1840–41 and 1849, and none were published between those dates, according to Miss Virginia Rugheimer, Librarian of the Charleston Library Society.

4. Sir George Cayley (1773–1857) is now generally called "The Father of British Aeronautics." For pictures of his balloons see Hodgson, *History of Aeronautics in Great Britain,* p. 300. [According to C. H. Gibbs-Smith, *Flight through the Ages* (1974), p. 22: "In the first half of the nineteenth century there was little useful activity in aviation except by Cayley, until W. S. Henson published his brilliantly prophetic design for a monoplane, 'Aerial Steam Carriage' (1843) which . . . did much to condition the thinking of later pioneers."]

5. With the preceding passage compare "Another Aerial Machine," *Alexander's Express Messenger,* February 21, 1844, cited in the introduction above:

"Mr. Henson's scheme of flight is founded upon the principle of an inclined plane, started from an eminence by an extrinsic force, applied and *continued* by the revolution of impinging vanes, in form and number resembling the sails of a windmill. In the experiments which were made in this gallery, (the Adelaide) with several models of Mr. Henson's construction, it was found that so far from *aiding* the machine in its flight, the operation of these vanes actually *impeded* its progress; inasmuch as it was always found to proceed to a greater distance by the mere force of acquired velocity (which is the only force it ever displayed,) than when the vanes were set in motion to aid it – a simple fact, which it is unnecessary to dilate upon. It is to the agency of this cause, namely, the broken continuity of surface, that, I have no doubt, is also to be ascribed the failure of the attempt of Sir George Cayley to propel a balloon of a somewhat similar shape to the present, which he made at the Polytechnic Institution a short while since, when he employed a series of revolving vanes, four in number, disposed at proper intervals around, but which were found ineffectual to move it."

6. Willis's Rooms, in King Street, St. James's, were built in 1765 by William Almack, whose niece, Mrs. Willis, inherited the place in 1781. These Assembly Rooms were the scene of Almack's Balls, mentioned by Poe in "Lionizing." The Royal Adelaide Gallery was in the Strand.

7. With this paragraph and the next compare the following passage from *Alexander's Express Messenger,* cited in n. 5:

"The balloon, is as before stated, an ellipsoid or solid oval; in length 13 feet 6 inches, and in height 6 feet 8 inches. It contains a volume of gas equal to about 320 cubic feet, which, in pure hydrogen, would enable it to support a weight of twenty-one pounds, which is about its real power when recently inflated, and before the gas has had time to become deteriorated. The whole weight of the machine and apparatus is seventeen pounds; consequently, says the projector, there is about four pounds to spare. Beneath the centre of the balloon, and about two thirds of its length, is a frame of light wood, answering to the hoop of an ordinary balloon; to which are attached the cords of the net which encloses the suspending vessel, and which serves to distribute the pressure of the appended weight equally over its whole surface, as well as to form an intermediate means of attachment for the rest of the apparatus. This consists of a car or basket in the centre . . . The Archimedean screw (by which the model is propelled) consists of an axis of hollow brass tube eighteen inches in length, through which, upon a semi-spiral of 15 degrees of inclination, are passed a series of radii or spokes of steel wire, two feet long, (thus projecting a foot on either side) and which being connected at their outer extremities by two bands of flattened wire, form the frame-work of the screw, which is completed by a covering of oiled silk cut into gores, and tightly stretched, so as to present as nearly uniform a surface as the nature of the case will permit. This screw is supported at either end of the axis by pillars of hollow brass tube descending from the hoop, in the lower extremities of which are the holes in which the pivots of the axis revolve. From the end of the axis which is next the car, proceeds a shaft of steel, which connects the Archimedean screw with the pinion of a piece of spring machinery seated in the car; by the operation of which it is made to revolve, and a progressive motion communicated to the whole apparatus. This spring is of considerable power, compared with its dimensions, being capable of raising about forty-five pounds upon a barrel of four inches' diameter after the first turn and gradually increasing as it is wound up. It weighs altogether, eight pounds six ounces. The rudder is a light frame of cane covered with silk, somewhat of the form of an elongated battledoor, about three feet long, and one foot wide, where it is largest. It weighs altogether only two ounces and a half . . . Being so contrived as to be capable of being turned *flat,* and also directed upwards or downwards as well as to the right or left, it enables the aeronaut to transfer the resistance of the air, which, in an inclined position, it must generate in its passage, to any side upon which he may desire to act, and thus give determination to the course of the balloon in an opposite direction."

The material in the *Express Messenger,* quoted in notes 5 and 7, is essentially the same as that given in parallel passages in Wilkinson's "Poe's 'Balloon Hoax' Once More" (*AL,* November 1960) as from *Remarks on the Ellipsoidal Balloon* . . . , the ultimate source of Poe's borrowings. [Wilkinson used the copy at the University of Michigan, where it is not now available for checking, but a copy has been located at the Science Reference Library in London, catalogued under Thomas Monck Mason.]

8. As observed in note 2 above, Mr. Osborne is Poe's invention – and so is Penstruthal, which is found in no atlas consulted.

9. The last two paragraphs are based on the ideas of Charles Green concerning the possibility of crossing the Atlantic in a balloon – "the result of observations made during two hundred and seventy-five ascents," according to the writer of "A Chapter on Science and Art" in *Burton's Magazine,* March 1840, who goes on to say: "Pure hydrogen must be discarded, as too subtle for our present means of retention. Balloons inflated with carburetted hydrogen (common coal gas) will retain a good inflation for a great length of time . . . [Green] has . . . travelled two thousand nine hundred miles with the same supply of gas, and could have continued its use for four months if necessary."

10. Poe's borrowings from Mason's *Account of the Late Aeronautical Expedition* . . . were recorded in parallel passages in Scudder's "Poe's 'Balloon Hoax' " (*AL,* May 1949) where the full indebtedness was first worked out. See Mason's *Account of the Late Aeronautical Expedition,* p. 11, and footnote:

"Provisions which had been calculated for a fortnight's consumption in case of emergency; ballast to the amount of upwards of a ton in weight, disposed in bags of different sizes, duly registered and marked, together with an unusual supply of cordage, implements, and other accessories to an aerial excursion, occupied the bottom of the car; while all around the hoop and elsewhere appended, hung cloaks, carpet-bags, barrels of wood and copper, coffee-warmer,* barometers, telescopes, lamps, wine jars and spirit flasks, with many other articles designed to serve the purposes of a voyage to regions where once forgotten, nothing could be again supplied."

"* A machine had been contrived for the purpose of warming coffee and other liquors, without the intervention of fire, by the means of slacked lime."

11. See Mason, *Account,* p. 9: "When a balloon ascends to navigate the atmosphere, independent of the loss of power occasioned by its own imperfections, an incessant waste of its resources in gas and ballast becomes the inevitable consequence of its situation. No sooner has it quitted the earth than it is immediately subjected to the influence of a variety of circumstances tending to create a difference in its weight; augmenting or diminishing, as the case may be, the power, by the means of which it is supported. The deposition or evaporation of humidity to the extent, in proportion to its size, of several hundred-weight; the alternate heating and cooling of its gaseous contents by the remotion or interposition of clouds between the object itself, and the influence of the solar rays, with a variety of other more secret, though not less powerful agencies, all so combine to destroy the equilibrium which it is the main object of the Aeronaut to preserve, that scarcely a moment passes without some call for his interposition, either to check the descent of the balloon by the relection of ballast, or to control its ascent by the proportionate discharge of gas; a process by which, it is unnecessary to observe, the whole power of the balloon, however great its dimensions, must in time be exhausted, and sooner or later terminate its career by succumbing to the laws of terrestrial gravitation."

12. For the merits of the guiderope, see Mason, *Account,* pp. 8, 9: "Great however as are the merits of Mr. Green's previous discoveries, they may be said to yield importance to that whereby he has succeeded in enabling the aeronaut to maintain the power of his balloon undiminished during the continuance of the most protracted voyage it could ever be required to perform ... By the simple contrivance of a rope of the requisite magnitude and extent, trailing on the ground beneath, (and if over the sea, with a sufficient quantity of liquid ballast contained in vessels floating on its surface,) have all these difficulties [i.e., the necessary loss of gas and ballast] been overcome, and all the features of the art completely and effectually reversed. Harnessed to the earth or ocean, by a power too great for her to resist, it is in vain the balloon endeavours to change the level of her onward course."

13. See Mason, *Account* p. 10n.: "The progress of the guide-rope being delayed to a certain extent by its motion over the more solid plane of the earth's surface, while the movement of the balloon is as freely as ever controlled by the propelling action of the wind, it is evident that the direction of the latter when in progress, must ever be in advance of the former; a comparison, therefore of the relative positions of these two objects by means of the compass, must at all

times indicate the exact direction of her course; while with equal certainty, an estimate can at once be obtained of the velocity with which she is proceeding, by observing the angle formed by the guide-rope, and the vertical axis of the machine. In proportion as this angle enlarges, an increase in the rate of the balloon may be infallibly inferred: and, vice versa, its diminution will be found to correspond exactly with the diminished velocity of her advance. When the rope is dependent perpendicularly, no angle of course is formed, and the machine may be considered as perfectly stationary, or at least endowed with a rate of motion too insignificant to be either appreciable or important."

14. Poe meant the English Channel (between Dover and Calais) here.

15. Weal-Vor House, like its owner, is mythical.

16. The Bristol Channel is between South Wales and the southwest tip of England, extending as far as Portsmouth.

17. See Mason, *Account,* p. 16: "In this situation [over the English Channel], we prepared to avail ourselves of those contrivances, the merits of which, as I have already stated, it was one of the main objects of our expedition to ascertain; and consequently, to provide against the loss of power by the increase of weight proceeding from the humidity of the atmosphere, naturally to be expected on the approach of night, we commenced lowering the copper vessels which we had provided for the occasion.

"Scarcely, however, had we completed our design, and were patiently awaiting the descent we had anticipated, when the faint sound of the waves beating against the shore again returned upon our ears, and awakened our attention. The first impression which this event was calculated to convey, was that the wind had changed, and that we were in the act of returning to the shores we had so shortly before abandoned. A glance or two, however, served to show us the fallacy of this impression; the well known lights of Calais . . . were already glittering beneath us."

18. Poe has characters put messages in bottles in "MS. Found in a Bottle," "Mellona Tauta," and *The Narrative of Arthur Gordon Pym.*

19. Compare the narrative following the accident in Poe's tale with the passage reproduced here to see how Mason's material was used by Poe to effect a dramatic reversal of direction and provide the crux of his story. In Mason's account the maneuver of the balloon set it "in the exact direction of crossing the straits" from England to France; in Poe's, it enabled the voyagers to make a new and daring decision to steer "due west."

From Mason's *Account,* p. 14: "Shortly after we had lost sight of the city of Canterbury, a considerable deviation appeared to have taken place in the direction of our route. Instead of pursuing our former line of south by east, which was that of the upper current, by means of which we had hitherto advanced, it became apparent that we were now rapidly bearing away upon one which tended considerably to the northward, and which, had we continued to remain within the limits of its influence, would have shortly brought us to sea, in the direction of the North Foreland. As it had all along been an object to proceed as near to Paris as circumstances would permit, we resolved to recover as soon as possible the advantages which a superior current had hitherto afforded us; and accordingly rose to resume a station upon our previous level. Nothing could exceed the beauty of this manoeuvre, or the success with which the balloon acknowledged the influence of her former associate. Scarcely had the superfluous burden been discharged proportioned to the effect required, when slowly she arose, and sweeping majestically around the horizon, obedient to the double impulse of her increasing elevation and the gradual change of current, brought us successively in sight of all those objects which we had shortly before left retiring behind us, and in a few minutes placed us almost vertically over the Castle of Dover, in the exact direction of crossing the straits between that town and Calais, where it is confined within its narrowest limits."

20. Mason, *Account,* pp. 13, 14: "During the latter period of this part of our voyage, the balloon . . . had continued so near the earth as to enable us, without much exertion, to carry on a conversation with such of the inhabitants as happened to be in our immediate vicinity."

21. See Mason, *Account,* p. 22: "The cold, during this part of the night especially, was certainly intense . . . Strange, however, as it may appear, . . . the effects produced upon our persons, undefended as they were by any extraordinary precautions, were by no means commensurate to the cause."

22. See Mason, *Account,* p. 16n: "I scarcely know whether it is an observation worthy of being committed to paper, that the sea, unless perhaps under circumstances of the most extraordinary agitation, does not in itself appear to be the parent of the slightest sound; unopposed by any material obstacle, an awful stillness seems to reign over its motions." And compare, also, Poe's "Dream-Land," lines 15–16: "Seas that restlessly aspire,/Surging, unto skies of fire."

23. Compare the famous lines, "One crowded hour of glorious life/Is worth an age without a name," quoted by Sir Walter Scott in chapter 34 of *Old Mortality* from a poem by Major Mordaunt in the Edinburgh *Bee,* October 12, 1791, and reprinted in the *Literary Digest,* 1920, page 38. The lines previously were generally supposed to be by Scott himself.

24. See Mason, *Account,* p. 34n: " . . . we frequently rose to an elevation of about twelve thousand feet, occasionally higher. At no time, however, did we experience the *slightest* effect upon our bodies, proceeding from the diminished pressure of the atmosphere." Cotopaxi, in Ecuador, 19,550 feet, in Poe's day was the highest mountain known. It is an active volcano, near Quito. See another mention of it in "Hans Phaall" in paragraph 24.

25. The Latin, meaning "Everything unknown is taken for magnificent," is from Tacitus, *Agricola,* XXX.

26. See Mason, *Account,* p. 21: "The sky, at all times darker when viewed from an elevation than it appears to those inhabiting the lower regions of the earth, seemed almost black with the intensity of night; while by contrast no doubt, and the remotion of intervening vapors, the stars, redoubled in their lustre, shone like sparks of the whitest silver scattered upon the jetty dome around us." Poe was writing hastily and did not notice that his source described a scene near midnight.

27. See Mason, *Account,* p. 23: "At this moment, while all around is im-

penetrable darkness and stillness, and darkness most profound, an unusual explosion issues from the machine above, followed instantaneously by a violent rustling of the silk, and all the signs which may be supposed to accompany the bursting of the balloon. In the same instant, the car as if suddenly detached from its hold, becomes subjected to a violent concussion, and appears at once to be in the act of sinking with all its contents into the dark abyss below . . . In a moment after all is tranquil and secure . . . The occurrence of this phenomenon . . . is, nevertheless, susceptible of the simplest resolution, and consists in the tendency to enlargement which the balloon experiences in rising from a low to a higher position in the atmosphere and the resistance to this enlargement occasioned by the network previously saturated with moisture, and subsequently congealed."

28. A packet from Liverpool arrived in New York on Saturday, April 13, but it was really the *Sheridan.* The error was made intentionally for verisimilitude.

29. Fort Moultrie is on Sullivan's Island in Charleston Harbor, where Poe was a soldier, 1827–1828. The island is the setting for "The Gold-Bug."

30. A dirigible balloon, the R 34, crossed the Atlantic in early July 1919. Its return trip took seventy-five hours, exactly Poe's figure. See the New York *Sun,* July 14, 1919, pointed out by Victor Paltsits for Phillips, *Poe the Man,* II, 873. Poe allowed his aeronauts to have very fair weather, *unusual* except for two brief periods in summer, and a very strong east wind, unusual at any time – small concessions indeed in fiction. Hervey Allen remarked in *Israfel* (1926), II, 588, that Poe "only anticipated the news by about a century."

UNSIGNED CONTRIBUTIONS TO THE *PUBLIC LEDGER*

These sketches were originally published in the Philadelphia *Public Ledger,* July 17, 18, and 19, 1844. In the *Columbia Spy* of August 14, Eli Bowen reprinted the second with the following introduction:

> A Rich Article. "Fun *is* fun," says the proverb. If the following article from the Philadelphia Ledger does not set our readers into a broad laugh, we know not human nature. From the style and manner, we should infer that the paper was written by Edgar A. Poe, who, it is whispered, indites many of the leaders of that able journal. It looks very much like him.

Few men were more likely to hear "whispers" about Poe than Bowen, to whose *Spy* he had been contributing in May and June of the same year. Poe did not deny the ascription of this article, so typically in his manner. It cannot be proved that Poe knew of

Bowen's remark, but, as Clarence S. Brigham said to me, the case is just short of absolute proof.*

The author of "A Moving Chapter" is surely that of its continuation. The third article, "Desultory Notes on Cats" in the *Ledger* of July 19, is also obviously closely akin to them, but nothing else of the kind is to be found in the paper. The three pieces were collected by Jacob E. Spannuth and me in Poe's *Doings of Gotham* (Pottsville, 1929), pp. 79–91.

[I]

A MOVING CHAPTER. — The *Omnibus* may be defined as a moveable house of public entertainment on strictly temperance principles, and four wheels. The word Omnibus is derived, or rather taken bodily from the Latin; and in view of that fact, we have made a painfully severe inquiry into the locomotive habits of the Romans, to find if they had the omnibus. But after profound researches, which would not have dishonored the industry of Niebuhr himself,[1] we arrived at no satisfactory conclusion. So we must leave that an open question for the antiquarian clubs. In modern times the discovery of the omnibus dates after that of the steamboat, and before that of the magnetic telegraph.[2] All three are united in a great cause, either the rapid conveyance of persons or ideas; the two first, however, frequently carrying persons without ideas, and the last being strictly confined, thus far, to carrying ideas without persons. But we are growing personal and ideal in our remarks, while our object is to be simply matter of fact. So we will not dilate on that head.

When the omnibus was first started (literally speaking) in Philadelphia, it was exclusively consecrated to the service of gentlemen weighing each twenty stone;[3] presidents of rich corporations, who had fallen irrevocably into fat, and who humanely thought that it was better to kill sorry public horses in dragging their heavy bodies over the stones, than to sacrifice a private pair periodically in that service. But by the multiplication of this public facility (we believe that is the word in use) other persons partook of the benefit; and the door (we speak figuratively now — the omnibus in hot

* See n. 3 below.

weather has no door) was opened to men less portly. Mothers or nurses also, with sleeping infants, would insinuate themselves into the omnibus; and it became a delicate question with the young gentlemen who takes the sixpences and soils the tickets,[4] whether the little affair of the *chargee* should go at half or whole price. But we believe, though our information is not accurate, never yet having been a mother, or even a nurse, that infants now go for nothing at all in the omnibus. This seems unkind on the part of the young gentleman, to estimate the moral and physical weight of the infant at nothing, when his own are not much. Next young ladies, who had no infants, would timorously venture into an omnibus; young men generally grew suddenly weak about the knees, and changed exercise into inertia in an omnibus. So all ages, sexes and conditions, ride now, where they used to walk; and we would not be surprised if the early accomplishment of using one's limbs (legs) were ultimately confined to newspaper carriers, porters, and pedestrians.

It is better to ride in an omnibus than to have your own carriage, because an omnibus cannot be upset, any more than a billiard-ball; neither can the horses run away. History records no example of an omnibus horse entertaining such an idea. Do we not often meet with an account of a rich man dying in a gutter, or in newspaper phrase, being dashed against a curbstone and killed instantly? But not from an omnibus, but from the private carriage, does this happen. So people, with or without brains to dash out, think of this when you meditate setting up a fine coach with a spirited pair.

The internal arrangements of an omnibus are superior to those of the old-fashioned stage coach. In a half-empty stage coach you cannot lie down. But in an omnibus, if there be one side full only, you can lie down on the other, and go to sleep, hat off and boots up. All the stuff in poetry and prose about quiet being necessary to sleep, you can practically deny. Monotony, not quiet, is the thing to put one to sleep. It is the quiet which wakes you up when the coach stops. We once heard of a man who had fallen asleep during a roaring thunder storm, and only waked up when the last tremendous clap (which struck the house) had just ceased. This loud fact sets the question at rest, if it be a question at all, which is a question. If you do not go to sleep in an omnibus, you should be careful as to your manners, for the word omnibus, translated, means, every body for himself.[5] If there be a modest, pretty girl within it, by all means put yourself directly opposite to her. Then an honest man is bound to have an open countenance; so open it upon her, and put her out of her countenance. If there be an old, infirm lady in the omnibus, do not move your feet as she endeavors to pass, but if you well nigh trip her up, it will be serviceable in reminding her of her declining years and strength, and thus help to reconcile her with fate. If there be a sick child, who complains, do you complain of people who bring sick children into an omnibus. If there be many passengers, delay them when you get in or out. A good plan is to require the young gentleman in attendance to change a five dollar note, just as you leave, and pay your fare. A wet umbrella and a dirty dog are useful in a full omnibus. When you enter and leave, tread upon the company's toes; it hurts their feelings, but yet makes an impression. Just now the omnibus is very useful. If a riot breaks out, you can ride into it in a few minutes;[6] you can also ride in an omnibus to Fairmount, and drink the pure warm water, just as it comes from the reservoir.[7] But as it is near dinner time we shall leave off writing, and take to riding in an Omnibus.

[II]

A MOVING CHAPTER CONTINUED. — In consideration of these times of popular movement, we ventured, yesterday, to say a few words on the people's coach and pair — the Omnibus. Following up the subject, we shall now offer a running commentary on the *Cab*, with the reader's kind permission.[8] This asking permission, however, after the thing is printed and poked under the reader's nose, is very much like humbug — but such is the fashion.

The derivation of the word *cab* is not quite certain. According to Dr. Lumberskull, of Gutt-stuffin University, the word comes from the lately discovered antediluvian Arabic. In that language, *caba* means *go-ahead* — hence a cab, a thing for going ahead.[9] But, with due deference to the doctor's erudition, we are inclined to think that the word comes from the Greek. In the Isle of Naxos, the word *kabos* means *tub*.[10] Now it is believed by some, and we are of that number, that the tub of the George Munday[11] of Greece, Diogenes, was not one of your vulgar washingtubs, but a circular box, on wheels, drawn, probably, by a donkey — possibly by a Newfoundland dog. This being the fact, the weight of evidence inclines to the Greek; for the word *kabos* is in Schrevilius,[12] and has not been lost, as we have shown, in the modern dialect. It probably floated, centuries ago, from the mainland to the island, where it has remained in use to this time. The word cab, however, sounds like English, inasmuch as it expresses the nature of the thing itself, for it has a squat, angular sound — cab! *Carriage,* an easy sound; *omnibus,* a heavy import. In this thing of the sound of words echoing their sense,[13] the English is remarkable. For example, *Christchurch-steeple* — a lofty, pointed sound; *sugarhousemolasses* — "linked sweetness, long drawn out,"[14] it strikes on the ear.

You can get into a difficulty gratis, at any time, but it requires twenty-five cents to get into a cab. The omnibus lines are as straight as those of a regiment; the lines of a cab are, on the contrary, all sorts; squares, rhomboids, cones, circles — whatever you are willing to pay for. As it is known that cabmen, in imitation of their illustrious ancestors, hackmen, are in a conspiracy to make all the money they can, and in which they differ, totally, from the rest of the world, the City Fathers have determined to put them down in this matter; accordingly, their prices are regulated by a special ordinance of the Select and Common Councils; so that gentlemen worth ten thousand a year cannot be ruined by being charged twelve cents too much cab-hire.

When it is considered that all the cabmen, without exception, are millionaires (of this fact we are confidentially assured), the wisdom of the ordinance is apparent. The aristocracy of apple women, of hot-corn venders, of charcoal men, of that particular man who makes such a devil of a noise with his "trallala! lemon ice-cream — and *the* vanilla, too!" should all read in this a severe lesson, that Law can protect the poor people in Chestnut and Walnut and Arch streets against their extortions. But we are deriving eloquence from a sense of indignation, while our desire is to be simply analytical.

The character of the cabman is soon summed up. If you approach within forty feet of one of them, he roars out "Cab, surr!" though you may at the time be looking out for an eclipse, or a lost trinket, in an opposite direction. The cabman, notwithstanding his wealth, dresses as if he is poor. His parsimony is further evinced in his manner, which seems to indicate that he does not get enough for his work. Actuated by a sneaking fondness for the root of all evil, he is willing to expose himself to all weathers, and all night, too, like the watchman; without a box to sleep in, or the privilege of boring you with execrable verses about sleet, and snow, and burglars, and all that, at Christmas time.[15] The cabman drives generally but one horse. It is obviously labor-saving machinery, if you can, to make one horse do the work of two. In case of a horse famine it would be well, therefore, to pass a horse law, operating upon all vehicles with two horses, taking up one of them – i. e., the horses. Seizing the horse would probably make him mad, and then he could be put to death under the statute against hydrophobia.

As the cab is heavy, and the rich driver is not light, not more than five persons, with their luggage, should drive up at night (after the horse has been on duty sixteen hours) from the foot of Chestnut street to Broad. There were some gentlemen who intended to start a "Society for the Suppression of Cruelty to Animals,"[16] and wishing to try how many passengers it would take to kill a horse in a given time, by way of scientific experiment, they got into a cab, about four too many, and the result was the cab overturned backwards. Now had the aforesaid gentlemen been, after the accident, drawn out, like Adam's wife, from the side, it would have been a humane experiment; but the back door coming on the ground, they were imprisoned in a lonely spot until muscular force was brought to their relief.

The manners which one should practice in a cab are easily told. When you enter, especially at night time, let your boots be filthy; plant them forthwith upon the opposite seat; and the next stranger, supposing her to be a lady in white satin, going to a ball, will remember that cab, though she has forgotten its number. As Americanism partakes largely of a defiance of law, just now,[17] you might occupy yourself by pitching the framed twenty-five ordinance out of the window. If you think yourself handsome, you may, in the day time, make mouths before the little looking-glass in the cab. It will be a lesson in human nature, showing its reflections under different circumstances. In consideration of the indignity which the cabman offers you, by emptying you out like a load of dirt at the back of a cart, you may very properly refuse to pay him a cent. If he ventures to bring the matter before the authorities, he will have to pay the costs, because the sympathy of republican power is never with extortion and aristocracy.

NOTES

[I]

1. Barthold Georg Niebuhr (1776–1831) was a German scholar of vast and varied learning, who, for his *Roman History* (English translation, 3 v., London, 1828–1842), studied monuments as well as literary sources.

2. Robert Fulton's steamboat, *Clermont,* made its first round trip between New York and Albany in August 1807; Samuel F. B. Morse sent his epoch-making message by telegraph between Washington and Baltimore on May 24, 1844. The new magnetic telegraph and steamboats are referred to as wonders in "The Thousand-and-Second Tale of Scheherazade."

3. Twenty stone is 280 pounds; use of the term, still current in England, was unusual in America, even in Poe's day. Its use, admittedly, does not strengthen the case for Poe as author of "A Moving Chapter."

4. To "soil the tickets" was obviously to cancel them; the word in this sense has not been recorded in dictionaries consulted. It may have been done with a drop of acid, a method sometimes used to cancel the stamps of private local posts.

5. Latin "omnibus" means primarily "for all," but may bear the humorous meaning given in the text.

6. There were serious anti-Catholic riots in Philadelphia in the summer of 1844. Members of the so-called American Party – the "Know-Nothings" – were concerned. The trouble began when a militia company, made up largely of Irish immigrants, stored rifles in the cellar of a Roman Catholic church, and rumors of a "Papist Rebellion" spread. The rumors were of course absurd, but some lives were lost in the violence. The newspapers were full of the troubles.

7. Fairmount Park is on the outskirts of the City of Philadelphia. Poe lived in the vicinity, at 2502 Coates Street in North Fairmount, for a time, in 1842 and early 1843. See Phillips, *Poe the Man,* I, 817.

[II]

8. Compare the *jeu d'esprit* "Cabs" from *Alexander's Weekly Messenger* of April 1, 1840, above.

9. Dr. Lumberskull of Gut-stuffin University – that is, Göttingen – reminds us of the imaginary learned Dutch worthies in "Hans Phaall" and "The Devil in the Belfry." The antediluvian Arabic "caba" is pure nonsense.

10. The word kabos, from the Hebrew *qab,* is a grain measure, used in the

Septuagint and in St. Luke 16:6 (translated "measure" in the King James Version). No vocabulary of the Naxian dialect has been found.

11. George Munday was a well-known eccentric in Philadelphia and its vicinity, who, for religious reasons, wore a beard. He was occasionally seen intoxicated. He was called "the hatless prophet" in a notice that he had been arrested for wife beating, in the New York *Evening Mirror,* July 21, 1846.

12. Cornelius Schrevelius (1615–1664), a Dutch scholar, compiled a *Lexicon Manuale,* Greco-Latin and Latin-Greek. First published in 1654, it was often reprinted for use in schools. *Schrevelius' Greek Lexicon translated into English,* 2nd edition, with added English and Greek Lexicon, was published in London in 1831, 3rd edition in 1836, and a 4th in 1841.

13. Compare Pope's *Essay on Criticism,* II, 165: "The sound must seem an echo to the sense."

14. The quotation is from Milton's "L'Allegro," line 140.

15. Night watchmen, like newspaper carriers, presented broadside poems to their patrons. Some printed specimens from Philadelphia are in the Harris Collection at Brown University.

16. See "The Literary Life of Thingum Bob, Esq.," note on ¶24. The movement for the protection of animals spread from England after the organization there in 1824 of the Society for the Prevention of Cruelty to Animals, which gained prestige by the addition of "Royal" to its title in 1840. In America the cause was among the mid-century reforms being agitated, but it was not until 1866 that the first American society with the same declared purpose was formed, by Henry Bergh, in New York.

17. Americanism here refers to the violence of the "Know-Nothing" party; see n. 6 above.

[III]

DESULTORY NOTES ON CATS. — Cats were first invented in the garden of Eden. According to the Rabbins, Eve had a pet cat, called Pusey, and from that circumstance arose a sect of cat-worshippers among the Eastern nations, called Puseyites, a sect which, it is said, is still in existence somewhere.[1] When rats began to be troublesome, Adam gave the first pair of cats six lessons in the art of catching them; and since then the knowledge has been retained. The Greeks spelled cat with a *k,* and the French put an *h* into it; the pure English scholar will not heed such ignorance, but will keep to the right orthography.[2] In the time of Chaucer,[3] cataract was spelt cat-erect; but what analogy there is between a cat getting up in the world and water falling down in it, it is difficult to say. The introduction of the cat into cat-aplasm, cat-egory, &c., is unauthorized;

it is without the knowledge or consent of the parties, and has no meaning. Cat-nip, on the contrary, has a signification; it bears the same relation to the animal economy of the cat that Pease's hoarhound candy does to that of the animal economy of man.[4] It is mentioned that a gentleman in the pursuit of knowledge under difficulties, wishes to know what is the reason that cats which have that within them which contains such divine melody, should make such execrable music themselves? The answer to this, perhaps, is simple. Cats are modest. They make no show of accomplishments. You never hear of a learned cat. Learned pigs, bears and dogs, who can tell what time of day it is, and how many spectators are present (which last is easily told, to the sorrow of the showman,) are common. But who ever heard of a learned cat? A cat pretends to no knowledge, not even to that of the piano and singing. If you kill her you may prepare a physical essence, so to speak, which, if stretched and resined, may have a divine effect.[5] It is probably the departed spirit refined down to a single string, and making simple melody, whereas, in the original, the strings were interlinked and confused, so that they produced necessarily discordant sounds; to say nothing of their being vulgarly alive, and in a raw state of nature.

This explanation seems clear. A young cat or kitten is graceful; her chief occupation is chasing her tail, but her tail will not stay chased. Very little children adore very little cats. But when the children, if boys, grow bigger, and learn the humanities at school, all about Draco,[6] Alexander and Cæsar, they change towards cats, and kill them whenever sport prompts them to do so. Among the saws, is one that persecution makes that thrive which it seeks to subdue. This is a slight mistake. In the case of rats, which cats persecute, persecution ever thins their numbers. It is only when persecution is half way, or has a spice of charity, that it does what the saw says. Not only in the case of rats, but of Indians, is this shown to be a false saw. The Indians have been persecuted with fire, whiskey and sword, and they are nearly exterminated. It is only when the cat is in love that she makes a fool of herself. It is then, that, forgetting all other considerations in the fullness of her heart, the cat plays, unconsciously, the troubadour. (We apply the feminine gender and pronoun to cats, because all cats are she; in the same way that all sluts and mares are called he, a peculiar beauty of the English language.)[7] The serenading cat makes a noise like an infant with the cholic, for which it is often mistaken. Both sexes of cats sport whiskers and moustaches; whether the actual she cats will ever change the fashion, as it applies to them, after it has so long prevailed, is doubtful. One of the brightest pages in English Annals, is the History of Whittington and his Cat.[8] We know a boy, who has a cat, and says he intends hereafter to be Mayor of Philadelphia. Not the slightest objection to it.

NOTES

Title: Poe's fondness for cats is well known. See cat behavior described in "Bon-Bon" and "Instinct vs Reason," and my introduction to "The Black Cat."

1. The reference to the Rabbins may be a sly allusion to the fact that cats are not mentioned in the Bible itself. "Puseyites" were the adherents of Edward Bouverie Pusey, Regius Professor of Hebrew at Oxford, who in 1843 had been suspended for two years, by the vice chancellor, from preaching before the university – an action that generated much controversy. Poe considered the storm raised about the beliefs of Pusey and his High Church associates to be a tempest in a teapot. See n. 17 on the 1845 version of "Lionizing"; and "Marginalia," number 3 (*Democratic Review,* November 1844, p. 485).

2. Greek for cat is *katos;* French, *le chat.* Poe has puns on "cat" in "Enigmatical and Conundrum-ical" (*Alexander's Weekly Messenger,* December 18, 1839) and in the *Saturday Museum,* April 1, 1843.

3. The reference here is pure nonsense. Poe almost never speaks of Chaucer. In reviewing Hall's *Book of Gems* (*SLM,* August 1836), Poe includes Chaucer in a list of English poets, and in a review of Chivers' poems in the *Broadway Journal,* August 2, 1845, he says that Chivers' work belongs "to the era of impulse – in contra-distinction to the era of criticism – to the Chaucerian rather than to the Cowperian days."

4. The Compound Extract of Hoarhound, made by John Pease and Son, 44 Division Street, New York, was widely sold nationally. Among the testimonials, in an advertisement in the New York *Brother Jonathan,* December 23, 1843, is one from Andrew Jackson. Hoarhound (horehound) drops are still used by some as cough drops.

5. Jokes about cats and violin strings made of catgut are commonplace, although the entrails really used are those of sheep.

6. Draco, an Athenian lawgiver of the Seventh Century before our era, wished to punish so many offenses by death that he is regarded as a monster of cruelty. His name means a big snake and it was punningly said "his were not the laws of a man but a dragon." Poe referred to "Draconian Laws" in "William Wilson."

7. The remark on the custom of referring to cats as "she," to dogs and horses as "he" is of interest. The phenomenon known as "unnatural gender" is common

in many languages, but is so rare in English that few of our grammars mention it. Boats of all kinds and cats are generally called "she" even now.

8. Richard Whittington (d. 1423) was a real person, and a friend of Henry V, who is said to have knighted him. He was a prominent merchant from about 1380 to 1423, and served three times as mayor of London. But the legends about him, familiar in the nursery and often printed in chapbooks, are what the author of "Desultory Notes on Cats" had in mind. According to these, Dick came to London as a poor boy and was employed in the kitchen of a wealthy man. There was an opportunity for members of the household to send items for sale in a trading vessel, and Dick had only his cat to offer. The ship went to a port in Barbary, where there was great need for cats, and the animal fetched a high price. Meanwhile, Dick was used badly by the cook, and determined to go home from the City. As he was walking away he heard the ringing of Bow Bells, which seemed to him to say: "Turn again, Whittington, Lord Mayor of London!" He obeyed, and soon was given the large sum received for his cat. With this as a beginning, he prospered greatly in trade, married an heiress, and in time became Lord Mayor.

THE ANGEL OF THE ODD

This is a bit of good-natured buffoonery, probably the most pleasantly absurd story Poe ever wrote. If we accept his own idea that the true basis of the comic is the combination of elements that do not belong together, we must regard "The Angel of the Odd" as a successful production.

It is also of interest in exemplifying Poe's love of experiment. In this tale the impossible incidents are throughout treated quizzically; and, at last, everything turns out to be a dream. Reviewing Dr. Robert Montgomery Bird's *Sheppard Lee* in the *Southern Literary Messenger,* September 1836, Poe had dismissed both the dream and complete jocularity as inferior methods in treatment of the incredible, but in 1844, he could not resist trying them out.*

Professor Gerald E. Gerber, in an article he courteously showed me before publication, pointed out that " 'The Angel of the Odd' . . . provides additional evidence of Poe's well-known dislike for the spirit of social reform," burlesquing "both the ideal of perfectibility and those reformers whose schemes were calculated to improve mankind."†

* A dream is hinted in "Some Words with a Mummy," but thereafter Poe avoided impossible subjects. His wild stories involving mesmerism are not really exceptions, for many of Poe's contemporaries thought they might be true.

† [See Gerber's paper, "Poe's Odd Angel," *Nineteenth Century Fiction,* June 1968, pp. 88–93.]

THE ANGEL OF THE ODD

As early as 1835, in "Lionizing," Poe had made fun of "a human-perfectibility man" along with other guests at Lady Blessington's party. Writing to Lowell on July 2, 1844, he said: "I have no faith in human perfectibility. I think that human exertion will have no appreciable effect upon humanity"; and on July 10 he wrote to Chivers, "Man is now only more active, not wiser nor more happy, than he was 6000 years ago." He summarized his opinion on reformers in 1849:

> The world is infested, just now, by a new sect of philosophers, who have not yet suspected themselves of forming a sect, and who, consequently, have adopted no name. They are the *Believers in everything Odd.* Their High Priest, in the East, is Charles Fourier – in the West, Horace Greeley . . . The only common bond among the sect, is Credulity: – let us call it Insanity at once, and be done with it.‡

Poe's impulse to write his story almost surely came from the newspaper article he quotes in his second paragraph. I found it in the Philadelphia *Public Ledger* of June 5, 1844. (See note 5 below.)

Gerber refers to a number of possible sources for ideas and details in Poe's story, ranging from "It's Very Odd," a story in *Blackwood's,* January 1829, through several books reviewed by Poe, to brief items in New York papers in the spring and summer of 1844, including one on "Progress of Social Questions" in the *Tribune* of June 8. Most significant of these sources is Cornelius Webbe's *The Man About Town* (Philadelphia, 1839), briefly noted in *Burton's,* October 1839, by Poe, who mentions for special commendation the chapter "Punning &c Made Easy." There is found an account of a transcendentalist Professor of Humanity from Leipzig, visiting England, who had his breeches repaired by "a little sporting slang tailor." When the job was completed, the tailor asked for "Eight and a Kick." The transcendentalist – who prided himself on his knowledge of English but did not know that "kick" was rhyming slang for sixpence – said, "Mein Gott! dat is very ott of him!" – then gave the tailor eight shillings and kicked him.

Webbe's moral is "a little learning is a dangerous thing," and Gerber thinks Poe played on the rest of Pope's couplet, "Drink deep or taste not the Pierian spring," not only with relation to

‡ "Fifty Suggestions" number 28, *Graham's Magazine,* June 1849, p. 363. Harrison, 14:179, misprints *Odd* as *Old,* thereby destroying the point.

Kirschenwasser but also to one of the "utopian excesses" of the time, Hydropathy.

Poe himself paid his respects to the water cure in the fifth letter of "Doings of Gotham," printed in the *Columbia Spy,* June 15, 1844, where he called its propounder, Vincent Priessnitz, "that monarch of charlatans." Priessnitz, a peasant, advocated the external and internal use of cold water for every ailment.§ The foes of liquor — the Washingtonians — also advocated at least the internal use of "Adam's ale." Poe's angel reverses things in substituting for plain water its namesake Kirschenwasser, a colorless but highly potent brandy, with results disastrous to the narrator of the story.

Poe's tale was probably written in the summer of 1844.*

TEXTS

(A) Columbian Magazine for October 1844 (2:158–161); *(B) Works,* IV (1856), 278–287.

Griswold's text *(B)* is used; he obviously had a revised form. Two words, omitted by accident, are restored in our text from the first printing *(A)*. The spelling "villanous" was accepted in Poe's day, and both authorized texts of this story use this spelling.

THE ANGEL OF THE ODD. [*B*]

AN EXTRAVAGANZA.

It was a chilly November afternoon. I had just consummated an unusually hearty dinner, of which the dyspeptic[a] *truffé*[a'] [1] formed not the least important item, and was sitting alone in the dining-room, with my feet upon the fender, and at my elbow a small table

§ Three enthusiasts for the regimen became friends of Poe later – Marie Louise Shew, who wrote *Water-Cure for Ladies* (1844), her brother-in-law Dr. Joel Shew, and Mrs. Mary Gove Nichols. They did not change Poe's attitude, and he ridiculed Hydropathy and other current fads in his "Literati" sketch, "Mary Gove," in *Godey's,* July 1846.

* Woodberry's comment on his listing of the tales (*Life,* 1909, II, 405) fails to take account of the fact that "The Angel of the Odd" is not mentioned as either published or unpublished in Poe's list of tales written up to May 28, 1844 in his letter of that date to Lowell.

---

a dispeptic *(A)* a' *truffe (A, B)*

which I had rolled up to the fire, and upon which were some apologies for dessert, with some miscellaneous bottles of wine, spirit and *liqueur*. In the morning I had been reading Glover's "Leonidas," Wilkie's[b] "Epigoniad," Lamartine's "Pilgrimage," Barlow's "Columbiad," [c]Tuckerman's "Sicily," and[c] Griswold's "Curiosities;" I am willing to confess, therefore, that I now felt a little stupid.[2] I made effort to arouse myself by aid of frequent Lafitte,[3] and, all failing, I betook myself to a stray newspaper in despair. Having carefully perused the column of "houses to let," and the column of "dogs lost," and then the two columns of "wives and apprentices runaway," I attacked with great resolution the editorial matter, and, reading it from beginning to end without understanding a syllable, conceived the possibility of its being Chinese, and so re-read it from the end to the beginning, but with no more satisfactory result. I was about throwing away, in disgust,

> This folio of four pages, happy work
> Which not even critics criticise,[4]

when I felt my attention somewhat aroused by the paragraph which follows:

"The avenues to death are numerous and strange. A London paper mentions the decease of a person from a singular cause. He was playing at 'puff the dart,' which is played with a long needle inserted in some worsted, and blown at a target through a tin tube. He placed the needle at the wrong end of the tube, and drawing his breath strongly to puff the dart forward with force, drew the needle into his throat. It entered the lungs, and in a few days killed him."[5]

Upon seeing this I fell into a great rage, without exactly knowing why. "This thing," I exclaimed, "is a contemptible falsehood — a poor hoax — the lees of the invention of some pitiable penny-a-liner — of some wretched concoctor of accidents in Cocaigne.[6] These fellows, knowing the extravagant gullibility of the age, set their wits to work in the imagination of improbable possibilities — of odd accidents, as they term them; but to a reflecting intellect (like mine," I added, in parenthesis, putting my forefinger unconsciously

---

b Wickliffe's *(A)* c . . . c and *(A)*

to the side of my nose,) "to a contemplative understanding such as I myself possess, it seems evident at once that the marvellous increase of late in these 'odd accidents' is by far the oddest accident of all. For my own part, I intend to believe nothing henceforward that has anything of the 'singular' about it."

"Mein Gott, den, vat a vool you bees for dat!" replied one of the most remarkable voices I ever heard. At first I took it for a rumbling in my ears — such as a man sometimes experiences when getting very drunk — but, upon second thought, I considered the sound as more nearly resembling that which proceeds from an empty barrel beaten with a big stick; and, in fact, this I should have concluded it to be, but for the articulation of the syllables and words. I am by no means naturally nervous, and the very few glasses of Lafitte which I had sipped served to embolden me no little, so that I felt nothing of trepidation, but merely uplifted my eyes with a leisurely movement, and looked carefully around the room for the intruder. I could not, however, perceive any one at all.

"Humph!" resumed the voice, as I continued my survey, "you mus pe so dronk as de pig, den, for not zee me as I zit here at your zide."

Hereupon I bethought me of looking immediately before my nose, and there, sure enough, confronting me at the table sat a personage nondescript, although not altogether indescribable. His body was a wine-pipe, or a rum puncheon, or something of that character, and had a truly Falstaffian air. In its nether extremity were inserted two kegs, which seemed to answer all the purposes of legs. For arms there dangled from the upper portion of the carcass two tolerably long bottles, with the necks outward for hands. All the head that I saw the monster possessed of was one of those Hessian canteens which resemble a large snuff-box with a hole in the middle of the lid.[7] This canteen (with a funnel on its top, like a cavalier cap slouched over the eyes) was set on edge upon the puncheon, with the hole toward myself; and through this hole, which seemed puckered up like the mouth of a very precise old maid, the creature was emitting certain rumbling and grumbling noises which he evidently intended for intelligible talk.

"I zay," said he, "you mos pe dronk as de pig, vor zit dare and not zee me zit ere; and I zay, doo, you mos pe pigger vool as de goose, vor to dispelief vat iz print in de print. 'Tiz de troof – dat it iz – eberry vord ob it."

"Who are you, pray?" said I, with much dignity, although somewhat puzzled; "how did you get here? and what is it you are talking about?"

"As vor ow I com'd ere," replied the figure, "dat iz none of your pizziness; and as vor vat I be talking apout, I be talk apout vat I tink proper; and as vor who I be, vy dat is de very ting I com'd here for to let you zee for yourzelf."

"You are a drunken vagabond," said I, "and I shall ring the bell and order my footman to kick you[d] into the street."

"He! he! he!" said the fellow, "hu! hu! hu! dat you can't do."

"Can't do!" said I, "what do you mean? – I can't do what?"

"Ring de pell;" he replied, attempting a grin with his little villanous mouth.

Upon this I made an effort to get up, in order to put my threat into execution; but the ruffian just reached across the table very deliberately, and hitting me a tap on the forehead with the neck of one of the long bottles, knocked me back into the arm-chair from which I had half arisen. I was utterly astounded; and, for a moment, was quite at a loss what to do. In the meantime, he continued his talk.

"You zee," said he, "it iz te bess vor zit still; and now you shall know who I pe. Look at me! zee! I am te *Angel ov te Odd*."

"And odd enough, too," I ventured to reply; "but I was always under the impression that an angel had wings."

"Te wing!" he cried, highly incensed, "vat I pe do mit te wing? Mein Gott! do you take me vor a shicken?"

"No – oh no!" I replied, much alarmed, "you are no chicken – certainly not."

"Well, den, zit still and pehabe yourself, or I'll rap you again mid me vist. It iz te shicken ab te wing, und te owl ab te wing, und te imp ab te wing, und te head-teuffel[8] ab te wing. Te angel ab *not* te wing, and I am te *Angel ov te Odd*."

---

d you out *(A)*

"And your business with me at present is — is" —

"My pizzness!"[e] ejaculated the thing, "vy vat a low bred[f] buppy you mos pe vor to ask a gentleman und an angel apout his pizziness!"

This language was rather more than I could bear, even from an angel; so, plucking up courage, I seized a salt-cellar which lay within reach, and hurled it at the head of the intruder. Either he dodged, however, or my aim was inaccurate; for all I accomplished was the demolition of the crystal which protected the dial of the clock upon the mantel-piece. As for the Angel, he evinced his sense of my assault by giving me two or three hard consecutive raps upon the forehead as before. These reduced me at once to submission, and I am almost ashamed to confess that either through pain or vexation, there came a few tears into my eyes.

"Mein Gott!" said the Angel of the Odd, apparently much softened at my distress; "mein Gott, te man is eder ferry dronk or ferry zorry. You mos not trink it so strong — you mos put te water in te wine. Here, trink dis, like a goot veller, und don't gry now — don't!"

Hereupon the Angel of the Odd replenished my goblet (which was about a third full of Port) with a colorless fluid that he poured from one of his hand bottles. I observed that these bottles had labels about their necks, and that these labels were inscribed "Kirschenwasser."[9]

The considerate kindness of the Angel mollified me in no little measure; and, aided by the water with which he diluted my Port more than once, I at length regained sufficient temper to listen to his very extraordinary discourse. I cannot pretend to recount all that he told me, but I gleaned from what he said that he was the genius who presided over the *contretemps*[g] of mankind, and whose business it was to bring about the *odd accidents* which are continually astonishing the skeptic. Once or twice, upon my venturing to express my total incredulity in respect to his pretensions, he grew very angry indeed, so that at length I considered it the wiser policy to say nothing at all, and let him have his own way. He talked

e pizziness!" *(A)*
f pred *(A)*
g *contre temps (A)*

on, therefore, at great length, while I merely leaned back in my chair with my eyes shut, and amused myself with munching raisins and filliping the stems about the room. But, by-and-by,[h] the Angel suddenly construed this behavior of mine into contempt. He arose in a terrible passion, slouched his funnel down over his eyes, swore a vast oath, uttered a threat of some character which I did not precisely comprehend, and finally made me a low bow and departed, wishing me, in the language of[i] the archbishop in Gil-Blas, *"beaucoup de bonheur et un peu plus de bon sens."*[10]

His departure afforded me relief. The *very*[j] few glasses of Lafitte that I had sipped had the effect of rendering me drowsy, and I felt inclined to take a nap of some fifteen or twenty minutes, as is my custom after dinner. At six I had an appointment of consequence, which it was quite indispensable that I should keep. The policy of insurance for my dwelling house had expired the day before; and, some dispute having arisen, it was agreed that, at six, I should meet the board of directors of the company and settle the terms of a renewal. Glancing upward at the clock on the mantel-piece, (for I felt too drowsy to take out my watch), I had the pleasure to find that I had still twenty-five minutes to spare. It was half past five; I could easily walk to the insurance office in five minutes; and my usual[k] siestas had never been known to exceed five and twenty. I felt sufficiently safe, therefore, and composed myself to my slumbers forthwith.

Having completed them to my satisfaction, I again looked toward the time-piece and was half inclined to believe in the possibility of odd accidents when I found that, instead of my ordinary fifteen or twenty minutes, I had been dozing only three; for it still wanted seven and twenty of the appointed hour. I betook myself again to my nap, and at length a second time awoke, when, to my utter amazement, it *still* wanted twenty-seven minutes of six. I jumped up to examine the clock, and found that it had ceased running. My watch informed me that it was half past seven; and, of course, having slept two hours, I was too late for my appointment. "It will make no difference," I said: "I can call at the office in the

h by and bye, *(A)*
i *Omitted (B) restored from A*
j very *(A)*
k usual post prandian *(A)*

morning and apologize; in the meantime what can be the matter with the clock?" Upon examining it I discovered that one of the raisin stems which I had[l] been filliping about the room during the discourse of the Angel of the Odd, had flown through the fractured crystal, and lodging, singularly enough, in the key-hole, with an end projecting outward, had thus arrested the revolution of the minute hand.

"Ah!" said I, "I see how it is. This thing speaks for itself. A natural accident, such as *will* happen now and then!"

I gave the matter no further[m] consideration, and at my usual hour retired to bed. Here, having placed a[n] candle upon a reading stand at the bed head, and having made an attempt to peruse some pages of the "Omnipresence of the Deity,"[11] I unfortunately fell asleep in less than twenty seconds, leaving the light burning as it was.

My dreams were terrifically disturbed by visions of the Angel of the Odd. Methought he stood at the foot of the couch, drew aside the curtains, and, in the hollow, detestable tones of a rum puncheon, menaced me with the bitterest vengeance for the contempt with which I had treated him. He concluded a long harangue by taking off his funnel-cap, inserting the tube into[o] my gullet, and thus deluging me with an ocean of Kirschenwässer, which he poured, in a continuous flood, from one of the long necked bottles that stood him instead of an arm. My agony was at length insufferable, and I awoke just in time to perceive that a rat had run off with the lighted candle from the stand, but *not* in season to prevent his making his escape with it through the[p] hole. Very soon, a strong suffocating odor assailed my nostrils; the house, I clearly perceived, was on fire. In a few minutes the blaze broke forth with violence, and in an incredibly brief period the entire building was wrapped in flames. All egress from my chamber, except through a window, was cut off. The crowd, however, quickly procured and raised a long ladder. By means of this I was descending rapidly, and in apparent safety, when a huge hog, about whose rotund stomach, and

---

l *Omitted (B) restored from A*
m farther *(A)*
n the *(A)*
o in *(A)*
p his *(A)*

indeed about whose whole air and physiognomy, there was something which reminded me of the Angel of the Odd — when this hog, I say, which hitherto had been quietly slumbering in the mud, took it suddenly into his head that his left shoulder needed scratching, and could find no more convenient rubbing-post than that afforded by the foot of the ladder. In an instant I was precipitated and had the misfortune to fracture my arm.

This accident, with the loss of my insurance, and with the more serious loss of my hair, the whole of which had been singed off by the fire, predisposed me to serious impressions, so that, finally, I made up my mind to take a wife. There was a rich widow disconsolate for the loss of her seventh husband,[q] and to her wounded spirit I offered the balm of my vows. She yielded a reluctant consent to my prayers. I knelt at her feet in gratitude and adoration. She blushed and bowed her luxuriant tresses into close contact with those supplied me, temporarily, by Grandjean.[12] I know not how the entanglement took place, but so it was. I arose with a shining pate, wigless; she in disdain and wrath, half buried in alien hair. Thus ended my hopes of the widow by an accident which could not have been anticipated, to be sure, but which the natural sequence of events had brought about.

Without despairing, however, I undertook the siege of a less implacable heart. The fates were again propitious for a brief period; but again a trivial incident interfered. Meeting my betrothed in an avenue thronged with the *élite*[r] of the city, I was hastening to greet her with one of my best considered bows, when a small particle of some foreign matter, lodging in the corner of my eye, rendered me, for the moment, completely blind. Before I could recover my sight, the lady of my love had disappeared — irreparably affronted at what she chose to consider my premeditated rudeness in passing her by ungreeted. While I stood bewildered at the suddenness of this accident, (which might have happened, nevertheless, to any one under the sun), and while I still continued incapable of sight, I was accosted by the Angel of the Odd, who proffered me his aid with a civility which I had no reason to expect.

---

q spouse, *(A)*

r *elite (A)*

He examined my disordered eye with much gentleness and skill, informed me that I had a drop in it,[13] and (whatever a "drop" was) took it out, and afforded me relief.

I now considered it high time[s] to die, (since fortune had so determined to persecute me), and accordingly made my way to the nearest river. Here, divesting myself of my clothes, (for there is no reason why we cannot die as we were born), I threw myself headlong into the current; the sole witness of my fate being a solitary crow that had been seduced into the eating of brandy-saturated corn, and so had staggered away from his fellows. No sooner had I entered the water than this bird took it into his head to fly away with the most indispensable portion of my apparel. Postponing, therefore, for the present, my suicidal design, I just slipped my nether extremities into the sleeves of my coat, and betook myself to a pursuit of the felon with all the nimbleness which the case required and its circumstances would admit. But my evil destiny attended me still. As I ran at full speed, with my nose up in the atmosphere, and intent only upon the purloiner of my property, I suddenly perceived that my feet rested no longer upon *terra-firma;* the fact is, I had thrown myself over a precipice, and should inevitably have been dashed to pieces but for my good fortune in grasping the end of a long guide-rope, which depended from a passing balloon.[14]

As soon as I sufficiently recovered my senses to comprehend the terrific predicament in which I stood or rather hung, I exerted all the power of my lungs to make that predicament known to the æronaut overhead. But for a long time I exerted myself in vain. Either the fool could not, or the villain would not perceive me. Meantime the machine rapidly soared, while my strength even more rapidly failed. I was soon[t] upon the point of resigning myself to my fate, and dropping quietly[u] into the sea, when my spirits were suddenly revived by hearing a hollow voice from above, which seemed to be lazily humming an opera air. Looking up, I perceived the Angel of the Odd. He was leaning with his arms folded, over the rim of the car; and with a pipe in his mouth, at which he puffed

s high time/time *(A)*
t *Omitted (A)*
u quiety *(B) misprint*

leisurely, seemed to be upon excellent terms with himself and the universe. I was too much exhausted to speak, so I merely regarded him with an imploring air.

For several minutes, although he looked me full in the face, he said nothing. At length removing carefully his meerschaum from the right to the left corner of his mouth, he condescended to speak.

"Who pe you," he asked, "und what der teuffel you pe do dare?"

To this piece of impudence, cruelty and affectation, I could reply only by ejaculating the monosyllable "Help!"

"Elp!" echoed the ruffian – "not I. Dare iz te pottle – elp yourself, und pe tam'd!"

With these words he let fall a heavy bottle of Kirschenwasser which, dropping precisely upon the crown of my head, caused me to imagine that my brains were entirely knocked out. Impressed with this idea, I was about to relinquish my hold and give up the ghost with a good grace, when I was arrested by the cry of the Angel, who bade me hold on.

"Old on!" he said; "don't pe in te urry – don't! Will you pe take de odder pottle, or ave you pe got zober yet and come to your zenzes?"

I made haste, hereupon, to nod my head twice – once in the negative, meaning thereby that I would prefer not taking the other bottle at present – and once in the affirmative, intending thus to imply that I *was* sober and *had* positively come to my senses. By these means I somewhat softened the Angel.

"Und you pelief, ten," he inquired, "at te last? You pelief, ten, in te possibility of te odd?"

I again nodded my head in assent.

"Und you ave pelief in *me,* te Angel of te Odd?"

I nodded again.

"Und you acknowledge tat you pe te blind dronk und te vool?"

I nodded once more.

"Put your right hand into your left hand preeches pocket, ten, in token ov your vull zubmizzion unto te Angel ov te Odd."

This thing, for very obvious reasons, I found it quite impossible to do. In the first place, my left arm had been broken in my fall from the ladder, and, therefore, had I let go my hold with the right hand, I must have let go altogether. In the second place, I could have no breeches until I[v] came across the crow. I was therefore obliged, much to my regret, to shake my head in the negative – intending thus to give the Angel to understand that I found it inconvenient, just at that moment, to comply with his very reasonable demand! No sooner, however, had I ceased shaking my head than –

"Go to der teuffel, ten!" roared the Angel of the Odd.

In pronouncing these words, he drew a sharp knife across the guide-rope by which I was suspended, and as we then happened to be precisely over my own house, (which, during my peregrinations, had been handsomely rebuilt,) it so occurred that I tumbled headlong down the ample chimney and alit upon the dining-room hearth.

Upon coming to my senses, (for the fall had very thoroughly stunned me,) I found it about four o'clock in the morning. I lay outstretched where I had fallen from the balloon. My head grovelled in the ashes of an extinguished fire, while my feet reposed upon the wreck of a small table, overthrown, and amid the fragments of a miscellaneous dessert, intermingled with a newspaper, some broken glasses and shattered bottles, and an empty jug of the Schiedam Kirschenwasser. Thus revenged himself the Angel of the Odd.

NOTES

1. A dish *truffé,* that is with truffles, is usually very rich.

2. The books mentioned are all dull, at least they were in Poe's opinion. Professor George Saintsbury called Richard Glover's *Leonidas* (1737) a "stupendous and terrible blank-verse epic." *The Epigoniad* (1757) is an epic on the Seven against Thebes by the "Scotch Homer," William Wilkie. The reading "Wickliffe" of the earliest version is puzzling, since a reference to the fourteenth-century English religious reformer, John Wycliffe, would be pointless. But it may have been a slip of the author or of his printer, since Charles A. Wickliffe of Kentucky was Postmaster General in Tyler's cabinet, 1841–1845, and the name was familiar. Lamartine's *Souvenirs d'Orient* was translated with the title *Pilgrimage to the Holy Land* (1835); Poe had no high regard for Lamartine – see "The Murders in the Rue Morgue," n. 18. Joel Barlow's *Columbiad* (Baltimore,

---

v we *(A)*

1807) is a huge volume by the Hartford Wit, an epic in heroic couplets on Columbus; a reference to it was canceled in "The Domain of Arnheim." Poe reviewed Henry T. Tuckerman's *Isabel, or Sicily: A Pilgrimage* (Philadelphia, 1839) in *Burton's,* July 1839, and mentioned it in "A Chapter on Autography" (*Graham's,* November 1841), where he called Tuckerman "a *correct* writer... but an insufferably tedious and dull one." Poe, however, seems to have liked Tuckerman personally after they met in 1845. Griswold, at the instigation of the publishers, compiled a 64-page independently numbered addition to increase the bulk of a two-column American reprinting of Isaac D'Israeli's popular and durable work. See *Curiosities of Literature, and The Literary Character Illustrated, by I.C.* [!] *D'Israeli... With Curiosities of American Literature, by Rufus W. Griswold*... New York, D. Appleton & Co., 1844, and the preface to Griswold's addition. See also Poe's comments on Griswold's appendix in his letters to the *Columbia Spy* dated June 18 and June 25, 1844 (*Doings of Gotham,* pp. 68–69 and p. 76) where he calls it "that last and greatest of all absurdities."

3. Château Lafite is usually considered the best of the red wines of Bordeaux. Poe mentioned it also in "Lionizing" and in early versions of "Bon-Bon." Not only in this story but always Poe spelled this wine "Lafitte," which makes it doubtful that he is here referring to *Lafitte, the Pirate of the Gulf,* a popular novel he reviewed unfavorably in *SLM,* August 1836.

4. The lines describing a newspaper are from Cowper's *Task,* IV, 50–51.

5. Save for the first line, the quotation about "puff-the-dart" I found almost verbatim, headed "Singular Death," in the Philadelphia *Public Ledger* of June 5, 1844. See my note in the London *N & Q,* January 3, 1931.

6. Cocaigne (or Cockaigne – see *OED*) is a humorous name for London, home of the Cockneys.

7. A Hessian canteen made of tinned iron, found in the Hut Camp of the Hessian Body Regiment at Arden Street, Manhattan, is now in the New-York Historical Society. It has a cylindrical body seven and three-quarters inches high and five and three-quarters wide – a little larger than a two-pound coffee can – with a spout one inch high and seven-eighths in diameter centered in the top. Gerber called attention to a being who appears first as a leaping mustard pot and then as a fairy among the supper dishes in *Anster Fair* (1812) by William Tennant. This portion of Tennant's mock-heroic poem was reprinted in the *New Mirror* (New York), May 4, 1844.

8. Head devil.

9. Kirschenwasser, cherry brandy, is made at Schiedam in Holland, and elsewhere in Europe, from unpitted whole cherries; it is more often called kirschwasser or kirsch.

10. The angel wishes the narrator "plenty of happiness and a little more good sense" in French of Poe's own. In Le Sage's *Gil Blas,* VII, iv, the archbishop wishes the hero "toutes sorts de prospérités avec un peu de goût" – taste.

11. Robert Montgomery's *Omnipresence of the Deity* (London, 1828), although it had twenty-six editions before 1855, is famed for dullness. Poe alludes to the soporific effect of the book in "Loss of Breath"; see n. 15 on that tale, and

see also "Never Bet the Devil Your Head," n. 20. In "Marginalia," number 83 (*Democratic Review,* December 1844), Poe says he can find no merit in "anything ever written by either of the Montgomeries."

12. Auguste Grandjean "hair comp." had an establishment at 1 Barclay Street, New York, according to the 1844 Directory. See also "Loss of Breath" for reference to the hair tonic made by him.

13. A drop in the eye means slightly intoxicated. Compare Robert Burns, "O Willie brewed a Peck o' Maut": "We are na fou', we're no that fou,/But just a drappie in our e'e."

14. The dirigibles *Victoria* in the "Balloon Hoax" and *Skylark* in "Mellonta Tauta" also have trailing guide ropes.

PREFACE TO MARGINALIA

The pleasant little Introduction to the series of miscellaneous paragraphs that Poe called "Marginalia" is to some extent integral to a collected edition of them, which there is reason to think Poe planned.* But it has also its place in our volumes containing his Tales and Sketches, since it is itself fiction. Poe really wrote almost no marginal notes in books he owned, and the very few discovered are all extremely brief.† His printed "Marginalia" are made up of extracts from his reviews, and some articles – mostly, but not all, brief – composed for the series, or revised extracts from the works of others that he found of special interest.

Poe published installments of "Marginalia" in various magazines, and on January 13, 1849 wrote to John R. Thompson proposing a new series in the *Southern Literary Messenger,* at "$2 per page." On January 31, Poe wrote Thompson that he was sending "eleven pages . . . done up in a *roll*"; he suggested that they be prefaced by a reprint of his original introduction, with a note say-

* Pages of the first installment (*Democratic Review,* November 1844, pp. 484–494) with revisions in Poe's hand, now in the library of the Johns Hopkins University (see *Ex Libris,* a Quarterly Leaflet, No. 2, January 1940), show that he was planning a reprint before July 1847. His manuscript changes in number 38 include, in the paragraph alluding to ten planetoids (p. 492, col. 1), the insertion of a footnote reading: "Now eleven – Astræa since discovered" (December 8, 1845), but no mention of Hebe, found July 1, 1847.

† A list of the few books now known to be from Poe's library will appear as an appendix to our collection of the "Marginalia" in a future volume of the present edition.

ing that it was a reprint.‡ The note in the *Messenger* of April 1849 reads:

> Some years since Mr. Poe wrote for several of the Northern magazines a series of critical brevities under the title of "Marginalia." They attracted great attention at the time and since, as characteristic of the author, and we are sure that our readers will be gratified at his resuming them in the Messenger. By way of introduction, we republish the original preface from the Democratic Review. — (*Ed., Mess.*)

Despite the signature, Poe probably composed this paragraph.

TEXTS

(A) Democratic Review, November 1844 (15:484–485); *(B)* Pages of the last, with slight autograph revisions, in the Johns Hopkins University Library; *(C) Southern Literary Messenger,* April 1849 (15:217–218); *(D) Works* (1850), III, 483–485.

Our text is from the *Southern Literary Messenger (C),* verbally the same as Griswold's version *(D).*

[PREFACE TO] MARGINALIA. [*C*]

In getting my books, I have been always solicitous of an ample margin; this not so much through any love of the thing in itself, however agreeable, as for the facility it affords me of pencilling suggested thoughts, agreements and differences of opinion, or brief critical comments in general. Where what I have to note is too much to be included within the narrow limits of a margin, I commit it to a slip of paper, and deposit it between the leaves; taking care to secure it by an imperceptible portion of gum tragacanth paste.

All this may be whim; it may be not only a very hackneyed, but a very idle practice; — yet I persist in it still; and it affords me pleasure; which is profit, in despite of Mr. Bentham with Mr. Mill on his back.[1]

This making of notes, however, is by no means the making of

‡ Mr. William H. Koester kindly sent me a copy of this unpublished letter. [It was published in 1973 by Professor Moldenhauer on page 71 of his *Descriptive Catalog of Edgar Allan Poe Manuscripts.*] The letter of "May 10, 1849" relating to "Marginalia," until recently ascribed to Poe, is now known to be a forgery. [See Ostrom in *American Literature,* January 1974, p. 576.]

mere *memoranda* — a custom which has its disadvantages, beyond doubt. *"Ce que je mets sur papier,"* says Bernardin de St. Pierre, *"je remets de ma mémoire, et par consequence je l'oublie;"* — and, in fact, if you wish to forget anything on[a] the spot, make a note that this thing is to be remembered.[2]

But the purely marginal jottings, done with no eye to the Memorandum Book, have a distinct complexion, and not only a distinct purpose, but none at all; this it is which imparts to them a value. They have a rank somewhat above the chance and desultory comments of literary chit-chat — for these latter are not unfrequently "talk for talk's sake,"[3] hurried out of the mouth; while the *marginalia* are deliberately pencilled, because the mind of the reader wishes to unburthen itself of a *thought;* — however flippant — however silly — however trivial — still a thought indeed, not merely a thing that might have been a thought in time, and under more favorable circumstances. In the *marginalia,* too, we talk only to ourselves; we therefore talk freshly — boldly — originally — with *abandonnement* — without conceit — much after the fashion of Jeremy Taylor, and Sir Thomas Browne, and Sir William Temple and the anatomical Burton, and that most logical analogist, Butler, and some other people of the old day,[4] who were too full of their matter to have any room for their manner, which being thus left out of question, was a capital manner, indeed, — a model of manners, with a richly marginalic air.

The circumscription of space, too, in these pencillings, has in it something more of advantage than[b] inconvenience. It compels us (whatever diffuseness of idea we may clandestinely entertain,) into Montesquieu-ism, into Tacitus-ism, (here I leave out of view the concluding portion of the "Annals,")[5] — or even into Carlyle-ism — a thing which, I have been told, is not to be confounded with your ordinary affectation and bad grammar.[6] I say "bad grammar," through sheer obstinacy, because the grammarians (who should know better) insist upon it that I should not. But then grammar is not what these grammarians will have it; and, being merely the analysis of language, with the result of this analysis, must be good or

a upon *(A) changed in B* b than of *(A, B)*

bad just as the analyst is sage or silly — just as he is a Horne Tooke or a Cobbett.[7]

But to our sheep.[8] During a rainy afternoon, not long ago, being in a mood too listless for continuous study, I sought relief from *ennui* in dipping here and there, at random, among the volumes of my library — no very large one, certainly, but sufficiently miscellaneous; and, I flatter myself, not a little *recherché*.[9]

Perhaps it was what the Germans call the "brain-scattering" humor of the moment; but, while the picturesqueness of the numerous pencil-scratches arrested my attention, their helter-skelteriness of commentary amused me. I found myself at length, forming a wish that it had been some other hand than my own which had so bedevilled the books, and fancying that, in such case, I might have derived no inconsiderable pleasure from turning them over. From this the transition-thought, (as Mr. Lyell, or Mr. Murchison, or Mr. Featherstonhaugh would have it,)[10] was natural enough: — there might be something even in *my* scribblings which, for the mere sake of scribbling, would have interest for others.

The main difficulty respected the mode of transferring the notes from the volumes — the context from the text — without detriment to that exceedingly frail fabric of intelligibility in which the context was imbedded. With all appliances to boot, with the printed pages at their back, the commentaries were too often like Dodona's oracles[11] — or those of Lycophron Tenebrosus[12] — or the essays of the pedant's pupils, in Quintillian,[13] which were "necessarily excellent, since even he (the pedant) found it impossible to comprehend them:" — what then, would become of it — this context — if transferred? — if translated? Would it not rather be *traduit* (traduced) which is the French synonyme, or *overzezet* (turned topsy-turvy) which is the Dutch one?[14]

I concluded, at length, to put extensive faith in the acumen and imagination of the reader: — this as a general rule. But, in some instances, where even faith would not remove mountains,[15] there seemed no safer plan than so to re-model the note as to convey at least the ghost of a conception as to what it was all about. Where, for such conception, the text itself was absolutely necessary, I could quote it; where the title of the book commented upon was indispensable, I could name it. In short, like a novel-hero dilemma'd, I made up my mind "to be guided by circumstances,"[16] in default of more satisfactory rules of conduct.

As for the multitudinous opinion expressed in the subjoined *farrago* — as for my present assent to all, or dissent from any portion of it — as to the possibility of my having, in some instances, altered my mind — or as to the impossibility of my not having altered it often — these are points upon which I say nothing, because upon these there can be nothing cleverly said. It may be as well to observe, however, that just as the goodness of your true pun is in the direct ratio of its intolerability, so is nonsense the essential sense of the Marginal Note.

NOTES

1. Jeremy Bentham was the leading utilitarian philosopher. Mill, here, is probably James Mill (1773–1836), Bentham's friend and follower and a vigorous opponent of romanticism; although James's more famous son, John Stuart Mill (1806–1873), the logician, who was also interested to some extent in Bentham's ideas, may be intended.

2. Saint-Pierre's remark has not been traced. [See Burton Pollin's paper on Poe and Saint-Pierre in *Romance Notes,* Spring 1971, p. 8.]

3. On "talk for talk's sake" compare *Doings of Gotham,* Letter I (May 14, 1844), and "Marginalia," number 109 (*Democratic Review,* December 1844, p. 592). "Talking just for the sake of talking" may be traced to Plato; see W. R. M. Lamb's translation of *Laches,* 196C (*LCL* edition, *Plato,* v. II, p. 67).

4. The names of the old moralists are familiar to most readers. Jeremy Taylor (1613–1667) is best known for his *Holy Living and Holy Dying* (1650–1651); Sir Thomas Browne (1605–1682) is best known for his *Urn-Burial* (1658), whence Poe took the motto for "The Murders in the Rue Morgue"; Sir William Temple (1628–1699), patron of Jonathan Swift, wrote a great deal — his best-known essays are included in *Miscellanea,* I and II (1680, 1692) — but if Poe had any particular work in mind, it is not to be identified. Robert Burton (1577–1640) wrote the famous *Anatomy of Melancholy,* published in 1621. Joseph Butler (1692–1752) first printed his extremely popular *Analogy of Religion Natural and Revealed* in 1736.

5. Poe's reference to the conciseness of Tacitus and Montesquieu comes from the eighteenth of Hugh Blair's *Lectures on Rhetoric* (1783); see "The Man That was Used Up," and its note 22. In "Pinakidia," number 161 (*SLM,* August 1836, p. 581), Poe mentions the "extreme prolixity" of the conclusion of the *Annals.*

6. Poe's poor opinion of Carlyle's style is frequently revealed. See "Never Bet the Devil Your Head," n. 13.

7. John Horne Tooke (1736–1812), vigorous promoter of parliamentary reform, was "an old-fashioned radical, who appealed to Magna Charta but ridiculed 'the rights of man' " *(Concise DNB),* but he was also the author of *Epea Pteroenta, or the Diversions of Purley* (2 parts, 1786 and 1798), largely on etymology, which established him as a philologist. A review – Poe's almost certainly – in the *Southern Literary Messenger,* August 1836, of Charles Richardson's *New Dictionary of the English Language* called Horne Tooke "the greatest of philosophical grammarians."

William Cobbett (1762–1835), virile writer, ardent champion of the working class, published an *English Grammar* in 1818 of which over ten thousand copies were sold. Poe despised him. (See review of Pue's *Grammar* in *Graham's,* July 1841, cited in "Never Bet the Devil Your Head," n. 25.)

8. "To our sheep," meaning "Let's get back to the matter in hand," has become a proverbial expression; it is traced back through Rabelais to line 1291: "Sus! Revenons à ces moutons!" in the fifteenth century French farce *Maître Pierre Pathelin.* See introduction and notes to Richard Holbrook's translation, *The Farce of Master Pierre Patelin* (Boston and New York, 1905).

9. *Recherché* – here – means "rare."

10. Charles Lyell (1797–1875), knighted in 1848, was one of the eminent geologists of his time. He lectured in America in 1841, and published *Travels in North America, with Geological Observations* in 1845.

Roderick Impey Murchison (1792–1871, knighted in 1846) was another eminent geologist, who in 1835 distinguished and named the Silurian System – the period of the earliest plants and land animals on the earth. In 1843 and 1844 there was animated discussion in the *American Journal of Science* and other periodicals of the fossil bird-like footprints found in the Connecticut Valley, and the opinions of Murchison and Lyell were sought. Lyell thought they were bird tracks; Murchison thought they might have been made by either birds or reptiles. (G. P. Merrill, *The First One Hundred Years of American Geology,* 1924, pp. 553–559.)

George William Featherstonhaugh, an Englishman of means and education, came to America as a young man, settled in Duanesburg, New York, and became one of the directors of the railroad from Albany to Schenectady, chartered in 1826; in 1831 he founded the short-lived *Monthly American Journal of Geology and Natural History* (New York). Subsequently he served as a government geologist in various parts of the United States, and in 1844 he published *An Excursion Through the Slave States,* an account of his survey of the Ozark country, made a decade before. (See indexed references in Merrill, cited above.)

11. At Dodona in Epirus was a grove of Zeus where the priests interpreted oracularly the rustling of the oak leaves. There is another reference to it in "Silence – a Fable."

12. Lycophron Tenebrosus, a Greek poet of Alexandria, was justly called "full of darkness" from the obscurity of his works.

13. For Quintilian's obscurantists, see his *Institutes,* VIII, ii, 18. Poe found both mentioned in Isaac D'Israeli's *Curiosities of Literature,* in the chapter on

"Professors of Plagiarism and Obscurity," and refers to them also, along with Carlyle, in the paragraphs on Emerson in "An Appendix of Autographs" (*Graham's Magazine,* January 1842).

14. Poe's intentional confusion here is compounded by what is probably a printer's error – z for *g* in *overgezet.*

15. Compare I Corinthians 13:2, ". . . and though I have all faith so that I could remove mountains . . ."

16. See Livy's *Annals,* xxii, xxxix, 9–10, for "guided by circumstances."

THE SWISS BELL-RINGERS

This *jeu d'esprit* is characteristically Poe's but was overlooked for more than a century. It was first printed in the New York *Evening Mirror* with an introductory note by N. P. Willis, in the issue of October 10, 1844, and was reprinted from the same type in the *Weekly Mirror* of the twelfth.

The introductory paragraph is a clear enough ascription to our author, for surely the *Mirror* had no "regular ally . . . of a very humorous turn" except Poe. In his long essay on "Maelzel's Chess-Player" (*SLM,* April 1836), Poe had discussed several elaborate mechanical toys, citing David Brewster's *Letters on Natural Magic* and the *Edinburgh Encyclopaedia,* and he had almost certainly observed other automata when Maelzel's Exhibition – which included a trumpeter – visited Richmond in December 1835.

Poe's new article was timely. The bell-ringers, "grandly calling themselves the Campanologians," first appeared in New York "between the farces" on September 12, 1844, at Niblo's, and "made a sensational hit." They appeared at the Tabernacle on October 7, 11, and 16, and again at Niblo's on November 7.* In the *Broadway Journal,* October 18, 1845, it was noted (2:231) that "The Bell Ringers, under the direction of Mr. Corbyn, have been literally coining money the past week in New-York, Boston and other places. They are at present in this city, and all who have not heard them,

* See George C. D. Odell, *Annals of the New York Stage,* V, 77, 145, and numerous further mentions. Odell comments (p. 77) on their opening at Niblo's: "This was the first performance of that kind of musical jugglery ever heard in New York, and our ancestors were astonished and delighted. For a while these people were as much discussed as had been Ole Bull or Castellan."

would do well to visit them this week, as they start *en route* for Mexico in a few days and will not return probably for two years." But they were soon back and continued to be popular entertainers in the New York area during the rest of the decade.

Our text is from the columns of the *Mirror*.

THE SWISS BELL-RINGERS

One of the regular allies of the Mirror, a man of a very humorous critical vein, has taken it into his head to prove the Swiss Bell-ringers to be an automaton. We have argued the point with him till we are tired, and have at last sent to beg a copy of their board-bill with affidavits that their stomachs are not wooden and *do kindly entertain* rolls and sausages. While these documents are coming, we publish the skeleton of our friend's hypothesis: —

The Swiss Bell-ringers. — The readers of the Mirror scarce need be told, — as most of them have seen and heard for themselves, — that the Swiss Bell-ringers enter, to the number of seven, white-plumed and fancifully costumed, and each armed with four or five hand-bells of various sizes, which they deposit on a cushioned table before them, retaining one in each hand, which they are continually changing for others in their armory, putting down and taking up with the rapidity of jugglers, and all the while ringing the changes upon them with a delicate harmony and precision, which are as perfect in a symphony of Haydn as in "Miss Lucy Long."[1] The writer alludes to them now only to say, that they may be heard again to-night, and to correct the *erroneous but common idea that these Bell-ringers are real living beings.* The writer is firmly convinced that they are ingenious pieces of mechanism, contrived on the principle of Maelzel's Automaton Trumpeter and Piano-forte player (exhibited here some years ago), but made so much more perfect and effective by the application to them of the same power which operates in the *Electro-Magnetic* Telegraph,[2] but which should here be called *Electro-tintinnabulic.*[3] A powerful electric battery under the stage communicates by a hidden wire with each of them, and its shocks are regulated and directed by the skilful musician and mechanician who secretly man[a]ges the whole affair. This explains the precision with which they all bow at the same instant, as if moved by the same soul (and so they are — an *electric* one), and keep such perfect time and order. For this reason, too, they arrange so carefully their surplus bells before them in such exact spots, just as Maelzel's Automaton Chess-player always insisted on the pieces being placed exactly on the centre of the squares, so that his mechanically-moved fingers might not miss them. Their very number shows that they were contrived in imitation of the music of the *seven* spheres,[4] and any lurking doubt of the truth of our theory will be at once removed by noticing how they *electrify* their hearers.

NOTES

1. "Miss Lucy Long" or "Take your time, Miss Lucy," a Negro minstrel song ascribed to Billy Whitlock by Sigmund Spaeth in his *History of Popular Music in America* (1948), p. 88, was long very popular. For a text, see *Heart Songs Dear to the American People,* ed. Joe M. Chapple, p. 289.

2. The telegraphic schemes of Samuel F. B. Morse were much in the public eye in 1844; his famous initial telegram had been sent from Washington to Baltimore on May 24 of that year. There are other references to the telegraph in "Moving Chapters" and "The Thousand-and-Second Tale of Scheherazade."

3. *Tintinnabulic* here means tintinnabulous. Compare "The Bells," line 11, and note concerning words related to tintinnabulation (Mabbott I, 435, 439).

4. The music of the spheres, says the *Century Dictionary* under "Harmony," is "according to the fancy of Pythagoras and his school, a music imperceptible to human ears, produced by the movements of the heavenly bodies... The seven planets produced severally the seven notes of the gamut."

BYRON AND MISS CHAWORTH

This is a "plate article" and was presumably written by Poe at the request of the publishers of the *Columbian Magazine,* who had an engraving in their possession. In Poe's day, everybody interested in literature knew the story of Byron's first love from the account of it in Thomas Moore's biography of Byron. There are patent allusions to it in Poe's tale "The Assignation."

In youth Poe made a manuscript copy of Byron's long poem "The Dream," written in 1816 after the collapse of his ill-starred marriage to Anne Isabella Milbanke, and recalling his bitter distress, years before, at the loss of his boyhood sweetheart, Mary Chaworth, who married a much older man. A century ago every lover of poetry who did not marry his first love had a fellow feeling for the disappointed Byron, and Poe was of their company. But Moore revealed that Byron was hurt by finding out that Mary Chaworth had made slighting remarks about him, including reference to his lameness. Poe in middle life reflected that the auspices for a really happy marriage to Mary Chaworth had not been wholly favorable.

The engraving that Poe wrote about, entitled "Byron & Miss Chaworth" and marked "Engraved Expressly for the Columbian Magazine," shows a boy and a girl in a garden — the boy writing on a paper held on his knee; the girl standing beside him, watching attentively. Both are quite young, and very serious.*

TEXTS

(A) Columbian Magazine for December 1844 (2:275); *(B) Works* (1850), III, 571–572, in "Marginalia," number CXC.†

The earlier version *(A)* has been preferred, since the changes in *(B)*, whether made by Griswold, or in a clipping marked by Poe, are merely to fit the piece into a book, in which the engraving itself was not to be reproduced.

BYRON AND MISS CHAWORTH. [A]

"Les anges," says Madame Dudevant, a woman who intersperses many an admirable sentiment amid a chaos of the most shameless and altogether objectionable fiction — *"Les anges ne sont plus*

* Below the picture are ascriptions to "H. Richter" and "C. Parker, Sc." — the latter, I suspect, G[eorge] Parker, an Englishman who came to America in 1833 and was still active here in 1868. The *Columbian's* plate was probably copied from an engraving by William Finden after a painting by Henry James Richter published in *The Byron Gallery* (London, 1833, often reprinted). Finden's plate is entitled "Love's Last Adieu" and is accompanied by lines 13–17 of that poem from Byron's early volume, *Hours of Idleness* (1807).

† To the material Poe called "Marginalia" or "Marginal Notes" when he published it in the *Democratic Review, Godey's, Graham's,* and the *Southern Literary Messenger,* "Griswold added, under the same title, short reviews and fragments of reviews selected by himself, apparently from Poe's minor writings in the magazines with which he had been editorially connected" (Stedman and Woodberry, *Works of . . . Poe,* VII, 1896, pp. 354–355). Thus the present piece, originally a "plate article" in the *Columbian Magazine,* is included by Griswold in what he calls "Marginalia, number CXC." Stedman and Woodberry in 1896 had not found the piece "in its original issue," but in 1902 Harrison printed it from the *Columbian* with its original title.

pures que le cœur d'un jeune homme qui aime en vérité." The angels are not more pure than the heart of a young man who loves with fervor.[1]

The hyperbole is scarcely less than true. It would be truth itself, were it averred of the love of him who is at the same time young and a poet. The boyish poet-love is indisputably that one of the human sentiments which most nearly realizes our dreams of the chastened voluptuousness of heaven.

In every allusion made by the author of "Childe Harold" to his passion for Mary Chaworth, there runs a vein of almost spiritual tenderness and purity, strongly in contrast with the gross earthliness pervading and disfiguring his ordinary love-poems. The Dream, in which the incidents of his parting with her when about to travel, are said to be delineated, or at least paralleled,[a] has never been excelled (certainly never excelled by him) in the blended fervor, delicacy, truthfulness and ethereality which sublimate and adorn it. For this reason, it may well be doubted if he has written anything so universally popular.

That his attachment for this "Mary" (in whose very name there indeed seemed to exist for him an "enchantment") was earnest, and long-abiding, we have every reason to believe. There are a hundred evidences of this fact, scattered not only through his own poems and letters, but in the memoirs of his relatives, and cotemporaries[2] in general. But that it *was* thus earnest and enduring, does not controvert, in any degree, the opinion that it was a passion (if passion it can properly be termed) of the most thoroughly romantic, shadowy and imaginative character. It was born of the hour, and of the youthful necessity to love, while it was nurtured by the waters and the hills, and the flowers and the stars. It had no peculiar regard to the person, or to the character, or to the reciprocating affection of Mary Chaworth. Any maiden, not immediately and positively repulsive, he would have loved, under the same circumstances of hourly and unrestricted communion, such as [b]our engraving shadows forth.[b] They met without restraint and without reserve. As mere children they sported together; in boyhood and girlhood they read

Title: *Omitted (B)*

a parralleled, *(A, B) misprint*

b . . . b the engravings of the subject show. *(B)*

from the same books, sang the same songs, or roamed, hand in hand, through the grounds of the conjoining estates. The result was not merely natural or merely probable, it was as inevitable as destiny itself.

In view of a passion thus engendered, Miss Chaworth, (who is represented as possessed of no little personal beauty and some accomplishments,) could not have failed to serve sufficiently well as the incarnation of the ideal that haunted the fancy of the poet. It is perhaps better, nevertheless, for the mere romance of the love-passages between the two, that their intercourse was broken up in early life and never uninterruptedly resumed in after years. Whatever of warmth, whatever of soul-passion, whatever of the truer nare[3] and essentiality of romance was elicited during the youthful association is to be attributed altogether to the poet. If *she* felt at all, it was only while the magnetism of *his* actual presence compelled her to feel. If *she* responded at all, it was merely because the necromancy of *his* words of fire could not do otherwise than exhort a response. In absence, the bard bore easily with him all the fancies which were the basis of his flame — a flame which absence itself but served to keep in vigor — while the less ideal but at the same time the less really substantial affection of his ladye-love, perished utterly and forthwith, through simple lack of the element which had fanned it into being. He to her, in brief, was a not unhandsome, and not ignoble, but somewhat portionless, somewhat eccentric and rather lame young man. She to him was the Egeria of his dreams[4] — the Venus Aphrodite that sprang, in full and supernal loveliness, from the bright foam upon the storm-tormented ocean of his thoughts.[5]

NOTES

Title: The title is as given here; below it is the ascription: "By Edgar A. Poe," and below that, in parentheses, *"See Engraving."*

1. The opening quotation Poe found in English, in a book he reviewed carefully in *Graham's* for April 1841 and often used as a source, R. M. Walsh's translation, *Conspicuous Living Characters of France,* p. 308. In the article on "George Sand" (who was legally Madame Dudevant), we read: "The author had elsewhere said, 'The angels are not more pure than the heart of a youth of twenty loving with fervour.' " The French author, now known to have been Louis-Léonard de Lo-

ménie, did not reveal exactly where George Sand made the observation, which Poe altered slightly and put into French of his own.

2. The form "cotemporary" was frequently used in Poe's time.

3. See "Diddling," n. 5, for comment on Poe's special use of this obsolete word.

4. For the nymph Egeria, who loved and counseled the Roman king and lawgiver, Numa Pompilius, see Livy, I, 19.

5. With the last sentences compare "To Frances" (Mabbott I, 236–237), lines 11–12: "Some ocean throbbing far and free/With storms."

THE LITERARY LIFE OF THINGUM BOB, ESQ.

This is one of Poe's comic stories — a witty satire on the world of magazine publishing in which the author himself lived. But much of the fun is local and ephemeral, and many of the jokes are lost on the reader who is not at home in that world.* Thomas Dunn English wrote:

> [Poe] once brought to me a manuscript entitled, I think, 'The Life of Thingum Bob', the late Literary Editor of 'Goosetherumfoodle.' This he assured me was a transcript of Graham's personal history. He read it to me, and though it was rather amusing, I could see that it was wholly imaginative slander, and gave none of Graham's history at all . . . Graham never resented the attack which he considered foolish.†

English later in life had mellowed, and we may accept this account as true, but it can hardly refer to the story as we have it.‡ Thingum Bob's narrative reflects the experiences of many editors and proprietors.

The general elements include the insertion of puffs in friendly newspapers — Poe had written them for T. W. White and for

* See the discussions by Sidney P. Moss, *Poe's Literary Battles* (1963), pp. 92, 182; William Whipple, "Poe, Clark, and Thingum Bob" (*AL,* November 1957). [See also Burton R. Pollin, "Poe's Mystification: Its Source in Fay's *Norman Leslie,*" *Mississippi Quarterly,* Spring 1970.]

† New York *Independent,* October 22, 1896.

‡ Graham was a combiner of periodicals, but he was rarely thought of as a writer of verse. He united *The Casket* and *Burton's Gentleman's Magazine* to form *Graham's Lady's and Gentleman's Magazine,* and he owned a share in the weekly Philadelphia *Saturday Evening Post.* The only poem by Graham discovered is "Winter" in *Godey's Lady's Book* for January 1873. There are, however, several glimpses of Graham and of his magazine in the *Lollipop* and its editor in the tale below.

William E. Burton. The latter seems to have bought a share of *Alexander's Weekly Messenger* partly to print puffs. The sure Graham elements include the boasting about high prices paid to contributors, especially for Cooper's story of a pocket-handkerchief, transparently burlesqued in Poe's story as "The Dish-Clout" by Fatquack.

There are also some patent references to the Clark brothers. Professor Whipple pointed out that Lewis Gaylord Clark had brought out the *Literary Remains* of his twin brother Willis (who died in 1841) – a book largely made up of the "Ollapodiana" papers contributed to the *Knickerbocker Magazine*. In that magazine for July 1844, in a comment on the *Literary Remains*, mention is made of Willis Gaylord Clark's ability to "write in every style, upon all classes and kinds of subject," and to gather from earlier authors "many a gem and fragment of intellectual gold, which he knew... how to polish and set among the jewels of his own intellect." He was not given to plagiarism but to apt quotation.

The earlier adventures of Thingum are conventional, but *Sargent's New Monthly Magazine* for February 1843 contains a possible specific source for one of them: a paper entitled "My First Article," ascribed to Samuel Samson, in which the protagonist culled passages from celebrated authors and succeeded in selling them, but was exposed by an unfriendly newspaper.

Poe probably wrote the first published version of his tale about October 1844, since it contains an allusion to something he did not know until late in September.§ Because his story might have been thought a personal matter by other editors, he played safe by sending it to Benjamin Blake Minor, who had only taken over the *Southern Literary Messenger* on July 15, 1843, and could hardly identify himself with such a veteran of the quill as Thingum Bob. Long afterward Minor printed a rambling account of asking Poe for contributions, stipulating "a monthly critical paper," but accepting the story at three dollars a printed page.* Poe must have been paid twenty-four dollars for eight pages.

§ See n. 46 below.

* See Minor's book called *The Southern Literary Messenger, 1834–1864* (1905), p. 132. Minor recalled the incident vaguely as if there were two stories, but I believe he had his old account books for what he paid.

In the Richmond periodical the story was not signed, but in the *Evening Mirror* of January 14, 1845, Poe inquired quizzically about its authorship. In *Graham's* for February 1845 (issued about January 15) Lowell listed it as by Poe; and in the *Broadway Journal* of July 26, Poe reprinted the piece with his own name.

TEXTS

(A) Southern Literary Messenger, December 1844 (10:719–727); *(B) Broadway Journal,* July 26, 1845 (2:33–39); *(C) Works,* IV (1856), 210–229.

Griswold's version *(C),* showing an auctorial change, is followed.

THE LITERARY LIFE OF THINGUM BOB, ESQ. [*C*]

LATE EDITOR OF THE "GOOSETHERUMFOODLE."

BY HIMSELF.

I AM now growing in years, and — since I understand that Shakespeare and Mr. Emmons[1] are deceased — it is not impossible that I may even die. It has occurred to me, therefore, that I may as well retire from the field of Letters and repose upon my laurels. But I am ambitious of signalizing my abdication of the literary sceptre by some important bequest to posterity; and, perhaps, I cannot do a better thing than just pen for it an account of my earlier career. My name, indeed, has been so long and so constantly before the public eye, that I am not only willing to admit the naturalness of the interest which it has everywhere excited, but ready to satisfy the extreme curiosity which it has inspired. In fact, it is no more than the duty of him who achieves greatness[2] to leave behind him, in his ascent, such landmarks as may guide others to be great. I propose, therefore, in the present paper, (which I had some idea of calling "Memoranda to serve for the Literary History of America,") to give a detail of[a] those important, yet feeble and tottering first steps, by which, at length, I attained the high road to the pinnacle of human renown.

Of one's *very* remote ancestors it is superfluous to say much. My

---

a to *(A)*

father, Thomas Bob, Esq., stood for many years at the summit of his profession, which was that of a merchant-barber,[3] in the city of Smug. His warehouse was the resort of all the principal people of the place, and especially of the editorial corps — a body which inspires all about it with profound veneration and awe. For my own part, I regarded them as gods, and drank in with avidity the rich wit and wisdom which continuously flowed from their august mouths during the process of what is styled "lather." My first moment of positive inspiration[b] must be dated from that ever-memorable epoch, when the brilliant conductor of the "Gad-Fly," in the intervals of the important process just mentioned, recited aloud, before a conclave of our apprentices, an inimitable poem in honor of the "Only Genuine Oil-of-Bob,"[4] (so called from its talented inventor, my father,) and for which effusion the editor of the "Fly" was remunerated with a regal liberality, by the firm of Thomas Bob and company, merchant-barbers.

The genius of the stanzas to the "Oil-of-Bob" first breathed into me, I say, the divine *afflatus*. I resolved at once to become a great man and to commence by becoming a great poet. That very evening I fell upon my knees at the feet of my father.

"Father," I said, "pardon me! — but I have a soul above lather. It is my firm intention to cut the shop. I would be an editor — I would be a poet — I would pen stanzas to the 'Oil-of-Bob.' Pardon me and aid me to be great!"[5]

"My dear Thingum," replied my father, (I had been christened Thingum after a wealthy relative so surnamed,) "My dear Thingum," he said, raising me from my knees by the ears — "Thingum, my boy, you're a trump, and take after your father in having a soul. You have an immense head, too, and it must hold a great many brains. This I have long seen, and therefore had thoughts of making you a lawyer. The business, however, has grown ungenteel, and that of a politician don't pay. Upon the whole you judge wisely; — the trade of[c] editor is best: — and if you can be a poet at the same time, — as most of the editors are, by the by,[6] — why you will kill two birds with one stone. To encourage

b inspiration, however, *(A)*

c of the *(A)*

you in the beginning of things, I will allow you a garret; pen, ink and paper; a rhyming dictionary; and a copy of the 'Gad-Fly.' I suppose you would scarcely demand any more."

"I would be an ungrateful villain if I did," I replied with enthusiasm. "Your generosity is boundless. I will repay it by making you the father of a genius."

Thus ended my conference with the best of men, and immediately upon its termination, I betook myself with zeal to my poetical labors; as upon these, chiefly, I founded my hopes of ultimate elevation to the editorial chair.

In my first[d] attempts at composition I found the stanzas to "The Oil-of-Bob" rather a draw-back than otherwise. Their splendor more dazzled than enlightened me. The contemplation of their excellence tended, naturally, to discourage me by comparison with my own abortions; so that for a long time I labored in vain. At length there came into my head one of those exquisitely original ideas which now and then *will* permeate the brain of a man of genius. It was this: — or, rather, thus was it carried into execution. From the rubbish of an old book-stall, in a very remote corner of the town, I got together several antique and altogether unknown or forgotten volumes. The bookseller sold them to me for a song. From one of these, which purported to be a translation of one Dante's "Inferno," I copied with remarkable neatness a long passage about a man named Ugolino, who had a parcel of brats. From another which contained a good many old[e] plays by some person whose name I forget, I extracted in the same manner, and with the same care, a great number of lines about "angels" and "ministers saying grace," and "goblins damned," and more besides of that sort. From a third, which was the composition of some blind man or other, either a Greek or a Choctaw — I cannot be at the pains of remembering every trifle exactly — I took about fifty verses beginning with "Achilles' wrath," and "grease," and something else. From a fourth, which I recollect was also the work of a blind man, I selected a page or two all about "hail" and "holy light;" and al-

d initial *(A)* e odd *(A)*

though a blind man has no business to write about light, still the verses were sufficiently good in their way.[7]

Having made fair copies of these poems I signed every one of them "Oppodeldoc," (a fine sonorous name,)[8] and, doing each up nicely in a separate envelope, I despatched one to each of the four principal Magazines, with a request for speedy insertion and prompt pay. The result of this well conceived plan, however, (the success of which would have saved me much trouble in afterlife,) served to convince me that some editors are not to be bamboozled, and gave the *coup-de-grâce*[f] (as they[g] say in France,) to my nascent hopes, (as they say in the city of the transcendentals.)[9]

The fact is, that each and every one of the Magazines in question, gave Mr. "Oppodeldoc" a complete using-up,[10] in the "Monthly Notices to Correspondents." The "Hum-Drum"[11] gave him a dressing after this fashion:

> " 'Oppodeldoc,' (whoever he is,) has sent us a long *tirade* concerning a bedlamite whom he styles 'Ugolino,'[h] who[i] had a great many children that[j] should have been all[k] whipped and sent to bed without their suppers.[12] The whole affair is exceedingly tame – not to say *flat*. 'Oppodeldoc,' (whoever he is,) is entirely devoid of imagination – and imagination, in our humble opinion, is not only the soul of[l] POESY, but also its very heart.[m] Oppodeldoc,' (Whoever he is,) has the audacity to demand of us, for his[n] twattle, a 'speedy insertion and prompt pay.' We neither insert nor purchase any stuff of the sort. There can be no doubt, however, that he would meet with a ready sale for all the balderdash he can scribble, at the office of either the 'Rowdy-Dow,' the 'Lollipop,' or the 'Goosetherumfoodle.' "

All this, it must be acknowledged, was very severe upon "Oppodeldoc" – but the unkindest cut was[o] putting the word POESY in small caps. In those five pre-eminent letters what a world of bitterness is there not involved![13]

But "Oppodeldoc" was punished with equal severity in the [p]"Rowdy-Dow," which spoke thus:[p]

---

f *coup-de-grace (A, B, C) accent supplied by editor*
g we *(A)*
h "Ugolino," *(C) misprint*
i and who *(A)*
j who *(A)*
k all well *(A)*
l of true *(A)*
m heart, and, (if we may so express ourselves,) its very gizzard. *(A)*
n this *(A)*
o was the *(A)*
p . . . p "Rowdy-dow." *(A)*

"We have [q]received a[q] most singular and insolent communication from a person, (whoever he is,) signing himself 'Oppodeldoc' – thus desecrating the greatness of the illustrious Roman Emperor so named. Accompanying the letter of 'Oppodeldoc,' (whoever he is,) we find sundry lines of most disgusting and unmeaning rant about 'angels and ministers of grace' – rant such as no madman short of a Nat Lee,[14] or an 'Oppodeldoc,' could possibly perpetrate. And for this trash of trash,[15] we are modestly requested to 'pay promptly.' No sir – no! We pay for nothing of *that* sort. Apply to the 'Hum-Drum,' the 'Lollipop,' or the 'Goosetherumfoodle.' These *periodicals* will undoubtedly accept any literary offal you may send them – and as undoubtedly *promise* to pay for it."

This was bitter indeed upon poor "Oppodeldoc;" but, in this instance, the weight of the satire falls upon the "Hum-Drum,"[r] the "Lollipop," and the "Goosetherumfoodle," who are pungently styled "*periodicals*" – in Italics, too – a thing that must have cut them to the heart.

Scarcely less savage was the [s]"Lollipop," which thus discoursed:[s]

"Some [t]*individual*, who[t] rejoices in the appellation 'Oppodeldoc,' (to what low uses are the names of the illustrious dead too often applied!) has enclosed us some fifty or sixty *verses* commencing after this fashion:

Achilles' wrath, to Greece the direful spring
Of woes unnumbered, &c., &c., &c., &c.

" 'Oppodeldoc,'[u] (whoever he is,) is respectfully informed that there is not a printer's devil in our office who is not in the daily habit of composing better *lines*. Those of 'Oppodeldoc' will not *scan*. 'Oppodeldoc' should learn to *count*. But why he should have[v] conceived the idea that *we*, (of all others, *we!*) would disgrace our pages with his ineffable nonsense is utterly beyond comprehension. Why, the absurd twattle is scarcely good enough for the 'Hum-Drum,' the 'Rowdy-Dow,' the 'Goosetherumfoodle' – things that are in the practice of publishing 'Mother Goose's Melodies' as original lyrics. And 'Oppodeldoc' (whoever he is,) has even the assurance to demand *pay* for this[w] drivel. Does 'Oppodeldoc,' (whoever he is,) know – is he aware that we could not be paid to insert it?"

As I perused this I felt myself growing gradually smaller and smaller, and when I came to the point at which the editor sneered at the poem as "*verses*," there was little more than an ounce of me left. As for "Oppodeldoc," I began to experience *compassion* for the poor fellow. But the "Goosetherumfoodle" showed, if possible,

---

q . . . q received," said that periodical, "a *(A)*
r "Humdrum," *(B, C) emended editorially*
s . . . s "Lollipop." *(A)*
t . . . t *individual*," said that journal, "who *(A)*
u "Oppodeldoc,' *(C) misprint*
v should have/shouldehave *(B) misprint*
w his *(A)*

less[x] mercy than the "Lollipop." [y]It was the "Goosetherumfoodle" that said:[y]

A wretched [z]poetaster, who[z] signs himself 'Oppodeldoc,' is silly enough to fancy that *we* will print and *pay for* a medley of incoherent and ungrammatical bombast which he has transmitted to us, and which commences with the following most *intelligible* line:

[a]'Hail, Holy Light! Offspring of Heaven, first born.'

"We[a] say, 'most *intelligible.*' 'Oppodeldoc,' (whoever he is,) will be kind enough to tell us, perhaps, how *'hail'* can be *'holy light.'* We always regarded it as *frozen rain.* Will he inform us, also, how frozen rain can be, at one and the same time, both 'holy light,' (whatever that is,) and an 'offspring?' – which latter term, (if we[b] understand any thing about English,) is only employed, with propriety, in reference to small babies of about six weeks old. But it is preposterous to descant upon such absurdity – although 'Oppodeldoc,' (whoever he is,) has the unparalleled effrontery to suppose that we will not only 'insert' his ignorant ravings, but (absolutely) *pay for them!*

"Now this is fine – it is rich! – and we have half a mind to punish this young scribbler for his egotism by really publishing his effusion,[c] *verbatim et literatim,* as he has written it. We could inflict[d] no punishment so severe, and we *would* inflict it, but for the boredom which we should cause our readers in so doing.

"Let 'Oppodeldoc,' (whoever he is,) send any future *composition* of like character to the 'Hum-Drum,' the 'Lollipop,' or the 'Rowdy-Dow.' *They* will 'insert' it. *They* 'insert' every month just such stuff. Send it to *them.*[e] WE are not to be insulted with impunity."[16]

This made an end of me; and as for the "Hum-Drum," the "Rowdy-Dow," and the "Lollipop," I never could comprehend how they survived it. The putting *them* in the smallest possible *minion,*[17] (that[f] was the rub – thereby insinuating their lowness – their baseness,) while[g] WE stood looking down upon them in gigantic capitals! – oh it was *too* bitter! – it was wormwood – it was gall.[18] Had I been either of these periodicals I would have spared no pains to have the "Goosetherumfoodle" prosecuted. It might have been done under the Act for the "Prevention of Cruelty to Animals."[19] As for "Oppodeldoc," (whoever he was,) I had by this time lost all patience with the fellow, and sympathized with him no longer. He was a fool, beyond doubt, (whoever he was,) and got not a kick more than he deserved.

---

x even less *(A)*
y . . . y *Omitted (A)*
z . . . z poetaster," said that eminent publication, "who *(A)*
a . . . a *New paragraph* "Hail, . . . first born, we *(A)*
b *we (A, B)*
c *effusion, (A)*
d inflict upon him *(A)*
e them. *(A) in smaller type*
f *that (A, B)*
g while the *(A)*

The result of my experiment with the old books, convinced me, in the first place, that "honesty is the best policy,"[20] and, in the second, that if I could not write better than Mr. Dante, and the two blind men, and the rest of the old set, it would, at least, be a difficult matter to write worse. I took heart, therefore, and determined to prosecute the "entirely original," (as they say on the covers of the magazines,) at whatever cost of study and pains.[21] I again placed before my eyes, as a model, the brilliant stanzas on "The Oil-of-Bob" by the editor of the "Gad-Fly," and resolved to construct an Ode on the same sublime theme, in rivalry of what had already been done.

With my first verse I had no material difficulty. It ran thus:

To[h] *pen an Ode upon the "Oil-of-Bob."*

Having carefully looked out, however, all the legitimate rhymes to "Bob," I found it impossible to proceed. In this dilemma I had recourse to paternal aid; and, after some hours of mature thought, my father and myself thus constructed the poem:

To[i] *pen an Ode upon the "Oil-of-Bob"*
Is all sorts of a job.
(Signed,) SNOB.[22]

To be sure, this composition was of no very great length — but I "have yet to learn" as they say in the Edinburgh Review, that the mere extent of a literary work has any thing to do with its merit. As for the Quarterly cant about "sustained effort,"[j] it is impossible to see the sense of it. Upon the whole, therefore, I was satisfied with the success of my maiden attempt, and now the only question regarded the disposal I should make of it. My father suggested that I should send it to the "Gad-Fly" — but there were two reasons which operated to prevent me from so doing. I dreaded the jealousy of the editor — and I had ascertained that he did not pay for original contributions. I therefore, after due deliberation, consigned the article to the more dignified pages of the "Lollipop," and awaited the event in anxiety, but with resignation.

h "To *(C) quotation mark deleted to follow A, B*

i "To *(C) quotation mark deleted to follow A, B*

j effort," and all that species of thing, *(A)*

In the very next published number I had the proud satisfaction of seeing my poem printed at length, as the leading article, with the following significant words, prefixed in italics and between brackets:

[*We call the attention of our readers to the subjoined admirable stanzas on "The Oil of Bob." We need say nothing of their sublimity, or of their pathos: — it is impossible to peruse them without tears. Those who have been nauseated with a sad dose on the same august topic from the goose-quill of the editor of the "Gad-Fly," will do well to compare the two compositions.*

P. S. We are consumed with anxiety to probe the mystery which envelops[k] *the evident pseudonym "Snob." May we*[l] *hope for a personal interview?*]

All this was scarcely more than justice, but it was, I confess, rather more than I had expected: — I acknowledged[m] this, be it observed, to the everlasting disgrace of my country and of mankind. I lost no time, however, in calling upon the editor of the "Lollipop," and had the good fortune to find this gentleman at home. He saluted me with an air of profound respect, slightly blended with a fatherly and patronizing admiration, wrought in him, no doubt, by my appearance of extreme youth and inexperience. Begging me to be seated, he entered at once upon the subject of my poem; — but modesty will ever forbid me to repeat the thousand compliments which he lavished upon me.[n] The eulogies of Mr. Crab, (such was the editor's name,) were, however, by no means fulsomely indiscriminate. He analyzed my composition with much freedom and great ability — not hesitating to point out a few trivial defects — a circumstance which elevated him highly in my esteem. The[o] "Gad-Fly" was, of course, brought upon the *tapis,* and I hope never to be subjected to a criticism so searching, or to rebukes so withering, as were bestowed by Mr. Crab upon that unhappy effusion. I had been accustomed to regard the editor of the "Gad-Fly" as something superhuman; but Mr. Crab soon disabused me of that idea. He set the literary as well as the personal character of the Fly (so Mr. C. satirically designated the rival editor,) in its true light. He, the Fly, was very little better than he should be. He had written infamous things. He was a penny-a-liner,[23] and a buffoon. He was a villain. He had composed a tragedy which set the whole country in a

k envelopes *(A)*
l we not *(A, B)*
m acknowledge *(A, B)*
n it. *(A)*
o The rival production of the editor of the *(A)*

guffaw, and a farce which deluged the universe in tears. Besides all this, he had[p] the impudence to pen what he meant for a lampoon upon himself, (Mr. Crab,) and the temerity to style him "an ass." Should I at any time wish to express my opinion to Mr. Fry,[q] the pages of the "Lollipop," Mr. Crab assured me, were at my unlimited disposal.[24] In the meantime, as it was very certain that I would be attacked in the Fly for my attempt at composing a rival poem on the[r] "Oil-of-Bob," he (Mr. Crab,) would take it upon himself to attend, pointedly, to my private and personal interests. If I were not made a man of at once, it should not be the fault of himself, (Mr. Crab.)

Mr. Crab having now paused in his discourse, (the latter portion of which I found it impossible to comprehend,) I ventured to suggest something about[s] the remuneration which I had been taught to expect for my poem, by an announcement on the cover of the "Lollipop," declaring that it, (the "Lollipop,") "insisted upon being permitted to pay exorbitant prices for all accepted contributions; — frequently expending more money for a single brief poem than the whole annual cost of the 'Hum-Drum,' the 'Rowdy-Dow,' and the 'Goosetherumfoodle' combined."

As I mentioned the word "remuneration," Mr. Crab first opened his eyes, and then his mouth, to quite a remarkable extent; causing his personal appearance to resemble that of a highly-agitated elderly duck in the act of quacking; — and in this condition he remained, (ever and anon pressing his hands tightly to his forehead, as if in a state of desperate bewilderment) until I had nearly[t] made an end of what I had to say.

Upon my conclusion, he sank back into[u] his seat, as if much overcome, letting his arms fall lifelessly by his side, but keeping his mouth still rigorously open, after the fashion of the duck. While I remained in speechless astonishment at behavior so alarming, he suddenly leaped to his feet and made a rush at the bell-rope; but just as he reached this, he appeared to have altered his intention, whatever it was, for he dived under a table and immediately re-

p had had *(A)*
q Fly, *(A)*
r on the/o *(B) misprint*
s in reference to *(A)*
t fairly *(A)*
u in *(A)*

appeared with a cudgel. This he was in the act of uplifting, (for what purpose I am at a loss to imagine,) when, all at once, there came a benign smile over his features, and he sank placidly back in his chair.

"Mr. Bob," he said, (for I had sent up my card before ascending myself,) "Mr. Bob, you are a young man, I presume — *very?*"

I assented; adding that I had not yet concluded my third lustrum.[25]

"Ah!" he replied, "very good! I see how it is — say no more![v] Touching this matter of compensation, what you observe is[w] very just: in fact it is excessively so. But ah — ah — the *first* contribution — the *first,* I say — it is never the Magazine custom to pay for — you comprehend, eh? The truth is, we are usually the *recipients* in such case." [Mr. Crab smiled blandly as he emphasized the word "recipients."] "For the most part, we are *paid* for the insertion of a maiden attempt — especially in verse. In the second place, Mr. Bob, the Magazine rule is never to disburse what we term in France the *argent comptant:*[26] — I have no doubt you understand. In a quarter or two after publication of the article — or in a year or two — we make no objection to giving our note at nine months: — provided always that we can so arrange our affairs as to be quite certain of a 'burst up'[27] in six. I really *do* hope, Mr. Bob, that you will look upon this explanation as satisfactory." Here Mr. Crab concluded, and the tears[x] stood in his eyes.

Grieved to the soul at having been, however innocently, the cause of pain to so eminent and so sensitive a man, I hastened to apologize, and to reassure him, by expressing my perfect coincidence with his views, as well as my entire appreciation of the delicacy of his position. Having done all this in a neat speech, I took leave.

One fine morning, very shortly afterwards, "I awoke and found myself famous."[28] The extent of my renown will be[y] best estimated by reference to the editorial opinions of the day. These opinions, it will be seen, were embodied in critical notices of the number of the "Lollipop" containing my poem, and are perfectly satisfactory,

v more. *(A)*
w is very proper and *(A)*
x tears positively *(A)*
y e *(B) misprint*

conclusive and clear with the exception, perhaps, of the hieroglyphical marks, "*Sep.* 15 — 1 *t.*"[z] appended to each of the critiques.[29]

The "Owl," a journal of profound sagacity, and well known for the deliberate gravity of its literary decisions — the "Owl," I say, spoke as follows:

" 'THE LOLLIPOP!' The October number of this delicious Magazine surpasses its predecessors, and sets competition at defiance. In the beauty of its typography and paper — in the number and excellence of its steel plates — as well as in the literary merit of its contributions — the 'Lollipop' compares with its slow-paced rivals as Hyperion with a Satyr.[30] The 'Hum-Drum,' the 'Rowdy-Dow,' and the 'Goosetherumfoodle,' excel, it is true, in braggadocio, but, in all other points, give us the 'Lollipop!'[a] How this celebrated journal can sustain its evidently tremendous expenses, is more than we can understand. To be sure, it has a circulation of 100,000, and its subscription-list has increased one-fourth during the last month;[31] but, on the other hand, the sums it disburses constantly for contributions are inconceivable. It is reported that Mr. Slyass received no less than thirty-seven and a half cents for his inimitable paper on 'Pigs.'[32] With Mr. CRAB, as editor, and with such names upon the list of contributors as SNOB and Slyass, there can be no such word as 'fail' for the 'Lollipop.' Go and subscribe. *Sep.* 15 — 1 *t.*"

I must say that I was gratified with this high-toned notice from a paper so respectable as the "Owl." The placing my name — that is to say, my *nom de guerre* — in priority of station to that of the great Slyass, was a compliment as happy as I felt it to be deserved.

My attention was next arrested by these paragraphs in the "Toad" — a print highly distinguished for its uprightness, and[b] independence — for its entire freedom from sycophancy and subservience to the givers of dinners:

"The 'Lollipop' for October is out in advance of all its contemporaries, and infinitely surpasses them, of course, in the splendor of its embellishments, as well as in the richness of its literary contents. The 'Hum-Drum,' the 'Rowdy-Dow,' and the 'Goosetherumfoodle' excel, we admit, in braggadocio, but, in all other points, give us the 'Lollipop.' How this celebrated Magazine can sustain its evidently tremendous expenses, is more than we can understand. To be sure, it has a circulation of 200,000, and its subscription list has increased one-third during the last fortnight, but on the other hand, the sums it disburses, monthly, for contributions, are fearfully great. We learn that Mr. Mumblethumb received no less than fifty cents for his late 'Monody in a Mud-Puddle.'[33]

---

z t."*(C)*
a 'Lollipop.' *(A)*
b *Omitted (A)*

"Among the original contributors to the present number we notice, (besides the eminent editor, Mr. CRAB,) such men as SNOB, Slyass, and Mumblethumb. Apart from the editorial matter, the most valuable paper, nevertheless, is, we think, a poetical gem by 'SNOB,' on the 'Oil-of-Bob' – but our readers must not suppose from the title of this incomparable *bijou,* that it bears any similitude to some balderdash on the same subject by a certain contemptible individual whose name is unmentionable to ears polite. The *present* poem 'On the Oil-of-Bob,' has excited universal anxiety and curiosity in respect to the owner of the evident pseudonym, 'Snob' – a curiosity which, happily, we have it in our power to satisfy. 'Snob' is the *nom-de-plume* of Mr. Thingum Bob, of this city, – a relative of the great Mr. Thingum, after whom he is named,) and otherwise connected with the most illustrious families of the State. His father, Thomas Bob, Esq., is on opulent merchant in Smug. *Sep.* 15 – 1 *t.*"

This generous approbation touched me to the heart – the more especially as it emanated from a source so avowedly – so proverbially pure as the "Toad." The word "balderdash," as applied to the "Oil-of-Bob" of the Fly, I considered singularly pungent and appropriate. The words "gem" and *"bijou,"* however, used in reference to my[c] composition, struck me as being, in some degree, feeble. They seemed to me to be deficient in force. They were not sufficiently *prononcés,* (as we have it in France).

I had hardly finished reading the "Toad," when a friend placed in my hands a copy of the "Mole," a daily, enjoying high reputation for the keenness of its perception about matters in general, and for the open, honest, above-ground style of its editorials. The "Mole" spoke of the "Lollipop" as follows:

"We have just received the 'Lollipop' for October, and *must* say that never before have we perused any single number of any periodical which afforded us a felicity so supreme. We speak advisedly. The 'Hum-Drum,' the 'Rowdy-Dow' and the 'Goosetherumfoodle' must look well to their laurels. These prints, no doubt, surpass every thing in loudness of pretension, but, in all other points, give us the 'Lollipop!' How this celebrated Magazine can sustain its evidently tremendous expenses, is more than we can comprehend. To be sure, it has a circulation of 300,000; and its subscription-list has increased one-half within the last week, but then the sum it disburses, monthly, for contributions, is astoundingly enormous. We have it upon good authority, that Mr. Fatquack received no less than sixty-two cents and a half for his late Domestic Nouvelette, the 'Dish-Clout.'[34]

"The contributors to the number before us are Mr.[d] CRAB, (the eminent editor,) SNOB, Mumblethumb, Fatquack, and others; but, after the inimitable compositions of the editor himself, we prefer a diamond-like effusion from the

c my own *(A)* d Mr. *omitted (A)*

pen of a[e] rising poet who writes over the signature[f] 'Snob' – a *nom de guerre* which we predict will one day extinguish the radiance of 'Boz,' 'SNOB,'[g] we learn, is a Mr. THINGUM BOB, Esq.,[h] sole heir of a wealthy merchant of this city, Thomas Bob, Esq., and a near relative of the distinguished Mr. Thingum. The title of Mr. B.'s admirable poem is the 'Oil-of-Bob' – a somewhat unfortunate name, by-the-by, as some contemptible vagabond connected with the penny press has already disgusted the town with a great deal of drivel upon the same topic. There will be no danger, however, of confounding the[i] compositions. *Sep.* 15 – 1 *t.*"

The generous approbation of so clear-sighted a journal as the "Mole" penetrated my soul with delight. The only objection which occurred to me was, that the terms "contemptible vagabond" might have been better written "*odious and* contemptible, *wretch, villain* and[j] vagabond." This would have sounded more gracefully, I think. "Diamond-like," also, was scarcely, it will be admitted, of sufficient intensity to express what the "Mole" evidently *thought* of the brilliancy of the "Oil-of-Bob."

On the same afternoon in which I saw these notices in the "Owl," the "Toad," and the "Mole" I happened to meet with a copy of the "Daddy-Long-Legs," a periodical proverbial for the extreme extent[k] of its understanding. And it was the "Daddy-Long-Legs" which spoke thus:

"The 'Lollipop'! ! This gorgeous Magazine is already before the public for October. The question of pre-eminence is forever put to rest, and hereafter it will be excessively preposterous in the 'Hum-Drum,' the 'Rowdy-Dow,' or the 'Goosetherumfoodle,' to make any farther spasmodic attempts at competition. These journals may excel the 'Lollipop' in outcry, but, in all other points, give us the 'Lollipop'![l] How this celebrated Magazine can sustain its evidently tremendous expenses, is past comprehension. To be sure it has a circulation of precisely half a million, and its subscription-list has increased seventy-five per cent, within the last couple of days; but then the sums it disburses, monthly, for contributions, are scarcely credible; we are cognizant of the fact, that Mademoiselle Cribalittle received no less than eighty-seven cents and a half for her late valuable Revolutionary Tale, entitled 'The York-Town Katy-Did, and the Bunker-Hill Katy-Didn't.'[m]

"The most able papers in the present number, are, of course, those furnished by the editor, (the eminent Mr. CRAB,) but there are numerous magnificent con-

---

e the *(A)*
f siguature *(B) misprint*
g "SNOB,' *(C)*
h Esq., *omitted (A, B)*
i the two *(A)*
j *and (A)*
k extent as well as solidity *(A)*
l 'Lollipop.' *(A)*
m Katy-Did'nt.' *(A, B, C)*

tributions from such names as SNOB, Mademoiselle Cribalittle,[35] Slyass, Mrs. Fibalittle, Mumblethumb, Mrs. Squibalittle, and last, though not least, Fatquack. The world may well be challenged to produce so rich a galaxy of genius.

"The poem over the signature 'SNOB' is, we find, attracting universal commendation, and, we are constrained to say, deserves, if possible, even more applause than it has received. The 'Oil-of-Bob' is the title of this masterpiece of eloquence and art. One or two of our readers *may* have a *very* faint, although sufficiently disgusting recollection of a poem (?) similarly entitled, the perpetration of a miserable penny-a-liner, mendicant, and cut-throat, connected in the capacity of scullion, we believe, with one of the indecent prints about the purlieus of the city; we beg them, for God's sake, not to confound the[n] compositions. The author of *the* 'Oil-of-Bob' is, we hear, THINGUM BOB, Esq., a gentleman of high genius, and a scholar. 'Snob' is merely a *nom-de-guerre*. *Sept.* 15 — 1 *t*."

I could scarcely restrain my indignation while I perused the concluding portions of this diatribe. It was clear to me that the yea-nay manner — not to say the gentleness — the positive forbearance with which the "Daddy-Long-Legs" spoke of that pig, the editor of the "Gad-Fly" — it was evident to me, I say, that this gentleness of speech could proceed from nothing else than a partiality for the Fly — whom it was clearly the intention of the "Daddy-Long-Legs" to elevate into reputation at my expense. Any one, indeed, might perceive, with half an eye, that, had the real design of the "Daddy" been what it wished to appear, it, (the "Daddy,") might have expressed itself in terms more direct, more pungent, and altogether more to the purpose. The words "penny-a-liner," "mendicant," "scullion," and "cut-throat," were epithets so intentionally inexpressive and equivocal, as to be worse than nothing when applied to the author of the very worst stanzas ever penned by one of the human race. We all know what is meant by "damning with faint praise,"[36] and, on the other hand, who could fail seeing through the covert purpose of the "Daddy" — that of glorifying with feeble abuse?

What the "Daddy" chose to say of the Fly, however, was no business of mine. What it said of myself *was*. After the noble manner in which the "Owl," the "Toad," the "Mole," had expressed themselves in respect to my ability, it was rather too much to be coolly[o] spoken of by a thing like the "Daddy-Long-Legs," as merely "a gentleman of high genius and a scholar." Gentleman indeed!

---

n the two *(A)*

o cooly *(B) misprint*

I made up my mind at once either to get a written apology from the "Daddy-Long-Legs," or to call it out.

Full of this purpose, I looked about me to find a friend whom I could entrust with a message to his Daddyship, and as the editor of the "Lollipop" had given me marked tokens of regard, I at length concluded to seek[p] assistance upon the present occasion.

I have never yet been able to account, in a manner satisfactory to my own understanding, for the *very* peculiar countenance and demeanor with which Mr. Crab listened to me, as I unfolded to him my design. He again went through the scene of the bell-rope and[q] cudgel, and did not omit the duck. At one period I thought he really intended to quack. His fit, nevertheless, finally subsided as before, and he began to act and speak in a rational way. He declined bearing the cartel, however, and in fact, dissuaded me from sending it at all; but was candid enough to admit that the "Daddy-Long-Legs" had been disgracefully in the wrong — more especially in what related to the epithets "gentleman and scholar."

Toward the end of this interview with Mr. Crab, who really appeared to take a paternal interest in my welfare, he suggested to me that I might turn an honest penny, and, at the same time,[r] advance my reputation, by occasionally playing Thomas Hawk for the "Lollipop."

I begged Mr. Crab to inform me who was Mr. Thomas Hawk and how it was expected that I should play him.

Here Mr. Crab again "made great eyes," (as we say in Germany,)[37] but at length, recovering himself from a profound attack of astonishment, he assured me that he employed the words "Thomas Hawk" to avoid the colloquialism, Tommy, which was low — but that the true idea was Tommy Hawk — or tomahawk — and that by "playing tomahawk" he referred to scalping, browbeating and otherwise using-up the herd of poor-devil authors.[38]

I assured my patron that, if this was all, I was perfectly resigned to the task of playing Thomas Hawk. Hereupon Mr. Crab desired me to use-up the editor of the "Gad-Fly" forthwith, in the fiercest style within the scope of my ability, and as a specimen of my powers.

---

p seek his *(A)*
q and the *(A)*
r time, materially *(A)*

This I did, upon the spot, in a review of the original "Oil-of-Bob," occupying thirty-six pages of the "Lollipop." I found playing Thomas Hawk, indeed, a far less onerous occupation than poetizing; for I went upon *system* altogether, and thus it was easy to do the thing thoroughly and well. My practice was this. I bought auction copies (cheap) of "Lord Brougham's Speeches," "Cobbett's Complete Works," the "New Slang-Syllabus," the "Whole Art of Snubbing," "Prentice's[s] Billingsgate," (folio edition,) [t]and "Lewis G. Clarke[t] on Tongue."[39] These works I cut up thoroughly with a curry-comb, and then, throwing the shreds into a sieve, sifted out carefully all that might be thought decent, (a mere trifle); reserving the hard phrases, which I threw into a large tin pepper-castor with longitudinal holes, so that an entire sentence could get through without material injury. The mixture was then ready for use. When called upon to play Thomas Hawk, I anointed a sheet of foolscap with the white of a gander's egg; then, shredding the thing to be reviewed as I had previously shredded the books, — only with more care, so as to get every word separate — I threw the latter shreds in with the former, screwed on the lid of the castor, gave it a shake, and so dusted out the mixture upon the egg'd foolscap; where it stuck.[40] The effect was beautiful to behold. It was captivating. Indeed, the reviews I brought to pass by this simple expedient have never been approached, and were the wonder of the world. At first, through bashfulness — the result of inexperience — I was a little put out by a certain inconsistency — a certain air of the *bizarre,* (as we say in France,) worn by the composition as a whole. All the phrases did not *fit,* (as we say in the Anglo-Saxon.) Many were quite awry. Some, even, were up-side-down; and there were none of them which were not, in some measure, injured in regard to effect, by this latter species of accident, when it occurred; — with the exception of Mr. [u]Lewis Clarke's[u] paragraphs, which were so vigorous, and altogether stout, that they seemed not particularly disconcerted by any extreme of position, but looked equally happy and satisfactory, whether on their heads, or on their heels.

What became of the editor of the "Gad-Fly," after the publica-

s Bennett's *(A)*
t . . . t "Prentice's Porcupiniana," and "John Neal *(A)*
u . . . u John Neal's *(A)*

tion of my criticism on his "Oil-of-Bob," it is somewhat difficult to determine. The most reasonable conclusion is, that he wept himself to death. At all events he disappeared instantaneously from the face of the earth, and no man has seen even the ghost of him since.

This matter having been properly accomplished, and the Furies appeased, I grew at once into high favor with Mr. Crab. He took me into his confidence, gave me a permanent situation as Thomas Hawk of the "Lollipop," and, as for the present, he could afford me no salary, allowed me to profit, at discretion, by his advice.

"My dear Thingum," said he to me one day after dinner, "I respect your abilities and love you as a son. You shall be my heir. When I die I will bequeath you the 'Lollipop.' In the meantime I will make a man of you — I *will* — provided always that you follow my counsel. The first thing to do is to get rid of the old bore."

"Boar?" said I inquiringly — "pig, eh? — [v]*aper?*[41] (as we say in Latin)[v] — who? — where?"

"Your father," said he.

"Precisely," I replied, — "pig."

"You have your fortune to make, Thingum," resumed Mr. Crab, "and that governor of yours is a millstone about your neck.[42] We must cut him at once." [Here I took out my knife.] "We must cut him," continued Mr. Crab, "decidedly and forever. He won't do — he *won't*. Upon second thoughts, you had better kick him, or cane him, or something of that kind."

"What do you say," I suggested modestly, "to my kicking him in the first instance, caning him afterwards, and winding up by tweaking his nose?"

Mr. Crab looked at me musingly for some moments, and then answered:

"I think, Mr. Bob, that what you propose would answer sufficiently well — indeed remarkably well — that is to say, as far as it went — but barbers are exceedingly hard to cut, and I think, upon the whole, that, having performed upon Thomas Bob the operations you suggest, it would be advisable to blacken, with your fists, both his eyes, very carefully and thoroughly, to prevent his ever

v . . . v *aper,* (as we say in Latin?) *(A)*

seeing you again in fashionable promenades. After doing this, I really do not perceive that you can do any more. However — it might be just as well to roll him[w] once or twice in the gutter, and then put him in charge of the police. Any time the next morning you can call at the watch-house and swear an assault."

I was much affected by the kindness of feeling towards me personally, which was evinced in this excellent advice of Mr. Crab, and I did not fail to profit by it forthwith. The result was, that I got rid of the old bore, and began to feel a little independent and gentleman-like. The want of money, however, was, for a few weeks, a source of some discomfort; but at length, by carefully putting to use my two eyes, and observing how matters went just in front of my nose, I perceived how the thing was to be brought about. I say "thing" — be it observed — for they tell me the Latin for it is *rem.* By the way, talking of Latin, can any one tell me[x] the meaning of *quocunque* — or what is the meaning of *modo?*[43]

My plan was exceedingly simple. I bought, for a song, a sixteenth of the "Snapping-Turtle:" — that was all. The thing was *done,* and I put money in my purse. There were some trivial arrangements afterwards, to be sure; but these formed no portion of the plan. They were a consequence — a result. For example, I bought pen, ink and paper, and put them into furious activity. Having thus completed a Magazine article, I gave it, for appellation, "FOL-LOL, *by the Author of* 'THE[y] OIL-OF-BOB,' " and enveloped it to the "Goosetherumfoodle." That journal, however, having pronounced it "twattle" in the "Monthly Notices to Correspondents," I reheaded the paper " 'Hey-Diddle-Diddle,' by THINGUM BOB, Esq., Author of the Ode on 'The Oil-of-Bob,' *and* Editor of the 'Snapping-Turtle.' " With this amendment, I re-enclosed it to the "Goosetherumfoodle," and, while I awaited a reply, published daily, in the "Turtle," six columns of what may be termed philosophical and analytical investigation of the literary merits of the "Goosetherumfoodle," as well as of the personal character[z] of the editor of the "Goosetherumfoodle." At the end of a week the "Goosetherumfoodle" discovered that it had, by some odd mistake,

w him over *(A)*
x me what is *(A)*
y 'THE *omitted (A)*
z turpitude *(A)*

"confounded a stupid article, headed 'Hey-Diddle-Diddle' and composed by some unknown ignoramus, with a gem of resplendent lustre similarly entitled, the work of Thingum Bob, Esq., the celebrated author of 'The Oil-of-Bob' " The "Goosetherumfoodle" deeply "regretted this very natural accident," and promised, moreover, an insertion of the *genuine* "Hey-Diddle-Diddle" in the very next number of the Magazine.

The fact is, I *thought* – I *really* thought – I thought at the time – I thought *then* – and have no reason for thinking otherwise *now* – that the "Goosetherumfoodle" *did* make a mistake. With the best intentions in the world, I never knew any thing that made as many singular mistakes as the "Goosetherumfoodle." From that day I took a liking to the "Goosetherumfoodle," and the result was I soon saw into the very depths of its literary merits, and did not fail to expatiate upon them, in the "Turtle," whenever a fitting opportunity occurred. And it is to be regarded as a very peculiar coincidence – as one of those positively *remarkable* coincidences which set a man to serious thinking – that just such a total revolution of opinion – just such entire *bouleversement,* (as we say in French,) – just such thorough *topsiturviness,* (if I may be permitted to employ a rather forcible term of the Choctaws,) as happened, *pro* and *con,* between myself on the one part, and the "Goosetherumfoodle" on the other, did actually again happen, in a brief period afterwards, and with precisely similar circumstances, in the case of myself and the "Rowdy-Dow," and in the case of myself and the "Hum-Drum."

Thus it was that, by a master-stroke of genius, I at length consummated my triumphs by "putting money in my purse,"[44] and thus may be said really and fairly to have commenced that brilliant and eventful career which rendered me illustrious, and which now enables me to say, with Chateaubriand, "I have made history" – *"J'ai*[a] *fait l'histoire."*[45]

I have indeed "made history." From the bright epoch which I now record, my actions – my works – are the property of mankind. They are familiar to the world. It is, then, needless for me to detail

a *I'ai (A, B, C) emended by the editor*

how, soaring rapidly, I fell heir to the "Lollipop" — how I merged this journal in the "Hum-Drum" — how again I made purchase of the "Rowdy-Dow," thus combining the three periodicals — how, lastly, I effected a bargain for the sole remaining rival, and united all the literature of the country in one magnificent Magazine, known everywhere as the

"Rowdy-Dow, Lollipop, Hum-Drum,
and
GOOSETHERUMFOODLE."

Yes; I have made history. My fame is universal. It extends to the uttermost ends of the earth. You cannot take up a common newspaper in which you shall not see some allusion to the immortal THINGUM BOB. It is Mr. Thingum Bob said so, and Mr. Thingum Bob wrote this, and Mr. Thingum Bob did that. But I am meek and expire with an humble heart. After all, what is it? — this indescribable something which men will persist in terming "genius?"[46] I agree with Buffon — with Hogarth — it is but *diligence* after all.[47]

Look at *me!* — how I labored — how I toiled — how I wrote! Ye Gods, did I *not* write? I knew not the word "ease." By day I adhered to my desk, and at night, a pale student, I consumed the midnight oil.[48] You should have seen me — you *should.* I leaned to the right. I leaned to the left. I sat forward. I sat backward. I sat upon end. I sat *tête*[b] *baissée,* (as they have it in the Kickapoo,) bowing my head close to the alabaster page. And, through all, I — *wrote.* Through joy and through sorrow, I — *wrote.* Through hunger and through thirst, I — *wrote.* Through good report and through ill report, I — *wrote.* Through sunshine and through moonshine, I — *wrote. What* I wrote it is unnecessary to say. The *style!* — that was the thing. I caught it from Fatquack — whizz! — fizz! — and I am giving you a specimen of it now.

NOTES

Title: Thingum Bob is equivalent to what-ye-may-call-it, but the family name is appropriate for a barber who cuts hair. In Thomas Moore's story *The*

---

b *tete (B, C)*

Fudge Family in England, a literary man is spoken of as "Lady Jane Thingum-bob's last novel's editor." See Burton Pollin's paper cited at p. 186, n. 21, above.

1. Richard Emmons, M.D., was born in Massachusetts in 1788. While living in Great Crossing, Kentucky, he completed *The Fredoniad, or Independence Preserved: An Epick Poem on the Late War of 1812* (1827); later, in Washington, he wrote another poem, *The Battle of Bunker Hill,* published posthumously in 1839. Commenting on the first of these, Timothy Flint, editor of the *Western Monthly Review* (Cincinnati), said in his issue for August 1828, "He [Emmons] is so glorious and unrivalled in the art of bathos, that one is delighted with the power that can so felicitously render any subject so superlatively ludicrous. But take the whole mass together, it is the most monstrous collection of maudlin, silly and incongruous verses, that ever were, or, we hope, ever will be put together." See Charles L. Squier's entertaining paper on *The Fredoniad* (*AL,* January 1961, pp. 446–454). Poe referred contemptuously to "Pop Emmons" in reviewing Griswold's *Poets and Poetry of America* (Philadelphia *Saturday Museum,* January 28, 1843) and again in the review of "Flaccus" (Thomas Ward, M.D.) in *Graham's* for March 1843, and he wrote of the absurdity of comparing Emmons to Homer in the *Broadway Journal's* "Editorial Miscellany," October 11, 1845.

2. Compare *Twelfth Night,* II, v: "Some are born great, some achieve greatness, and some have greatness thrust upon 'em." See also n. 45 below.

3. The term merchant-barber parallels merchant-banker and merchant-tailor.

4. The "Gad-Fly," and the poem, are referred to frequently below. Byron mentions Oil of Macassar in *Don Juan,* I, xvii, 8. Poe ridiculed fancy names for hair tonics in "Loss of Breath."

5. With this and the preceding paragraph, compare the first few paragraphs of "Lionizing."

6. Poetical editors in Poe's time included Bryant, E. C. Pinkney, G. P. Morris, N. P. Willis, W. G. Simms, W. G. Clark, J. S. DuSolle, Epes Sargent, J. H. Hewitt, Griswold, and Poe himself. The list also might include English, Whittier, Whitman, and Lowell.

7. For these gleanings see *Inferno,* canto 33; *Hamlet,* I, iv, 39–40; Pope's *Iliad,* I, 1; and *Paradise Lost,* III, 1.

8. Opodeldoc is an age-old preparation of soap, alcohol, camphor, and essential oils, used by barbers as well as horse-doctors and others. "Dr. Steer's Opodeldoc" was one of the widely advertised nostrums with extravagant claims held in contempt by Poe. [See Burton Pollin's analysis, "Poe's Literary Use of 'Oppodeldoc' and Other Patent Medicines," *Poe Studies,* December 1971.]

9. The city of the transcendentals is presumably Boston.

10. Poe used this expression a number of times in connection with blasting reviews. See our comment and footnote on p. 377 above.

11. Poe has the name *Hum-Drum* twice as of a magazine in his "Autography" (1836), and refers to the *North American Quarterly Humdrum,* parodying the *North American Review,* in "Never Bet the Devil Your Head."

12. The sons of Dante's Ugolino were starved to death.

13. Compare this phrase with a series of like ones, "What a world of merriment," etc., in "The Bells" (Mabbott I, 435ff).

14. Nathaniel Lee (1653–1692) wrote bombastic tragedies and died insane.

15. With "trash of trash" compare "An Enigma" for Mrs. Lewis, line 5: "Trash of all trash!" (Mabbott I, 425).

16. Compare the motto on Montresor's arms in "The Cask of Amontillado": *Nemo me impune lacessit.*

17. Minion is a small printing type — about 10½ lines to the inch, according to the *Century Dictionary*.

18. For "the wormwood and the gall" see Lamentations 3:19.

19. An Act of Parliament for the Prevention of Cruelty to Animals, proposed by an Irishman called "Humanity Dick" (Richard Martin), received the assent of George IV, July 22, 1822 (*Natural History Magazine,* December 1967). See also "Moving Chapters," n. 16.

20. "Honesty is the best policy" has been traced to 1599.

21. So many old magazines used selected material that those that did not advertised their policy.

22. The name "Snob" suggests Thingum's attitude, but I have actually found a "Discourse on Pigs" signed "Snob" in the New York *Sunday Atlas,* August 30, 1840.

23. A "penny-a-liner" is a hack writer who works for small pay.

24. "Mr. Fry" in the *Broadway Journal* and in Griswold's text may be a misprint, but Poe sometimes changed slightly the names of persons who annoyed him; for example, "Thomas Dunn Brown" for Dr. English.

25. A lustrum is five years; Poe was fond of the word, using it also in "Metzengerstein," "Eleonora," "Three Sundays in a Week," "Morella," and "The Colloquy of Monos and Una."

26. *Argent comptant* means ready money.

27. To "burst up" (colloquial) is to fail, to become bankrupt; hence "a burst up" means a bankruptcy.

28. The quotation is from Byron's "Memoranda" of 1812, quoted by Thomas Moore in his *Life of Byron* after Letter XCI.

29. The mark "*Sep.* 15 – 1 *t.*" identifies a paid advertisement to be inserted one time only on September 15 when most monthly magazines for October appeared.

30. For a comparison of Hyperion with a satyr see *Hamlet,* I, ii, 140.

31. The circulation figure of 100,000 is, of course, highly exaggerated. *Graham's Magazine,* not completely a literary journal, had the largest circulation of its day, between 35,000 and 37,000 (Heartman and Canny, p. 201). The *Broadway Journal* had probably less than 1,000 (see Quinn, p. 456).

32. See note 22 above. The reference to the eminence of Slyass may be a thrust at Bryant, whose work Poe privately thought overrated.

33. Mumblethumb's "Monody" may suggest Emerson's "Threnody," but Coleridge wrote a "Monody on a Teakettle." Poems with strange titles seem to have been common, especially in the *Knickerbocker;* among them are: "To a Pair of Old Earrings" by Mary E. Hewitt, December 1842; "Apostrophe to an Old Hat" by John G. Saxe, January 1844; and "Ode to an Old Pair of India Rubbers" ascribed to Seatsfield, September 1844.

34. Fatquack's "Dish-Clout" refers to Cooper's "Autobiography of a Pocket Handkerchief," published serially in *Graham's* for January to April 1843. Cooper himself did not allow this potboiler to appear in book form while he lived.

35. Mademoiselle Cribalittle is almost surely the formidable Mrs. E. F. Ellet, widely (and justly) accused of plagiarism, and interested in stories of the American Revolution. The other female writers I cannot identify firmly.

36. For "Damn with faint praise" see Pope's *Epistle to Dr. Arbuthnot,* line 201.

37. "To make great eyes" is a German idiom for incredulity.

38. Poe mentioned "poor-devil authors" several times. See "Some Secrets of the Magazine Prison House," n. 4.

39. All the abusive writers are real. Henry Peter, Lord Brougham – see p. 358, n. 5 – was famed for ridicule, sarcasm, and invective in Parliament. Poe reviewed collections of his writings in *Burton's* and *Graham's.* William Cobbett, the Utilitarian and radical – see "Preface to Marginalia," n. 4 – called one paper he published in Philadelphia *Porcupine's Gazette.* George Dennison Prentice (1802–1870) founded the *Louisville Journal* in Kentucky in 1831. Collections of his writings called *Prenticeana* appeared in 1860 and 1870. He once paid his respects to Poe for calling Carlyle an ass by the remark that Poe was "a better judge of asses than men like Carlyle." Lewis Gaylord Clark, in the *Knickerbocker Magazine* for October 1843, p. 392, quoted the last sally with approval.

In revising his tale, Poe removed two names from his list. One was John Neal's. That peppery critic was always friendly to Poe. The other, James Gordon Bennett, founder of the *New York Herald,* was a sensational journalist. I suspect that Poe later came to be on better terms with him than in 1844. Reference to folio editions of Prentice and of Bennett is a special joke. Both men edited daily newspapers, which of course were folios.

40. A similar method of composition was described humorously as one for making Latin verses by Père de Cerceau in *Réflexions sur la poésie françois* (1718): put all the terms of a phrase in a hat, and take them out at random. See Alfred G. Engstrom in *Modern Language Notes,* June 1958.

41. *Aper* is wild boar, not old bore.

42. See St. Matthew 18:6 for "a millstone . . . hanged about his neck."

43. The allusion is to Horace, *Epistles,* I, i, 65–66, *rem facias . . . quocumque modo,* which means "make money in any way."

44. See Iago's urgent advice in *Othello,* I, iii: "Put money in thy purse."

45. Chateaubriand's remark, "I have made history," is in the *New-York Mirror,* May 24, 1834, in a translation of a section of his autobiography then recently printed in the *Revue des deux mondes,* August 1, 1832. It is in the complete work, *Mémoires d'outre tombe* (Paris, 1860), VI, 382. One who reads Chateaubriand's remark in the original context may feel that the context inspired the first paragraph of Poe's tale.

46. A personal joke in one phrase was pointed out to me by A. H. Quinn. James Russell Lowell wrote "Mr. Poe has that indescribable something which men have agreed to call genius" in the sketch of the author published in *Graham's Magazine* for February 1845. Poe had read that sketch in manuscript soon after Lowell wrote on September 27, 1844, that he was sending it "by a private hand" (see Woodberry, *Life,* II, 100).

47. The great French naturalist Buffon said, "Le génie, c'est la patience" in his *Discours sur la style* (1753), and elsewhere. The English artist William Hogarth said to Gilbert Cooper, "Genius is but labor and diligence," according to William Seward's *Biographiana* (1799), II, 293. Poe referred to the remarks of Buffon and Hogarth also in a review of Anthon's *Sallust* in the *Southern Literary Messenger,* May 1836; and one of Bulwer's *Night and Morning* in *Graham's* for April 1841.

48. See John Gay, *Fables,* "Introduction," lines 15–16, "... hath thy toil/ O'er books consumed the midnight oil?"

THE THOUSAND-AND-SECOND TALE OF SCHEHERAZADE

This tale, in the tradition of the Arabian Nights, is one of Poe's most amusing stories. He was well aware that many of the discoveries of modern scholars and achievements of modern scientists put to shame the magic tales that delighted our ancestors. He commented on occasion that whereas doubt of what seemed extraordinary had long been fashionable, in his day the advanced thinker tended to believe, rather than to disbelieve, something told him.*

The story of Scheherazade is known to every reader, and is, as Poe told it, from the old sources. The author of *The Thousand Nights and One Night* is unnamed, his date is uncertain, his orig-

* This point is made in Poe's articles on the "Beet-root" (December 18, 1839) and "Credulity" (May 6, 1840) in *Alexander's Weekly Messenger;* both are reprinted in Clarence S. Brigham's paper on Poe's contributions to the *Messenger,* cited on p. 477 above.

inality is negligible. Again and again, he says, "I tell the tale as 'twas told to me." For over a hundred years it has been clear that the stories exist in old manuscripts; and some were, at least in the last century, still told by professional storytellers in the bazaars of the East.

The stories were introduced into Europe in a French version by Antoine Galland, early in the eighteenth century, and were almost immediately translated into many other languages. An English translation from Galland's French was available by 1713.

In "Pinakidia," number 27 (*SLM,* August 1836, p. 575), Poe quoted from James Montgomery's *Lectures on Literature* a query: "Who does not turn with absolute contempt from the rings and gems, and filters, and caves and genii of Eastern Tales as from the trinkets of a toyshop, and the trumpery of a raree-show?" — and replied to the question himself: "What man of genius but must answer 'Not I.' "†

The impulse to write this tale in an Arabian Nights framework almost certainly came from an article headed "Prairie and Mountain Life: The Petrified Forest" in the Saint Louis *Weekly Reveille,* November 18, 1844.‡ The article repeats the story of a simple Frenchman with a trading party, who ruined his hatchet trying to cut firewood from a petrified tree. A member of the party had been accustomed to entertain his comrades at the campfire by reading aloud from a copy of the Arabian Nights, and "the effect produced upon the Frenchman" by his own experience, and the similar experience of a companion, "was to make him believe, implicitly, in all the stories he had ever heard read before from the Arabian Nights. And nothing ever after could convince him that the flying palaces of Aladdin, the wonderful caverns and transcendent gardens, the abodes of the Genii, and the wonderful floral extravagance of the

† Montgomery's lectures, delivered in 1830 and 1831, were often reprinted. Poe undoubtedly knew an earlier edition, but the sentence quoted may be found on p. 147 of Harper's edition, *Lectures on General Literature, Poetry, &c* (New York, 1838). The quotation is given again in "Marginalia," number 19 (*Democratic Review,* November 1844, p. 487), with even more vigorous denunciation of James and Robert Montgomery. Poe's dislike of the brothers was frequently revealed.

‡ The *Reveille* was edited by Joseph M. Field, a friend of Poe's. The story synopsized here was reprinted in *Simmond's Colonial Magazine,* February 1845, about the time Poe's tale was published.

fairies, was anything but most solemn truth, set down in a book."

In Poe's tale, the oriental ruler's doubt of the factual probably comes from a piece headed "Oriental Incredulity," copied from the *Boston Traveller* in the Philadelphia *Saturday Evening Post,* September 4, 1841. It reports that an Englishman told a Turk how swiftly trains ran between Manchester and Liverpool. The Turk said, "That's a lie." The Englishman said he had seen it. "I don't believe it a bit more for that," answered the Turk, nothing daunted.

Poe gathered his factual wonders from many sources, but was helped to a number of items by Dr. Dionysius Lardner's *Course of Lectures* (New York, 1842). Poe satirized the lecturer in "Three Sundays in a Week," and attacked him in "Marginalia," number 38 (*Democratic Review,* November 1844, pp. 491–493), but found that his work had its uses for a writer of fiction.

The story was probably written very late in 1844, and sold almost immediately. Slight additions were made in each of the two later authorized publications.

TEXTS

(A) Godey's Magazine and Lady's Book for February 1845 (30:61–67); *(B) Broadway Journal,* October 25, 1845 (2:235–240); *(C) Works* (1850), I, 131–149.

Griswold's version *(C),* which has auctorial additions, is followed.

It was this tale that suffered most from typographical errors in some of the later printings of *Works.* See the discussion of these errors in the note on Griswold's edition, under Sources.

THE THOUSAND-AND-SECOND TALE OF SCHEHERAZADE. [*C*]

Truth is stranger than fiction. — *Old Saying.*

Having had occasion, lately, in the course of some Oriental investigations, to consult the *Tellmenow Isitsöornot,* a work which (like the Zohar of Simeon Jochaides)[a] is scarcely known at all,[1] even in Europe, and which has never been quoted, to my knowledge, by any American — if we except, perhaps, the author of the "Curiosities

a Ischaides) *(A) misprint*

of American Literature;"[2] —having had occasion, I say, to turn over some pages of the first-mentioned very remarkable work, I was not a little astonished to discover that the literary world has hitherto been strangely in error respecting the fate of the vizier's daughter, Scheherazade, as that fate is depicted in the "Arabian Nights;" and that the *dénouement*[b] there given, if not altogether inaccurate, as far as it goes, is at least to blame in not having gone very much farther.

For full information on this interesting topic, I must refer the inquisitive reader to the "Isitsöornot" itself; but, in the mean time, I shall be pardoned for giving a summary of what I there discovered.

It will be remembered, that, in the usual version of the tales, a certain monarch, having good cause to be jealous of his queen, not only puts[c] her[d] to death, but makes a vow, by his beard and the prophet, to espouse each night the most beautiful maiden in his dominions, and the next morning to deliver her up to the executioner.

Having fulfilled this vow for many years to the letter, and with a religious punctuality and method that conferred great credit upon him as a man of devout feelings and excellent sense, he was interrupted one afternoon (no doubt at his prayers) by a visit from his grand vizier, to whose daughter, it appears, there had occurred an idea.

Her name was Scheherazade, and her idea was, that she would either redeem the land from the depopulating tax upon its beauty, or perish, after the approved fashion of all heroines, in the attempt.

Accordingly, and although we do not find it[e] to be leap-year, (which makes the sacrifice more meritorious,) she deputes her father, the grand vizier, to make an offer to the king of her hand. This hand the king eagerly accepts — (he had intended to take it at all events, and had put off the matter from day to day, only through fear of the vizier,) — but, in accepting it now, he gives all parties very distinctly to understand, that, grand vizier or no grand vizier, he has not the slightest design of giving up one iota of his vow or of

---

b *denouement (A); dénoument (B); denouément (C)*

c put *(A)*

d her immediately *(A)*

e it stated *(A)*

his privileges. When, therefore, the fair Scheherazade insisted upon marrying the king, and did actually marry him despite[f] her father's excellent advice not to do anything of the kind – when she would and did marry him, I say, will I nill I, it was with her beautiful black eyes as thoroughly open as the nature of the case would allow.

It seems, however, that this politic damsel (who had been reading Machiavelli, beyond doubt,) had a very ingenious little plot in her mind.[3] On the night of the wedding, she contrived, upon I forget what specious pretence,[g] to have her sister occupy a couch sufficiently near that of the royal pair to admit of easy conversation from bed to bed; and, a little before cock-crowing, she took care to awaken the good monarch, her husband, (who bore her none the worse will because he intended to wring her neck on the morrow,) – she managed to awaken[h] him, I say, (although, on account of a capital conscience and an easy digestion, he slept well,) by the profound interest of a story (about a rat and a black cat, I think,) which she was narrating (all in an under-tone, of course,) to her sister. When the day broke, it so happened that this history was not altogether finished, and that Scheherazade, in the nature of things, could not finish it just then, since it was high time for her to get up and be bowstrung – a thing very little more pleasant than hanging, only a trifle more genteel![i]

The king's curiosity, however, prevailing, I am sorry to say, even over his sound religious principles, induced him for this once to postpone the fulfilment of his vow until next morning, for the purpose and with the hope of hearing that night how it fared in the end with the black cat (a black cat, I think it was)[4] and the rat.

The night having arrived, however, the lady Scheherazade not only put the finishing stroke to the black cat and the rat, (the rat was blue,) but before she well knew what she was about, found herself deep in the intricacies of a narration, having reference (if I am not altogether mistaken) to a pink horse (with green wings) that went, in a violent[j] manner, by clockwork, and was wound up with an indigo key. With this history the king was even more profoundly

f in despite of *(A)*
g pretenee, *(B) misprint*
h awake *(A)*
i genteel. *(A, B)*
j violet *(A, B) misprint*

interested than with the other — and, as the day broke before its conclusion, (notwithstanding all the queen's endeavors to get through with it in time for the bowstringing,) there was again no resource but to postpone that ceremony as before, for twenty-four hours. The next night there happened a similar accident with a similar result; and then the next[k] — and then again the next; so that, in the end, the good monarch, having been unavoidably deprived of all opportunity to keep his vow during a period of no less than one thousand and one nights, either forgets it altogether by the expiration of this time, or gets himself absolved of it in the regular way, or, (what is more probable) breaks it [l]outright, as well as[l] the head of his father confessor. At all events, Scheherazade, who, being lineally descended from Eve, fell heir, perhaps, to the whole seven baskets of talk, which the latter lady, we all know, picked up from under the trees in the garden of Eden;[5] Scheherazade, I say, finally triumphed, and the tariff upon beauty was repealed.

Now, this conclusion (which is that of the story as we have it upon record) is, no doubt, excessively proper and pleasant — but, alas! like a great many pleasant things, is more pleasant than true; and I am indebted altogether to the "Isitsöornot" for the means of correcting the error. *"Le mieux,"* says a French proverb, *"est l'ennemi du bien,"*[6] and, in mentioning that Scheherazade had inherited the seven baskets of talk, I should have added, that she put them out at compound interest until they amounted to seventy-seven.[m]

"My dear sister," said she, on the thousand-and-second night, (I quote the language of the "Isitöornot" at this point, *verbatim,*) "my dear sister," said she, "now that all this little difficulty about the bowstring has blown over, and that this odious tax is so happily repealed, I feel that I have been guilty of[n] great indiscretion in withholding from you and the king (who, I am sorry to say, snores — a thing[o] no gentleman would do,) the full conclusion of the history of Sinbad the sailor. This person went through numerous other and more interesting adventures than those which I related;

k next night *(A)*
l . . . l outright with *(A)*
m seventeen. *(A)*
n of a *(A)*
o thing that *(A)*

but the truth is, I felt sleepy on the particular night of their narration, and so was seduced into cutting them short — a grievous piece of misconduct, for which I only trust that Allah will forgive me. But even yet it is not too late to remedy my great neglect — and as soon as I have given the king a pinch or two in order to wake him up so far that he may stop making that horrible noise, I will forthwith entertain you (and him if he pleases) with the sequel of this very remarkable story."

Hereupon the sister of Scheherazade, as I have it from the "Isitsöornot," expressed no very particular intensity of gratification; but the king having been sufficiently pinched, at length ceased snoring, and finally said "Hum!" and then "Hoo!" when the queen understanding these words (which are no doubt[p] Arabic) to signify that he was all attention, and would do his best not to snore any more — the queen, I say, having arranged these matters to her satisfaction, re-entered thus, at once, into the history of Sinbad the sailor:

" 'At length, in my old age,' (these are the words of Sinbad himself, as retailed by Scheherazade,) — 'at length, in my old age, and after enjoying many years of tranquillity at home, I became once more possessed with a desire of visiting foreign countries; and one day, without acquainting any of my family with my design, I packed up some bundles of such merchandise as was most precious and least bulky, and, engaging a porter to carry them, went with him down to the sea-shore, to await the arrival of any chance vessel that might convey me out of the kingdom into some region which I had not as yet explored.

" 'Having deposited the packages upon the sands, we sat down beneath some trees, and looked out into the ocean in the hope of perceiving a ship, but during several hours we saw none whatever. At length I fancied that I could hear a singular buzzing or humming sound — and the porter, after listening awhile, declared that he also could distinguish it. Presently it grew louder, and then still louder, so that we could have no doubt that the object which caused it was approaching us. At length, on the edge of the horizon, we discovered a black speck, which rapidly increased in size until we

p doubt capital *(A)*

made it out to be a vast monster, swimming with a great part of its body above the surface of the sea. It came towards us with inconceivable swiftness, throwing up huge waves of foam around its breast, and illuminating all that part of the sea through which it passed, with a long line of fire that extended far off into the distance.[7]

" 'As the thing drew near we saw it very distinctly. Its length was equal to that of three of the loftiest trees that grow, and it was as wide as the great hall of audience in your palace, O most sublime and munificent of the caliphs. Its body, which was unlike that of ordinary fishes, was as solid as a rock, and of a jetty blackness throughout all that portion of it which floated above the water, with the exception of a narrow blood-red streak that completely begirdled it. The belly, which floated beneath the surface, and of which we could get only a glimpse now and then as the monster rose and fell with the billows, was entirely covered with metallic scales, of a color like that of the moon in misty weather. The back was flat and nearly white, and from it there extended upwards of six[q] spines, about half the length of the whole body.

" 'This horrible creature had no mouth that we could perceive; but, as if to make up for this deficiency, it was provided with at least four score of eyes, that protruded from their sockets like those of the green dragon-fly, and were arranged all around the body in two rows, one above the other, and parallel to the blood-red streak, which seemed to answer the purpose of an eyebrow. Two or three of these dreadful eyes were much larger than the others, and had the appearance of solid gold.

" 'Although this beast approached us, as I have before said, with the greatest rapidity, it must have been moved altogether by necromancy — for it had neither fins like a fish nor web-feet like a duck, nor wings like the sea-shell which is blown along in the manner of a vessel;[8] nor yet did it writhe itself forward as do the eels. Its head and its tail were shaped precisely alike, only, not far from the latter, were two small holes that served for nostrils, and through which the monster puffed out its thick breath with prodigious violence, and with a shrieking, disagreeable noise.

q of six/four *(A)*; six *(B)*

" 'Our terror at beholding this hideous thing was very great; but it was even surpassed by our astonishment, when, upon getting a nearer look, we perceived upon the creature's back a vast number of animals about the size and shape of men, and altogether much resembling them, except that they wore no garments (as men do,) being supplied (by nature, no doubt,) with an ugly, uncomfortable covering, a good deal like cloth, but fitting so tight to the skin, as to render the poor wretches laughably awkward, and put them apparently to severe pain. On the very tips of their heads were certain square-looking boxes, which, at first sight, I thought might have been intended to answer as turbans, but I soon discovered that they were excessively heavy and solid, and I therefore concluded they were contrivances designed, by their great weight, to keep the heads of the animals steady and safe upon their shoulders. Around the necks of the creatures were fastened black collars, (badges of servitude, no doubt,) such as we keep on our dogs, only much wider and infinitely stiffer — so that it was quite impossible for these poor victims to move their heads in any direction without moving the body at the same time; and thus they were doomed to perpetual contemplation of their noses — a view puggish and snubby in a wonderful if not positively in an awful degree.

" 'When the monster had nearly reached the shore where we stood, it suddenly pushed out one of its eyes to a great extent, and emitted from it a terrible flash of fire, accompanied by a dense cloud of smoke, and a noise that I can compare to nothing but thunder. As the smoke cleared away, we saw one of the odd man-animals standing near the head of the large beast with a trumpet in his hand, through which (putting it to his mouth) he presently addressed us in loud, harsh, and disagreeable accents, that, perhaps, we should have mistaken for language, had they not come altogether through the nose.

" 'Being thus evidently spoken to, I was at a loss how to reply, as I could in no manner understand what was said; and in this difficulty I turned to the porter, who was near swooning through affright, and demanded of him his opinion as to what species of monster it was, what it wanted, and what kind of creatures those were that so swarmed upon its back. To this the porter replied, as well as he could for trepidation, that he had once before heard of this sea-beast; that it was a cruel demon, with bowels of sulphur and blood of fire, created by evil genii as the means of inflicting misery upon mankind; that the things upon its back were vermin, such as sometimes infest cats and dogs, only a little larger and more savage; and that these vermin had their uses, however evil — for, through the torture they caused the beast by their nibblings and stingings, it was goaded into that degree of wrath which was requisite to make it roar and commit ill, and so fulfil the vengeful and malicious designs of the wicked genii.

" 'This account determined me to take to my heels, and, without once even looking behind me, I ran at full speed up into the hills, while the porter ran equally fast, although nearly in an opposite direction, so that, by these means, he finally made his escape with my bundles, of which I have no doubt[r] he took excellent care — although this is a point I cannot determine, as I do not remember that I ever beheld him again.

" 'For myself, I was so hotly pursued by a swarm of the men-vermin (who had come to the shore in boats) that I was very soon overtaken, bound hand and foot, and conveyed to the beast, which immediately swam out again into the middle of the sea.

" 'I now bitterly repented my folly in quitting[s] a comfortable home to peril my life in such adventures as this; but regret being useless, I made the best of my condition, and exerted myself to secure the good-will of the man-animal that owned the trumpet, and who appeared to exercise authority over its fellows. I succeeded so well in this endeavor that, in a few days, the creature bestowed upon me various tokens of its favor, and, in the end, even went to the trouble of teaching me the rudiments of what it was vain enough to denominate its language; so that, at length, I was enabled to converse with it readily, and came to make it comprehend the ardent desire I had of seeing the world.

" '*Washish squashish squeak, Sinbad, hey-diddle diddle, grunt unt grumble, hiss, fiss, whiss,*' said he to me, one day after dinner — but I beg a thousand pardons, I had forgotten that your majesty is not conversant with the dialect of the Cock-neighs,[9] (so the man-

r doubt that *(A)* s quitiing *(B) misprint*

animals were called; I presume because their language formed the connecting link between that of the horse and that of the rooster.) With your permission, I will translate. *'Washish squashish,'* and so forth: — that is to say, 'I am happy to find, my dear Sinbad, that you are really a very excellent fellow; we are now about doing a thing which is called circumnavigating the globe; and since you are so desirous of seeing the world, I will strain a point and give you a free passage upon the back of the beast.' "

When the Lady Scheherazade had proceeded thus far, relates the "Isitsöornot," the king turned over from his left side to his right, and said —

"It is, in fact, *very* surprising, my dear queen, that you omitted, hitherto, these latter adventures of Sinbad. Do you know I think them exceedingly entertaining and strange?"

The king having thus expressed himself, we are told, the fair Scheherazade resumed her history in the following words: —

"Sinbad went on in this manner, with his narrative[t] — 'I thanked the man-animal for its kindness, and soon found myself very much at home on the beast, which swam at a prodigious rate through the ocean; although the surface of the latter is, in that part of the world, by no means flat, but round like a pomegranate, so that we went — so to say — either up hill or down hill all the time.' "

"That, I think, was very singular," interrupted the king.

"Nevertheless, it is quite true," replied Scheherazade.

"I have my doubts," rejoined the king; "but, pray, be so good as to go on with the story."

"I will," said the queen. " 'The beast,' continued Sinbad,[u] 'swam, as I have related, up hill and down hill, until, at length, we arrived at an island, many hundreds of miles in circumference, but which, nevertheless, had been built in the middle of the sea by a colony of little things like caterpillars.' "*[10]

"Hum!" said the king.

" 'Leaving this island,' said Sinbad — (for Scheherazade, it must be understood, took no notice of her husband's ill-mannered ejacu-

* The coralites.

t narrative to the caliph *(A, B)* u Sinbad to the caliph, *(A, B)* lation) — 'leaving this island, we came to another where the forests were of solid stone, and so hard that they shivered to pieces the finest-tempered axes with which we endeavored to cut them down.' "†[11]

"Hum!" said the king, again; but Scheherazade, paying him no attention, continued in the language of Sinbad.

" 'Passing beyond this last island, we reached a country where there was a cave that ran to the[w] distance of thirty or forty miles within the bowels of the earth, and that contained a greater number of far more spacious and more magnificent palaces than are to be found in all Damascus and Bagdad. From the roofs of these palaces there hung myriads of gems, like diamonds, but larger than men; and in among the streets of towers and pyramids and temples, there

† "One of the most remarkable natural curiosities in Texas is a petrified forest, near the head of Pasigono[u'] river. It consists of several hundred trees, in an erect position, all turned to stone. Some trees, now growing, are partly petrified. This is a startling fact for natural philosophers, and must cause them to modify the existing theory of petrifaction." — *Kennedy.*

[v] This account, at first discredited, has since been corroborated by the discovery of a completely petrified forest, near the head waters of the Chayenne, or Chienne river, which has its source in the Black Hills of the rocky chain.

There is scarcely, perhaps, a spectacle on the surface of the globe more remarkable, either in a geological or picturesque point of view, than that presented by the petrified forest, near Cairo. The traveller, having passed the tombs of the caliphs, just beyond the gates of the city, proceeds to the southward, nearly at right angles to the road across the desert to Suez, and, after having travelled some ten miles up a low barren valley, covered with sand, gravel, and sea shells, fresh as if the tide had retired but yesterday, crosses a low range of sandhills, which has for some distance run parallel to his path. The scene now presented to him is beyond conception singular and desolate. A mass of fragments of trees, all converted into stone, and when struck by his horse's hoof ringing like cast iron, is seen to extend itself for miles and miles around him, in the form of a decayed and prostrate forest. The wood is of a dark brown hue, but retains its form in perfection, the pieces being from one to fifteen feet in length, and from half a foot to three feet in thickness, strewed so closely together, as far as the eye can reach, that an Egyptian donkey can scarcely thread its way through amongst them, and so natural that, were it in Scotland or Ireland, it might pass without remark for some enormous drained bog, on which the exhumed trees lay rotting in the sun. The roots and rudiments of the branches are, in many cases, nearly perfect, and in some the worm-holes eaten under the bark are readily recognisable. The most delicate of the sap vessels, and all the finer portions of the centre of the wood, are perfectly entire, and bear to be examined with the strongest magnifiers. The whole are so thoroughly silicified as to scratch glass and be capable of receiving the highest polish. — *Asiatic Magazine.*[v]

---

u' Pasigno *(A, B, C) misprint*

v . . . v *Omitted (A, B)*

w a *(A)*

flowed immense rivers as black as ebony, and swarming with fish that had no eyes.' "‡[12]

"Hum!" said the king.

" 'We then swam into a region of the sea where we found a lofty mountain, down whose sides there streamed torrents of melted metal, some of which were twelve miles wide and sixty miles long;§[13] while from an abyss on the summit, issued so vast a quantity of ashes that the sun was entirely blotted out from the heavens,[14] and it became darker than the darkest midnight; so that when we were even at the distance of a hundred and fifty miles from the mountain, it was impossible to see the whitest object, however close we held it to our eyes.' "*

"Hum!" said the king.

" 'After quitting this coast, the beast continued his voyage until we met with a land in which the nature of things seemed[y] reversed — for we here saw a great lake, at the bottom of which, more than a hundred feet beneath the surface of the water, there flourished in full leaf a forest of tall and luxuriant trees.' "†

"Hoo!" said the king.

[z]" 'Some hundred miles farther on brought us to a climate where the atmosphere was so dense as to sustain iron or steel, just as our own does feathers.' "‡[15]

‡ The Mammoth Cave of Kentucky.

§ In Iceland, 1783.

* "During the eruption of Hecla in 1766, clouds of this kind produced such a degree of darkness that, at Glaumba, which is more than fifty leagues from the mountain, people could only find their way by groping. During the eruption of Vesuvius, in 1794, at Caserta, four leagues distant, people could only walk by the light of torches. On the first of May, 1812, a cloud of volcanic ashes and sand, coming from a volcano in the island of St. Vincent covered the whole of Barbadoes, spreading over it so intense a darkness[x] that, at mid-day, in the open air, one could not perceive the trees or other objects near him, or even a white handkerchief placed at the distance of six inches from the eye." — *Murray,* p. 215, *Phil. edit.*

† "In the year 1790, in the Caraccas, during an earthquake, a portion of the granite soil sank and left a lake eight hundred yards in diameter, and from eighty to a hundred feet deep. It was a part of the forest of Aripao which sank, and the trees remained green for several months under the water." — *Murray,* p. 221.

‡ The hardest steel ever manufactured may, under the action of a blowpipe, be reduced to an impalpable powder, which will float readily in the atmospheric air.

---

x darknesr *(B) misprint*

y was altogether *(A);* seem *(B) misprint*

z . . . z *Omitted (A, B)*

"Fiddle de dee," said the king.[z]

" 'Proceeding still in the same direction, we presently arrived at the most magnificent region in the whole world. Through it there meandered a glorious river for several thousands of miles. This river was of unspeakable depth, and of a transparency richer than that of amber. It was from three to six miles in width; and its banks, which arose on either side to twelve hundred feet in perpendicular height, were crowned with ever-blossoming trees, and perpetual sweet-scented flowers, that made the whole territory one gorgeous garden; but the name of this luxuriant land was the kingdom[a] of Horror, and to enter it was inevitable death.' "§[16]

"Humph!" said the king.

" 'We left this kingdom[b] in great haste, and, after some days, came to another, where we were astonished to perceive myriads of monstrous animals with horns resembling scythes upon their heads. These hideous beasts dig for themselves vast caverns in the soil, of a funnel shape, and line the sides of them with rocks, so disposed one upon the other that they fall instantly, when trodden upon by other animals, thus precipitating them into the monsters' dens, where their blood is immediately sucked, and their carcasses afterwards hurled contemptuously out to an immense distance from the[c] caverns of death.' "*[17]

"Pooh!"[d] said the king.

" 'Continuing our progress, we perceived a district abounding with vegetables that grew not upon any soil, but in the air.†[18] There were others that sprang from the substance of other vegetables;‡[19] others that derived their sustenance from the bodies of

§ The region of the Niger. See *Simmond's "Colonial Magazine."*

* The *Myrmeleon* – lion-ant. The term "monster" is equally applicable to small abnormal things and to great, while such epithets as "vast" are merely comparative. The cavern of the myrmeleon is *vast* in comparison with the hole of the common red ant. A grain of silex is, also, a "rock."

† The *Epidendron, Flos Aeris*[e] of the family of the *Orchideæ,* grows with merely the surface of its roots attached to a tree or other object, from which it derives no nutriment – subsisting altogether upon air.

‡ The *Parasites,* such as the wonderful *Rafflesia Arnoldi.*[f]

a kindom *(B) misprint*
b kindom *(B) misprint*
c "the *(B, C)*
d "Pish!" *(A)*
e *Acris, (A) misprint*
f *Arnoldii, (A); Arnaldii, (B, C) misprint, corrected editorially*

living animals;§[20] and then, again, there were others that glowed all over with intense fire;* [j]others that moved from place to place at pleasure;†[j] [21] and what is still more wonderful, we discovered flowers that lived and breathed and moved their limbs at will, and had, moreover, the detestable passion of mankind for enslaving other creatures, and confining them in horrid and solitary prisons until the fulfillment of appointed tasks.' "‡[22]

"Pshaw!" said the king.

" 'Quitting this land, we soon arrived at another in which the bees and the birds are mathematicians of such genius and erudition,

§ *Schouw* advocates a class of plants that grow upon living animals — the *Plantæ Epizoæ*. Of this class are the *Fuci* and *Algæ*.

[g] *Mr. J. B. Williams, of Salem, Mass.*, presented the "National Institute," with an insect from New Zealand, with the following description: — " '*The Hotte,*' a decided caterpillar, or worm, is found growing at the foot of the *Rata* tree, with a plant growing out of its head. This most peculiar and most extraordinary insect travels up both the *Rata* and *Perriri*[h] trees, and entering into the top, eats its way, perforating the trunk of the tree until it reaches the root, it then comes out of the root, and dies, or remains dormant, and the plant propagates out of its head; the body remains perfect and entire, of a harder substance than when alive. From this insect the natives make a coloring for tattooing."[g]

* In mines and natural caves we find a species of cryptogamous[i] *fungus* that emits an intense phosphorescence.

† The orchis, scabius and vallisneria.[k]

‡ "The corolla of this flower, *(Aristolochia Clematitis,)* which is tubular, but terminating upwards in a ligulate limb, is inflated into a globular figure at the base. The tubular part is internally beset with stiff hairs, pointing downwards. The globular part contains the pistil, which consists merely of a germen and stigma, together with the surrounding stamens. But the stamens, being shorter than even the germen, cannot discharge the pollen so as to throw it upon the stigma, as the flower stands always upright till after impregnation. And hence, without some additional and peculiar aid, the pollen must necessarily fall down to the bottom of the flower. Now, the aid that nature has furnished in this case, is that of the *Tipula*[l] *Pennicornis,* a small insect, which, entering the tube of the corolla in quest of honey, descends to the bottom, and rummages[m] about till it becomes quite covered with pollen; but, not being able to force its way out again, owing to the downward position of the hairs, which converge to a point like the wires of a mouse-trap, and being somewhat impatient of its confinement, it brushes backwards and forwards, trying every corner, till, after repeatedly traversing the stigma, it covers it with pollen sufficient for its impregnation, in consequence of which the flower soon begins to droop, and the hairs to shrink to the side of the tube, effecting an easy passage for the escape of the insect." — *Rev. P. Keith — "System of Physiological Botany."*

---

g . . . g *Omitted (A)*
h *Puriri in OED*
i crytogamous *(B) misprint*
j . . . j *Omitted (A, B)*
k valisneria. *(C) misprint, corrected editorially*
l *Tiputa (B, C) misprint, corrected from A*
m rumages *(B) misprint*

that they give daily instructions in the science of geometry to the wise men of the empire. The king of the place having offered a reward for the solution of two very difficult problems, they were solved upon the spot – the one by the bees, and the other by the birds; but the king keeping their solutions a secret, it was only after the most profound researches and labor, and the writing of an infinity of big books, during a long series of years, that the men-mathematicians at length arrived at the identical solutions which had been given upon the spot by the bees and by the birds.' "§[23]

"Oh my!" said the king.

" 'We had scarcely lost sight of this empire when we found ourselves close upon another, from whose shores there flew over our heads a flock of fowls a mile in breadth, and two hundred and forty miles long; so that, although they flew a mile during every minute, it required no less than four hours for the whole flock to pass over us – in which there were several millions of millions of fowls.' "*[24]

"Oh fy!" said the king.

" 'No sooner had we got rid of these birds, which occasioned us great annoyance, than we were terrified by the appearance of a fowl of another kind, and infinitely larger than even the rocs which I met in my former voyages; for it was bigger than the biggest of the domes upon your seraglio, oh, most Munificent of Caliphs. This

§ The bees – ever since bees were – have been constructing their cells with just such sides, in just such number, and at just such inclinations, as it has been demonstrated (in a problem involving the profoundest mathematical principles) are the very sides, in the very number, and at the very angles, which will afford the creatures the most room that is compatible with the greatest stability of structure.

During the latter part of the last century, the question arose among mathematicians – "to determine the best form that can be given to the sails of a windmill, according to their varying distances from the revolving vanes, and likewise from the centres of[n] revolution." This is an excessively complex problem; for it is, in other words, to find the best possible position at an infinity of varied distances, and at an infinity of points on the arm. There were a thousand futile attempts to answer the query on the part of the most illustrious mathematicians; and when, at length, an undeniable solution was discovered, men found that the wings of a bird had given it with absolute precision, ever since the first bird had traversed the air.

* He observed a flock of pigeons passing betwixt Frankfort and the Indiana territory, one mile at least in breadth; it took up four hours in passing; which, at the rate of one mile per minute, gives a length of 240 miles; and, supposing three pigeons to each square yard, gives 2,230,272,000 pigeons – *"Travels in Canada and the United[o] States," by Lieut. F. Hall.*

n of the *(C) emended from A and B* o U. *(A, B)*

terrible fowl had no head that we could perceive, but was fashioned entirely of belly, which was of a prodigious fatness and roundness, of a soft looking substance, smooth, shining and striped with various colors. In its talons, the monster was bearing away to his[p] eyrie in the heavens, a house from which it had knocked off the roof, and in the interior of which we distinctly saw[q] human beings, who, beyond doubt, were in a state of frightful despair at the horrible fate which awaited them. We shouted with all our might, in the hope of frightening the bird into letting go of[r] its prey; but it merely gave a snort or puff, as if of rage, and then let fall upon our heads a heavy sack which proved to be filled with sand!' "[s][25]

"Stuff!" said the king.

" 'It was just after this adventure that we encountered a continent of immense extent and of prodigious solidity, but which, nevertheless, was supported entirely upon the back of a sky-blue cow that had no fewer than four hundred horns.' "†[26]

"*That,* now, I believe," said the king, "because I have read something of the kind before, in a book."

" 'We passed immediately beneath this continent, (swimming in between the legs of the cow,) and, after some hours, found ourselves in a wonderful country indeed, which, I was informed by the man-animal, was his own native land, inhabited by things of his own species. This elevated the man-animal very much in my esteem; and in fact, I now began to feel ashamed of the contemptuous familiarity with which I had treated him; for I found that the man-animals in general were a nation of the most powerful magicians, who lived with worms in their brains,‡[27] which, no doubt, served to stimulate them by their painful writhings and wrigglings to the most miraculous efforts of imagination.' "

"Nonsense!" said the king.

" 'Among the[u] magicians, were domesticated several animals of

† "The earth is upheld by a cow of a blue color, having horns four hundred in number." — *Sale's Koran.*

‡ "The *Entozoa,* or intestinal worms, have repeatedly been observed in the muscles, and in the cerebral substance[t] of men." — *See Wyatt's Physiology,* p. 143.

p its *(A)*
q saw several *(A)*
r *Omitted (A)*
s sand.' " *(A, B)*
t substencee *(B) misprint*
u these *(A)*

very singular kinds; for example, there was a huge horse whose bones were iron and whose blood was boiling water. In place of corn, he had black stones for his usual food; and yet, in spite[v] of so hard a diet, he was so strong and swift that he would drag a load more weighty than the grandest temple in this city, at a rate surpassing that of the flight of most[w] birds.' "§[28]

"Twattle!" said the king.

" 'I saw, also, among these people a hen without feathers, but bigger than a camel; instead of flesh and bone she had iron and brick; her blood, like that of the horse, (to whom, in fact, she was nearly related,) was boiling water; and like him she ate nothing but wood or black stones. This hen brought forth very frequently, a hundred chickens in the day; and, after birth, they took up their residence[y] for several weeks within the stomach of their mother.' "*[29]

"Fal lal!" said the king.

" 'One of this nation of mighty conjurors created a man out of brass and wood, and leather, and endowed him with such ingenuity that he would have beaten at chess, all the race of mankind with the exception of the great Caliph, Haroun Alraschid.†[30] Another of these magi constructed (of like material) a creature that put to shame even the genius of him who made it; for so great were its reasoning powers that, in a second, it performed calculations of so vast an extent that they would have required the united labor of fifty thousand fleshly[a] men for a year.‡[31] But a still more wonderful conjuror fashioned for himself a mighty thing that was neither man nor beast, but which had brains of lead, intermixed with a black matter like pitch, and fingers that it employed with such incredible speed and dexterity that it would have had no trouble in writing out twenty thousand copies of the Koran in an hour; and

[x] § On the great Western Railway, between London and Exeter, a speed of 71 miles per hour has been attained. A train weighing 90 tons was whirled from Puddington to Didcot (53 miles,) in 51 minutes.[x]

* The *Eccaleobion.*[z]

† Maelzel's Automaton Chess-player.

‡ Babbage's Calculating Machine.

---

v despite *(A)*

w some *(A)*

x . . . x *Omitted (A, B)*

y residenco *(B) misprint*

z *Eccalobeion. (A, B, C) misprint, corrected editorially*

a fleshy *(C) misprint, corrected from A, B*

this with so exquisite a precision, that in all the copies there should not be found one to vary from another by the breadth of the finest hair. This thing was of prodigious strength, so that it erected or overthrew the mightiest empires at a breath; but its powers were[b] exercised equally[c] for evil and for good.' "[32]

"Ridiculous!" said the king.

" 'Among this nation of necromancers there was also one who had in his veins the blood of the salamanders; for he made no scruple of sitting down to smoke his chibouc in a red-hot oven until his dinner was thoroughly roasted upon its floor.§[33] Another had the faculty of converting the common metals into gold, without even looking at them during the process.*[34] Another had such a[d] delicacy of touch that he made a wire so fine as to be invisible.†[35] Another had such quickness of perception that he counted all the separate motions of an elastic body, while it was springing backwards and forwards at the rate of nine hundred millions of times in a second.' "‡[36]

"Absurd!" said the king.

" 'Another of these magicians, by means of a fluid that nobody ever yet saw, could make the corpses of his friends brandish their arms, kick out their legs, fight, or even get up and dance at his will.§[37] Another had cultivated his voice to so great an extent that he could have made himself heard from one end of the earth to the other.*[38] [e]Another had so long an arm that he could sit down in Damascus and indite a letter at Bagdad — or indeed at any distance whatsoever.†[e][39] Another commanded the lightning to come down to

§ *Chabert,* and, since him, a hundred others.

* The Electrotype.

† *Wollaston* made a platinum for the field of views in a telescope, a wire one eighteen-thousandth part of an inch in thickness. It could be seen only by means of the microscope.

‡ Newton demonstrated that the retina beneath the influence of the violet ray of the spectrum, vibrated 900,000,000 of times in a second.

§ The Voltaic pile.

* The Electro Telegraph transmits intelligence instantaneously — at least so far as regards any distance upon the earth.

† The Electro Telegraph Printing Apparatus.

---

b powers were/power was *(A, B)*

c exercised equally/equally exercised *(A)*

d *Omitted (A, B)*

e . . . e *Omitted (A)*

him out of the heavens, and it came at his call; and served him for a plaything when it came.[40] Another took two loud sounds and out of them made a silence. Another constructed a deep darkness out of two brilliant lights.‡[41] [g]Another made ice in a red-hot furnace.§[g42] Another directed the sun to paint his portrait,[i] and the sun did.*[43] Another took this luminary with the moon and the planets, and having first weighed them with scrupulous accuracy, probed into their depths and found out the solidity of the substance of which they are made. But the whole nation is, indeed, of so surprising a necromantic ability, that not even their infants, nor their commonest cats and dogs have any difficulty in seeing objects that do not exist at all, or that for twenty millions of[j] years before the birth of the nation itself, had been blotted out from the face of creation.' "†[44]

‡ Common experiments in Natural Philosophy. [f]If two red rays from two luminous points be admitted into a dark chamber so as to fall on a white surface, and differ in their length by 0.0000258 of an inch, their intensity is doubled. So also if the difference in length be any whole-number multiple of that fraction. A multiple by 2¼, 3¼, &c., gives an intensity equal to one ray only; but a multiple by 2½, 3½, &c., gives the result of total darkness. In violet rays similar effects arise when the difference in length is 0.0000157 of an inch; and with all other rays the results are the same – the difference varying with a uniform increase from the violet to the red.

Analogous experiments in respect to sound produce analogous results.[f]

§ Place a platina crucible over a spirit lamp, and keep it a red heat; pour in some sulphuric acid, which, though the most volatile of bodies at a common temperature, will be found to become completely fixed in a hot crucible, and not a drop evaporates — being surrounded by an atmosphere of its own, it does not, in fact, touch the sides. A few drops of water are now introduced, when the acid immediately coming in contact with the heated sides of the crucible, flies off in sulphurous acid vapor, and so rapid is its progress, that the caloric[h] of the water passes off with it, which falls a lump of ice to the bottom; by taking advantage of the moment before it is allowed to re-melt, it may be turned out a lump of ice from a red-hot vessel.

* The Daguerreotype.

† Although light travels 167,000[k] miles in a second, the distance of [l]61 Cygni, (the only star whose distance is ascertained,)[l] is so inconceivably great, that its rays would require [m]more than ten[m] years to reach the earth. For stars beyond this, 20 – or even 1000 years – would be a moderate estimate. Thus, if they had been annihilated 20, or 1000 years ago, we might still see them to-day, by the light which *started* from their surfaces, 20 or 1000 years in the past time. That many which we see daily are really extinct, is not impossible – not even improbable.

f . . . f *Omitted (A, B)*
g . . . g *Omitted (A)*
h chaloric *(B) misprint*
i portraitt, *(B) misprint*
j millions of/thousand *(A, B)*
k 200,000 *(A, B)*
l . . . l what we *suppose* to be the nearest fixed star (Sirius) *(A, B)* [suppose *not italicized in B*]
m . . . m *at least* three *(A, B)*

"Preposterous!" said the king.

" 'The wives and daughters of these incomparably great and wise magi,' " continued Scheherazade, without being in any manner disturbed by these frequent and most ungentlemanly interruptions on the part of her husband — " 'the wives and daughters of these eminent conjurors are every thing that is accomplished and refined; and would be every thing that is interesting and beautiful, but for an unhappy fatality that besets them, and from which not even the miraculous powers of their husbands and fathers has, hitherto, been adequate to save. Some fatalities come in certain shapes, and some in others — but this of which I speak, has come in the shape of a[o] crotchet.' "

"A what?" said the king.

" 'A crotchet,' " said Scheherazade. " 'One of the evil genii who are perpetually upon the watch to inflict ill, has put it into the heads of these accomplished ladies that the thing which we describe as personal beauty, consists altogether in the protuberance of the region which lies not very far below the small of the back. Perfection of loveliness, they say, is in the direct ratio of the extent of this hump. Having been long possessed of this idea, and bolsters being cheap in that country, the days have long gone by since it was possible to distinguish a woman from a dromedary —' "[45]

"Stop!" said the king — "I can't stand that, and I won't. You have already given me a dreadful headache with your lies. The day, too, I perceive, is beginning to break. How long have we been married? —— my[p] conscience is getting to be troublesome again. And then that dromedary touch — do you take me for a fool? Upon the whole, you might as well get up and be throttled."

These words, as I learn from the Isitsöornot, both grieved and astonished Scheherazade; but, as she knew the king to be a man of scrupulous integrity, and quite unlikely to forfeit his word, she sub-

[n] The elder Herschel maintains that the light of the faintest nebulæ seen through his great telescope, must have taken 3,000,000 years in reaching the earth. Some, made visible by Lord Ross' instrument must, then, have required at least 20,000,000.[n]

n . . . n *Omitted (A, B)*
o a horrible *(A)*
p ——my/Besides, my *(A)*

mitted to her fate with a good grace. She derived, however, great consolation, (during the tightening of the bowstring,) from the reflection that much of the history remained still untold, and that the petulance of her brute of a husband had reaped for him a most righteous reward,[46] in depriving him of many inconceivable adventures.

NOTES

Motto: Compare Byron's *Don Juan,* XIV, CI, 1, and see *Politian,* V, 40; "How to Write a Blackwood Article" at n. 16; "A Tale of the Ragged Mountains," and "Von Kempelen and His Discovery."

1. Unlike the *Tellmenow Isitsöornot,* the *Zohar* is a real work, mentioned as Poe describes it in the first edition of Irving's classic, *A History of New York by Dietrich Knickerbocker* (1809), Book IV, chapter 4, paragraph 12. Known since the last part of the thirteenth century, the *Zohar* is a collection of esoteric material long ascribed to a second century rabbi, Simeon ben Jochai (Jochiades); it is one source of the Kabbala.

2. The "Curiosities" referred to was supplied by Griswold for an American edition of Isaac D'Israeli's *Curiosities of Literature* (1844) and is also mentioned in "The Angel of the Odd" at n. 3 and in *Doings of Gotham,* Letter VI.

3. Compare Butler's couplet in *Hudibras,* I, i, 741–742: "There is a Machiavelian plot,/Tho' ev'ry nare olfact it not" – used as the motto to "The Folio Club."

4. For other special mention of black cats, see "Instinct vs Reason," "The Black Cat," and "Desultory Notes on Cats."

5. Says the *New-York Mirror,* May 30, 1835, in an article captioned "The Ladies": "The Rabbins ought to be ashamed of themselves for their scandalous libel, in saying that ten baskets of chatter were let down from heaven, and that the women appropriated nine of them." The story is given in other forms in other periodicals of the time.

6. "The better is the enemy of the good" is from one of the *Contes Moreaux* of Voltaire, written in 1772 (Beuchot edition, 1828), XVI, 407, "Dans ses écrits un sage Italien/Dit que le mieux est l'ennemi du bien." Adolph Bowski, in the New York *Times Book Review,* August 21, 1921, says that "Il meglio e l'inimico del bene" is an old Italian proverb.

7. The monster described is a battleship propelled by steam and manned by sailors. The first steamship of the United States Navy to be driven by a screw propeller, the *Princeton,* was new in 1844. Despite subsequent worthy service, it is chiefly remembered as the scene of a gun explosion on February 28, 1844 that killed two cabinet officers.

8. For another reference to the sea animal called the argonaut or paper nautilus, see "Parody on Drake" and note (Mabbott, I, 301–302).

9. Cockneys. The quotation, obviously, is meaningless gibberish.

10. A corallite is a fossil coral. Poe spoke of "the coral worm" in "Instinct vs Reason," and of "the corralliferi" in "Julius Rodman."

11. This wonder is from the *Weekly Reveille* cited in the introduction. The first paragraph of Poe's footnote follows verbatim – ascription and all – the head-note to the article on "Prairie and Mountain Life." The source is Chapter V of William Kennedy's *Texas* (London, 1841), I, 120, or p. 69 in the New York 1844 reprint.

The second paragraph of the long footnote was added in Griswold's edition, but came from the same article in the *Reveille:* "That the forest exists there, at the head of the Chayenne river, in the vicinity of the Black Hills, is as certain as that there are no stone trees around St. Louis, and very few wooden ones on the Platte." The spelling today is Cheyenne.

The third paragraph, also added in Griswold's edition, came from the *Asiatic Journal,* 3 ser. III, 359, August, 1844 – a short article headed "Petrified Forest near Cairo."

12. The Mammoth Cave, known before 1800, was the subject of at least three books possibly known to Poe, which were published respectively by Nahum Ward in 1816; Edmund F. Lee in 1835, and Alexander Bullett in 1844.

13. The lava flow of 1783 from the Laki fissure in Iceland is recognized as the greatest in recorded history. The note on Iceland and the subsequent notes on Hekla (in Iceland) and other volcanic explosions, and on the earthquake at Caracas in Venezuela, are from Hugh Murray's *Encyclopaedia of Geography* (1836), I, 215, 217, and 221.

14. Compare "To M. L. Shew," lines 3–4, "The blotting utterly from out high heaven/The sacred sun."

15. This item was added in Griswold's edition. Poe's source for powdered steel is undiscovered.

16. Poe's source is a series of four articles by Richard Mouat in *Simmond's Colonial Magazine,* June-September 1844 (II, 138, 311, 416, and III, 115), called "A Narrative of the Niger Expedition."

17. See Thomas Wyatt's *Synopsis of Natural History,* p. 135. The lion-ant is also mentioned in Poe's "Instinct vs Reason," and in "Julius Rodman," Chapter III.

18. See Patrick Keith's *System of Physiological Botany* (1816), II, 429, with credit to "Willdenow, *Princ. Bot.,* 263." The Epidendron is also mentioned in "How to Write a Blackwood Article" at n. 28, and in "Eleonora." A specimen, which had an odor like vanilla, was exhibited at a meeting of the Horticultural Society described in an article reprinted in the Philadelphia *Public Ledger,* July 22, 1839 from the *Baltimore Patriot.* See Cornelia Varner, in the *Journal of English and Germanic Philology,* January 1933, p. 78.

19. The *Rafflesia Arnoldi* is a giant parasitic plant, a blossom without stalk or leaves, measuring three feet across – the largest flower known. It was discovered in Sumatra in 1818.

20. Joachim Frederik Schouw (1789–1852) was a Danish botanist, some of whose writings were translated into English.

The National Institute, founded in 1840 at Washington, D.C., was a forerunner and urgent proponent of the Smithsonian Institution. Many of the communications it received were published in newspapers in Washington and elsewhere. John B. Williams of Salem was for a time United States consul at Auckland, New Zealand. His gift, in 1844, of the "Hotté, a remarkable insect or worm," further described in words followed almost verbatim in Poe's note, is recorded in the third *Bulletin* of the Institute (1845), page 369. Notes concerning a second gift from Williams appear in the fourth *Bulletin* (1846), pages 483, 493, 506–507.

21. This group was added in Griswold's edition. The orchis, or orchid, needs no comment. The scabius, or scabious, is any one of more than 70 species of the teasel family, supposedly remedial for scabies, or mange; some kinds are the Mourning Bride, the Horseweed, and the Daisy Fleabane. The "Valisnerian lotus" is mentioned in "Al Aaraaf," I, 74; the correct spelling is Vallisneria.

22. In the footnote, Poe quotes from Keith (cited in n. 18 above), vol. II, p. 354.

23. Compare "Instinct vs Reason" on the perfect construction of the bees' honeycomb.

24. Tremendous flights of passenger pigeons darkening the sky were a familiar spectacle in the Middle West through much of the nineteenth century. The last survivor of the species died in the Cincinnati Zoo in 1914.

25. The monster is a balloon with car, which discharges ballast.

26. See also "Lionizing" for a "Grand Turk's" discussion of these legends. Poe's exact source is uncertain; it is not in the Koran itself.

27. The reference should be to Wyatt's *Synopsis of Natural History,* p. 143. Poe refers to the *Entozoa* in an article in *Alexander's Weekly Messenger,* April 15, 1840, and in a review of Charles Lamb in the *Broadway Journal,* September 13, 1845. The scientist first observing the phenomenon was a Philadelphian, Professor John Morgan (1735–1789), who published "Of a Living Snake in a Living Horse's Eye" in the *Transactions of the American Philosophical Society* (1787). Compare "the animalculae which infest the brain" in "The Island of the Fay."

28. See the introductory note on the speed of trains.

29. The Eccaleobion (a word formed from Greek, meaning "that which brings forth life") was being demonstrated in New York in the summer of 1844. It had been shown in London some five years earlier. Cornelia Varner (cited in n. 18) printed a notice from the Philadelphia *Public Ledger* of May 23, 1839, which says: "A London paper states that a curious exhibition, under the name of 'Eccaleobion,' is about to be opened in Pall-Mall"; it may have been brought to America the same year. The *Monthly Review* (London), for November 1839, reviews and quotes from *The Eccaleobion. A Treatise on Artificial Incubation. By William Bucknell. Published for the Author* – a pamphlet describing "an exhibition that has been established in London and is in practical operation – viz. the hatching of chickens by artificial heat . . . on a scale that might produce a hundred birds every day." The *New-York Tribune* for May 23, 1844 (p. 3, col. 7) carried an advertisement under the heading "ECCALEOBION. – HATCHING EGGS BY

STEAM," saying: "The proprietor of this wonderful invention . . . is happy to announce the re-opening of the Exhibition at No. 285 Broadway, opposite Washington Hall, from 9 a.m. until sunset daily," with some further words of praise. A brief statement of hours and prices – "Tickets 25 cts. Children 12½ cts." – was repeated almost daily for months. On June 10, the *Tribune* carried a paragraph (p. 2, col. 7):

> The greatest curiosity that ever was in the United States is the wonderful Eccaleobion, 285 Broadway, displaying the laws established by the creator for the production of life. The idea of producing life by machinery is certainly worthy of attention. The curious and reflecting mind may have food for his thoughts. And no person can go from the Eccaleobion dissatisfied What would our forefathers have thought had they been told that for 25¢ they could see *chickens hatched by steam?* Their first thought would be, "We'll go and see it."

N. P. Willis was impressed, and wrote some paragraphs in which he commented:

> The chirruping of chickens saluted our ears as we opened the door, and we observed that a corner of the room was picketed off, where a dozen or two of these *pseudo*-orphans (who had lost their mother by not having been suffered to have one), were pecking at gravel and evidently doing well . . . It began to look very much as if mothers were a superfluity.

See his *Complete Prose Works* (1846), p. 676.

30. The footnote was added in Griswold's edition. See Poe's essay on "Maelzel's Chess-Player" (*SLM,* April 1836), and a book on the subject by the Poe scholar, Henry Ridgely Evans, 1939. The machine's ability to defeat the redoubtable Haroun Alraschid is perhaps suggested by a story – repeated by Evans, p. 28 – that Maelzel's hidden player, William Schlumberger, took a hint *not* to checkmate the venerable Charles Carroll of Carrollton.

31. Charles Babbage, professor of mathematics at Cambridge, wanted a machine to help him prepare tables of logarithms, and traveled about Europe studying mechanical processes. Discouraged by withdrawal of government aid, he had not finished his labors after eighteen years; but a machine to add, subtract, divide, and multiply was perfected, according to an article, "Difference Machines," in the *Edinburgh Review,* July 1834. Poe, in his essay on "Maelzel's Chess-Player" refers to Babbage on the basis of statements he ascribes to Brewster's *Letters on Natural Magic.*

32. The "thing" is, of course, the printing press, which was rapidly developed during the eighteen-thirties and forties through innovation after innovation by the Hoe Company of New York. Willis hailed "The Mirror Steam-Press" soon after its installation in the summer of 1844. See his *Complete Works* (1846), p. 725: "Now (thanks to Mr. Hoe), we have a steam-press, which *puts up three fingers for a sheet of white paper, pulls it down into its bosom, gives it a squeeze that makes an impression, and then lays it into the palm of an iron hand which deposites it evenly on a heap – at the rate of two thousand an hour!*"

33. Poe from here on takes many notes from Dionysius Lardner's *Course of Lectures.* The account of John Xavier Chabert is from page 25. In London, Chabert sat in an oven, but had protection between himself and the floor upon which he broiled a beefsteak.

34. "Electrotype" is defined by the *Century Dictionary* as "a copy in metal (precipitated by galvanic action, usually in the form of a thin sheet) of any engraved or molded surface." Lardner (p. 36) touched on the process of electrotyping, then comparatively new. To Poe it seems to have suggested alchemy.

35. William Hyde Wollaston (1766–1828), English scientist who made many important contributions to chemistry, physics, and optics, discovered the means of making platinum available for industrial use. Lardner, p. 35, gave as Wollaston's estimate the figure Poe mentions. Poe referred to "Wollaston's wires" in "Marginalia," number 129 (*Godey's,* August 1845, p. 50).

36. Lardner (pp. 40–41) discussed vibrations of the retina, but Poe's figure is not mentioned there and may have been Poe's own calculation from other data.

37. Lardner, pp. 11–12, discussed the Voltaic Pile, invented by and named for Count Alessandro Volta (1745–1827), which by chemical action between two dissimilar metals produced electricity like that produced by the Galvanic battery. See the effects of the Galvanic battery as described in "Loss of Breath," "Premature Burial," and "Some Words with a Mummy."

38. The practicality of Morse's telegraph was strikingly demonstrated by Morse's message transmitted from Washington to Baltimore on May 24, 1844.

39. This item was added in the *Broadway Journal* text. Lardner, pp. 18–19, said that Morse had demonstrated an experimental instrument in 1837. He had 153 miles of wire when *Brother Jonathan* published an article on his experiments, October 28, 1843. He had indeed thought of a printing telegraph before he planned transmitting an audible signal.

40. Franklin's kite?

41. Two examples of waves canceling each other – a phenomenon described by Lardner on p. 40. The explanatory paragraph was added to the footnote in Griswold's edition.

42. This item – added in the *Broadway Journal* – is taken practically verbatim from an article headed "Production of Ice in a Red Hot Crucible" in the *Weekly Reveille,* November 18, 1844, credited to a "Mining Journal."

43. The daguerreotype, invented by L. J. M. Daguerre of Paris, was first published in 1839. Poe was already much interested in daguerreotypes when he wrote about them in *Alexander's Weekly Messenger* of January 15 and May 6, 1840.

44. Poe's very significant changes in text and footnotes revealed by the variants suggest the tremendous advances being made in the science of astronomy. He had clearly made use of Lardner's information in the first version of his tale, but in the final version, which may have been prepared in 1848 or 1849, he incorporated much more detailed, more accurate, and more awesomely impressive information, some of which he used also in *Eureka,* which he was writing in 1847.

45. For other comments on the absurdity of bustles, see "The Spectacles" and "Mellonta Tauta."

46. Compare "A righteous man's reward," St. Matthew 10:41.

SOME WORDS WITH A MUMMY

In this story Poe made fun of the craze for Egyptology that swept our Eastern cities at the time he wrote, and incidentally he satirized the smug belief in Progress which he distrusted as fallacious.

Modern Egyptology began with the discovery in 1799 of the Rosetta Stone, inscribed in hieroglyphic, demotic, and Greek characters, which provided a key to the decipherment of hieroglyphic inscriptions and thus to early Egyptian history. It was not until the second quarter of the nineteenth century, however, that the results of intensive study by devoted scholars, made possible by the work of J. F. Champollion, became available to the English-speaking public through Sir James Wilkinson's *Manners and Customs of the Ancient Egyptians* (2 v., 1837, 1841) and, in America, through the lectures of George Robins Gliddon. The excitement engendered by the new discoveries, presented as they were in comparison with familiar biblical accounts, was further stimulated by comments and controversy in the press.

One of the principal sources of Poe's tale was *Ancient Egypt,* developed from lectures by Gliddon delivered in Boston in December 1842 and January 1843. First published as an Extra of the *New World* (numbers 68 and 69) early in April 1843, it was many times reprinted. Gliddon, born in England, had been for years consul of the United States in Cairo and was considered an authority on contemporary Egypt. He was deeply interested in Egyptian antiquities; about 1836 helped found the Egyptian Society of Cairo; and through personal contacts with visiting archeologists and correspondence had followed as well as he could — at his distance from the centers of scholarly publication — the progress of Egyptian studies. "It is the object of the present essay," he said in his introductory chapter, "to give a summary of the RESULTS of Hieroglyphical researches, after a brief explanation of the process by which these results have been achieved." During a stay in England in 1841 he had published an *Appeal to the Antiquaries of Europe, on the Destruction of the Monuments of Egypt,* deploring the reckless spoliation of tombs and temples to make way for "improvements" under the "progressive" pasha Mohammed Ali.

Another significant source drawn on by Poe was an article in the *Westminster Review* for July 1841, quoted in the New York *Journal of Commerce,* September 2, 1841, and in the *New-York Tribune* of December 21. This article, in the course of discussing Wilkinson's *Manners and Customs of the Ancient Egyptians,* Ippolito Rossellini's notable and handsomely illustrated work on monuments of Egypt and Nubia (Pisa, 1840), and an anonymous *Egyptian History deduced from Monuments still in existence* (London, 1841), gives a great deal of detailed information from the works reviewed.

For other details, Poe made copious use of the *Encyclopaedia Americana,* especially the articles on "Mummies" and "Embalming."*

Other sources have been suggested. As a boy Poe probably saw the mummy belonging to the Boston Medical College, when it was exhibited in the senate chamber of the Capitol at Richmond, beginning on December 23, 1823.† The idea that the ancients were far more advanced scientifically than has generally been supposed was propounded by Louis Dutens in 1766. He believed they knew about electricity, telescopes, microscopes, and the circulation of the blood.‡ Experiments in revival by galvanic batteries are discussed in "Loss of Breath," and in "The Premature Burial." Lucille King (cited above) found in the *New-York Mirror,* January 21, 1832, "A Letter from a Revived Mummy" which is a possible source for one feature of Poe's story. The "Letter" tells of an English soldier, rendered insensible by a blow on the head, preserved in a museum in Brussels for a hundred years, and then sent to New York, where several efforts were made to revive him, the last being the application of a galvanic battery. At the *third* exhibition, the

* See Lucille King, *Texas Studies in English* (1930), 10:134f; she presents an illuminating array of parallel passages. [For a later discussion see B. Pollin, "Poe's 'Some Words with a Mummy' Reconsidered," *Emerson Society Quarterly,* Fall 1970, with additional information about *The Mummy,* a play Poe may have seen.]

† See Agnes M. Bondurant, *Poe's Richmond* (1942), p. 142. Admission was twenty-five cents, and a season ticket was fifty cents. I have a pamphlet of four pages, "E. Conrad, printer," issued by the exhibitors, which says the mummy, in two sarcophagi, came from a catacomb near Thebes.

‡ *Recherches sur l'origine des découvertes attribuées aux moderns* (1766).

mummy leaped to his feet, and shouted, "Hurrah for merry England!" The close parallel to Allamistakeo's conduct when revived by Dr. Ponnonner is unmistakable.§

"Some Words with a Mummy" must have been finished in the fall or early winter of 1844, for it was named as accepted in the *Columbian Magazine* for January 1845. It did not appear there, however, but was later published in Colton's *American Review,* which probably paid better.

TEXTS

(A) American Review: A Whig Journal, April 1845 (1:363–370); *(B) Broadway Journal,* November 1, 1845 (2:251–256); *(C) Works* (1850), II, 438–454.

The *Broadway Journal* text *(B)* is to be preferred, I believe, and is used here. The Griswold change of "astonished" for "ashamed" in *Works (C)* was probably auctorial, and I have adopted it as did my predecessors, Stedman and Woodberry, and Harrison in the Virginia edition.

SOME WORDS WITH A MUMMY. [*B*]

THE SYMPOSIUM[a] of the preceding evening had been a little too much for my nerves. I had a wretched headache, and was desperately drowsy. Instead of going out, therefore, to spend the evening as I had proposed, it occurred to me that I could not do a wiser thing than just eat a mouthful of supper and go immediately to bed.

A *light* supper of course. I am exceedingly fond of Welsh rabbit.[b] More than a pound at once, however, may not [c]at all times be[c] advisable. Still, there can be no material objection to two. And

§ Still another source was suggested by John Nichol, in his article on Henry Glassford Bell in the *Dictionary of National Biography,* as a story called "The Living Mummy" in Bell's *My Old Portfolio* (1832). Nichol suggested a highly probable source for "Morella" in another of Bell's stories, but resemblances between Bell's and Poe's mummies are negligible. Both tales involve catalepsy; but Poe's is about an Egyptian, who was embalmed alive and revived; Bell's about a Dutchman about to be embalmed, who regained consciousness just in time to escape certain death. Poe shows no acquaintance with a once well-known novel called *The Mummy* by Mrs. Jane Webb Loudon (London, 1827). The notion of deliberately embalming a live person has not been found prior to Poe's tale.

---

a *symposium (C)*
b rarebit. *(A)*
c . . . c be at all times *(A)*

really between two and three, there is merely a single unit of difference. I ventured, perhaps, upon four. My wife will have it five; — but, clearly, she has confounded two very distinct affairs. The abstract number, five, I am willing to admit; but, concretely, it has reference to bottles of Brown Stout, without which, in the way of condiment, Welsh rabbit[d] is to be eschewed.[1]

Having thus concluded a frugal meal, and donned my night-cap, with the serene hope of enjoying it till[e] noon the next day, I placed my head upon the pillow, and through the aid of a capital conscience, fell into a profound slumber forthwith.

But when were the hopes of humanity fulfilled? I could not have completed my third snore when there came a furious ringing at the street-door bell, and then an impatient thumping at the knocker, which awakened me at once. In a minute afterward, and while I was still rubbing my eyes, my wife thrust in my face a note from my old friend, Doctor Ponnonner.[2] It ran thus:

Come to me by all means, my dear good friend, as soon as you receive this. Come and help us to rejoice. At last, by long persevering diplomacy, I have gained the assent of the Directors of the City Museum, to my examination of the Mummy — you know the one I mean.[3] I have permission to unswathe it and open it, if desirable. A few friends only will be present — you, of course. The Mummy is now at my house, and we shall begin to unroll it at eleven to-night.

Yours ever,

PONNONNER.

By the time I had reached the "Ponnonner," it struck me that I was as wide awake as a man need be. I leaped out of bed in an ecstasy, overthrowing all in my way; dressed myself with a rapidity truly marvellous; and set off, at the top of my speed, for the Doctor's.

There I found a very eager company assembled. They had been awaiting me with much impatience; the Mummy was extended upon the dining table; and the moment I entered, its examination was commenced.

It was one of a pair brought, several years previously, by Cap-

---

d rarebit *(A)* e until *(A)*

tain Arthur Sabretash,[4] a cousin of Ponnonner's, from a tomb near Eleithias,[5] in the Lybian Mountains, a considerable distance above Thebes on the Nile. The grottoes at this point, although less magnificent than the Theban sepulchres, are of higher interest, on account of affording more numerous illustrations of the private life of the Egyptians. The chamber from which our specimen was taken, was said to be very rich in such illustrations; the walls being completely covered with fresco paintings and bas-reliefs, while statues, vases, and Mosaic work of rich patterns, indicated the vast wealth of the deceased.[6]

The treasure had been deposited in the Museum precisely in the same[f] condition in which Captain Sabretash had found it; — that is to say, the coffin had not been disturbed. For eight years it had thus stood, subject only externally to public inspection. We had now, therefore, the complete Mummy at our disposal; and to those who are aware how very rarely the unransacked antique reaches our shores, it will be evident, at once, that we had great reason to congratulate ourselves upon our good fortune.

Approaching the table, I saw on[g] it a large box, or case, nearly seven feet long, and perhaps three feet wide, by two feet and a half deep. It was oblong — not coffin-shaped. The material was at first supposed to be the wood of the sycamore (*platanus*),[7] but, upon cutting into it, we found it to be pasteboard, or more properly, *papier maché,* composed of papyrus. It was thickly ornamented with paintings, representing funeral scenes, and other mournful subjects, interspersed among which, in every variety of position, were certain series of hieroglyphical characters intended, no doubt, for the name of the departed. By good luck, Mr. Gliddon[8] formed one of our party; and he had no difficulty in translating the letters, which were simply phonetic,[9] and represented the word, *Allamistakeo.*

We had some difficulty in getting this case open without injury, but, having at length accomplished the task, we came to a second, coffin-shaped, and very considerably less in size than the exterior one, but resembling it precisely in every other respect. The interval

f *Omitted (A)* g upon *(A)*

between the two was filled with resin, which had, in some degree, defaced the colors of the interior box.

Upon opening this latter (which we did quite easily,) we arrived at a third case, also coffin-shaped, and varying from the second one in no particular, except in that of its material, which was cedar, and still emitted the peculiar and highly aromatic odor of that wood. Between the second and the[h] third case there was no interval; the one fitting accurately within the other.

Removing the third case, we discovered and took out the body itself. We had expected to find it, as usual, enveloped in frequent rolls, or bandages, of linen, but, in place of these, we found a sort of sheath, made of papyrus, and coated with a layer of plaster, thickly gilt and painted. The paintings represented subjects connected with the various supposed duties of the soul, and its presentation to different divinities, with numerous identical human figures, intended, very probably, as portraits of the person[i] embalmed. Extending from head to foot, was a columnar, or perpendicular inscription in phonetic hieroglyphics, giving again his name and titles, and the names and titles of his relations.

Around the neck thus ensheathed,[j] was a collar of cylindrical glass beads, diverse in color, and so arranged as to form images of deities, of the scarabæus, etc., with the winged globe. Around the small of the waist was a similar collar, or belt.

Stripping off the papyrus, we found the flesh in excellent preservation, with no perceptible odor. The color was reddish. The skin was hard, smooth and glossy. The teeth and hair were in good condition. The eyes (it seemed) had been removed, and glass ones substituted, which were very beautiful and wonderfully life-like, with the exception of somewhat too determined a stare. The finger and toe[k] nails were brilliantly gilded.

Mr. Gliddon was of opinion, from the redness of the epidermis, that the embalmment[l] had been effected altogether by asphaltum; but, on[m] scraping the surface with a steel instrument, and throwing

h *Omitted (A)*
i persons *(B, C) misprint, corrected from A*
j unsheathed, *(C) misprint*
k the *(B, C) misprint, corrected from A*
l embalment *(B, C) misprint*
m upon *(A)*

into the fire some of the powder thus obtained, the flavor of camphor and other sweet-scented gums became apparent.

We searched the corpse very carefully for the usual openings through which the entrails are extracted, but, to our surprise, we could discover none. No member of the party was at that period aware that entire or unopened mummies are not unfrequently met. The brain it was customary to withdraw through the nose; the intestines through an incision in the side; the body was then shaved, washed, and salted; then laid aside for several weeks, when the operation of embalming, properly so called, began.

As no trace of an opening could be found, Doctor Ponnonner was preparing his instruments for dissection, when I observed that it was then past two o'clock. Hereupon it was agreed to postpone the internal examination until the next evening; and we were about to separate for the present, when some one suggested an experiment or two with the Voltaic pile.[10]

The application of electricity to a Mummy[n] three or four thousand years old at the least, was an idea, if not very sage, still sufficiently original, and we all caught at[o] it at once. About one tenth in earnest and nine tenths in jest, we arranged a battery in the Doctor's study, and conveyed thither the Egyptian.

It was only after much trouble that we succeeded in laying bare some portions of the temporal muscle which appeared of less stony rigidity than other parts of the frame, but which, as we had anticipated, of course, gave no indication of galvanic susceptibility when brought in contact with the wire. This the first trial, indeed, seemed decisive, and, with a hearty laugh at our own absurdity, we were bidding each other good night, when my eyes, happening to fall upon those of the Mummy, were there immediately riveted in amazement. My brief glance, in fact, had sufficed to assure me that the orbs which we had all supposed to be glass, and which were originally noticeable for a certain wild stare, were now so far covered by the lids that only a small portion of the *tunica albuginea* remained visible.

With a shout I called attention to the fact, and it became immediately obvious to all.

---

n Mummy some *(A)* o *Omitted (C)*

I cannot say that I was *alarmed* at the phenomenon, because "alarmed" is, in my case, not exactly the word. It is possible, however, that, but for the Brown Stout, I might have been a little nervous. As for the rest of the company, they really made no attempt at concealing the downright fright which possessed them. Doctor Ponnonner was a man to be pitied. Mr. Gliddon, by some peculiar process, rendered himself invisible. Mr. Silk Buckingham, I fancy, will scarcely be so bold as to deny that he made his way, upon all fours, under the table.[11]

After the first shock of astonishment, however, we resolved, as a matter of course, upon farther experiment forthwith. Our operations were now directed against the great toe of the right foot. We made an incision over the outside of the exterior *os sesamoideum pollicis pedis,* and thus got at the root of the *abductor* muscle. Re-adjusting the battery, we now applied the fluid to the bisected nerves — when, with a movement of exceeding life-likeness,[p] the Mummy first drew up its right knee so as to bring it nearly in[q] contact with the abdomen, and then, straightening the limb with inconceivable force, bestowed a kick upon Doctor Ponnonner which had the effect of discharging that gentleman, like an arrow from a catapult, through a window into the street below.[12]

We rushed out *en masse* to bring in the mangled remains of the victim, but had the happiness to meet him upon the staircase, coming up in an unaccountable hurry, brimfull of the most ardent philosophy, and more than ever impressed with the necessity of prosecuting our experiments with rigor and with zeal.

It was by his advice, accordingly, that we made, upon the spot, a profound incision into the tip of the subject's nose, while the Doctor himself, laying violent hands upon it, pulled it into vehement contact with the wire.

Morally and physically — figuratively and literally — was the effect electric. In the first place, the corpse opened its eyes and winked very rapidly for several minutes, as does Mr. Barnes[13] in the pantomime; in the second place, it sneezed; in the third, it sat upon end; in the fourth, it shook its fist in Doctor Ponnonner's

---

p life-likeliness, *(A)* q into *(A)*

face; in the fifth, turning to Messieurs[r] Gliddon and Buckingham, it addressed them, in very capital Egyptian, thus:

"I must say, gentlemen, that I am as much surprised as I am mortified, at your behaviour. Of Doctor Ponnonner nothing better was to be expected. He is a poor little fat fool who *knows* no better. I pity and forgive him. But you, Mr. Gliddon – and you, Silk – who have travelled and resided in Egypt until one might imagine you to the manor born[14] – you, I say, who have been so much among us that you speak Egyptian fully [s]as well, I think, as[s] you write your mother tongue – you, whom I have [t]always been[t] led to regard as the firm friend of the mummies – I really did anticipate more gentlemanly conduct from *you.* What am I to think of your standing quietly by and seeing me thus unhandsomely used? What am I to suppose by your permitting Tom, Dick and Harry to strip me of my coffins, and my clothes, in this wretchedly cold climate? In what light (to come to the point) am I to regard your aiding and abetting that miserable little villain, Doctor Ponnonner, in pulling me by the nose?"

It will be taken for granted, no doubt, that upon hearing this speech under the circumstances, we all either made for the door, or fell into violent hysterics, or went off in a general swoon. One of these things was, I say, to be expected. Indeed each and all of these lines of conduct might have been very plausibly pursued. And, upon my word, I am[u] at a loss to know[v] how or why it was that we pursued neither the one or[w] the other. But, perhaps, the true reason is to be sought in the spirit of the age, which proceeds by the rule of contraries altogether, and is now usually admitted as the solution of everything in the way of paradox and impossibility. Or, perhaps, after all, it was only the Mummy's exceedingly natural and matter-of-course air that divested his words of the terrible. However this may be, the facts are clear, and no member of our party betrayed any very particular trepidation, or seemed to consider that any thing had gone very especially wrong.

For my part I was convinced it was all right, and merely stepped

r Messiurs *(B) misprint*
s . . . s as well as *(A)*
t . . . t been always *(A)*
u am somewhat *(A)*
v explain *(A)*
w nor *(A)*

aside, out of the range of the Egyptian's fist. Doctor Ponnonner thrust his hands into his breeches' pockets, looked hard at the Mummy, and grew excessively red in the face. Mr. Gliddon stroked his whiskers and drew up the collar of his shirt. Mr. Buckingham hung down his head, and put his right thumb into the left corner of his mouth.

The Egyptian regarded him with a severe countenance for some minutes, and at length, with a sneer, said:

"Why don't you speak, Mr. Buckingham? Did you hear what I asked you, or not? *Do* take your thumb out of your mouth!"[x]

Mr. Buckingham, hereupon, gave a slight start, took his right thumb out of the left corner of his mouth, and, by way of indemnification, inserted his[y] left thumb in the right corner of the aperture above-mentioned.

Not being able to get an answer from Mr. B., the figure turned peevishly to Mr. Gliddon, and, in a peremptory tone, demanded in general terms what we all meant.

Mr. Gliddon replied at great length, in phonetics; and but for the deficiency of[z] American printing-offices in hieroglyphical type, it would afford me much pleasure to record here, in the original, the whole of his very excellent[a] speech.

I may as well take this occasion to remark, that all the subsequent conversation in which the Mummy took a part, was carried on in[b] primitive Egyptian, through the medium (so far as concerned myself and[c] other untravelled members of the company) — through the medium, I say, of Messieurs[d] Gliddon and Buckingham, as interpreters. These gentlemen spoke the mother-tongue of the mummy with inimitable fluency and grace; but I could not help observing that (owing, no doubt, to the introduction of images entirely modern, and, of course, entirely novel to the stranger,) the two travelers were reduced, occasionally, to the employment of sensible forms for the purpose of conveying a particular meaning. Mr. Gliddon, at one period, for example, could not make the

x mouth." *(A)*
y the *(A)*
z of the *(A)*
a capital *(A)*
b in the *(A)*
c and the *(A)*
d Messiurs *(B) misprint*

Egyptian comprehend the term "politics," until he sketched upon the wall, wth a bit of charcoal, a little carbuncle-nosed gentleman, out at elbows, standing upon a stump, with his left leg drawn back, his right arm thrown forward, with the[e] fist shut, the eyes rolled up toward Heaven, and the mouth open at an angle of ninety degrees. Just in the same way Mr. Buckingham failed to convey the absolutely modern idea, "wig,"[f] until, (at Doctor Ponnonner's suggestion,) he grew very pale in the face, and consented to take off his own.[15]

It will be readily understood that Mr. Gliddon's discourse turned chiefly upon the vast benefits accruing to science from the unrolling and disembowelling of mummies; apologizing, upon this score, for any disturbance that might have been occasioned *him*, in particular, the individual Mummy called Allamistakeo; and concluding with a mere hint, (for it could scarcely be considered more,) that, as these little matters were now explained, it might be as well to proceed with the investigation intended. Here Doctor Ponnonner made ready his instruments.

In regard to the latter suggestions of the orator, it appears that Allamistakeo had certain scruples of conscience, the nature of which I did not distinctly learn; but he expressed himself satisfied with the apologies tendered, and, getting down from the table, shook hands with the company all round.

When this ceremony was at an end, we immediately busied ourselves in repairing the damages which our subject had sustained from the scalpel. We sewed up the wound in his temple, bandaged his foot, and applied a square inch of black plaster to the tip of his nose.

It was now observed that the Count, (this was the title, it seems, of Allamistakeo,) had a slight fit of shivering – no doubt from the cold. The doctor immediately repaired to his wardrobe, and soon returned with a black dress coat, made in Jennings' best manner,[16] a pair of sky-blue plaid pantaloons with straps, a pink gingham *chemise*, a flapped vest of brocade, a white sack overcoat, a walking cane with a hook, a hat with no brim, patent-leather boots, straw-

e his *(C)* f "whig," *(C)*

colored kid gloves, an eye-glass, a pair of whiskers, and a waterfall cravat. Owing to the disparity of size between the Count and[g] doctor, (the proportion being as two to one,) there was some little difficulty in adjusting these habiliments upon the person of the Egyptian; but when all was arranged, he might have been said to be dressed. Mr. Gliddon, therefore, gave him his arm, and led him to a comfortable chair by the fire, while the doctor rang the bell upon the spot and ordered a supply of cigars and wine.

The conversation soon grew animated. Much curiosity was, of course, expressed in regard to the somewhat remarkable fact of Allamistakeo's still remaining alive.

"I should have thought," observed Mr. Buckingham, "that it is high time you were dead."

"Why," replied the Count, very much astonished, "I am little more than seven hundred years old. My father lived a thousand, and was by no means in his dotage when he died."

Here ensued a brisk series of questions and computations, by means of which it became evident that the antiquity of the Mummy had been grossly misjudged. It had been five thousand and fifty years, and some months, since he had been consigned to the catacombs at Eleithias.[17]

"But my remark," resumed Mr. Buckingham, "had no reference to your age at the period of interment; (I am willing to grant, in fact, that you are still a young man,) and my allusion was to the immensity of time during which, by your own showing, you must have been done up in asphaltum."

"In what?" said the Count.

"In asphaltum," persisted Mr. B.

"Ah, yes; I have some faint notion of what you mean; it might be made to answer, no doubt, — but in my time we employed scarcely anything else than the Bichloride of Mercury."[18]

"But what we are especially at a loss to understand," said Doctor Ponnonner, "is how it happens that, having been dead and buried in Egypt five thousand years ago, you are here to-day all alive, and looking so delightfully well."

---

g and the *(A, C)*

"Had I been, as you say, *dead,*" replied the Count, "it is more than probable that dead I should still be; for I perceive you are yet in the infancy of Galvanism, and cannot accomplish with it what was a common thing among us in the old days. But the fact is, I fell into catalepsy, and it was considered by my best friends that I was either dead or should be; they accordingly embalmed me at once — I presume you are aware of the chief principle of the embalming process?"

"Why, not altogether."

"Ah, I perceive; — a deplorable condition of ignorance! Well, I cannot enter into details just now: but it is necessary to explain that to embalm, (properly speaking,) in Egypt, was to arrest indefinitely *all* the animal functions subjected to the process. I use the word "animal" in its widest sense, as including the physical not more than the moral and *vital* being. I repeat that the leading principle of embalmment[h] consisted, with us, in the immediately arresting, and holding in perpetual *abeyance, all* the animal functions subjected to the process. To be brief, in whatever condition the individual was, at the period of embalmment,[i] in that condition he remained. Now, as it is my good fortune to be of the blood of the Scarabæus,[j] I was embalmed *alive,* as you see me at present."[19]

"The blood[k] of the Scarabæus!"[20] exclaimed Doctor Ponnonner.

"Yes. The Scarabæus was the *insignium,* or[l] the "arms," of a very distinguished and a[m] very rare patrician family. To be "of the blood of the Scarabæus," is merely to be one of that family of which the Scarabæus is the *insignium.*[21] I speak figuratively."

"But what has this to do with your being alive?"

"Why it is the general custom, in Egypt, to deprive a corpse, before embalmment,[n] of its bowels and brains; the race of the Scarabæi alone did not coincide with the custom. Had I not been a Scarabæus, therefore, I should have been without bowels and brains; and without either it is inconvenient to live."

---

h embalment *(B, C) misprint*
i embalment, *(B, C) misprint*
j *Scarabœus, (A, B, C) With the exception of the first occurrence in paragraph 13, all texts have this form. All have been corrected, as have the plural forms*
k bloood *(C) misprint*
l on *(A)*
m *Omitted (C)*
n embalment, *(B, C) misprint*

"I perceive that;" said Mr. Buckingham, "and I presume that all the *entire* mummies that come to hand are of the race of Scarabæi."

"Beyond doubt."

"I thought," said Mr. Gliddon very meekly, "that the Scarabæus was one of the Egyptian gods."

"One of the Egyptian *what?*" exclaimed the Mummy, starting to its feet.

"Gods!" repeated the traveler.

"Mr. Gliddon, I really am astonished[o] to hear you talk in this style," said the Count, resuming his chair. "No nation upon the face of the earth has ever acknowledged more than[p] *one god.* The Scarabæus, the Ibis, etc., were with us, (as similar creatures have been with others) the symbols, or *media,* through which we offered worship to a[q] Creator too august to be more directly approached."[22]

There was here a pause. At length the colloquy was renewed by Doctor Ponnonner.

"It is not improbable, then, from what you have explained," said he, "that among the catacombs near the Nile, there may exist other mummies of the Scarabæus tribe, in a condition of vitality."

"There can be no question of it," replied the Count; "all the Scarabæi embalmed accidentally while alive, are alive now.[r] Even some of those *purposely* so embalmed, may have been overlooked by their executors, and still remain in the tombs."

"Will you be kind enough to explain," I said, "what you mean by 'purposely so embalmed'?"

"With great pleasure," answered the Mummy, after surveying me leisurely through his eye-glass – for it was the first time I had ventured to address him a direct question.

"With great pleasure," said he.[s] "The usual duration of man's life, in my time, was about eight hundred years. Few men died, unless by most extraordinary accident, before the age of six hundred; few lived longer than a decade of centuries; but eight were

o ashamed *(A, B)*
p than the *(A)*
q the *(A, C)*
r alive now./alive. *(C)*
s said he./he said. *(C)*

considered the natural term.[23] After the discovery of the embalming principle, as I have already described it to you, it occurred to our philosophers that a laudable curiosity might be gratified, and, at the same time, the interests of science much advanced, by living this natural term in instalments. In the case of history, indeed, experience demonstrated that something of this kind was indispensable. An[t] historian, for example, having attained the age of five hundred, would write a book with great labor and then get himself carefully embalmed; leaving instructions to his executors *pro tem.*, that they should cause him to be revivified after the lapse of a certain period — say five or six hundred years. Resuming existence at the expiration of this term,[u] he would invariably find his great work converted into a species of hap-hazard notebook — that is to say, into a kind of literary arena for the conflicting guesses, riddles, and personal squabbles of whole herds of exasperated commentators. These guesses, etc., which passed under the name of annotations or emendations, were found so completely to have enveloped, distorted, and overwhelmed the text, that the author had to go about with a lantern[24] to discover his own book. When discovered, it was never worth the trouble of the search.[25] After re-writing it throughout, it was regarded as the bounden duty of the historian to set himself to work, immediately,[v] in correcting from his own private knowledge and experience, the traditions of the day concerning the epoch at which he had originally lived. Now this process of re-scription and personal rectification, pursued by various individual sages, from time to time, had the effect of preventing our history from degenerating into absolute fable."

"I beg your pardon," said Doctor Ponnonner at this point, laying his hand gently upon the arm of the Egyptian — "I beg your pardon, sir, but may I presume to interrupt you for one moment?"

"By all means, *sir,*" replied the Count, drawing up.

"I merely wished to ask you a question," said the Doctor. "You mentioned the historian's personal correction of *traditions* respect-

t A *(A)*
u time, *(C)*
v forthwith, *(A)*

ing his own epoch. Pray, sir, upon an average, what proportion of these Kabbala were usually found to be right?"[26]

"The Kabbala, as you properly term them, sir, were generally discovered to be precisely on a par with the facts recorded in the un-re-written histories themselves; – that is to say, not one individual iota of either, was ever known, under any circumstances, to be not totally and radically wrong."

"But since[w] it is quite clear," resumed the Doctor, "that at least five thousand years have elapsed since your entombment, I take it for granted that your histories at that period, if not your traditions, were sufficiently explicit on that one topic of universal interest, the Creation, which took place, as I presume you are aware, only about ten centuries before."[27]

"Sir!" said[x] Count Allamistakeo.

The Doctor repeated his remarks, but it was only after much additional explanation, that the foreigner could be made to comprehend them. The latter at length said, hesitatingly:

"The ideas you have suggested are to me, I confess, utterly novel. During my time I never knew any one to entertain so singular a fancy as that the universe (or this world if you will have it so) ever had a beginning at all. I remember, once, and once only, hearing something remotely hinted, by a man of many speculations, concerning the origin *of the human race;* and by this individual the very word *Adam,* (or Red Earth) which you make use of, was employed.[28] He employed it, however, in a generical sense, with reference to the[y] spontaneous germination from rank soil (just as a thousand of the lower *genera* of creatures are germinated) – the spontaneous germination, I say, of five vast hordes of men, simultaneously upspringing in five distinct and nearly equal divisions of the globe."[29]

Here, in general, the company shrugged their shoulders, and one or two of us touched our foreheads with a very significant air. Mr. Silk Buckingham, first glancing slightly at the occiput and then at the sinciput[z] of Allamistakeo, spoke as follows: –

w as *(A)*
x said the *(C)*
y *Omitted (A)*
z siniciput *(B, C) misprint, corrected from A*

"The long duration of human life in your time, together with the occasional practice of passing it, as you have explained, in instalments, must have had, indeed, a strong tendency to the general development and conglomeration of knowledge. I presume, therefore, that we are to attribute the marked inferiority of the old Egyptians in all particulars of science, when compared with the moderns, and more especially with the Yankees, altogether to the superior solidity of the Egyptian skull."

"I confess again," replied the Count with much suavity, "that I am somewhat at a loss to comprehend you; pray, to what particulars of science do you allude?"

Here our whole party, joining voices, detailed, at great length, the assumptions of phrenology and the marvels of animal magnetism.

Having heard us to an end, the Count proceeded to relate a few anecdotes, which rendered it evident that prototypes of Gall and Spurzheim[30] had flourished and faded in Egypt so long ago as to have been nearly forgotten, and that the manœuvres of Mesmer[a] were really very contemptible tricks when put in collation with the positive miracles of the Theban *savans,* who created lice and a great many other similar things.[31]

I here asked the Count if his people were able to calculate eclipses. He smiled rather contemptuously, and said they were.[32]

This put me a little out, but I began to make other inquiries in regard to his astronomical knowledge, when a member of the company, who had never as yet opened his mouth, whispered in my ear that, for information on this head, I had better consult Ptolemy, (whoever Ptolemy is) as well as one Plutarch *de facie lunæ.*[33]

I then questioned the Mummy about burning-glasses and lenses, and, in general, about the manufacture of glass; but I had not made an end of my queries before the silent member again touched me quietly on the elbow, and begged me for God's sake to take a peep at Diodorus Siculus. As for the Count, he merely asked me, in the way of reply, if we moderns possessed any such microscopes as would enable us to cut cameos in the style of the

---

a Mesmerism *(A)*

Egyptians. While I was thinking how I should answer this question, little Doctor Ponnonner committed himself in a very extraordinary way.

"Look at our architecture!" he exclaimed, greatly to the indignation of both the travelers, who pinched him black and blue to no purpose.

"Look," he cried with enthusiasm, "at the Bowling-Green Fountain in New York! or if this be too vast a contemplation, regard for a moment the Capitol at Washington, D. C.!" – and the good little medical man went on to detail very minutely the proportions of the fabric to which he referred. He explained that the portico alone was adorned with no less than four and twenty columns, five feet in diameter, and ten feet apart.[34]

The Count said that he regretted not being able to remember, just at that moment, the precise dimensions of any one of the principal buildings of the city of Aznac,[35] whose foundations were laid in the night of Time, but the ruins of which were still standing, at the epoch of his entombment, in a vast plain of sand to the westward of Thebes. He recollected, however, (talking of porticoes) that one affixed to an inferior palace in a kind of suburb called Carnac, consisted of a hundred and forty-four columns, thirty-seven feet each in circumference, and twenty-five[b] feet apart. The approach to[c] this portico, from the Nile, was through an avenue two miles long, composed of sphynxes, statues and obelisks, twenty, sixty, and a hundred feet in height. The palace itself (as well as he could remember) was, in one direction, two miles long, and might have been, altogether, about seven in circuit. Its walls were richly painted all over, within and without, with hieroglyphics. He would not pretend to *assert* that even fifty or sixty of the Doctor's Capitols might have been built within these walls, but he was by no means sure that two or three hundred of them might not have been squeezed in with some trouble. That palace at Carnac was an insignificant little building after all. He, (the Count) however, could not conscientiously refuse to admit the ingenuity, magnificence, and superiority of the Fountain

b twent-five *(A) misprint* c of *(C)*

at the Bowling-Green, as described by the Doctor. Nothing like it, he was forced to allow, had ever been seen in Egypt or elsewhere.

I here asked the Count what he had to say to our railroads.

"Nothing," he replied, "in particular." They were rather slight, rather ill-conceived, and clumsily put together. They could not be compared, of course, with the vast, level, direct, iron-grooved causeways, upon which the Egyptians conveyed entire temples and solid obelisks of a hundred and fifty feet in altitude.

I spoke of our gigantic mechanical forces.

He agreed that we knew something in that way, but inquired how I should have gone to work in getting up the imposts on the lintels of even the little palace at Carnac.

This question I concluded not to hear, and demanded if he had any idea of Artesian wells; but he simply raised his eye-brows; while Mr. Gliddon[d] winked at me very hard, and said, in a low tone, that one had been recently discovered by the engineers employed to bore for water in the Great Oasis.

I then mentioned our steel; but the foreigner elevated his nose, and asked me if our steel could have executed the sharp carved[e] work seen on the obelisks, and which was wrought altogether by edge-tools of copper.[36]

This disconcerted us so greatly that we thought it advisable to vary the attack to Metaphysics. We sent for a copy of a book called the "Dial,"[37] and read out of it a chapter or two about something which is not very clear, but which the Bostonians call the Great Movement or Progress.

The Count merely said that Great Movements were awfully common things in his day, and as for Progress it was [f]at one time[f] quite a nuisance, but it never progressed.

We then spoke of the great beauty and importance of Democracy, and were at much trouble in impressing the Count with a due sense of the advantages we enjoyed in living where there was suffrage *ad libitum,* and no king.

d Gliddon, *(A, B) comma deleted to follow C*

e curved *(B) misprint, corrected from A, B*

f . . . f *Omitted (A)*

He listened with marked interest, and in fact seemed not a little amused. When we had done, he said that, a great while ago, there had occurred something of a very similar sort. Thirteen Egyptian provinces determined all at once to be free, and so set a magnificent example to the rest of mankind. They assembled their wise men, and concocted the most ingenious constitution it is possible to conceive. For a while they managed remarkably well; only their habit of bragging was prodigious. The thing ended, however, in the consolidation of the thirteen states, with some fifteen or twenty others, into[g] the most odious and insupportable despotism that ever was heard of upon the face of the Earth.

I asked what was the name of the usurping tyrant.

As well as the Count could recollect, it was *Mob*.[38]

Not knowing what to say to this, I raised my voice, and deplored the Egyptian ignorance of steam.

The Count looked at me with much astonishment, but made no answer. The silent gentleman, however, gave me a violent nudge in the ribs with his elbows — told me I had sufficiently exposed myself for once — and demanded if I was really such a fool as not to know that the modern steam engine is derived from the invention of Hero, through Solomon de Caus.[39]

We were now in imminent danger of being discomfited; but, as good luck would have it, Doctor Ponnonner, having rallied, returned to our rescue, and inquired if the people of Egypt would seriously pretend to rival the moderns in the all-important particular of dress.

The Count, at this, glanced downward[h] to the straps of his pantaloons, and then, taking hold of the[i] end of one of his coattails, held it up close to his eyes for some minutes. Letting it fall, at last, his mouth extended itself very gradually from ear to ear; but I do not[j] remember that he said anything in the way of reply.

Hereupon we recovered our spirits, and the Doctor, approaching the mummy with great dignity, desired it to say candidly, upon its honor as a gentleman, if the Egyptians had compre-

g in *(C)*
h downwards *(C)*
i the extreme *(A)*
j do not/don't *(A)*

hended, at *any* period, the manufacture of either Ponnonner's lozenges, or Brandreth's pills.[40]

We looked, with profound anxiety, for an answer; – but in vain. It was not forthcoming. The Egyptian blushed and hung down his head. Never was triumph more consummate; never was defeat borne with so ill a grace. Indeed I could not endure the spectacle of the poor Mummy's mortification. I reached my hat, bowed to him stiffly, and took leave.

Upon getting home I found it past four o'clock, and went immediately to bed.[k] It is now ten, A.M. I have been up since seven, penning these memoranda for the benefit of my family and of mankind. The former I shall behold no more. My wife is a shrew. The truth is, I am heartily sick of this life and of the nineteenth century in general. I am convinced that everything is going wrong. Besides, I am anxious to know who will be President in 2045. As soon, therefore, as I shave and swallow a cup of coffee, I shall just step over to Ponnonner's and get embalmed for a couple of hundred years.

NOTES

1. A Welsh rabbit, made of melted cheese, was generally considered indigestible and conducive of nightmares. This is Poe's hint to matter-of-fact readers that the story is all a dream. Brown stout is defined in the *Century Dictionary* as a superior kind of porter.

2. Ponnonner is obviously " 'Pon honor!"

3. There was no "City Museum" in New York when Poe's tale was written, but P. T. Barnum, buying out two rival privately owned establishments, had opened his long-famous American Museum early in 1842.

4. Captain Sabretash may owe his name to a series of articles in *Fraser's Magazine,* March 1838, January and August 1839, addressed to Oliver Yorke, the mythical editor of *Fraser's,* by "Captain Orlando Sabertash" (Major General John Mitchell, 1785–1859) [or to a column called "Gayeties and Gravities" in the *New-York Mirror,* November 12, 1842, signed "Captain Sabretash"; this note courtesy of B. Pollin]. A sabretache (variously spelled) according to the *OED* is a leather satchel suspended on the left side by long straps from the sword belt of a cavalry officer. The *OED* quotes an example from Lever, *Charles O'Malley,* which was reviewed by Poe in *Graham's,* March 1842.

5. The city was called Nuben by the Ancient Egyptians, by the Greeks usually Eileithyia, and is now El Kab.

---

k to bed./to-bed. *(C) misprint*

6. Most of the details in this paragraph and the next nine come from the article "Mummies" in the *Encyclopaedia Americana* (1836), vol. IX, pp. 89–90, quoted here:

"Numerous caves or grottoes [containing mummies and artifacts] are found in the two mountainous ridges which run nearly parallel with the Nile from Cairo to Syene. Some of the most remarkable of these tombs are those in the vicinity of ancient Thebes, in the Lybian mountains, many of which were examined by Belzoni, and those near Eleithias (described by Hamilton), farther up the river, which, though less splendid than Theban sepulchres, contain more illustrations of the private life of the Egyptians. The sepulchral chambers are almost entirely covered with fresco paintings and bass-reliefs, and frequently contain statues, vases, &c.... Those of private individuals vary according to the wealth of the deceased, but are often very richly ornamented. Many of these tombs have been ransacked by Arabs for the purpose of plunder, and great numbers of the mummies destroyed for the rosin or asphaltum they contain, which is sold to advantage in Cairo . . .

"The bodies of the rich and the great underwent the most complicated operations, and were laboriously adorned with all kinds of ornaments. Embalmers of different ranks and duties extracted the brain through the nostril, and the entrails through an incision in the side; the body was then shaved, washed, and salted, and, after a certain period, the process of *embalming* [see n. 18, below], properly speaking, began. The whole body was then steeped in balsam, and wrapped up in linen bandages; each finger and toe was separately enveloped, or sometimes sheathed in a gold case, and the nails were often gilded. The bandages were then folded round each of the limbs, and finally round the whole body, to the number of 15–20 thicknesses. The head was the object of particular attention; it was sometimes enveloped in several folds of fine muslin; the first was glued to the skin, and the others to the first; the whole was then coated with a fine plaster. A collar of cylindrical glass beads of different colors, is attached to the mask which covers the head, and with it is connected a tunic of the same material. The beads, both in the collar and tunic, are so arranged as to form images of divinities, of the scarabæus, the winged globe, &c. Instead of this, the mummy is sometimes contained in a sort of sheath, made of paper or linen, and coated with a layer of plaster, on which are paintings and gilding. These paintings represent subjects relating to the duties of the soul, its presentation to the different divinities; and a perpendicular hieroglyphical inscription in the centre gives the name of the deceased, and of his relations, his titles, &c. The whole is then placed in the coffin. Those mummies which have been examined present very different appearances. One class has an opening in the left side, under the armpit, and in another the body is whole. Some of those which have been opened have been dried by vegetable and balsamic substances, others by salt. In the former case, aromatic gums or asphaltum were used (the gums, when thrown into the fire, give out an aromatic odor); in these the teeth and hair are generally preserved; but if exposed to the air, they are soon affected. Those prepared with asphalt are of a reddish color and are in good preservation . . . The coffin is usually of sycamore, cedar, or pasteboard; the case is entire, and covered, within and without, by paintings, representing funeral scenes, and a great variety of other subjects: the name of the deceased is also repeated on them in hieroglyphic characters. The cover, which is also entire, is ornamented in the same manner, and contains, too, the countenance of the deceased in relief, painted, and often gilded. The breast is covered with a large collar; a perpendicular inscription occupies the centre, and funeral scenes the sides. The coffin is often enclosed in a second, and even third case, each of which is also ornamented with similar representations."

7. The American sycamore is *Platanus occidentalis;* the Egyptian tree is *Ficus sycamorus.*

8. For Gliddon, who may have been in New York when Poe's tale was written, see the introduction above.

9. Poe is right about phonetic characters. From the earliest times the Egyptians, who employed several hundred hieroglyphics, had a complete set that could represent specific *sounds* (what we now term phonemes) although they did not abandon pictograms – and ideograms (see Gliddon's *Ancient Egypt,* pp. 6–7).

10. For the Voltaic Pile see "The Thousand-and-Second Tale of Scheherazade," n. 37.

11. Compare the conduct of Dr. Maillard in "The System of Doctor Tarr and Professor Fether." James Silk Buckingham (1786–1855), after some years as a journalist in India, traveled extensively in the Near East and published books on his travels in Palestine (1822), Syria (1825), Mesopotamia (1827), Assyria, Media, and Persia (1830). Returning to England, he became an active proponent of social reforms and of temperance, was a member of Parliament for Sheffield, 1832–1837, then spent nearly four years traveling and lecturing in America. He subsequently published *America: Historical, Descriptive, and Statistic, including a Journey through the Northern or Free States* (1841); *The Slave States of America* (1842); *The Eastern and Western States of America* (1842), and similar descriptions of his travels in Canada. Poe mentioned him with respect among authors of "valuable books of eastern travel" in his review of J. L. Stephens' *Arabia Petraea* (*New York Review,* October 1837), but something [probably, as Burton Pollin points out in his paper cited in the introduction above, Buckingham's harsh criticism of slavery and the attitude toward it in the Southern states] antagonized Poe, who later referred to Buckingham only contemptuously. See "Mellonta Tauta" for other references.

12. When Dr. Andrew Ure, of Glasgow, applied the galvanic battery to a man who had been hanged, one leg was thrown out so as almost to overturn an assistant, one spectator fainted, and others fled. The reference to the medico's account of this in *The Medical Repository,* January 1820, was given by Robert Lee Rhea in *University of Texas Studies* (1930), 10:145f.

13. John Barnes was a celebrated comedian at the Park Theatre, New York, and elsewhere, for at least twenty-five years before 1841. Odell (*Annals of the New York Stage,* IV, 67) calls him a low comedian and says of him in 1836, "Two more concienceless gaggers and muggers never played together than Reeve and Barnes . . . audiences howled their joy."

14. Compare *Hamlet,* I, iv, 14–16:

> But to my mind, though I am a native here
> And to the manner born, it is a custom
> More honor'd in the breach than the observance.

"*Manner* here is sometimes understood as *manor* (which was formerly also spelled *manner*), and is often changed to *manor* in the quotation to make the phrase applicable to locality" – *Century Dictionary.*

15. The change to "whig" in Griswold's text may be a misprint or may be an intentional pun related to "politics" – another example of Poe's "mystification." The *Westminster Review* article, p. 11, devotes a whole paragraph to "Barber-Surgeons," including the following statement:

> To prove the proficiency in their art of the Theban *perruquiers,* we need only to refer to the specimen which may be seen in the British Museum . . . It is in an entire state of preservation, as if it came yesterday from the barber's shop. It exactly resembles the wigs worn by females of quality, delineated on the tombs, as also on the female Egyptian statues. It is of immense size; as large as those worn by fashionable gallants in the time of Charles II, or by our learned judges (often to their great annoyance) at the present time. It is of a glossy auburn, and differs from the modern style in having the plaits beneath and the ringlets above.

16. William T. Jennings & Co., 231 Broadway, at the American Hotel, opposite the Park Fountain, New York, ran what is called by N. P. Willis (*New Mirror,* January 27, 1844), "the emporium of 'bang-up' toggery," and dealt in ready-made clothes, at low cash prices.

17. Allamistakeo was entombed in 3204 B.C. Deciphering the hieroglyphic inscriptions had made it possible to push back Egyptian history for literally thousands of years.

18. See the following excerpt from the article "Embalming" in the *Encyclopaedia Americana* (1836), vol. IV, p. 487:

> The intestines are taken out of the body, and the brains out of the head, and the cavities filled up with a mixture of balsamic herbs, myrrh and others of the same kind; the large blood-vessels and other vessels are injected with balsams dissolved in spirits of wine; the body is rubbed hard with spirits of the same kind, &c. (See *Mummies.*) The ancient Egyptians removed the viscera from the large cavities, and replaced them with aromatic, saline and bituminous substances, and also enveloped the outside of the body in cloths impregnated with similar materials . . . Impregnation of the animal body with corrosive sublimate appears to be the most effectual means of preserving it, excepting immersion in spirits. The impregnation is performed by the injection of a strong solution, consisting of about four ounces of bichloride of mercury to a pint of alcohol, into the blood-vessels, and, after the viscera are removed, the body is immersed, for three months, in the same solution, after which it dries easily, and is almost imperishable.

(The actual injection of such a solution into a living body would of course be fatal.)

19. I find that one Dr. Grusselbach of Upsala seriously discussed live embalming. My source is a note in the *Berrien County Record* of Buchanan, Michigan, February 3, 1870. The story may, like so many newspaper fillers, be far older, and may even perhaps have been known to Poe.

20. *Scarabaeus* is a genus of Old World beetles, one of which, *Scarabaeus*

sacer, through its habit of rolling a ball of dung across the sand to its burrow, came to be popularly associated with the sun-god Khepri (from *khepes,* "to bring into existence"), who rolled the sun across the sky. The beetle, called the *kheper* beetle, provided the hieroglyph for the sun-god's name. Stone representations of the insect, called scarabs, were the commonest amulets in Egypt. Tens of thousands are still in existence. (See "The Gold-Bug" for a living scarab.)

21. The word *insignium* is incorrect; the singular of *insignia* should be *insigne,* but Poe may never have seen it.

22. Poe's discussion of Egyptian monotheism is based on statements of Egyptologists of his day. The early Egyptians had a set of three major and six minor divinities for each district. When Egypt was united, at the dawn of history, there was much identification, and indeed the sun was the chief god almost everywhere. The hymn of Akhnaten to the Solar Disc, Aten, as sole divinity, was not known in Poe's day, but that differs far less radically than many modern historians suppose from the texts in honor of Amon-Ra, the sun-god of Thebes, with whose powerful priesthood Akhnaten quarreled. Philosophical Egyptians held a basically monotheistic view, but to what extent ordinary folk regarded gods as individuals is not sure. The sacred animals, that so amazed such Romans as Juvenal, were in some cases theophanies – a divinity sometimes taking residence in a living body. The Egyptian religion was highly ethical, and human sacrifice was abhorred by the time of the pyramid builders.

23. See Genesis 5 for the ages of the antediluvian patriarchs. In the Septuagint, some of the ages are given differently, allowing more time for early history.

24. The allusion – going about with a lantern – is to the story that Diogenes of Sinope, the Cynic, went about Athens by day with a lantern, searching for someone meriting the name of a man. See Diogenes Laertius, VI, "Diogenes," Section 6. The story is usually told that he sought "an honest man."

25. Remarks on the unreliability of historians are commonplace. On April 18, 1775, Johnson, as Boswell records, said, "all the colouring, all the philosophy of history is conjecture." In the *Curiosities of Literature* (9th edition, 1834, II, 179), " 'Critical Sagacity' and 'Happy Conjecture' or, Bentley's Milton," Isaac D'Israeli writes of "that 'true conjectural critic' whose practice a Portuguese satirist so greatly admired: by which means, if he be only followed up by future editors, we might have that immaculate edition, in which little or nothing should be found of the original!"

26. The Kabbala is a mystic commentary on the Talmud; Poe uses the term here and elsewhere as a type of the mysterious or incredible. See n. 1 on "The Imp of the Perverse."

27. The date 4004 B.C. was set by James Ussher (1581–1656), Archbishop of Armagh, who worked out in his *Annales Veteris et Novi Testamenti* a biblical chronology, standard in authorized editions of the English Bible for more than two centuries. Gliddon, in his *Ancient Egypt* (p. 33) sought tactfully to win the pious to accept the evidence of the new discoveries that human history extends much farther into the past by citing tables prepared by "the learned Hales" (William, professor of oriental languages at Trinity College, Dublin) to show that

"for the three most important events recorded in the Old Testament, i.e., the Creation, the Deluge, and the Exodus, the inquirer after truth is lost in a chaos of 300 different, published human opinions on the eras of the same events; opinions conflicting with each other!"

28. Gliddon, pp. 28–29, reproduces from Champollion's *Grammaire egyptienne* (1836–41) a picture accompanied by hieroglyphic text translated as "Knum, the Creator, on his wheel moulds the divine members of Osiris (the type of man) in the shining house of life." Gliddon comments, "He moulds man; in Hebrew, ADAM, the first man, meaning both *man* and *red earth,* or clay," and compares Isaiah 64:8, "But now, O Lord, thou art our father; we are the clay, and thou our potter; and we all are the work of thy hand." Red earth as the meaning of Adam is given by Byron in *The Deformed Transformed,* I, i, 385, and a footnote.

29. For spontaneous generation see Lucretius, *De Rerum Natura,* V, 797–798. Johann Friedrich Blumenbach (1752–1840), professor at Göttingen – called the founder of physical anthropology – in the second edition (1781) of his treatise *On the Natural Variety of Mankind* named the five principal races as the Caucasian, Asiatic, American, Ethiopian, and Malay – a division long standard.

30. Gall and Spurzheim wrote on phrenology; Mesmer on animal magnetism. See "The Imp of the Perverse," n. 2, and "A Tale of the Ragged Mountains," introduction and n. 3.

31. For the Theban *savans,* compare the magicians in Exodus 8.

32. With this and the next three paragraphs compare the *Westminster Review* article, p. 32, commenting on the eighteenth Theban dynasty:

> The practical, chemical, astronomical, and mechanical knowledge which they shared with the priestly (scientific) colleges was in some respects equal to, in some respects greater than, our own. They made glass in great profusion (Diodorus Siculus), and burning glasses and lenses for telescopes. They must have cut their delicate cameos by the aid of microscopes. Ptolemy describes an astrolobe; they calculated eclipses; they said that the moon was diversified by sea and land (Plutarch *de facie lunae*).

33. Claudius Ptolemaeus, the geographer and astronomer (second century A.D.), was born and studied in Egypt. The treatise of Plutarch is "On the face of the moon."

34. The Bowling Green Fountain in New York was a monument of bad taste, built by Aaron P. Price, master-mason for the contractor, Assistant Alderman Pettigrew. It was first exhibited on July 4, 1843, illuminated by sixteen bat wing gas lights. It is described in the *New York Herald* of the sixth, and there is a woodcut in the *New World,* June 17, 1843. Poe ridiculed it in the first letter of *Doings of Gotham,* published in the *Columbia Spy,* May 18, 1844; and again in a review of George Jones's *Ancient America* in the *Aristidean* for March 1845. The Capitol at Washington is minutely described in a plate article, unsigned, in *Burton's,* November 1839, which I now (December 12, 1958) assign to Poe on the strength of the letter to Burton, June 1, 1840, and this passage in "Some Words with a Mummy."

35. Aznac is purely imaginary, but the description of Karnak is factual.

36. With the foregoing paragraphs, compare the *Westminster Review,* pp. 32–33:

> They possessed the art of tempering copper tools so as to cut the hardest granite with the most minute and brilliant precision. This art we have lost... our tools would not cut such stone with the precision of outline which the inscriptions retain to the present day. Again, what mechanical means had they to raise and fix the enormous imposts on the lintels of their temples as at Karnac?... That they were familiar with the principle of Artesian wells, has been lately proved by engineering investigations carried on while boring for water in the Great Oasis. That they were acquainted with the principle of the railroad is obvious, that is to say, they had artificial causeways, levelled, direct, and grooved (the grooves being anointed with oil), for the conveyance from great distances of enormous blocks of stone, entire stone temples, and colossal statues half the height of the monument. Remnants of iron, it is said, have been found in these grooves. Finally, M. Arago has argued that they not only possessed a knowledge of steam power... but that the modern steam engine is derived through Solomon de Caus, the predecessor of Worcester, from the invention of Hero, the Egyptian engineer.

37. *The Dial* was the chief organ of the Transcendentalists; for other criticisms of Progress, see "Never Bet the Devil Your Head," and "The Colloquy of Monos and Una."

38. See a reference to the tyrant "Mob" in "Mellonta Tauta."

39. See n. 36. Hero of Alexandria (circa 170 B.C.) described his machine in his *Pneumatica;* Solomon de Caus planned an engine in 1615; he was preceded by Giambattista della Porta, in 1601.

40. Brandreth's Pills were widely advertised; they are also mentioned in "How to Write a Blackwood Article," where see n. 17.

TALES: 1845–1846

SOME SECRETS OF THE MAGAZINE PRISON-HOUSE

This bitter piece has in it enough of fictional narrative to justify inclusion among the Tales and Sketches. It appeared unsigned in the *Broadway Journal* of February 15, 1845, but was acknowledged by the penciled initial *"P"* in the file of the paper that Poe gave to Mrs. Whitman in 1848. Griswold overlooked it, but Ingram collected it in 1875.

The presence of an autobiographical element is mentioned by Woodberry and by Miss Phillips.* Poe had indeed probably been victimized in a prize contest in his youth; and T. W. White paid him (before Poe became his editor) only after publication; but both Graham and Godey always paid Poe on receipt of his manuscripts.

The Philadelphia *Sun,* February 19, 1845, commented on "Some Secrets" as too harsh. A reply, obviously by Poe, in the *Broadway Journal* of February 22 was as follows:

> The editor of the Philadelphia Sun has misunderstood our remarks on the Magazines; we certainly bear them no ill will, and do not see how they can possibly interfere with our own circulation. We thought that we paid them a very high compliment in saying that they were the best, almost the only patrons of our native writers. We are extremely happy to learn that *Graham* paid *Cooper* fifteen hundred dollars in seventeen months, and that *Godey* keeps almost as many ladies in his pay as the Grand Turk; but we have heard of writers, whose articles are certainly equal to any thing of *Cooper's* that we have seen in Graham, to whom that munificent publisher pays nothing.

James Fenimore Cooper was paid highly by Graham, and for inferior work. There is a veiled reference in "The Literary Life of Thingum Bob" to Cooper's "Autobiography of a Pocket Handkerchief," which Cooper himself never republished as a book, although later editors have done so.

In the *Broadway Journal* of March 1, 1845, there was another comment, headed "Graham's Magazine," and presumably by Briggs:

* Stedman-Woodberry edition, IX (1895), 380; and Phillips, *Poe the Man,* II, 944. See also my introduction to "The Coliseum" (Mabbott I, 227).

We have ample reason to believe that we did the publisher of Graham's Magazine an injustice last week in respect to his paying contributors. We are assured that he has uniformly paid liberally where pay has been asked, and that during the last three or four years he has paid more to American authors than any other publisher in the country.

Of course, Poe, who had edited *Graham's,* disapproved of the authors who did not *ask* for payment.

TEXTS

(A) Broadway Journal, February 15, 1845 (1:103–104); *(B) Works* edited by J. H. Ingram (1875), III, 508–511.

The original publication *(A),* which is the only authorized text, is followed. The sketch was omitted by Griswold. Ingram's example in collecting it – its first appearance in a book – was followed by Stedman and Woodberry, *Works* (1894–95), IX, 344–349; and Harrison, *Complete Works* (1902), XIV, 160–163.

SOME SECRETS OF THE MAGAZINE PRISON-HOUSE. [*A*]

The want of an International Copy-Right Law, by rendering it nearly impossible to obtain anything from the booksellers in the way of remuneration for literary labor, has had the effect of forcing many of our very best writers into the service of the Magazines and Reviews, which with a pertinacity that does them credit, keep up in a certain or uncertain degree the good old saying, that even in the thankless field of Letters the laborer is worthy of his hire.[1] How – by dint of what dogged instinct of the honest and proper, these journals have contrived to persist in their paying practices, in the very teeth of the opposition got up by the Fosters and Leonard Scotts,[2] who furnish for eight dollars any four of the British periodicals for a year, is a point we have had much difficulty in settling to our satisfaction, and we have been forced to settle it, at last, upon no more reasonable ground than that of a still lingering *esprit de patrie.* That Magazines can live, and not only live but thrive, and not only thrive but afford to disburse money for original contributions, are facts which can only be solved, under the circumstances, by the really fanciful but still agreeable supposition, that there is somewhere still existing an ember not altogether quenched among the fires of good feeling for letters and literary men, that once animated the American bosom.

It would *not do* (perhaps this is the idea) to let our poor devil authors absolutely starve, while we grow fat, in a literary sense, on the good things of which we unblushingly pick the pocket of all Europe: it would not be exactly the thing *comme il faut*,[3] to permit a positive atrocity of this kind: and hence we have Magazines, and hence we have a portion of the public who subscribe to these Magazines (through sheer pity), and hence we have Magazine publishers (who sometimes take upon themselves the duplicate title of "editor *and* proprietor,") – publishers, we say, who, under certain conditions of good conduct, occasional puffs, and decent subserviency at all times, make it a point of conscience to encourage the poor devil author[4] with a dollar or two, more or less as he behaves himself properly and abstains from the indecent habit of turning up his nose.

We hope, however, that we are not so prejudiced or so vindictive as to insinuate that what certainly does look like illiberality on the part of them (the Magazine publishers) is really an illiberality chargeable to *them*. In fact, it will be seen at once, that what we have said has a tendency directly the reverse of any such accusation. These publishers pay *something* – other publishers nothing at all. Here certainly is a difference – although a mathematician might contend that the difference might be infinitesimally small. Still, these Magazine editors and proprietors *pay* (that is the word), and with your true poor-devil author the smallest favors are sure to be thankfully received. No: the illiberality lies at the door of the demagogue-ridden public, who suffer their anointed delegates (or perhaps arointed – which is it?)[5] to insult the common sense of them (the public) by making orations in our national halls on the beauty and conveniency of robbing the Literary Europe on the highway, and on the gross absurdity in especial of admitting so unprincipled a principle, that a man has any right and title either to his own brains or the flimsy material that he chooses to spin out of them, like a confounded caterpillar as he is. If anything of this gossamer character stands in need of protection, why we have our hands full at once with the silk-worms and the *morus multicaulis*.[6]

But if we cannot, under the circumstances, complain of the absolute illiberality of the Magazine publishers (since pay they do), there is at least one particular in which we have against them good grounds of accusation. Why (since pay they must) do they not pay with a good grace, and *promptly*. Were we in an ill humor at this moment, we could a tale unfold which would erect the hair on the head of Shylock.[7] A young author, struggling with Despair itself in the shape of a ghastly poverty, which has no alleviation — no sympathy from an every-day world, that cannot understand his necessities, and that would pretend not to understand them if it comprehended them ever so well — this young author is politely requested to compose an article, for which he will "be handsomely paid." Enraptured, he neglects perhaps for a month the sole employment which affords him the chance of a livelihood, and having starved through the month (he and his family) completes at length the month of starvation and the article, and despatches the latter (with a broad hint about the former) to the pursy "editor" and bottle-nosed "proprietor" who has condescended to honor him (the poor devil) with his patronage. A month (starving still), and no reply. Another month — still none. Two months more — still none. A second letter, modestly hinting that the article may not have reached its destination — still no reply. At the expiration of six additional months, personal application is made at the "editor and proprietor" 's office. Call again. The poor devil goes out, and does not fail to call again. Still call again; — and call again is the word for three or four months more. His patience exhausted, the article is demanded. No — he can't have it — (the truth is, it was too good to be given up so easily) — "it is in print," and "contributions of this character are never paid for (it is a *rule* we have) under six months after publication. Call in six months after the issue of your affair, and your money is ready for you — for we are business men, ourselves — prompt." With this the poor devil is satisfied, and makes up his mind that the "editor and proprietor" is a gentleman, and that of course he (the poor devil) will wait as requested. And it is supposable that he would have waited if he could — but Death in the meantime would not. He dies, and by the good luck of his decease (which came by starvation) the fat "editor and proprietor" is fatter henceforward and for ever to the amount of five and twenty dollars, very cleverly saved, to be spent generously in canvas-backs and champagne.[8]

There are two things which we hope the reader will not do, as he runs over this article: first, we hope that he will not believe that we write from any personal experience of our own, for we have only the reports of actual sufferers to depend upon, and second, that he will not make any personal application of our remarks to any Magazine publisher now living, it being well known that they are all as remarkable for their generosity and urbanity, as for their intelligence, and appreciation of Genius.

NOTES

Title: Poe has in mind some of the words of the Ghost in *Hamlet,* I, v, quoted in n. 7 below.

1. See St. Luke 10:7, "The laborer is worthy of his hire."

2. Theodore Foster published New York reprints of British magazines; some of his reprints were reviewed in the *Southern Literary Messenger,* April and December 1835. Leonard Scott & Co. of 112 Fulton Street printed similar piracies in 1845.

3. "As it should be." Poe also used this common French phrase in "The Duc de L'Omelette."

4. Poe referred to "poor devil authors" in a review of *A Continuation of the Memoirs of Charles Mathews* in *Burton's,* January 1840; in "The Literary Life of Thingum Bob," and again in the late sketch "A Reviewer Reviewed."

5. See *Macbeth,* I, iii, 6, "Aroint thee, witch."

6. The *Morus multicaulis* is one of the mulberries upon the leaves of which silkworms are fed. For several years there had been a feverish speculative interest in the culture of silkworms in the United States. A large part of the Annual Report of the American Institute of New York for 1844 was devoted to meetings, discussions, and papers dealing with the silkworm industry.

7. Compare the speech of the Ghost in *Hamlet,* I, v, 13–20:

"But that I am forbid
To tell the secrets of my prison-house,
I could a tale unfold whose lightest word
. . . [would make] . . .
Thy knotted and combined locks to part
And each particular hair to stand on end,
Like quills upon the fearful porpentine."

Shylock, however, is usually played in a long wig; it would be hard to make *his* hair stand on end. (Compare the motto for "A Tale of Jerusalem.")

8. Poe, amusingly enough, was to assume the title Editor and Proprietor in the *Broadway Journal* of October 25, 1845.

THE POWER OF WORDS

This latest of Poe's three imaginary dialogues of blessed spirits in heaven is usually considered the best. Like "The Conversation of Eiros and Charmion" (see p. 451) it is laid in the future, after the destruction of the world. The piece was discussed enthusiastically by C. Alphonso Smith (*Poe: How to Know Him,* pp. 333–334) who explained that Agathos inducts Oinos "into the methods of creation" by "a leap of fantasy over the walls of analytic reason."

Briefly, "The Power of Words" is a prose poem with various philosophical concerns, perhaps best synopsized by Quinn (*Poe,* p. 469):

> Poe faced in this story the problem of creation and took the position that God created only in the beginning. Through the conversation of Oinos and Agathos, he depicted the future life where the soul's unquenchable desire to *know* is recognized as its greatest happiness, and therefore the soul's search for knowledge is never ceasing. He also expressed the idea of the conservation of force in poetic terms. As no thought can perish, so no act is without infinite result. Since every vibration once set in motion is eternal, the power of the word once spoken is also everlasting.

As the Cosmos is unified, every atom is related to every other atom. Poe said in *Eureka* (paragraph 67):

> If I venture to displace, even by the billionth part of an inch, the microscopical speck of dust which lies now upon the point of my finger, what is the character of that act upon which I have adventured? I have done a deed which shakes the Moon in her path, which causes the Sun to be no longer the Sun, and which alters forever the destiny of the multitudinous myriads of stars that roll and glow in the majestic presence of their Creator.

In his Drake-Halleck review (*SLM,* April 1836), referring to "the sense of the beautiful, of the sublime, and of the mystical," he had said, "Thence spring immediately admiration of the fair flowers, the bright valleys and rivers and mountains of the Earth — and love of the gleaming stars and other burning glories of

Heaven – and, mingled up inextricably with this love and this admiration of Heaven and Earth, the unconquerable desire – to *know*." This desire he made an integral part of the action in three of his tales. Twice at least the narrator is saved by his mind's activity, by his "curiosity to penetrate the mysteries," but salvation is more in the nature of a by-product than a goal – "not in knowledge is happiness, but in the acquisition of knowledge," Agathos says.

Poe did not need a source for the desire to know any more than for the love of Heaven, but he must surely have read in *The Loves of the Angels* by his favorite Moore the lines from the "Second Angel's Story":

> The wish to know – that endless thirst,
> Which even by quenching is awaked,
> And which becomes or blest or curst,
> As is the fount whereat 'tis slaked –
> Still urged me onward, with desire
> Insatiate, to explore, inquire.

It may be relevant to recall that Poe's interest in "the Future Condition of Man" mentioned in his letter to George Bush, January 4, 1845, was of long standing. "The Conversation of Eiros and Charmion" (*Burton's,* December 1839), "The Colloquy of Monos and Una" (*Graham's,* August 1841), and "Mesmeric Revelation" (*Columbian Magazine,* August 1844) would reappear in the small volume of *Tales* (1845) before the end of July. "The Power of Words" was probably completed by the early spring of 1845, for it must have been in the editor's hands in April for publication, about the middle of May, in the *Democratic Review* for June.

TEXTS

(A) Democratic Review, June 1845 (16:602–604); *(B) Broadway Journal,* October 25, 1845 (2:243–244); *(C) Works* (1850), II, 271–275.

Griswold's text *(C)* which is verbally like *(B)* is followed.

THE POWER OF WORDS. [C]

Oinos. – Pardon, Agathos, the weakness of a spirit new-fledged with immortality!

Agathos. – You have spoken nothing, my Oinos,[1] for which pardon is to be demanded. Not even here is knowledge a thing of intuition. For wisdom, ask of the angels freely, that it may be given![2]

Oinos. — But in this existence, I dreamed that I should be at once cognizant of all things, and thus at once happy in being cognizant of all.

Agathos. — Ah, not in knowledge is happiness, but in the acquisition of knowledge![3] In for ever knowing, we are for ever blessed; but to know all, were the curse of a fiend.

Oinos. — But does not The Most High know all?

Agathos. — *That* (since he is The Most Happy) must be still the *one* thing unknown even to HIM.

Oinos. — But, since we grow hourly in knowledge, must not *at last* all things be known?

Agathos. — Look down into the abysmal distances! — attempt to force the gaze down the multitudinous vistas of the stars,[4] as we sweep slowly through them thus — and thus — and thus! Even the[a] spiritual vision, is it not at all points arrested by the continuous golden walls of the universe? — the walls of the myriads of the shining bodies that mere number has appeared to blend into unity?

Oinos. — I clearly perceive that the infinity of matter is no dream.

Agathos. — There are *no* dreams in Aidenn[5] — but it is here whispered that, of this infinity of matter, the *sole* purpose is to afford infinite springs, at which the soul may allay the thirst *to know* which is for ever unquenchable within it — since to quench it, would be to extinguish the soul's self.[6] Question me then, my Oinos, freely and without fear. Come! we will leave to the left the loud harmony of the Pleiades, and swoop outward from the throne into the starry meadows beyond Orion, where, for pansies and violets, and heart's-ease, are the beds of the triplicate and triple-tinted suns.[7]

Oinos. — And now, Agathos, as we proceed, instruct me! — speak to me in the earth's familiar tones![8] I understood not what

a the keen *(A)*

you hinted to me, just now, of the modes or of the methods of what, during mortality, we were accustomed to call Creation. Do you mean to say that the Creator is not God?

Agathos. — I mean to say that the Deity does not create.

Oinos. — Explain!

Agathos. — In the beginning *only,* he created. The seeming creatures which are now, throughout the universe, so perpetually springing into being, can only be considered as the mediate or indirect, not as the direct or immediate results of the Divine creative power.

Oinos. — Among men, my Agathos, this idea would be considered heretical in the extreme.

Agathos. — Among angels, my Oinos, it is seen to be simply true.

Oinos. — I can comprehend you thus far — that certain operations of what we term Nature, or the natural laws, will, under certain conditions, give rise to that which has all the *appearance* of creation. Shortly before the final overthrow of the earth, there were, I well remember, many very successful experiments in what some philosophers were weak enough to denominate the creation of animalculæ.[9]

Agathos. — The cases of which you speak were, in fact, instances of the secondary creation — and of the *only* species of creation which has ever been, since the first word spoke into existence the first law.

Oinos. — Are not the starry worlds that, from the abyss of nonentity, burst hourly forth into the heavens — are not these stars, Agathos, the immediate handiwork of the King?

Agathos. — Let me endeavor, my Oinos, to lead you, step by step, to the conception I intend. You are well aware that, as no thought can perish, so no act is without infinite result. We moved our hands, for example, when we were dwellers on the earth, and, in so doing, we gave vibration to the atmosphere which engirdled it. This vibration was indefinitely extended, till it gave impulse to every particle of the earth's air, which thenceforward, *and for ever,* was actuated by the one movement of the hand. This fact the mathematicians of our globe well knew. They made the special effects, indeed, wrought in the fluid by special impulses, the subject of exact calculation — so that it became easy to determine in what precise period an impulse of given extent would engirdle the orb, and impress (for ever) every atom of the atmosphere circumambient. Retrograding, they found no difficulty, from a given effect, under given conditions, in determining the value of the original impulse. Now the mathematicians who saw that the results of any given impulse were absolutely endless — and who saw that a portion of these results were accurately traceable through the agency of algebraic analysis — who saw, too, the facility of the retrogradation — these men saw, at the same time, that this species of analysis itself, had within itself a capacity for indefinite progress — that there were no bounds conceivable to its advancement and applicability, except within the intellect of him who advanced or applied it. But at this point our mathematicians paused.

Oinos. — And why, Agathos, should they have proceeded?

Agathos. — Because there were some considerations of deep interest beyond. It was deducible from what they knew, that to a being of infinite understanding — one to[b] whom the *perfection* of the algebraic analysis lay unfolded — there could be no difficulty in tracing every impulse given the air — and the ether through the air — to the remotest consequences at any even infinitely remote epoch of time. It is indeed demonstrable that every such impulse *given the air,* must, *in the end,* impress every individual thing that exists *within the universe;* — and the being of infinite understanding — the being whom we have imagined — might trace the remote undulations of the impulse — trace them upward and onward in their influences upon all particles of all matter — upward and onward for ever in their modifications of old forms — or, in other words, *in their creation of new* — until he found them reflected — unimpressive *at last* — back from the throne of the Godhead. And not only could such a being do this, but at any epoch, should a given result be afforded him — should one of these numberless comets,[c] for example, be presented to his inspection — he could have no difficulty in determining, by

b one to/to one *(A)*

c *nebulae, (A)*

the analytic retrogradation, to what original impulse it was due. This power of retrogradation in its absolute fulness and perfection – this faculty of referring at *all* epochs, *all* effects to *all* causes – is of course the prerogative of the Deity alone – but in every variety of degree, short of the absolute perfection, is the power itself exercised by the whole host of the Angelic Intelligences.

Oinos. – But you speak merely of impulses upon the air.

Agathos. – In speaking of the air, I referred only to the earth: but the general proposition has reference to impulses upon the ether – which, since it pervades, and alone pervades all space, is thus the great medium of *creation.*

Oinos. – Then all motion, of whatever nature, creates?[d]

Agathos. – It must: but a true philosophy has long taught that the source of all motion is thought – and the source of all thought is ––

Oinos. – God.[10]

Agathos. – I have spoken to you, Oinos, as to a child of the fair Earth which lately perished – of impulses upon the atmosphere of the Earth.

Oinos. – You did.

Agathos. – And while I thus spoke, did there not cross your mind some thought of the *physical power of words?* Is not every word an impulse on the air?

Oinos. – But why, Agathos, do you weep – and why, oh why do your wings droop as we hover above this fair star – which is the greenest and yet most terrible of all we have encountered in our flight? Its brilliant flowers look like a fairy[e] dream – but its fierce volcanoes like the passions of a turbulent heart.

Agathos. – They *are!* – they *are!* This wild star – it is now three centuries since, with clasped hands,[f] and with streaming eyes, at the feet of my beloved – I spoke it – with a few passionate sentences – into birth. Its brilliant flowers *are* the dearest of all unfulfilled dreams, and its raging volcanoes *are* the passions of the most turbulent and unhallowed of hearts.[11]

---

d creates. *(A)*
e faëry *(A)*
f hand, *(A)*

TALES: 1845–1846

NOTES

Title: Poe used the phrase in his "Marginalia," number 150 (*Graham's*, March 1846, p. 117), in the poem "To Marie Louise," and in a letter to Helen Whitman, of October 1, 1848, but in these instances he referred only to the power or lack of power of words to embody thoughts. (See Mabbott I, 408, where the "Marginalia" number is given incorrectly as 149.) The phrase had been used as a title for one of the "Fragments" of Letitia E. Landon, of whose poems Poe was fond in his youth.

1. Oinos here means "One" as in the tale "Shadow," where see my comment on the rare Greek word. Agathos means "Good."

2. Compare St. Matthew 7:7, "Ask and it shall be given you."

3. See the introduction above.

4. Compare "multitudinous thunders" in Poe's "Lines after Elizabeth Barrett" (Mabbott I, 377–378).

5. Compare "The Conversation of Eiros and Charmion": "Dreams are with us no more"; and see n. 2 on that tale for Aidenn.

6. See the introduction above, and "MS. Found in a Bottle" where at n. 25 the narrator says that "a curiosity to penetrate the mysteries of these awful regions predominates even over my despair." Also in "A Descent into the Maelström" at n. 16, "in the very jaws of the gulf . . . I became possessed with the keenest curiosity about the whirl itself. I positively felt a *wish* to explore its depths." Finally, in "The Pit and the Pendulum" on page 686, the despairing narrator says, "I had little object – certainly no hope – in these researches [into the dimensions of the dungeon] but a vague curiosity prompted me to continue them," and at n. 17 his "soul took a wild interest in trifles."

7. Compare Job 9:9, "Which maketh Arcturus, Orion and Pleiades." C. Alphonso Smith (in *Poe: How to Know Him*, p. 33) calls this last sentence "unsurpassed in ancient or modern English prose." Walt Whitman in youth admired, and wrote sketches in the manner of, Poe's dialogues of angels, and it seems to me possible that he had Poe's phrasing in mind when he wrote in the thirty-third section of the "Song of Myself": "I visit the orchards of spheres and look at the product,/And look at quintillions ripen'd and look at quintillions green."

8. Compare "The Conversation of Eiros and Charmion": ". . . let us converse of familiar things in the old familiar language of the world. . ."

9. The allusion is probably to the reports of mites (of the genus Acarus) found in a solution connected with experiments in electro-crystallization made by Andrew Crosse in 1837. These experiments are mentioned in the article on Ancient Egyptians in the *Westminster Review,* July 1841, used by Poe in "Some Words with a Mummy" and cited in the introduction to that tale. The following passage from the *Westminster,* referring to the contest of the Egyptian *sophoi* with Moses before Pharaoh, is pertinent here:

> Three of the miracles of their natural magic (see Sir D. Brewster) the jugglers of the East can and do now perform. In the fourth, an attempt to pro-

> duce the lowest form of life, they fail. From the whole statement, one inference is safe, that the daring ambition of the priestly chemists and anatomists had been led from the triumphs of embalming and chicken-hatching (imitating and assisting the production of life) to a Frankenstein experiment on the vital fluid and on the principle of life itself, perhaps to experiments like those correctly or incorrectly ascribed to Mr. Crosse, in the hope of creating, not reviving, the lowest form of animal life.

Compare "Some Words with a Mummy" at n. 31.

10. Much of the foregoing argument is akin to the argument in "Mesmeric Revelation" following the question "What then is God?"

11. Compare "Ulalume," line 13, "These were days when my heart was volcanic"; and see also Poe's letter of October 1, 1848 to Helen Whitman: "It is the most spiritual of love that I speak, even if I speak it from the depths of the most passionate of hearts."

THE IMP OF THE PERVERSE

This is one of Poe's great stories, although not one of the most popular. Benjamin De Casseres (1873–1945), a fine American critic, too little remembered now, said that Poe's profundity is

> best illustrated in his little *Imp of the Perverse* . . . We've all got that "imp" in us. It makes us do things we ought not to do. It whispers to us to lean as far over a cliff as we can. It literally forces us to wound a friend with an insult. It shouts in our mental ear "Do it! do it!" when we have resolved not to do it. What or who is this Imp of the Perverse? Poe doesn't tell us for he cannot. It is one of the insoluble mysteries of the soul . . . Why should Nature, which does everything to cause us to fight for self-survival, put a voice – or an imp – in our soul that deliberately advises us to destroy ourselves? . . . You – and I – know that imp.*

Poe knew that imp himself. In his early album verses for "Elizabeth" he wrote of his "innate love of contradiction," and anyone familiar with Poe's life will recall instances of impulsive actions that brought him into needless difficulties. He had already recognized this compelling perverseness in his powerful tale "The Black Cat." Poe's dark views were not understood by some of his contemporaries.†

* *New York Journal-American,* August 23, 1944, quoted by permission.

† In the *Broadway Journal,* December 6, 1845, Poe quoted from a Princeton magazine, *The Nassau Monthly* for December 1845, a notice describing "The Imp of the Perverse" as "humbug philosophical."

Poe's title and the main theme — and even a connection with phrenology — clearly have their inspiration in a passage in the twenty-second chapter of Lady Georgiana Fullerton's novel *Ellen Middleton* (1844). There Ellen, who feels herself responsible, through accident rather than intention, for the death of her young cousin, is in a room with persons who knew her secret and taunt her.

> "The organ of destructiveness must be strong in you," observed Mr. Escourt ... Again an icy chill ran through me ... I felt that I was making an odious speech, I saw in [my husband] Edward's face an expression almost of disgust. I felt that I was sinking every moment in his opinion; perhaps losing ground in his affections ... A spirit of reckless defiance took possession of me, — and I completely lost my head. A torrent of words burst from my lips, of which I hardly knew the meaning ... like Samson ... I was dragging down ... the ruin which had so long hung over my head.

Poe's "Marginalia" number 52 gave high praise to *Ellen Middleton* in the *Democratic Review,* December 1844, page 582. There he remarked that the author's style "has, now and then, an odd Gallicism — such as 'she lost her head,' meaning she grew crazy." This observation makes it certain that he knew the cited paragraph in the novel.‡

The means of the murder executed by Poe's protagonist after the rejection of "a thousand schemes" was probably suggested by an article in the *New Monthly Magazine,* December 1839. He was familiar with this periodical and indebted to its pages for other inspirations.

The first version of Poe's story must have been in Graham's hands at least two months before it appeared in his magazine, issued about June 15, 1845. The other version differs so much that I suspect it was rewritten from memory for its second printing. In the *Broadway Journal,* August 9, 1845, Poe said, "Mr. Robert Hamilton [of Boston] is getting ready 'The May-Flower' of which we have seen some specimen sheets." Poe's tale appeared in that annual later in the year.

‡ A connection between Poe's story and *Ellen Middleton* was first pointed out in an anonymous volume, *The Rambles and Reveries of an Art-Student in Europe* (Philadelphia, 1855), p. 36.

THE IMP OF THE PERVERSE

TEXTS

(A) Graham's Magazine for July 1845 (27[incorrectly numbered 28]: 1–3; *(B) The May-Flower for 1846*, pp. 11–22; *(C) Works* (1850), I, 353–359.

Griswold, whose text we print, shows one variant from *The May-Flower (B)* which I think auctorial.

THE IMP OF THE PERVERSE. [*C*]

In the consideration of the faculties and impulses — of the *prima mobilia* of the human soul, the phrenologists have failed to make room for a propensity which, although obviously existing as a radical, primitive, irreducible sentiment, has been equally overlooked by all[a] the moralists who have preceded them. In the pure arrogance of the reason, we have all overlooked it. We have suffered its existence to escape our senses, solely through want of belief — of faith; — whether it be faith in Revelation, or faith in the Kabbala.[b1] [c]The idea of it has never[c] occurred to us, simply because of its[d] supererogation. We saw no *need* [e]of the impulse — for the propensity.[e] We could not perceive its necessity. We could not understand, that is to say, we could not have understood, had the notion of this *primum mobile* ever obtruded [f]itself; — we could not have understood[f] in what manner it might be made to further the objects of humanity, either temporal or eternal. It cannot be denied that [g]phrenology and, in great measure, all metaphysicianism have[g] been concocted *à priori*. The intellectual or logical man, rather than the understanding or observant man, set himself to imagine designs — to dictate purposes to God. Having thus fathomed,[h] to his satisfaction, the intentions of Jehovah, out of these intentions he built[i] his innumerable systems of mind. In the matter of phrenology, for example, we first determined, naturally enough, that it was the design of the[j] Deity that man should eat. We then assigned to man an organ of alimentiveness, and this organ is the scourge with[k]

---

a *Omitted (A)*
b inner teachings of the spirit. *(A)*
c . . . c Its idea has not *(A)*
d its seeming *(A, B)*
e . . . e for the propensity in question. *(A)*
f . . . f itself — *(A)*
g . . . g all metaphysicianism has *(A)*; phrenology, and in a great measure, all metaphysicianism, *(C) repunctuated to follow B*
h fathomed *(C) comma added from B*
i reared *(A)*
j *Omitted (A)*
k by *(A)*

which the[l] Deity compels [m]man, will-I nill-I, into eating.[m] Secondly,[n] having settled it to be God's will that man should continue his species, we discovered an organ of amativeness, forthwith. And so with combativeness, with ideality, with causality, with constructiveness, — so, in short, with every organ, whether representing a propensity, a moral sentiment, or a faculty of the pure intellect. And in these arrangements of the *principia* of human action, the Spurzheimites,[2] whether right or wrong, in part, or upon the whole, have but followed, in principle, the footsteps of their predecessors; deducing and establishing every thing from the preconceived destiny of man, and upon the ground of the objects[o] of his Creator.

It would have been [p]wiser, it would have been safer to classify, (if classify we must,)[p] upon the basis of what man usually or occasionally did, and was always occasionally doing, rather than upon the basis of what we took it for granted the Deity intended him to do. If we cannot comprehend God in his visible works, how then in his inconceivable thoughts, that call the works into being? If we cannot understand him in his objective creatures, how then in his substantive moods and phases of creation?

Induction, *à posteriori,* would have brought phrenology to admit, as an innate and primitive principle of human action, a paradoxical something, which[q] we may call [r]*perverseness,* for want of a more characteristic term.[r] In the sense I intend, it is, in fact, a *mobile* without motive, a motive not *motivirt.* Through its promptings we act without comprehensible object; or, if this shall be understood as a contradiction in terms, we may so far modify the proposition as to say, that through its promptings we act, for the reason that we should *not.* In theory, no reason can be more unreasonable; but, in fact,[s] there is none more[t] strong. With certain minds, under certain conditions,[u] it becomes absolutely irresistible. I am not more certain[v] that I breathe, than that the assurance[w] of

---

l *Omitted (A)*
m . . . m man to his food. *(A)*
n Again, *(A)*
o *objects (A)*
p . . . p safer — if classify we must — to classify *(A)*
q which, for want of a better term, *(A)*
r . . . r *Perverseness. (A)*
s reality *(A)*
t so *(A)*
u circumstances, *(A)*
v sure *(A)*
w conviction *(A)*

the wrong or error[x] of any[y] action is often the one unconquerable *force* which impels us, and alone impels us to its prosecution. Nor will this overwhelming tendency to do wrong for the wrong's sake, admit of analysis, or resolution into ulterior elements. It is a radical, a primitive impulse — elementary. It will be said, I am aware, that when we persist in acts because we feel[z] we should *not* persist in them, our conduct is but a modification of that which ordinarily springs from the *combativeness*[a] of phrenology. But a glance will show the fallacy of this idea. The phrenological combativeness has for its essence, the necessity of self-defence. It is our safeguard against injury. Its principle regards our well-being; and thus the desire to be well[a'] is[b] excited simultaneously with [c]its development. It follows, that the desire to be well must be excited simultaneously with[c] any principle which shall be merely a modification of combativeness, but in the case of that something which I term *perverseness,*[d] the desire to be well is not only not[e] aroused, but a strongly antagonistical sentiment exists.[f]

An appeal to one's own heart is, after all, the best reply to the sophistry just noticed. No one who trustingly consults [g]and thoroughly questions[g] his own soul, will be disposed to deny the entire radicalness of the propensity in question. It is not more incomprehensible than distinctive.[h] There lives no man who at some period[h'] has not been tormented, for example, by an earnest desire to tantalize a listener by circumlocution. The speaker[i] is aware that he displeases; he has every intention to please; he is usually curt, precise, and clear; the most laconic and luminous language is struggling for utterance upon his tongue; it is only with difficulty that he restrains himself from giving it flow; he dreads and deprecates the anger of him whom he addresses; yet,[j] the thought strikes him,

x impolicy *(A)*
y an *(A)*
z feel that *(A)*
a Combativeness *(A)*
a′ well, *(C) comma deleted to follow A, B*
b must be *(A)*
c . . . c *Omitted (A)*
d Perverseness, *(A)*
e *not (A)*
f prevails. *(A)*
g . . . g *Omitted (A)*
h distinct. *(A)*
h′ period, *(C) comma deleted to follow B*
i speaker, in such case, *(A)*
j yet a shadow seems to flit across the brain, and suddenly *(A)*

that[k] by certain involutions and parentheses, this[l] anger may be engendered. That single thought is enough. The impulse increases to a wish, the wish to a desire, the desire to an uncontrollable longing, and the longing, [m](to the deep regret and mortification of the speaker, and[m] in defiance of all consequences,) is indulged.

We[n] have a task before us which must be speedily performed. We know that it will be ruinous to make delay. The most important crisis of our life calls, trumpet-tongued,[3] for immediate energy and action. We glow, we are consumed with eagerness to commence the work, [o]with the anticipation of whose glorious result our whole souls are on fire.[o] It must, it shall be undertaken to-day, and yet we put it off until to-morrow; and why? There is no answer, except that we feel *perverse,* using[p] the word with no comprehension of the principle. To-morrow arrives, and with it a more impatient anxiety to do our duty, but with this very increase of anxiety arrives, also, a nameless, a positively fearful because unfathomable, craving for delay. This craving gathers strength as the moments fly. The last hour for action is at hand. We tremble with the violence of the conflict within us, — of the definite with the indefinite — of the substance with the shadow. But, if the contest have proceeded thus far, it is the shadow which prevails, — we struggle in vain. The clock strikes, and is the knell of our welfare. At[q] the same time, it[r] is the chanticleer-note to the ghost[s] that has so long overawed us. It flies — it disappears — we are free.[4] The old energy returns. We will labor *now*. Alas, it is *too late!*

We[t] stand upon the brink of a precipice. We peer into the abyss — we grow sick and dizzy. Our first impulse is to shrink from the [u]danger. Unaccountably[u] we remain. By slow degrees our sickness, and dizziness, and horror, become merged in a cloud of unnameable feeling.[5] By gradations, still more imperceptible, this cloud assumes shape, as did the vapor from the bottle out of which arose the genius

k strikes him, that/strikes that, *(A)*
l *Omitted (A)*
m . . . m *Omitted (A)* [*no parentheses in A*]
n Again: — We *(A)*
o . . . o and our whole souls are on fire with anticipation of the glorious result. *(A)*
p employing *(A)*
q welfare. At/welfare, but at *(A)*
r *Omitted (A)*
s Thing *(A)*
t And yet again: — We *(A)*
u . . . u danger, and yet, unaccountably, *(A)*

in the Arabian Nights.[6] But out of this *our* cloud upon[v] the precipice's edge, there grows into palpability, a shape, far more terrible than any genius, or any demon of a tale, and yet it is but a thought,[w] although [x]a fearful one, and[x] one which chills the very marrow of our bones with the fierceness of the delight of its horror. It is merely the idea of what would be our sensations during the sweeping precipitancy of a fall from such a height. And this fall — this rushing annihilation — for the very reason that it involves that one most ghastly and loathsome of all the most ghastly and loathsome images of death and suffering which have ever presented themselves to our imagination — [y]for this very cause[y] do we now the most vividly[z] desire it. And because our reason violently[a] deters us from the brink, *therefore,* do we the more impetuously[b] approach it. There is no passion in nature [c]so demoniacally impatient,[c] as that[d] of him, who shuddering upon the edge of a precipice, thus meditates a plunge. To indulge[e] for a moment, in any attempt at *thought,* is to be inevitably lost; for reflection but urges us to forbear, and *therefore* it is, I say, that we *cannot.* If there be no friendly arm to check us, or if we fail in a sudden effort to prostrate[f] ourselves backward from the abyss,[g] we plunge, and are destroyed.

Examine these and similar actions as we will, we shall find them resulting solely from the spirit of the *Perverse.* We perpetrate them merely because we feel that we should *not.* Beyond or behind this, there is no [h]intelligible principle: and we might, indeed, deem this perverseness[h] a direct instigation of the [i]arch-fiend, were it not occasionally known to operate in furtherance of good.[i]

I have said[j] thus much, that [k]in some measure I may answer your question[k] — that I may explain to you why I am here — that I may assign [l]to you something that shall have at least the faint aspect of a

v on *(A)*
w *Thought, (A)*
x . . . x *Omitted (A)*
y . . . y *for this very cause (A)*
z impetuously *(A)*
a most strenuously *(A)*
b unhesitatingly *(A)*
c . . . c of so demoniac an impatience *(A)*
d the passion *(A)*
e indulge, even *(A)*
f throw *(A)*
g danger, and so out of its sight, *(A)*
h . . . h principle that men, in their fleshly nature, can understand; and were it not occasionally known to operate in furtherance of good, we might deem the anomalous feeling *(A)*
i . . . i Arch-fiend. *(A)*
j premised *(A)*
k . . . k I may be able, in some degree, to give an intelligible answer to your queries *(A)*
l . . . l something like a reason *(A)*

cause[l] for my wearing these fetters, and for[m] my[n] tenanting this cell of the condemned. Had I not been thus prolix, you might either have misunderstood me altogether, or, with the rabble, have[o] fancied me mad. [p]As it is, you will easily perceive that I am one of the many uncounted victims of the Imp of the Perverse.[p]

It is impossible that any deed could have been wrought with a[q] more thorough deliberation. For weeks, for months, I pondered upon the means of the murder. I rejected a thousand schemes, because their accomplishment involved a *chance* of detection. At length, in reading some French memoirs, I found an account of a nearly fatal illness that occurred to Madame Pilau, through the agency of a candle accidentally poisoned.[7] The idea struck my fancy at once. I knew my victim's habit of reading in bed. I knew, too, that his apartment was narrow and ill-ventilated. But I need not vex you with impertinent details. I need not describe the easy artifices by which I substituted, in his bed-room[r] candlestand, a wax-light of my own making, for the one which I there found. The next morning he was discovered[s] dead in his bed, and the coroner's[t] verdict was, — "Death by the visitation of God."

Having inherited his estate, all went well[u] with me for years. The idea of detection never [v]once entered my brain.[v] Of the remains of the fatal taper, I had myself carefully [w]disposed. I had left no[w] shadow of a clue by which it would be possible to convict, or even to suspect me of the crime. It is inconceivable how rich a sentiment of satisfaction arose in my bosom as I reflected upon my absolute[x] security. For a very long period of time, I [y]was accustomed to revel[y] in this sentiment. It afforded me[z] more real delight than all the mere worldly advantages accruing from my sin. But there[a] arrived at length an epoch, from which the[b] pleasurable feeling[c] grew, by scarcely perceptible gradations, into a haunting and harassing [d]thought. It[d] harassed because it haunted. I could scarcely get rid

m *Omitted (A)*
n *Omitted (A)*
o you might have *(A, B)*
p . . . p *Omitted (A)*
q *Omitted (A)*
r *Omitted (A)*
s *Omitted (A)*
t *Omitted (A)*
u merrily *(A)*
v . . . v obtruded itself. *(A)*
w . . . w disposed, nor had I left the *(A)*
x *absolute (A)*
y . . . y reveled *(A)*
z me, I believe, *(A)*
a But there/There *(A)*
b from which the/after which this *(A)*
c feeling took to itself a new tone, and *(A)*
d . . . d thought — a thought that *(A)*

of it for an instant. It is quite a common thing to be thus annoyed with[e] the ringing in our ears, or rather in our[f] memories, of the burthen[g] of some[h] ordinary song, or some unimpressive snatches from an opera. Nor will we be less tormented if[i] the song in itself be good, or the opera air meritorious. In this manner, at last, I would perpetually catch[j] myself pondering upon my[k] security, and[l] repeating, in a low, under-tone, the [m]phrase, "I am safe."[m]

One day, whilst[n] sauntering along[o] the streets, I arrested myself in the act of murmuring, half aloud, these customary syllables. In a fit of petulance,[p] I re-modelled them thus: — "I am safe — I am safe —[q]yes — if I be not fool enough to make open confession!"[q]

No sooner had I spoken[r] these words, than I felt an icy chill creep to my heart. I had had[s] some experience in these[t] fits of perversity, [u](whose nature I have been at some trouble to explain,)[u] and I remembered well,[v] that in no [w]instance, I had[w] successfully resisted their attacks. And now my own casual self-suggestion, that I might possibly be[x] fool enough [y]to confess the murder of which I had been guilty,[y] confronted me, as if the very ghost of him whom[z] I had murdered — and beckoned me on to death.

At first, I made an[a] effort to shake off this nightmare of the soul. I[b] walked vigorously — [c]faster — still faster — at length I ran.[c] I felt a maddening[d] desire to shriek aloud. Every succeeding wave of thought overwhelmed me with new terror, for, alas! [e]I well, too

---

e by *(A)*
f or rather in our/or *(A)*
g burden *(A)*
h an *(A)*
i though *(A)*
j find *(A)*
k my impunity and *(A)*
l and very frequently would catch myself *(A)*
m . . . m phrases "I am safe — I am safe." *(A)*
n while *(A)*
o listlessly about *(A)*
p petulance at my indiscretion *(A)*
q . . . q yes, *if I do not prove fool enough to make open confession.*" *(A)*
r uttered *(A)*
s had (long ago, during childhood) *(A)*
t those *(A)*
u . . . u whose nature I have been at so much trouble in explaining, *(A)*
v well, *omitted (A)*
w . . . w instance had I *(A)*
x prove *(A)*
y . . . y to make open confession — *(A)*
z *Omitted (A)*
a strong *(A)*
b I whistled — I laughed aloud — I *(A)*
c . . . c faster and still faster. At length I saw — or fancied that I saw — a vast and formless shadow that seemed to dog my footsteps, approaching me from behind, with a cat-like and stealthy pace. It was then that I *ran.* *(A)*
d wild *(A)*
e . . . e I understood too well that to *think,* in my condition, was to be undone. *(A)*

well understood that, to *think,* in my situation, was to be lost.[e] I still quickened my pace.[f] I bounded like a madman through the crowded thoroughfares. At length,[g] the populace took the[h] alarm, and pursued me.[i] I felt *then*[j] the consummation of my fate. Could I have torn out my tongue, I would have done it — but a rough voice[k] resounded in my ears — a[l] rougher grasp seized me by the shoulder.[m] I turned — I gasped for breath. For a moment, I experienced all the pangs of suffocation; I became blind, and deaf, and giddy;[8] and [n]then, some invisible fiend, I thought, struck me with his broad[n] palm upon the back.[9] The[o] long-imprisoned secret burst forth from my soul.[10]

They say that I spoke with a[p] distinct enunciation, but with marked[q] emphasis and passionate hurry, as if in dread of interruption before concluding the brief but pregnant sentences that consigned me to the hangman and to hell.

[r]Having related all that was necessary for the fullest judicial conviction, I fell prostrate in a swoon.

But why shall I say more? To-day I wear these chains, and am *here.* To-morrow I shall be fetterless! — *but where?*[r]

NOTES

Title: Poe's title has literally the same meaning as Lady Fullerton's "spirit of reckless defiance" in the passage quoted in my introduction, but is an example of Poe's imaginative mastery of phrase.

1. The Kabbala (cabbala, cabala) is specifically an esoteric Hebraic theosophy based on Holy Writ and the Talmud. It was developed during the Middle Ages and transmitted orally for many generations. Poe used the term on several occasions to mean something highly abstruse.

2. Spurzheimites were followers of Dr. Johann Gaspar Spurzheim, a German codiscoverer with Dr. Franz Josef Gall of the principles of phrenology. He came to the United States and died at Boston, November 10, 1832. Thomas Dunn English wrote his medical thesis on phrenological relations to medicine. Poe spoke

f steps. *(A)*
g At length,/But now *(A)*
h *Omitted (A)*
i me *omitted (A)*
j I felt *then*/Then — then I felt *(A)*
k voice from some member of the crowd now *(A)*
l ears — a/ears, and a *(A)*
m arm. *(A)*
n . . . n at this instant it was no mortal hand, I knew, that struck me violently with a broad and massive *(A)*
o At that blow the *(A)*
p *Omitted (A)*
q *Omitted (A)*
r . . . r *Omitted (A)*

with much respect of phrenology in his earlier years; but, as what he says in the present story suggests, he came to distrust its validity. He removed an allusion to it from "The Murders in the Rue Morgue," and another from "The Black Cat." He did, however, continue to use some of its special vocabulary, as did Walt Whitman. See "Poe and Phrenology," by Edward Hungerford in *American Literature,* November 1930.

3. For "trumpet-tongued" see *Macbeth,* I, vii, 19; the expression is also used in *Politian,* VI, 23 (see Mabbott I, 293), and in the "Literati" sketch of Caroline Kirkland in *Godey's* for August 1846.

4. Many ghosts must return to their graves at cock-crow, before dawn, as is recounted in *Hamlet,* I, i, 147–156.

5. Compare a passage on the fascination of precipices in *Arthur Gordon Pym,* chapter xxiv. [In connection with this paragraph, see "The Self-Destructive Fall: A Theme from Shakespeare used in *Pym* and 'The Imp of the Perverse,' " by B. Pollin, *Études Anglaises,* T. XXIX, No. 2 (1976).]

6. The bottle imp is in the "Story of the Fisherman," one of the best known in the Arabian Nights. Compare also Poe's poem "Alone," lines 20–22, "And the cloud that took the form/ . . . Of a demon in my view."

7. The Madame Pilau Poe refers to appears in "An Oddity of the Seventeenth Century," by Mrs. [Catherine] Gore, in the *New Monthly Magazine,* December 1839. The sketch states that this very ugly woman was "the privileged Mrs. Grundy of the French capital during the ascendancy of Cardinal Richelieu," and after recounting some lively adventures, says "At eighty-six years of age Madame Pilau was near coming to an untimely end from lighting a taper at a poisoned candle, composed by some lackeys for the purpose of stupefying one of their comrades." She only recovered because of a physician's "prompt administration of an antidote." George Lyman Kittredge, in *Witchcraft* (1929), p. 347, tells of a poisoned candle made by one Roland Jenks in 1579.

8. Compare "Tamerlane," line 57, "Rendered me mad and deaf and blind."

9. The supernatural blow recalls an incident in the *Iliad,* where Apollo disabled Patroclus. In Pope's *Iliad,* XVI, 954, we read:

> For lo! the God in dusky clouds enshrin'd,
> Approaching, dealt a staggering blow behind.

To Poe's earlier version of "The Imp of the Perverse" the original Greek, *Iliad,* XVI, 791–792, is even closer:

> *Στῆ δ'ὄπιθε, πλῆξέν τε μετάφρενον, εὐρέε τ'ὤμω*
> *Χειρὶ καταπρηνεῖ. στρεφεδίνηθεν δέ οἱ ὄσσε.*

There is evidence in "A Reviewer Reviewed" that Poe remembered lines from Homer as late as 1849.

10. Compare "The Tell-Tale Heart" at n. 13 and the excerpt (p. 790) from Webster's speech referred to in that note.

THE FACTS IN THE CASE OF M. VALDEMAR

This repulsive masterpiece develops further one of the themes – mesmerism of the dying – previously used in "Mesmeric Revelation." It is not surprising to learn that at least one editor rejected it,* but it is surprising that many early readers believed the story, which Poe had never expected.

The setting of Poe's story comes from a factual letter from Dr. A. Sidney Doane of 32 Warren Street, New York, printed in the *Broadway Journal* of February 1, 1845, of which the more pertinent portions may be quoted:

> On the 16th of January I was requested by my friend Dr. S. Vital Bodinier, recently from Paris, to witness the extirpation of a tumor from the neck of a female, which he said would be performed without her consciousness, and without suffering, "while she was in a *magnetic sleep,*" he having operated twice under similar circumstances in Paris, and with success.
>
> ... I went to No. – Chambers street, previous to the hour appointed for the operation (which was half-past one), in order to witness the process of putting the female to sleep. After being in the house about five minutes, the patient came into the basement room and seated herself in an easy chair. She seemed extremely bright and nowise sleepy, with a rosy cheek, black eyes, and dark hair. After an inquiry or two as to her health, and feeling her pulse, which was natural, Dr. B. proceeded to make what are termed "magnetic passes," and so successfully, that in five minutes the eyelids drooped, and in ten minutes – say at twenty minutes of twelve – she was sound asleep. I learned from Dr. B. that she had been placed in this state some ten or twelve times previously, with a view to secure her entire insensibility ... I left the patient at twelve o'clock, still sleeping soundly.
>
> I returned to the house at quarter past one, in company with Prof. J. W. Francis and Mr. J. S. Redfield, the publisher. A few moments after, we were joined by Drs. Mott, Delafield, J. Kearney Rodgers, Taylor, Nelson, Dr. Alfaro, a highly distinguished physician from Madrid, Mr. Parmly the dentist, and one or two others. Descending to the basement, we found the patient still asleep ... [The tumor] was the size of a pullet's egg, and the operation occupied two and a half minutes only ... [The patient] continued to sleep on quietly and calmly through the whole of it. Dr. Bodinier seemed to be operating rather upon a cadaver than on a living being ... I ... went again to the house at ten minutes past four. She was still sleeping, but at quarter past four, the time indicated, she was *demagnetized* by Dr. B., Drs. Taylor, Parmly, and others being present. I im-

* Poe refers to the rejection in the still unprinted manuscript, "The Living Writers of America" (now in the Pierpont Morgan Library), but he does not name the editor.

mediately inquired, "How she felt?" She answered, "rather tired." "Had she suffered during her sleep?" She said, "No." "Had she been cut?" She replied "No, the operation was to be performed the next day," as Dr. B. had previously stated to her would be the case. She was now shown the tumor, at which she seemed much surprised and gratified. Since that time the patient has recovered rapidly, and to-day, Thursday, one week since the operation, the wound is entirely healed, and she has resumed her duties in the family.

Another probable source is a statement in the fourth edition (London, 1844) of Chauncey Hare Townshend's *Facts in Mesmerism* – a work for which Poe had high regard. In his "Notice" to that edition (p. xvi) Townshend said:

I have watched the effects of mesmeric treatment upon a suffering friend, who was dying of that most fearful disorder – Lumbar Abscess. Unfortunately, through various hindrances, Mesmerism was not resorted to till late in the progress of the disease, so that, of course, that it should effect a cure was out of the question . . . I have no hesitation in saying, that, under God, the life of my friend, R. T. was prolonged, at least, two months by the action of Mesmerism.†

A third source, pointed out as long ago as 1855,‡ is the conclusion (p. 119) of *The Seeress of Prevorst* (1845), translated by Catherine Crowe from the German of Justinus Andreas Kerner – poet, spiritualist, and chief physician of Weinsberg. He described the death of the Seeress:

She often called loudly for me, though I was absent at the time; and once, when she appeared dead, someone having uttered my name, she started into life again, and seemed unable to die, – the magnetic relation between us being not yet broken. She was, indeed, susceptible to magnetic influences, to the last; for, when she was already cold and her jaws stiff, her mother having made three passes over her face, she lifted her eyelids and moved her lips. At ten o'clock, her sister saw a tall bright form enter the chamber, and, at the same instant, the dying woman uttered a loud cry of joy; her spirit then seemed to be set free. After a short interval, her soul also departed; leaving behind it a totally irrecognizable husk – not a single trace of her former features remaining.

An American edition of *The Seeress of Prevorst* in paper covers, published by Harper & Brothers, was advertised in the *Broadway Journal* of August 2, 1845, for twenty-five cents.

The climate of belief in the wonderful accomplishments of Dr. Mesmer has been mentioned in my introduction to "Mes-

† Quoted by Lind in "Poe and Mesmerism," cited on p. 1024 above.

‡ In an anonymous work, *Rambles and Reveries of an Art-Student* (Philadelphia, Thomas T. Watts, 1855), pp. 37f.

meric Revelation." The far wilder tale of the imaginary Valdemar found credence too. A writer in the *New-York Daily Tribune* of December 10, 1845, observed that the story was "of course a romance" but that "several good matter-of-fact citizens" had been sorely puzzled by it. He concluded, "It is a pretty good specimen of Poe's style of giving an air of reality to fictions . . . but whoever thought it a veracious recital must have the bump of Faith large, very large indeed."

Poe reprinted the paragraph from the *Tribune* in the *Broadway Journal* of December 13, 1845, with an ironical rejoinder:

> For our parts we find it difficult to understand how any dispassionate transcendentalist can doubt the facts as we state them; they are by no means so incredible as the marvels which are hourly narrated, and believed, on the topic of Mesmerism. *Why* cannot a man's death be postponed indefinitely by Mesmerism? *Why* cannot a man talk after he is dead? *Why? – Why?* – that is the question; and as soon as the Tribune has answered it to our satisfaction we will talk to it farther.

The author followed this up by reprinting his story in the *Broadway Journal* of December 20, 1845, with a quizzical introduction:

> *The Facts in the case of M. Valdemar.*
>
> An article of ours, thus entitled, was published in the last number of Mr. Colton's "American Review," and has given rise to some discussion – especially in regard to the truth or falsity of the statements made. It does not become *us*, of course, to offer one word on the point at issue. We have been requested to reprint the article, and do so with pleasure. We leave it to speak for itself. We may observe, however, that there are a certain class of people who pride themselves upon Doubt, as a profession. – *Ed. B. J.*

Meanwhile, on December 16, 1845, Robert Collyer, the eminent Mesmerist, wrote Poe from Boston: "Your account of M. Valdemar's case has been universally copied in this city, and has created a very great sensation." He requested a reply "for publication, in order to put at rest the growing impression that your account is merely a *splendid creation* of your own brain, not having any truth in fact." Collyer added that he had sent an account to London for a spiritualist periodical called *The Zoist,* which apparently disregarded it. Poe printed Collyer's letter in the *Broadway Journal* of December 27, 1845, with an amusing reply:

We have not doubt that Mr. Collyer is perfectly correct in all that he says – and all that he desires us to say – but the truth is, there was a very small modicum of truth in the case of M. Valdemar – which, in consequence, may be called a hard case – *very* hard for M. Valdemar, for Mr. Collyer, and ourselves. If the story was not true, however, it should have been – and perhaps "The Zoist" may discover that it *is* true after all.

The British press, whether alerted by Collyer or someone else, was soon busy. The *London Morning Post* on January 5, 1846 printed the story from the *American Review,* with a heading "Mesmerism in America," including a suggestion that it was fiction.§ But the weekly *Popular Record of Modern Science* (which had previously reprinted "Mesmeric Revelation"), in the issue of January tenth reprinted and gave some credence to the story of Valdemar.

It was then published as a pamphlet, *Mesmerism "in articulo mortis,"** with a prefatory note worth quoting:

Advertisement.

The following astonishing narrative first appeared in the *American Magazine,* a work of some standing in the United States, where the case has excited the most intense interest.

The effects of mesmeric influence, in this case, were so astounding, so contrary to all past experience, that no one could have possibly anticipated the final result. The narrative, though only a plain recital of facts, is of so extraordinary a nature as almost to surpass belief. It is only necessary to add, that credence is given to it in America, where the occurrence took place.

Nor was this all. On November 30, 1846, Arch Ramsay, "druggist, of Stonehaven," Scotland, wrote Poe, asking if the pamphlet was a hoax. In reply, the author wrote on December 30, 1846, " 'Hoax' *is* precisely the word suited to M. Valdemar's case... The article... is now circulating in France.† Some few persons believe it – but *I* do not – and don't you." On April 14, 1847, the obtuse Ramsay wrote, "I thought you could at once affirm or deny it... this appears not to be the case."‡

§ [An earlier appearance is now known to have been in the *Sunday Times* (London), January 4, 1846. This was located in 1974 by Ian Walker. Poe had written to Joseph M. Field, June 15, 1846, saying "The Times! – the matter of fact 'Times!' – copies the 'Valdemar Case.' "]

* This is the true first edition, though pirated; see below.

† No French version printed in Poe's lifetime has been found.

‡ Both of Ramsay's letters are printed by Harrison, 17:268 and 284.

The comment of Poe's friend Philip Pendleton Cooke was of another nature. He wrote on August 4, 1846:

> The "Valdemar Case" I read in a number of your Broadway Journal last winter – as I lay in a Turkey blind, muffled to the eyes in overcoats, &c., and pronounce it without hesitation the most damnable, vraisemblable, horrible, hair-lifting, shocking, ingenious chapter of fiction that any brain ever conceived, or hands traced. That gelatinous, viscous sound of man's voice! there never was such an idea before. The story scared me in broad day, armed with a double-barrel Tryon Turkey gun. What would it have done at midnight in some old ghostly country-house?§

On March 11, 1847, Poe wrote George W. Eveleth, " 'The Valdemar Case' was a hoax, of course."

In *Graham's Magazine* for March 1848 (pp. 178–179), Poe devoted an installment of his "Marginalia" to the reception abroad of the two stories of mesmerism of the dying.* He ridiculed both the *London Morning Post* and the *Popular Record* for discussions written confidently without any investigation in New York.

TEXTS

(A) American Review: A Whig Journal, December 1845 (2:561–565); *(B) Broadway Journal,* December 20, 1845 (2:365–368); *(C)* Mrs. Whitman's copy of the last with a manuscript revision, 1848; *(D) Works* (1850), I, 121–130.

Our text follows *C,* which was not available to Griswold; in it Poe corrected four of the twelve misprints, and in the last sentence changed putrescence to putridity.

Reprints

Spirit of the Times (Philadelphia), December 23, 24, 1845, from the *Broadway Journal;* and the following from the *American Review* (the first text): *Sunday Times* (London), January 4, 1846, as "Mesmerism in America: Astounding and Horrifying Narrative"; the *Morning Post* (London), January 5, 1846, as "Mesmerism in America"; the *Popular Record of Modern Science* (London), January 10, 1846, as "Mesmerism in America. Death of M. Valdemar of New York" (copied from the *Morning Post*); *Boston Museum,* August 18, 1849.

Separate Printing

MESMERISM/"in articulo mortis."/Astounding & Horrifying Narrative,/ shewing the extraordinary power of mesmerism/in arresting the/Progress of

§ Harrison, 17:262; Woodberry, *Life,* II, 205.

* This is the first item in Griswold's collection of the "Marginalia" (*Works,* III, 486–488), and number 200 in the present edition. Harrison inadvertently omitted it.

THE CASE OF M. VALDEMAR

Death./By Edgar A. Poe, Esq./of New York. London: Short & Co., 8, King Street, Bloomsbury, 1846. 16 pp.

Reprints Not Located

The copies referred to by Collyer in his letter quoted in the introduction have not yet been found.

Philip Pendleton Cooke, in an article on Poe in *SLM*, January 1848, says, "The editor of the Baltimore Visiter republished it as a statement of facts, and was at pains to vouch for Mr. Poe's veracity."

THE FACTS IN THE CASE OF M. VALDEMAR. [*C*]

Of course I shall not pretend to consider it any matter for wonder, that the extraordinary case of M. Valdemar has excited discussion. It would have been a miracle had it not — especially under the circumstances. Through the desire of all parties concerned, to keep the affair from the public, at least for the present, or until we had farther opportunities for investigation — through our endeavors to effect this — a garbled or exaggerated account made its way into society, and became the source of many unpleasant misrepresentations, and, very naturally, of a great deal of disbelief.

It is now rendered necessary that I give the *facts* — as far as I comprehend them myself. They are, succinctly, these:

My attention, for the last three years, had been repeatedly drawn to the subject of Mesmerism; and, about nine months ago, it occurred to me, quite suddenly, that in the series of experiments made hitherto, there had been a very remarkable and most unaccountable omission: — no person had as yet been mesmerized *in articulo mortis*. It remained to be seen, first, whether, in such condition, there existed in the patient any susceptibility to the magnetic influence; secondly, whether, if any existed, it was impaired or increased by the condition; thirdly, to what extent, or for how long a period, the encroachments of Death might be arrested by the process. There were other points to be ascertained, but these most excited my curiosity — the last in especial, from the immensely important character of its consequences.

Title: The Facts of M. Valdemar's Case (*A*)

In looking around me for some subject by whose means I might test these particulars, I was brought to think of my friend, M. Ernest Valdemar, the well-known compiler of the "Bibliotheca Forensica," and author (under the *nom de plume* of Issachar Marx) of the Polish versions of "Wallenstein" and "Gargantua."[1] M. Valdemar, who has resided principally at Harlaem,[a] N. Y., since the year 1839, is (or was) particularly noticeable for the extreme spareness of his person – his lower limbs much resembling those of John Randolph;[2] and, also, for the whiteness of his whiskers, in violent contrast to the blackness of his hair – the latter, in consequence, being very generally mistaken for a wig. His temperament was markedly nervous, and rendered him a good subject for mesmeric experiment. On two or three occasions I had put him to sleep with little difficulty, but was disappointed in other results which his peculiar constitution had naturally led me to anticipate. His will was at no period positively, or thoroughly, under my control, and in regard to *clairvoyance,* I could accomplish with him nothing to be relied upon. I always attributed my failure at these points to the disordered state of his health. For some months previous to my becoming acquainted with him, his physicians had declared him in a confirmed phthisis. It was his custom, indeed, to speak calmly of his approaching dissolution, as of a matter neither to be avoided nor regretted.

When the ideas to which I have alluded first occurred to me, it was of course very natural that I should think of M. Valdemar. I knew the steady philosophy of the man too well to apprehend any scruples from *him;* and he had no relatives in America who would be likely to interfere. I spoke to him frankly upon the subject; and, to my surprise, his interest seemed vividly excited. I say to my surprise; for, although he had always yielded his person freely to my experiments, he had never before given me any tokens of sympathy with what I did. His disease was of that character which would admit of exact calculation in respect to the epoch of its termination in death; and it was finally arranged between us that he would send for me about twenty-four hours before the period announced by his physicians as that of his decease.

a Harlem, *(D)*

THE CASE OF M. VALDEMAR

It is now rather more than seven months since I received, from M. Valdemar himself, the subjoined note:

MY DEAR P——,

You may as well come *now*. D—— and F——[3] are agreed that I cannot hold out beyond to-morrow midnight; and I think they have hit the time very nearly.

VALDEMAR.

I received this note within half an hour after it was written, and in fifteen minutes more I was in the dying man's chamber. I had not seen him for ten days, and was appalled by the fearful alteration which the brief interval had wrought in him. His face wore a leaden hue; the eyes were utterly lustreless; and the emaciation was so extreme that the skin had been broken through by the cheek-bones. His expectoration was excessive. The pulse was barely perceptible. He retained, nevertheless, in a very remarkable manner, both his mental power and a certain degree of physical strength. He spoke with distinctness — took some palliative medicines without aid — and, when I entered the room, was occupied in penciling memoranda in a pocket-book.[4] He was propped up in the bed by pillows. Doctors D——and F——were in attendance.

After pressing Valdemar's hand, I took these gentlemen aside, and obtained from them a minute account of the patient's condition. The left lung had been for eighteen months in a semi-osseous or cartilaginous state, and was, of course, entirely useless for all purposes of vitality. The right, in its upper portion, was also partially, if not thoroughly, ossified, while the lower region was merely a mass of purulent tubercles, running one into another. Several extensive perforations existed; and, at one point, permanent adhesion to the ribs had taken place. These appearances in the right lobe were of comparatively recent date. The ossification had proceeded with very unusual rapidity; no sign of it had been discovered a month before, and the adhesion had only been observed during the three previous days. Independently of the phthisis, the patient was suspected of aneurism of the aorta; but on this point the osseous symptoms rendered an exact diagnosis impossible. It was the opinion of both physicians that M. Valdemar would die about midnight on the morrow (Sunday). It was then seven o'clock on Saturday evening.

On quitting the invalid's bed-side to hold conversation with myself, Doctors D——and F——had bidden him a final farewell. It had not been their intention to return; but, at my request, they agreed to look in upon the patient about ten the next night.

When they had gone, I spoke freely with M. Valdemar on the subject of his approaching dissolution, as well as, more particularly, of the experiment proposed. He still professed himself quite willing and even anxious to have it made, and urged me to commence it at once. A male and a female nurse were in attendance; but I did not feel myself altogether at liberty to engage in a task of this character with no more reliable witnesses than these people, in case of sudden accident, might prove. I therefore postponed operations until about eight the next night, when the arrival of a medical student with whom I had some acquaintance, (Mr. Theodore L——l,)[5] relieved me from farther embarrassment. It had been my design, originally, to wait for the physicians; but I was induced to proceed, first, by the urgent entreaties of M. Valdemar, and secondly, by my conviction that I had not a moment to lose, as he was evidently sinking fast.

Mr. L——l was so kind as to accede to my desire that he would take notes of all that occurred; and it is from his memoranda that what I now have to relate is, for the most part, either condensed or copied *verbatim.*

It wanted about five minutes[b] of eight when, taking the patient's hand, I begged him to state, as distinctly as he could, to Mr. L——l, whether he (M. Valdemar) was entirely willing that I should make the experiment of mesmerizing him in his then condition.

He replied feebly, yet quite audibly, "Yes, I wish to be mesmerized" — adding immediately afterwards, "I fear you have deferred it too long."

While he spoke thus, I commenced the passes which I had already found most effectual in subduing him. He was evidently

---

b minntes *(B, C) misprint*

influenced with the first lateral stroke of my hand across his forehead; but although I exerted all my powers, no farther perceptible effect was induced until some minutes after ten o'clock, when Doctors D——and F——called, according to appointment. I explained to them, in a few words, what I designed, and as they opposed no objection, saying that the patient was already in the death agony, I proceeded without hesitation – exchanging, however, the lateral passes for downward ones, and directing my gaze entirely into the right eye of the sufferer.

By this time his pulse was imperceptible and his breathing was stertorous,[c] and at intervals of half a minute.

This condition was nearly unaltered for a quarter of an hour. At the expiration of this period, however, a natural although a[d] very deep sigh escaped the bosom of the dying man, and the stertorous[e] breathing ceased – that is to say, its stertorousness[f] was no longer apparent; the intervals were undiminished. The patient's extremities were of an icy coldness.

At five minutes[g] before eleven I perceived unequivocal signs of the mesmeric influence. The glassy roll of the eye was changed[h] for that expression of uneasy *inward* examination which is never seen except in cases of sleep-waking,[6] and which it is quite impossible to mistake. With a few rapid lateral passes I made the lids quiver, as in incipient sleep, and with a few more I closed them altogether. I was not satisfied, however, with this, but continued the manipulations vigorously, and with the fullest exertion of the will, until I had completely stiffened the limbs of the slumberer, after placing them in a seemingly easy position. The legs were at full length; the arms were nearly so, and reposed on[i] the bed at a moderate distance from the loins. The head was very slightly elevated.

When I had accomplished this, it was fully midnight, and I requested the gentlemen present to examine M. Valdemar's condition. After a[j] few experiments, they admitted him to be in an

---

c stertorious, *(D)*
d Omitted *(A)*
e stertorious *(D)*
f stertoriousness *(D)*
g miutes *(B, C) misprint*
h exchanged *(A)*
i upon *(A)*
j a very *(A)*

unusually[k] perfect state of mesmeric trance. The curiosity of both the physicians was greatly excited. Dr. D——resolved at once to remain with the patient all night, while Dr. F——took leave with a promise to return at day-break. Mr. L——l[l] and the nurses remained.

We left M. Valdemar entirely undisturbed until about three o'clock in the morning, when I approached him and found him in precisely the same condition as when Dr. F—— went away — that is to say, he lay in the same position; the pulse was imperceptible; the breathing was gentle (scarcely noticeable, unless through the application of a mirror to the lips); the eyes were closed naturally; and the limbs were as rigid and as cold as marble. Still, the general appearance was certainly not that of death.

As I approached M. Valdemar I made a kind of half effort to influence his right arm into pursuit of my own, as I passed the latter gently to and fro above his person. In such experiments with this patient I had never perfectly succeeded before, and assuredly I had little thought of succeeding now; but to my astonishment, his arm very readily, although feebly, followed every direction I assigned it with mine. I determined to hazard a few words of conversation.

"M. Valdemar," I said, "are you asleep?" He made[m] no answer, but I perceived a tremor about the lips, and was thus induced to repeat the question, again and again. At its third repetition, his whole frame was agitated by a very slight shivering; the eye-lids unclosed themselves so far as to display a white line of the[n] ball; the lips moved sluggishly, and from between them, in a barely audible whisper, issued the words:

"Yes; — asleep now. Do not wake me! — let me die so!"

I here felt the limbs and found them as rigid as ever. The right arm, as before, obeyed the direction of my hand. I questioned the sleep-waker again:

"Do you still feel pain in the breast, M. Valdemar?"

The answer now was immediate, but even less audible than before:

---

k unusally *(B, C) misprint*
l L —— l/L ——— *(A)*
m made me *(A)*
n a *(D) misprint*

"No pain — I am dying."

I did not think it advisable to disturb him farther just then, and nothing more was said or done until the arrival of Dr. F——, who came a little before sunrise, and expressed unbounded astonishment at finding the patient still alive. After feeling the pulse and applying a mirror to the lips, he requested me to speak to[o] the sleep-waker again. I did so, saying:

"M. Valdemar, do you still sleep?"

As before, some minutes elapsed ere a reply was made; and during the interval the dying man seemed to be collecting his energies to speak. At my fourth repetition of the question, he said very faintly, almost inaudibly:

"Yes; still asleep — dying."

It was now the opinion, or rather the wish, of the physicians, that M. Valdemar should be suffered to remain undisturbed in his present apparently tranquil condition, until death should supervene — and this, it was generally agreed, must now take place within a few minutes. I concluded, however, to speak to him once more, and merely repeated my previous question.

While I spoke, there came a marked change over the countenance of the sleep-waker. The eyes rolled themselves slowly open, the pupils disappearing upwardly; the skin generally assumed a cadaverous hue, resembling not so much parchment as white paper; and the circular hectic spots which, hitherto, had been strongly defined in the centre of each cheek, *went out* at once. I use this expression, because the suddenness of their departure put me in mind of nothing so much as the extinguishment of a candle by a puff of the breath. The upper lip, at the same time, writhed itself away from the teeth, which it had previously covered completely;[7] while the lower jaw fell with an audible jerk, leaving the mouth widely extended, and disclosing in full view the swollen and blackened tongue. I presume that no member of the party then present had been unaccustomed to death-bed horrors; but so hideous beyond conception was the appearance of M. Valdemar at this moment, that there was a general shrinking back from the region of the bed.

---

o with *(A)*

I now feel that I have reached a point of this narrative at which every reader will be startled into positive disbelief. It is my business, however, simply to proceed.

There was no longer the faintest sign of vitality in M. Valdemar; and concluding him to be dead, we were consigning him to the charge of the nurses, when a strong vibratory motion was observable in the tongue. This continued for perhaps a minute. At the expiration of this period, there issued from the distended and motionless jaws a voice — such as it would be madness in me to attempt describing. There are, indeed, two or three epithets which might be considered as applicable to it in part; I might say, for example, that the sound was harsh, and broken and hollow; but the hideous whole is indescribable, for the simple reason that no similar sounds have ever jarred upon the ear of humanity. There were two particulars, nevertheless, which I thought then, and still think, might fairly be stated as characteristic of the intonation — as well adapted to convey some idea of its unearthly peculiarity. In the first place, the voice seemed to reach our ears — at least mine — from a vast distance, or from some deep cavern within the earth.[p8] In the second place, it impressed me (I fear, indeed, that it will be impossible to make myself comprehended) as gelatinous or glutinous matters impress the sense of touch.

I have spoken both of "sound" and of "voice." I mean to say that the sound was one of distinct — of even wonderfully, thrillingly distinct — syllabification.[q] M. Valdemar *spoke* — obviously in reply to the question I had propounded to him a few minutes before. I had asked him, it will be remembered, if he still slept. He now said:

"Yes; — no; — I *have been* sleeping — and now — now — *I am dead.*"

No person present even affected to deny, or attempted to repress, the unutterable,[r] shuddering horror which these few words, thus uttered, were so well calculated to convey. Mr. L——l (the student) swooned. The nurses immediately left the chamber, and could not be induced to return. My own impressions I would

p earth, *(B, C) misprint*
q syllibification. *(D) misprint*
r unuterable, *(B) misprint, corrected in C*

not pretend to render intelligible to the reader. For nearly an hour, we busied ourselves, silently — without the utterance of a word — in endeavors to revive Mr.[s] L——l. When he came to himself, we addressed ourselves again to an investigation of M. Valdemar's condition.

It remained in all respects as I have last described it, with the exception that the mirror no longer afforded evidence of respiration. An attempt to draw blood from the arm[t] failed. I should mention, too, that this limb was no farther subject to my will. I endeavored in vain to make it follow the direction of my hand. The only real indication,[u] indeed, of the mesmeric influence, was now found in the vibratory movement of the tongue, whenever I addressed M. Valdemar a question. He seemed to be making an effort at reply, but had no longer sufficient volition. To queries put to him by any other person than myself he seemed utterly insensible — although I[v] endeavored to place each member of the company in mesmeric *rapport* with him. I believe that I have now related all that is necessary to an understanding of the sleep-waker's state at this epoch. Other nurses were procured; and at ten o'clock I left the house in company with the two physicians and Mr. L——l.

In the afternoon we all called again to see the patient. His condition remained precisely the same. We had now some discussion as to the propriety and feasibility of awakening him; but we had little difficulty in agreeing that no good purpose would be served by so doing. It was evident that, so far, death (or what is usually termed death) had been arrested by the mesmeric process. It seemed clear to us all that to awaken M. Valdemar would be merely to insure his instant, or at least his speedy dissolution.

From this period until the close of last week — *an interval of nearly seven months* — we continued to make daily calls at M. Valdemar's house, accompanied, now and then, by medical and other friends. All this time the sleep-waker remained *exactly* as I have last described him. The nurses' attentions were continual.

It was on Friday last that we finally resolved to make the ex-

s Mr, *(B, C) misprint*
t arm *not clear (B) corrected in C*
u indicatiom *(B, C) misprint*
v I *missing (B) corrected in C*

periment of awakening, or attempting to awaken him; and it is the (perhaps) unfortunate result of this latter experiment which has given rise to so much discussion in private circles – to so much of what I cannot help thinking unwarranted popular feeling.[w]

For the purpose of relieving M. Valdemar from the mesmeric trance, I made use of the customary passes. These, for a time, were unsuccessful. The first indication of revival was afforded by a partial descent of the iris. It was observed, as especially remarkable, that this lowering of the pupil was accompanied by the profuse out-flowing of a yellowish ichor (from beneath the lids) of a pungent and highly offensive odor.

It now was[x] suggested that I should[y] attempt to influence the patient's arm, as heretofore. I made the attempt and failed. Dr. F––then intimated a desire to have me put a question. I did so as follows:

"M. Valdemar, can you explain to us what are your feelings or wishes now?"

There was an instant return of the hectic circles on the cheeks; the tongue quivered, or rather rolled violently in the mouth (although the jaws and lips remained rigid as before;) and at length the same hideous voice which I have already described, broke forth:

"For God's sake! – quick! – quick! – put me to sleep – or, quick! – waken me! – quick! – *I say to you that I am dead!*"[9]

I was thoroughly unnerved, and for an instant remained undecided what to do. At first I made an endeavor to re-compose the patient; but, failing in this through total abeyance of the will, I retraced my steps and as earnestly struggled to awaken him. In this attempt I soon saw that I should be successful – or at least I soon fancied that my success would be complete – and I am sure that all in the room were prepared to see the patient awaken.

For what really occurred, however, it is quite impossible that any human being could have been prepared.

As I rapidly made the mesmeric passes,[z] amid ejaculations of

---

w eeling. *(B) misprint, corrected in C*

x now was/was now *(A)*

y sdould *(B, C) misprint*

z pasess, *(B, C) misprint*

"dead! dead!" absolutely *bursting* from the tongue and not from the lips of the sufferer, his whole frame at once — within the space of a single minute, or even less, shrunk — crumbled — absolutely *rotted* away beneath my hands. Upon the bed, before that whole company, there lay a nearly liquid mass of loathsome — of detestable putridity.[a10]

NOTES

Title: The name Valdemar may have been suggested by mention in the *Southern Literary Messenger,* July 1835, of a play, "Valdemar, or the German Exiles, by Mr. T –, actor, scene-painter and tavern-keeper of Montreal," in an article, "My First Night in a Watchhouse," by Edward V. Sparhawk. This mention was pointed out to me by David K. Jackson. Mrs. Nellie Reiss, reference librarian of McGill University, found that *Waldemar* by Mr. Turnbull was often performed about 1821 in Montreal. Turnbull came from England to Boston about 1799, and later settled in Canada. He is clearly the "Mr. T –" mentioned by Sparhawk, for his scene-painting is recorded.

1. Poe's original *may* have been Piero Maroncelli (1795–August 1, 1846). He was a translator (from the Italian) and in 1846, according to Poe's sketch in "The Literati" (*Godey's,* June 1846), was "suffering from severe illness, and from this it can scarcely be expected that he will recover." See Angeline H. Lograsso, "Poe's Piero Maroncelli" (*PMLA,* September 1943). The "Bibliotheca Forensica" is made up, and its compiler's pseudonym is jocular; Issachar means "He brings gifts," but in Genesis 49:14, we are told that Jacob, blessing his sons, said, "Issachar is a strong ass, couching down between two burdens." Schiller's tragedy, and the work of Rabelais, in Poe's opinion, were burdensome.

2. Poe must have himself seen the cadaverous Virginia statesman, John Randolph of Roanoke (1773–1833), who was often in Richmond.

3. Readers may well have expanded P as Poe; F as Dr. John W. Francis, president of the Academy of Medicine and one of Poe's Literati, who was the poet's own physician; and D as Dr. John W. Draper, the best-known professor in the Medical School of New York University. Poe did not like Draper, who is mentioned slightingly in "Von Kempelen and His Discovery." According to Poe's letter of June 26, 1849 to Eveleth, Draper was satirized in *Eureka.*

4. A pocket-book here means a notebook, as usual at the time, as in "Diddling."

5. L — — l has not been identified.

6. Sleep-waking is the mesmeric state, not a misprint for sleep-walking, as was sometimes supposed in England. See "Mesmeric Revelation," n. 1.

---

a putrescence. *(A, B, D)*

7. Compare "Berenicë": "The teeth . . . with the pale lips writhing about them"; and "The Pit and the Pendulum": "I saw the lips of the black-robed judges . . . I saw them writhe with a deadly locution."

8. Roderick Usher painted a picture of "a vault or tunnel" which suggested that "this excavation lay at an exceeding depth below the surface of the earth."

9. With the passage above, beginning with "It was on Friday last," compare the account quoted from *The Seeress of Prevorst* in the introduction above.

10. This gruesome passage has a parallel in the thirteenth chapter of *Arthur Gordon Pym.*

THEATRICAL RATS

The rats infesting the leading theater of New York were well known and frequently mentioned in the press. In the *New Mirror* of July 15, 1843, there was a dull satirical story about them signed "B." – "RATS ATTEND! MASS MEETING AT THE PARK THEATRE . . . Your rights are in jeopardy! Your privileges are threatened!" – and so on; and on October 31, 1845, the *Evening Mirror* printed a note describing a man with a French inscription on his hat – *"Mort aux Rats!"* – carrying a pole with several dead rats hanging from it and some cages with live ones at his side, obviously seeking patronage. The note ended with the quip, "Will no one send him to the Park Theatre?"

The following paragraph was printed in a column headed "The Drama" in the *Broadway Journal* of November 1, 1845 (2:259–260). Poe was then its sole editor, and hence obviously the author of the "quaint and curious" little *jeu d'esprit.*

[THEATRICAL RATS]

The well-known company of rats at the Park Theatre understand, it is said, their cue perfectly. It is worth the price of admission to see their performance. By long training they know precisely the time when the curtain rises, and the exact degree in which the audience is spellbound by what is going on. At the sound of the bell they sally out; scouring the pit for chance peanuts and orange-peel. When, by the rhyming couplets, they are made aware that the curtain is about to fall, they disappear — through respect for the moving heels of the audience. Their temerity is regulated by the intensity of the performers. A profitable engagement might be made, we think, with "the celebrated Dog Billy."[1]

NOTES

1. The dog was in the act of William Cole, a contortionist, known as the India Rubber Man, or the Chinese Nondescript, who appeared at P. T. Barnum's American Museum in 1844 and 1845. There are numerous references to Cole's "sagacious" or "wonderful" dog in the newspapers of the time. For examples see the *Sunday Times,* April 14, 1844; the *New-York Tribune,* March 1, 1845; G. C. D. Odell, *Annals of the New York Stage,* IV, 333, 417, and passim. An advertisement in the *Sunday Times and Messenger,* May 5, 1844, calls him "the dog Billy."

THE SPHINX

This slight story is based mainly on the old idea that things are not always what they seem, and a realization that our senses may sometimes mislead us even when they function normally. It is not surprising that an imaginative author should reflect on relative size. Giants and dwarfs are the themes of countless folk stories — and of *Gulliver's Travels.* Poe presents us with a monster horrendous indeed.

Poe's chief source was the book he had helped compile, Thomas Wyatt's *Synopsis of Natural History* (1839), which he quoted directly in the story below.* There is a remote connection between the sphinx and the beetle in "The Gold-Bug," but the latter is partly made up, and the sphinx exists in nature.

The story is of some biographical interest, as it is the only article Poe is known to have sold to his friend Timothy Shay Arthur, who published it in his magazine about December 15, 1845 and reprinted it in his *Home Magazine* for November 1855.† The story was also reproduced in *The American Keepsake for*

* For Wyatt's book, see "The Murders in the Rue Morgue," n. 35.

† See Warren G. French, "T. S. Arthur . . . Champion of Poe," in *Tennessee Studies in Literature,* 5:35–41 (1960).

1851, an annual that included two stories by Arthur, author of *Ten Nights in a Barroom;* this circumstance suggests that Anna Wilmot, who edited the gift book, may have obtained Poe's tale from Arthur.

TEXTS

(A) Arthur's Ladies' Magazine for January 1846 (5: 15–16); *(B) The American Keepsake for 1851,* pp. 50–56; *(C) Works* (1850), II, 433–438.

The Griswold version *(C)* showing several auctorial revisions is followed.

THE SPHINX. [*C*]

DURING the dread reign of the Cholera in New-York,[1] I had accepted the invitation of a relative to spend a fortnight with him in the retirement of his *cottage orné*[a] on the banks of the Hudson. We had here around us all the ordinary means of summer amusement; and what with rambling in the woods, sketching, boating, fishing, bathing, music and books, we should have passed the time pleasantly enough, but for the fearful intelligence which reached us every morning from the populous city. Not a day elapsed which did not bring us news of the decease of some acquaintance. Then, as the fatality increased, we learned to expect daily the loss of some friend. At length we trembled at the approach of every messenger. The very air from the South seemed to us redolent with death.[2] That palsying thought, indeed, took entire possession of my soul. I could neither speak, think, nor dream of anything else. My host was of a less excitable temperament, and, although greatly depressed in spirits, exerted himself to sustain my own. His richly philosophical intellect was not at any time affected by unrealities. To the substances of terror he was sufficiently alive, but of its shadows he had no apprehension.

His endeavors to arouse me from the condition of abnormal gloom into which I had fallen, were frustrated in[b] great measure, by certain volumes which I had found in his library. These were

a *ornée (A, B, C)* b in a *(B)*

of a character to force into germination whatever seeds of hereditary superstition lay latent in my bosom. I had been reading these books without his knowledge, and thus he was often at a loss to account for the forcible impressions which had been made upon my fancy.

A favorite topic with me was the popular belief in omens — a belief which, at this one epoch of my life, I was almost seriously disposed to defend. On this subject we had long and animated discussions — he maintaining the utter groundlessness of faith in such matters — I contending that a popular sentiment arising with absolute spontaneity — that is to say, without apparent traces of suggestion — had in itself the unmistakeable elements of truth, and was entitled to [c]much respect.[c]

The fact is, that soon after my arrival at the cottage, there had occurred to myself an incident so entirely inexplicable, and which had in it so much of the portentous character, that I might well have been excused for regarding it as an omen. It appalled, and at the same time so confounded and bewildered me, that many days elapsed before I could make up my mind to communicate the circumstance to my friend.

Near the close of an exceedingly warm day, I was sitting, book in hand, at an open window, commanding, through a long vista of the river banks, a view of a distant hill, the face of which nearest my position, had been denuded, by what is termed a land-slide, of the principal portion of its trees. My thoughts had been long wandering from the volume before me to the gloom and desolation of the neighboring city. Uplifting my eyes from the page, they fell upon the naked face of the hill, and upon an object — upon some living monster of hideous conformation, which very rapidly made its way from the summit to the bottom, disappearing finally in the dense forest below. As this creature first came in sight, I doubted my own sanity — or at least the evidence of my own eyes; and many minutes passed before I succeeded in convincing myself that I was neither mad nor in a dream. Yet when I describe the monster, (which I distinctly saw, and calmly surveyed through

---

c . . . c as much respect, as that intuition which is the idiosyncrasy of the individual man of genius. *(A, B)*

the whole period of its progress,) my readers, I fear, will feel more difficulty in being convinced of these points than even I did myself.

Estimating the size of the creature by comparison with the diameter of the large trees near which it passed — the few giants of the forest which had escaped the fury of the land-slide — I concluded it to be far larger than any ship of the line in existence. I say ship of the line, because the shape of the monster suggested the idea — the hull of one of our seventy-fours[4] might convey a very tolerable conception of the general outline. The mouth of the animal was situated at the extremity of a proboscis some sixty or seventy feet in length, and about as thick as the body of an ordinary elephant. Near the root of this trunk was an immense quantity of black shaggy hair — more than could have been supplied by the coats of a score of buffaloes; and projecting from this hair downwardly and laterally, sprang two gleaming tusks not unlike those of the wild boar, but of infinitely greater dimension. Extending forward, parallel with the proboscis, and on each side of it, was a gigantic staff, thirty or forty feet in length, formed seemingly of pure crystal, and in shape a perfect prism: — it reflected in the most gorgeous manner the rays of the declining sun. The trunk was fashioned like a wedge with the apex to the earth. From it there were outspread two pairs of wings — each wing nearly one hundred yards in length — one pair being placed above the other, and all thickly covered with metal scales; each scale apparently some ten or twelve feet in diameter. I observed that the upper and lower tiers of wings were connected by a strong chain. But the chief peculiarity of this horrible thing, was the representation of a *Death's Head,* which covered nearly the whole surface of its breast, and which was as accurately traced in glaring white, upon the dark ground of the body, as if it had been there carefully designed by an artist. While I regarded this terrific animal, and more especially the appearance on its breast, with a feeling of horror and awe — with a sentiment of forthcoming evil, which I found it impossible to quell by any effort of the reason, I perceived the huge jaws at the extremity of the proboscis, suddenly expand themselves, and from them there proceeded a sound so loud and so expressive of wo, that it struck upon my nerves like a knell, and as the monster disappeared at the foot of the hill, I fell at once, fainting, to the floor.

Upon recovering, my first impulse of course was, to inform my friend of what I had seen and heard — and I can scarcely explain what feeling of repugnance it was, which, in the end, operated to prevent me.

At length, one evening, some three or four days after the occurrence, we were sitting together in the room in[d] which I had seen the apparition — I occupying the same seat at the same window, and he lounging on a sofa near at hand. The association of the place and time impelled me to give him an account of the phenomenon. He heard me to the end — at first laughed heartily — and then lapsed into an excessively grave demeanor, as if my insanity was a thing beyond suspicion. At this instant I again had a distinct view of the monster — to which, with a shout of absolute terror, I now directed his attention. He looked eagerly — but maintained that he saw nothing — although I designated minutely the course of the creature, as it made its way down the naked face of the hill.

I was now immeasurably alarmed, for I considered the vision either as an omen of my death, or, worse, as the forerunner of an attack of mania. I threw myself passionately back in my chair, and for some moments buried my face in my hands. When I uncovered my eyes, the apparition was no longer visible.[e]

My host, however, had in some degree resumed the calmness of his demeanor, and questioned me very rigorously[f] in respect to the conformation of the visionary creature. When I had fully satisfied him on this head, he sighed deeply, as if relieved of some intolerable burden, and went on to talk, with what I thought a cruel calmness, of various points of speculative philosophy, which had heretofore formed subject of discussion between us. I remember his insisting very especially (among other things) upon the idea that the[g] principal source of error in all human investigations, lay in the liability of the understanding to under-rate or to over-

d *Omitted (A)*
e apparent. *(A, B)*
f vigorously *(A, B)*
g a *(A, B)*

value the importance of an object, through mere misadmeasurement of its propinquity. "To estimate properly, for example," he said, "the influence to be exercised on mankind at large by the thorough diffusion of Democracy, the distance of the epoch at which such diffusion may possibly be accomplished, should not fail to form an item in the estimate.[5] Yet can you tell me one writer on the subject of government, who has ever thought this particular branch of the subject worthy of discussion at all?"

He here paused for a moment, stepped to a book-case, and brought forth one of the ordinary synopses of Natural History. Requesting me then to exchange seats with him, that he might the better distinguish the fine print of the volume, he took my arm-chair at the window, and, opening the book, resumed his discourse very much in the same tone as before.

"But for your exceeding minuteness," he said, "in describing the monster, I might never have had it in my power to demonstrate to you what it was. In the first place, let me read to you a school-boy account of the genus *Sphinx,* of the family *Crepuscularia,* of the order *Lepidoptera,* of the class of *Insecta* — or insects. The account runs thus:

" 'Four membranous wings covered with little colored scales of a metallic appearance; mouth forming a rolled proboscis, produced by an elongation of the jaws, upon the sides of which are found the rudiments of mandibles[h] and downy palpi; the inferior wings retained to the superior by a stiff hair; antennæ[i] in the form of an elongated club, prismatic; abdomen pointed. The Death's-headed Sphinx has occasioned much terror among the vulgar, at times, by the melancholy kind of cry which it utters, and the insignia of death which it wears upon its corslet.' "[6]

He here closed the book and leaned forward in the chair, placing himself accurately in the position which I had occupied at the moment of beholding "the monster."

"Ah, here it is!" he presently exclaimed — "it is reascending the face of the hill, and a very remarkable looking creature, I admit it to be. Still, it is by no means so large or so distant as you imag-

h manibles *(C) misprint, corrected from A, B*

i anteunœ *(A);* autennœ *(C) misprint, corrected from B*

ined it; for the fact is that, as it wriggles its way up this thread,[j] which some spider has wrought along the window-sash, I find it to be about the sixteenth of an inch in its extreme length, and also about the sixteenth of an inch distant from the pupil of my eye."

NOTES

1. When Poe wrote, the most recent epidemic of cholera in New York was that of 1832.

2. Compare Poe's "Serenade," lines 14–15, "And earth, and stars, and sea, and sky/Are redolent of sleep."

3. Compare this passage and its variant with Dupin's dictum in "The Mystery of Marie Rogêt" at the reference to n. 81: "Now, the popular opinion, under certain conditions, is not to be disregarded. When arising of itself – when manifesting itself in a strictly spontaneous manner – we should look upon it as analogous with that *intuition* which is the idiosyncrasy of the individual man of genius."

4. A seventy-four is a fighting ship with seventy-four guns.

5. If this is the sentiment of the author, as it well may be, it represents a considerable relaxation of the uncompromising statement in "The Colloquy of Monos and Una" five years before (p. 610 above): "Alas! we had fallen upon the most evil of all our evil days . . . Among other odd ideas, that of universal equality gained ground, and in the face of analogy and of God – in despite of the loud warning voice of the laws of *gradation* so visibly pervading all things in Earth and Heaven – wild attempts at an omni-prevalent Democracy were made." Nor is there here any of that satire of "suffrage *ad libitum*" we find in "Some Words with a Mummy" preceding n. 38. I take a view contrary to that of A. H. Quinn, who suggested (*Poe,* p. 499) that the author's purpose in the story was to criticize the dangers of democracy. The statement here is rather a gentle and philosophical admonition not to judge the democratic experiment too hastily, through a "misadmeasurement of its propinquity."

6. Poe abridges somewhat but otherwise quotes almost verbatim from the discussion of Insects in Thomas Wyatt's *Synopsis of Natural History,* pp. 138–139:

"ORDER VII. LEPIDOPTERA. Four membranous wings covered with little coloured scales; mouth forming a rolled proboscis, produced by an elongation of the jaws, upon the sides of which are found the rudiments of mandibles and downy palpi . . . FAMILY II. CREPUSCULARIA. Wings, . . . the inferior one retained to the superior by a stiff hair; antennæ in the form of an elongated club . . . GENUS SPHINX. Antennæ prismatic and terminating in hairs; wings long and horizontal; abdomen pointed. The Death's-headed Sphinx has occasioned much terror in certain countries by the kind of cry which it utters, and the insignia of death upon its corselet."

Compare the imaginary insect in "The Gold-Bug," and see Carroll Laverty in *American Literature,* March 1940.

---

j hair, *(A, B)*

TALES: 1845–1846

THE CASK OF AMONTILLADO

This is one of the undeniably great stories, by some critics regarded as the finest of all Poe's tales of horror. It is unsurpassed for subtly ironic touches. The theme is a successful crime, and to many readers it has merely the fascination of one of the unsolved murder stories perennially retold in Sunday newspapers. But Poe made it plain that a moral can be most effectively introduced into a story by subtlety; and "The Cask," on its surface completely amoral, is perhaps the most moral of his Tales. The murderer at the end remembers that his victim rests in peace. That is something the criminal had been unable to do for fifty years.

Poe probably had long considered a story of this kind. In reviewing for *Burton's Magazine,* February 1840, a novel called *The Spitfire* — one of the nautical tales of Frederick Chamier (1796–1870) — he wrote, "Villains do not always, nor even generally, meet with punishment and shame in reality, and we should have been pleased if Captain Chamier had courageously departed from this common-place fiction and uncommon reality, and exhibited the success of an impudent rogue . . . [instead of attempting to invest] the character of a pirate and a cut-throat with the attributes of a hero and a deserving man."

A challenge was offered here, as in the themes of "Berenicë" and "William Wilson." But it was several years before the challenge was met. In 1846 the occasion arose; a bitter quarrel developed between Poe and the cohorts of the vengeful Mrs. Ellet led by Thomas Dunn English and Hiram Fuller.* Fuller attacked Poe in a libelous article in the *New-York Mirror* for May 26; English, reacting to Poe's contemptuous "Literati" sketch in *Godey's* for July (on sale in mid-June), struck back venomously in the *Mirror* for June 23, and the hostilities continued for months. Poe longed for revenge, and indeed his extremely immoderate "Reply to English" (in the *Spirit of the Times* for

* See A. H. Quinn's account (*Poe,* chapter 16, especially pages 497–498 and 501–505); Poe's letters written to a number of friends between June 15, 1846 and March 11, 1847, with Professor Ostrom's illuminating notes; and on the Poe-English quarrel, T. O. Mabbott and W. H. Gravely, Jr., in the *Princeton University Library Chronicle,* V (1944), 107.

July 10) buried that worthy under an avalanche of words.† That "The Cask of Amontillado," published in the first issue of *Godey's* after the last installment of the "Literati" papers, was the working out of his immediate emotions can hardly be doubted.‡

Poe's story is skillfully told; the offenses of the victim are not revealed. There was insult, there was injury; one phrase about "the lady Fortunato" suggests that a woman may have been concerned. But were we fully informed about what Fortunato did our sympathies would be involved — we might pity him, or some might say "it served him right." As it is, we are merely spectators of a terrible incident. If pity and terror are aroused, it is by the darker side of human nature *per se,* exemplified in people whom we have not met.

Poe had an interest in burial alive,§ and knew of it as a punishment. Roman Vestal Virgins, so sacred that it was sacrilege to shed their blood, were immured if proved to be unchaste — something that almost never happened. In Scott's *Marmion,* the runaway nun, Constance de Beverley, captured in disguise as a pageboy, suffers this fate.*

Poe's most immediate source for this element of his tale, however, is obviously "A Man Built in a Wall," by Joel T. Headley, first published in the *Columbian Magazine* for August 1844 — the number containing Poe's "Mesmeric Revelation" — and collected in Headley's *Letters from Italy* (1845), a book advertised in the *Broadway Journal,* June 28, 1845.† Headley reported that in the Italian town of Don Giovanni, with a party of other visitors to the Church of St. Lorenzo, he was shown a niche in the church wall containing a skeleton discovered by workmen some years before

† Poe's "Reply," dated June 27, was sent to Godey, who "communicated" it to Du Solle and paid ten dollars for its publication.

‡ This was first pointed out by Albert Mordell in *The Erotic Motive in Literature* (1919), p. 233. The idea occurred independently to others and was developed — perhaps over-developed — by Francis B. Dedmond (*Modern Language Quarterly,* June 1954), who gives a detailed account of blows and counter-blows in the press and cites many other references.

§ Compare "Berenicë," "The Fall of the House of Usher," and "The Premature Burial."

* Scott's last note for Canto II tells of the bones of an immured person found in the ruins of the Abbey of Coldingham.

† Pointed out by Joseph S. Schick in *American Literature,* March 1934.

and left undisturbed. "The frame indicates a powerful man," says Headley,

> and though it is but a skeleton, the whole attitude and aspect give one the impression of a death of agony . . . An English physician was with me, and inured to skeletons as he was, his countenance changed as he gazed on it . . . he made no reply to the repeated questions I put him, but kept gazing, as if in a trance. It was not till after we left that he would speak of it, and then his voice was low and solemn, as if he himself had seen the living burial. Said he, *"That man died by suffocation,* and he was built up alive in that wall . . . He was packed into the rough wall, and built over, beginning at the feet" . . . By the dim light of lamps, whose rays scarcely reached the lofty ceiling, the stones were removed before the eyes of the doomed man, and measurement after measurement taken, to see if the aperture was sufficiently large . . . At length the opening was declared large enough, and he was lifted into it. The workman began at the feet, and with his mortar and trowel built up with the same carelessness he would exhibit in filling any broken wall. The successful enemy stood leaning on his sword – a smile of scorn and revenge on his features – and watched the face of the man he hated, but no longer feared . . . It was slow work fitting the pieces nicely, so as to close up the aperture with precision . . . With care and precision the last stone was fitted in the narrow space – the trowel passed smoothly over it – a stifled groan, as if from the centre of a rock, broke the stillness – one strong shiver, and all was over. The agony had passed – revenge was satisfied, and a secret locked up for the great revelation day.

A more famous story analogous to Poe's is "La Grande Bretêche" by Honoré de Balzac. This tells of a jealous husband who, learning that his wife's lover is hidden in a closet, had it walled up in the presence of the lady. An acknowledged adaptation of Balzac's story appeared in the *Democratic Review,* November 1843.

Another probable source has been pointed out in the story "Apropos of Bores" (*New-York Mirror,* December 2, 1837) "related by the late Joseph Jekyll, Esq." He had attended a party where a gentleman began by request to recount his adventure in the wine-vaults of Lincoln's Inn. Having secured safe cellarage there for several pipes of wine from Madeira, he went with a porter to visit the vast cellars of Lincoln's-Inn-square, twenty feet beneath the square and one hundred and fifty feet from "any dwelling, or populous resort." The pipes stored there were in perfect condition, but an accident occurred, extinguishing the visitors' candle. Groping in the dark, they found the door, but the porter turned the key "with such force that it snapped, the head remaining inextricably secured in the wards." When the seriousness of their predicament became clear the porter lamented bitterly, but then proposed "Let us stave in one of the wine-pipes . . . that we may forget, in the excitement of wine, the horrible death that awaits us." They decided against this step, but became more and more convinced that "our mortal remains would not be discovered, until every trace of identity was destroyed." The narrator finally remarked, "I seized the arm of my companion, and — "

Here one of the guests at the party, noted for his obtuseness, asked loudly, "How do you think, Jekyll, I should have got out?" "You would have bored your way out, to be sure," Jekyll answered. But at this moment the butler announced that "the ladies were waiting tea for us." Hence Jekyll never learned how the men in the vault escaped, but the story may well have contributed to Poe's underground descriptions.‡

On several occasions Poe took up a challenge to tell a story some other writer could not finish. Here he used from his several sources the vast vault, the pipe of wine, the bones, and the intoxication, but he transmuted his material as only a man of genius can.

The setting of Poe's story is not stated; to me it seems French, at a time when rapiers were still worn.§ The name of Poe's narrator, Montresor, is that of an old French family;* he lived in his ancestral domicile (although he did speak of it as "my palazzo") and he remarked that Fortunato was "in painting and gemmary . . . like his countrymen . . . a quack" — hardly what a fellow Italian would say.

Fortunato's name is significant, meaning fated as well as lucky;

‡ [Burton Pollin, *Discoveries in Poe,* pp. 24, 29–30, 31, makes a case for Poe's indebtedness to Victor Hugo's *Notre-Dame de Paris* both in its description of the "subterraneous vaults" used as dungeons below the Palais de Justice and in a brief single passage he thinks may have suggested to Poe the name Fortunato, the basic idea of self-destructive drunkenness, and the word "cask" in both title and plot.]

§ A good many people, however, have supposed that the scene was Italy; one even suggested that the locale was Venice.

* Montrésor — John — was also the name of a British military engineer with a long and distinguished service (1754–1778) in the American colonies, constructing fortifications. In the area of New York City he was regarded as a villain, said to be the original of Montraville, the fictional seducer of Charlotte Temple in Susannah Haswell Rowson's famous novel, and known to have been the bearer from Howe to the American lines of the news of the execution of Nathan Hale.

Luchesi's name is from that of a Baltimore personage discussed in my notes on "Why the Little Frenchman Wears His Hand in a Sling." Further comments on these names and on other details are to be found in the endnotes below. Mention of several supposed sources – really peripheral analogues – can be relegated to a footnote here.†

Poe's story was probably written in the late summer or early fall of 1846.

TEXTS

(A) Godey's Magazine and Lady's Book for November 1846 (33:216–218); *(B) Works* (1850), I, 346–352.

Griswold's version *(B)* is followed; it shows several important auctorial changes.

THE CASK OF AMONTILLADO. [*B*]

The thousand injuries of Fortunato I had borne as I best could; but when he ventured upon insult, I vowed revenge. You, who so well know the nature of my soul, will not suppose, however, that I gave utterance to a threat. *At length* I would be avenged; this was a point definitively settled – but the very definitiveness with which it was resolved[a] precluded the idea of risk. I must not only punish, but punish with impunity. A wrong is unredressed when retribution overtakes its redresser. It is equally unredressed when the avenger fails to make himself felt as such to him who has done the wrong.[1]

† Dedmond (*N & Q*, London, May 10, 1952) mentioned "A Tun of Red Wine," in *Burton's Gentleman's Magazine,* May 1838, in which a party of soldiers, entering a cellar where there had been a combat, find a dead man in a tun of red wine. Killis Campbell (*Mind of Poe,* p. 70) compared Bulwer's *Last Days of Pompeii,* Book IV, chapter 13, where victims are locked behind doors in vaults. It is doubtful that Poe ever knew of a "Parisian bravo" named Poulailler who walled up an unfaithful follower, mentioned by Alan Lang Strout in the *London Times Literary Supplement,* January 8, 1938 – or of the legend of an immurement on an island in Boston Harbor, told by Edward Rowe Snow in the *Yankee,* April 1961.

a resolved, *(B) comma deleted to follow A*

It must be understood[b] that neither by word nor deed had I given Fortunato cause to doubt my good will. I continued, as was my wont, to smile in his face, and he did not perceive that my smile *now* was at the thought of his immolation.

He had a weak point — this Fortunato — although in other regards he was a man to be respected and even feared. He prided himself on[c] his connoisseurship in wine. Few Italians have the true virtuoso spirit. For the most part their enthusiasm is adopted to suit the time and opportunity — to practise imposture upon the British and Austrian *millionaires*. In painting and gemmary Fortunato, like his countrymen, was a quack[2] — but in the matter of old wines he was sincere. In this respect I did not differ from him materially; I was skilful in the Italian vintages myself, and bought largely whenever I could.

It was about dusk, one evening during the supreme madness of the carnival season,[3] that I encountered my friend. He accosted me with excessive warmth, for he had been drinking much. The man wore motley. He had on a tight-fitting parti-striped dress, and his head was surmounted by the conical cap and bells. I was so pleased to see him[d] that I thought I should never have done wringing his hand.

I said to him — "My dear Fortunato, you are luckily met. How remarkably well you are looking to-day![e] But I have received a pipe of what passes for Amontillado, and I have my doubts."[4]

"How?" said he. "Amontillado? A pipe? Impossible! And in the middle of the carnival!"

"I have my doubts," I replied; "and I was silly enough to pay the full Amontillado price without consulting you in the matter. You were not to be found, and I was fearful of losing a bargain."

"Amontillado!"

"I have my doubts."

"Amontillado!"

"And I must satisfy them."

"Amontillado!"

---

b understood, *(B) comma deleted to follow A*

c upon *(A)*

d him, *(B) comma deleted to follow A*

e to-day. *(A)*

"As you are engaged, I am on my way to Luchesi.[f5] If any one has a critical turn, it is he. He will tell me —"

"Luchesi[g] cannot tell Amontillado from Sherry."[6]

"And yet some fools will have it that his taste is a match for your own."

"Come, let us go."

"Whither?"

"To your vaults."

"My friend, no; I will not impose upon your good nature. I perceive you have an engagement. Luchesi[h] —"

"I have no engagement; – come."

"My friend, no. It is not the engagement, but the severe cold with which I perceive you are afflicted. The vaults are insufferably damp. They are encrusted with nitre."

"Let us go, nevertheless. The cold is merely nothing. Amontillado! You have been imposed upon. And as for Luchesi,[i] he cannot distinguish Sherry from Amontillado."

Thus speaking, Fortunato possessed himself of my [j]arm. Putting[j] on a mask of black silk, and drawing a *roquelaire*[7] closely about my person, I suffered him to hurry me to my palazzo.

There were no attendants at home; they had absconded to make merry in honor of the time. I had told them that I should not return until the morning, and had given them explicit orders not to stir from the house. These orders were sufficient, I well knew, to insure their immediate disappearance, one and all, as soon as my back was turned.[8]

I took from their sconces two flambeaux, and giving one to Fortunato, bowed him through several suites of rooms to the archway that led into the vaults. I passed down a long and winding staircase, requesting him to be cautious as he followed. We came at length to the foot of the descent, and stood together on[k] the damp ground of the catacombs of the Montresors.

The gait of my friend was unsteady, and the bells upon his cap jingled as he strode.

f Luchresi. *(A)*
g Luchresi *(A)*
h Luchresi *(A)*
i Luchresi, *(A)*
j . . . j arm; and putting *(A)*
k upon *(A)*

"The pipe," said he.

"It is farther on," said I; "but observe the white web-work which gleams from these cavern walls."

He turned towards me, and looked into my eyes with two filmy orbs that distilled the rheum of intoxication.

"Nitre?" he asked, at length.

"Nitre," I replied. "How long have you had that cough?"

"Ugh! ugh! ugh! – ugh! ugh! ugh! – ugh! ugh! ugh! – ugh! ugh! ugh! – ugh! ugh! ugh!"

My poor friend found it impossible to reply for many minutes.

"It is nothing," he said, at last.

"Come," I said, with decision, "we will go back; your health is precious. You are rich, respected, admired, beloved; you are happy, as once I was. You are a man to be missed. For me it is no matter. We will go back; you will be ill, and I cannot be responsible. Besides, there is Luchesi[1] —"

"Enough," he said; "the cough is a mere nothing; it will not kill me. I shall not die of a cough."

"True – true," I replied; "and, indeed, I had no intention of alarming you unnecessarily – but you should use all proper caution. A draught of this Medoc will defend us from the damps."[9]

Here I knocked off the neck of a bottle which I drew from a long row of its fellows that lay upon the mould.

"Drink," I said, presenting him the wine.

He raised it to his lips with a leer. He paused and nodded to me familiarly, while his bells jingled.

"I drink," he said, "to the buried that repose around us."

"And I to your long life."[10]

He again took my arm, and we proceeded.

"These vaults," he said, "are extensive."

"The Montresors," I replied, "were a great and numerous family."

"I forget your arms."[11]

"A huge human foot d'or, in a field azure; the foot crushes a serpent rampant whose fangs are imbedded in the heel."[12]

"And the motto?"

---

1 Luchresi *(A)*

"Nemo me impune lacessit."[13]

"Good!" he said.

The wine sparkled in his eyes and the bells jingled. My own fancy grew warm with the Medoc. We had passed through[m] walls of piled bones,[n] with casks and puncheons intermingling, into the inmost recesses of the catacombs. I paused again, and this time I made bold to seize Fortunato by an arm above the elbow.

"The nitre!" I said; "see, it increases. It hangs like moss upon the vaults. We are below the river's bed.The drops of moisture trickle among the bones. Come, we will go back ere it is too late. Your cough —"

"It is nothing," he said; "let us go on. But first, another draught of the Medoc."

I broke and reached him a flaçon[o] of De Grâve.[14] He emptied it at a breath. His eyes flashed with a fierce light. He laughed and threw the bottle upwards with a gesticulation I did not understand.

I looked at him in surprise. He repeated the movement – a grotesque one.

"You do not comprehend?" he said.

"Not I," I replied.

"Then you are not of the brotherhood."

"How?"

"You are not of the masons."

"Yes, yes," I said, "yes, yes."

"You? Impossible! A mason?"

"A mason," I replied.

"A sign," he said.[p]

"It is this," I answered, producing [q]a trowel from beneath the folds of my *roquelaire*.[q]

"You jest," he exclaimed, recoiling a few paces.[15] "But let us proceed to the Amontillado."

"Be it so," I said, replacing the tool beneath the cloak, and again offering him my arm. He leaned upon it heavily. We continued our route[r] in search of the Amontillado. We passed through a

---

m through long *(A)*
n skeletons, *(A)*
o flaçon *(A, B)*
p said, "a sign." *(A)*
q . . . q from beneath the folds of my *roquelaire* a trowel. *(A)*
r rout *(A)*

range of low arches, descended, passed on, and descending again, arrived at a deep crypt, in which the foulness of the air caused our flambeaux rather to glow than flame.

At the most remote end of the crypt there appeared another less spacious. Its walls had been lined with human remains, piled to the vault overhead, in the fashion of the great catacombs of Paris.[16] Three sides of this interior crypt were still ornamented in this manner. From the fourth[s] the bones had been thrown down, and lay promiscuously upon the earth, forming at one point a mound of some size. Within the wall thus exposed by the displacing of the bones, we perceived a still interior recess,[t] in depth about four feet, in width three, in height six or seven. It seemed to have been constructed for no especial use within itself, but formed merely the interval between two of the colossal supports of the roof of the catacombs, and was backed by one of their circumscribing walls of solid granite.

It was in vain that Fortunato, uplifting his dull torch, endeavored to pry into the depth of the recess. Its termination the feeble light did not enable us to see.

"Proceed," I said; "herein is the Amontillado. As for Luchesi[u] ——"

"He is an ignoramus," interrupted my friend, as he stepped unsteadily forward, while I followed immediately at his heels. In an instant he had reached the extremity of the niche, and finding his progress arrested by the rock, stood stupidly bewildered. A moment more and I had fettered him to the granite. In its surface were two iron staples, distant from each other about two feet, horizontally. From one of these depended a short chain, from the other a padlock. Throwing the links about his waist, it was but the work of a few seconds to secure it. He was too much astounded to resist. Withdrawing the key I stepped back from the recess.

"Pass your hand," I said, "over the wall; you cannot help feeling the nitre. Indeed it is *very* damp. Once more let me *implore* you to return. No? Then I must positively leave you. But I must first render you all the little attentions in my power."

---

s fourth side *(A)*
t crypt or recess, *(A)*
u Luchresi *(A)*

"The Amontillado!" ejaculated my friend, not yet recovered from his astonishment.

"True," I replied; "the Amontillado."

As I said these words I busied myself among the pile of bones of which I have before spoken. Throwing them aside, I soon uncovered a quantity of building stone and mortar. With these materials and with the aid of my trowel, I began vigorously to wall up the entrance of the niche.[17]

I had scarcely laid the first tier of the masonry when I discovered that the intoxication of Fortunato had in a[v] great measure worn off. The earliest indication I had of this was a low moaning cry from the depth of the recess. It was *not* the cry of a drunken man. There was then a long and obstinate silence. I laid the second tier, and the third, and the fourth; and then I heard the furious vibrations[w] of the chain. The noise lasted for several minutes, during which, that I might hearken to it with the more satisfaction, I ceased my labors and sat down upon the bones. When at last the clanking subsided, I resumed the trowel, and finished without interruption the fifth, the sixth, and the seventh tier. The wall was now nearly upon a level with my breast. I again paused, and holding the flambeaux over the mason-work, threw a few feeble rays upon the figure within.

A succession of loud and shrill screams, bursting suddenly from the throat of the chained form, seemed to thrust me violently back. For a brief moment I hesitated — I trembled. Unsheathing my rapier, I began to grope with it about the recess: but the thought of an instant reassured me. I placed my hand upon the solid fabric of the catacombs, and felt satisfied. I reapproached the wall. I replied to the yells of him who clamored. I re-echoed — I aided — I surpassed them in volume and in strength. I did this, and the clamorer grew still.

It was now midnight, and my task was drawing to a close. I had completed the eighth, the ninth, and the tenth tier. I had finished a portion of the last and the eleventh; there remained but a single stone to be fitted and plastered in. I struggled with its weight; I

---

v *Omitted (A)*   w vibration *(A)*

placed it partially in its destined position. But now there came from out the niche a low laugh that erected the hairs upon my head. It was succeeded by a sad voice, which I had difficulty in recognising as that of the noble Fortunato. The voice said —

"Ha! ha! ha! — he! he![x] — a very good joke indeed — an excellent jest. We will have many a rich laugh about it at the palazzo — he! he! he! — over our wine — he! he! he!"

"The Amontillado!" I said.

"He! he! he! — he! he! he! — yes, the Amontillado.[18] But is it not getting late? Will not they be awaiting us at the palazzo, the Lady Fortunato and the rest? Let us be gone."

"Yes," I said, "let us be gone."

"For the love of God, Montresor!"

"Yes," I said, "for the love of God!"

But to these words I hearkened in vain for a reply. I grew impatient. I called aloud —

"Fortunato!"

No answer. I called again —

"Fortunato!"

No answer still. I thrust a torch through the remaining aperture and let it fall within. There came forth in return only a jingling of the bells. My heart grew [y]sick — on account of[y] the dampness of the catacombs.[z] I hastened to make an end of my labor. I forced the last stone into its position; I plastered it up. Against the new masonry I re-erected the old rampart of bones. For the half of a century no mortal has disturbed them. *In pàce requiescat!*[19]

NOTES

Title: Amontillado is a very fine light-colored variety of Xeres or Sherry, chiefly from Jerez de Frontera in the south of Spain. For a conjecture regarding Poe's choice of this particular brand for use in his tale see n. 18 below.

1. Woodberry (*Life,* II, 231) characterized Poe's tale as "a tale of Italian vengeance," without further comment (compare n. 27 to "The Pit and the Pendulum," p. 700 above). "Italian vengeance" had for centuries indicated an implacable demand for retribution. This first paragraph of the present tale outlines

x he! he! *(A)*

y . . . y sick; it was *(A)*

z catacombs that made it so. *(A)*

the traditionally recognized requirements of that demand. The second sentence suggests that the narrator, Montresor – probably on his deathbed – addresses a father confessor, but Poe's many subtleties have generated endless discussion, by serious readers, of the person or persons addressed, and of Montresor's fundamental motive.

2. Italy was in Poe's day a great center for production of bogus works of art. Montresor's words prove that he was not himself an Italian.

3. Somewhere it has been suggested that Poe conceived the tale during the Carnival season. The Carnival is elaborately celebrated in Italy and France, and, of course, in America as the Mardi Gras, especially at New Orleans and Mobile. But in 1846 Shrove Tuesday fell on February 24, and it is not probable that "The Cask" was written so early in that year. The Carnival in New York the previous year, as described in the *Broadway Journal,* February 22, 1845, consisted merely of a few sideshows and refreshment stands on Broadway and a good deal of sleighing.

4. Note that Montresor has not claimed to be an expert on *Spanish* wines.

5. This name is spelled "Luchresi" (Look-crazy) in the first version. Dedmond, cited in the introduction, thought it represented Hiram Fuller. For the name Luchesi see p. 471, n. 5, above.

6. The difficulty of telling Amontillado from (ordinary) Sherry is mentioned in the 1845 versions of "Lionizing." A pipe is a large cask, containing two hogsheads; note the word in "Apropos of Bores," quoted in the introduction above.

7. The *roquelaire* (*roquelaure*) is a knee-length cloak, mentioned also in "The Man of the Crowd" at n. 12.

8. Compare similar orders to servants in "The Purloined Letter," at n. 6.

9. Médoc (a French wine) is reputedly hygienic, not fatiguing the head or stomach. See Cora, Rose and Bob Brown, *Wine Cook Book* (1934), p. 310. The therapeutic value of Médoc is also alluded to in "Bon-Bon." Commentators unaware of the medicinal value of the wine have been puzzled by Poe's selection. See the *Explicator,* November 1966.

10. The toast is ironic.

11. Fortunato's forgetfulness of Montresor's arms is subtly insulting. (This note is from Sculley Bradley.)

12. W. M. Forrest (*Biblical Allusions in Poe*) saw a reminiscence of the prophecy of Genesis 3:14–15: "And the Lord God said unto the serpent . . . I will put enmity between thee and the woman . . . and her seed . . . shall bruise thy head, and thou shalt bruise his heel."

13. The motto, "No one provokes me with impunity," is actually the ancient motto of Scotland and that of the Scottish Order of the Thistle. See also on p. 34 above "The Duc de L'Omelette": " 'Sir!' replied the Duc, 'I am not to be insulted with impunity!' " – and a similar declaration in "The Literary Life of Thingum Bob, Esq." Poe may have seen the following verses in Carey and Hart's edition of *The Noctes Ambrosianae of "Blackwood"* (4 v., Philadelphia, 1843, I, 128) or in the magazine itself (December 1822, p. 702):

"You ask me, kind Hunt, why does Christopher North
For his crest Thistle, Shamrock, and Rose blazon forth?
The answer is easy: his pages disclose
The splendour, the fragrance, the grace of the Rose;
Yet so humble, that he, though of writers the chief,
In modesty vies with the Shamrock's sweet leaf;
Like the Thistle! – Ah, Leigh, you and I must confess it,
NEMO ME (is his motto) IMPUNE LACESSET."

These sources spell "lacessit" with an "e" but the "i" is correct.

14. De Grâve or Grâves is the name given wines from a city and region of the Bordeaux district of France, known for its gravelly soil. Most of them are white, but a few are red. The name here may well be chosen for a grim pun on the English word grave. Queen Elizabeth made a jest of this kind according to Bacon's *Apophthegms* (Spedding edition) 78.(12): "When the Archduke did raise his siege from Grave, the then secretary came to Queen Elizabeth; and the Queen, having intelligence first, said to the secretary, *Wot you what? The Archduke is risen from the Grave.* He answered, *What, without the trumpet of the Archangel?* The Queen replied; *Yes, without sound of trumpet.*"

15. Poe was not a Mason. The excellent Poe scholar, Dr. Henry Ridgely Evans, a 32° Mason, who was much interested in Continental as well as British and American Masonry, told me he knew of nothing at all like Fortunato's gesture. That is made up; the trowel is ironic, revealing Montresor as a *practical* mason, rather than a member of a fraternal Masonic lodge.

16. The catacombs of Paris are not so famous as those of Rome, but they probably are what Poe actually had in mind. [B. Pollin, *Discoveries,* p. 34, quotes a letter on "The Catacombs of Paris" that appeared in the "Editor's Table" of the *Knickerbocker* for March 1838 that Poe very likely read.] However, efforts to fix the geography of a work of pure fiction do not seem necessary.

17. Compare the process described in the following paragraphs with Headley's imaginative account quoted in the introduction above.

18. Commenting on the many repetitions of the word Amontillado, Professor Charles W. Steele, in the *Explicator,* April 1960, suggested that Poe – who took courses in both Spanish and Italian at the University of Virginia – might have had a pun in mind, since the Italian *ammonticchiato* and the Spanish *amontanado* both in sound remotely resemble the name of the wine and both mean "collected in a heap." He goes on to say: "The implication of Montresor's pun can be understood ... As the climax of the story is reached he causes his victim to repeat the word *amontillado* (with its inherent play on words) a final time, as if to assure himself that his subtle and superior wit has been fully appreciated ... The idea of a pun cannot be dismissed. 'Collected in a heap' suits very well the pile of bricks revealed at the climax of the story. Poe was an inveterate punster; already a grim pun on 'mason' is surely recognizable ... "

19. The jingling was a knell. Montresor's heart grew sick at his first murder, but he at once dismissed the twinge of his rudimentary conscience. The last words are also ironic. Fortunato had rested in peace for fifty years; Montresor

must always have feared being found out. This view was taken by Robert H. Fossum in the *Explicator,* November 1958. In the same periodical for November 1961, Dorothy Norris Foote argued that Montresor failed to make clear to his victim the reason for revenge. I accept the idea that Montresor did *not* escape punishment; but Marvell Felheim in the London *Notes and Queries,* October 1954, took the opposite view, as did Vincent Buranelli in his *Edgar Allan Poe* (1961), p. 72. These questions, however, like those mentioned in note 1, will probably always remain moot.

THE DOMAIN OF ARNHEIM

This tale is an expansion of "The Landscape Garden" of 1842.* Poe set great store by it, and wrote to Helen Whitman on October 18, 1848, "Meantime I enclose . . . 'The Domain of Arnheim' which happens to be at hand, and which, moreover, expresses *much of my soul.*" On the copy of the New York *Columbian Magazine* Poe sent Mrs. Whitman he wrote, "This story contains more of myself and of my inherent tastes and habits of thought than anything I have written." Mrs. Whitman believed that Poe had decided to expand his story on reading some account of William Beckford's famous estate at Fonthill, Wiltshire.†

Since the story is mentioned as accepted in "Notices to Correspondents" of the *Columbian Magazine* for January 1847, it must have been completed for submission in November or early December 1846.

TEXTS

(A) Manuscript, late 1846; *(B) Columbian Lady's and Gentleman's Magazine* for March 1847 (7:123–129); *(C) Works* (1850), I, 388–403.

* The annotation of that tale should be consulted. The first fifteen paragraphs of the present tale correspond substantially to the twelve paragraphs of the earlier story.

† See Caroline Ticknor, *Poe's Helen* (1916), p. 273. The inscribed copy of the magazine has disappeared, but Miss Ticknor printed Poe's note from a transcript made by Mrs. Whitman for Stéphane Mallarmé. [More immediately Poe knew about and perhaps even watched the construction of Edwin Forrest's country villa, "Fonthill Castle," on a beautiful prominence overlooking the Hudson not far from his own Fordham Cottage. According to the New York Landmarks Preservation Commission, it was built in 1846, and is believed to have been influenced by William Beckford's Fonthill Abbey in England. The romantic Gothic castle is now the Elizabeth Seton Library of the College of Mount St. Vincent in the Riverdale section of the Bronx. (Note contributed by Patricia Edwards Clyne.)]

THE DOMAIN OF ARNHEIM

Griswold's version *(C)* is chosen as the text for this edition, but two misprints have been corrected.

The manuscript is of two rolls, the second now somewhat damaged, as indicated in the list of variants. I first examined it in the auction room of Stan V. Henkels of Philadelphia, who sold it July 1, 1920, lot 331. It is now in the William H. Koester Collection in the Humanities Research Center Library of the University of Texas. [Thanks are due Professor Joseph J. Moldenhauer for a final check of this manuscript, and with his permission we quote his description of it from his *Descriptive Catalog of Edgar Allan Poe Manuscripts:*

> Black ink on pale blue paper, faintly ruled, in sheets of varying lengths (usually 12 inches) and measuring 3 15/16 inches wide. The sheets are numbered and wafered vertically into two rolls, the first comprising 17 sheets of text, plus two short sheets on which appear title, author's name, and epigraph from Giles Fletcher. Roll I ends with the words " 'man and God.' " Roll II contains 14 sheets, the first numbered "19" and commencing "him to abandon the idea." One sheet (p. 18), containing two paragraphs and part of a third of printed text, is missing from the manuscript. Roll II ends with the words "violets, tulips," the final sheet of manuscript (p. 32) has been torn away. Both rolls are somewhat smudged on their outer surfaces, and suffer from slight tears in addition to the loss of sheets at the beginning and end of roll II.]

A comparison with the variants will make the missing portions clear. In the variants deletions in the manuscript are indicated by angle brackets < >, insertions by arrows ↑ ↓.

It is from the manuscript that the *Columbian Magazine,* March 1847, printed and, while Poe's punctuation and capitalization were not followed in all cases, the verbal variants seem to indicate that Poe revised the tale in proof. Poe capitalized Nature, Beauty, etc., in the manuscript, and beside the quotation in paragraph 12 he wrote "smaller type."

A comparison of the earlier sketch, "The Landscape Garden," with its paragraphs incorporated in "The Domain of Arnheim" shows that Poe did a thorough job of tightening up, eliminating adjectives and using more specific phrases in the later version. He improved the punctuation, and he also made certain additions, all indicated in the notes.

THE DOMAIN OF ARNHEIM. [*C*]

The garden like a lady fair was cut,
  That lay as if she slumbered in delight,
And to the open skies her eyes did shut.
  The azure fields of Heaven were 'sembled right
  In a large round set with the flowers of light.
The flowers de luce and the round sparks of dew
That hung upon their azure leaves did shew
Like twinkling stars that sparkle in the evening blue.

Giles Fletcher.

Title *The title and* By Edgar A. Poe *under it are in printed letters. The tale is in script. (A)*

FROM his cradle to his grave a gale of prosperity bore my friend Ellison along.[1] Nor do I use the word prosperity in its mere worldly sense. I mean it as synonymous with happiness. The person of whom I speak seemed born for the purpose of foreshadowing the doctrines of Turgot,[a] Price, Priestley[b] and Condorcet[c] – of exemplifying by individual instance what has been deemed the chimera of the perfectionists.[2] In the brief existence of Ellison I fancy that I have seen refuted the dogma, that in man's very nature lies some hidden principle, the antagonist of bliss. An anxious examination of his career has given me to understand that, in general, from the violation of a few simple laws of humanity arises the wretchedness of mankind – that as a species we have in our possession the as yet unwrought elements of content – and that, even now, in the present darkness and madness of all thought on the great question of the social condition, it is not impossible that man, the individual, under certain unusual and highly fortuitous conditions, may be happy.

With opinions such as these my young friend, too, was fully imbued; and thus it is worthy of observation that the uninterrupted enjoyment which distinguished his life was, in great measure, the result of preconcert. It is, indeed, evident that with less of the instinctive philosophy which, now and then, stands so well in the stead of experience, Mr. Ellison would have found himself precipitated, by the very extraordinary success[d] of his life, into the common vortex of unhappiness which yawns for those of pre-eminent endowments.[3] But it is by no means my object to pen an essay on happiness. The ideas of my friend may be summed up in a few words. He admitted but four elementary principles, or, more strictly, conditions, of bliss. That which he considered chief was (strange to say!) the simple and purely physical one of free exercise in the open air. "The health," he said, "attainable by other means is scarcely worth the name." He instanced the ecstasies[e] of the fox-hunter, and[f] pointed to the tillers of the earth, the only people who, as a class, can be

a Turgôt, *(A, B)*
b Priestly *(A, B, C) corrected editorially*
c Condorcêt *(A, B)*
d successes *(A, B)*
e ecstacies *(A, B, C)*
f and <he> *(A)*

fairly considered happier than others. His second condition was the love of woman. His third, and most difficult of realization, was the contempt of ambition. His fourth was an object of unceasing pursuit; and he held that, other things being equal, the extent of attainable happiness was in proportion to the spirituality of this object.[4]

Ellison was remarkable in the continuous profusion of good gifts lavished upon him by fortune. In personal grace and beauty he exceeded all men. His intellect was of that order to which the acquisition of knowledge is less a labor than an intuition and a necessity. His family was one of the most illustrious of the empire. His bride was the loveliest and most devoted of women. His possessions had been always ample; but, on the attainment of his majority,[g] it was discovered that one of those extraordinary freaks of fate had been played in his behalf which startle the whole social world amid which they occur, and seldom fail radically to alter the moral constitution of those who are their objects.[4a]

It appears that about a hundred years before Mr. Ellison's coming of age, there had died, in a remote province, one Mr. Seabright Ellison. This gentleman had amassed a princely fortune, and, having no immediate connections, conceived the whim of suffering his wealth to accumulate for a century after his decease. Minutely and sagaciously directing the various modes of investment, he bequeathed the aggregate amount to the nearest of blood, bearing the name Ellison, who should be alive at the end of the hundred years. Many attempts had been made to set aside this singular bequest; their *ex post facto* character rendered them abortive; but the attention of a jealous government was aroused, and a legislative act finally obtained, forbidding all similar accumulations. This act, however, did not prevent young Ellison from entering into possession, on his twenty-first birth-day, as the heir of his ancestor Seabright, of a fortune of *four hundred and fifty millions of dollars.*[*][5]

* An incident, similar in outline to the one here imagined, occurred, not very long ago, in England. The name of the fortunate heir was Thelluson. I first saw an account of this matter in the "Tour" of Prince Puckler Muskau, who makes the sum inherited *ninety millions of pounds,* and justly observes that "in the contemplation of so vast a

---

g <one and twentieth year> ↑majority↓ *(A)*

When it had become known that such was the enormous wealth inherited, there were, of course, many speculations as to the mode of its disposal. The magnitude and the immediate availability of the sum bewildered all who thought on the topic. The possessor of any *appreciable* amount of money might have been imagined to perform any one of a thousand things. With riches merely surpassing those of any citizen, it would have been easy to suppose him engaging to supreme excess in the fashionable extravagances of his time — or busying himself with political intrigue — or aiming at ministerial power — or purchasing increase of nobility — or collecting large museums of *virtu*[6] — or playing the munificent patron of letters, of science, of art — or endowing, and bestowing his name upon extensive institutions of charity. But for the inconceivable wealth in the actual possession of the heir, these objects and all ordinary objects were felt to afford too limited a field. Recourse was had to figures, and these but sufficed to confound. It was seen that, even at three per cent., the annual income of the inheritance amounted to no less than thirteen millions and five hundred thousand dollars; which was one million and one hundred and twenty-five thousand per month; or thirty-six thousand nine hundred and eighty-six per day; or one thousand five hundred and forty-one per hour; or six and twenty dollars for every minute that flew. Thus the usual track of supposition was thoroughly broken up. Men knew not what to imagine. There were some who even conceived that Mr. Ellison would divest himself of at least one half of his fortune, as of utterly superfluous opulence — enriching whole troops of his relatives by division of his superabundance. To the nearest of these he did, in fact, abandon the very unusual wealth which was his own before the inheritance.[6a]

I was not surprised, however, to perceive that he had long made up his mind on a point which had occasioned so much discussion to his friends. Nor was I greatly astonished at the nature of his deci-

sum, and of the services to which it might be applied, there is something even of the sublime." To suit the views of this article I have followed the Prince's statement, although a grossly exaggerated one. The germ, and, in fact, the commencement of the present paper was published many years ago — previous to the issue of the first number of Sue's admirable *"Juif Errant,"* which may possibly have been suggested to him by Muskau's account.[5a]

sion.[6b] In regard to individual charities he had satisfied his conscience. In the possibility of any improvement, properly so called, being effected by man himself in the general condition of man, he had (I am[h] sorry to confess it) little faith. Upon the whole, whether happily or unhappily, he was thrown back, in very great measure, upon self.[6c]

In the widest and noblest sense he was a poet. He comprehended, moreover, the true character, the august aims, the supreme majesty and dignity of the poetic sentiment. The fullest, if not the sole proper satisfaction of this sentiment he instinctively felt to lie in the creation of novel forms of beauty. Some peculiarities, either in his early education, or in the nature of his intellect, had tinged with what is termed materialism all his ethical speculations; and it was this bias, perhaps, which led him to believe that the most advantageous at least, if not the sole legitimate field for the poetic exercise, lies in the creation of novel moods of purely *physical* loveliness. Thus it happened[i] he became neither musician nor poet — if we use this latter term in its every-day acceptation. Or it might have been that he neglected to become either, merely in pursuance of his idea that in contempt of ambition is to be found one of the essential principles of happiness on earth. Is it not, indeed, possible that, while a high order of genius[j] is necessarily ambitious, the highest is above that which is termed ambition? And may it not thus happen that many far greater than Milton have contentedly remained "mute and inglorious?"[7] I believe that the world has never seen — and that, unless through some series of accidents goading the noblest order of mind into distasteful exertion, the world will never see — that full extent of triumphant execution, in the richer domains of art, of which the human nature is absolutely capable.

Ellison became neither musician nor poet; although no man lived more profoundly enamored of music and poetry. Under other circumstances than those which invested him, it is not impossible that he would have become a painter. Sculpture, although in its nature rigorously poetical, was too limited in its extent and consequences, to have occupied, at any time, much of his attention. And I

h am <, perhaps,> *(A)*
i happened that *(A)*
j <ambition> ↑genius↓ *(A)*

have now mentioned all the provinces in which the common understanding of the poetic sentiment has declared it capable of expatiating. But Ellison maintained that the richest, the truest and most natural, if not altogether the most extensive province, had been unaccountably neglected. No definition had spoken of the landscape-gardener as of the poet; yet it seemed to my friend that the creation of the landscape-garden offered to the proper Muse the most magnificent of opportunities. Here, indeed, was the fairest field for the display of imagination in the endless combining of forms of novel beauty; the elements to enter into combination being, by a vast superiority, the most glorious which the earth could afford. In the multiform and multicolor of the flower and the trees,[k] he recognised the most direct and energetic efforts of Nature at physical loveliness. And in the direction or concentration of this effort — or, more properly, in its adaptation to the eyes which were to behold it on[l] earth — he perceived that he should be employing the best means — laboring to the greatest advantage — in the fulfilment, not only of his own destiny as poet,[7a] but of the august purposes for which the Deity had implanted the poetic sentiment in man.

"Its adaptation to the eyes which were to behold it on earth." In his explanation of this phraseology, Mr. Ellison did much toward solving what has always seemed to me an enigma: — I mean the fact (which none but the ignorant dispute) that no such combination[m] of scenery exists[n] in nature as the painter of genius may produce. No such paradises are to be found in reality as have glowed on the canvass of Claude.[8] In the most enchanting of natural landscapes, there will always be found a defect or an excess — many excesses and defects. While the component parts may defy[o], individually, the highest skill of the artist, the arrangement of these parts will always be susceptible of improvement. In short, no position can be attained on the wide surface of the *natural* earth, from which an artistical eye, looking steadily, will not find matter of offence in what is termed the "composition" of the landscape. And yet how unintelligible is this! In all other matters we are justly instructed to regard nature as

k tree, *(A)*
l <upon> ↑on↓ *(A)*
m combinations *(A)*
n exist *(A)*
o <exceed> ↑defy↓ *(A)*

supreme. With her details we shrink from competition. Who shall presume to imitate the colors of the tulip, or to improve the proportions of the lily of the valley? The criticism which says, of sculpture or portraiture, that here nature is to be exalted or idealized rather than imitated, is in error. No pictorial or sculptural combinations of points of human loveliness do more than approach the living and breathing beauty.[9a] In landscape alone is the principle of the critic true; and, having felt its truth here, it is but the headlong spirit of generalization which has led him to pronounce it true throughout all the domains of art. Having, I say, *felt* its truth here; for the feeling is no affectation or chimera. The mathematics afford no more absolute demonstrations than the sentiment of his art yields the artist. He not only believes, but positively knows, that such and such apparently arbitrary arrangements of matter constitute and alone constitute the true beauty. His reasons, however, have not yet been matured into expression. It remains for a more profound analysis than the world has yet seen, fully to investigate and express them. Nevertheless he is confirmed in his instinctive opinions by the voice of all his brethren. Let a "composition" be defective; let an emendation be wrought in its mere arrangement of form; let this emendation be submitted to every artist in the world; by each will its necessity be admitted. And even far more than this: in remedy of the defective composition, each insulated member of the fraternity would have suggested the identical emendation.

I repeat that in landscape arrangements alone is the physical nature susceptible of exaltation, and that, therefore, her susceptibility of improvement at this one point, was a mystery I had been unable to solve.[9b] My own thoughts on the subject had rested in the idea that the primitive intention of nature would have so arranged the earth's surface as to have fulfilled at all points man's sense of perfection in the beautiful, the sublime, or the picturesque; but that this primitive intention had been frustrated by the known geological disturbances — disturbances of form and color-grouping, in the correction or allaying of which lies the soul of art. The force of this idea was much weakened, however, by the necessity which it involved of considering the disturbances abnormal and unadapted[p]

---

p inadapted *(A)*

to any purpose. It was Ellison who suggested that they were prognostic of *death.* He thus explained: — Admit the earthly immortality of man to have been the first intention. We have then the primitive arrangement of the earth's surface adapted to his blissful estate, as not existent but designed. The disturbances were the preparations for his subsequently conceived deathful condition.

"Now," said my friend, "what we regard as exaltation of the landscape may be really such, as respects only the mortal[q] or human *point of view.* Each alternation of the natural scenery may possibly effect a blemish in the picture, if we can suppose this picture viewed at large — in mass — from some point distant from the earth's surface, although not beyond the limits of its atmosphere. It is easily understood that what might improve a closely scrutinized detail, may[r] at the same time injure a general or more distantly observed effect. There *may* be a class of beings, human once, but now invisible to humanity, to whom, from afar, our disorder may seem order — our unpicturesqueness picturesque; in a word, the earth-angels, for whose scrutiny more especially than[s] our own, and for whose death-refined appreciation of the beautiful, may have been set in array by God the wide landscape-gardens of the hemispheres."

In the course of discussion, my friend quoted some passages from a writer on landscape-gardening, who has been supposed to have well treated his theme:[10]

"There are properly but two styles of landscape-gardening, the natural and the artificial. One seeks to recall the original beauty of the country, by adapting its means to the surrounding scenery; cultivating trees in harmony with the hills or plain of the neighboring land; detecting and bringing into practice those nice relations of size, proportion and color which, hid from the common observer, are revealed everywhere to the experienced student of nature. The result of the natural style of gardening[s'] is seen rather in the absence of all defects and incongruities — in the prevalence of a healthy harmony and order — than in the creation of any special wonders or miracles. The artificial style has as many varieties as there are

q moral *(C) misprint, corrected from A, B*

r <might> ↑may↓ *(A)*

s than for *(A)*

s′ gardening, *(C) comma deleted to follow A, B*

different tastes to gratify. It has a certain general relation to the various styles of building. There are the stately avenues and retirements of Versailles; Italian terraces; and a various mixed old English style, which bears some relation to the domestic Gothic or English Elizabethan architecture. Whatever may be said against the abuses of the artificial landscape-gardening, a mixture of pure art in a garden scene adds to it a great beauty. This is partly pleasing to the eye, by the show of order and design, and partly moral. A terrace, with an old moss-covered balustrade, calls up at once to the eye the fair forms that have passed there in other days. The slightest exhibition of art is an evidence of care and human interest."

"From what I have already observed," said Ellison, "you will understand that I reject the idea, here expressed, of recalling the original beauty of the country. The original beauty is never so great as that which may be introduced. Of course, everything depends on the selection of a spot with capabilities.[11] What is said about detecting and bringing into practice nice relations of size, proportion, and color, is one of those mere vaguenesses of speech which serve to veil inaccuracy of thought. The phrase quoted may mean anything, or nothing, and guides in no degree. That the true result of the natural style of gardening is seen rather in the absence of all defects and incongruities than in the creation of any special wonders or miracles, is a proposition better suited to the grovelling apprehension of the herd than to the fervid dreams of the man of genius. The negative merit suggested appertains to that hobbling criticism which, in letters, would elevate Addison into apotheosis. In truth, while that virtue which consists in the mere avoidance of vice appeals directly to the understanding, and can thus be circumscribed in *rule,* the loftier virtue, which flames in creation, can be apprehended in its results alone. Rule applies but to the merits of denial — to the excellencies[t] which refrain. Beyond these, the critical art can but suggest. We may be instructed to build a "Cato," but[u] we are in vain told *how* to conceive a Parthenon or an "Inferno."[12a] The thing done, however; the wonder accomplished; and the capacity for apprehension becomes universal. The sophists of the negative school

t excellences *(A)*

u <or a "Columbiad"> but *(A)*

who, through inability to create, have scoffed at creation, are now found the loudest in applause. What, in its chrysalis condition of principle, affronted their demure reason, never fails, in its maturity of accomplishment, to extort admiration from their instinct[v] of beauty.

"The author's observations on the artificial style," continued Ellison, "are less objectionable. A mixture of pure art in a garden scene adds to it a great beauty. This is just; as also is the reference to the sense of human interest. The principle expressed is incontrovertible — but there *may* be something beyond it. There may be an object in keeping with the principle — an object unattainable by the means ordinarily possessed by individuals, yet which, if attained, would lend a charm to the landscape-garden far surpassing that which a sense of merely human interest could bestow. A poet, having very unusual pecuniary resources, might, while retaining the necessary idea of art, or culture, or, as our author expresses it, of interest, so imbue his designs at once with extent and novelty of beauty, as to convey the sentiment of spiritual interference. It will be seen that, in bringing about such result, he secures all the advantages of interest or *design,* while relieving his work of the harshness or technicality of the worldly *art.* In the most rugged of wildernesses — in the most savage of the scenes of pure nature — there is apparent the *art* of a creator; yet this art is apparent to reflection only; in no respect has it the obvious force of a feeling. Now let us suppose this sense of the Almighty design to be *one step depressed* — to be brought into something like harmony or consistency with the sense of human art — to form an intermedium between the two: — let us imagine, for example, a landscape whose combined vastness and definitiveness — whose united beauty, magnificence, and *strangeness,*[13] shall convey the idea of care, or culture, or superintendence, on the part of beings superior, yet akin to humanity — then the sentiment of *interest* is preserved, while the art intervolved is made to assume the air of an intermediate or secondary nature — a nature which is not God, nor an emanation from God, but which still is nature in the sense of the handiwork of the angels that hover between man and God."[14]

v <instict> ↑instinct↓ *(A)*

[w]It was in devoting his enormous wealth to the embodiment of a vision such as this — in the free exercise in the open air ensured by the personal superintendence of his plans — in the unceasing object which these plans afforded — in the high spirituality of the object — in the contempt of ambition which it enabled him truly to feel — in the perennial springs with which it gratified, without possibility of satiating, that one master passion of his soul, the thirst for beauty; above all, it was in the sympathy of a woman, not unwomanly, whose loveliness and love enveloped his existence in the purple atmosphere of Paradise, that Ellison thought to find, *and found*, exemption from the ordinary cares of humanity, with a far greater amount of positive happiness than ever glowed in the rapt daydreams of De Staël.[x][15]

I despair of conveying to the reader any distinct conception of the marvels which my friend did actually accomplish.[16] I wish to describe, but am disheartened by the difficulty of description, and hesitate between detail and generality. Perhaps the better course will be to unite the two in their extremes.

Mr. Ellison's first step regarded, of course, the choice of a locality; and scarcely had he commenced thinking on this point, when the luxuriant nature of the Pacific Islands arrested his attention. In fact, he had made up his mind for a voyage to the South Seas, when a night's reflection induced[w] him to abandon the idea. "Were I misanthropic," he said, "such a *locale* would suit me. The thoroughness of its insulation and seclusion, and the difficulty of ingress and egress, would in such case be the charm of charms; but as yet I am not Timon.[17] I wish the composure but not the depression of solitude. There must remain with me a certain control over the extent and duration of my repose. There will be frequent hours in which I shall need, too, the sympathy of the poetic in what I have done. Let me seek, then, a spot not far[y] from a populous city — whose vicinity, also, will best enable me to execute my plans."

In search of a suitable place so situated, Ellison travelled for several years, and I was permitted to accompany him. A thousand spots with which I was enraptured he rejected without hesitation,

w . . . w *Portion of the manuscript (A) missing*

x Stäel. *(B);* Stael. *(C)*

y not far/*not far (A)*

for reasons which satisfied me, in the end, that he was right. We came at length to an elevated table-land of wonderful fertility and beauty, affording a panoramic prospect very little less in extent than that of Ætna,[18] and, in Ellison's opinion as well as my own, surpassing the far-famed view from that mountain in all the true elements of the picturesque.

"I am aware," said the traveller, as he drew a sigh of deep delight after gazing on this scene, entranced, for nearly an hour, "I know that here, in my circumstances, nine-tenths of the most fastidious of men would rest content. This panorama is indeed glorious, and I should rejoice in it but for the excess of its glory. The taste of all the architects I have ever known leads them, for the sake of 'prospect,' to put up buildings on hill-tops. The error is obvious. Grandeur in any of its moods, but especially in that of extent, startles, excites — and then fatigues, depresses. For the occasional scene nothing can be better — for the constant view nothing worse. And, in the constant view, the most objectionable phase of grandeur is that of extent; the worst phase of extent, that of distance. It is at war with the sentiment and with the sense of *seclusion* — the sentiment and sense which we seek to humor in 'retiring to the country.' In looking from the summit of a mountain we cannot help feeling *abroad* in the world. The heart-sick avoid distant prospects as a pestilence."

It was not until toward the close of the fourth year of our search that we found a locality with which Ellison professed himself satisfied. It is, of course, needless to say *where* was the[z] locality. The late death of my friend, in causing his[a] domain to be thrown open to certain classes of visiters, has given to *Arnheim* a species of secret and subdued if not solemn celebrity, similar in kind, although infinitely superior in degree, to that which so long distinguished Fonthill.[19]

The usual approach to Arnheim was by the river. The visiter left the city in the early morning. During the forenoon he passed between shores of a tranquil and domestic beauty, on which grazed innumerable sheep, their white fleeces spotting[b] the vivid green of rolling meadows. By degrees the idea of cultivation subsided into

z this *(A, B)*
a his <wierd> *(A)*
b <gleaming against> ↑spotting↓ *(A)*

that of merely pastoral care. This slowly became merged in a sense of retirement — this again in a consciousness of solitude. As the evening approached, the channel grew more narrow; the banks more and more precipitous; and these latter were clothed in richer, more profuse, and more sombre foliage. The water increased in transparency. The stream took a thousand turns, so that at no moment could its gleaming surface be seen for a greater distance than a furlong. At every instant the vessel seemed imprisoned within an enchanted circle, having insuperable and impenetrable walls of foliage, a roof of ultra-marine satin, and *no* floor — the keel balancing itself with admirable nicety on that of a phantom bark which, by some accident having been turned upside down, floated in constant company with the substantial one, for the purpose of sustaining it.[c] The channel now became a *gorge* — although the term is somewhat[d] inapplicable, and I employ it merely because the language has no word which better represents the most striking — not the most distinctive — feature of the scene. The character of gorge was maintained only in the height and parallelism of the shores; it was lost altogether in their other traits. The walls of the ravine (through which the clear water still tranquilly flowed) arose to an elevation of a hundred and occasionally of a hundred and fifty feet, and inclined so much toward each other as, in a great measure, to shut out the light of day; while the long plume-like moss which depended densely from the intertwining shrubberies overhead, gave the whole chasm an air of funereal gloom. The windings became more frequent and intricate, and seemed often as if returning in upon themselves, so that the voyager had long lost all idea of direction. He was, moreover, enwrapt in an exquisite sense of the strange. The thought of nature still remained, but her character seemed to have undergone modification; there was a weird[e] symmetry, a thrilling uniformity, a wizard propriety in these her works. Not a dead branch — not a withered leaf — not a stray pebble — not a patch of the brown earth was anywhere visible. The crystal water welled up against the clean granite, or the unblemished moss, with a sharpness of outline that delighted while it bewildered the eye.[20]

Having threaded the mazes of this channel for some hours,[21] the

---

c it. <in mid-air.> *(A)* *(A)*
d <in great measure> ↑somewhat↓
e wierd *(A, B, C)*

gloom deepening every moment, a sharp and unexpected turn of the vessel brought it suddenly, as if dropped from heaven, into a circular basin of very considerable extent when compared with the width of the gorge. It was about two hundred yards in diameter, and girt in at all points but one — that immediately fronting the vessel as it entered — by hills equal in general height to the walls of the chasm, although of a thoroughly different character. Their sides sloped from the water's edge at an angle of some forty-five degrees, and they were clothed from base to summit — not a perceptible point escaping — in a drapery of the most gorgeous flower-blossoms; scarcely a green leaf being visible among the sea of odorous and fluctuating color. This basin was of great depth, but so transparent was the water that the bottom, which seemed to consist of a thick mass of small round alabaster pebbles, was distinctly visible by glimpses[f] — that is to say, whenever the eye could permit itself *not* to see, far down in the inverted heaven, the duplicate blooming of the hills. On these latter there were no trees, nor even shrubs of any size. The impressions wrought on the observer were those of richness, warmth, color, quietude, uniformity, softness, delicacy, daintiness, voluptuousness, and a miraculous extremeness of culture that suggested dreams of a new race of fairies, laborious, tasteful, magnificent, and fastidious; but as the eye[g] traced upward the myriad-tinted slope, from its sharp junction with the water to its vague termination amid the folds of over-hanging cloud, it became, indeed, difficult not to fancy a panoramic cataract of rubies, sapphires, [h]opals and golden onyxes,[h] rolling silently out of the sky.[22]

The visiter, shooting suddenly into this bay from out the gloom of the ravine, is delighted but astounded by the full orb of the declining[i] sun, which he had supposed to be already far below the horizon, but which now confronts him, and forms the sole termination of an otherwise limitless vista seen through another chasm-like rift in the hills.

But here the voyager quits the vessel which has borne him so far, and descends into a light canoe of ivory, stained with arabesque

f <gleams> ↑glimpses↓ *(A)*
g <vision> ↑eye↓ *(A)*
h . . . h <onyxes, and golden opals,> ↑opals, and golden onyxes,↓ *(A)*
i <setting> ↑declining↓ *(A)*

devices in vivid scarlet, both within and without. The poop and beak of this boat arise[j] high above the water, with sharp points, so that the general form is that of an irregular crescent. It lies on the surface of the bay with the proud grace of a swan. On its ermined floor resposes a single feathery paddle of satin-wood; but no oarsman or attendant is to be seen. The guest is bidden to be of good cheer[23] — that the fates will take care of him. The larger vessel disappears, and he is left alone in the canoe, which lies apparently motionless in the middle of the lake. While he considers what course to pursue, however, he becomes aware of a gentle movement in the fairy bark.[24] It slowly swings itself around until its prow points toward the sun. It advances with a gentle but gradually accelerated velocity, while the slight ripples it creates seem to break about the ivory sides in divinest[k] melody — seem to offer the only possible explanation of the soothing yet melancholy music for whose unseen origin the bewildered voyager looks around him in vain.

The canoe steadily proceeds, and the rocky gate of the vista is approached, so that its depths can be more distinctly seen. To the right arise a chain of lofty hills rudely and luxuriantly wooded. It is observed, however, that the trait of exquisite *cleanness* where the bank dips into the water, still prevails. There is not one token of the usual river *debris*. To the left the character of the scene is softer and more obviously artificial. Here the bank slopes upward from the stream in a very gentle ascent, forming a broad sward of grass of a texture resembling nothing so much as velvet, and of a brilliancy of green which would bear comparison with the tint of the purest emerald.[25] This *plateau* varies in width from ten to three hundred yards; reaching from the river bank[l] to a wall, fifty feet high, which extends, in an infinity of curves, but following the general direction of the river, until lost in the distance to the westward. This wall is of one continuous rock, and has been formed by cutting perpendicularly the once rugged precipice of the stream's southern bank; but no trace of the labor has been suffered to remain. The chiselled stone has the hue of ages and is profusely overhung and

j rise *(A, B)*
k divinist *(C) corrected from A, B*
l brink *(A, B)*

overspread with the ivy, the coral honeysuckle, the eglantine, and the clematis. The uniformity of the top and bottom lines of the wall is fully relieved by occasional trees of gigantic height, growing singly or in small groups, both along the *plateau* and in the domain behind the wall, but in close proximity to it; so that frequent limbs (of the black walnut especially) reach over and dip their pendent extremities into the water. Farther back within the domain, the vision is impeded by an impenetrable screen of foliage.

These things are observed during the canoe's gradual approach to what I have called the gate of the vista. On drawing nearer to this, however, its chasm-like appearance vanishes; a new outlet from the bay is discovered to the left — in which direction the wall is also seen to sweep, still following the general course of the stream. Down this new opening the eye cannot penetrate very far, for the stream, accompanied by the wall, still bends to the left, until both are swallowed up by the leaves.

The boat, nevertheless, glides magically into the winding channel; and here the shore opposite the wall is found to resemble that opposite the wall in the straight vista. Lofty hills, rising occasionally into mountains, and covered with vegetation in wild luxuriance, still shut in the scene.

Floating gently onward, but with a velocity slightly augmented, the voyager, after many short turns, finds his progress apparently barred by a gigantic [m]gate or rather door[m] of burnished gold, elaborately carved and fretted, and reflecting the direct rays of the now fast-sinking sun with an effulgence that seems to wreath the whole surrounding forest in flames. This gate is inserted in the lofty wall; which here appears to cross the river at right angles. In a few moments, however, it is seen that the main body of the water still sweeps in a gentle and extensive curve to the left, the wall following it as before, while a stream of considerable volume, diverging from the principal one, makes its way, with a slight ripple, under the door[n], and is thus hidden from sight. The canoe falls into the lesser channel and approaches the gate. Its ponderous wings are slowly and musically expanded. The boat glides between them, and com-

m . . . m <Saracenic gate-way>↑ gate or, rather, door↓ *(A)*

n <gate-way> ↑door↓ *(A)*

mences a rapid descent into a vast amphitheatre entirely begirt with[o] purple mountains, whose bases are laved by a gleaming river throughout the full extent of their circuit. Meantime the whole Paradise of Arnheim bursts upon the view. There is a gush of entrancing melody; there is an oppressive sense of strange sweet odor; – there is a dream-like intermingling to the eye of tall slender Eastern trees[26] – bosky shrubberies – flocks of golden and crimson birds – lily-fringed lakes – meadows of violets, tulips, [p]poppies, hyacinths and tuberoses – long intertangled lines of silver streamlets – and, upspringing confusedly from amid all, a mass of semi-Gothic, semi-Saracenic architecture, sustaining itself as if by miracle in mid air; glittering in the red sunlight with a hundred oriels, minarets, and pinnacles; and seeming the phantom handiwork, conjointly, of the Sylphs, of the Fairies, of the Genii, and of the Gnomes.[p][27]

NOTES

Title: Arnheim was the name of the ancestral home of the heroine of Scott's *Anne of Geierstein* (1829), whose family dabbled in magic. Poe calls the heroine of "Berenicë" a "sylph amid the shrubberies of Arnheim . . . a Naiad among its fountains." See John Robert Moore, "Poe's Reading of Anne of Geierstein," *AL,* January 1951, for a consideration of Poe's indebtedness to Scott's novel.

Motto: This is repeated from "The Landscape Garden," with minor changes in punctuation. It is stanza 42 of Fletcher's poem, "Christ's Victorie on Earth" (1610).

1–15. For notes 1–15 see the corresponding notes on "The Landscape Garden." Notes 4a–12a and 16ff. below pertain only to the present tale.

4a. In "The Landscape Garden" there is no paragraph break at this point.

5a. Poe's footnote is substantially the same as that in "The Landscape Garden" except for the last sentence, which was added in the present tale. Poe's statement is correct. "The Landscape Garden," printed in 1842, did precede Eugene Sue's *Wandering Jew,* which was published in parts in 1844 and 1845.

6a. This sentence does not appear in "The Landscape Garden."

6b. The rest of this paragraph is new in the present tale.

6c. In "The Landscape Garden" there is no paragraph break before the next sentence.

7a. The rest of this sentence is new in the present tale.

9a. Some words that were in "The Landscape Garden," including a couplet quoted from Byron, are omitted here.

---

o <by> ↑with↓ *(A)* *in the manuscript (A)*

p . . . p *All save* tuberoses – *torn away*

9b. Beginning with the next sentence, there are significant changes in this and the next paragraph, with the idea of death explicitly introduced.

12a. Except for the "Inferno," the works of art are changed from those in "The Landscape Garden." Addison's *Cato* (1713) is a sententious tragedy. A reference to Joel Barlow's dull epic, *The Columbiad* (1807), is canceled in the manuscript. (Barlow's poem is also mentioned in "The Angel of the Odd.") Poe seems to have discussed Dante's "Inferno" with Mrs. Sarah Anna Lewis at about the time he wrote "The Domain of Arnheim." See her sonnet "Beneath the Elm" (1879), reprinted in J. H. Ingram's *Life,* p. 448, from the New York *Home Journal,* February 11, 1880.

16. With this sentence the new part of the story begins.

17. Embittered by ingratitude, Timon of Athens in the Shakespearean play went off by himself to live in a cave.

18. The view from Mount Aetna is also mentioned in *Eureka.* It was much talked about because of a celebrated account (perhaps partly fictional) in Patrick Brydone's *Tour Through Sicily and Malta* (1773).

19. "Fonthill Abbey" in Wiltshire, an extreme example of romantic Gothic, was built in the 1790's for William Beckford, author of *Vathek.* Its tall tower collapsed within a generation and the "abbey" fell into ruin, but it has continued to be referred to as a type of "picturesque" magnificence.

20. [It has been pointed out that Poe may have "borrowed extensively" from Thomas Cole's very popular series of paintings, *The Voyage of Life,* exhibited in Boston in 1840 and in New York in 1841, for the details of this river journey. Not only Cole's explanatory notes but the canvasses themselves may have contributed details. For a study of these possible sources, see Jeffrey A. Hess, "Sources and Aesthetics of Poe's Landscape Fiction," *American Quarterly,* September 1970.]

21. Compare the river's "mazy courses" in "Eleonora," and "playful maziness" in Poe's early poem "To the River —."

22. With the last sentence compare lines 932–933 of Milton's *Comus,* "May thy billows roll ashore/The beryl and the golden ore," which Poe discussed in "Marginalia," number 41 (*Democratic Review,* November 1844, p. 493).

23. See St. Matthew 9:2, "Son, be of good cheer."

24. In Isaac D'Israeli's *Curiosities of Literature,* "Dreams at the Dawn of Philosophy," an automatic boat is described: "The house of Winstanley . . . must have been the wonder of the age . . . There was an arbor in the garden, by the side of a canal; you had scarcely seated yourself when you were sent out afloat to the middle of the canal – from whence you could not escape till this man of art and science wound you up to the arbor." Henry Winstanley, a gentleman of Essex, built the first Eddystone Light, called Winstanley's Tower, and was among those lost when the great storm of November 20, 1703 swept it away. This catastrophe may have suggested Poe's story of "The Light-House."

25. Compare "Julius Rodman," chapter III, "the grass resembled a robe of the softest green velvet."

26. Compare "The Island of the Fay" at note 11: "The trees were lithe . . . of eastern figure and foliage"; and "The Poetic Principle," in the penultimate paragraph: "the slanting of tall, Eastern trees."

27. See the "Sonnet to Science" as adapted for the first version (1841) of "The Island of the Fay," lines 13–14: "The elfin from the grass, the dainty fay,/ The witch, the sprite, the goblin, where are they?"

TALES: 1847–1849

MELLONTA TAUTA and A REMARKABLE LETTER

This story — part of which was entirely rewritten in the form now called "A Remarkable Letter" — satirized the future as seen from the present. There is obviously a kinship to "Some Words with a Mummy," where the present is ridiculed as seen from the past. These stories deal with three favorite ideas of Poe — that history is unreliable, that democracy degenerates into mob rule, and that belief in progress is fallacious.*

The third attitude is illustrated by Poe's remarks in his letter of July 10, 1844, to Dr. Thomas Holley Chivers:

> I disagree with you in what you say of Man's advance towards perfection. Man is now only more active, not wiser, nor more happy, than he was 6000 years ago. To say that we are better than our progenitors, is to make the foregone ages only the rudiment of the present and future; whereas each individual man is the rudiment of a future (material, *not* spiritual) being. It were to suppose God unjust to suppose those who have died before us possessed of less advantage than ourselves.

Comment on dishonest politicians of the last century is needless. But Poe's method here of presenting the corruption of history is complicated. Almost but not quite everything is mixed up for the characters, whom it is convenient to call the Futurians. Some very great men are remembered correctly. Kepler and Newton are unforgotten, but even Francis Bacon is confused with James Hogg, a minor Scottish poet of Poe's own time. Many of the jokes were more apparent to Poe's first readers than they are today; but some, even in 1848, were probably private jokes for Poe himself, for whom any absurd combination was, *per se,* funny.

There is much that is serious in the story. The Futurians are callous toward individual suffering in a terrible way,† but there is

* Other tales dealing with one or more of these ideas are "The Colloquy of Monos and Una," "The Angel of the Odd," "The Thousand-and-Second Tale of Scheherazade," and "The Sphinx."

† See note 10 below.

also a plea for imaginative thinking in science. Poe made more of the latter in the second form of his tale.

The history of the publication in two forms is curious. Poe had "Mellonta Tauta" finished before January 17, 1848, when he wrote Louis A. Godey that he had an article "imaginative – not critical" which he thought might please him, and which must have been accepted and paid for at once. It was the last thing Godey bought from the author.

When Poe delivered his lecture on "The Universe" at the New York Society Library on February 3, 1848, he quoted material from paragraphs 7–13 of the story, entirely reworked and expanded. This was quite justifiable in a lecture, and Poe probably expected the original tale to appear by mid-March, in Godey's magazine for April. But Godey delayed, and the tale was still unpublished when the quoted paragraphs were included in the slightly revised lecture issued in book form as *Eureka* in July 1848.

Poe seems to have forgotten about the matter, for about January 21, 1849, he wrote Annie Richmond, "I see Godey advertises an article by me, but I am at a loss to know what it is." The *Lady's Book* for February 1849, containing "Mellonta Tauta," came out about January 15. It is unlikely that Godey read *Eureka,* but he must have found out about the duplication, and been displeased. Sometime after April 28, Poe again wrote to Annie: "then (on account of his oppression and insolence) I was obliged to quarrel, finally, with . . . ." (This letter is known to us only through publication by Ingram; see Ostrom, *Letters,* II, 437 and 539. The name has been printed only as a blank, but only "Godey" will fit in with what we know of the situation.) It is pleasant to add that Godey made up with Poe early in July 1849.‡

TEXTS

Mellonta Tauta

(A) Godey's Lady's Book for February 1849 (38:133–138); *(B) Works,* IV (1856), 288–301.

The first printed version *(A)* is followed with correction of three misprints. Griswold's version *(B)* shows no auctorial changes or corrections; but, to make

‡ See Poe's letter of July 19, 1849, to Mrs. Clemm; and Quinn, *Poe,* p. 621.

a text that he thought more appropriate to publication in a book, that editor omitted the introductory letter, not observing that it was integral to the story.

The erroneous accents on *"à priori"* and *"à posteriori"* were omitted in *B.*

A Remarkable Letter

(A) Eureka (1848), pp. 10–21; *(B)* Bishop Hurst's copy of *Eureka* with manuscript revisions (1849), now in the collection of Mr. H. Bradley Martin; *(C) Works* (1850), II, 119–127.

There are two copies of Poe's book in which he made revisions, but only the copy that was once in the collection of Bishop Hurst has changes in the pages containing the *jeu d'esprit*, hence that text *(B)* is given. Griswold gave an unrevised copy of *Eureka* to his printer, and his version *(C)* can be disregarded.

MELLONTA TAUTA. [*A*]

To the Editors of the Lady's Book:—

I have the honor of sending you, for your magazine, an article which I hope you will be able to comprehend rather more distinctly than I do myself. It is a translation, by my friend, Martin Van Buren Mavis,[1] (sometimes called the "Poughkeepsie[a] Seer,") of an odd-looking MS. which I found, about a year ago, tightly corked up in a jug floating in the *Mare Tenebrarum* — a sea well described by the Nubian geographer,[2] but seldom visited, now-a-days, except by the transcendentalists and divers for crotchets.[3]

Truly yours,

Edgar A. Poe.

On board Balloon "Skylark,"
April 1, 2848.[4]

Now, my dear friend — now, for your sins, you are to suffer the infliction of a long gossiping letter. I tell you distinctly that I am going to punish you for all your impertinences by being as tedious, as discursive, as incoherent and as unsatisfactory as possible. Besides, here I am, cooped up in a dirty balloon, with some one or two hundred of the *canaille,* all bound on a *pleasure* excursion, (what a funny idea some people have of pleasure!) and I have no prospect

The Letter is omitted from B

a Toughkeepsie *(A) emended for sense, since Poe wrote capital P and T alike*

of touching *terra firma* for a month at least. Nobody to talk to. Nothing to do. When one has nothing to do, then is the time to correspond with one's friends. You perceive, then, why it is that I write you this letter — it is on account of my *ennui* and your sins.

Get ready your spectacles and make up your mind to be annoyed: I mean to write at you every day during this odious voyage.

Heigho! when will any *Invention* visit the human pericranium? Are we forever to be doomed to the thousand inconveniences of the balloon? Will *nobody* contrive a more expeditious mode of progress? This jog-trot movement, to my thinking, is little less than positive torture. Upon my word, we have not made more than a hundred miles the hour since leaving home! The very birds beat us — at least some of them. I assure you that I do not exaggerate at all. Our motion, no doubt, seems slower than it actually is — this on account of our having no objects about us by which to estimate our velocity, and on account of our going *with*[b] the wind. To be sure, whenever we meet a balloon we have a chance of perceiving our rate, and then, I admit, things do not appear so very bad. Accustomed as I am to this mode of traveling, I cannot get over a kind of giddiness whenever a balloon passes us in a current directly overhead. It always seems to me like an immense bird of prey about to pounce upon us and carry us off in its claws. One went over us this morning about sunrise, and so nearly overhead that its drag-rope actually brushed the net-work suspending our car, and caused us very serious apprehension.[5] Our captain said that if the material of the bag had been the trumpery varnished "silk" of five hundred or a thousand years ago, we should inevitably have been damaged. This silk, as he explained it to me, was a fabric composed of the entrails of a species of earth-worm. The worm was carefully fed on mulberries — a kind of fruit resembling a water-melon — and, when sufficiently fat, was crushed in a mill.[6] The paste thus arising was called *papyrus* in its primary state, and went through a variety of processes until it finally became "silk." Singular to relate, it was once much admired as an article of *female dress!* Balloons were also very generally constructed from it. A better kind of material, it appears, was subsequently found in the

b with *(B)*

down surrounding the seed-vessels of a plant vulgarly called *euphorbium,* and at that time botanically termed milk-weed.[7] This latter kind of silk was designated as silk-buckingham,[8] on account of its superior durability, and was usually prepared for use by being varnished with a solution of gum caoutchouc — a substance which in some respects must have resembled the *gutta percha* now in common use. This caoutchouc was occasionally called India rubber or rubber of whist, and was no doubt one of the numerous *fungi.* Never tell me again that I am not at heart an antiquarian.

Talking of drag-ropes — our own, it seems, has this moment knocked a man overboard from one of the small magnetic propellers that swarm in ocean below us — a boat of about six thousand tons,[9] and, from all accounts, shamefully crowded. These diminutive barques should be prohibited from carrying more than a definite number of passengers. The man, of course, was not permitted to get on board again, and was soon out of sight, he and his life-preserver. I rejoice, my dear friend, that we live in an age so enlightened that no such a thing as an individual is supposed to exist.[10] It is the mass for which the true Humanity cares. By the by, talking of Humanity, do you know that our immortal Wiggins[11] is not so original in his views of the Social Condition and so forth, as his contemporaries are inclined to suppose? Pundit assures me that the same ideas were put, nearly in the same way, about a thousand years ago, by an Irish philosopher called Furrier,[12] on account of his keeping a retail shop for cat-peltries and other furs. Pundit *knows,* you know; there can be no mistake about it. How very wonderfully do we see verified, every day, the profound observation of the Hindoo Aries Tottle (as quoted by Pundit) — "Thus must we say that, not once or twice, or a few times, but with almost infinite repetitions, the same opinions come round in a circle among men."[13]

April 2. — Spoke to-day the magnetic cutter in charge of the middle section of floating telegraph wires. I learn that when this species of telegraph was first put into operation by Horse, it was considered quite impossible to convey the wires over sea; but now we are at a loss to comprehend where the difficulty lay![14] So wags the world. *Tempora mutantur* — excuse me for quoting the Etruscan. What *would* we do without the Atalantic[c] telegraph?[15] (Pundit says Atlantic was the ancient adjective.) We lay to a few minutes to ask the cutter some questions, and learned, among other glorious news, that civil war is raging in Africia, while the plague is doing its good work beautifully both in Yurope and Ayesher.[16] Is it not truly remarkable that, before the magnificent light shed upon philosophy by Humanity, the world was accustomed to regard War and Pestilence as calamities? Do you know that prayers were actually offered up in the ancient temples to the end that these *evils* (!) might not be visited upon mankind? Is it not really difficult to comprehend upon what principle of interest our forefathers acted? Were they so blind as not to perceive that the destruction of a myriad of individuals is only so much positive advantage to the mass![17]

April 3. — It is really a very fine amusement to ascend the rope-ladder leading to the summit of the balloon-bag and thence survey the surrounding world. From the car below, you know, the prospect is not so comprehensive — you can see little vertically. But seated here (where I write this) in the luxuriously-cushioned open piazza of the summit, one can see everything that is going on in all directions. Just now, there is quite a crowd of balloons in sight, and they present a very animated appearance, while the air is resonant with the hum of so many millions of human voices. I have heard it asserted that when Yellow or (as Pundit *will* have it) Violet, who is supposed to have been the first æronaut,[18] maintained the practicability of traversing the atmosphere in all directions, by merely ascending or descending until a favorable current was attained, he was scarcely hearkened to at all by his cotemporaries, who looked upon him as merely an ingenious sort of madman, because the philosophers (?)[d] of the day declared the thing impossible. Really now it does seem to me *quite* unaccountable how anything so obviously feasible could have escaped the sagacity of the ancient *savans*. But in all ages the great obstacles to advancement in Art have been opposed by the so-called men of science. To be sure, *our* men of science are not quite so bigoted as those of old: — oh, I have

c Atlantic *(B)*

d philosophers (!) *(B)*

something *so* queer to tell you on this topic.[19] Do you know that it is not more than a thousand years ago since the metaphysicians consented to relieve the people of the singular fancy that there existed but *two possible roads for the attainment of Truth!* Believe it if you can! It appears that long, long ago, in the night of Time, there lived a Turkish philosopher (or Hindoo possibly) called Aries Tottle. This person introduced, or at all events propagated what was termed the deductive or *à priori* mode of investigation. He started with what he maintained to be *axioms* or "self-evident truths," and thence proceeded "logically" to results. His greatest disciples were one Neuclid and one Cant.[20] Well, Aries Tottle flourished supreme until the advent of one Hog, surnamed the "Ettrick Shepherd," who preached an entirely different system, which he called the *à posteriori* or *in*ductive.[21] His plan referred altogther to Sensation. He proceeded by observing, analyzing and classifying facts — *instantiæ naturæ,* as they were affectedly called — into general laws. Aries Tottle's mode, in a word, was based on *noumena;* Hog's on *phenomena.* Well, so great was the admiration excited by this latter system that, at its first introduction, Aries Tottle fell into disrepute; but finally he recovered ground, and was permitted to divide the realm of Truth with his more modern rival. The *savans* now maintained that the Aristotelian and *Baconian* roads were the sole possible avenues to knowledge. "Baconian," you must know, was an adjective invented as equivalent to Hog-ian and more euphonious and dignified.

Now, my dear friend, I do assure you, most positively, that I represent this matter fairly, on the soundest authority; and you can easily understand how a notion so absurd on its very face must have operated to retard the progress of all true knowledge — which makes its advances almost invariably by intuitive bounds.[22] The ancient idea confined investigation to *crawling;* and for hundreds of years so great was the infatuation about Hog especially, that a virtual end was put to all thinking properly so called. No man dared utter a truth for[e] which he felt himself indebted to his *Soul* alone. It mattered not whether the truth was even *demonstrably* a

e to *(A, B) emended for sense and on the basis of the parallel sentence in* "A Remarkable Letter."

truth, for the bullet-headed *savans* of the time regarded only *the road* by which he had attained it. They would not even *look* at the end. "Let us see the means," they cried, "the means!" If, upon investigation of the means, it was found to come neither under the category Aries (that is to say Ram) nor under the category Hog, why then the savans went no farther, but pronounced the "theorist" a fool, and would have nothing to do with him or his truth.

Now, it cannot be maintained, even, that by the crawling system the greatest amount of truth would be attained in any long series of ages, for the repression of *imagination* was an evil not to be compensated for by any superior *certainty* in the ancient modes of investigation. The error of these Jurmains, these Vrinch, these Inglitch and these Amriccans, (the latter, by the way, were our own immediate progenitors,)[23] was an error quite analogous with that of the wiseacre who fancies that he must necessarily see an object the better the more closely he holds it to his eyes.[24] These people blinded themselves by details. When they proceeded Hoggishly, their "facts" were by no means always facts — a matter of little consequence had it not been for assuming that they *were* facts and must be facts because they appeared to be such. When they proceeded on the path of the Ram, their course was scarcely as straight as a ram's horn, for they *never had* an axiom which was an axiom at all. They must have been very blind not to see this, even in their own day; for even in their own day many of the long "established" axioms had been rejected. For example — *"Ex nihilo nihil fit;"*[25] "a body cannot act where it is not;" "there cannot exist antipodes;" "darkness cannot come out of light" — all these, and a dozen other similar propositions, formerly admitted without hesitation as axioms, were, even at the period of which I speak, seen to be untenable. How absurd in these people, then, to persist in putting faith in "axioms" as immutable bases of Truth! But even out of the mouths of their soundest reasoners it is easy to demonstrate the futility, the impalpability of their axioms in general. Who *was* the soundest of their logicians? Let me see! I will go and ask Pundit and be back in a minute . . . . Ah, here we have it! Here is a book written nearly a thousand years ago and lately translated from the Inglitch — which, by the way, appears to have been the rudiment of the Amriccan. Pundit says it is decidedly the cleverest ancient work on its topic, Logic. The author (who was much thought of in his day) was one Miller, or Mill; and we find it recorded of him, as a point of some importance, that he had a mill-horse called Bentham. But let us glance at the treatise![26]

Ah! — "Ability or inability to conceive," says Mr. Mill, very properly, "is in no case to be received as a criterion of axiomatic truth." What *modern* in his senses would ever think of disputing this truism? The only wonder with us must be, how it happened that Mr. Mill conceived it necessary even to hint at anything so obvious. So far good — but let us turn over another page. What have we here? — "Contradictories cannot both be true — that is, cannot co-exist in nature." Here Mr. Mill means, for example, that a tree must be either a tree or not a tree — that it cannot be at the same time a tree and not a tree. Very well; but I ask him *why*. His reply is this — and never pretends to be anything else than this — "Because it is impossible to conceive that contradictories can both be true." But this is no answer at all, by his own showing; for has he not just admitted as a truism that "ability or inability to conceive is *in no case* to be received as a criterion of axiomatic truth?"

Now I do not complain of these ancients so much because their logic is, by their own showing, utterly baseless, worthless and fantastic altogether, as because of their pompous and imbecile proscription of all *other* roads of Truth, of all *other* means for its attainment than the two preposterous paths — the one of creeping and the one of crawling — to which they have dared to confine the Soul that loves nothing so well as to *soar*.[27]

By the by, my dear friend, do you not think it would have puzzled these ancient dogmaticians to have determined by *which* of their two roads it was that the most important and most sublime of *all* their truths was, in effect, attained? I mean the truth of Gravitation. Newton owed it to Kepler. Kepler admitted that his three laws were *guessed at* — these three laws of all laws which led the great Inglitch mathematician to his principle, the basis of all physical principle — to go behind which we must enter the Kingdom of Metaphysics. Kepler guessed — that is to say, *imagined*.[28] He was essentially a "theorist" — that word now of so much sanctity, formerly an epithet of contempt. Would it not have puzzled these old moles,[29] too, to have explained by which of the two "roads" a cryptographist unriddles a cryptograph of more than usual secrecy, or by which of the two roads Champollion directed mankind to those enduring and almost innumerable truths which resulted from his deciphering the Hieroglyphics?[30]

One word more on this topic and I will be done boring you. Is it not *passing* strange that, with their eternal prating about *roads* to Truth, these bigoted people missed what we now so clearly perceive to be the great highway — that of Consistency? Does it not seem singular how they should have failed to deduce from the works of God the vital fact that a perfect consistency *must be* an absolute truth! How plain has been our progress since the late announcement of this proposition! Investigation has been taken out of the hands of the ground-moles and given, as a task, to the true and only true thinkers, the men of ardent imagination. These latter *theorize.* Can you not fancy the shout of scorn with which my words would be received by our progenitors were it possible for them to be now looking over my shoulder? These men, I say, *theorize;* and their theories are simply corrected, reduced, systematized — cleared, little by little, of their dross of inconsistency — until, finally, a perfect consistency stands apparent which even the most stolid admit, because it *is* a consistency, to be an absolute and an unquestionable *truth.*

April 4. — The new gas is doing wonders, in conjunction with the new improvement with gutta percha. How very safe, commodious, manageable, and in every respect convenient are our modern balloons! Here is an immense one approaching us at the rate of at least a hundred and fifty miles an hour. It seems to be crowded with people — perhaps there are three or four hundred passengers — and yet it soars to an elevation of nearly a mile, looking down upon poor us with sovereign contempt. Still a hundred or even two hundred miles an hour is slow traveling, after all. *Do* you remember our flight on the railroad across the Kanadaw continent?[31] — fully three hundred miles the hour — *that* was traveling. Nothing to be seen, though — nothing to be done but flirt, feast and dance in the magnificent saloons. Do you remember what an odd sensation was experienced when, by chance, we caught a glimpse of external objects while the cars were in full flight? Everything seemed unique — in one mass.[32] For my part, I cannot say but that I preferred the traveling by the slow train of a hundred miles the hour. Here we were permitted to have glass windows — even to have them open — and something like a distinct view of the country was attainable. . . . . . . Pundit says that *the route* for the great Kanadaw railroad must have been in some measure marked out about nine hundred years ago![33] In fact, he goes so far as to assert that actual traces of a road are still discernible — traces referable to a period quite as remote as that mentioned. The track, it appears, was *double* only; ours, you know, has twelve paths; and three or four new ones are in preparation. The ancient rails were very slight, and placed so close together as to be, according to modern notions, quite frivolous, if not dangerous in the extreme. The present width of track — fifty feet — is considered, indeed, scarcely secure enough. For my part, I make no doubt that a track of some sort *must* have existed in very remote times, as Pundit asserts; for nothing can be clearer, to my mind, than that, at some period — not less than seven centuries ago, certainly — the Northern and Southern Kanadaw continents were *united;*[34] the Kanawdians, then, would have been driven, by necessity, to a great railroad across the continent.

April 5. — I am almost devoured by *ennui.* Pundit is the only conversible person on board; and he, poor soul! can speak of nothing but antiquities. He has been occupied all day in the attempt to convince me that the ancient Amriccans *governed themselves!* — did ever anybody hear of such an absurdity? — that they existed in a sort of every-man-for-himself confederacy, after the fashion of the "prairie dogs" that we read of in fable.[35] He says that they started with the queerest idea conceivable, viz: that all men are born free and equal — this in the very teeth of the laws of *gradation* so visibly impressed upon all things both in the moral and physical universe. Every man "voted," as they called it — that is to say, meddled with public affairs — until, at length, it was discovered that what is everybody's business is nobody's, and that the "Republic" (so the absurd thing was called) was without a government at all. It is related, however, that the first circumstance which disturbed, very particularly, the self-complacency of the philosophers who constructed this "Republic," was the startling discovery that universal suffrage gave opportunity for fraudulent schemes, by means of which any desired number of votes might at any time be polled, without the possibility of prevention or even detection, by any party which should be merely villainous enough not to be ashamed of the fraud. A little reflection upon this discovery sufficed to render evident the consequences, which were that rascality *must* predominate — in a word, that a republican government *could* never be anything but a rascally one. While the philosophers, however, were busied in blushing at their stupidity in not having foreseen these inevitable evils, and intent upon the invention of new theories, the matter was put to an abrupt issue by a fellow of the name of *Mob*, who took everything into his own hands and set up a despotism, in comparison with which those of the fabulous Zeros and Hellofagabaluses were respectable and delectable.[36] This Mob (a foreigner, by the by), is said to have been the most odious of all men that ever encumbered the earth. He was a giant in stature — insolent, rapacious, filthy; had the gall of a bullock with the heart of an hyena and the brains of a peacock. He died, at length, by dint of his own energies, which exhausted him. Nevertheless, he had his uses, as everything has, however vile, and taught mankind a lesson which to this day it is in no danger of forgetting — never to run directly contrary to the natural analogies. As for Republicanism, no analogy could be found for it upon the face of the earth — unless we except the case of the "prairie dogs," an exception which seems to demonstrate, if anything, that democracy is a very admirable form of government — for dogs.

April 6. — Last night had a fine view of Alpha Lyræ,[37] whose disk, through our captain's spyglass, subtends an angle of half a degree, looking very much as our sun does to the naked eye on a misty day. Alpha Lyræ, although so *very* much larger than our sun, by the by, resembles him closely as regards its spots, its atmosphere, and in many other particulars. It is only within the last century, Pundit tells me, that the binary relation existing between these two orbs began even to be suspected. The evident motion of our system in the heavens was (strange to say!) referred to an orbit about a prodigious star in the centre of the galaxy. About this star, or at all events about a centre of gravity common to all the globes of the Milky Way and supposed to be near Alcyone[38] in the Pleiades, every one of these globes was declared to be revolving, our own performing the circuit in a period of 117,000,000 of years! *We,* with our present lights, or vast telescopic improvements and so forth, of course find it difficult to comprehend *the ground* of an idea such as this. Its first propagator was one Mudler.[39] He was led, we must presume, to this wild hypothesis by mere analogy in the first instance; but, this being the case, he should have at least adhered to analogy in its development. A great central orb *was,* in fact, suggested; so far Mudler was consistent. This central orb, however, dynamically, should have been greater than all its surrounding orbs taken together. The question might then have been asked — "Why do we not see it?" — *we,* especially, who occupy the mid region of the cluster — the very locality *near* which, at least, must be situated this inconceivable central sun. The astronomer, perhaps, at this point, took refuge in the suggestion of non-luminosity; and here analogy was suddenly let fall. But even admitting the central orb non-luminous, how did he manage to explain its failure to be rendered visible by the incalculable host of glorious suns glaring in all directions about it? No doubt what he finally maintained was merely a centre of gravity common to all the revolving orbs — but here again analogy must have been let fall. Our system revolves, it is true, about a common centre of gravity, but it does this in connection with and in consequence of a material sun whose mass more than counterbalances the rest of the system. The mathematical circle is a curve composed of an infinity of straight lines; but this idea of the circle — this idea of it which, in regard to all earthly geometry, we consider as merely the mathematical, in contradistinction from the practical, idea — is, in sober fact, the *practical* conception which alone we have any right to entertain in respect to those Titanic circles with which we have to deal, at least in fancy, when we suppose our system, with its fellows, revolving about a point in the centre of the galaxy. Let the most vigorous of human imaginations but attempt to take a single step towards the comprehension of a circuit so unutterable! It would scarcely be paradoxical to say that a flash of lightning itself, traveling *forever* upon the circumference of this inconceivable circle, would still *forever* be traveling in a straight line. That the path of our sun along such a circumference — that the direction of our system in such an orbit — would, to any human perception, deviate in the slightest degree from a straight line even in a million of years, is a proposition not to be entertained; and yet these ancient astronomers were absolutely cajoled, it appears, into believing that a decisive curvature had become apparent during the brief period of their astronomical history — during the mere point — during the utter nothingness of two or three thousand years! How incomprehensible, that considerations such as this did not at once indicate to them the true state of affairs — that of the binary revolution of our sun and Alpha Lyræ around a common centre of gravity!

April 7. — Continued last night our astronomical amusements. Had a fine view of the five Neptunian[f] asteroids,[40] and watched with much interest the putting up of a huge impost on a couple of lintels in the new temple at Daphnis in the moon.[41] It was amusing to think that creatures so diminutive as the lunarians and bearing so little resemblance to humanity, yet evinced a mechanical ingenuity so much superior to our own. One finds it difficult, too, to conceive the vast masses which these people handle so easily, to be as light as our reason tells us they actually are.

April 8. — Eureka! Pundit is in his glory. A balloon from Kanadaw spoke us to-day and threw on board several late papers: they contain some exceedingly curious information relative to Kanawdian or rather to Amriccan antiquities. You know, I presume, that laborers have for some months been employed in preparing the ground for a new fountain at Paradise, the emperor's principal pleasure garden.[42] Paradise, it appears, has been, *literally* speaking, an island time out of mind — that is to say, its northern boundary was always (as far back as any records extend) a rivulet, or rather a very narrow arm of the sea. This arm was gradually widened until it attained its present breadth — a mile. The whole length of the

f Nepturian *(A, B) emended for sense*

island is nine miles; the breadth varies materially. The entire area (so Pundit says) was, about eight hundred years ago, densely packed with houses, some of them twenty stories high; land (for some most unaccountable reason) being considered as especially precious just in this vicinity. The disastrous earthquake, however, of the year 2050, so totally uprooted and overwhelmed the town (for it was almost too large to be called a village) that the most indefatigable of our antiquarians have never yet been able to obtain from the site any sufficient data (in the shape of coins, medals or inscriptions) wherewith to build up even the ghost of a theory concerning the manners, customs, &c. &c. &c., of the aboriginal inhabitants. Nearly all that we have hitherto known of them is, that they were a portion of the Knickerbocker tribe of savages infesting the continent at its first discovery by Recorder Riker, a knight of the Golden Fleece.[43] They were by no means uncivilized, however, but cultivated various arts and even sciences after a fashion of their own. It is related of them that they were acute in many respects, but were oddly afflicted with a monomania for building what, in the ancient Amriccan, was denominated "churches" – a kind of pagoda instituted for the worship of two idols that went by the names of Wealth and Fashion. In the end, it is said, the island became, nine-tenths of it, church. The women, too, it appears, were oddly deformed by a natural protuberance of the region just below the small of the back – although, most unaccountably, this deformity was looked upon altogether in the light of a beauty. One or two pictures of these singular women have, in fact, been miraculously preserved. They look very odd, *very* – like something between a turkey-cock and a dromedary.[44]

Well, these few details are nearly all that have descended to us respecting the ancient Knickerbockers. It seems, however, that while digging in the centre of the emperor's garden, (which, you know, covers the whole island,) some of the workmen unearthed a cubical and evidently chiseled block of granite, weighing several hundred pounds. It was in good preservation, having received, apparently, little injury from the convulsion which entombed it. On one of its surfaces was a marble slab with (only think of it!) *an inscription – a legible inscription.* Pundit is in ecstasies. Upon detaching the slab, a cavity appeared, containing a leaden box filled with various coins, a long scroll of names, several documents which appear to resemble newspapers, with other matters of intense interest to the antiquarian! There can be no doubt that all these are genuine Amriccan relics belonging to the tribe called Knickerbocker. The papers thrown on board our balloon are filled with fac-similes of the coins, MSS., typography, &c. &c. I copy for your amusement the Knickerbocker inscription on the marble slab: — [45]

This Corner Stone of a Monument to the
Memory of
GEORGE WASHINGTON,
was laid with appropriate ceremonies on the
19TH DAY OF OCTOBER, 1847,
the anniversary of the surrender of
Lord Cornwallis
to General Washington at Yorktown,
A.D. 1781,
under the auspices of the
Washington Monument Association of the
city of New York.

This, as I give it, is a verbatim translation done by Pundit himself, so there *can* be no mistake about it. From the few words thus preserved, we glean several important items of knowledge, not the least interesting of which is the fact that a thousand years ago *actual* monuments had fallen into disuse — as was all very proper — the people contenting themselves, as we do now, with a mere indication of the design to erect a monument at some future time; a corner stone being cautiously laid by itself "solitary and alone" (excuse me for quoting the great Amriccan poet Benton!)[46] as a guarantee of the magnanimous *intention.* We ascertain, too, very distinctly, from this admirable inscription, the how, as well as the where and the what, of the great surrender in question. As to the *where,* it was Yorktown (wherever that was), and as to the *what,* it was General Cornwallis (no doubt some wealthy dealer in corn). *He* was surrendered. The inscription commemorates the surrender of — what? — why, "of Lord Cornwallis." The only question is what could the savages wish him surrendered for. But when we remember that these savages were undoubtedly cannibals, we are led to the conclusion that they intended him for sausage. As to the *how* of the surrender, no language can be more explicit. Lord Cornwallis was surrendered (for sausage) "under the auspices of the Washington Monument Association" – no doubt a charitable institution for the depositing of corner-stones. —— But, Heaven bless me! what is the matter? Ah, I see – the balloon has collapsed, and we shall have a tumble into the sea. I have, therefore, only time enough to add that, from a hasty inspection of the fac-similes of newspapers, &c. &c., I find that *the* great men in those days among the Amriccans, were one John, a smith, and one Zacchary, a tailor.[47]

Good bye, until I see you again. Whether you ever get this letter or not is a point of little importance, as I write altogether for my own amusement. I shall cork the MS. up in a bottle, however, and throw it into the sea.

Yours everlastingly,

PUNDITA.

NOTES

Title: The title phrase, meaning "These things are in the future," is from the *Antigone* of Sophocles, line 1333. Poe probably found it together with the translation as one of the quotations preceding Book IX of Bulwer's *Ernest Maltravers* (1837). For *Tales* (1845), he inserted it as the motto for "The Colloquy of Monos and Una." Poe certainly saw W. Dinneford's disastrous production of Sophocles' play in English in New York – see "The Antigone at Palmo's," *Broadway Journal,* April 12, 1845 – but I doubt that he read it in Greek.

1. By Martin Van Buren Mavis Poe meant the "Poughkeepsie Seer," Andrew Jackson Davis (1826–1910), as was observed by Kendall B. Taft in *American Literature,* January 1955. (The spelling "Toughkeepsie" – see variants – *may* have been auctorial "mystification.") Under mesmerism Davis practiced "clairvoyant" healing from about 1843, and between November 28, 1845 and January 25, 1847 he delivered, in Manhattan, 157 lectures while in a state of mesmeric trance; subsequently he "preached social reconstruction as going hand in hand with spiritual regeneration," gave modern spiritualism much of its phraseology, and first formulated its underlying principles (see *DAB*). In the eleventh of "Fifty Suggestions" (*Graham's,* May 1849) Poe said "There surely can*not* be more things in Heaven and Earth than are dreamt of (oh, Andrew Jackson Davis!) in *your* philosophy."

2. For the term *Mare Tenebrarum* (Sea of Shadows, an old name for the Atlantic Ocean), and for the Nubian Geographer, see "Eleonora," n. 4.

3. The *OED* lists, among derived and figurative meanings of the word crotchet, "a whimsical fancy . . . a fanciful device, mechanical, artistic, or literary." Compare "The Thousand-and-Second Tale of Scheherazade" at n. 45.

4. The setting was a thousand years in the future, for the story was written in 1848; but the letter begins on April Fool's Day, as did the adventure of Poe's earlier balloonist, Hans Phaall.

5. The English balloonist Charles Green (1785–1870) – see "The Balloon Hoax" – is credited with introducing the dragrope (also called guide rope), hung from a balloon to trail along the ground and serve, according to Webster, as "a variable ballast, a brake, or a mooring line." One was used by Poe's voyagers in "The Balloon Hoax" and one by an aeronaut in "The Angel of the Odd."

6. An allusion to the feverish interest in sericulture that raged for several years after 1838. See "Some Secrets of the Magazine Prison-House," n. 6.

7. The botany is intentional nonsense. Euphorbium is an extremely acid gum obtained from spurge *(Euphorbia),* and has no close relation to milkweed *(Asclepias).* Spurge was supposed to cure warts, and is the source of the word expurgate.

8. J. Silk Buckingham was a British traveler, satirized in "Some Words with a Mummy" (see n. 11), in Poe's criticism of Miss Barrett (1845), and in "Marginalia," number 288 (*SLM,* July 1849, p. 416).

9. The first American transatlantic steamers, 1,750 tons each, were put into service between New York and Bremen in 1847.

10. This callous cruelty is intentionally brought in to suggest that the advancements of the future are accompanied by retrogressions – Poe's idea being that Progress is illusory.

11. Wiggins is obviously a philosopher of the future. It is absurd to try to identify him with any writer of Poe's day.

12. Furrier is François-Marie-Charles Fourier, the French socialist, founder of communities called phalanxes; Brook Farm was modeled on his plans. There is another joke in calling him Irish, since "Frenchman" was in Poe's day a humorous name for Irishman.

13. The quotation is from Aristotle's *Meteorologia,* I, iii, as Professor James H. Reid, S. J. told me.

14. Horse is Samuel Finley Breese Morse (1791–1872), inventor of the electric telegraph, referred to also in "The Thousand-and-Second Tale of Scheherazade." Notice that in his prophecy Poe did not envision the Atlantic cable (successfully completed in 1866) as being laid under the ocean, but afloat.

15. The Latin quotation, "Times change and we change with them," is often ascribed (as it was by John Lyly in *Euphues*) to Ovid. Modern reference works call it a sage remark of Lothair, Holy Roman Emperor (840–855), recorded by Borbonius.

16. Etruscan (above) is for Latin; Africa, Europe, and Asia are transparent.

17. See note 10.

18. Here the reference is probably to Charles Green, mentioned above.

19. The material from this point to the end of the entry for April 3 was presented in elaborated form, adorned with several extra bits of "mystification," in "A Remarkable Letter."

20. Euclid and Kant are hardly *disciples* of Aristotle!

21. Francis Bacon is deliberately confused with James Hogg (1770–1835), a Scottish dialect poet called the Ettrick Shepherd, of whom we learn much from the *Noctes Ambrosianae* of *Blackwood's Magazine.*

22. Here Poe stresses the importance of intuition and imagination. Compare the striking change of wording in "A Remarkable Letter" at n. 5.

23. Germans, French, English, and Americans are patent.

24. On holding something too close to see it well, compare "The Murders in the Rue Morgue" (p. 545 above) and "The Sphinx."

25. "Out of nothing nothing is made" – a very old thought – the basis of Epicurean physics – uttered in Greek about 595 B.C. by the poet Alcaeus (Fragment 173) and repeated, with variations in phrasing, in several languages down through more than two thousand years. The concise Latin form Poe quotes he may have found in Henry Fielding's "Essay on Nothing," section 1 (c. 1750): "There is nothing falser than the old proverb which . . . is in everyone's mouth: *Ex nihilo nihil fit.* Thus translated by Shakespeare . . . 'Nothing can come of nothing.' " See *King Lear,* I, 1, 90.

26. John Stuart Mill (1806–1873) is confused with Joe Miller (1684–1738), the reputed compiler of the celebrated joke book. Poe's slighting references to the utilitarian theories of Jeremy Bentham, who disliked poetry, are frequent. The last three quotations above, as well as those in the following paragraph, are adapted from John Stuart Mill, *System of Logic,* Book II, "Of Reasoning," sections 5–7. I quote the 10th edition, London, 1879, pp. 276 and 311:

"There was a time when men of the most cultivated intellects, and the most emancipated from the dominion of early prejudice, could not credit the existence of antipodes; were unable to conceive, in opposition to old association, the force of gravity acting upwards instead of downwards. The Cartesians long rejected the Newtonian doctrine of the gravitation of all bodies toward one another, on the faith of a general proposition, the reverse of which seemed to them to be inconceivable – the proposition that a body cannot act where it is not . . .

"When Mr. Spencer says that while looking at the sun a man cannot conceive that he is looking into darkness, he should have said that a man cannot *believe* that he is doing so."

27. Compare "To Helen [Whitman]," lines 4 and 5, "A full-orbed moon, that, like thine own soul, soaring,/Sought a precipitate pathway up through heaven . . ." Compare the elaboration in "A Remarkable Letter" at n. 8.

28. The discussion of Newton and Kepler is serious.

29. For the phrase "old mole," see *Hamlet,* I, v, 162.

30. See the introduction and notes to "Some Words with a Mummy" for the background of Poe's somewhat imperfect knowledge of Champollion and ancient Egyptian writing. The French savant did *guess* that Coptic was akin to the language of the Pharaohs.

31. Kanadaw (Canada) is the Futurians' generic name for the Americas.

32. "Unique" in this sense is now obsolete. Compare "The Pit and the Pendulum" at n. 24. Poe uses "unique mass" as descriptive of unparticled matter in "Mesmeric Revelation."

33. In 1844 Asa Whitney (1797–1872), a New York businessman with some experience in China, convinced of the benefits a transcontinental railway would produce for the whole country, presented a plan to Congress for a railroad that would run from Lake Michigan to the Pacific. Unsuccessful but tenacious, for the next seven years he conducted a vigorous, unremitting campaign of education in promotion of the project through the press, public meetings, addresses to state legislatures, and contacts with individual congressmen – but the first transcontinental line was not completed until May 10, 1869.

34. The Panama Canal, severing the continents, was first opened to traffic on August 15, 1914.

35. The prairie dog (*Cynomys ludovicianus*) is really a rodent, akin to the squirrels. The following account is abridged from a chapter called "A Republic of Prairie Dogs" in *A Tour of the Prairies* by Washington Irving, which was copied in a review, presumably by E. V. Sparhawk (*SLM,* April 1835):

"A burrow, or village, as it is termed, of prairie dogs, had been discovered . . . about a mile from the camp . . . The prairie dog is . . . one of the curiosities of the far West, about which travellers delight to tell marvellous tales, endowing him at times with something of the politic and social habits of a rational being, and giving him systems of civil government and domestic economy, almost equal to what they used to bestow upon the beaver.

"The prairie dog is an animal of the coney kind, and about the size of a rabbit . . . He is very gregarious, living in large communities, sometimes of several acres in extent, where innumerable little heaps of earth show the entrances to the subterranean cells of the inhabitants, and the well beaten tracks, like lanes and streets, show their mobility and restlessness . . . They would seem to be continually full of sport, business and public affairs . . . Sometimes . . . they pass half the night in revelry, barking or yelping with short, quick, yet weak tones, like those of very young puppies . . .

"This little inhabitant of the prairies . . . appears to be a subject of much whimsical speculation and burlesque remarks, among the hunters of the far West."

36. Zero is for Nero. Hellofagabalus is for Heliogabalus (more properly Elagabalus), a Roman Emperor mentioned also in "William Wilson" and "Four Beasts in One" (note 12). Although sexually depraved, wasteful, and a religious fanatic, he was not cruel. The tyrant Mob is referred to in "Some Words with a Mummy," at n. 38.

37. Alpha Lyrae is Vega; see "Ligeia," n. 14.

38. Alcyone is the central star of the Pleiades in Taurus.

39. Johann Heinrich von Mädler (1794–1874), a German astronomer, in 1846 published *Die Centralsonne,* propounding a system of all the solar systems of the Galaxy revolving about a central orb. The discussion that follows is much elaborated in paragraphs 212–225 of *Eureka.*

40. Neptunian asteroids are minor planets, which might be found in the future, near Neptune. The original magazine reading (Nepturian) is clearly a misprint; Poe does not meaninglessly confuse the names of heavenly bodies in the story.

41. Poe planned to discuss the inhabitants of the moon in "Hans Phaall," had he continued it. Daphnis is not the real name of any lunar formation now recorded. In Greek mythology Diana, the moon goddess, was the patron of the shepherd Daphnis. By 2848 a city in the moon may be named for him.

42. Paradise means park; the reference (reminiscent of Kubla Khan's stately pleasure dome) is to the Park Fountain, near City Hall in New York; the island is Manhattan.

43. Richard Riker (1773–1842) was a New York politician, to whom Fitz-Greene Halleck addressed his once famous poem, "To the Recorder." The Order of the Golden Fleece was the highest decoration of the Holy Roman Empire. Poe hints that Riker, who was widely suspected of grafting, had fleeced the people of their gold.

44. Poe also ridiculed bustles in "The Spectacles" and in "The Thousand-and-Second Tale of Scheherazade."

45. The proponents of a "suitable" monument had been trying since the beginning of a subscription list in 1843 to raise funds for the project. The goal remained far out of sight, however, and in 1847 it was hoped that the laying of a cornerstone would stimulate further contributions. Elaborate ceremonies accompanied the dedication, including a parade, cannon, speeches, and George Pope Morris's ode, sung by 500 voices "with great *éclat*." The *New-York Daily Tribune,* October 20, 1847, carried a glowing account of the affair. But the proposed monument never took shape, and Henry Kirke-Brown's equestrian bronze statue of Washington, in Union Square, was not unveiled until 1856. See James Grant Wilson, *Memorial History of . . . New York* (1893), III, 454.

46. The phrase "solitary and alone" occurs in Laurence Sterne's *Sentimental Journey,* chapter xxxi, "Paris," but Poe and his contemporaries undoubtedly associated it with Thomas Hart Benton (1782–1858), senator from Missouri, who had used it in a brief but emphatic speech of 1837. Referring to his stalwart three-year fight to have a resolution censuring President Jackson for removing federal deposits from the Bank of the United States "expunged" from the record, just before the "expunging" vote was taken Benton "uttered the following well-known words which have become imperishably associated with his name: 'Solitary and alone I set this ball in motion.' " See the *United States Magazine and Democratic Review* for October 1837, p. 83. [Burton Pollin calls attention to this reference and others in "Politics and History in Poe's 'Mellonta Tauta': Two Allusions Explained," *Studies in Short Fiction,* Fall 1971, in which he sketches the contemporary background of Poe's tale.] Benton, in the course of his long and distinguished political career, had, on numerous issues, voted in opposition to his fellow Democrats; in 1848 he refused to take sides in a split in the Democratic Party over the choice of a presidential candidate and thereafter was politically isolated.

47. The references are to the commonest name, John Smith; and to that of President Zachary Taylor, recently elected when Poe wrote.

[A REMARKABLE LETTER (*B*)]

[Excerpted from paragraphs 11–25 of *Eureka*]

And now, before proceeding to our subject proper, let me beg the reader's attention to an extract or two from a somewhat remarkable letter, which appears to have been found corked in a bottle and floating on the *Mare Tenebrarum* — an ocean well described by the Nubian geographer, Ptolemy Hephestion,[1] but little frequented in modern days unless by the Transcendentalists and some other divers for crotchets. The date of this letter, I confess, surprises me even more particularly than its contents; for it seems to have been written in the year *two* thousand eight hundred and forty-eight. As for the passages I am about to transcribe, they, I fancy, will speak for themselves.

"Do you know, my dear friend," says the writer, addressing, no doubt, a contemporary — "Do you know that it is scarcely more than eight or nine hundred years ago since the metaphysicians first consented to relieve the people of the singular fancy that there exist *but two practicable roads to Truth*?[2] Believe it if you can! It appears, however, that long, long ago, in the night of Time, there lived a Turkish philosopher called Aries and surnamed Tottle." [Here, possibly, the letter-writer means Aristotle; the best names are wretchedly corrupted in two or three thousand years.] "The fame of this great man depended mainly on[a] his demonstration that sneezing is a natural provision, by means of which over-profound thinkers are enabled to expel superfluous ideas through the nose;[3] but he obtained a scarcely less valuable celebrity as the founder, or at all events as the principal propagator, of what was termed the *de*ductive or *à priori* philosophy. He started with what he maintained to be axioms, or self-evident truths: — and the now well understood fact that *no* truths are *self*-evident, really does not make in the slightest degree against his speculations: — it was sufficient for his purpose that the truths in question were evident at all. From axioms he proceeded, logically, to results. His most illustrious disciples were one Tuclid, a geometrician," [meaning Euclid] "and

---

Title: Editorially supplied from the narrative itself.

a upon *(A, C)*

one Kant, a Dutchman, the originator of that species of Transcendentalism which, with the change merely of a C for a K, now bears his peculiar name.[4]

"Well, Aries Tottle flourished supreme, until the advent of one Hog, surnamed 'the Ettrick shepherd,' who preached an entirely different system, which he called the *à posteriori* or *in*ductive. His plan referred altogether to sensation. He proceeded by observing, analyzing, and classifying facts – *instantiæ, Naturæ,* as they were somewhat affectedly called – and arranging them into general laws. In a word, while the mode of Aries rested on *noumena,* that of Hog depended on *phenomena;* and so great was the admiration excited by this latter system that, at its first introduction, Aries fell into general disrepute. Finally, however, he recovered ground, and was permitted to divide the empire of Philosophy with his more modern rival: – the savans contenting themselves with proscribing all *other* competitors, past, present, and to come; putting an end to all controversy on the topic by the promulgation of a Median law, to the effect that the Aristotelian and Baconian roads are, and of right ought to be, the sole possible avenues to knowledge: – 'Baconian,' you must know, my dear friend," adds the letter-writer at this point, "was an adjective invented as equivalent to Hog-ian, while[b] more dignified and euphonious.

"Now I do assure you most positively" – proceeds the epistle – "that I represent these matters fairly; and you can easily understand how restrictions so absurd on their very face must have operated, in those days, to retard the progress of true Science, which makes its most important advances – as all History will show – by seemingly intuitive *leaps.*[5] These ancient ideas confined investigation to crawling; and I need not suggest to you that crawling, among varieties of locomotion, is a very capital thing of its kind; – but because the snail[c] is sure of foot, for this reason must we clip the wings of the eagles? For many centuries, so great was the infatuation, about Hog especially, that a virtual stop was put to all thinking, properly so called. No man dared utter a truth for which he felt himself indebted to his soul alone. It mattered not whether

b and at the same time *(A, C)* c tortoise *(A, C)*

the truth was even demonstrably such; for the dogmatizing philosophers of that epoch regarded only *the road* by which it professed to have been attained. The end, with them, was a point of no moment, whatever: – 'the means!' they vociferated – 'let us look at the means!' – and if, on scrutiny of the means, it was found to come neither under the category Hog, nor under the category Aries (which means ram), why then the savans went no farther, but, calling the thinker 'a fool' and branding him a 'theorist,' would never, thenceforward, have any thing to do either with *him* or with his truths.

"Now, my dear friend," continues the letter-writer, "it cannot be maintained that by the crawling system, exclusively adopted, men would arrive at the maximum amount of truth, even in any long series of ages; for the repression of imagination was an evil not to be counterbalanced even by *absolute* certainty in the snail processes. But their certainty was very far from absolute. The error of our progenitors was quite analogous with that of the wiseacre who fancies he must necessarily see an object the more distinctly, the more closely he holds it to his eyes. They blinded themselves, too, with the impalpable, titillating Scotch snuff of *detail;* and thus the boasted facts of the Hog-ites were by no means always facts – a point of little importance but for the assumption that they always *were.* The vital taint, however, in Baconianism – its most lamentable fount of error – lay in its tendency to throw power and consideration into the hands of merely perceptive men – of those inter-Tritonic minnows,[6] the microscopical savans – the diggers and pedlers of minute *facts,* for the most part in physical science – facts all of which they retailed at the same price on[d] the highway; their value depending, it was supposed, simply upon the *fact of their fact,* without reference to their applicability or inapplicability in the development of those ultimate and only legitimate facts, called Law.

"Than the persons" – the letter goes on to say – "Than the persons thus suddenly elevated by the Hog-ian philosophy into a station for which they were unfitted – thus transferred from the

---

d upon *(A, C)*

sculleries into the parlors of Science — from its pantries into its pulpits — than these individuals a more intolerant — a more intolerable set of bigots and tyrants never existed on the face of the earth. Their creed, their text and their sermon were, alike, the one word *'fact'* — but, for the most part, even of this one word, they knew not even the meaning. On those who ventured to *disturb* their facts with the view of putting them in order and to use, the disciples of Hog had no mercy whatever. All attempts at generalization were met at once by the words 'theoretical,' 'theory,' 'theorist' — all *thought,* to be brief, was very properly resented as a personal affront to themselves. Cultivating the natural sciences to the exclusion of Metaphysics, the Mathematics, and Logic, many of these Bacon-engendered philosophers — one-idead, one-sided and lame of a leg — were more wretchedly helpless — more miserably ignorant, in view of all the comprehensible objects of knowledge, than the veriest unlettered hind[7] who proves that he knows something at least, in admitting that he knows absolutely nothing.

"Nor had our forefathers any better right to talk about *certainty,* when pursuing, in blind confidence, the *à priori* path of axioms, or of the Ram. At innumerable points this path was scarcely as straight as a ram's-horn. The simple truth is, that the Aristotelians erected their castles on[e] a basis far less reliable than air; *for no such things as axioms ever existed or can possibly exist at all.* This they must have been very blind, indeed, not to see, or at least to suspect; for, even in their own day, many of their long-admitted 'axioms' had been abandoned: — *'ex nihilo nihil fit,'* for example, and a 'thing cannot act where it is not,' and 'there cannot be antipodes,' and 'darkness cannot proceed from light.' These and numerous similar propositions formerly accepted, without hesitation, as axioms, or undeniable truths, were, even at the period of which I speak, seen to be altogether untenable: — how absurd in these people, then, to persist in relying upon a basis, as immutable, whose mutability had become so repeatedly manifest!

"But, even through evidence afforded by themselves against themselves, it is easy to convict these *à priori* reasoners of the

e upon *(A, C)*

grossest unreason — it is easy to show the futility — the impalpability of their axioms in general. I have now lying before me" — it will be observed that we still proceed with the letter — "I have now lying before me a book printed about a thousand years ago. Pundit assures me that it is decidedly the cleverest ancient work on its topic, which is 'Logic.' The author, who was much esteemed in his day, was one Miller, or Mill; and we find it recorded of him, as a point of some importance, that he rode a mill-horse whom he called Jeremy Bentham: — but let us glance at the volume itself!

"Ah! — 'Ability or inability to conceive,' says Mr. Mill very properly, 'is *in no case* to be received as a criterion of axiomatic truth.' Now, that this is a palpable truism no one in his senses will deny. *Not* to admit the proposition, is to insinuate a charge of variability in Truth itself, whose very title is a synonym of the Steadfast. If ability to conceive be taken as a criterion of Truth, then a truth to *David* Hume would very seldom be a truth to *Joe;*[8] and ninety-nine hundredths of what is undeniable in Heaven would be demonstrable falsity upon Earth. The proposition of Mr. Mill, then, is sustained. I will not grant it to be an *axiom;* and this merely because I am showing that *no* axioms exist; but, with a distinction which could not have been cavilled at even by Mr. Mill himself, I am ready to grant that, *if* an axiom *there be,* then the proposition of which we speak has the fullest right to be considered an axiom — that no *more* absolute axiom *is* — and, consequently, that any subsequent proposition which shall conflict with this one primarily advanced, must be either a falsity in itself — that is to say no axiom — or, if admitted axiomatic, must at once neutralize both itself and its predecessor.

"And now, by the logic of their own propounder, let us proceed to test any one of the axioms propounded. Let us give Mr. Mill the fairest of play. We will bring the point to no ordinary issue. We will select for investigation no common-place axiom — no axiom of what, not the less preposterously because only impliedly, he terms his secondary class — as if a positive truth by definition could be either more or less positively a truth: — we will select, I say, no axiom of an unquestionability so questionable as is to be found in Euclid. We will not talk, for example, about such propositions as that two straight lines cannot enclose a space, or that the whole is greater than any one of its parts. We will afford the logician *every* advantage. We will come at once to a proposition which he regards as the acme of the unquestionable — as the quintessence of axiomatic undeniability. Here it is: — 'Contradictions cannot *both* be true — that is, cannot cöexist in nature.' Here Mr. Mill means, for instance, — and I give the most forcible instance conceivable — that a tree must be either a tree or *not* a tree — that it cannot be at the same time a tree *and* not a tree: — all which is quite reasonable of itself and will answer remarkably well as an axiom, until we bring it into collation with an axiom insisted upon a few pages before — in other words — words which I have previously employed — until we test it by the logic of its own propounder. 'A tree,' Mr. Mill asserts, 'must be either a tree or *not* a tree.' Very well: — and now let me ask him, *why*. To this little query there is but one response: — I defy any man living to invent a second. The sole answer is this: — 'Because we find it *impossible to conceive* that a tree can be any thing else than a tree or not a tree.' This, I repeat, is Mr. Mill's sole answer: — he will not *pretend* to suggest another: — and yet, by his own showing, his answer is clearly no answer at all; for has he not already required us to admit, *as an axiom,* that ability or inability to conceive is *in no case* to be taken as a criterion of axiomatic truth? Thus all — absolutely *all* his argumentation is at sea without a rudder. Let it not be urged that an exception from the general rule is to be made, in cases where the 'impossibility to conceive' is so peculiarly great as when we are called upon to conceive a tree *both* a tree and *not* a tree. Let no attempt, I say, be made at urging this sotticism; for, in the first place, there are no *degrees* of 'impossibility,' and thus no one impossible conception can be *more* peculiarly impossible than another impossible conception: — in the second place, Mr. Mill himself, no doubt after thorough deliberation, has most distinctly, and most rationally, excluded all opportunity for exception, by the emphasis of his proposition, that, *in no case,* is ability or inability to conceive, to be taken as a criterion of axiomatic truth: — in the third place, even were exceptions admissible at all, it remains to be shown how any exception is admissible *here.* That a tree can be both a tree and not a tree, is an idea which the angels, or the devils, *may* entertain, and which no doubt many an earthly Bedlamite, or Transcendentalist, *does.*

"Now I do not quarrel with these ancients," continues the letter-writer, "*so much* on account of the transparent frivolity of their logic – which, to be plain, was baseless, worthless and fantastic altogether – as on account of their pompous and infatuate proscription of all *other* roads to Truth than the two narrow and crooked paths – the one of creeping and the other of crawling – to which, in their ignorant perversity, they have dared to confine the Soul – the Soul which loves nothing so well as to soar in those regions of illimitable intuition which are utterly incognizant of *'path.'*[9]

"By the bye, my dear friend, is it not an evidence of the mental slavery entailed upon those bigoted people by their Hogs and Rams,[f] that in spite of the eternal prating of their savans about *roads* to Truth, none of them fell, even by accident, into what we now so distinctly perceive to be the broadest, the straightest and most available of all mere roads – the great thoroughfare – the majestic highway of the *Consistent?* Is it not wonderful that they should have failed to deduce from the works of God the vitally momentous consideration that *a perfect consistency can be nothing but an absolute truth?* How plain – how rapid our progress since the late announcement of this proposition! By its means, investigation has been taken out of the hands of the ground-moles, and given as a duty, rather than as a task, to the true – to the *only* true thinkers – to the generally-educated men of ardent imagination. These latter – our Keplers – our Laplaces – [10] 'speculate' – 'theorize' – these are the terms – can you not fancy the shout of scorn with which they would be received by our progenitors, were it possible for them to be looking over my shoulders as I write? The Keplers, I repeat, speculate – theorize – and their theories are merely corrected – reduced – sifted – cleared, little by little, of their chaff of inconsistency – until at length there stands apparent an unencumbered *Consistency* – a consistency which the most stolid admit – because it *is* a consistency – to be an absolute and an unquestionable *Truth.*

f Eams *(C) misprint*

"I have often thought, my friend, that it must have puzzled these dogmaticians of a thousand years ago, to determine, even, by which of their two boasted roads it is that the cryptographist attains the solution of the more complicate cyphers — or by which of them Champollion guided mankind to those important and innumerable truths which, for so many centuries, have lain entombed amid the phonetical hieroglyphics of Egypt. In especial, would it not have given these bigots some trouble to determine by which of their two roads was reached the most momentous and sublime of *all* their truths — the truth — the fact of *gravitation?* Newton deduced it from the laws of Kepler. Kepler admitted that these laws he *guessed* — these laws whose investigation disclosed to the greatest of British astronomers that principle, the basis of all (existing) physical principle, in going behind which we enter at once the nebulous kingdom of Metaphysics. Yes! — these vital laws Kepler *guessed* — that is to say, he *imagined* them. Had he been asked to point out either the *de*ductive or *in*ductive route by which he attained them, his reply might have been — 'I know nothing about *routes* — but I *do* know the machinery of the Universe. Here it is. I grasped it with *my soul* — I reached it through mere dint of *intuition.* Alas, poor ignorant old man! Could not any metaphysician have told him that what he called 'intuition' was but the conviction resulting from *de*ductions or *in*ductions of which the processes were so shadowy as to have escaped his consciousness, eluded his reason, or bidden defiance to his capacity of expression? How great a pity it is that some 'moral philosopher' had not enlightened him about all this! How it would have comforted him on his death-bed to know that, instead of having gone intuitively and thus unbecomingly, he had, in fact, proceeded decorously and legitimately — that is to say Hog-ishly, or at least Ram-ishly — into the vast halls where lay gleaming, untended, and hitherto untouched by mortal hand — unseen by mortal eye — the imperishable and priceless secrets of the Universe!

"Yes, Kepler was essentially a *theorist;* but this title, *now* of so much sanctity, was, in those ancient days, a designation of supreme contempt. It is only *now* that men begin to appreciate that divine old man — to sympathize with the prophetical and poetical rhapsody of his ever-memorable words. For *my* part," continues the unknown correspondent, "I glow with a sacred fire when I even think of them, and feel that I shall never grow weary of their repetition: — in concluding this letter, let me have the real pleasure of transcribing them once again: — *'I care not whether my work be read now or by posterity. I can afford to wait a century for readers when God himself has waited six thousand years for an observer. I triumph. I have stolen the golden secret of the Egyptians. I will indulge my sacred fury.'* "[11]

Here end my quotations from this very unaccountable [g]if not[g] impertinent epistle; and perhaps it would be folly to comment, in any respect, upon the chimerical, not to say revolutionary, fancies of the writer — whoever he is — fancies so radically at war with the well-considered and well-settled opinions of this age.

NOTES

Most of the allusions are discussed in the notes on "Mellonta Tauta" above, but several of Poe's references, different in "A Remarkable Letter," are identified below.

1. This is intentional confusion: Ptolemy Hephestion (or son of Hephestion), a Greek mythographer (see "Berenicë," n. 9), was *not* the Nubian Geographer (see "Eleonora," n. 4). Compare the introductory paragraph of "Mellonta Tauta."

2. Compare "Mellonta Tauta" at n. 19.

3. Aristotle, in *Problemata,* xxxiii, 9, said that sneezing comes from the head, the "seat of reason." Compare "Bon-Bon" at n. 19.

4. Immanuel Kant was *ein Deutscher,* a German, but not *ein Hollander,* a Dutchman.

5. Compare "Mellonta Tauta" at n. 22. Poe's change in wording strengthens his point by making it startlingly clear. On knowledge by intuition see "A Chapter of Suggestions" (*The Opal* for 1845), number 8: "The intuitive and seemingly casual perception by which we often attain knowledge, when reason herself falters and abandons the effort, appears to resemble the sudden glancing at a star, by which we see it more clearly than by a direct gaze; or the half-closing the eyes in looking at a plot of grass, the more fully to appreciate the intensity of its green." See also "The Murders in the Rue Morgue," n. 30.

6. Inter-Tritonic minnows are little fishes swimming among Tritons — monstrous denizens of the deep — whose vastness is beyond their comprehension.

---

g . . . g and, perhaps, somewhat *(A, C)*

7. Compare Milton, *Comus,* lines 171–173:

"... riot and ill managed merriment
Such as the jocund flute, or gamesome pipe
Stirs up among the base unlettered hinds ..."

8. David Hume (1711–1776) was the great Scottish historian and empiric philosopher; Joseph Hume (1777–1855) was long a radical leader in the House of Commons, and proposed many reforms in Church and State. He was certainly an eccentric, but noted for his integrity.

9. See "Mellonta Tauta," n. 27.

10. The allusion is to Pierre-Simon, Marquis de Laplace (1749–1827), celebrated French astronomer and mathematician.

11. Poe here had in mind remarks of Johann Kepler (1571–1630), discoverer of the "laws" of planetary motion known by his name and basic to the development of modern astronomy, in a letter written after he had confirmed the validity of his third law. An account of the episode by Sir David Brewster appeared in his small volume *The Martyrs of Science, or, the Lives of Galileo, Tycho Brahe, and Kepler* (London, 1841). In the Harper edition of 1843, p. 217, one reads:

"This law, as he himself informs us, first entered his mind on the 8th of March, 1618; but, having made an erroneous calculation, he was obliged to reject it. He resumed the subject on the 15th of May; and, having discovered his former error, he recognised with transport the absolute truth of a principle which for seventeen years had been the object of his incessant labours. The delight which this grand discovery gave him had no bounds. 'Nothing holds me,' says he; 'I will indulge in my sacred fury; I will triumph over mankind by the honest confession that I have stolen the golden vases of the Egyptians to build up a tabernacle for my God, far away from the confines of Egypt. If you forgive me I rejoice; if you are angry, I can bear it. The die is cast; the book is written, to be read either now or by posterity, I care not which. It may well wait a century for a reader, as God has waited six thousand years for an observer.' "

One of Brewster's acknowledged sources, John Elliot Drinkwater Bethune's *Life of Kepler* (1830) in the Library of Useful Knowledge, was first cited in connection with Poe by Margaret Alterton in *Origins of Poe's Critical Theory,* pp. 142–143. Poe may have found his material in either Brewster or Bethune, or in another translation, since Kepler's rhapsodic outburst was well known to students of astronomy.

A PREDICTION

This short piece deserves a place among Poe's Tales and Sketches because of its imaginative character and its avowed connection with "The Conversation of Eiros and Charmion."

Poe never printed it, but on February 29, 1848, included a manuscript copy in the postscript to a letter addressed to George

W. Eveleth. The body of the letter was mainly concerned with the lecture on "The Universe" which Poe had delivered on February 3 and was to publish in revised form as *Eureka* in July. The postscript contained, besides "A Prediction," some less speculative comments on the solar system, and has been in print, somewhat incompletely, since 1895.

Poe could not have composed "A Prediction" in the form that has reached us until he had heard about the discovery of Neptune. The new planet was first seen by Johann Gottfried Galle at Berlin on September 23, 1846, and a satellite was noticed three weeks later. News must have taken from two to four weeks to reach America.

An earlier version of "A Prediction" may have been written in which Uranus was mentioned as the most remote planet, as Poe's words suggest, but his notorious inaccuracy about dates makes his phrase "penned . . . several years ago" of doubtful value.

TEXTS

(A) Manuscript, February 29, 1848; *(B)* Transcript of the manuscript by George W. Eveleth, October 1, 1878; *(C) Works,* edited by Stedman and Woodberry, vol. IX (1895), pp. 293–295; *(D)* New York *Methodist Review,* January 1896 (78: 9–11); *(E) Complete Works,* edited by Harrison (1902), XVI, 337–339, as part of "Poe's Addenda to 'Eureka.' "

The transcript *(B)* sent in a letter to John H. Ingram in 1878, now number 41 among his papers at the University of Virginia, is necessarily followed, since the original manuscript *(A)* no longer accompanies Poe's letter in the Pierpont Morgan Library and has not been seen since 1896. There is reason to think this text is complete. [We are indebted to Edmund Berkeley, Jr., Curator of the Manuscripts Department of the Alderman Library at the University of Virginia for a recent collation.] The two versions first published *(C* and *D)* are from later transcripts by Eveleth, who silently omitted small portions in each case. Harrison's text *(E)* is a composite making use of both the early printed forms, but neither of these included the final sentence, which is now first printed.

A PREDICTION. [*B*]

By the bye, lest you infer that my views, in detail, are the same with those advanced in the *Nebular Hypothesis,*[a] [1] I venture to offer a few addenda, the substance of which was penned, though[a′] never printed, several years ago, under the head of — A Prediction.

a Nebular Hypothesis, *(C)* a′ but *(C)*

A PREDICTION

As soon as the[a″] next century it will be entered in *the books,*[b] that the Sun was originally condensed *at once*[c] (not gradually, according to the supposition of Laplace) into[d] his smallest size; that, thus condensed, he rotated on an axis; that this axis of rotation was not the centre of his figure, so that he not only rotated, but revolved in an elliptical orbit (the rotation and revolution are one; but I separate them for convenience of illustration); that, thus formed and thus revolving, he was on fire [e](in the same way that a volcano and an ignited meteoric stone are on fire)[e] and sent into space his substance in [f]the form of[f] vapor, this vapor reaching farthest on the side of the larger[g] hemisphere, partly on account of the largeness, but principally because the force of the fire was greater here; that, in due time, this vapor, not necessarily carried then to the place now occupied by Neptune, condensed into Neptune;[h] that the planet[i] took, as a matter of necessity,[j] the same figure that[k] the Sun had, which figure made his rotation a revolution in an elliptical orbit; that, in consequence of such revolution — in consequence of his being *carried backward* at each of the *daily*[1] revolutions — the velocity of his *annual* revolution is not so great as it would be, if it depended solely upon the Sun's velocity of rotation (Kepler's Third Law);[2] that his figure, by influencing his rotation — the heavier half, as it turns downward toward the Sun, gains an impetus sufficient to carry it by[m] the direct line of attraction, and thus to *throw outward* the centre of gravity — gave him power to save himself from falling to the [n]Sun (and, perhaps, to work himself gradually outward to the position he now holds);[n] that he received, through a series of ages, the Sun's heat, which penetrated to his centre, causing [o]volcanic eruptions[o] eventually, and thus throwing off vapor; and which evaporated substances upon his surface, till finally[p] his moons and his gaseous ring (if it is true that he has a ring)[3] were produced; that these moons took elliptical forms, rotated and revolved "both under one," were

a″ the beginning of the *(C, D, E)*
b the books *(D, E)*
c at once *(D, E)*
d to *(D, E)*
e . . . e *Omitted (C, D, E)*
f . . . f *Omitted (D, E)*
g larger (equatorial) *(D, E)*
h that planet; *(C, D, E)*
i the planet/Neptune *(C, D, E)*
j course, *(D, E)*
k which *(D, E)*
l daily *(D, E)*
m past *(D, E)*
n . . . n Sun; *(D, E)*
o . . . o volcanoes *(C, D, E)*
p *Omitted (C)*

kept in their *monthly* orbits by the centrifugal force acquired in their *daily*[q] orbits, and required a longer time to make their monthly revolutions than they would have required[q'] if they had had no daily revolutions.

I have said enough, without referring to the other planets, to give you an inkling of my hypothesis, which is all I intended to do. I did not design to offer any evidence of its reasonableness; since I have not, in fact, any collected, excepting as it is flitting, in the shape of a shadow, to and fro within my brain.

You perceive that I hold to the idea that our Moon[r] must rotate upon her axis oftener than she revolves round her primary, the same being the case with the satellites[s] accompanying Jupiter, Saturn and Uranus.

Since the penning, a closer analysis of the matter contained has led me to modify somewhat my opinion as to the origin of the satellites — that is, I think[s'] now that these came, not from vapor sent off in volcanic burnings[t] and by simple diffusion under the solar rays, but from rings of it which were left in the inter-planetary spaces, after the precipitation of the primaries. There is no insuperable obstacle in the way of the conception that aerolites[u] and "shooting-stars" have their source in matter which has gone off from [v]the Earth's surface and from out her bowels;[v] but it is hardly supposable that a sufficient quantity could be produced thus to make a body so large as, by centrifugal force resulting from rotation, to withstand the absorptive power of its parent's rotation. The event implied may take place not until the planets have become flaming suns — *from an accumulation of their own Sun's caloric, reaching from centre to circumference,*[w] *which shall, in the lonesome latter days,*[4] *melt all the elements*[x] *and dissipate the solid foundations out as a scroll!*[5] [y](Please substitute the idea for that in "Conversation of Eiros and Charmion").[y] [6]

---

q daily (moon-day) *(C)*
q' *Omitted (C)*
r moon *(D, E)*
s moons *(C, D, E)*
s' hold *(C, D, E)*
t eruptions *(C, D, E)*
u meteoric stones *(C, D, E)*
v . . . v volcanoes, and by common evaporation; *(C, D, E)*
w *surface, (C, D, E)*
x *'elements' (D, E)*
y . . . y *Omitted (C, D, E)*

NOTES

Title: Supplied from the introductory paragraph. Poe's letter of February 29, 1848, with its postscript, was apparently the fifth item in a series of transcripts Eveleth sent to Ingram in one mailing. The letter proper begins near the foot of page 10, ends on page 12 with Poe's signature, and is followed on the next line by the paragraph ("By the bye . . .") introducing the postscript. Professor Ostrom (*Letters*, II, 525, note on letter 263) points out that the original manuscript of Poe's letter, now in the Morgan Library, consists of two pages, with "the last line of the letter, the close, and the signature all being written on the same line at the foot of the page," thus the paragraph introducing the postcript began on a new page, and – from the evidence of Eveleth's closely written transcript – probably without a heading. Mr. Ostrom also mentions that the introductory paragraph was first printed by Ingram (II, 141–142), in his 1880 biography of Poe.

1. The Nebular Hypothesis is that of Pierre-Simon, Marquis de Laplace (1749–1827) who published his *Mécanique Céleste* between 1799 and 1825. The translation (1829–1839) by Nathaniel Bowditch is a famous work of early American scholarship. This hypothesis is referred to again in "A Remarkable Letter."

2. Johann Kepler's Third Law is: "The square of the time of revolution of any planet about the Sun is proportional to the cube of its mean distance from the Sun." It was stated in Kepler's *Harmonici mundi* (1619).

3. Neptune now is known to have no ring. The existence of his second moon was long doubted, but was finally confirmed in 1949 by G. P. Kuiper, who found it on a photograph made May 1, 1949 with the 82-inch reflector at McDonald Observatory in Texas. (I am indebted to Professor Stanley P. Wyatt for these details.) The two moons are now named Triton and Nereid. Triton (the larger, and the first discovered) is retrograde.

4. Compare "The Conqueror Worm," lines 1–2, "a gala night/Within the lonesome latter years."

5. Compare also Isaiah 34:4, "And all the host of heaven shall be dissolved, and the heavens shall be rolled together as a scroll"; and Revelation 6:14, "The heaven departed as a scroll when it is rolled together."

6. In "The Conversation of Eiros and Charmion" (1839) Poe suggested that a comet with an affinity for nitrogen might cause a final general conflagration. See the commentary on that story.

A WOULD-BE CRICHTON

This little story is old in substance, and tells again something generally told of the famous Cambridge Professor Richard Porson (1759–1808), as noted for classical learning as for Bacchanalian prowess.* Once, when traveling, Porson met a boastful fellow who quoted freely from Aeschylus, Sophocles, and Euripides. Porson produced the complete works of the three Greek tragedians from his pockets, and confounded the pretender, who could locate none of the passages he had cited.

Oddly enough, Poe once saved a friend from a similar experience. Mrs. Whitman, discussing Poe's "habitual courtesy and good nature . . . in domestic and social life," said, "At one of the soirées . . . A lady, noted for her great lingual attainments, wishing to . . . check . . . the vanity of a young author, proposed inviting him to translate . . . a difficult passage in Greek, of which . . . she knew him to be profoundly ignorant, although given to a . . . display of Greek quotations in his published writings. Poe's earnest and persistent remonstrance against this piece of *méchanceté* alone averted the embarrassing test."†

Poe's paragraph was in one of the manuscripts of "Marginalia" he had just sent to the *Southern Literary Messenger,* as he reported in a letter to Annie Richmond about January 21, 1849.

TEXTS

(A) Southern Literary Messenger, April 1849 (15:220), "Marginalia," no. 207; *(B) Works* (1850), III, 517, "Marginalia," no. LXIII.

Griswold's text *(B)* is followed; it shows three slight changes, none verbal and one a correction of an obvious misprint.

[A WOULD-BE CRICHTON (*B*)]

Here is a good idea for a Magazine paper: — let somebody "work it up:" — A flippant pretender to universal acquirement — a would-be Crichton[1] — engrosses, for an hour or two,[a] perhaps, the attention

* Poe probably saw the Porson anecdote in Charles Caleb Colton's once popular compilation, *Lacon, or Many Things in Few Words* (1821–1822); see p. 387 in the New York stereotyped edition (1849), published by Poe's friend William Gowans. Colton (1780–1832) visited America in 1828. Poe mentioned him in "Marginalia," number 46 (*Democratic Review,* December 1844, p. 581).

† See Sarah Helen Whitman, *Edgar Poe and His Critics* (1860), pp. 25–26. The salon was probably that of Miss Anne C. Lynch, and the female linguist almost surely Mrs. Ellet. The young author is unidentified, even by conjecture.

a *Comma omitted (A)*

of a large company — most of whom are profoundly impressed by his knowledge. He is very witty, in especial, at the expense of a modest young gentleman, who ventures to make no reply, and who, finally, leaves the room as if overwhelmed with confusion; — the Crichton greeting his exit with a laugh. Presently he returns, followed by a footman carrying an armful[b] of books. These are deposited on the table. The young gentleman, now, referring to some penciled[c] notes which he had been secretly taking during the Crichton's display of erudition, pins the latter to his statements, each by each, and refutes them all in turn, by reference to the very authorities cited by the egotist himself — whose ignorance at all points is thus made apparent.

NOTES

Title: Supplied from text.

1. "The admirable Crichton rose like a meteor upon the literary horizon of Europe, and his career was as brilliant and as brief," said an editorial note in the *New-York Mirror*, September 10, 1836, introducing a passage from W. Harrison Ainsworth's forthcoming novel *Crichton*, which the Harpers published in New York in 1837. James Crichton (1560?–1682?), M.A. of St. Andrews University in 1575, whose appellation was accorded in 1652 by his biographer, Sir Thomas Urquhart, reputedly knew ten languages, was an accomplished swordsman, athlete, and horseman, wrote poetry in Latin and Italian, and served for a time in the French army. During travels in Europe he distinguished himself in debates on questions of science and religion with leading scholars in Paris, Genoa, Venice, and Padua. In Mantua, intending to enter the service of the Duke, he was killed in a street brawl.

LANDOR'S COTTAGE

This charming description of a beautiful little home in the country has in it a pervading element of poetic autobiography. It is laid in a part of our country that Poe knew well, for he was living amidst the scenery that inspired the many artists of the Hudson River School. In the summer of 1848 he apparently made a tour of one or two of the Hudson River counties, about which he wanted

b armfull *(A)* c pencilled *(A)*

to write an account with the hope that his friend Eli Bowen, the Pennsylvania editor, might publish it.* The house itself is simply Poe's own Fordham cottage, idealized only a little for his glowing word picture.

A brief description of the residence in 1846, as a visitor recalled it, may be welcome here, since the cottage was removed from its original site early in the present century. Mrs. Mary Gove Nichols found Poe, Virginia, and Mrs. Clemm

> living in a little cottage at the top of a hill. There was an acre or two of greensward, fenced in about the house, as smooth as velvet and as clean as the best kept carpet. There were some grand old cherry-trees in the yard, that threw a massive shade around them. The house had three rooms – a kitchen, a sitting-room, and a bed-chamber over the sitting-room. There was a piazza in front of the house that was a lovely place to sit in summer . . . There was no cultivation, no flowers – nothing but the smooth greensward and the majestic trees . . . The floor of the kitchen was white as wheaten flour. A table, a chair, and a little stove that it contained seemed to furnish it completely. The sitting-room floor was laid with check matting; four chairs, a light stand, and a hanging book-shelf completed its furniture.†

Poe once said to Mrs. Whitman that he intended writing a pendant to "The Domain of Arnheim" in which the most charming effects should be attained by artistic combinations of familiar and unvalued materials.‡ His idea for this sequel began to take shape when in his long letter of October 18, 1848 to his fiancée he wrote:

> I suffered my imagination to stray with you, and with the few who love us both, to the banks of some quiet river, in some lovely valley of our land. Here, not *too* far secluded from the world, we exercised a taste controlled by no conventionalities, but the sworn slave of a Natural Art, in the building for ourselves a cottage which no human being could ever pass without an ejaculation of wonder at its strange, wierd, and incomprehensible yet most simple beauty. Oh, the sweet and gorgeous, but not often rare flowers in which we half buried it! – the grandeur

* See his letter to Bowen, October 18, 1848 (*American Notes & Queries,* January 1965, and in Ostrom's "Fourth Supplement to the Letters of Poe" *(AL,* January 1974). Poe says, "I am willing to accept your offer about the correspondence . . . *provided* you decline the *tour* etc, as I suggested." The manuscript is now in the Richard Gimbel Collection, The Free Library of Philadelphia.

† "Reminiscences" in the London *Sixpenny Magazine,* February 1863, reprinted as a separate pamphlet in 1931, and important sections more conveniently in Woodberry's *Life* (1909), II, 214 and 433.

‡ See her letter of December 15, 1864, to George W. Eveleth, whose transcript, made October 1, 1878, is in the Ingram Collection, number 96.

of the little-distant magnolias and tulip-trees which stood guarding it – the luxurious velvet of its lawn – the lustre of the rivulet that ran by the very door – the tasteful yet quiet comfort of the interior – the music – the books – the unostentatious pictures – and, above all, the love – the *love* that threw an unfading *glory* over the whole! – Ah Helen! my heart is, *indeed, breaking* and I must now put an end to these divine dreams.§

Instead of putting an end to the dreams, however, he was soon at work on an expanded version. From its setting he excluded magnolia trees, none of which grew north of Philadelphia in his day.

About January 21, 1849, Poe, who tended to report promptly on such matters to his friend Mrs. Charles Richmond, of Lowell and Westford, Massachusetts, whom he called "Annie," wrote to her that "Landor's Cottage" was finished "not long ago," with "something about Annie in it,"* and had been turned in to Israel Post's New York *American Metropolitan Magazine.* Publication was expected in its third number, that for March. But the magazine collapsed with its second number, and on March 23, Poe wrote Annie that the tale was "returned upon my hands unprinted." In a letter sent to the same lady in April or May, Poe wrote that the Boston *Flag of Our Union* had it. That paper paid in advance, but was dilatory in printing "Landor's Cottage," which, although not the latest story he wrote, was the last to appear in Poe's lifetime.

In the last paragraph of "Landor's Cottage" as first published, Poe mentioned that he had some idea of writing a sequel. It is practically sure that he did not compose it, but there is some reason to believe he made some plans for it. During his last summer he often visited Duncan Lodge, the home of the Mackenzie family, with whom his sister Rosalie resided, in Richmond, Virginia. Discussing Poe's project of his magazine *The Stylus,* Susan Archer Talley Weiss writes that "he even commenced arranging a Table of Contents for the first number of the magazine; and Mrs. [William]

§ Woodberry in his *Life* (1909), II, 275, called this passage an extract from "Landor's Cottage," but the reference to magnolias, eliminated from the longer story, establishes the priority of the letter. The text follows the original manuscript in the Josiah K. Lilly, Jr. Collection at Indiana University. The part of the letter containing the account of the poet's daydream was first printed by William Fearing Gill in *The Life of Edgar Allan Poe* (1877), pages 217–218.

* "Something about Annie" is the description of the lady in the text below at note 19.

Mackenzie told me how he one morning spent an hour in her room taking from her information, notes and *data* for an article which he intended to appear in one of its earliest numbers."† A discussion of the arrangement of furniture and flowers in a larger home than the two described in "Philosophy of Furniture" and "Landor's Cottage" might well have fitted into a sequel.

TEXTS

(A) Boston *Flag of Our Union* for June 9, 1849; *(B) Works* (1850), I, 404–416.

Griswold's version *(B)* is followed, although it, like the first printing, is marred by misprints. The two changes in the final paragraph may have been made by Griswold, the first to fit the piece into a book publication, the second because it referred to a "possible" sequel that the author did not write. If the literary executor made these changes, I think he was performing his proper function.

LANDOR'S COTTAGE. [*B*]

A PENDANT TO "THE DOMAIN OF ARNHEIM."

DURING a pedestrian tour last summer, through one or two of the river counties of New York, I found myself, as the day declined, somewhat embarrassed about the road I was pursuing.[1] The land undulated very remarkably; and my path, for the last hour, had wound about and about so confusedly, in its effort to keep in the valleys, that I no longer knew in what direction lay the sweet village of B———, where I had determined to stop for the night.[2] The sun had scarcely *shone* — strictly speaking — during the day, which, nevertheless, had been unpleasantly warm. A smoky mist, resembling that of the Indian summer, enveloped all things, and, of course, added to my uncertainty. Not that I cared much about the matter. If I did not hit upon the village before sunset, or even before dark, it was more than possible that a little Dutch farmhouse, or something of that kind, would soon make its appearance — although, in fact, the neighborhood (perhaps on account of being

† *Home Life of Poe* (1907), p. 198. Poe set great store by "The Domain of Arnheim" and "Landor's Cottage," and it may well be that it was in similar quiet stories that he hoped that "in prose he might yet surpass what he had already accomplished," as Mrs. Weiss records in *Scribner's* for March 1878.

more picturesque than fertile) was very sparsely inhabited.[a] At all events, with my knapsack for a pillow, and my hound as a sentry, a bivouac in the open air was just the thing which would have amused me. I sauntered on, therefore, quite at ease — Ponto[3] taking charge of my gun — until at length, just as I had begun to consider whether the numerous little glades that led hither and thither were intended to be paths at all. I was conducted by one of the most promising of them into an unquestionable carriage-track. There could be no mistaking it. The traces of light wheels were evident; and although the tall shrubberies and overgrown undergrowth met overhead, there was no obstruction whatever below, even to the passage of a Virginian mountain wagon — the most aspiring vehicle, I take it, of its kind.[4] The road, however, except in being open through the wood — if wood be not too weighty a name for such an assemblage of light trees — and except in the particulars of evident wheel-tracks —bore no resemblance to any road I had before seen. The tracks of which I speak were but faintly perceptible — having been impressed upon the firm, yet pleasantly moist surface of — what looked more like green Genoese velvet than anything else.[5] It was grass, clearly — but grass such as we seldom see out of England — so short, so thick, so even, and so vivid in color. Not a single impediment lay in the wheel-route — not even a chip or dead twig. The stones that once obstructed the way had been carefully *placed* — not thrown — along the sides of the lane, so as to define its boundaries at bottom with a kind of half-precise, half-negligent, and wholly picturesque definition. Clumps of wild flowers grew everywhere, luxuriantly, in the interspaces.

What to make of all this, of course I knew not. Here was *art* undoubtedly — *that* did not surprise me — all roads, in the ordinary sense, are works of art; nor can I say that there was much to wonder at in the mere *excess* of art manifested; all that seemed to have been done, might have been done *here* — with such natural "capabilities" (as they have it in the books on Landscape Gardening) — with very little labor and expense.[6] No; it was not the amount but the *character* of the art which caused me to take a seat on one of the blossomy

---

a inhahited. *(A) misprint*

stones and gaze up and down this fairy-like avenue for half an hour or more in bewildered admiration. One thing became more and more evident the longer I gazed: an artist, and one with a most scrupulous eye for form, had superintended all these arrangements. The greatest care had been taken to preserve a due medium between the neat and graceful on the one hand, and the *pittoresque,* in the true sense of the Italian term,[7] on the other. There were few straight, and no long uninterrupted lines. The same effect of curvature or of color, appeared twice, usually, but not oftener, at any one point of view. Everywhere was variety in uniformity. It was a piece of "composition," in which the most fastidiously critical taste could scarcely have suggested an emendation.

I had turned to the right as I entered this road, and now, arising, I continued in the same direction. The path was so serpentine, that at no moment could I trace its course for more than two or three paces in advance. Its character did not undergo any material change.

Presently the murmur of water fell gently upon my ear — and in a few moments afterwards, as I turned with the road somewhat more abruptly than hitherto, I became aware that a building of some kind lay at the foot of a gentle declivity just before me. I could see nothing distinctly on accout of the mist which occupied all the little valley below. A gentle breeze, however, now arose, as the sun was about descending; and while I remained standing on the brow of the slope, the fog gradually became dissipated into wreaths, and so floated[b] over the scene.

As it came fully into view — thus *gradually* as I describe it — piece by piece, here a tree, there a glimpse of water, and here again the summit of a chimney, I could scarcely help fancying that the whole was one of the ingenious illusions sometimes exhibited under the name of "vanishing[c] pictures."[8]

By the time, however, that the fog had thoroughly disappeared, the sun had made its way down behind the gentle hills, and thence, as if with a slight *chassez* to the south, had come again fully into sight; glaring with a purplish lustre through a chasm that entered the valley from the west. Suddenly, therefore — and as if by the

b floated from *(A)* c varnishing *(A, B) misprint*

hand of magic — this whole valley and everything in it became brilliantly visible.

The first *coup d'œil,* as the sun slid into the position described, impressed me very much as I have been impressed when a boy, by the concluding scene of some well-arranged theatrical spectacle or melodrama. Not even the monstrosity of color was wanting; for the sunlight came out through the chasm, tinted all orange and purple; while the vivid green of the grass in the valley was reflected more or less upon all objects, from the curtain of vapor that still hung overhead, as if loth to take its total departure from a scene so enchantingly beautiful.

The little vale into which I thus peered down from under the fog-canopy, could not have been more than four hundred yards long; while in breadth it varied from fifty to one hundred and fifty, or perhaps two hundred. It was most narrow at its northern extremity, opening out as it tended southwardly, but with no very precise regularity. The widest portion was within eighty yards of the southern extreme. The slopes which encompassed the vale could not fairly be called hills, unless at their northern face. Here a precipitous ledge of granite arose to a height of some ninety feet; and, as I have mentioned, the valley at this point was not more than fifty feet wide; but as the visiter proceeded southwardly from this cliff, he found on his right hand and on his left, declivities at once less high, less precipitous, and less rocky. All, in a word, sloped and softened to the south; and yet the whole vale was engirdled by eminences, more or less high, except at two points. One of these I have already spoken of. It lay considerably to the north of west, and was where the setting sun made its way, as I have before described, into the amphitheatre, through a cleanly cut natural cleft in the granite embankment: this fissure might have been ten yards wide at its widest point, so far as the eye could trace it. It seemed to lead up, up, like a natural causeway, into the recesses of unexplored mountains and forests. The other opening was directly at the southern end of the vale. Here, generally, the slopes were nothing more than gentle inclinations, extending from east to west about one hundred and fifty yards. In the middle of this extent was a depression, level with the ordinary floor of the valley. As regards vegetation, as well as in respect to every thing else, the scene *softened and sloped* to the south. To the north — on the craggy precipice — a few paces from the verge — upsprang the magnificent trunks of numerous hickories, black walnuts, and chestnuts, interspersed with occasional oak; and the strong lateral branches thrown out by the walnuts especially, spread far over the edge of the cliff. Proceeding southwardly, the explorer saw, at first, the same class of trees, but less and less lofty and Salvatorish in character;[9] then he saw the gentler elm, succeeded by the sassafras and locust — these again by the softer linden, red-bud, catalpa, and maple — these yet again by still more graceful and more modest varieties. The whole face of the southern declivity was covered with wild shrubbery alone — an occasional silver willow or white poplar excepted. In the bottom of the valley itself — (for it must be borne in mind that the vegetation hitherto mentioned grew only on the cliffs or hill-sides) — were to be seen three insulated trees. One was an elm of fine size and exquisite form: it stood guard over the southern gate of the vale. Another was a hickory, much larger than the elm, and altogether a much finer tree, although both were exceedingly beautiful: it seemed to have taken charge of the north-western entrance, springing from a group of rocks in the very jaws of the ravine, and throwing its graceful body, at an angle of nearly forty-five degrees, far out into the sunshine of the amphitheatre. About thirty yards east of this tree stood, however, the pride of the valley, and beyond all question the most magnificent tree I have ever seen, unless, perhaps, among the cypresses of the Itchiatuckanee.[10] It was a triple-stemmed tulip tree — the *Liriodendron Tulipiferum* — one of the natural order of magnolias.[11] Its three trunks separated from the parent at about three feet from the soil, and diverging very slightly and gradually, were not more than four feet apart at the point where the largest stem shot out into foliage: this was at an elevation of about eighty feet. The whole height of the principal division was one hundred and twenty feet. Nothing can surpass in beauty the form, or the glossy, vivid green of the leaves of the tulip tree. In the present instance they were fully eight inches wide; but their glory was altogether eclipsed by the gorgeous splendor of the profuse blossoms. Conceive, closely congregated, a million of the largest and most resplendent tulips! Only thus can the reader get any idea of the picture I would convey. And then the stately grace of the clean, delicately-granulated columnar stems, the largest four feet in diameter, at twenty from the ground. The innumerable blossoms, mingling with those of other trees scarcely less beautiful, although infinitely less majestic, filled the valley with more than Arabian perfumes.[12]

The general floor of the amphitheatre was *grass* of the same character as that I had found in the road: if anything, more deliciously soft, thick, velvety, and miraculously green. It was hard to conceive how all this beauty had been attained.

I have spoken of the two openings into the vale. From the one to the north-west issued a rivulet, which came, gently murmuring and slightly foaming, down the ravine, until it dashed against the group of rocks out of which sprang the insulated hickory. Here, after encircling the tree, it passed on a little to the north of east, leaving the tulip tree some twenty feet to the south, and making no decided alteration in its course until it came near the midway between the eastern and western boundaries of the valley. At this point, after a series of sweeps, it turned off at right angles and pursued a generally southern direction — meandering as it went — until it became lost in a small lake of irregular figure (although roughly oval), that lay gleaming near the lower extremity of the vale. This lakelet was, perhaps, a hundred yards in diameter at its widest part. No crystal could be clearer than its waters. Its bottom, which could be distinctly seen, consisted altogether of pebbles brilliantly white. Its banks, of the emerald grass already described, *rounded*, rather than sloped, off into the clear heaven below; and *so* clear was this heaven, so perfectly, at times, did it reflect all objects above it, that where the true bank ended and where the mimic one commenced, it was a point of no little difficulty to determine.[13] The trout, and some other varieties of fish, with which this pond seemed to be almost inconveniently crowded, had all the appearance of veritable flying-fish. It was almost impossible to believe that they were not absolutely suspended in the air. A light birch canoe that lay placidly on the water, was reflected in its minutest fibres with a fidelity unsurpassed by the most exquisitely polished mirror. A small island, fairly laughing with flowers in full bloom, and affording little more space than just enough for a picturesque little building, seemingly a fowl-house — arose from the lake not far from its northern shore — to which it was connected by means of an inconceivably light-looking and yet very primitive bridge. It was formed of a single, broad and thick plank of the tulip wood. This was forty feet long, and spanned the interval between shore and shore with a slight but very perceptible arch, preventing all oscillation. From the southern extreme of the lake issued a continuation of the rivulet, which, after meandering for, perhaps, thirty yards, finally passed through the "depression" (already described) in the middle of the southern declivity, and tumbling down a sheer precipice of a hundred feet, made its devious and unnoticed way to the Hudson.

The lake was deep — at some points thirty feet — but the rivulet seldom exceeded three, while its greatest width was about eight. Its bottom and banks were as those of the pond — if a defect could have been attributed to them, in point of picturesqueness, it was that of excessive *neatness*.

The expanse of the green turf was relieved, here and there, by an occasional showy shrub, such as the hydrangea, or the common snow-ball, or the aromatic seringa; or, more frequently, by a clump of geraniums blossoming gorgeously in great varieties. These latter grew in pots which were carefully buried in the soil, so as to give the plants the appearance of being indigenous. Besides all this, the lawn's velvet was exquisitely spotted with sheep — a considerable flock of which roamed about the vale, in company with three tamed deer, and a vast number of brilliantly-plumed ducks. A very large mastiff seemed to be in vigilant attendance upon these animals, each and all.

Along the eastern and western cliffs — where, towards the upper portion of the amphitheatre, the boundaries were more or less precipitous — grew ivy in great profusion — so that only here and there could even a glimpse of the naked rock be obtained. The northern precipice, in like manner, was almost entirely clothed by grape-vines of rare luxuriance; some springing from the soil at the base of the cliff, and others from ledges on its face.

The slight elevation which formed the lower boundary of this little domain, was crowned by a neat stone wall, of sufficient height to prevent the escape of the deer. Nothing of the fence kind was observable elsewhere; for nowhere else was an artificial enclosure needed: — any stray sheep, for example, which should attempt to make its way out of the vale by means of the ravine, would find its progress arrested, after a few yards' advance, by the precipitous ledge of rock over which tumbled the cascade that had arrested my attention as I first drew near the domain. In short, the only ingress or egress was through a gate[d] occupying a rocky pass in the road, a few paces below the point at which I stopped to reconnoitre the scene.

I have described the brook as meandering very irregularly through the whole of its course. Its two *general* directions, as I have said, were first from west to east, and then from north to south. At the *turn,* the stream, sweeping backwards, made an almost circular *loop,* so as to form a peninsula which was *very* nearly an island, and which included about the sixteenth of an acre. On this peninsula stood a dwelling-house — and when I say that this house, like the infernal terrace seen by Vathek, *"était[e] d'une architecture inconnue dans les annales de la terre,"*[14] I mean, merely, that its *tout ensemble* struck me with the keenest sense of combined novelty and propriety — in a word, of *poetry* — (for, than in the words just employed, I could scarcely give, of poetry in the abstract, a more rigorous definition) — and I do *not* mean that the merely *outré*[f] was perceptible in any respect.

In fact, nothing could well be more simple — more utterly unpretending than this cottage. Its marvellous *effect* lay altogether in its artistic arrangement *as a picture.*[15] I could have fancied, while I looked at it, that some eminent landscape-painter had built it with his brush.

The point of view from which I first saw the valley, was not *altogether,* although it was nearly, the best point from which to survey[g] the house. I will therefore describe it as I afterwards saw it — from a position on the stone wall at the southern extreme of the amphitheatre.

The main building was about twenty-four feet long and sixteen

d grate *(A, B) misprint*
e *etait (B)*
f *outre (B)*
g servey *(B) misprint*

broad — certainly not more. Its total height, from the ground to the apex of the roof, could not have exceeded eighteen feet.[16] To the west end of this structure was attached one about a third smaller in all its proportions: — the line of its front standing back about two yards from that of the larger house; and the line of its roof, of course, being considerably depressed below that of the roof adjoining. At right angles to these buildings, and from the rear of the main one — not exactly in the middle — extended a third compartment, very small — being, in general, one third less than the western wing. The roofs of the two larger were very steep — sweeping down from the ridge-beam with a long concave curve, and extending at least four feet beyond the walls in front, so as to form the roofs of two piazzas. These latter roofs, of course, needed no support; but as they had the *air* of needing it, slight and perfectly plain pillars were inserted at the corners alone. The roof of the northern wing was merely an extension of a portion of the main roof. Between the chief building and western wing arose a very tall and rather slender square chimney of hard Dutch bricks, alternately black and red: — a slight cornice of projecting bricks at the top. Over the gables, the roofs also projected very much: — in the main building about four feet to the east and two to the west. The principal door was not exactly in the main division, being a little to the east — while the two windows were to the west. These latter did not extend to the floor, but were much longer and narrower than usual — they had single shutters like doors — the panes were of lozenge form, but quite large. The door itself had its upper half of glass, also in lozenge panes — a moveable shutter secured it at night. The door to the west wing was in its gable, and quite simple — a single window looked out to the south. There was no external door to the north wing, and it, also, had only one window to the east.

The blank wall of the eastern gable was relieved by stairs (with a balustrade) running diagonally across it — the ascent being from the south. Under cover of the widely projecting eave these steps gave access to a door leading into the garret, or rather loft — for it was lighted only by a single window to the north, and seemed to have been intended as a store-room.

The piazzas of the main building and western wing had no

floors, as is usual; but at the doors and at each window, large, flat, irregular slabs of granite lay imbedded[h] in the delicious turf, affording comfortable footing in all weather. Excellent paths of the same material — not *nicely* adapted, but with the velvety sod filling frequent intervals between the stones, led hither and thither from the house, to a crystal spring about five paces off, to the road, or to one or two out-houses that lay to the north, beyond the brook, and were thoroughly concealed by a few locusts and catalpas.

Not more than six steps from the main door of the cottage stood the dead trunk of a fantastic pear-tree, so clothed from head to foot in the gorgeous bignonia blossoms that one required no little scrutiny to determine what manner of sweet thing it could be. From various arms of this tree hung cages of different kinds.[17] In one, a large wicker cylinder with a ring at top, revelled a mocking bird; in another, an oriole; in a third, the impudent bobolink[i] — while three or four more delicate prisons were loudly vocal with canaries.

The pillars of the piazza were enwreathed in jasmine and sweet honeysuckle; while from the angle formed by the main structure and its west wing, in front, sprang a grape-vine of unexampled luxuriance. Scorning all restraint, it had clambered first to the lower roof — then to the higher; and along the ridge of this latter it continued to writhe on, throwing out tendrils to the right and left, until at length it fairly attained the east gable, and fell trailing over the stairs.

The whole house, with its wings, was constructed of the old-fashioned Dutch shingles — broad, and with unrounded corners. It is a peculiarity of this material to give houses built of it the appearance of being wider at bottom than at top — after the manner of Egyptian architecture; and in the present instance, this exceedingly picturesque effect was aided by numerous pots of gorgeous flowers that almost encompassed the base of the buildings.

The shingles were painted a dull gray; and the happiness with which this neutral tint melted into the vivid green of the tulip-tree leaves that partially overshadowed the cottage, can readily be conceived by an artist.

---

h embedded *(A)*

i bobalink *(A, B) misprint*

From the position near the stone wall, as described, the buildings were seen at great advantage — for the south-eastern angle was thrown forward — so that the eye took in at once the whole of the two fronts, with the picturesque eastern gable, and at the same time obtained just a sufficient glimpse of the northern wing, with parts of a pretty roof to the spring-house, and nearly half of a light bridge that spanned the brook in the near vicinity of the main buildings.

I did not remain very long on the brow of the hill, although long enough to make a thorough survey of the scene at my feet. It was clear that I had wandered from the road to the village, and I had thus good traveller's[j] excuse to open the gate before me, and inquire my way, at all events; so, without more ado, I proceeded.

The road, after passing the gate, seemed to lie upon a natural ledge, sloping gradually down along the face of the north-eastern cliffs. It led me on to the foot of the northern precipice, and thence over the bridge, round by the eastern gable to the front door. In this progress, I took notice that no sight of the out-houses could be obtained.

As I turned the corner of the gable, the mastiff bounded towards me in stern silence, but with the eye and the whole air of a tiger. I held him out my hand, however, in token of amity — and I never yet knew the dog who was proof against such an appeal to his courtesy. He not only shut his mouth and wagged his tail, but absolutely offered me his paw — afterwards extending his civilities to Ponto.

As no bell was discernible, I rapped with my stick against the door, which stood half open. Instantly a figure advanced to the threshold — that of a young woman about twenty-eight years of age — slender, or rather slight, and somewhat above the medium height. As she approached, with a certain[k] *modest decision* of step altogether indescribable, I said to myself, "Surely here I have found the perfection of natural, in contradistinction from artificial *grace*." The second impression which she made on me, but by far the more vivid of the two, was that of *enthusiasm*. So intense an expression of *romance*, perhaps I should call it, or of unworldliness, as that which gleamed from her deep-set eyes, had never so sunk into my heart of

---

j travellers' *(B) misprint, corrected from A*

k *cartain (A) misprint*

hearts before.[18] I know not how it is, but this peculiar expression of the eye, wreathing itself occasionally into the lips, is the most powerful, if not absolutely the *sole* spell, which rivets my interest in woman. *"Romance,"* provided my readers fully comprehend what I would here imply by the word — "romance" and "womanliness" seem to me convertible terms: and, after all, what man truly *loves* in woman, is, simply, her *womanhood.* The eyes of Annie (I heard some one from the interior call her "Annie, darling!") were "spiritual gray;" her hair, a light chestnut: this is all I had time to observe of her.[19]

At her most courteous of invitations, I entered — passing first into a tolerably wide vestibule. Having come mainly to *observe,* I took notice that to my right as I stepped in, was a window, such as those in front of the house; to the left, a door leading into the principal room; while, opposite me, an *open* door enabled me to see a small apartment, just the size of the vestibule, arranged as a study, and having a large *bow* window looking out to the north.[20]

Passing into the parlor, I found myself with *Mr. Landor* — for this, I afterwards found, was his name. He was civil, even cordial in his manner; but just then, I was more intent on observing the arrangements of the dwelling which had so much interested me, than the personal appearance of the tenant.

The north wing, I now saw, was a bed-chamber: its door opened into the parlor. West of this door was a single window, looking towards the brook. At the west end of the parlor, were a fire-place, and a door leading into the west wing — probably a kitchen.

Nothing could be more rigorously simple than the furniture of the parlor.[21] On the floor was an ingrain carpet, of excellent texture — a white ground, spotted with small circular green figures. At the windows were curtains of snowy white jaconet muslin: they were tolerably full, and hung *decisively,* perhaps rather formally, in sharp, parallel plaits to the floor — *just* to the floor. The walls were papered with a French paper of great delicacy — a silver ground, with a faint green cord running zig-zag throughout.[22] Its expanse was relieved merely by three of Julien's exquisite lithographs *à*[1]

---

1 *a (B)*

trois crayons,[23] fastened to the wall without frames. One of these drawings was a scene of Oriental luxury, or rather voluptuousness; another was a "carnival piece," spirited beyond compare; the third was a Greek female head — a face so divinely beautiful, and yet of an expression so provokingly indeterminate, never before arrested my attention.

The more substantial furniture consisted of a round table, a few chairs (including a large rocking-chair,)[24] and a sofa, or rather "settee:" its material was plain maple painted a creamy white, slightly interstriped with green — the seat of cane. The chairs and table were "to match;" but the *forms* of all had evidently been designed by the same brain which planned "the grounds:" it is impossible to conceive anything more graceful.

On the table were a few books; a large, square, crystal bottle of some novel perfume; a plain, ground-glass *astral* (not solar) lamp, with an Italian shade; and a large vase of resplendently-blooming flowers. Flowers indeed of gorgeous colors and delicate odor, formed the sole mere *decoration* of the apartment. The fire-place was nearly filled with a vase of brilliant geranium. On a triangular shelf in each angle of the room stood also a similar vase, varied only as to its lovely contents. One or two smaller *bouquets*[m] adorned the mantel; and late violets clustered about the open windows.

It is not the purpose of this work[n] to do more than give, in detail, a picture of Mr. Landor's residence — *as I found it.*[o]

NOTES

Title: Poe is less likely to have had Walter Savage Landor in mind than "William Landor," the pseudonym by which he knew Horace Binney Wallace (1817–1852), whose novel *Stanley* (1838) he often used. (There is a convenient summary in "Poe's Borrowings from H. B. Wallace," G. E. Hatvary, *American Literature,* November 1966.)

1. He presumably walked from Fordham — in Westchester County in his day — through Putnam County on its north and into Dutchess County, where Poughkeepsie is situated. He seems to have met the spiritualist Andrew Jackson Davis, who lived in that city. See the notes on "Mellonta Tauta."

---

m *boquets (A, B)*
n paper *(A)*
o *After this* How he made it what it was — and *why,* with some particulars of Mr. Landon [*sic*] himself — may, *possibly* form the subject of another article. *(A)*

2. The village has not been identified.

3. Ponto was at one time a common canine name. It was also the name of the narrator's dog in R. M. Bird's *Sheppard Lee,* reviewed by Poe in 1836.

4. Mountain wagons were large, had oversized brakes, wheels forty-four and fifty-two inches high, and a body over ten feet by three and a half. Some could haul up to three and a half tons. See M. M. Mathews, *A Dictionary of Americanisms* (1951). I cannot find that the wagons used in Virginia had any distinctive features, but Poe may have ridden in such a wagon in his childhood.

5. For other references to grass like green velvet see "Julius Rodman," chapter III, and "The Domain of Arnheim," at n. 25; for references to the fine velvet of Genoa, see *Politian,* VIII, 52, and "Bon-Bon," at n. 8.

6. See the notes on "The Landscape Garden" and "The Domain of Arnheim" for Poe's interest in the work of the American landscape gardener A. J. Downing. See note 11 on the former tale for the celebrated English practitioner of the art, nicknamed "Capability" Brown.

7. Literally, in the style of a painter. Although he refers to "the Italian term," Poe uses the French form; most of the English and American "books on Landscape Gardening" referred to the "picturesque" as contrasted with the "natural" style. Compare "The Landscape Garden," near n. 8, for the tenet that "no such combinations of scenery exist in Nature as the painter of genius has the power to produce." For further development of the significance of art in the enhancement of natural beauty, see "The Domain of Arnheim." For an illuminating article on the implications of this doctrine see Robert D. Jacobs, "Poe's Earthly Paradise," in the *American Quarterly,* Fall 1960. [On Poe's change from description of dream landscapes to description of observed phenomena, see Alvin Rosenfeld's paper in *Studies in Short Fiction,* Spring 1967.]

8. "Vanishing pictures" were often shown by stage magicians.

9. The allusion is to Salvator Rosa (1615–1673) of the Neapolitan School, famed for pictures of wild scenes in the Apennines. He is named in "Morning on the Wissahiccon."

10. The creek Poe had in mind may be the Ichawaynochaway; it flows into the Flint River in Baker County, Georgia.

11. Poe mentioned the huge flowering tulip trees also in "Morning on the Wissahiccon" and "The Gold-Bug," where one is incorrectly, for the sake of plot, placed near Sullivan's Island. A. J. Downing's detailed description of the tulip tree is quoted in the *Arcturus* review (June 1841) of his book, immediately before the long passage quoted by Poe in "The Landscape Garden." Unlike the related magnolia, tulip trees flourish in and near Manhattan Island. Poe gives the name in correct Latin; botanists use the form *tulipifera.*

12. The Arabian perfumes are of course famous, especially remembered for the guilty queen's mention in *Macbeth,* V, i: "All the perfumes of Arabia will not sweeten this little hand." Compare "Marginalia," number 48 (*Democratic Review,* December 1844, p. 581): "I believe that odors have an altogether idiosyncratic force, in affecting us through association; a force differing *essentially* from that of objects addressing the touch, the taste, the sight, or the hearing."

13. Compare Poe's lines, "So blended bank and shadow there/That each seemed pendulous in air," as he adapted them in "The Island of the Fay" from his early poem "The Doomed City" (1831); see Mabbott I, 199–200.

14. The French phrase means "was of an architecture unknown in the annals of the world." It is correctly quoted from William Beckford's original French version of *Vathek,* but Poe probably took it from Wallace's *Stanley* (1838), I, 154. The same quotation was also used by Poe in a review of *Ancient America* by George Jones, in the *Aristidean* for March 1845.

15. See text at n. 7, and n. 7 above.

16. Haldeen Braddy, *Glorious Incense* (1953), p. 29, observes that the dimensions of the cottage are similar to those of Poe's cottage at Fordham. Miss Phillips observed this in *Poe the Man* (1926), II, 1290. Resemblance of the cottage to some in Currier and Ives prints has been noticed, but they are later than Poe's tale, and of course likewise inspired by real cottages near the Hudson River. See Henry S. Canby, *Classic Americans* (1931), pp. 272–273.

17. Poe was interested in tame birds; his close friend in Philadelphia, Henry Beck Hirst, ran a shop selling them, and wrote *The Book of Cage Birds* (1842) about them. A visitor to Fordham reported:

> Poe had somehow caught a full grown bob-o'-link. He had put him in a cage, which he had hung on a nail driven into the trunk of a cherry-tree . . . [The bird] was as restless as his jailer, and sprang continually in a fierce, frightened way, from one side of the cage to the other . . . Poe was bent on training him . . . [said he,] "You are wrong in wishing me to free the bird. He is a splendid songster, and as soon as he is tamed will delight our home with his musical gifts."

This comes from Mrs. Mary Gove Nichols, quoted in Woodberry's *Life* (1909), II, 433.

18. The phrase "heart of hearts" is a favorite with Poe; used also in *Politian,* VI, 57; "To My Mother," line 7; and a letter of October 1, 1848 to Helen Whitman. Compare "heart of heart" in *Hamlet,* III, ii, 78.

19. The description of Mrs. Richmond seems to be factual. Her gray eyes are thought to be responsible for a change in line 23 of "To One in Paradise"; see also the poem "For Annie" (Mabbott I, 214–216 and 452–461). Unhappily no picture of Mrs. Richmond when she knew Poe seems to be available. That shown by Miss Phillips, II, 1294, is much later.

20. There is no bow window in the Fordham cottage.

21. With the description of this parlor, contrast the "small and not ostentatious chamber" described in "Philosophy of Furniture."

22. The wallpaper was that of a room in Mrs. Whitman's home in Providence. She refers to this, mentioning the zigzag pattern, in a letter of December 15, 1864, to G. W. Eveleth, and another of April 24, 1874, to Ingram. See the Ingram List, numbers 96 and 147.

23. The artist mentioned is the French painter and lithographer, Bernard-Romain Julien (1802–1871). The prints now cannot be exactly identified. In her

delightful reminiscences of her visit to Fordham in 1847, in the *Home Journal,* July 21, 1860, Mary Elizabeth Bronson LeDuc told how Poe assured her cheerfully that a print of a pretty girl on the wall was "not the lost Lenore." See Carroll D. Laverty in *American Literature,* May 1948.

24. Poe's rocking chair is preserved at the Fordham cottage. Mrs. Clemm gave it to Mrs. Rebecca Cromwell, whose daughter Susan married Josiah Valentine, a nephew of Poe's landlord, John Valentine. Their son William Henry Valentine presented the relic for exhibition at the cottage. See Phillips, *Poe the Man* (1926), II, 1544, where there is a photograph of the chair.

HOP-FROG

This is one of Poe's great tales of horror, but few can regard it as one of his best. It seems far inferior to the kindred "Cask of Amontillado" in sublety. There the motive for revenge is never fully revealed; in "Hop-Frog" the motive is made all too clear. The reader is expected to sympathize with the murderous dwarf, but the vengeance is too much for poetic justice. The story is notable mainly as a terrible exposition of the darkness of a human soul.

Our knowledge of the genesis, composition, and publication of the story is practically complete.

Poe's three principle sources are definitely known. Many readers must recognize the story of the disaster at a royal masquerade as something related in the 138th chapter of the *Chronicles* of Froissart. Poe did not go to Froissart, but to the files of his own *Broadway Journal,* where he found the incident from Froissart associated with an accident to a young dancer in a single article. That was "Barbarities of the Theater," initialled E.A.D. (for Evert A. Duyckinck in the issue of February 1, 1845.

According to Froissart, during a wedding party at the court of Charles VI of France in 1385 a group of five courtiers dressed as wild men (*sauvages,* familiar to us in heraldry), with long hair covering their bodies, wearing kirtles of leaves, and chained together, entered a room where ladies were dancing. All torches had at first been removed at the suggestion of one of the party, Sir Evan of Foix; but the Duke of Orleans came late, accompanied by torchbearers. One came too close to a masker, the long artificial hair of the suits caught fire, and all save one were killed. The King had accompanied them, but was not fastened, and escaped when the Duchess of Berry threw the train of her dress over him. Duyckinck compared with this episode the sad death of a young English girl, Miss Clare Webster, in a burletta called "The Revolt of the Harem" at Drury Lane Theater, London. She was wearing a thin voluminous costume which took fire from a footlight.

The third principal element in the tale, the jester, was suggested by a story called "Frogère and the Emperor Paul"* which tells that Czar Paul I pretended to exile his jester, a Parisian comedian, to Siberia, but really had him merely driven a long way in a closed carriage and brought back to court. The jester later was among those who in 1801 found the Emperor murdered.† The dwarf's deformity is known in nature.

The manner of chaining apes described is not mentioned by any authorities consulted, and since it is integral to the plot, may well be invented on the basis of the captive wild men described by Froissart.

The tale was finished on February 7, 1849, as Poe related in a letter of the next day to Annie Richmond, wherein he remarked that the owner of the Boston *Flag* had offered him five dollars a Graham page, and he had accepted, "to get out of my pecuniary difficulties." Poe calls it "5 prose pages" and the price must have been twenty-five dollars.

TEXTS

(A) The Flag of Our Union (Boston), March 17, 1849; *(B) Works* (1850), II, 455–464.

Griswold's version *(B)* is followed. He seems to have had a clipping with auctorial emendations and corrections. Two of the latter were misunderstood — the word "Caryatides" was too much for the printers — and these now have been corrected editorially. The formsheet of the *Flag* used double for single quotation marks and vice versa, but the form was normalized by Griswold.

* Signed P. in the London *New Monthly Magazine* of June 1830. This, A. H. Quinn (*Poe,* p. 596) pointed out, is in the same volume of the magazine as Bulwer's "Monos and Daimonos," on which Poe founded his "Silence — a Fable."

† It is not likely that Poe knew of the assassination of a Duke of Münsterberg in Silesia by his fool shortly before 1400. That story Thomas Lovell Beddoes found in Karl Friedrich Flögel's *Geschichte der Hofnarren* (1789), and made the basis of *Death's Jestbook,* a poetic drama not printed until 1850.

HOP-FROG

HOP-FROG. [*B*]

I never knew any one so keenly alive to a joke as the king was. He seemed to live only for joking. To tell a good story of the joke kind, and to tell it well, was the surest road to his favor. Thus it happened that his seven ministers were all noted for their accomplishments as jokers. They all took after the king, too, in being large, corpulent, oily men, as well as inimitable jokers.[1] Whether people grow fat by joking, or whether there is something in fat itself which predisposes to a joke, I have never been quite able to determine; but certain it is that a lean joker is a *rara avis in terris.*[2]

About the refinements, or, as he called them, the "ghosts" of wit, the king troubled himself very little. He had an especial admiration for *breadth* in a jest, and would often put up with *length,* for the sake of it. Over-niceties wearied him. He would have preferred Rabelais's "Gargantua," to the "Zadig" of Voltaire:[3] and, upon the whole, practical jokes suited his taste far better than verbal ones.

At the date of my narrative, professing jesters had not altogether gone out of fashion at court. Several of the great continental "powers" still retained their "fools," who were motley, with caps and bells, and who were expected to be always ready with sharp witticisms, at a moment's notice, in consideration of the crumbs that fell from the royal table.[4]

Our king, as a matter of course, retained his "fool." The fact is, he *required* something in the way of folly — if only to counterbalance the heavy wisdom of the seven wise men who were his ministers — not to mention himself.

His fool, or professional jester, was not *only* a fool, however. His value was trebled in the eyes of the king, by the fact of his being also a dwarf and a cripple. Dwarfs were as common at court, in those days, as fools; and many monarchs would have found it difficult to get through their days (days are rather longer at court than elsewhere) without both a jester to laugh *with,* and a dwarf to laugh *at.*[5] But, as I have already observed, your jesters, in ninety-nine cases out of a hundred, are fat, round[a] and unwieldy — so

---

Title: Hop-Frog: or, The Eight Chained Orang-Outangs. *(A)*

a sound *(A) misprint*

that it was no small source of self-gratulation with our king that, in Hop-Frog (this was the fool's name,) he possessed a triplicate treasure in one person.[6]

I believe the name "Hop-Frog" was *not* that given to the dwarf by his sponsors at baptism, but it was conferred upon him, by general consent of the seven ministers, on account of his inability to walk as other men do. In fact, Hop-Frog could only get along by a sort of interjectional gait — something between a leap and a wriggle — a movement that afforded illimitable amusement, and of course consolation, to the king, for (notwithstanding the protuberance of his stomach and a constitutional swelling of the head) the king, by his whole court, was accounted a capital figure.

But although Hop-Frog, through the distortion of his legs, could move only with great pain and difficulty along a road or floor, the prodigious muscular power which nature seemed to have bestowed upon his arms, by way of compensation for deficiency in the lower limbs, enabled him to perform many feats of wonderful dexterity, where trees or ropes were in question, or anything else to climb. At such exercises he certainly much more resembled a squirrel, or a small monkey, than a frog.

I am not able to say, with precision, from what country Hop-Frog originally came. It was from some barbarous region, however, that no person ever heard of — a vast distance from the court of our king. Hop-Frog, and a young girl very little less dwarfish than himself (although of exquisite proportions, and a marvellous dancer,) had been forcibly carried off from their respective homes in adjoining provinces, and sent as presents to the king, by one of his ever-victorious generals.

Under these circumstances, it is not to be wondered at that a close intimacy arose between the two little captives. Indeed, they soon became sworn friends. Hop-Frog, who, although he made a great deal of sport, was by no means popular, had it not in his power to render Trippetta many services; but *she*, on account of her grace and exquisite beauty (although a dwarf,)[7] was universally admired and petted: so she possessed much influence; and never failed to use it, whenever she could, for the benefit of Hop-Frog.

On some grand state occasion — I forget what — the king determined to have a masquerade; and whenever a masquerade, or anything of that kind, occurred at our court, then the talents both of Hop-Frog and Trippetta were sure to be called in play.[8] Hop-Frog, in especial, was so inventive in the way of getting up pageants, suggesting novel characters, and arranging costume, for masked balls, that nothing could be done, it seems, without his assistance.

The night appointed for the *fête* had arrived. A gorgeous hall had been fitted up, under Trippetta's eye, with every kind of device which could possibly give *éclat*[b] to a masquerade. The whole court was in a fever of expectation. As for costumes and characters, it might well be supposed that everybody had come to a decision on such points. Many had made up their minds (as to what *rôles* they should assume) a week, or even a month, in advance; and, in fact, there was not a particle of indecision anywhere — except in the case of the king and his seven ministers. Why *they* hesitated I never could tell, unless they did it by way of a joke. More probably, they found it difficult, on account of being so fat, to make up their minds. At all events, time flew; and, as a last resource, they sent for Trippetta and Hop-Frog.

When the two little friends obeyed the summons of the king, they found him sitting at his wine with the seven members of his cabinet council; but the monarch appeared to be in a very ill humor. He knew that Hop-Frog was not fond of wine; for it excited the poor cripple almost to madness; and madness is no comfortable feeling. But the king loved his practical jokes, and took pleasure in forcing Hop-Frog to drink and (as the king called it) "to be merry."[9]

"Come here, Hop-Frog," said he, as the jester and his friend entered the room: "swallow this bumper to the health of your absent friends [here Hop-Frog sighed,] and then let us have the benefit of your invention. We want characters — *characters,* man — something novel — out of the way. We are wearied with this everlasting sameness. Come, drink! the wine will brighten your wits."

---

b *éclât (A, B)*

Hop-Frog endeavored, as usual, to get up a jest in reply to these advances from the king; but the effort was too much. It happened to be the poor dwarf's birthday, and the command to drink to his "absent friends"[10] forced the tears to his eyes. Many large, bitter drops fell into the goblet as he took it, humbly, from the hand of the tyrant.

"Ah! ha! ha! ha!" roared the latter, as the dwarf reluctantly drained the beaker. "See what a glass of good wine can do! Why, your eyes are shining already!"

Poor fellow! his large eyes *gleamed,* rather than shone; for the effect of wine on his excitable brain was not more powerful than instantaneous. He placed the goblet nervously on the table, and looked round upon the company with a half-insane stare. They all seemed highly amused at the success of the king's *"joke."*

"And now to business," said the prime minister, a *very* fat man.

"Yes," said the king; "come, Hop-Frog, lend us your assistance. Characters, my fine fellow; we stand in need of characters — all of us — ha! ha! ha!" and as this was seriously meant for a joke, his laugh was chorused by the seven.

Hop-Frog also laughed, although feebly and somewhat vacantly.

"Come, come," said the king, impatiently, "have you nothing to suggest?"

"I am endeavoring to think of something *novel,*" replied the dwarf, abstractedly, for he was quite bewildered by the wine.

"Endeavoring!" cried the tyrant, fiercely; "what do you mean by *that?* Ah, I perceive. You are sulky, and want more wine. Here, drink this!" and he poured out another goblet full and offered it to the cripple, who merely gazed at it, gasping for breath.

"Drink, I say!" shouted the monster, "or by the fiends —"

The dwarf hesitated. The king grew purple with rage. The courtiers smirked. Trippetta, pale as a corpse, advanced to the monarch's seat, and, falling on her knees before him, implored him to spare her friend.

The tyrant regarded her, for some moments, in evident wonder at her audacity. He seemed quite at a loss what to do or say —

how most becomingly to express his indignation. At last, without uttering a syllable, he pushed her violently from him, and threw the contents of the brimming goblet in her face.

The poor girl got up as best she could, and, not daring even to sigh, resumed her position at the foot of the table.

There was a dead silence for about a[c] half a minute, during which the falling of a leaf, or of a feather, might have been heard. It was interrupted by a low, but harsh and protracted *grating* sound which seemed to come at once from every corner of the room.

"What – what – *what* are you making that noise for?" demanded the king, turning furiously to the dwarf.

The latter seemed to have recovered, in great measure, from his intoxication, and looking fixedly but quietly into the tyrant's face, merely ejaculated:

"I – I? How could it have been me?"

"The sound appeared to come from without," observed one of the courtiers. "I fancy it was the parrot at the window, whetting his bill upon his cage-wires."

"True," replied the monarch, as if much relieved by the suggestion; "but, on the honor of a knight, I could have sworn that it was the gritting of this vagabond's teeth."

Hereupon the dwarf laughed (the king was too confirmed a joker to object to any one's laughing), and displayed a set of large, powerful, and very repulsive teeth. Moreover, he avowed his perfect willingness to swallow as much wine as desired. The monarch was pacified; and having drained another bumper with no very perceptible ill effect, Hop-Frog entered at once, and with spirit, into the plans for the masquerade.

"I cannot tell what was the association of idea," observed he, very tranquilly, and as if he had never tasted wine in his life, "but *just after* your majesty had struck the girl and thrown the wine in her face – *just after* your majesty had done this, and while the parrot was making that odd noise outside the window, there came into my mind a capital diversion – one of my own country frolics

---

c *Omitted (A)*

– often enacted among us, at our masquerades: but here it will be new altogether. Unfortunately, however, it requires a company of eight persons, and –"

"Here we *are!*" cried the king, laughing at his acute discovery of the coincidence; "eight to a fraction – I and my seven ministers. Come! what is the diversion?"

"We call it," replied the cripple, "the Eight Chained Ourang-Outangs, and it really is excellent sport if well enacted."[11]

"*We* will enact it," remarked the king, drawing himself up, and lowering his eyelids.

"The beauty of the game," continued Hop-Frog, "lies in the fright it occasions among the women."

"Capital!" roared in chorus the monarch and his ministry.

"*I* will equip you as ourang-outangs," proceeded the dwarf; "leave all that to me. The resemblance shall be so striking, that the company of masqueraders will take you for real beasts – and of course, they will be as much terrified as astonished."

"O, this is exquisite!" exclaimed the king. "Hop-Frog! I will make a man of you."

"The chains are for the purpose of increasing the confusion by their jangling. You are supposed to have escaped, *en masse,* from your keepers. Your majesty cannot conceive the *effect* produced, at a masquerade, by eight chained ourang-outangs, imagined to be real ones by most of the company; and rushing in with savage cries, among the crowd of delicately and gorgeously habited men and women. The *contrast* is inimitable."

"It *must* be," said the king: and the council arose hurriedly (as it was growing late), to put in execution the scheme of Hop-Frog.

His mode of equipping the party as ourang-outangs was very simple, but effective enough for his purposes. The animals in question had, at the epoch of my story, very rarely been seen in any part of the civilized world; and as the imitations made by the dwarf were sufficiently beast-like and more than sufficiently hideous, their truthfulness to nature was thus thought to be secured.

The king and his ministers were first encased in tight-fitting stockinet shirts and drawers. They were then saturated with tar. At this stage of the process, some one of the party suggested feathers; but the suggestion was at once overruled by the dwarf, who soon convinced the eight, by ocular demonstration, that the hair of such a brute as the ourang-outang was much more efficiently represented by *flax*. A thick coating of the[d] latter was accordingly plastered upon the coating of tar.[12] A long chain was now procured. First, it was passed about the waist of the king, *and tied;* then about another of the party, and also tied; then about all successively, in the same manner. When this chaining arrangement was complete, and the party stood as far apart from each other as possible, they formed a circle; and to make all things appear natural, Hop-Frog passed the residue of the chain, in two diameters, at right angles, across the circle, after the fashion adopted, at the present day, by those who capture Chimpanzees, or other large apes, in Borneo.

The grand saloon in which the masquerade was to take place, was a circular room, very lofty, and receiving the light of the sun only through a single window at top. At night (the season for which the apartment was especially designed,) it was illuminated principally by a large chandelier, depending by a chain from the centre of the sky-light, and lowered, or elevated, by means of a counter-balance as usual; but (in order not to look unsightly) this latter passed outside the cupola and over the roof.

The arrangements of the room had been left to Trippetta's superintendence;[e] but, in some particulars, it seems, she had been guided by the calmer judgment of her friend the dwarf. At his suggestion it was that, on this occasion, the chandelier was removed. Its waxen drippings (which, in weather so warm, it was quite impossible to prevent,) would have been seriously detrimental to the rich dresses of the guests, who, on account of the crowded state of the saloon, could not *all* be expected to keep from out its centre — that is to say, from under the chandelier. Additional sconces were set in various parts of the hall, out of the way; and a flambeau, emitting sweet odor, was placed in the right hand of each of the Caryatides[f] that stood against the wall — some fifty or sixty altogether.[13]

---

d this *(A)*
e superintendance *(B) misprint*
f Caryabides *(A)*; Caryaides *(B) misprints*

The eight ourang-outangs, taking Hop-Frog's advice, waited patiently until midnight (when the room was thoroughly filled with masqueraders) before making their appearance. No sooner had the clock ceased striking, however, than they rushed, or rather rolled in, all together — for the impediment of their chains caused most of the party to fall, and all to stumble as they entered.

The excitement among the masqueraders was prodigious, and filled the heart of the king with glee. As had been anticipated, there were not a few of the guests who supposed the ferocious-looking creatures to be beasts of *some* kind in reality, if not precisely ourang-outangs. Many of the women swooned with affright; and had not the king taken the precaution to exclude all weapons from the saloon, his party might soon have expiated their frolic in their blood. As it was, a general rush was made for the doors; but the king had ordered them to be locked immediately upon his entrance; and, at the dwarf's suggestion, the keys had been deposited with *him*.

While the tumult was at its height, and each masquerader attentive only to his own safety — (for, in fact, there was much *real* danger from the pressure of the excited crowd,) — the chain by which the chandelier ordinarily hung, and which had been drawn up on its removal, might have been seen very gradually to descend, until its hooked extremity came within three feet of the floor.

Soon after this, the king and his seven friends, having reeled about the hall in all directions, found themselves, at length, in its centre, and, of course, in immediate contact with the chain. While they were thus situated, the dwarf, who had followed closely at their heels, inciting them to keep up the commotion, took hold of their own chain at the intersection of the two portions which crossed the circle diametrically and at right angles. Here, with the rapidity of thought, he inserted the hook from which the chandelier had been wont to depend; and, in an instant, by some unseen agency, the chandelier-chain was drawn so far upward as to take the hook out of reach, and, as an inevitable consequence, to drag the ourang-outangs together in close connection, and face to face.

The masqueraders, by this time, had recovered, in some measure, from their alarm; and, beginning to regard the whole matter as a well-contrived pleasantry, set up a loud shout of laughter at the predicament of the apes.

"Leave them to *me!*" now screamed Hop-Frog, his shrill voice making itself easily heard through all the din. "Leave them to *me.* I fancy *I* know them. If I can only get a good look at them, *I* can soon tell who they are."

Here, scrambling over the heads of the crowd, he managed to get to the wall; when, seizing a flambeau from one of the Caryatides,[g] he returned, as he went, to the centre of the room — leaped,[h] with the agility of a monkey, upon the king's head — and thence clambered a few feet up the chain — holding down the torch to examine the group of ourang-outangs, and still screaming, "*I* shall soon find out who they are!"

And now, while the whole assembly (the apes included) were convulsed with laughter, the jester suddenly uttered a shrill whistle; when the chain flew violently up for about thirty feet — dragging with it the dismayed and struggling ourang-outangs, and leaving them suspended in mid-air between the sky-light and the floor.[14] Hop-Frog, clinging to the chain as it rose, still maintained[i] his relative position in respect to the eight maskers, and still (as if nothing were the matter) continued to thrust his torch down towards them, as though endeavoring to discover who they were.

So thoroughly astonished were the whole company at this ascent, that a dead silence, of about a minute's duration, ensued. It was broken by just such a low, harsh, *grating* sound, as had before attracted the attention of the king and his councillors, when the former threw the wine in the face of Trippetta. But, on the present occasion, there could be no question as to *whence* the sound issued. It came from the fang-like teeth of the dwarf, who ground them and gnashed them as he foamed at the mouth, and glared, with an expression of maniacal rage, into the upturned countenances of the king and his seven companions.

"Ah, ha!" said at length the infuriated jester. "Ah, ha! I begin

---

g Caryabides *(A);* Caryaides *(B)* *misprints*

h leaping, *(A)*

i maintaining *(A)*

to see who these people *are*, now!" Here, pretending to scrutinize the king more closely, he held the flambeau to the flaxen coat which enveloped him, and which instantly burst into a sheet of vivid flame. In less than half a minute the whole eight ourang-outangs were blazing fiercely, amid the shrieks of the multitude who gazed at them from below, horror-stricken, and without the power to render them the slightest assistance.

At length the flames, suddenly increasing in virulence, forced the jester to climb higher up the chain, to be out of their reach; and, as he made this movement, the crowd again sank, for a brief instant, into silence. The dwarf seized his opportunity, and once more spoke:

"I now see *distinctly*," he said, "what manner of people these maskers are. They are a great king and his seven privy-councillors — a king who does not scruple to strike a defenceless girl, and his seven councillors who abet him in the outrage. As for myself, I am simply Hop-Frog, the jester — and *this is my last jest*."

Owing to the high combustibility of both the flax and the tar to which it adhered, the dwarf had scarcely made an end of his brief speech before the work of vengeance was complete. The eight corpses swung in their chains, a fetid, blackened, hideous, and indistinguishable mass. The cripple hurled his torch at them, clambered leisurely to the ceiling, and disappeared through the skylight.

It is supposed that Trippetta, stationed on the roof of the saloon, had been the accomplice of her friend in his fiery revenge, and that, together, they effected their escape to their own country: for neither was seen again.

NOTES

1. The King reminds one a little of George IV, who indulged in coarse practical jokes. Poe called him "that filthy compound of all that is bestial — that lazar-house of all moral corruption," in a review of Charles James Lever's *Charles O'Malley*, in *Graham's* for March 1842.

2. "A rare bird in the world" is from Juvenal, *Satires*, VI, 165; Poe used it also in "Philosophy of Furniture" at n. 11.

3. A reference in "The Facts in the Case of M. Valdemar" (see n. 1) seems to make fun of Rabelais; Poe's own liking for Voltaire's *Zadig* is shown by his

modeling M. Dupin upon that character (see introduction to "The Murders in the Rue Morgue").

4. For "crumbs that fell from the rich man's table" see St. Luke 16:21.

5. Poe wrote of laughing *with* or *at* someone also in a review of *Madrid in 1835* in the *Southern Literary Messenger,* October 1836; and again in "The Oblong Box," at n. 7.

6. Hop-Frog is said to resemble David Ritchie, the original of Sir Walter Scott's *Black Dwarf.* I have also seen an eighteenth century print of a certain Sir Jeffrey Dunstan who was similarly deformed. [Charles Lombard, in *Poe Studies,* December 1970, points out Poe's apparent indebtedness to Victor Hugo – not only for suggestions from Quasimodo of *Notre Dame de Paris* but also from characters in the earlier novels, *Han d'Islande* and *Bug-Jargal.*]

7. Tripetta seems to be from French "tripette," something of slight value, but the name suggests dancing. Curiously, Poe seems not to have known the distinction between a dwarf, like Hop-Frog, and a midget, like Trippetta.

8. Masquerades were popular in Poe's day.

9. Hop-Frog reacts to wine as Poe did on occasion. "Drink and be merry" is from St. Luke 12:19.

10. "Absent friends" is probably quoted because the King had just said it; but it was a customary toast at banquets.

11. One of my students suggested that Hop-Frog is perhaps thought of as coming from Borneo, where ourang-outangs dwell. For Poe's interest in these apes see the notes on "The Murders in the Rue Morgue," and "The System of Doctor Tarr and Professor Fether."

12. The costumes are thus described by Froissart: "A squire of Normandy, called Hogreymen of Gensay . . . devised six coats made of linen cloth, covered with pitch, and thereon flax like hair . . . When they were thus arrayed in these said coats, and sewed fast in them, they seemed like wild savages, full of hair from the top of the head to the sole of the foot. This device pleased well the French King." The squire was one of those killed.

13. Caryatides are columns in the form of female captives. They commemorate the women of Caryae in Laconia, whom the Spartans condemned to servitude at hard labor. The King's taste for them fits in with his harsh treatment of Trippetta.

14. The last of Poe's hanging lamps. See "King Pest," n. 13.

VON KEMPELEN AND HIS DISCOVERY

This is Poe's prose comment on the Gold Rush to California which inspired his "Eldorado" in verse.* Gold was found on

* See *Poems* (Mabbott I), 461–465.

January 24, 1848 by James Wilson Marshall in the raceway of a sawmill constructed by Captain John Augustus Sutter on the South Fork of the American River in California. The discovery is recorded in the San Francisco *Californian* of March 15, 1848. The Gold Rush came very late in that year and in 1849. That the transmutation of the baser into precious metals would be possible in the nineteenth century was asserted by "Dr. Girianger, of Göttingen," according to the article "Alchymy" in Isaac D'Israeli's *Curiosities of Literature.*

Experience had shown Poe that unwary readers could believe in imaginary miracles of mesmerism. He concluded that such people might swallow an account of a chemist who really made gold. The piece was finished by March 8, 1849, when Poe wrote to E. A. Duyckinck:

> If you have looked over the Von Kempelen article which I left with your brother, you will have fully perceived its drift. I mean it as a kind of "exercise", or experiment, in the plausible or verisimilar style. Of course, there is *not one* word of truth in it from beginning to end. I thought that such a style, applied to the gold-excitement, could not fail of effect. My sincere opinion is that nine persons out of ten (even among the best-informed) will *believe* the quiz (provided the design does not leak out before publication) and that thus, acting as a sudden, although of course a very temporary *check* to the gold-fever, it will create a *stir* to some purpose . . .
>
> I believe the quiz is the first deliberate literary attempt of the kind on record. In the story of Mrs Veal, we are permitted, now and then, to perceive a tone of *banter.* In "Robinson Crusoe" the design was far more to please, or excite, than to deceive by verisimilitude . . . In my "Valdemar Case" (which *was* credited by many) I had not the slightest idea that any person should credit it as any thing more than a "Magazine-paper" – but here the whole strength is laid out in verisimilitude.

Poe offered the hoax to Duyckinck for the New York *Literary World,* "for $10, or, in fact, whatever you think you can afford." He asked Duyckinck not to reveal the secret, and to return the piece if he felt "shy" about it, and added that the agent of the *Flag of Our Union* would give him fifteen dollars for it, but it would then "be quite thrown away." It was.

Poe's trap was laid only for the credulous. For the rest, his exercise in the verisimilar practically avoided the veracious. He was at no pains to mislead the analytic. He referred in the story itself to his hero as "connected, in some way, with Maelzel," whose chessplayer involved only theatrical magic. The localities in Bremen mentioned are found in no map of that city. The scientists mentioned are men of international reputation whose scientific discussions of the savant from Utica would soon be found not to exist; and the English name of the chemical compound to which Von Kempelen's discovery was akin is the broadest hint of all. There are also direct and indirect allusions to several friends of Poe which I think were calculated to amuse them. All these and other whimsical elements in the story are discussed in the notes below.†

TEXTS

(A) The Flag of Our Union (Boston), April 14, 1849; *(B) Works* (1850), I, 102–109.

Griswold's version *(B)* is followed as it shows two apparently auctorial changes. *The Flag of Our Union* text *(A)* reverses the usual custom of printing single quotations within, double without. This earlier text is, however, superior in punctuation, and a number of improvements in our text have been made from it. The spelling of Sir Humphry Davy's given name is permitted to remain as Poe always spelled it.

VON KEMPELEN AND HIS DISCOVERY. [*B*]

After the very minute and elaborate paper by Arago, to say nothing of the summary in "Silliman's Journal," with the detailed statement just published by Lieutenant Maury,[1] it will not be supposed, of course, that in offering a few hurried remarks in reference to Von Kempelen's discovery, I have any design to look at the subject in a *scientific* point of view. My object is simply, in the first place, to say a few words of Von Kempelen himself (with whom, some years ago, I had the honor of a slight personal acquaintance,) since everything[a] which concerns him must necessarily, at this moment, be of interest; and, in the second place, to look in a general way, and speculatively, at the *results* of the discovery.

† Poe's story and its component parts were discussed by Professor Burton R. Pollin, "Poe's Von Kempelen . . . Sources and Significance," in *Études Anglaises*, January-March 1967. [This article was revised for ***Discoveries in Poe*** and presents a full treatment of Poe's story.]

a every thing *(B) emended to follow A*

It may be as well, however, to premise the cursory observations which I have to offer, by denying, very decidedly, what seems to be a general impression (gleaned, as usual in a case of this kind, from the newspapers,) viz.: that this discovery, astounding as it unquestionably is, is *unanticipated.*

By reference to the "Diary of Sir Humphrey Davy," (Cottle and Munroe, London, pp. 150,)[2] it will be seen at pp. 53 and 82, that this illustrious chemist had not only conceived the idea now in question, but had actually made *no inconsiderable progress, experimentally,* in the very *identical analysis* now so triumphantly brought to an issue by Von Kempelen, who,[b] although he makes not the slightest allusion to it, is, *without doubt* (I say it unhesitatingly, and can prove it, if required,) indebted to the "Diary" for at least the first hint of his own undertaking. Although a little technical, I cannot refrain from appending two passages from the "Diary," with one of Sir Humphrey's equations. [As we have not the algebraic signs necessary, and as the "Diary" is to be found at the Athenæum Library, we omit here a small portion of Mr. Poe's manuscript. — Ed.][3]

The paragraph from the "Courier and Enquirer,"[4] which is now going the rounds of the press, and which purports to claim the invention for a Mr. Kissam, of Brunswick, Maine,[5] appears to me, I confess, a little apocryphal, for several reasons; although there is nothing either impossible or very improbable in the statement made. I need not go into details. My opinion of the paragraph is founded principally upon its *manner.* It does not *look* true. Persons[c] who are narrating *facts,* are seldom so particular as Mr. Kissam seems to be, about day and date and precise location. Besides, if Mr. Kissam actually *did* come upon the discovery he says he did, at the period designated — nearly eight years ago — how happens it that he took no steps, *on the instant,* to reap the immense benefits which the merest bumpkin must have known would have resulted to him individually, if not to the world at large, from the discovery? It seems to me quite incredible that any man, of common understanding, could have discovered what Mr. Kissam says he did, and yet

b who *(B) comma added from A* c People *(A)*

have subsequently acted so like a baby — so like an owl — as Mr. Kissam *admits* that he did. By-the-way, who *is* Mr. Kissam? and is not the whole paragraph in the "Courier and Enquirer" a fabrication got up to "make a talk?" It must be confessed that it has an amazingly moon-hoax-y air.[6] Very little dependence is to be placed upon it, in my humble opinion; and if I were not well aware, from experience, how very easily men of science are *mystified,* on points out of their usual range of inquiry, I should be profoundly astonished at finding so eminent a chemist as Professor Draper,[7] discussing Mr. Kissam's (or is it Mr. Quizzem's?) pretensions to this discovery, in so serious a tone.

But to return to the "Diary" of Sir Humphrey Davy.[8] This pamphlet was *not* designed for the public eye, even upon the decease of the writer, as any person at all conversant with authorship may satisfy himself at once by the slightest inspection of the style. At page 13, for example, near the middle, we read, in reference to his researches about the protoxide of azote: "In less than half a minute the respiration being continued, diminished gradually and *were* succeeded by analogous to gentle pressure on all the muscles." That the *respiration* was not "diminished," is not only clear by the subsequent context, but by the use of the plural, "were." The sentence, no doubt, was thus intended: "In less than half a minute, the respiration [being continued, these feelings] diminished gradually, and were succeeded by [a sensation] analogous to gentle pressure on all the muscles."[9] A hundred similar instances go to show that the MS. so inconsiderately published, was merely a *rough note-book,* meant only for the writer's own eye; but an inspection of the pamphlet will convince almost any thinking person of the truth of my suggestion. The fact is, Sir Humphrey Davy was about the last man in the world to *commit himself* on scientific topics. Not only had he a more than ordinary dislike to quackery, but he was morbidly afraid of *appearing* empirical; so that, however fully he might have been convinced that he was on the right track in the matter now in question, he would never have spoken *out,* until he had everything[d] ready for the most practical demon-

d every thing *(B) emended to follow A*

stration. I verily believe that his last moments would have been rendered wretched, could he have suspected that his wishes in regard to burning this "Diary" (full of crude speculations) would have been unattended to; as, it seems, they were. I say "his wishes," for that he meant to include this note-book among the miscellaneous papers directed "to be burnt," I think there can be no manner of doubt. Whether it escaped the flames by good fortune or by bad, yet remains to be seen. That the passages quoted above, with the other similar ones referred to, gave Von Kempelen *the hint,* I do not in the slightest degree question; but I repeat, it yet remains to be seen whether this momentous discovery itself (*momentous* under any circumstances,) will be of service or disservice to mankind at large. That Von Kempelen and his immediate friends will reap a rich harvest, it would be folly to doubt for a moment. They will scarcely be so weak as not to *"realize,"* in time, by large purchases of houses and land, with other property of *intrinsic* value.

In the brief account of Von Kempelen which appeared in the "Home Journal,"[10] and has since been extensively copied, several misapprehensions of the German original seem to have been made by the translator, who professes to have taken the passage[e] from a late number of the Presburg "Schnellpost."[11] *"Viele"* has evidently been misconceived (as it often is,) and what the translator renders by "sorrows," is probably *"lieden,"* which, in its true version, "sufferings," would give a totally different complexion to the whole account; but, of course, much of this is merely guess, on my part.[12]

Von Kempelen, however, is by no means "a misanthrope," in appearance, at least, whatever he may be in fact. My acquaintance with him was casual altogether; and I am scarcely warranted in saying that I know him at all; but to have seen and conversed with a man of so *prodigious* a notoriety as he has attained, or *will* attain in a few days, is not a small matter, as times go.

"The Literary World"[13] speaks of him, confidently, as a *native* of Presburg (misled, perhaps, by the account in the "Home Journal,") but I am pleased in being able to state *positively,* since I have it from his own lips, that he was born in Utica, in the State

---

e passages *(A)*

of New York,[14] although both his parents, I believe, are of Presburg descent. The family is connected, in some way, with Mäelzel, of Automaton-chess-player memory. [If we are not mistaken, the name of the *inventor* of the chess-player was either Kempelen, Von Kempelen, or something like it. – Ed.][15] In person, he is short and stout, with large, *fat,* blue eyes, sandy hair and whiskers, a wide but pleasing mouth, fine teeth, and I think a Roman nose. There is some defect in one of his feet.[16] His address is frank, and his whole manner noticeable for *bonhommie.* Altogether, he looks, speaks and acts as little like "a misanthrope" as any man I ever saw. We were fellow-sojourners for a week, about six years ago, at Earl's Hotel, in Providence, Rhode Island;[17] and I presume that I conversed with him, at various times, for some three or four hours altogether. His principal topics were those of the day; and nothing that fell from him led me to suspect his scientific attainments. He left the hotel before me, intending to go to New York, and thence to Bremen; it was in the latter city that his great discovery was first made public; or, rather, it was there that he was first suspected of having made it. This is about all that I personally know of the now immortal Von Kempelen; but I have thought that even these few details would have interest for the public.

There can be little question that most of the marvellous rumors afloat about this affair[f] are pure inventions, entitled to about as much credit as the story of Aladdin's lamp; and yet, in a case of this kind, as in the case of the discoveries in California, it is clear that the truth *may be* stranger than fiction.[18] The following anecdote, at least, is so well authenticated, that we may receive it implicitly.

Von Kempelen had never been even tolerably well off during his residence at Bremen; and often, it was well known, he had been put to extreme shifts, in order to raise trifling sums. When the great excitement occurred about the forgery on the house of Gutsmuth & Co., suspicion was directed towards Von Kempelen, on account of his having purchased a considerable property in Gasperitch Lane, and his refusing, when questioned, to explain how

---

f affair, *(B) comma deleted to follow A*

he became possessed of the purchase money. He was at length arrested, but nothing decisive appearing against him, was in the end set at liberty.[19] The police, however, kept a strict watch upon his movements, and thus discovered that he left home frequently, taking always the same road, and invariably giving his watchers the slip in the neighborhood of that labyrinth of narrow and crooked passages known by the flash-name[20] of the "Dondergat." Finally, by dint of great perseverance, they traced him to a garret in an old house of seven stories, in an alley called Flätplatz; and, coming upon him suddenly, found him, as they imagined, in the midst of his counterfeiting operations. His agitation is represented as so excessive that the officers had not the slightest doubt of his guilt. After hand-cuffing him, they searched his room, or rather rooms; for it appears he occupied all the *mansarde*.[g] [21]

Opening into the garret where they caught him[h] was a closet, ten feet by eight, fitted up with some chemical apparatus, of which the object has not yet been ascertained. In one corner of the closet was a very small furnace, with a glowing fire in it, and on the fire a kind of duplicate crucible — two crucibles connected by a tube. One of these crucibles was nearly full of *lead* in a state of fusion, but not reaching up to the aperture of the tube, which was close to the brim. The other crucible had some liquid in it, which, as the officers entered, seemed to be furiously dissipating in vapor. They relate that, on finding himself taken, Von Kempelen seized the crucibles with both hands (which were encased in gloves that afterwards turned out to be asbestic), and threw the contents on the tiled floor. It was now that they hand-cuffed him; and, before proceeding to ransack the premises, they searched his person, but nothing unusual was found about him, excepting a paper parcel, in his coat pocket, containing what was afterwards ascertained to be a mixture of antimony and some *unknown substance,* in nearly, but not quite, equal proportions. All attempts at analyzing the unknown substance have, so far, failed, but that it will ultimately be analyzed, is not to be doubted.

Passing out of the closet with their prisoner, the officers went

---

g *mausarde (A, B) misprint* h him, *(B) comma deleted to follow A*

through a sort of ante-chamber, in which nothing material was found, to the chemist's sleeping-room. They here rummaged some drawers and boxes, but discovered only a few papers, of no importance, and some good coin, silver and gold. At length, looking under the bed, they saw *a large, common hair trunk, without hinges, hasp, or lock,* and with the top lying carelessly *across* the bottom portion. Upon attempting to draw this trunk out from under the bed, they found that, with their united strength (there were three of them, all powerful men), they "could not stir it one inch." Much astonished at this, one of them crawled under the bed, and looking into the trunk, said:

"No wonder we couldn't move it – why, it's full to the brim of old bits of brass!"

Putting his feet, now, against the wall, so as to get a good purchase, and pushing with all his force, while his companions pulled with all theirs, the trunk, with much difficulty, was slid out from under the bed, and its contents examined. The supposed brass with which it was filled was all in small, smooth pieces, varying from the size of a pea to that of a dollar; but the pieces were irregular in shape, although all more or less flat – looking, upon the whole, "very much as lead looks when thrown upon the ground in a molten state, and there suffered to grow cool." Now, not one of these officers for a moment suspected this metal to be anything *but* brass. The idea of its being *gold* never entered their brains, of course; how *could* such a wild fancy have entered it? And their astonishment may be well conceived, when next day it became known, all over Bremen, that the "lot of brass" which they had carted so contemptuously to the police office, without putting themselves to the trouble of pocketing the smallest scrap, was not only gold – real gold – but gold far finer than any employed in coinage – gold, in fact, absolutely pure, virgin, without the slightest appreciable alloy!

I need not go over the details of Von Kempelen's confession (as far as it went) and release, for these are familiar to the public. That he has actually realized, in spirit and in effect, if not to the letter, the old chimera of the philosopher's stone, no sane person is at liberty to doubt. The opinions of Arago are, of course, entitled to the greatest consideration; but he is by no means infallible; and what he says of *bismuth,* in his report to the academy, must be taken *cum grano salis.*[22] The simple truth is, that up to this period, *all* analysis has failed; and until Von Kempelen chooses to let us have the key to his own published enigma, it is more than probable that the matter will remain, for years, *in statu quo.* All that as[i] yet can fairly be said to be known, is, that *"pure gold can be made at will, and very readily, from lead, in connection with certain other substances, in kind and in proportions, unknown."*

Speculation, of course, is busy as to the immediate and ultimate results of this discovery — a discovery which few thinking persons will hesitate in referring to an increased interest in the matter of gold generally, by the late developments in California; and this reflection brings us inevitably to another — the exceeding *inopportuneness* of Von Kempelen's analysis. If many were prevented from adventuring to California, by the mere apprehension that gold would so materially diminish in value, on account of its plentifulness in the mines there, as to render the speculation of going so far in search of it a doubtful one — what impression will be wrought *now,* upon the minds of those about to emigrate, and especially upon the minds of those actually in the mineral region, by the announcement of this astounding discovery of Von Kempelen? a discovery which declares, in so many words, that beyond its intrinsic worth for manufacturing purposes, (whatever that worth may be), gold now is, or at least soon will be (for it cannot be supposed that Von Kempelen can *long* retain his secret) of no greater *value* than lead, and of far inferior value to silver. It is, indeed, exceedingly difficult to speculate prospectively upon the consequences of the discovery; but one thing may be positively maintained — that the announcement of the discovery six months ago[j] would have had material influence in regard to the settlement of California.

In Europe, as yet, the most noticeable results have been a rise of two hundred per cent. in the price of lead, and nearly twenty-five per cent. in that of silver.

---

i that as/that *(B) emended to follow A* j ago, *(B) comma deleted to follow A*

VON KEMPELEN AND HIS DISCOVERY

NOTES

1. The supposed publications are all imaginary, but the persons were real scholars of note, whose names were well known in Poe's day. Dominique-François Arago (1786–1853), a celebrated physicist and astronomer, was probably the most prominent of French scientists in 1849. Benjamin Silliman's *American Journal of Science and Arts,* founded in 1818 at New Haven by the professor of chemistry and natural history at Yale College, was already one of the important scientific journals of the world. Lieutenant Matthew Fontaine Maury (1806–1873), who was a contributor to the *Southern Literary Messenger* under the pen-name of Harry Bluff, in 1847 and 1848 had just published the first of his famous wind and current charts and the companion sailing instructions which were to shorten materially the sailing time between ports in many parts of the world.

2. The reference to Davy's "Diary" is wholly fictitious, but Poe may have seen a footnote in Harper's 1842 edition of Bulwer's *Zanoni* saying "Mr. D'Israeli, in his 'Curiosities of Literature' (Article Alchem.), after quoting the sanguine judgments of modern chymists as to the transmutation of metals, observes... 'Sir Humphrey Davy told me that he did not consider this undiscovered art as impossible...'"

3. In the bracketed passage Poe's reference must be to the Boston Athenaeum – a library that still flourishes – since the explanation is ascribed to the pen of the editor of the Boston *Flag of Our Union,* in which the tale appeared. There was no subscription library called Atheneum in New York, and institutions of the name in Providence and Baltimore can have nothing to do with the case. For dealing with a problem by means of an editorial explanation in brackets, see "The Mystery of Marie Rogêt" at n. 120.

4. The *Morning Courier and New York Enquirer* was edited by James Watson Webb, a friend of Poe in later years. He raised a fund for the poet at the Metropolitan Club after Virginia Poe's death in 1847, according to Griswold's "Ludwig" article in the *New-York Tribune,* October 9, 1849 – a statement I see no reason to doubt. (See Harrison, *Complete Works,* I, 354.)

5. Brunswick, Maine, was the residence of Poe's young correspondent George W. Eveleth, for whose amusement the reference was probably inserted. The name Kissam is slightly ludicrous and was chosen for the pun on Quizzem.

6. Obviously a reference to Richard Adams Locke's Moon Hoax; see "The Balloon Hoax," introduction, p. 1066.

7. John William Draper was a professor at New York University and a leading scientist, whose improvements in the chemistry of Daguerre's photography shortened exposure time enough to make possible the first daguerreotype portrait (1839). Poe did not like Draper, and told Eveleth, in a letter of June 26, 1849, that he was satirized in *Eureka.* Poe may have enjoyed representing Draper as a dupe.

8. [As indicated in note 2 above, the "Diary" mentioned was Poe's invention, but Thomas Hall demonstrated, in "Poe's Use of a Source" (*Poe Newsletter,* October 1968), that the material for the ensuing discussion actually came from a

paragraph in Davy's *Collected Works,* III: "Researches Concerning Nitrous Oxide" (London, 1839).]

9. Azote was Lavoisier's name for nitrogen; its protoxide (N_2O) is, in common parlance, laughing gas.

[Davy's paragraph found by Mr. Hall on p. 272 of the volume cited reads as follows:

> "Having previously closed my nostrils and exhausted my lungs, I breathed four quarts of nitrous oxide from and into a silk bag. The first feelings were similar to those produced in the last experiment; but in less than half a minute, the respiration being continued, they diminished gradually, and were succeeded by a sensation analogous to gentle pressure on all the muscles, attended by a highly pleasurable thrilling, particularly in the chest and the extremities. The objects around me became dazzling and my hearing more acute. Towards the last inspirations, the thrilling increased, the sense of muscular power became greater, and at last an irresistible propensity to action was indulged in; I recollect but indistinctly what followed; I know that my motions were various and violent.
>
> "These effects very soon ceased after respiration. In ten minutes, I had recovered my natural state of mind. The thrilling in the extremities, continued longer than the other sensations."

Poe's contribution here to the effectiveness of his tale was his skillful manipulation of Davy's phrases.]

10. The New York *Home Journal,* founded in 1846 by Morris and Willis after they left the *New-York Mirror,* was always friendly to Poe.

11. Pressburg (now Bratislava, Czechoslovakia) was reputedly a home of magic; compare "Morella" at n. 1. The newspaper named has not been found, and I think it a namesake of the New York *Deutsche Schnellpost* – which had been mentioned in the *Broadway Journal* of August 30, 1845, and was still being published in 1849.

12. Poe used his scraps of German hard. Where he found *viele* (many) has not been discovered, but the comment on *Leiden* – which he misspelled and failed to capitalize as a substantive – came from a footnote in Sarah Austin's translation of Prince Pückler-Muskau's *Tour* (1833), p. 388. There one finds a critical mention of Goethe's *Sorrows of Werther* and Mrs. Austin's note: "The translation of the title is of a piece with all the rest. *Leiden* does not mean *sorrows,* but *sufferings.*" Poe had used the note earlier in "Marginalia," number 174 (*Democratic Review,* July 1846, p. 32).

13. The *Literary World* was the weekly edited by Evert Duyckinck and his brother George, to whom Poe had offered the tale of Von Kempelen.

14. Many German families were settled in Utica, but Poe probably chose it because it was the site of the New York State Insane Asylum, opened in 1843.

15. The famous "automaton" chess-player exhibited by J. N. Maelzel was indeed the invention of Wolfgang von Kempelen (1734–1804), a native of Pressburg. Poe described and analyzed the device, which despite its exhibitor's claims depended on human agency, in the *Southern Literary Messenger* for April 1836. The bracketed editorial interjection here is of course Poe's own.

16. The defect of Poe's protagonist's foot is a jocular hint of diablerie. Compare "Never Bet the Devil Your Head" at n. 19.

17. The Earl House, 67 North Main Street, Providence, was kept by Robert Earl at the time Poe lectured there on December 20, 1848; but "six years ago" in the 1844 Directory, Mr. Earl was listed as keeper of the City Hotel, 25 Broad Street.

18. Compare the motto of "The Thousand-and-Second Tale of Scheherazade" and the note on it.

19. In William Godwin's *St. Leon,* the hero's wealth without explicable source more than once causes his arrest; but he did learn of the true philosopher's stone, which is also the elixir of life, from a mysterious stranger; whereas Von Kempelen seems to be an investigating scientist rather than an "adept" in forbidden lore.

The German names in this paragraph are made up. [For a discussion see *Discoveries in Poe,* p. 174.]

20. Poe here makes a very neat reference in the "plausible or verisimilar style" when he calls these sinister passages by the flash-name of "Dondergat." He obviously means a name in the flash language, identified by *OED* and the *Century Dictionary* as thieves' cant or slang. [The word flash-name is listed as a Poe coinage in *Poe, Creator of Words* (1974) by B. Pollin.]

21. The *mansarde* is the top story, under the roof.

22. *Cum grano salis* means literally "with a grain of salt" – and signifies something to be doubted, but there is a joke here also, since bismuth is metallic and forms salts.

X-ING A PARAGRAB

This anecdote is by no means original with Poe. Stories are common about strange-looking articles resulting from the printers' custom of substituting X for a letter for which type is lacking. One called "No O's" appeared as translated from the French in the *New-York Mirror,* March 5, 1836; and another, "Xtraordinary Play upon Xes," is in the same paper of September 12, 1840.*

The name of the town in Poe's story was surely inspired by a paper on which he commented in the *Evening Mirror,* January 11, and the *Weekly Mirror,* January 18, 1845 (1:27):

THE ALPHADELPHIA TOCSIN. – (Phoebus, what a name, to fill the sounding trump of future fame!) – is the title of a new journal published at Al-

* See Killis Campbell, *Mind of Poe,* p. 167. Heartman and Canny, *Bibliography* (1943), p. 173, refer to some similar paragraph in the Philadelphia *Citizen Soldier* in 1843 (1:35).

phadelphia, Michigan, and "devoted to the interest of the laboring classes;" by which we presume are intended the classes who have to pronounce every morning the great appellation of the paper itself. Such a work should not want editors, and accordingly we are informed that it has *eight.* What on earth is the meaning of Alphadelphia? – is the "Alphadelphia Tocsin" the Tocsin of the city of double A's? – if so, the idea is too easily slipped into A double S.†

The Alphadelphian Association was founded on December 14, 1843 by fifty-six persons under the leadership of Dr. H. R. Schetterly of Ann Arbor. A site for their Fourierite community was chosen on the southeast corner of the township of Comstock, Kalamazoo County, Michigan. There meetings were held from March 21, 1844 to April 30, 1848, and there the *Tocsin* was published.‡

Poe's story was probably written not long before publication.

TEXTS

(A) The Flag of Our Union (Boston), May 12, 1849; *(B)* in *The Spanish Galleon* by J. H. Ingraham (Boston, 1849), pp. 92–95; *(C) Works,* IV (1856), 260–266.

The text chosen is Griswold's *(C).* Text *B* is merely a reprint from the *Flag* types, used as filler for an edition of Ingraham's romance about Captain Kidd, issued by F. Gleason at the *Flag* office. The only copy of this edition located is now in the William H. Koester Collection at the University of Texas. Other Gleason printings of the book do not include Poe's tale. See Heartman and Canny's *Bibliography* (1943), p. 126, for an explanation. All texts are inconsistent in the use of Tea-Pot or Tea-pot. We silently normalize the usage for our text, and record in the variants some verbal and punctuation emendations from the first printing.

X-ING A PARAGRAB. [*C*]

As it is well known that the "wise men" came "from the East,"[1] and as Mr. Touch-and-go Bullet-head[2] came from the East, it

† Poe used his paragraph again in "Marginalia," number 172, in the *Democratic Review,* July 1846, p. 31. The parenthetical comment is an inaccurate quotation from Byron's *English Bards and Scotch Reviewers,* lines 399–400.

‡ No copy of any issue of the paper can now be found, but see the article by A. D. P. Van Buren, contributed to Samuel W. Durant's *History of Kalamazoo County* (1880), pp. 369–371, and *Michigan Pioneer and Historical Society Historical Collections,* 5:406–412 (1882). Van Buren quotes some very bad verses from the paper. This information was sent to me by courtesy of Margaret I. Smith, Reference Librarian, University of Michigan.

follows that Mr. Bullet-head was a wise man; and if collateral proof of the matter be needed, here we have it — Mr. B. was an editor. Irascibility was his sole foible; for in fact the obstinacy of which men accused him was anything but his *foible,* since he justly considered it his *forte.*[3] It was his strong point — his virtue; and it would have required all the logic of a Brownson[4] to convince him that it was "anything else."

I have shown that Touch-and-go Bullet-Head was a wise man; and the only occasion on which he did not prove infallible, was when, abandoning that legitimate home for all wise men, the East,[5] he migrated to the city of Alexander-the-Great-o-nopolis, or some place of a similar title, out West.

I must do him the justice to say, however, that when he made up his mind finally to settle in that town, it was under the impression that no newspaper, and consequently no editor, existed in that particular section of the country. In establishing "The Tea-Pot," he expected to have the field all to himself.[6] I feel confident he never would have dreamed of taking up his residence in Alexander-the-Great-o-nopolis, had he been aware that, in Alexander-the-Great-o-nopolis, there lived a gentleman named John Smith (if I rightly remember), who, for many years, had there quietly grown fat in editing and publishing the "Alexander-the-Great-o-nopolis Gazette." It was solely, therefore, on account of having been misinformed, that Mr. Bullet-head found himself in Alex —— suppose we call it Nopolis,[7] "for short" — but, as he *did* find himself there, he determined to keep up his character for obst — for firmness, and remain. So remain he did; and he did more; he unpacked his press, type, etc., etc., rented an office exactly opposite to[a] that of the "Gazette," and, on the third morning after his arrival, issued the first number of "The Alexan" — that is to say, of "The Nopolis Tea-Pot:" — as nearly as I can recollect, this was the name of the new paper.

The leading article, I must admit, was brilliant — not to say severe. I was especially bitter about things in general — and as for the editor of "The Gazette," he was torn all to pieces in particular. Some of Bullet-head's remarks were really so fiery that I have al-

a *Omitted (A, B)*

ways, since that time, been forced to look upon John Smith, who is still alive, in the light of a salamander. I cannot pretend to give *all* the Tea-Pot's paragraphs *verbatim,* but one of them run thus:

"Oh, yes! — Oh,[b] we perceive! Oh, no doubt! The editor over the way is a genius — Oh,[c] my! Oh, goodness, gracious! — what *is* this world coming to? *Oh, tempora! Oh, Moses!*"[8]

A philippic at once so caustic and so classical, alighted like a bombshell among the hitherto peaceful citizens of Nopolis. Groups of excited individuals gathered at the corners of the streets. Every one awaited, with heartfelt anxiety, the reply of the dignified Smith. Next morning it appeared, as follows:

"We quote from 'The Tea-Pot' of yesterday the subjoined paragraph: — '*Oh,* yes! *Oh,* we perceive! *Oh,* no doubt! *Oh,* my! *Oh,* goodness! *Oh,* tempora! *Oh,* Moses!' Why, the fellow is all O! That accounts for his reasoning in a circle, and explains why there is neither beginning nor end to him, nor to anything that he says. We really do not believe the vagabond can write a word that hasn't an O in it. Wonder if this O-ing is a habit of his? By-the-by, he came away from Down-East in a great hurry. Wonder if he *O's* as much there as he does here? '*O!* it is pitiful.' "[d] [9]

The indignation of Mr. Bullet-head at these scandalous insinuations, I shall not attempt to describe. On the eel-skinning[10] principle, however, he did not seem to be so much incensed at the attack upon his integrity as one might have imagined. It was the sneer at his *style* that drove him to desperation. What! —*he,*[e] Touch-and-go Bullet-head! — not able to write a word without an O in it! He would soon let the jackanapes see that he was mistaken. Yes! he would let him see how *much* he was mistaken, the puppy! He, Touch-and-go Bullet-head, of Frogpondium,[11] would let Mr. John Smith perceive that he, Bullet-head, could indite, if it so pleased him, a whole paragraph — ay! a whole article — in which that contemptible vowel should not *once* — not even *once* — make its appearance. But no; — that would be yielding a point to the said John Smith. *He,* Bullet-head, would make *no* alteration in his style, to suit the caprices of any Mr. Smith in Christendom.

---

b Oh *(C) comma added from A, B*

c O, *(C) emended from A, B*

d pitiful?" ' *(A, B)*

e *he (C) comma added from A, B*

Perish so vile a thought! The O forever! He would persist in the O. He would be as O-wy as O-wy could be.

Burning with the chivalry of this determination, the great Touch-and-go, in the next "Tea-Pot," came out merely with this simple but resolute paragraph, in reference to this unhappy affair:

"The editor of the 'Tea-Pot' has the *honor* of advising the editor of 'The Gazette' that he, (the 'Tea-Pot,') will take an opportunity,[f] in to-morrow morning's paper, of convincing him, (the 'Gazette,') that he, (the 'Tea-Pot,') both can and will be[g] *his own master,* as regards style; — he (the 'Tea-Pot') intending to show him, (the 'Gazette,') the supreme, and indeed the withering contempt with which the criticism of him, (the 'Gazette,') inspires the independent bosom of him, (the 'Tea-Pot,') by composing for the especial gratification (?) of him, (the 'Gazette,') a leading article, of some extent, in which the beautiful vowel — the emblem of Eternity — yet so offensive[h] to the hyper-exquisite delicacy of him, (the 'Gazette,') shall most certainly *not be avoided* by his (the 'Gazette's') most obedient, humble servant, the 'Tea-Pot.' 'So much for Buckingham!' "[12]

In fulfilment of the awful threat thus darkly intimated rather than decidedly enunciated, the great Bullet-head, turning a deaf ear to all entreaties for "copy," and simply requesting his foreman to "go to the d—— l," when he (the foreman) assured him (the "Tea-Pot!") that it was high time to "go to press:" turning a deaf ear to everything, I say, the great Bullet-head sat up until daybreak, consuming the midnight oil, and absorbed in the composition of the really unparalleled paragraph, which follows:

"So, ho, John! how now? Told you so, you know. Don't crow, another time, before you're out of the woods! Does your mother *know* you're out? Oh, no, no! — so go home at once, now, John, to your odious old woods of Concord![13] Go home to your woods, old owl, — go! You wont?[14] Oh, poh, poh, John, don't do so! You've *got* to go, you know! So go at once, and don't go slow; for nobody owns you here, you know. Oh, John, John, if you *don't* go you're

f opportunity *(C) comma added from A, B*

g *be (A, B)*

h inoffensive *(C) misprint corrected from A, B*

no *homo* — no! You're only a fowl, an owl; a cow, a sow; a doll, a poll;[i] a poor, old, good-for-nothing-to-nobody, log, dog, hog, or frog, come out of a Concord bog. Cool, now — cool! *Do* be cool, you fool! None of your crowing, old cock! Don't frown so — don't! Don't hollo, nor howl, nor growl, nor bow-wow-wow! Good Lord, John, how you *do* look! Told you so, you know — but stop rolling your goose of an old poll about so, and go and drown your sorrows in a bowl!"[15]

Exhausted, very naturally, by so stupendous an effort, the great Touch-and-go could attend to nothing farther that night. Firmly, composedly, yet with an air of conscious power, he handed his MS. to the devil in waiting,[16] and then, walking leisurely home, retired, with ineffable dignity, to bed.

Meantime the devil to whom the copy was entrusted, ran up stairs to his "case," in an unutterable hurry, and forthwith made a commencement at "setting" the MS. "up."

In the first place, of course, — as the opening word was "So" — he made a plunge into the capital S hole and came out in triumph with a capital S. Elated by this success, he immediately threw himself upon the little-*o* box with a blindfold impetuosity — but who shall describe his horror when his fingers came up without the anticipated letter in their clutch? who shall paint his astonishment and rage at perceiving, as he rubbed his knuckles, that he had been only thumping them to no purpose, against the bottom of an *empty* box. Not a single little-*o* was in the little-*o* hole; and, glancing fearfully at the capital-*O* partition, he found *that,* to his extreme terror, in a precisely similar predicament. Awe-stricken, his first impulse was to rush to the foreman.

"Sir!" said he, gasping for breath, "I can't never set up nothing without no o's."[j]

"*What* do you mean by that?" growled the foreman, who was in a very ill-humor at being kept up so late.

"Why, sir, there beant an *o* in the office, neither a big un nor a little un!"

"What — what the d — l has become of all that were in the case?"

---

i Poll; *(A, B)* j *o*'s." *(A, B)*

"I don't know, sir," said the boy, "but one of them ere G'zette devils is bin prowling bout here all night, and I spect *he's* gone and cabbaged em every one."

"Dod rot him! I haven't a doubt of it," replied the foreman, getting purple with rage — "but I tell you what you do, Bob, that's a good boy — you go over the first chance you get and hook every one of their i's[k] and (d — n them!) their izzards."

"Jist so," replied Bob, with a wink and a frown — *"I'll* be into em, *I'll* let em know a thing or two; but in de meantime, that ere paragrab? *Mus* go in to-night, you know — else there'll be the d — l to pay, and — "

"And not a *bit* of pitch hot,"[17] interrupted the foreman, with a deep sigh and an emphasis on the "bit." "Is it a *very* long paragraph, Bob?"

"Shouldn't call it a *wery* long paragrab," said Bob.

"Ah, well, then! do the best you can with it! we *must* get to press," said the foreman, who was over head and ears in work; "just stick in some other letter for *o*, nobody's going to read the fellow's trash, any how."

"Wery well," replied Bob, "here goes it!" and off he hurried to his case; muttering as he went — "Considdeble vell, them ere expressions, perticcler for a man as doesn't[l] swar. So I's to gouge out all their eyes, eh? and d —— n all their gizzards![18] Vell! this here's the chap as is jist able *for* to do it." The fact is, that although Bob was but twelve years old and four feet high, he was equal to any amount of fight, in a small way.

The exigency here described is by no means of rare occurrence in printing-offices; and I cannot tell how to account for it, but the fact is indisputable, that when the exigency *does* occur, it almost always happens that *x* is adopted as a substitute for the letter deficient. The true reason, perhaps, is that *x* is rather the most superabundant letter in the cases, or at least *was* so in old times — long enough to render the substitution in question an habitual thing with printers. As for Bob, he would have considered it heretical to employ any other character, in a case of this kind, than the *x* to which he had been accustomed.

---

k *i's" (A, B)*

l doesen't *(C) misprint*

"I *shell* have to *x* this ere paragrab," said he to himself, as he read it over in astonishment, "but it's jest about the awfulest *o*-wy paragrab I ever *did* see:" so *x* it he did, unflinchingly, and to press it went *x-ed*.

Next morning,[m] the population of Nopolis were taken all aback by reading, in "The Tea-Pot," the following extraordinary leader:

"Sx hx, Jxhn! hxw nxw![n] Txld yxu sx, yxu knxw. Dxn't crxw, anxther time, befxre yxu're xut xf the wxxds! Dxes yzur mxther *knxw* yxu're xut? Xh, nx, nx! sx gx hxme at xnce, nxw, Jxhn, tx yxur xdixus xld wxxds xf Cxncxrd! Gx hxme tx yxur wxxds, xld xwl, — gx! Yxu wxnt? Xh, pxh, pxh, Jxhn, dxn't[o] dx sx! Yxu've *gxt* tx gx, yxu knxw! sx gx at xnce, and dxn't gx slxw; fxr nxbxdy xwns yxu here, yxu knxw.Xh, Jxhn, Jxhn, if yxu *dxn't* gx yxu're nx *hxmx* — nx! Yxu're xnly a fxwl, an xwl; a cxw, a sxw; a dxll, a pxll;[p] a pxxr xld gxxd-fxr-nxthing-tx-nxbxdy lxg, dxg, hxg, xr frxg, cxme xut xf a Cxncxrd bxg. Cxxl, nxw — cxxl! Dx be cxxl, yxu fxxl! Nxne xf yxur crxwing, xld cxck! Dxn't frxwn sx — dxn't! Dxn't hxllx, nxr hxwl, nxr grxwl, nxr bxw-wxw-wxw! Gxxd Lxrd, Jxhn, hxw yxu *dx* lxxk! Txld yxu sx, yxu knxw, but stxp rxlling yxur gxxse xf an xld pxll abxut sx, and gx and drxwn yxur sxrrxws in a bxwl!"

The uproar occasioned by this mystical and cabalistical article, is not to be conceived. The first definite idea entertained by the populace was, that some diabolical treason lay concealed in the hieroglyphics; and there was a general rush to Bullet-head's residence, for the purpose of riding him on a rail; but that gentleman was nowhere to be found. He had vanished, no one could tell how; and not even the ghost of him has ever been seen since.

Unable to discover its legitimate object, the popular fury at length subsided; leaving behind it, by way of sediment, quite a medley of opinion about this unhappy affair.

One gentleman thought the whole an X-ellent joke.

Another said that, indeed, Bullet-head had shown much X-uberance of fancy.

---

m morning *(C) comma added from A, B*

n nxw? *(A, B)*

o dxnt *(C) changed to conform to A, B, and C text below*

p Pxll; *(A, B)*

A third admitted him X-entric, but no more.

A fourth could only suppose it the Yankee's design to X-press, in a general way, his X-asperation.

"Say, rather, to set an X-ample to posterity," suggested a fifth.

That Bullet-head had been driven to an extremity,[q] was clear to all; and in fact, since *that* editor could not be found, there was some talk about lynching the other one.

The more common conclusion, however, was, that the affair was, simply, X-traordinary and in-X-plicable. Even the town mathematician confessed that he could make nothing of so dark a problem. X, everybody knew, was an unknown quantity; but in this case (as he properly observed), there was an unknown quantity of X.

The opinion of Bob, the devil (who kept dark "about his having X-ed the paragrab"), did not meet with so much attention as I think it deserved, although it was very openly and very fearlessly expressed. He said that, for his part, he had no doubt about the matter at all, that it was a clear case, that Mr. Bullet-head never *could*[r] be persvaded[s] fur to drink like other folks, but vas *con*tinually a-svigging o' that ere blessed XXX ale,[19] and, as a naiteral consekvence, it just[t] puffed him up savage, and made him X (cross) in the X-treme.

NOTES

1. The wise men from the East (or Magi) are mentioned in the second chapter of St. Matthew.

2. Touchandgo appears as a personal name in Thomas Love Peacock's *Crotchet Castle* (1831); Bullet-head was a favorite term with Poe, applied to Thomas Dunn English in a letter to F. W. Thomas, September 8, 1844, and to Lewis Gaylord Clark in the "Literati" (*Godey's*, September 1846).

3. Compare "Three Sundays in a Week" at n. 15.

4. Poe featured Orestes Augustus Brownson in "A Chapter on Autography," and mentioned him in "Mesmeric Revelation"; see n. 5 on that tale. The present reference is to the argument in Brownson's novel, *Charles Elwood, or The Infidel Converted* (1840).

5. Compare Poe's remark in a letter of February 14, 1849, to F. W. Thomas:

q x-tremity, *(A, B)*
r *vould (A, B)*
s pursvaded *(A, B)*
t jist *(A, B)*

"That conceited booby, the East – which is by no means the East out of which came the wise men mentioned in Scripture!" Down East meant all of New England, for Poe.

6. *The Tea-Pot* was obviously tempestuous and spouted hot air. In the *Saturday Evening Post,* September 3 and 10, 1842, are references to a controversy with Major P. R. Freas, editor of the *Germantown Telegraph,* with a threat, "to ask why he is like a teapot."

7. Nopolis means, humorously, "no city."

8. A misquotation from the opening of Cicero's first oration against Catiline, "O tempora, o mores." See Poe's early satire, so entitled, among the Poems (Mabbott I, 8).

9. "*O!* it is pitiful" is adapted from Thomas Hood's "The Bridge of Sighs" (1844), line 46. Poe recited the poem in his lecture on "The Poetic Principle," and it probably suggested the meter of "For Annie."

10. The term "eel-skinning" is an Americanism with so many rich connotations that it is difficult to know what Poe means here. In this case, "Let everybody skin their own eels." (See *The Macmillan Book of Proverbs, Maxims, and Famous Phrases,* 1948.)

11. Frogpondium was Poe's name for Boston. The Frog Pond is still a feature of Boston Common.

12. The quotation is from the rearrangement of Shakespeare's *Richard III,* Act IV, scene IV, made by Colley Cibber (c. 1700). It is scene iii in Cibber's version, which was that usually acted in Poe's day:

ENTER CATESBY

Cat. My Liege, the Duke of Buckingham is taken.
Rich. Off with his head. So much for Buckingham.

Poe showed himself familiar with Cibber's version in "The Duc De L'Omelette," at n. 23.

13. Concord, Massachusetts, was the home of Emerson, Alcott, and other Transcendentalists.

14. The spelling of "won't" without an apostrophe seems to have been tolerated.

15. "Drown your sorrows in a bowl" is an old familiar saying, which goes back at least to the *Anacreontea,* number 38.

16. *Printer's* devil, of course.

17. "The devil to pay and no pitch hot," is a proverbial term for inevitable trouble. *The Macmillan Book of Proverbs, Maxims, and Famous Phrases* (1948) quotes an example from Sir Walter Scott, *The Pirate* (1821), chapter 36, and explains that "the proverb in this form is supposed to refer to the difficulty of 'paying' or caulking the seam near a ship's keel, called the 'devil.' "

18. Bob confuses *i's* and *z's* (izzards) with eyes and gizzards.

19. Ale marked XXX is of excellent quality.

A REVIEWER REVIEWED

This *jeu d'esprit* was composed during the last months of Poe's life. His leaf of "Memoranda for Philadelphia" reminded him to get an epigram from *Graham's* on his trip south, and he undoubtedly meant the one quoted near the beginning of "A Reviewer Reviewed." The holograph manuscript is unfinished, although we clearly have all there ever was of it. It came into the hands of Rufus Wilmot Griswold from Poe's trunk, and the editor's son, W. M. Griswold, sold it with other Poeana, in New York in 1896.* Shortly before the sale an arrangement was made to publish it as a syndicated newspaper article on Sunday, March 15, 1896, in the *New York Journal* and other newspapers. The method of publication chosen was regrettable, because all of one significant paragraph and part of another were silently omitted by the syndicators. This abridged version was reprinted by Miss Phillips,† but has been completely ignored by almost all later writers on Poe. I saw the manuscript when Dr. A. S. W. Rosenbach owned it, but for text here I follow a photocopy graciously given by the present owner, Mr. H. Bradley Martin.

"A Reviewer Reviewed" is apparently the latest of Poe's numerous articles designed to call attention to his own growing reputation as an author. It has enough of the element of fiction in it to justify its collection among the Tales and Sketches. The device of praise grudgingly given, and with some dispraise by a severe critic, must have amused Poe. On the manuscript he wrote, "For Graham's Magazine," as if he had hoped it might appear there. It is fair to say that he may have decided the thing was too extravagant, and abandoned it. Yet he did not destroy it.‡

The evidence of Poe's authorship, which I regard as conclusive, can be summed up briefly. He used a pseudonym when he felt it

* Bangs & Co., sale of April 11, 1896, lot 97. Complete authentication by both R. H. Stoddard and G. E. Woodberry was given there.

† *Poe the Man* (1926), II, 961–967. Killis Campbell in his *Mind of Poe* (1933), p. 229, commented on this imperfect version, and accepted it as a composition by Poe, with slight reservations. The parts Campbell never saw (indicated by "*m . . . m*" and "*o . . . o*" in the list of variants) are those most unmistakably Poe's.

‡ Griswold's edition omitted all unfinished material. Harrison never mentioned "A Reviewer Reviewed," and probably did not know of its existence.

would serve his purpose.§ It was nothing new for him to ridicule his own methods – he did that in "How to Write a Blackwood Article." The most telling evidence is that the uses of "drop" and "upon" censured as solecisms are "corrected" in Poe's own copy (the Lorimer Graham copy) of *The Raven and Other Poems* and *Tales* bound as one. Who else would have picked out precisely those items in 1849?*

The text below is the first complete publication of "A Reviewer Reviewed."

TEXTS

(A) Manuscript, summer 1849; *(B) New York Journal,* March 15, 1896, p. 26 (abridged); *(C)* Mary E. Phillips, *Edgar Allan Poe the Man* (1926), II, 961–967, from the last.

The manuscript *(A)* is of eight unnumbered but consecutive pages approximately 8 by 10 inches with a small left-hand margin. The seventh page is not filled, a space being left after the "Sonnet to Zante," and on the eighth page the final paragraph is written between blank spaces. Hence, it is clear that the unfinished manuscript contains all that was written of Poe's article.

The manuscript *(A),* without emendation, is followed, by courtesy of the owner, Mr. H. Bradley Martin. The first publication *(B)* was in a syndicated article, simultaneously published in several Sunday papers throughout the nation.

None of the italicizations in the manuscript *(A)* are carried in texts *B* and *C.*

For Graham's Magazine.

A REVIEWER REVIEWED.

BY WALTER G. BOWEN.

> As we rode along the valley we saw a herd of
> *asses* on the top of one of the mountains – how
> they viewed and *reviewed* us!
> Sterne – "Letter from France."

Mr Editor – In a late number of your widely circulated Magazine I had the satisfaction of reading an epigram which appeared to me, and to your subscribers generally, if I am not very

§ "Walter G. Bowen" is obviously a pseudonym. Poe was in correspondence in 1844 and 1848 with the Pennsylvania editor, Eli Bowen; Francis Bowen wrote for the *North American Review;* but no record of a Walter Bowen has been found.

* Students may ask if there be any kinship between "A Reviewer Reviewed" and the letter of "Outis," which forms part of the controversy of 1845 known as "The Longfellow War." "Outis" (Nobody) was the author of a letter "written in a clever imitation of Poe's manner" (Quinn, *Poe,* p. 454) defending Longfellow and James Aldrich from Poe's charge of plagiarism made in a review (*Evening Mirror,* January 20 and 21, 1845) of *The Waif,* an anthology of minor poets, edited by Longfellow.

much mistaken, to be not less well aimed and fairly driven home to the mark, than righteously deserved. It was in these words,

On P—, the Versifier, reviewing his own Verses.[1]

When critics scourged him there was scope
  For self-amendment and for hope;
Reviewing his own verses, he
  Has done the deed — *felo de se.*

I am glad to perceive that there is at least one editor of a Magazine who is not so tied up in Mr Poe's interest as to be afraid of expressing an honest opinion of him as a literary man, but I do assure you that not only myself but a great many others were astonished beyond measure at finding that you had the courage to insert the epigram, good as it was. Your putting it in however, has elevated you not a little in the public opinion, and has encouraged me to hope that you will do me the favor of publishing this Review of the Reviewer, especially as what I ask is merely in the way of perfectly fair and above board retaliation for what Mr P. upon one or two occasions has seen fit to say of some unpretending poems of mine, as well as of a novel by my brother-in-law.[2] And as for the truth and justice of what I shall write, I trust that on that score there will be no one to offer objection, as I do not intend to say a single word that shall not be accompanied *by the proof.* Mr Poe, to say nothing of my own case, has done little else than "ride rough shod" over what he is in the facetious habit of denominating the "poor devil authors" of the land,[3] and I presume that neither you nor any body else will think it unreasonable that, sooner or later, he should have the bitter chalice of criticism returned to his own lip — provided always and of course that the thing is done fairly, honorably, and with no trick or subterfuge — in a word, provided that the criticism be *just.*

To follow Mr Poe's own apparently frank mode of reviewing, I will begin by putting the merits of my author "in the fairest light." I shall not pretend to deny then that he has written several pieces of very considerable merit, and that some of these pieces

---

Actually it was "A Reviewer Reviewed" that led Miss Phillips (*Poe the Man,* II, 956ff.) to identify "Outis" as Poe himself. H. W. L. Dana (Longfellow's grandson) and I, independently, and for still different reasons, came to the conclusion that "Outis" was Poe. Killis Campbell dissented in his *Mind of Poe,* p. 229, but, as noted above, he never saw a complete copy of "A Reviewer Reviewed."

have attracted, partly of their own accord and partly through the puffing of his friends, an unusual degree of notoriety. Among these I feel called upon to mention his Tales published by Wiley & Putnam,[4] and especially the one called "The Murder in the Rue Morgue," which I learn has been reprinted and highly complimented in Paris,[5] and "The Gold Bug"[6] which Martin Farquhar Tupper justly praises,[7] as well as the "Descent into the Maelstroom,"[8] and several other stories, all of which I am willing to admit display great power of analysis and imagination. "The Facts in the Case of Mr Valdemar" have perhaps made a greater "sensation" than anything else he has written, and has, I understand, not only gone the complete rounds of the London press, from the Morning Post down, but has been printed in pamphlet form in London, Paris and Vienna.[9] The ingenuity and general merit of his "Raven" I do not wish to detract from, although I certainly do not think quite so highly of it as Miss Barrett [a]or as Mr Willis[a] professes to do; nor as Mr P[b] himself does, if we are to judge by the laudatory criticism on it which he lately published in "Graham," a criticism which displayed, perhaps, more analysis than modesty.[10] Some of his shorter poems are also praiseworthy, and his "Sleeper" and "Dreamland" are in my opinion better than the Raven, although in a different way. Of his criticisms I have not so much to observe in the way of commendation. They show scholarship, and the peculiar analytic talent which is the ruling feature in everything he writes. They are also remarkable for that Quixotic kind of courage which induces people of Mr P's[c] temperament to be perpetually tilting at something – although it too often happens that the something is a windmill;[11] and there is one good point about them which it would be unjust to omit; and that is, they show no respect for persons. They are seldom aimed at small game. On the other hand they seem to me bitter in the extreme, captious, fault-finding, and unnecessarily severe. Mr. P.[d] has been so often complimented for his powers of sarcasm that he thinks it incumbent upon him[e] to keep up his reputation in that line by

a ↑or as Mr. Willis↓ *(A)*
b Poe *(B, C)*
c Poe's *(B, C)*
d Poe *(B, C)*
e himself *(B, C)*

sneers upon all occasions and downright abuse. As for the beauties of a work, he appears to have made up his mind to neglect them altogether, or when he condescends to point one out, or to quote it, his compliments, however well they begin, are always sure to end with a point, or barb, which it is easy to mistake for satire in disguise. Real, honest, heartfelt praise is a thing not to be looked for in a criticism by Mr Poe. Even when it is[f] his evident intention to be partial, to compliment in an extravagant manner some of his *lady* friends (for he never compliments a gentleman) there always seems to be something constrained, and shall I say malicious, at the bottom of the honey cup. These blemishes render his critical judgments of little value. [g]They may be read for their pungency, but all the honesty they ever contain may be placed upon the point of a cambric needle.[g]

Before proceeding with some very serious literary accusations which I have to make on my own part against Mr Poe, it may be as well, perhaps, to call his attention to something which has been said about him in the "London Literary Gazette." I wish to see if he will vouchsafe a reply to it. Mr P.[h] has pointed out, in his late "Literati", a number of *scientific* blunders on the part of Mr. Richard Adams Locke,[12] and perhaps the public may have some curiosity to know how he will account for his own. The "Gazette" referred to is of the date of March 14th 1846.

> "*To the Editor of the Literary Gazette* — Sir, Having just read a review of Edgar Poe's Romances in the *Literary Gazette* of January p 101,[13] allow me to advert to a curious misconception in[i] a scientific point of view which the author has fallen into. In describing his whirling in the Maelstroom he says — 'On looking out when half way down, the boat appeared *hanging* as if by magic *upon the interior surface* of a funnel of vast circumference and prodigious depth' &c. . . . My gaze fell instinctively *downwards* . . . . . . The smack hung on the *inclined surface of the pool which sloped at an angle* of more than forty-

f ↑is↓ *(A)*
g . . . g *Omitted (B, C)*
h Poe *(B, C)*
i <page 101> in *(A)*

five degrees; so that we *seemed* to be lying on our beam ends.' &c. . . . .

Now, with all deference I would submit, first, That our only notions of *up* or *down* are derived from the direction of gravity; when therefore the direction of gravity is changed by centrifugal force, *that* direction will still *appear* to be down. 2d. That our only sense of motion is relative; when therefore all that is visible is rotating along with ourselves, we shall have no sense of motion; and in few cases do we ever *ourselves* appear to be the moving objects (witness the case of railway travelling). The only apparent motion will be the slight *difference of motion* between the various objects and ourselves. Whence it appears that the gentleman in the predicament described would, on looking about him, see a vast funnel of water apparently *laid on its side,* with its lower side horizontal, at which lower part his boat would *always appear to be lying;* the heavens appearing *at one end horizontally* and *apparently rotating;* while the chaotic abyss and foam would be at the opposite end; the waters appearing (full of local currents no doubt) stretching in a miraculous archway or tunnel, almost motionless, about and over the boat, and apparently supported by nothing; and objects nearer the entrance would appear to rotate vertically in a *slowly* retrograde direction; while objects would appear to have an opposite rotation, more and more rapid, towards the[j] misty tumultuous end; the real velocity of the whole being unperceived, except by the contrary apparent rotation of the heavens. This would, indeed, be a wondrous spectacle, though scarcely sufficing to induce a personal experiment by your humble servant,

William Petrie."

So much for Mr Petrie, and leaving Mr Poe to reply to him, I will just here put in a point for myself, although I confess it has been suggested to me by a friend at my elbow. It is this — In accounting for his hero's escape from the Maelstrom, [k]Mr P.[k] quotes Archimedes *"De Incidentibus in Fluido"* lib 2. for the following

j the <mis> *(A)* k . . . k ↑Mr. P.↓ *(A)*

fact, viz: that "a cylinder swimming in a vortex, offers more resistance to its suction and is drawn in with greater difficulty than an equally bulky body of any form whatsoever." Now[l] the friend at my elbow asserts roundly, first, that the fact stated is no fact at all and is contrary to known laws, and secondly that there is no such passage in the second book of Archimedes as the one referred to. Thirdly he says that *no such passage, nor any resembling it, is in Archimedes at all, and that he defies Mr Poe to point it out.*[14]

[m]With Mr Poe's general *style* no great fault can be justly found. He has the rare merit of distinctness and simplicity, and can be forcible enough upon occasion; but as he has a most unmannerly habit of picking flaws in the grammar of other people, I feel justified in showing him that he is far from being immaculate himself. Not long ago I remember his sneering at some one for using the verb "drop" in an active sense, but at page 14 of his Tales (Wiley & Putnam edition) he commits the very same blunder — e.g — "As sure as you *drop* that beetle I'll break your neck." Again at page 18 — "Was it this eye or that through which you *dropped* the beetle?" "As[n] sure as you *let fall* that beetle" would be proper. An apple drops, but we let an apple fall. At page 34 he uses "except," with gross impropriety, for "unless" — a common error. E.g — "I found that it was impossible to retain a seat *upon* it *except* in one particular position." "*Upon*" in this sentence is also improperly employed for "*on*." This error is very usual with Mr Poe. At page 25 there are no less than five instances of it — e.g — "I doubted not that heat had been the agent in bringing to light *upon* the parchment the skull which I saw designed *upon* it." The *up* is properly used only where *action* appears. An apple, for instance, lies *on* a table; but we place an apple *up*on a table.[15] Even in the Preface to his Poems, where we are forced to suppose him careful if ever, he is guilty of inaccurate construction. For example — "If what I have written is to circulate at all, I am naturally anxious that it should circulate as I wrote it." Now here the sentence should obviously be — "I am naturally anxious that what I have written should circulate as I wrote it, if it circulate at all." Or — "I am

l <Not> ↑Now↓ *(A)*

m . . . m *Paragraph omitted (B, C)*

n <At page 34 he> "As *(A)*

naturally anxious that what I have written, if it is to circulate at all, should circulate as I wrote it."[16] But a truce with these trifles – and yet they are the very kind of *trifles* which Mr P. is so fond of exposing in other people.[m]

The truth is, I have something more serious to speak of. The great *point* which Mr Poe has become notorious for making is that of *plagiarism*, and in his elaborate reply to *"Outis"* in the earlier numbers of the "Broadway Journal," he was at great pains to demonstrate what a plagiarism is, and by what chain of reasoning it could be established.[17] My own purpose at present is simply to copy a few parallel passages, leaving it for the public to decide whether they do or do not come properly under the head of *wilful and deliberate literary theft.*

At page 24 of Mr P's last volume of Poems (Wiley & Putnam's edition) in a song called Eulalie, is the passage,

> Now Doubt – now Pain
> Come never again
> For her soul *gives me sigh for sigh.*[18]

In Tom Moore's "Last Rose of Summer" we find it thus,

> No flower of her kindred,
> No rose-bud is nigh,
> To reflect back her blushes
> *Or give sigh for sigh.*

The author of the lines which follow I cannot *name* just now, but I give them because there are doubtless many of my readers who can. *Some* poet, however, is speaking of a traitor to his country and wishes him doomed

> *to dwell*
> Full in the sight of Paradise
> *Beholding Heaven yet feeling Hell.*

In "Al Aaraaf," at page 69 of the Poems, we read

> And there oh may my weary spirit *dwell*
> *Apart from Heaven's eternity, and yet how far from Hell!*[19]

One of Mr Poe's most admired passages is this, forming the

conclusion of the poem called "The City in the Sea," and to be found at page 22 –

> And when, amid no earthly moans
>   Down, down, that town shall settle hence
> *Hell rising from a thousand thrones*
>   *Shall do it reverence.*

But unfortunately Mrs Sigourney, in a little poem called "Musing Thoughts," first published in "The Token," for 1829, has the lines,

> *Earth slowly rising from her thousand thrones*
> *Did homage* to the Corsican.[20]

[o]Mr Poe has also been much praised for these[p] lines, found at page 63 of the Poems,

> A dome[q] by linked light from Heaven let down
> Sat gently on these columns as a crown.[21]

Every classical scholar however[r] must remember the Gods' Council of Homer, beginning ’Ηὼς μὲν κροκόπεπλος ἐκίδνατο πᾶσαν ἐπ’ αἶαν, and the lines which Pope translates (I have not the original by me)

> Let down our golden everlasting chain
> Whose strong embrace holds Heaven and Earth and Main.[o]

That Mr Poe has in many cases obtained *help* from the more obscure classics is, I fancy, no more than a legitimate inference from so glaringly obvious an *imitation* as this, which we find at page 20.

> *Sonnet to Zante*
> Fair isle that, from the fairest of all flowers,
>   Thy gentlest of all gentle names dost take!
> How many memories of what radiant hours
>   At sight of thee and thine at once awake!
> How many scenes of what departed bliss!
>   How many thoughts of what entombed hopes
> How many visions of a maiden that is
>   No more – no more upon thy verdant slopes!
> No more! alas that magical sad sound
>   Transforming all! Thy charms shall please no more –

o . . . o *Omitted (B, C)*
p the↑se↓ *(A)*
q <dome> <↑chain↓> ↑dome↓ *(A)*
r ↑however↓ *(A)*

Thy memory *no more!* Accursed ground
  Henceforth I hold thy flower-enamelled shore,
O hyacinthine isle! O purple Zante!
  Isola d'oro! Fior di Levante![22]

Here I might safely pause; but it would not be quite proper to omit all mention of this critic's facility at *imitation!* in prose as well as verse. In his story of "Hans Phaall" published in his "Tales of the Grotesque and Arabesque," but originally appearing in the first volume of the "Southern Literary Messenger"[23]

[*No more was written.*]

NOTES

Title: No source is needed for so obvious a phrase, but it may be noted that "The Reviewer Reviewed" was the heading given in *Blackwood's Magazine,* June 1828, to a letter to the editor humorously but vigorously criticizing a review in the *Edinburgh Review* for January 1828. The criticism was of substance, but also of style and of many specific abuses of grammar and syntax.

Motto: The motto Poe took from *Stanley* (1838), I, 102. This work by Horace Binney Wallace, whom Poe knew only as "William Landor," gives the incorrect reference to Sterne; the passage is really in *Tristram Shandy,* VI, 1. Poe used it also in "Marginalia," number 145 (*Godey's,* September 1845, p. 122) and number 211 (*SLM,* April 1849, p. 221).

1. The epigram, signed W., appeared in *Graham's* for December 1846; Poe's "Philosophy of Composition" had been published in the April issue.

2. This allusion is probably "mystification."

3. For other mentions of "poor devil authors," see "Some Secrets of the Magazine Prison-House," n. 4.

4. *Tales* was published in June 1845.

5. Two pirated and abridged translations of "The Murders in the Rue Morgue," one signed G. B. in *La Quotidienne,* June 11, 12, 13, 1846, and another by Old Nick (E. D. Forgues) in *Le Commerce,* October 12, led to a famous lawsuit in Paris. See pp. 525–526 above.

6. All authorized texts hyphenate "Gold-Bug." See introduction to that tale above.

7. Martin Farquhar Tupper's review of the *Tales* appeared under the heading "American Romance" in the London *Literary Gazette,* January 31, 1846.

8. The spelling "Maelstroom" (from Petrie's letter quoted below as it was printed in the *Literary Gazette*) may reflect Poe's peculiar diaeresis over the "o." Note that in the paragraph following Petrie's letter there is no mark over the "o."

9. The London *Morning Post,* January 5, 1846, carried the Valdemar story as "Mesmerism in America," with a note that the editor thought it fiction. It also appeared in the *Popular Record of Modern Science,* London, January 10, 1846, a paper which had previously copied "Mesmeric Revelation" (see the London *Notes and Queries,* November 21, 1942), and separately as *Mesmerism "In Articulo Mortis"* (London, 1846). No German or French version printed while Poe was alive has been found.

10. The praise of Willis in the *Evening Mirror,* January 29, 1845, and that of Miss Barrett in her famous letter to Poe of April 1846 (now in the Berg Collection), are quoted by most of Poe's biographers. Poe's own article on "The Raven" is "The Philosophy of Composition" (*Graham's,* April 1846).

11. Poe wrote of his own "Quixotic sense of the honorable" to Mrs. Whitman, October 18, 1848.

12. Poe's sketch of Locke was in *Godey's Lady's Book* for October 1846. In it Poe pointed out errors in the Moon Hoax perpetrated by Locke in 1835.

13. The review cited is that by Tupper; see n. 7 above.

14. See "A Descent into the Maelström," n. 21.

15. The "errors" cited are from "The Gold-Bug." Poe corrected most of them in the J. Lorimer Graham copy of his volume of 1845, which is the source of our text; see the variants.

16. These instances of inaccurate construction were marked by Poe for correction in his copy. (See reproduction, Mabbott I, 579.)

17. Poe's replies to "Outis" are in the *Broadway Journal,* March 8 to April 5, 1845. "Outis" was, in my opinion, probably Poe himself, something "A Reviewer Reviewed" tends to confirm. Poe had a very gentle and sensible comment on plagiarism in his "Literati" sketch of James Aldrich (*Godey's,* July 1846); see also "Marginalia," number 160 (*Democratic Review,* April 1846, p. 270).

18. "Eulalie," lines 14–16; see Mabbott 1:349–350.

19. See Thomas Moore, *Lalla Rookh,* "The Fire Worshippers":

> Just Prophet, let the damn'd one dwell
> Full in the sight of Paradise,
> Beholding heav'n and feeling hell!

The other quotation is from "Al Aaraaf," II, 172–173 (Mabbott 1:111).

20. Lines 45–46 of Lydia H. Sigourney's "Musing Thoughts," alluding to Napoleon, are quoted. The poem was published in *The Token for 1829,* pp. 75–77. See "The City in the Sea," lines 52–53 and note, Mabbott 1:202, 204.

21. See "Al Aaraaf," II, 20–21 (Mabbott 1:106). The Greek that follows is the first line of the eighth book of the *Iliad,* and means, "Dawn yellow-robed spread over all the earth"; the English quotation is from Pope's *Iliad,* VIII, 25–26. Both quotations are correct, even to the Greek accents.

22. What minor classic Poe connected with his Zante sonnet is not known; the context shows it was something in Greek or Latin. See Mabbott 1:310–312.

23. "Hans Phaall – A Tale" (in *SLM,* June 1835); "Hans Phaall" (in *Tales*

of the Grotesque and Arabesque, 1840). Poe's borrowings in this tale from *Rees's Cyclopaedia* (of which John Allan bought a set in 1810) were discussed in *Modern Language Notes,* December 1930, by Meredith Neill Posey.

THE LIGHT-HOUSE

This is the last of Poe's tales of terror, and was never finished. It was probably planned as a companion piece to "A Descent into the Maelström," and like that story is laid in the Land of the Midnight Sun.

Marked advances in industrial technology in the first half of the nineteenth century had generated public interest and awareness. Increasing maritime commerce called for the multiplication of safety measures, and both the new technical journals and periodicals of general circulation discussed problems of the lighthouse service and reported on the construction of one major tower after another.* Poe's lighthouse, however, is imaginary, although Alan Stevenson, beginning in 1838, built one at Skerryvore, off the west coast of Scotland, that is somewhat like it. Presumably Poe consulted an encyclopedia on the subject, as I have done.†

The most famous disaster to a lighthouse occurred on November 20, 1703, when a great storm swept away the first Eddystone light — a timber structure — and several persons in it, including its builder, Henry Winstanley.‡ That Poe's lighthouse was doomed

* The third number of Colton's *American Review,* March 1845, contained an article critical of "Our Light-House System," with the local collectors of customs as the responsible officials, and compared it unfavorably with that of Britain, where England's lighthouses were governed by Trinity House of Deptford Stroud; Scotland's, by the Commissioner of Northern Lights; and Ireland's, by the Corporation for Improving and Preserving the Port of Dublin. Poe's mention of the Consistory may have been suggested by knowledge of the existence of these boards.

† But an article in the London *Quarterly Review* for March 1849, reprinted in *Littell's Living Age* for July 7, reviewed Stevenson's *Account of the Skerryvore Lighthouse* (1848), retrospectively commenting on Robert Stevenson's *Account of the Bell Rock Lighthouse* (1824) and John Smeaton's *Narrative of the Building of the Eddystone Lighthouse with Stone* (2nd ed., 1813). Smeaton's was the third at the site, completed in 1759. It was the first to use stone throughout, with each piece dovetailed into the one next to it, a practice adopted and improved upon by the Stevensons and other later engineers. [See B. Pollin, *Discoveries in Poe,* pp. 150–151 and 273 for other specific references.]

‡ See "The Domain of Arnheim," n. 24, for a suggestion that Poe took some interest in Winstanley.

to fall cannot be doubted, but whether the dog, whose great strength is emphasized, was to save only the diary, or his master too, must be left to the reader's imagination.

The manuscript came with Poe's papers to R. W. Griswold. It consists of four leaves — long narrow strips — the first having a space at the top for a title and the author's name; the last, some space at the bottom where nothing was written. Since the script is the very neat hand characteristic of Poe's last years and the style, clear and direct, almost without ornament, is one that is common toward the end of his career, I believe that the tale is unfinished, not because Poe gave it up, but because he was at work upon it and was prevented from completing it by his sudden death. Griswold's son sold the first leaf in 1896,§ but the family retained the other pages, which Woodberry was allowed to print in 1909. The first page was again auctioned in the Stephen H. Wakeman Sale,* when a text was inaccurately printed. The last three pages were given to Harvard by Griswold's grandchildren. Meanwhile, I printed a complete text in 1942.

TEXTS

(A) Manuscript: sheet 1 in the Berg Collection, New York Public Library, sheets 2, 3, and 4 in the Houghton Library, Harvard University; *(B)* George E. Woodberry, *The Life of Edgar Allan Poe* (1909), II, 397–399 (sheets 2, 3, and 4); *(C)* London *Notes and Queries,* April 25, 1942 (182:226–227); *(D) Selected Poetry and Prose of Edgar Allan Poe* (ed. T. O. Mabbott, 1951), pp. 344–345.

The manuscript *(A)* is followed for our text, and by the kind permission of Mrs. Lola Szladits of the Berg Collection and Mr. W. H. Bond of the Houghton Library a reproduction of all four sheets is included in this volume. It is the first time the entire manuscript has been so presented in one place.

[The sheets obviously belong together and at Mrs. Szladits' suggestion we have asked Mr. Bond to describe them.]

"The Light-House" is written on four strips of light blue machine-made paper, basically (like all machine-made paper) wove, but showing faint traces of a dandy-roll apparently intended to give it the appearance of laid paper. None of the pieces contains a watermark. The strips are all the same width — 102 mm. scant or 3 15/16″. The strip numbered 1 is 310 mm. or 12 3/8″ long; the strip numbered 2 is 289 mm. or 11 3/8″ long; that numbered 3 is 316 mm. or 12 7/16″

§ Auction of Bangs & Co., New York, April 11, 1896.

* American Art Association, New York, April 29, 1924, lot 964. It is now in the Berg Collection.

long; that numbered 4 is 251 mm. or 9 7/8″, and is not cut square at the bottom. The paper is ruled in blue on both sides, the rules being 5/16″ apart or 8 mm. They are written on rectos only. Leaves 2 and 4 show traces of black adhesive, possibly some kind of wafer, across the top on the verso; leaf 3 shows similar traces across the top of the recto and was evidently formerly fastened thereby to the verso of leaf 2.

[THE LIGHT-HOUSE (*A*)]

Jan 1 — 1796.[a] This day — my first on the light-house — I make this entry in my Diary, as agreed on with De Grät.[b1] As regularly as I *can* keep the[c] journal, I will — but there is no telling what may happen to a man all alone as I am — I may get sick, or worse . . . . .[d] So far well! The cutter had a narrow escape — but why dwell on that, since I am *here,* all safe? My spirits are beginning to revive already, at the mere thought of being — for once in my life at least — thoroughly *alone;*[2] for, of course, Neptune,[3] large as he is, is not to be taken into consideration as "society".[e] Would to Heaven I had ever found in "society" one half as much *faith* as in this poor dog: — in such case I and "society" might never have parted — even for the[f] year . . .[g] What most[h] surprises me, is the difficulty De Grät[i] had in getting me the appointment — and I a noble of the realm! It could not be that the Consistory had any doubt of my ability to manage the light. *One* man had attended *it*[j] before now — and got on quite as well as the three that are usually put in. The duty is a mere nothing; and the printed instructions are as plain as possible. It never would[k] have done to let Orndoff accompany me. I never should have made any way with my book as long as he was within reach of me, with his intolerable gossip — not to mention that everlasting meërschaum.[l4] Besides, I wish to be *alone* . . . . . .[m] It is strange that I never observed, until this moment, how

---

Title: *Untitled (A);* [The Lighthouse.] *(C)*

a *Jan.* 1—1796. *(C); Jan. 1*—1796. *(D)*

b DeGrät. *(C, D)*

c this *(C)*

d worse . . . *(C);* worse. . . . *(D)*

e "society." *(C, D)*

f a *(C, D)*

g year. . . . *(D)*

h more *(C)*

i DeGrät. *(C, D)*

j it *(C, D)*

k never would/would never *(D)*

l meerschaum. *(C)*

m *alone. . . . (B, D);* alone . . . *(C)*

dreary a sound that word has — "alone"! I could half fancy there was some peculiarity in the echo of these cylindrical walls — but oh, no! — this[n] is all nonsense. I do believe I am going to get nervous about my insulation. *That* will never do. I have not forgotten De Grät's[o] prophecy. Now for a scramble to the lantern and a good look around to "see what I can see" . . . .[p] To see what I can see indeed! — not very much. The swell is subsiding a little, I think — but the cutter will have a rough passage home, nevertheless. She will hardly get within sight of the Norland[q5] before noon to-morrow — and yet it can hardly be more than 190 or 200 miles.

Jan. 2.[r] I have passed this day in a species of ecstasy that I find it impossible to describe. My passion for solitude could scarcely have been more thoroughly gratified. I do not say *satisfied;* for I believe I should never be satiated with such delight as I have experienced to-day . . . .[s] The wind lulled about[t] day-break, and by the afternoon the sea had gone down materially . . . . .[u] Nothing to be seen, with the telescope even, but ocean and sky, with an occasional gull.

Jan. 3.[v] A dead calm all day. Towards evening, the sea looked very much like glass. A few sea-weeds came in sight; but besides them absolutely *nothing* all day — not even the slightest speck of cloud . . . .[w] Occupied myself in exploring the light-house . . . .[x] It is a very lofty one — as I find to my cost when I have to ascend its interminable stairs — not quite 160 feet, I should say, from the low-water mark to the top of the lantern. From the bottom *inside* the shaft, however, the distance to the summit is 180 feet at least: — thus the floor is 20 feet below the surface of the sea, even at low-tide . . . . . .[y] It seems to me that the hollow interior at the bottom should have been filled in with solid masonry. Undoubtedly the whole would have been thus rendered more *safe:* — but what am I thinking about?[z] A structure such as this is safe enough under any

n that *(D)*
o DeGrät's *(C, D)*
p see." . . . *(B, C);* see." . . . . *(D)*
q Nordland *(C)*
r *Jan.* 2. *(B, C)*
s to-day. . . . *(B, D);* to-day . . . *(C)*
t after *(C)*
u materially. . . . *(B, D);* materially . . . *(C)*
v *Jan.* 3. *(B, C)*
w cloud. . . . *(B, C);* cloud . . . *(D)*
x light-house . . . *(C)*
y low-tide. . . . *(B, D);* low-tide . . . *(C)*
z about. *(D)*

circumstances. I should feel myself secure in it during the fiercest hurricane that ever raged — and yet I have heard seamen say that, occasionally, with a wind at South-West, the sea has been known to run higher here than any where with the single exception of the Western opening of the Straits of Magellan. No mere sea, though, could accomplish anything with this solid iron-riveted wall — which, at 50 feet from high-water mark, is four feet thick, if one inch . . . .[a] The basis on which the structure rests seems to me to be chalk . . . . . .[b]

Jan 4.[c]

NOTES

Title: Supplied by Woodberry, in 1909.

1. De Grät may mean "They wept," in Norwegian; in German it suggests a fishbone, as Professor Eric Carlson wrote me. [Professor Pollin suggests that the name may come from Poe's acquaintance James De Graw, for whom see Mabbott I, 387–388.]

2. The theme of the love of solitude had already been used by Poe in the third chapter of "The Journal of Julius Rodman," "A Tale of the Ragged Mountains," "Morning on the Wissahiccon," and the poem "Alone" (Mabbott I, 146–147).

3. There is a dog named Neptune in "The Journal of Julius Rodman." The name seems especially appropriate in "The Light-House," however, where the dog is apparently destined to play an important part.

4. Monsieur Dupin also smoked a meerschaum pipe; see "The Purloined Letter."

5. Nordland is a county in northwest Norway, wherein are located the Lofoten Islands, mentioned in "A Descent into the Maelström"; "norland" — sometimes capitalized — has the more general meaning of land or country to the north. The *OED* cites as an example: "As the storm-wind blows bleakly from the norland" — line 1707 of Elizabeth Barrett Barrett's long poem "A Drama of Exile" (*Poems,* London, 1844). Poe reviewed the American edition, *The Drama of Exile and Other Poems* (1844), in the *Broadway Journal* for January 4 and 11, 1845.

---

a inch. . . . *(B, D);* inch . . . *(C)*
b chalk. . . . *(B, D)*
c *Jan.* 4 *(B); Jan.* 4. *(C); Jan. 4. (D)*

THE LIGHT-HOUSE MANUSCRIPT

The Berg Collection and Houghton Library

The following pages reproduce in full size the four long numbered strips of the original. To fit our pages the reproduction of each strip is cut in half.

Jan 1 — 1796. This day — my first on the light-house — I make this entry in my Diary, as agreed on with De Grät. As regularly as I can keep the journal, I will — but there is no telling what may happen to a man all alone as I am — I may get sick, or worse. . . . So far well! The cutter had a narrow escape — but why dwell on that, since I am here, all safe? My spirits are beginning to revive already, at the mere thought of being — for once in my life at least — thoroughly alone; for, of course, Neptune, large as he is, is not to be taken into consideration as "society". Would to Heaven I had ever found in "society" one half as much faith as in this poor dog: — in such case I and "society" might never have parted — even for the year . . . What most surprises me, is the difficulty De Grät had in getting me the appointment — and I a noble of the realm! It could not be that the Consistory had any doubt of my ability to manage the light. One man has attended it before now — and got on quite as well as

The Berg Collection

2.

the three that are usually put in. The duty is a mere nothing; and the printed instructions are as plain as possible. It never would have done to let Orndoff accompany me. I never should have made any way with my book as long as he was within reach of me, with his intolerable gossip – not to mention that everlasting meërschaum. Besides, I wish to be alone..... It is strange that I never observed, until this moment, how dreary a sound that word has – "alone"! I could half fancy there was some peculiarity in the echo of these cylindrical walls – but

oh, no! — this is all nonsense. I do
believe I am going to get nervous a-
bout my insulation. That will never
do. I have not forgotten De Grät's prophecy. Now for a scramble to the lantern and a good look around to "see
what I can see" . . . .
To see what I can see indeed! — not very much. The swell is subsiding a little,
I think — but the cutter will have a
rough passage home, nevertheless. She
will hardly get within sight of the Norland before noon to-morrow — and yet
it can hardly be more than 190 or
200 miles.

Jan. 2. I have passed this day in
a species of ecstasy that I find it im-

The Houghton Library

3

possible to describe. My passion for solitude could scarcely have been more thoroughly gratified. I do not say _satisfied_; for I believe I should never be satiated with such delight as I have experienced to-day........ The wind lulled about day-break, and by the afternoon the sea had gone down materially...... Nothing to be seen, with the telescope even, but ocean and sky, with an occasional gull.

Jan. 3. A dead calm all day. Towards evening, the sea looked very much like glass. A few sea-weeds came in sight; but besides them absolutely _nothing_ all day — not even the slightest speck of cloud....... Occupied myself in exploring the light-house.... It is a very lofty one — as I find to my cost when I have to ascend its interminable stairs — not quite 160 feet, I should say, from the low-water mark to the top of the lantern. From the bottom <u>inside</u> the shaft, however, the distance to the summit is 180 feet at least: — thus the floor is 20 feet below the surface of the sea, even at low-tide. ..... It seems to me that the hollow interior at the bottom should have been filled in with solid masonry. Undoubtedly the whole would have been thus rendered more <u>safe</u>: — but what am I thinking about? A structure such as this is safe enough under any circumstances. I should feel myself se-

The Houghton Library

cure in it during the fiercest hurricane that ever raged —— and yet I have heard seamen say that, occasionally, with a wind at South-West, the sea has been known to run higher here than any where with the single exception of the Western opening of the Straits of Magellan. No mere sea, though, could accomplish anything with this solid iron-riveted wall – which, at 50 feet from high-water mark, is four feet thick, if one inch. . . . . . .
The basis on which the structure rests seems to me to be chalk . . . . .

Jan 4.

SOURCES

SOURCES OF TEXTS COLLATED

Titles are given as in the source. Titles and text designations in square brackets are those under which the tales are discussed in this edition.

MANUSCRIPT COLLECTIONS

Free Library of Philadelphia
The Murders in the Rue <Trianon-Bas> Morgue [The Murders in the Rue Morgue, *A*]
[Summer and Winter]

Houghton Library, Harvard University
The Folio Club [*A*]
The Light-House [*A*] (leaves 2, 3 and 4)
Also, in the Widener Memorial Room, the Pedder copy of *Tales of the Grotesque and Arabesque* (1840) with a manuscript change in The Devil in the Belfry [*C*]

Henry E. Huntington Library and Art Gallery
Morella [*A*]
Also the annotated copy of the *Broadway Journal* given to Helen Whitman

Johns Hopkins University Library
Preface to "Marginalia" [*B*] pages of the *Democratic Review,* November 1844, with slight autograph revisions

New York Public Library
Manuscript Division: Thou Art the Man [*A*]
Berg Collection: The Light-House [*A*] (Leaf 1)

Pierpont Morgan Library
The System of Doctor Tarr and Professor Fether [*A*]
A Tale of the Ragged Mountains [*A*]

Poe Foundation
Manuscript fragment [Silence. – A Fable, *A*] housed in the State Library, Richmond, Virginia

University of Texas: Humanities Research Center Library
The Domain of Arnheim [*A*]
The Spectacles [*B*]
Also the J. Lorimer Graham copy of *Tales* (1845)

Collection of H. Bradley Martin, Esq.
Epimanes [Four Beasts in One, *A*]

SOURCES OF TEXTS COLLATED

Bishop Hurst copy of *Eureka* with manuscript changes by Poe [A Remarkable Letter, *B*]
A Reviewer Reviewed
Also PHANTASY-PIECES, and the Duane *Messengers*

POE'S OWN COLLECTIONS

PUBLISHED VOLUMES

Tales of the Grotesque and Arabesque. 2 vols. Philadelphia: Lea and Blanchard, 1840 (issued in November 1839). Dedication to Colonel William Drayton.

Lea and Blanchard, in a letter to Poe on September 28, 1839 (now in the Boston Public Library), agreed to print a small edition of 750 copies, the copyright to remain with Poe, who was to have a few copies for distribution but no royalties. William A. Charvat, who had access to the "cost book," cleared up details about number and cost of this edition in "A Note on Poe's 'Tales of the Grotesque and Arabesque,' " *Publisher's Weekly,* November 23, 1946.

An early notice of the published collection appeared in the *United States Gazette,* December 5, 1839. On December 28, 1839, the *New-York Mirror* carried a short laudatory review, reprinted in Eric W. Carlson's *Recognition of Edgar Allan Poe* (1966). The book was also noticed favorably by Sarah Josepha Hale in *Godey's Lady's Book* for January 1840, but either because it came on the market during the severe depression of 1840–1844 or for other reasons, it did not sell well. [In his forthcoming "Poe in Philadelphia, 1838–1844: A Documentary Record" Dwight Thomas records that the widely circulated *Saturday Courier* carried a favorable advance notice on November 2; that on December 5 the Philadelphia *Public Ledger* mentioned the publication, and that on the same date the *Pennsylvania Inquirer,* as did the *United States Gazette,* gave the *Tales* a laudatory review. There was a scathing review in the *Boston Notion,* December 14, reprinted by Burton R. Pollin in *English Language Notes,* September 1970.]

This first published collection of Poe's tales, although a commercial failure, was a milestone in his career, as Heartman and Canny (p. 53) stated. It contains a Preface, twenty-five tales, and an Appendix in the following order:

Volume I: Preface [*sole text*]; Morella [*D*]; Lionizing [*B*]; William Wilson [*C*]; The Man that was Used Up. A Tale of the Late Bugaboo and Kickapoo Campaign [*B*]; The Fall of the House of Usher [*B*]; The Duc de L'Omelette [*C*]; MS. Found in a Bottle [*D*]; Bon-Bon [*C*]; Shadow. A Fable [*C*]; The Devil in the Belfry [*B*]; Ligeia [*B*]; King Pest. A Tale Containing an Allegory [*C*]; The Signora Zenobia *and* The Scythe of Time [How to Write a Blackwood Article, *B*].

Volume II: Epimanes [Four Beasts in One, *C*]; Siope. A Fable [In the Manner of the Psychological Autobiographists] [Silence, *C*]; Hans Phaall*; A Tale of Jerusalem [*C*]; Von Jung [Mystification, *B*]; Loss of Breath [*C*]; Metzengerstein [*D*]; Berenice [*C*]; Why the Little Frenchman Wears His Hand in a Sling [*B*]; The Visionary [The Assignation, *D*]; The Conversation of Eiros and Charmion [*B*]; Appendix [*6 pp., concerning Hans Phaall*].

——— [Copy given to the Misses Pedder, now in the Widener Memorial

* To appear in Volume IV.

Room at Harvard University]. This contains a manuscript note added by Poe in The Devil in the Belfry [*C*].

The Prose Romances of Edgar A. Poe ... Uniform Serial Edition. Each number complete in itself. No. I. Containing The Murders in the Rue Morgue and The Man that was Used Up. Philadelphia: William H. Graham, 1843.

The size of the edition is unknown, the price as indicated on the title page was 12½ cents for this first of what was intended to be a series of pamphlets. Further numbers did not appear, and only five copies of No. I, complete with title page, are known to exist. See *Edgar Allan Poe/Prose Romances* ... Photographic Facsimile Edition prepared by George E. Hatvary and Thomas O. Mabbott (1968) for details.

Ephemeral as it seems to have been, the book did not go unnoticed. It was advertised for sale in the Philadelphia *Public Ledger,* July 20, 1843, and noticed in *Godey's* for September and in the *New-York Mirror* of September 9, 1843, which carried the following:

> We greet heartily the publication in numbers of "The Prose Romances of Edgar A. Poe;" but few writers of fiction are at all comparable with this fine author for clearness of plot and individuality of character. No. 1 contains a most thrilling story, entitled, "The Murders in the Rue Morgue," and a laughable sketch, which, to illustrate the truth of our commendatory remarks, we subjoin. [There follows a reprint of "The Man that was Used Up."]

The texts collated are The Murders in the Rue Morgue [*C*] and The Man that was Used Up [*D*].

Tales by Edgar A. Poe. New York: Wiley and Putnam, 1845. (Wiley and Putnam Library of American Books, number 2).

This volume, without dedication or Preface, was issued late in June. On Thursday, June 26, 1845, the *New-York Daily Tribune* carried on page 3, under Books, the following: "Also just published. Tales by Edgar A. Poe. 1 vol. beautifully printed in large clear type, on fine paper – 50 cents."

The selection of twelve tales had been made by Evert A. Duyckinck, choosing, Woodberry felt, "from Poe's numerous and uneven stories those on which his fame has proved itself to be founded" (*Life,* II, 146). This was only partly true, and Poe in a letter to Duyckinck of January 8, 1846, said he was anxious to have another volume, "a far better one than the first – containing, for instance, Ligeia ..." However, he revised the stories chosen very carefully. In "The Fall of the House of Usher" alone he made more than fifty changes, including the addition of the motto. After advance notices in the *New-York Daily Tribune* on June 18 and 21, and the "just published" notice of the 26th, *Tales* was advertised in the *Broadway Journal* on June 28 and July 19 as number II in Wiley & Putnam's Library of American Books, stating, "This excellent collection will include the most characteristic of the peculiar series of Tales written by Mr. Poe." On July 11 Margaret Fuller had published in the *New-York Daily Tribune* a brief, on the whole appreciative, review, and by mid-November Poe was able to say (in a letter to Duyckinck, November 13, 1845) that he had sold 1500 copies. He was to receive 8¢ a copy.

There were other issues of *Tales,* with no textual changes:

SOURCES OF TEXTS COLLATED

Tales. London: Wiley and Putnam, 1845. This edition was made up of the American sheets with an English title page tipped in. Copies with the date 1846 are known.

Tales. 1845, bound with *The Raven and Other Poems*. The book of poems was published in November 1845. "From documentary evidence it now seems possible to assign the middle of February 1846, as the possible date of combination" (Heartman and Canny, p. 98). Poe's presentation copies to Mrs. Browning and Mrs. Whitman, and his own personal copy (now known as the J. Lorimer Graham copy), are all of this state.

Incorporating the emendations Poe made in the J. Lorimer Graham copy, I have used all twelve tales of this collection as master texts for this edition. As they appear in the book, they are: The Gold-Bug [*B*]; The Black Cat [*B*]; Mesmeric Revelation [*B*]; Lionizing [*E*]; The Fall of the House of Usher [*D*]; A Descent into the Maelström [*B*]; The Colloquy of Monos and Una [*D*]; The Conversation of Eiros and Charmion [*D*]; The Murders in the Rue Morgue [*D*]; The Mystery of Marie Roget [*B*]; The Purloined Letter [*B*]; The Man of the Crowd [*B*].

——— [The J. Lorimer Graham copy with revisions as late as 1849].† The tales affected are The Gold-Bug [*C*]; Mesmeric Revelation [*C*]; A Descent into the Maelström [*C*]; The Murders in the Rue Morgue [*E*]; The Mystery of Marie Roget [*C*]; The Purloined Letter [*C*]; The Man of the Crowd [*C*].

Tales. New York: John Wiley, 161 Broadway, and 13 Paternoster Row, London, 1849. A re-issue, with cancel title of the 1845 *Tales*.‡

Eureka: A Prose Poem. New York: Geo. P. Putnam, 1848.

——— Bishop Hurst copy with manuscript changes by Poe. I have used this copy as the source of my text for "A Remarkable Letter."

POE'S COLLECTION NOT IN BOOK FORM

PHANTASY-PIECES. This copy of the first volume of the *Tales of the Grotesque and Arabesque* (from which title page and preliminary matter have been removed) was annotated by the author in 1842 to serve as copy for a projected later edition, and contains a manuscript table of contents and title page (see illustrations). Poe was unsuccessful in finding a publisher. The marked volume I is now owned by Mr. H. Bradley Martin. A limited facsimile edition issued by George

†See my edition of *The Raven and Other Poems,* Facsimile Text Society, Columbia University Press (1942), where I describe Poe's compound book on p. xvi, and the J. Lorimer Graham copy of it on pp. xviii and xix. This famous copy, in which *The Raven and Other Poems* is bound ahead of *Tales,* is now at the University of Texas at Austin, and I am indebted to Mrs. June Moll for final verification of Poe's changes.

‡ For further bibliographical details of *Tales* (1845) the student is referred to Heartman and Canny, *A Bibliography of . . . Poe* (1943), and to William B. Todd, "The Early Issues of Poe's *Tales* (1845)," *Texas University Library Chronicle,* Fall 1967.

Blumenthal is mentioned in the Yale List, under number 150. The tales showing changes are Morella [*E*]; Lionizing [*C*]; William Wilson [*D*]; The Man that was Used Up. A Tale of the Late Bugaboo and Kickapoo Campaign [*C*]; The Fall of the House of Usher (The Fall of *deleted on running heads*) [*C*]; The Duc de L'Omelette [*D*]; MS. Found in a Bottle [*E*]; Bon-Bon [*D*]; Shadow. A Fable [*D*]; The Devil in the Belfry [*D*]; Ligeia [*C*]; King Pest [*D*]; How to Write a Blackwood Article *and* A Predicament [How to Write a Blackwood Article, *C*].

ANTHOLOGIES PREPARED DURING POE'S LIFETIME
(in chronological order)

The Gift: A Christmas and New Year's Present for 1836. ed. Miss Leslie (Philadelphia: E. L. Carey & A. Hart, copr. 1835): Manuscript Found in a Bottle [MS. Found in a Bottle, *B*].

The Baltimore Book, A Christmas and New Year's Present. ed. W. H. Carpenter and T. S. Arthur (Baltimore: Bayley and Burns, 1838, pub. in 1837): Siope. A Fable [Silence, *B*].

The Gift: A Christmas and New Year's Present for 1840. ed. Miss Leslie (Philadelphia: Carey & Hart, copr. 1839): William Wilson [*A*].

The Gift: A Christmas and New Year's Present for 1842. (Philadelphia: Carey & Hart, copr. 1841): Eleonora [*A*].

The Gift: A Christmas and New Year's Present. MDCCCXLIII. (Philadelphia: Carey and Hart, copr. 1842): The Pit and the Pendulum [*A*].

The Gift: A Christmas, New Year, and Birthday Present. MDCCCXLV. (Philadelphia: Carey and Hart, copr. 1844): The Purloined Letter [*A*].

The Opal: A Pure Gift for the Holy Days. ed. N. P. Willis (New-York: John C. Riker, 1844, no copyright date): Morning on the Wissahiccon [*A*].

The Mayflower for MDCCCXLVI. ed. Robert Hamilton (Boston: Saxton & Kelt, copr. 1845): The Imp of the Perverse [*B*].

The Prose Writers of America. ed. Rufus Wilmot Griswold (Philadelphia: Carey and Hart, 1847, copr. 1846): The Fall of the House of Usher [*E*].

The American Keepsake for 1851. ed. Anna Wilmot (New York: Cornish, Lamport and Company, copr. 1850): The Sphinx [*B*].

GRISWOLD'S EDITION OF POE'S WORKS

The Works of the Late Edgar Allan Poe. Edited by Rufus W. Griswold. 4 vols. (New York: J. S. Redfield, 1850–1856). Volumes I and II were announced in the *New-York Daily Tribune* as ready Thursday morning, January 10, 1850. I am indebted to the officials of the Henry W. and Albert A. Berg Collection of the New York Public Library for permission to use their copy of this first issue as the source of my texts from *Works.*§

§ These volumes were reprinted, according to Heartman and Canny (p. 132), fifteen times between 1850 and 1864. At some time after 1853, something happened,

SOURCES OF TEXTS COLLATED

Volume I. Tales (1850): The Unparalleled Adventure of one Hans Pfaall;* The Gold-Bug [*D*]; The Balloon Hoax [*B*]; Von Kempelen and His Discovery [*B*]; Mesmeric Revelation [*D*]; The Facts in the Case of M. Valdemar [*D*]; The Thousand-and-Second Tale of Scheherazade [*C*]; MS. Found in a Bottle [*G*]; A Descent into the Maelström [*D*]; The Murders in the Rue Morgue [*F*]; The Mystery of Marie Roget [*D*]; The Purloined Letter [*D*]; The Black Cat [*D*]; The Fall of the House of Usher [*F*]; The Pit and the Pendulum [*C*]; The Premature Burial [*C*]; The Masque of the Red Death [*C*]; The Cask of Amontillado [*B*]; The Imp of the Perverse [*C*]; The Island of the Fay [*C*]; The Oval Portrait [*C*]; The Assignation [*F*]; The Tell-Tale Heart [*C*]; The Domain of Arnheim [*C*]; Landor's Cottage [*B*]; William Wilson [*F*]; Berenice [*E*]; Eleonora [*C*]; Ligeia [*G*]; Morella [*H*]; Metzengerstein [*E*].

Volume II. Poems and Tales (1850): The Power of Words [*C*]; The Colloquy of Monos and Una [*C*]; The Conversation of Eiros and Charmion [*E*]; Shadow – A Parable [*F*]; Silence – A Fable [*E*]; Philosophy of Furniture [*C*]; A Tale of Jerusalem [*E*]; A Tale of the Ragged Mountains [*D*]; The Spectacles [*D*]; The Duc de L'Omelette [*F*]; The Oblong Box [*C*]; King Pest. A Tale Containing an Allegory [*F*]; Three Sundays in a Week [*C*]; The Devil in the Belfry [*F*]; Lionizing [*F*]; The Man of the Crowd [*D*]; Never Bet the Devil Your Head. A Tale with a Moral [*C*]; Thou Art the Man [*C*]; The Sphinx [*C*]; Some Words with a Mummy [*C*]; Hop-Frog [*B*]; Four Beasts in One; the Homo-cameleopard [*E*]; Why the Little Frenchman wears His Hand in a Sling [*D*]; Bon-Bon [*F*].

Volume III. The Literati, Marginalia, etc. (1850): A Would-Be Crichton [*B*].

Volume IV. Arthur Gordon Pym, &. (1856): The System of Doctor Tarr and Professor Fether [*C*]; The Literary Life of Thingum Bob, Esq. [*C*]; How to Write a Blackwood Article *and* A Predicament [How to Write a Blackwood Article, *E*]; Mystification [*D*]; X-ing a Paragrab [*C*]; Diddling Considered as one of the Exact Sciences [*C*]; The Angel of the Odd [*B*]; Mellonta Tauta [*B*]; Loss of Breath [*E*]; The Man that Was Used Up [*F*]; The Business Man [*C*]; The Landscape Garden [*C*].

---

some accident to the type, to introduce a number of new errors, especially in Volume I between pages 131 and 213. These errors are recorded as Griswold's in the variants of Harrison's *Complete Works of Poe* (1902). Apparently one of the "defective" later copies of *Works* was used for collation, and the errors in it were, no doubt, one of the reasons R. A. Stewart (Harrison II, 299) called the *Works* "very defective in typography." The texts therein are not free from errors, but a comparison of the original 1850 *Works* texts with the original *Broadway Journal* texts shows by far more typographical errors in the latter.

Harrison distrusted Griswold and all his works, and preferred the periodicals when it was possible to use them, although he accepted the extensive changes of "The Balloon Hoax" and several other pieces. Griswold's tampering with texts of letters discredits him badly. But no evidence of mistreatment of the texts of the tales can be found, and, after all, the man had no motive to alter Poe's fiction.

* To appear in Volume IV.

NEWSPAPERS AND MAGAZINES

LATER BOOKS
(first printing in book form)

J. H. Ingraham, *The Spanish Galleon* (Boston, 1849): X-ing a Paragrab [*B*].
Edmund Clarence Stedman and George Edward Woodberry, editors. *The Works of Edgar Allan Poe* (10 vols. Chicago, 1894–95): A Prediction [*C*].
James A. Harrison, ed. *The Complete Works of Edgar Allan Poe* (New York: Thomas Y. Crowell and Company, 1902): The Folio Club [*B*].
George E. Woodberry, *The Life of Edgar Allan Poe* (Boston and New York: Houghton Mifflin Company, 1909): The Light-House [*B*].
T. O. Mabbott, ed. *The Selected Poetry and Prose of Edgar Allan Poe*. The Modern Library (New York: Random House, 1951): The Light-House [*D*].

NEWSPAPERS AND MAGAZINES
(in alphabetical order)

Alexander's Weekly Messenger (Philadelphia). While Poe was at *Burton's,* his co-editor and proprietor of the magazine, William E. Burton, was associated from December 1839 to May 1840 with a newspaper called *Alexander's Weekly Messenger* and for a time, *Alexander's Express Messenger*. Poe, among other things, contributed to it his first series of solutions of cryptograms and two pieces included in our collection of tales: Instinct vs Reason – A Black Cat; and Cabs.
American Monthly Magazine (New York, Philadelphia, Boston): Von Jung, the Mystific [Mystification, *A*].
American Museum of Science, Literature, and the Arts (Baltimore): Ligeia [*A*]; The Psyche Zenobia (*with* The Scythe of Time) [How to Write a Blackwood Article, *A*].
American Review: A Whig Journal (New York). This periodical, whose editor, George Hooker Colton, was the first to accept and print "The Raven," carried the first printing of Some Words With a Mummy [*A*]; and The Facts of M. Valdemar's Case [The Facts in the Case of M. Valdemar, *A*].
Arthur's Ladies' Magazine (Philadelphia): The Sphinx [*A*].

Baltimore Saturday Visiter: MS. Found in a Bottle [*A*].
Broadway Journal (New York). Poe wrote for this journal from its founding in January 1845; he became co-editor in March; and the issue of October 25 had "Edgar A. Poe, Editor and Proprietor" at its masthead. But the magazine, which had a circulation of less than 1000 subscribers (Quinn, *Poe,* p. 456), lost money and terminated with the issue of January 3, 1846. Poe's contributions were numerous, many of them revised and reissued earlier pieces. He used the signature Edgar A. Poe for thirty of the forty-three pieces of fiction he printed in the *Broadway Journal,* Littleton Barry for five, and left eight pieces unsigned.

The tales are listed here in the order of their appearance: Some Secrets of the Magazine Prison-House [*A*]; Some Passages in the Life of a Lion [Lionizing, *D*]; Berenice [*D*]; Bon-Bon [*E*]; The Oval Portrait [*B*]; House

Furniture [Philosophy of Furniture, *B*]; Three Sundays in a Week [*B*]; The Pit and the Pendulum [*B*]; Eleonora [*B*]; Shadow – A Parable [*E*]; The Assignation [*E*]; The Premature Burial [*B*]; Morella [*F*]; How to Write a Blackwood Article [*D*]; The Masque of the Red Death [*B*]; The Literary Life of Thingum Bob, Esq. [*B*]; The Business Man [*B*]; The Man that was Used Up [*E*]; Never Bet the Devil Your Head. A Moral Tale [*B*]; The Tell-Tale Heart [*B*]; William Wilson [*E*]; Why the Little Frenchman Wears His Hand in a Sling [*C*]; Silence – A Fable [*D*]; Diddling Considered as One of the Exact Sciences [*B*]; The Landscape Garden [*B*]; A Tale of Jerusalem [*D*]; Ligeia [*E*]; The Island of the Fay [*B*]; MS. Found in a Bottle [*F*]; The Duc de L'Omelette [*E*]; King Pest. A Tale Containing an Allegory [*E*]; The Thousand-and-Second Tale of Scheherazade [*B*]; The Power of Words [*B*]; Some Words With a Mummy [*B*]; Theatrical Rats [*A*]; The Devil in the Belfry [*E*]; The Spectacles [*C*]; A Tale of the Ragged Mountains [*C*]; Four Beasts in One – The Homo-Cameleopard [*D*]; The Oblong Box [*B*]; The Facts in the Case of M. Valdemar [*C*]; Mystification [*C*]; Loss of Breath [*D*].

——— Also copy given to Mrs. Sarah Helen Whitman with manuscript revisions. Poe penciled the initial P. beside a number of unsigned things in this copy, which is now in the Huntington Library. The tales with revisions are Morella [*G*]; Ligeia [*F*]; The Facts in the Case of M. Valdemar [*C*].

Burton's Gentleman's Magazine (Philadelphia). In May 1839 Poe became co-editor with William E. Burton, the proprietor. Besides many reviews and the anonymous serial, "The Journal of Julius Rodman," before he was discharged late in May of 1840 Poe contributed to this magazine the following tales: The Man that Was Used Up [*A*]; The Fall of the House of Usher [*A*]; William Wilson. A Tale [*B*]; Morella. A Tale [*D*]; The Conversation of Eiros and Charmion [*A*]; Peter Pendulum, the Business Man [The Business Man, *A*]; The Philosophy of Furniture [*A*].

Columbian Lady's and Gentleman's Magazine (New York): Mesmeric Revelation [*A*]; The Angel of the Odd – An Extravaganza [*A*]; Byron and Miss Chaworth [*A*]; The Domain of Arnheim [*B*].

Democratic Review: see *United States Magazine and Democratic Review.*

Dollar Newspaper (Philadelphia): The Gold-Bug [*A*]; The Spectacles [*A*]; The Premature Burial [*A*].

Evening Mirror (New York): The Swiss Bell-Ringers.

Flag of Our Union (Boston). By 1849 this cheap but well-printed popular weekly was Poe's chief market. He had no regard for it, but it paid well. The following tales appeared first in its pages: Hop-Frog [*A*]; Von Kempelen and His Discovery [*A*]; X-ing a Paragrab [*A*]; Landor's Cottage [*A*].

Godey's Magazine and Lady's Book (Philadelphia). For *Godey's* Poe wrote criticisms; the famous series, The Literati of New York City; and the following tales: The Visionary [The Assignation, *A*]; A Tale of the Ragged Mountains [*B*]; The Oblong Box [*A*]; "Thou Art the Man!" [*B*]; The Thousand-and-Second Tale of Scheherazade [*A*]; The Cask of Amontillado [*A*]; Mellonta Tauta [*A*].

NEWSPAPERS AND MAGAZINES

Graham's Magazine (Philadelphia). Late in 1840, George R. Graham purchased *Burton's Gentleman's Magazine* and combined it with his *Casket* to form *Graham's Magazine*. Probably recommended by Burton, Poe began his contributions with the first number in December, and was announced as one of the editors in February 1841. In January 1842, after a misunderstanding, Poe resigned and with the May number ceased to be a regular editor. The tales that appeared in *Graham's* were: The Man of the Crowd [*A*]; The Murders in the Rue Morgue [*B*]; A Descent into the Maelström [*A*]; The Island of the Fay [*A*]; The Colloquy of Monos and Una [*A*]; Never Bet Your Head. A Moral Tale [Never Bet the Devil Your Head, *A*]; Life in Death [The Oval Portrait, *A*]; The Mask of the Red Death. A Fantasy [The Masque of the Red Death, *A*]; The Imp of the Perverse [*A*]; The System of Dr. Tarr and Prof. Fether [*B*].

Ladies' Companion, familiarly known as Snowden's (New York): The Landscape Garden [*A*]; The Mystery of Marie Roget [*A*].

Methodist Review (New York): A Prediction [*D*].

New World (New York): Ligeia [*D*].
Notes and Queries (London): The Light-House [*D*].

Pioneer (Boston): The Tell-Tale Heart [*A*].
Public Ledger (Philadelphia): Moving Chapters; Desultory Notes on Cats.

Saturday Chronicle (Philadelphia): The Devil in the Belfry. An Extravaganza [*A*].

Saturday Courier (Philadelphia). The first five of the following tales, not having won in the contest conducted by the *Courier* for which they were submitted, were published anonymously (see Mabbott, I, 543): Metzengerstein [*A*]; The Duke de L'Omelette [*A*]; A Tale of Jerusalem [*A*]; A Decided Loss [*A*]; The Bargain Lost [*A*]; later another story appeared, Raising the Wind; or Diddling Considered as one of the Exact Sciences [Diddling, *A*].

Saturday Evening Post (Philadelphia): A Dream; A Succession of Sundays [Three Sundays in a Week, *A*]; The Black Cat [*A*].

Saturday Museum (Philadelphia): The Destruction of the World. (A Conversation between two Departed Spirits.) [The Conversation of Eiros and Charmion, *C*].

Southern Literary Messenger (Richmond). From the spring of 1835 Poe was a contributor, and from December 1835 to January 1837, editor. For it he wrote tales, articles, and book reviews in great number. It was his criticism that attracted attention and increased the sales of the magazine. The tales printed were: Berenice – A Tale [*A*]; Morella – A Tale [*B*]; Lion-izing. A Tale [*A*]; The Visionary – A Tale (The Assignation, *B*]; Bon-Bon – A Tale [*A*]; Loss of Breath. A Tale a la Blackwood [*A*]; King Pest the First. A Tale Containing an Allegory – By – [*A*]; Shadow. A Fable – By – [*A*]; MS. Found in a Bottle [*C*]; Metzengerstein. A Tale in Imitation of the German [*B*]; The Duc de L'Omelette [*B*]; Autography [*A*]; Epimanes [Four Beasts in One, *B*]; A Tale of Jerusalem [*B*]; The Literary Life of Thingum Bob, Esq. Late Editor of the "Goosetherumfoodle" By Himself [*A*]; [Preface to] Marginalia [*C*]; A Would-Be Crichton [*A*].

——— [The Duane copy of volumes I and II of the *Southern Literary Messenger,* with penciled changes in Poe's hand, presumably made in 1839 to provide printer's copy for *Tales of the Grotesque and Arabesque* (1840), since all the changes indicated were adopted in that edition.] The bound volumes were owned for some time by William J. Duane and later by J. H. Whitty. They were examined by Woodberry, who made no use of them. I collated them before 1925, and again in 1968 when the "Duane *Messengers,*" now owned by H. Bradley Martin, were loaned for my use to the Grolier Club of New York City. The tales affected are: Berenice – A Tale [*B*]; The Visionary – A Tale [The Assignation, *C*]; Bon-Bon – A Tale [*B*]; Loss of Breath. A Tale a la Blackwood [*B*]; King Pest the First. A Tale Containing an Allegory – By – [*B*]; Shadow. A Fable [*B*]; Metzengerstein. A Tale in Imitation of the German [*C*].

United States Magazine and Democratic Review (New York): [Preface to] Marginalia [*A*]; The Power of Words [*A*].

OTHER WORKS FREQUENTLY USED

INCLUDING POE'S SOURCES MOST OFTEN CITED

Alterton, Margaret. *Origins of Poe's Critical Theory.* University of Iowa Humanistic Studies, volume II, number 3. Published by the University, Iowa City, 1925.

Bandy, William T. *A Tentative Checklist of Translations of Poe's Works.* Madison, Wisconsin, 1959.

Bielfeld, Jacob Friedrich, baron. *Les Premiers Traits de l'érudition universelle, ou Analyse abrégée de toutes les sciences, des beaux-arts et des belles-lettres.* 3 vols., Leide: S. & J. Luchtmans, 1767.

——— *L'Erudition universelle, ou Analyse abrégée . . . par M. le Baron de Bielfeld.* 4 vols., Berlin, 1768. [Publisher not named.]

——— *The Elements of Universal Erudition, containing an Analytical Abridgment of the Sciences, Polite Arts, and Belles Lettres, by Baron Bielfeld . . . translated from the last edition printed at Berlin.* By W. Hooper, M.D. . . . Printed by G. Scott for J. Robson and B. Law . . . 3 vols., London, 1770.

Poe drew frequently from Bielfeld, and cited the 1767 edition in his review of Moore's *Alciphron.* Pagination differs, but book, chapter, and section numbers are the same in the three editions listed.

Bryant, Jacob. *A New System; or, An Analysis of Antient Mythology.* A compendium of ancient lore based on great erudition, pointing out similarities between "Gentile" legends and Old Testament narratives in an endeavor to confirm the Scriptural accounts and to prove the common origin of mankind. Bryant laid emphasis on etymology (often erroneous), a defect criticized by many of his contemporaries, who nevertheless greatly respected him for his learning. Poe probably used the third edition (1807).

Campbell, Killis. *The Mind of Poe and Other Studies.* Cambridge, Massachusetts: Harvard University Press, 1933. Seven important articles by the leading Poe authority of his day.

Chivers, Thomas Holley. *Chivers' Life of Poe.* Edited with an Introduction by Richard Beale Davis. New York: E. P. Dutton & Co., Inc. 1952.

Chivers, Thomas Holley. *The Complete Works of Thomas Holley Chivers.* Edited by E. L. Chase and L. P. Parks. Vol. I. Providence, R. I.: Brown University Press, 1957.

Coleridge, Henry Nelson. *Introductions to the Study of the Greek Classic Poets.* Philadelphia: Carey and Lea, 1831. Poe's immediate source for some of his classical references.

Disraeli, Benjamin. *Vivian Grey.* [First edition.] 5 vols. London: H. Colburn, 1826. Influential in Poe's early tales.

D'Israeli, Isaac. *Curiosities of Literature.* 6th ed. in 3 vols. London: J. Murray, 1817, and subsequent editions.

The first series in this collection of "anecdotes, characters, sketches, and observations, literary, critical, and historical" was issued by Murray in 1791 and reprinted in Philadelphia the same year. Revised repeatedly with numerous changes, augmented and rearranged, frequently combined with one or another of the author's other works – his essay on "The Literary Character" and others – it went through edition after edition in both England and America. Poe showed his familiarity with it as early as his review of *Paul Ulric* (*SLM,* February 1836), mentioned it in "Pinakidia" the following August, and was undoubtedly indebted to it for suggestions throughout his career. A one-volume American abridgment (1844) included "Curiosities of American Literature" by R. W. Griswold.

Gordan, John D. *Edgar Allan Poe . . . A Catalogue of First Editions, Manuscripts, Autograph Letters, from the Berg Collection.* New York: The New York Public Library, 1949.

Griswold, Rufus Wilmot, ed. *The Works of the Late Edgar Allan Poe, with a Memoir by Rufus Wilmot Griswold and Notices of His Life and Genius by N. P. Willis and J. R. Lowell.* New York: J. S. Redfield. vols. I–III, 1850; vol. IV, 1856. The "Memoir" appeared first in vol. III, but was moved to vol. I in subsequent issues.

Griswold, Rufus Wilmot. *Passages from the Correspondence and Papers of Rufus W. Griswold.* Cambridge, Massachusetts: W. M. Griswold, 1898. Most of the originals are now in the Boston Public Library, which issued a catalogue in its periodical *More Books* and its successor, *The Boston Public Library Quarterly,* between March 1941 and April 1951.

Harrison, James A., ed. *The Complete Works of Edgar Allan Poe.* 17 vols. New York: Thomas Y. Crowell & Company, 1902: the "Virginia Edition." Volume 1, biography, and volume 17, letters, were also issued as *Life and Letters of Edgar Allan Poe* (2 vols., New York: Crowell, 1902–1903).

Heartman, Charles F., and James R. Canny, compilers. *A Bibliography of the First Printings of the Writings of Edgar Allan Poe.* Revised edition. Hattiesburg, Miss.: The Book Farm, 1943. In spite of the errors that remain in the revised edition, this work is invaluable for the student of the works of Poe.

Indiana List. "The J. K. Lilly Collection of Edgar Allan Poe," by David A. Randall, in the *Indiana University Bookman,* March 1960.

Ingram, John H. *Edgar Allan Poe: His Life, Letters and Opinions.* 2 vols. London: John Hogg, 1880. The first serious and comprehensive biography of Poe. Ingram, an Englishman, zealously collected and preserved a great deal of source material from Poe's contemporaries. He published many articles and an edition of Poe in four volumes.

Ingram List. See Miller, John Carl.

Mabbott, Thomas Ollive, ed. *Collected Works of Edgar Allan Poe.* vol. I, *Poems.* Cambridge, Massachusetts: The Belknap Press of Harvard University Press, 1969. One of the unusual features of this edition of Poe's poems is the "Annals," a 43-page account of Poe's life year by year.

Miller, John Carl. *John Henry Ingram's Poe Collection at the University of*

Virginia: A Calendar... Charlottesville: University of Virginia Press, 1960. Cited as the Ingram List, it is an extremely valuable checklist of manuscripts, letters and clippings.

Moldenhauer, Joseph J. *A Descriptive Catalog of Edgar Allan Poe Manuscripts in the Humanities Research Center Library, The University of Texas at Austin.* [Austin, Texas, 1973; A *Texas Quarterly* Supplement.] This has been a valuable tool for the assisting editors.

Mott, Frank Luther. *A History of American Magazines, 1741–1850.* New York and London: D. Appleton and Company, 1930. The first of five volumes, it presents not only a general history but individual sketches with precise listings of dates, title changes, editors, publishers, and other specific information concerning the significant magazines of the period it covers.

New-York Mirror. This "weekly journal devoted to literature and the fine arts," went through several phases and confusing changes of title. It was founded in 1823 as the *New-York Mirror and Ladies' Gazette* by George Pope Morris, who during the best parts of its life was its editor or publisher or both, with a succession of associates. In 1831, the year it was joined by Nathaniel Parker Willis, it dropped the last part of its title in favor of the description quoted above. Financial troubles brought about its demise at the end of 1842. It was revived by Morris and Willis in April 1843 as the *New Mirror,* which flourished until October 1844 when, to avoid the high postal rates on magazines, it became a daily newspaper – the *Evening Mirror* – with the *Weekly Mirror* as an adjunct. With the beginning of the daily, Hiram Fuller was made a third partner. Poe, who had been engaged as a critical writer in September 1844, left in February 1845 for the *Broadway Journal.* In the same month Willis, and a little later Morris, also withdrew, and the glory was departed, although Fuller continued the weekly as the *New York Mirror* until 1847.

Ostrom, John Ward, ed. *The Letters of Edgar Allan Poe.* 2 vols. Cambridge, Massachusetts: Harvard University Press, 1948. Mr. Ostrom published two supplements (*AL,* November 1952 and March 1957, 24:358–366 and 29:79–86 respectively) before the publication of a new edition of *The Letters*... (Gordian Press, New York, 1966). This edition contains a photographic reproduction of the 1948 edition followed by a supplementary section that includes the material in the first and second supplements mentioned above and additional material forming a third supplement. In January 1974 (*AL* 45:513–536) Mr. Ostrom published a fourth supplement.

Phillips, Mary Elizabeth. *Edgar Allan Poe: The Man.* 2 vols. Chicago-Philadelphia-Toronto: The John C. Winston Company, 1926. Presents important source material but must be used with discretion.

Poe, Edgar Allan. (For further information on books by Poe, see Sources of Texts Collated, and Index.) His separately published volumes in chronological order are:

Tamerlane and Other Poems. Boston, 1827.
Al Aaraaf, Tamerlane, and Minor Poems. Baltimore, 1829.
Poems. Second Edition. New York, 1831.

The Narrative of Arthur Gordon Pym. New York, 1838.
The Conchologist's First Book. Philadelphia, 1839.
Tales of the Grotesque and Arabesque. Philadelphia, 1840.
Prose Romances No. 1. Philadelphia, 1843.
Tales. New York, 1845.
The Raven and Other Poems. New York, 1845.
Mesmerism "in articulo mortis" (pirated). London, 1846.
Eureka: A Prose Poem. New York, 1848.

Poe Newsletter, Pullman, Washington. Editor, G. R. Thompson. Volume I, number 1, April 1968. Twice a year this publication supplies current articles and bibliographies on the works of Poe. The name was changed to *Poe Studies* with the issue of June 1971 (Volume IV, number 1).

Pollin, Burton R. *Dictionary of Names and Titles in Poe's Collected Works.* New York: Da Capo Press, 1968. Based upon *The Complete Works of Edgar Allan Poe,* ed. James A. Harrison, 1902. This has been a most valuable tool for the assisting editors.

Pollin, Burton R. *Discoveries in Poe*. Notre Dame, Indiana: University of Notre Dame Press, 1970. A selection of twelve of the most substantial of Mr. Pollin's numerous articles. The emphasis is on Poe's multiple sources and their complex relationships in his works.

Quinn, Arthur Hobson. *Edgar Allan Poe: A Critical Biography*. New York and London: D. Appleton-Century Company, 1941. A distinguished piece of scholarship, indispensable to the student of Poe's life and works.

Quinn, Arthur Hobson, and Richard H. Hart, eds. *Edgar Allan Poe: Letters and Documents in the Enoch Pratt Free Library.* New York: Scholars' Facsimiles and Reprints, 1941.

" 'Quoth the Raven': An Exhibition of the work of Edgar Allan Poe . . . from the collections of H. Bradley Martin and Colonel Richard Gimbel," *The Yale University Library Gazette,* 33:138–189 (April 1959). Cited as the Yale List.

Robertson, John W. *Bibliography of the Writings of Edgar A. Poe.* 2 vols. San Francisco: Russian Hill Private Press. Edwin & Robert Grabhorn, 1934. Peculiarly useful for its reproductions of title pages and other documents.

Smith, Horatio. *Zillah; a Tale of the Holy City*. 4 vols. London: Henry Colburn, New Burlington Street, 1828.

Stedman, Edmund Clarence, and George Edward Woodberry. *The Works of Edgar Allan Poe*. 10 vols. Chicago, 1894–95. There are later printings with different pagination.

Wallace, Horace Binney ("William Landor"). *Stanley, or the Recollections of a Man of the World*. 2 vols. Philadelphia: Lea and Blanchard, 1838. A novel.

Willis, Nathaniel Parker. *Prose Works* in *Complete Works*. New York: J. S. Redfield, Clinton Hall, 1846.

Woodberry, George Edward. *Edgar Allan Poe*. Boston: Houghton Mifflin and Company, 1885 (American Men of Letters series).

Woodberry, George Edward. *The Life of Edgar Allan Poe, personal and literary, with his chief correspondence with men of letters.* 2 vols. Boston and New

York: Houghton Mifflin Company, 1909. A thorough revision and expansion of the 1885 biography, judicious, appreciative of Poe's genius, and beautifully written. Woodberry was not well informed about Poe's early life, but his book is indispensable for the serious student.

Wyllie, John Cook. "A List of the Texts of Poe's Tales," *Humanistic Studies in Honor of John Calvin Metcalf*. New York: Columbia University Press, 1941. A convenient list of "all authoritative texts of Poe's tales of which the compiler has any knowledge." In general only the "Duane *Messenger*" texts with Poe's manuscript changes are omitted.

Yale List. See "Quoth the Raven," above.

SUPPLEMENTARY NOTE

Three of Poe's well-known series must be added to the foregoing list. Because of their close connection with the tales they are frequently cited in these volumes.

"Pinakidia," *Southern Literary Messenger,* August 1836, pp. 573–582. Three introductory paragraphs and 172 separate items taken, as Poe states, "from the confused mass of marginal notes and entries in a commonplace book." This early compilation, mined repeatedly for later works, will appear in a succeeding volume of the *Collected Works* where the items are numbered to follow the original sequence. It differs slightly from that in Harrison's 1902 edition.

"The Doings of Gotham," a series of seven newsletters about life in New York, written between May 14 and June 25, 1844, and printed in the *Columbia Spy,* Columbia, Pennsylvania. They may be seen in *Doings of Gotham, as described in a series of letters to the editors of the Columbia Spy, together with various editorial comments and criticisms by Poe now first collected* by Jacob E. Spannuth, with a preface, introduction and comments by Thomas Ollive Mabbott. Pottsville, Pennsylvania, Jacob E. Spannuth, Publisher, 1929.

"Marginalia," seventeen installments in four magazines: *Democratic Review,* November and December 1844, April and July 1846 (July not in Harrison); *Godey's Lady's Book* as "Marginal Notes," August and September 1845; *Graham's Magazine,* March, November, and December 1846, January, February, and March 1848 (March not in Harrison); *Southern Literary Messenger,* April, May, June, July, and September 1849.

See "Preface to Marginalia," pages 1113–1116, for Poe's description of this series. As in "Pinakidia," the separate items have been numbered in sequence as they will appear in a succeeding volume of the *Collected Works.*

INDEX

OF NAMES AND TITLES IN COMMENTARY

Anonymous works and works by Poe, except for his letters and reviews, are indexed under title or subject; other works are indexed under the author's name. Poe's letters and reviews are indexed under the name of the addressee or author reviewed, and also under POE *by categories. An asterisk (*) following an entry indicates that it will be found also in the list of Sources of Texts Collated. A small* n *prefixed to a number* (390 n19) *refers to a particular note on the page indicated; a small* n *following a page number* (719n) *indicates a footnote on that page.*

INDEX

INDEX

INDEX

INDEX

INDEX

INDEX

INDEX

INDEX

INDEX

INDEX

INDEX

INDEX

University of Illinois Press
1325 South Oak Street
Champaign, IL 61820-6903
WWW.PRESS.UILLINOIS.EDU